# Philosophers Speak of God

# Philosophers Speak of God

*By*

Charles Hartshorne

*and*

William L. Reese

THE UNIVERSITY OF CHICAGO PRESS
CHICAGO & LONDON

THE UNIVERSITY OF CHICAGO PRESS, CHICAGO 60637
The University of Chicago Press, Ltd., London W.C. 1

# Prologue: *Deity as Inclusive Process and Tragic Love*

## I. MAHANAM BRATA BRAHMACHARI

For Sankara there is only one truth, and that is the Absolute. . . . It is neither creator, nor preserver, nor savior, nor providence. For all these expressions presuppose relation, and the Absolute is beyond relations. The realm of relation is the realm of phenomena for Sankara, and hence theology belongs to the phenomenal world. . . . When the Absolute limits itself, it becomes God.

Different, however, is the view of Ramanuja and very different is that of Sri Jiva. For Ramanuja, the Absolute itself is a personality. . . . He is the Providence and the Lord. . . . Sankara places God below the Absolute and prefers to call him the lower Brahman. Ramanuja makes them identical and puts them on the same throne. . . . Sri Jiva places God above and beyond the Absolute. This perhaps appears illogical. How can there be anything beyond the Absolute?

For Sri Jiva . . . the Absolute Being is all-existence, all-knowledge, and all-joy. Sri Jiva can express it in one word. The Absolute Reality is love. It is this nature of the Absolute that accounts for its unceasing expressiveness. The nature of perfect Love is to overflow. So far as the Absolute is a perfect Being, it is steady, calm, and immutable, but so far as the outburst of Love is concerned, it is a mobile, flexible, and dynamic substance. Due to perfect integrity, the Absolute is a Being, and due to indomitable impetus for expressiveness, it is a Becoming. Since it is a Becoming, it has a "life" and a "history." . . . Because of the exuberance of fulness, the permanent being becomes fluent.

Krisnadas, a contemporary follower of Sri Jiva, writes that God is full and perfect in his Love and has no room to grow, but it is a mystery that he grows without cessation. In this process of never ending augmentation all the values of joyful delight that are realized remain conserved with Him for all time.

[Doctoral thesis, "The Philosophy of Sri Jiva Goswami (Vaisnava Vedanta of the Bengal School)" (Swift Hall Library, University of Chicago, 1937).]

## II. A. N. WHITEHEAD

All realization is finite, and there is no perfection which is the infinitude of all perfections. Perfections of divers types are among themselves discordant. . . .

This principle of intrinsic incompatibility has an important bearing upon our conception of the nature of God. The concept of impossibility such that God himself cannot surmount it, has been for centuries quite familiar to theologians. . . . But curiously enough, so far as I know, this notion of incompatibility has never been applied to ideals in the Divine realization. We must conceive the Divine Eros as the active entertainment of all ideals, with the urge to their finite realization, each in its due season. Thus a process must be inherent in God's nature whereby his infinity is acquiring realization.

[*Adventures of Ideas*, pp. 330 and 357.]

The ascription of mere happiness, and of arbitrary power to the nature of God is a profanation. This nature . . . receives into its unity the scattered effectiveness of realized activities, transformed by the supremacy of its own ideals. The result is Tragedy, Sympathy, and the Happiness evoked by actualized heroism.

Of course we are unable to conceive

the experience of the Supreme Unity of Existence. But these are the human terms in which we can glimpse the origin of that drive towards limited ideals of perfection which haunts the Universe. This immortality of the World of Action, derived from its transformation in God's nature, is beyond our imagination to conceive. The various attempts at description are often shocking and profane. What does haunt our imagination is that the immediate facts of present action pass into permanent significance for the Universe. The insistent notion of Right and Wrong, Achievement and Failure, depends upon this background. Otherwise every activity is merely a passing whiff of insignificance.

[*The Philosophy of Alfred North Whitehead*, ed. P. A. Schilpp, pp. 697-98.]

## III. NICOLAS BERDYAEV

[There is a] continuation by man of the creation of the world . . . man, who is able to enrich the very divine life itself. . . .

[*The Russian Idea*, p. 243.]

Is all tragedy that of fate, or is a Christian tragedy possible? Traditional theology is afraid of the very idea of it, though it is curious that the religion of the Cross should deny tragedy. . . . Christianity reveals freedom which is the primary source of tragedy. . . . Tragedy . . . need not necessarily be a conflict between good and evil, the divine and the diabolical. . . . The most tragic situations in life are conflicts between values which are equally noble and lofty. And this implies that tragedy exists within the Divine life itself. . . . We can only reconcile ourselves to the tragedy of the world because

God suffers in it too. God shares his creatures' destiny.

[*The Destiny of Man*, pp. 41-42 and 40.]

## IV. SØREN KIERKEGAARD

The minds of men so often yearn for might and power, and their thoughts are constantly being drawn to such things, as if by their attainment all mysteries would be resolved. Hence they do not even dream that there is sorrow in heaven as well as joy. . . . The learner is in error, and that by reason of his own guilt. . . . Men sometimes think that this might be a matter of indifference to God, since he does not stand in need of the learner. But in this we forget . . . that God loves the learner. And just as that kingly grief of which we have spoken can be found only in a kingly soul, and is not even named in the language of the multitude of men, so the entire human language is so selfish that it refuses even to suspect the existence of such a grief. But for that reason God has reserved it to himself, this unfathomable grief: to know that he may repel the learner . . . that the learner has brought destruction upon himself.

[*Philosophical Fragments*, pp. 23 and 21.]

## V. G. T. FECHNER

Is not that the best God for us who bears within himself our good fortune and misfortune? . . . What would he be if he looked upon our misery merely from the outside, as we look upon the misery of a beggar in rags to whom we throw a penny? . . . God does not view your pain merely from the outside, but he feels it along with you yourself . . . and is kept incessantly busy effecting the removal of evil.

[*Zend-Avesta*, p. 249.]

# Preface

This work aims to present—by selections from some fifty writers ranging in time and space from Lao-tse, Plato, and Sankara to Whitehead, Berdyaev, and Radhakrishnan—the chief philosophical conceptions of deity. It also aims to aid readers in estimating the validity of these conceptions. The work is thus two things: (1) a book of readings in philosophical theology—the first of its kind—and (2) a systematic analysis and evaluation of theistic (and atheistic) ideas.

1. There are anthologies of philosophy, and of religious writings or sacred scriptures, but not of philosophical treatments of the central religious idea. Out of the vast array of writings by philosophers dealing with the nature and existence of God, sample texts (some of them not elsewhere available in English) have been chosen, representing the principal concepts of deity which a new analytic classification shows to be logically possible. By this means the material is reduced to manageable proportions, and yet no major concept is omitted. The coverage is thus relatively objective; passages are included not merely because the editors agree with them, or like them, but because, taken together, they acquaint the student with the totality of views among which, or something like them, anyone seeking a philosophical solution of the religious problem must decide. Highly skeptical or atheistic views are also included.

2. The classification of doctrines employed is shown to have historical as well as systematic significance and is made the key to an interpretation of the meaning of the historical development. Each selection is prefaced by a sympathetic introduction from which criticism has been largely excluded; but it is followed in most cases by a critical commentary devoted to the frank statement of such objections as the editors deem valid. Thus selections expressing the classical conceptions are first presented; the student is given opportunity to see the various views positively and from the inside, and yet he is not left without help in the task of comparative evaluation. In the general Introduction an argument is outlined for the superiority of one of the main types of conception, which we term "panentheism" or "surrelativism." Its chief recent representative among philosophers is Whitehead, but we trace it back to Plato, Ramanuja, and Schelling; and something like it can be found in most of the outstanding theologians of recent times—Berdyaev, Nygren, Niebuhr, and even, to a lesser extent, Barth. The book is designed partly as a historico-systematic argument pointing to a definite conclusion.

Thus this volume is, we think, unique in two respects: in the adequacy with which man's efforts to think rationally, or with intellectual responsibility, about deity are covered through samplings of the great texts, old and new; and in the evaluation of this historical panorama from the standpoint of certain prevalent views in current metaphysics and philosophy of religion which have not yet had time to embody themselves very extensively in historical and scholarly surveys.

What is the use of such an undertaking?

The quantity of works in which great philosophic minds have set down thoughts about deity is so vast, and these works are written in so many languages, from so many points of view, and at so many periods of time, that a student going into a library to look into the matter for himself, to ascertain what great intellects have actually done with this problem, confronts an overwhelming task. As a result he usually contents himself with a few samples, chosen either at random or according to the religious and philosophical convictions or interests of himself or his teacher or adviser. This has two disadvantages. First, he does not discover the full range of alternatives which the toil of generations over the civilized world bequeaths to us for our acceptance or rejection. This range of alternatives, however, is precisely our chief heritage in this matter. For if we could learn what *can* be believed, and for what reasons or upon what arguments, and still be unable to determine what is true, then the task of religious philosophy must for us be entirely hopeless. For we would have been furnished with every philosophical resource, save that which only we ourselves can provide, namely, our own judgment. But everyone who has had philosophical experience knows that to attempt to think out for one's self, without help from one's ancestors, the range of possible doctrines is hardly a feasible enterprise.

The second disadvantage of the usual procedure is that the possibilities which random or prejudiced sampling of the literature will be apt to miss are likely to be important. This is a subject in which strong prejudices have nearly always been operative. The histories and comparative studies have been written with a good deal of bias. Authors of various "orthodox" allegiances, and this includes multitudes of very learned men, have done what they could to make certain posibilities for thought appear to be *the* possibilities. Not that they have done anything so crude as to limit the possibilities to their own tenets. This would have been too manifestly illegitimate and would not have satisfied their own or anyone's conscience. They have done something more subtle and insidious. Not only is it usual to limit the inquiry almost entirely to our Western culture, and indeed (especially among European scholars) sometimes largely to one's own country, but there is the even worse tendency to set up artificially limited options such as theism and pantheism, or infinite God and finite God, or immutable and mutable God—and many more. In every such case, analysis discloses that one may believe in God while being about equally far from (or near to) the positions mentioned, as customarily construed. God may, in some aspect, be infinite and, in some other aspect, finite; and the same holds with respect to the predicate "mutable" or the pantheistic predicate "coextensive with reality," or "includes all things within his own being." In all intellectual fields one meets the phenomenon of half-truths confronting one another, agreeing only in this: that all alike deny the whole truth, which is more subtle and many-sided than any one of them alone. When something like the whole truth is expressed, the half-truth addicts pounce upon it almost as one man with charges of compromise, evasion, or confusion. It lacks the sort of dramatic trenchancy which men so love to defend—and attack.

The obstacles to fair sampling of the history of thought which have just been outlined are inherent in the problem, and we can claim no immunity. But we have at least reflected upon these obstacles and have, we trust, overcome them sufficiently to render this work a uniquely comprehensive book of theistic meditation. We have, it is true, attempted no posture of impartiality as between various doctrines. Such a posture tends to be either an affectation or a confession of incompetence. On the one hand, if we, surveying for many years the history of theistic speculations, were able to draw no conclusion for ourselves, how could we ask students to do so? And if nothing followed from the study to which we invite them, why should they undertake it? On the other hand, if we have drawn conclusions but conceal them, it of course would follow, not so much that the student would be spared exposure to their influence, as that he would undergo this influence without warning as to its character. We propose through our Introduction to give him fair notice of the "bias" of this work.

In the choice of selections our guiding idea has been that we wish to exhibit the whole outline of what men have thought—in a philosophically disciplined way—about the central religious problem. We have also given weight to the testimony of scholars with whose philosophical or religious creeds we disagree concerning the relative importance of various thinkers. We have included, as recognized spokesmen of groups whom we have not the right to ignore, Aquinas, Maimonides, and Sankara. But we have also insisted upon a hearing for many thinkers, especially of the last hundred and fifty years, who have not wholly identified themselves with any great religious body of doctrine, but whose intellectual abilities are to be taken seriously, and who seem to us to have contributed penetrating analyses not simply duplicating earlier ones and to have achieved positive insights, partly through their comparative freedom with respect to bodies of religious doctrine. Such are Schelling, Fechner, and, in a very different vein, Feuerbach. No doubt glaring omissions, not justified by any principle, and dubious inclusions could with plausibility be charged against us. The literature is vast.

With some exceptions we have felt compelled to rely upon existing translations of non-English sources. Fechner's great chapter xi of his *Zend-Avesta*, only three pages of which have previously been rendered into English (in Lowrie's *The Religion of a Scientist*), seemed to us too valuable and too unjustly neglected to omit; so we have translated some twenty pages of it. The Nietzsche, Zeller, and portions of the Kant translations are also our own; while the passages from Lequier and Pfleiderer, and the admirable Fock paraphrases of Socinus, are here, so far as we know, presented for the first time in English.

There is no simple way of describing the division of labor between the two author-editors. Every chapter and almost every main aspect of the book contains the work of both. Chapters ii and viii–x were primarily Mr. Reese's responsibility. The prefatory notes and commentaries concerning Plato (chap. i), Peirce, Watts (chap. vii), Brightman (chap. viii), Alexander, Berman, Ames, Cattell (chap. ix), and Nietzsche (chap. xiii) are almost entirely of his authorship as are also considerable portions of the discussions of Aristotle (chap. ii), Philo (chap. iii), Plotinus (chap. iv), Fechner, Weiss (chap. vii), James, Ehrenfels (chap. viii), and certain additional prefatory notes as that for Wieman (chap. x). Mr. Reese, too, in most of these and some other cases largely selected the passages and throughout the book performed much of the editorial detail work. Mr. Hartshorne wrote the general Introduction and a majority of the commentaries and prefatory notes. The translation of Fechner was first made by Mr. Reese but was revised jointly. The plan of the book grew out of discussions between us, and without intensive joint effort neither it nor anything much like it could have been conceived or executed.

Since the book is too long for thorough study in a single course (unless continued for a whole year), teachers assigning it will doubtless wish to select certain parts for emphasis. For instance, one might omit all but one or two key figures in each of the longer chapters or in Part Three. The student would thus acquire an outline knowledge of the panorama of theistic and antitheistic doctrines, while also receiving some suggestions at least of how much there remains for him to know. Obviously other plans could be followed. We believe that the book is sufficiently rich in the variety and high quality of the included materials to be of permanent value to any serious student. He therefore need not object to the fact that its scope may exceed the needs of a single course. The selections should of course be supplemented, where possible, by further reading in the works of the authors found most significant. With this understanding the book offers a design for adult education in the subject, not merely a brief initiation into it.

In transcribing texts or existing translations, we have usually adhered to the wording, punctuation, and spelling of the authors or translators. Only a few obvious slips have been corrected. To modify punctuation in a work such as this is a complicated and, to judge by the disastrous results sometimes achieved, a hazardous undertaking. In the case of some authors who wrote the English of an earlier century, but wrote it wonderfully well, such as Hume or George Eliot (Mary Anne Evans, who so brilliantly and eloquently translated Feuerbach), one hesitates to make any changes (all the more because the first-mentioned of these has been sadly mutilated by the sense-destroying punctuation of one of his modern editors).

In all cases a new section number means a new locus in the text. This device thus takes the place, where it occurs, of ellipses indicating omission (except where the new passage does not begin with the first word of a sentence) and also facilitates the furnishing of references at the ends of selections and in our commentaries.

The subheadings employed in the selections are our own (except where marked by asterisks). Their function is to suggest some of the principal ideas which the passages chosen seem to us to express and to compensate so far as possible for the loss of continuity and background inevitable in an anthology of this type. The subheadings are almost the only form of editorial interpretation in which we have indulged within the series of passages from a given author. (In some few cases an explanatory word or phrase has been inserted in brackets. Where previous translators or editors have used this practice, we have sometimes, to avoid confusion with our own bracketed insertions, reduced the previous brackets to parentheses—which some of the translators themselves use for editorial inserts.)

# Acknowledgments

We are grateful to Professors Gustave E. von Grünebaum and George V. Bobrinskoy for some corrections in connection with al-Ghazzali and Hindu pantheism, respectively. For substantial assistance in the interpretation of Aristotle, we must thank Dr. Alan Gewirth. But, for the most part, we have dared to rely upon our own research, inadequate though it must be over so vast a field. Considerable portions of the manuscript were read by Dorothy C. Hartshorne, to whom we are deeply indebted for many corrections and improvements in style.

The following publishers, authors, and editors have kindly granted us permission to use (in some instances translate) selections from the authors and publications specified.

Abingdon-Cokesbury Press: E. S. Brightman, *The Problem of God*

George Allen & Unwin, Ltd.: Leibniz (trans. by Bertrand Russell and G. E. Moore), passages cited in *The Philosophy of Leibniz*, by B. Russell; B. Varisco, *Know Thyself* (trans. by G. Salvadori); S. Radhakrishnan, *An Idealist View of Life*

American Scandinavian Foundation and the Princeton University Press: Kierkegaard, *Philosophical Fragments* (trans. by D. F. Swenson)

Appleton-Century-Crofts, Inc.: Josiah Royce, *Studies in Good and Evil*

G. Bell & Sons, Ltd.: Philo Judæus, *Works* trans. by C. D. Yonge); Plotinus, *Complete Works* (trans. by K. S. Guthrie); Schopenhauer, *Essays* (trans. by Belford Bax)

Benziger Brothers: Thomas Aquinas, *The Summa theologica* (trans. by Fathers of the English Dominican Province)

The Clarendon Press (Oxford): Sankara (trans. by G. Thibaut), in *The Sacred Books of the East* (ed. by M. Müller), Vols. XXXIV and XXXVIII; Ramanuja (trans. by G. Thibaut), *ibid.*, Vol.

XLVIII; Plato, *Dialogues* (trans. by B. Jowett); Aristotle, *Works* (trans. by B. Jowett); J. Stenzel, *Plato's Method of Dialectic* (trans. by D. J. Allan); M. Iqbal, *The Reconstruction of Religious Thought in Islam*; Rhys Davids (trans.), *The Buddhist Suttas*

T. & T. Clark, Publishers: M. Buber, *I and Thou* (trans. by R. G. Smith)

Librairie Armand Colin: J. Lequier, *La Recherche d'une première vérité*

Columbia University Press: Schelling, *Ages of the World* (trans. by F. deW. Bolman)

Conference on Science, Philosophy, and Religion: Paul Weiss, "God and the World," in *Science, Philosophy, and Religion: A Symposium* (1941)

Andrew Dakers, Ltd.: Lao-tse, *Tao Tê Ching* (trans. by H. Ould)

E. P. Dutton & Company: Augustine, *Confessions* (trans. by E. B. Pusey); F. von Hügel, *Essays and Addresses*; Spinoza, *Ethics* (trans. by A. Boyle)

Dr. Mildred Focht: Chr. Ehrenfels, *Cosmogonie* (trans. by M. Focht)

Walter de Gruyter & Co. (successors to Georg Reimer Verlag): O. Pfleiderer, *Grundriss der christlichen Glaubenslehre*

Harper & Brothers: L. Berman, *Behind the Universe*

Harvard University Press: C. S. Peirce, *Collected Papers*; H. A. Wolfson, *Spinoza*; H. C. Warren, *Buddhism in Translation*

Hogarth Press: S. Freud, *The Future of an Illusion* and *Civilization and Its Discontents*

Henry Holt & Company: E. S. Ames, *Religion*; A. Schweitzer, *Out of My Life and Thought*

Library of Living Philosophers, Inc.: A. N. Whitehead, "Immortality," in *The Philosophy of Alfred North Whitehead*

Liveright Publishing Corporation: S. Freud, *The Future of an Illusion*

Longmans, Green & Company: W. James, *Essays on Faith and Morals* and *A Pluralistic Universe*

Longmans, Green & Company, Ltd.: Kant, *Critique of Practical Reason* (trans. by T. K. Abbott)

The Macmillan Company (New York): S. Alexander, *Space, Time, and Deity;* N. Berdyaev, *The Russian Idea;* A. N. Whitehead, *Adventures of Ideas, Process and Reality,* and *Religion in the Making*

The Macmillan Company (London): Origenes, *Selections* (trans. by R. B. Tollinton)

Thomas Nelson & Sons, Ltd.: R. B. Cattell, *Psychology and the Religious Quest*

Max Niemeyer Verlag: Hans Bauer, *Die Dogmatik des Alghazzali's*

W. W. Norton & Company: S. Freud, *A New Series of Introductory Lectures on Psycho-analysis*

The Open Court Publishing Company: Asvaghosha, *Discourse on the Awakening of Faith in the Mahayana* (trans. by T. Suzuki); Anselm, *Proslogium* (trans. by S. N. Deane); Descartes, *Meditations* (trans. by J. Veitch); Leibniz, *Discourse on Metaphysics and Correspondence with Arnauld* (trans. by G. R. Montgomery); Kant, *Prolegomena* (trans. by P. Carus)

Oxford Press (London): R. Davids (trans.), *The Sacred Books of Buddhism,* Vol. II

Pantheon Books: R. Jeffers, *Selected Poetry*

Princeton University Press: Kierkegaard, *Philosophical Fragments* (trans. by D. F. Swenson)

Reisland, O. R., Verlagsbuchhandlung: E. Zeller, *Die Philosophie der Griechen,* Vol. III, Part I

*Review of Religion, The:* Charles Hartshorne, "The Mathematical Analysis of Theism"

Routledge and Kegan Paul, Ltd.: Maimonides, *Guide for the Perplexed* (trans. by M. Friedländer)

Stephen Royce: Josiah Royce, *The Conception of God*

P. A. Schilpp: W. R. Dennes, "Preface to an Empiricist Philosophy of Religion," in *College of the Pacific Publications in Philosophy,* Vol. III

Albert Schweitzer: Schweitzer, *Christianity and the Religions of the World*

Charles Scribner's Sons: N. Berdyaev, *The Destiny of Man* (trans. by N. Duddington); J. H. Breasted, *The Dawn of Conscience*

Society for the Promotion of Christian Knowledge: R. Davids (trans.), *Buddhism*

The University of Chicago Press: Descartes, "Reply to Objections," in *From Descartes to Kant* (ed. by T. V. Smith and Marjorie Grene); J. M. P. Smith and E. J. Goodspeed (eds.), *The Complete Bible: An American Translation;* H. N. Wieman, *The Source of Human Good*

Paul Weiss: Weiss, article published by the Conference on Science, Philosophy, and Religion (see above)

# Table of Contents

# Introduction: *The Standpoint of Panentheism*

## A. THE LAW OF POLARITY

A principal aim of this sourcebook is to exhibit a pattern in the history of rational reflection about God. Some will say we have imposed this pattern upon the material; but we rather think we have found it there—or, at least, that we have found something like it. We also think the pattern points a moral, a lesson taught by man's intellectual and religious history. The lesson is that man's reason, here as elsewhere, tends toward oversimplifications, which it can overcome only through more or less painful disillusionment with initial, all-too-neat and easy formulas. Whitehead's maxim, "Seek simplicity—and mistrust it," applies to all intellectual inquiry, no matter how exalted its subject matter. Accordingly, we should be grateful to our theological and philosophical ancestors who sought simplicity in their notions about God and thus took a necessary first step in our behalf. (Examples will be found in many chapters of this book.) It is harder to feel gratitude toward their contemporary disciples who have not yet reached the stage of mistrust, and who employ the "method of tenacity" in defense of ancient ideas. Still, the question is difficult, we all share more or less in similar weaknesses, and there is perhaps a need that some should continue to call attention, with the effectiveness derived from partisanship, to the earlier stages in the development of theistic thought, without which, or something equally one-sided, more adequate notions could probably not have been achieved.

It is true that the idea of "God," that is (to give a preliminary definition), the supremely excellent or all-worshipful being, first reaches vivid consciousness in an emotional and practical, not in an explicitly logical or analytic, form and that this preanalytic form is not particularly simple. There is a wealth of expression, often highly poetic, not wholly consistent, of feelings and imperatives of behavior, with a relative absence of definition, analysis, or demonstration. But the dearth of logical technique is partly compensated for by a richness of insight into the fundamental experiences from which alone a meaningful idea of God can be derived. If nothing is sharply defined in primitive theism, neither perhaps is anything wholly or sharply excluded, almost the entire testimony of life in its universal aspects being given a hearing—although not, for all that, without one-sided emphasis upon, or relative neglect of, certain aspects. The Old Testament, the Hymns of Ikhnaton, and the Upanishads are examples of this primitive theism.

Then come the early attempts to define, analyze, complete, and purify. Aristotle, Philo, and Sankara are outstanding representatives of this phase. As generally happens, the analyses are at first somewhat crude and one-sided. It is comparatively easy to say: God is strong rather than weak; hence in all relations cause, not effect, acting, not acted upon or "passive." He overflows into innumerable consequences and derivatives but does not himself derive anything from others or depend upon them. Secure and trustworthy "beyond shadow of turning," he is therefore eternal, not temporal; necessary, not contingent or accidental; wholly actual and in no respect potential. Further, he is spiritual, not corporeal; simple, not a compound (for then something must have put him together); absolute, or wholly independent, not relative or dependent. The method here is this: taking each pair of ultimate contraries, such as one and many, permanence and change, being and becoming, necessity and contingency, the self-sufficient or nonrelative versus the dependent or relative, the actual versus the potential, one decides in each case which member of the pair is good or admirable and then attributes it (in some supremely excellent or transcendent form) to deity, while wholly denying the contrasting term. What we propose to call "classical theism" is, in the West, the chief product of this method; in the Orient, its chief product is pantheism. The difference between the two is that theism admits the reality of plurality, potentiality, becoming—as a secondary form of existence "outside" God, in no way constitutive of his reality; whereas pantheism, properly so called, supposes that, although God includes all within himself, still, since he cannot be really complex, or mutable, such categories can only express human ignorance or illusion. Thus, common to theism and pantheism is the doctrine of the invidious nature of categorical contrasts. One pole of each contrary is regarded as more excellent than the other, so that the supremely excellent being cannot be described by the other and inferior pole. At once the dilemma results: either there is something outside of deity, so that the total real is deity-and-something-else, a whole of which deity is merely one constituent; or else the allegedly inferior pole of each categorical contrast is an illusory conception. Theism takes one horn of the dilemma; pantheism, the other. The dilemma, however, is artificial; for it is produced by the assumption that the highest form of reality is to be indicated by separating or purifying one pole of the ultimate contrasts from the other pole.

An obvious objection to this assumption is that it is at best problematic whether the "superior" pole retains its meaning under such treatment; whether "unity," for example, means anything, save as either a member or an integration of a plurality; whether "being" can conceivably be more or less than a factor in the becoming of experience and its objects, from which becoming we must have abstracted it; whether necessity is anything merely in its own terms rather than as a common element of all possibilities (that which would be absent in no possible case); whether activity and passivity are not likewise essentially correlative, passivity being the way in which an individual's activity takes account of, renders itself appropriate to, the activities of others; and whether actuality is not essentially the realization of potency and the ground of potentialities for further actualization, the implication being that an actuality so rich and complete that nothing further was possible would be a contradiction in terms.

There seems a good deal of support in experience, logic, and intellectual history for what Morris Cohen called the "Law of Polarity." According to this law, ultimate contraries are correlatives, mutually interdependent, so that nothing real can be described by the wholly one-sided assertion of simplicity, being, actuality, and the like, each in a "pure" form, devoid and independent of complexity, becoming, potentiality, and related contraries. This principle of polarity, which may be traced back through Hegel to Heraclitus and Plato, is violated by the procedure usual in some theistic and pantheistic schools. For, as explained above, these schools hold that the superior unity and actuality of deity consists in the sheer absence or "unreality" in him of multiplicity and potentiality. Thus he alone (is the implication) illustrates the superior pole of basic conceptions in their "purity," free from all mixture with the contrasting conceptions. Whereas unity, in the ordinary case, is entangled with plurality, being with becoming, in the supreme case (which for this very reason is not "unity" or "being" in altogether

*theism / pantheism*

the same sense) the superior pole is not thus entangled with its contrary. What this amounts to is that God is asserted to be an absolute exception to the Law of Polarity. It is all summed up in the Thomistic phrase, "pure actuality" (*actus purus*)—or in the more modern expression, "the absolute"—implying a being *solely* actual, or *wholly* nonrelative. This may be called the "monopolar" conception of deity—and the principle involved, that of "monopolarity."

The issue is subtle for the reason hinted at in the parentheses fifteen lines above. Theologians and philosophers did not say simply and baldly: "Of such pairs of contrasting ideas as actual-potential, simple-compound, and the rest, the first in each pair is to be accepted and the other rejected, with reference to deity." Rather, it was commonly held that no human concept whatever applies literally or "univocally" to God but at most analogically. Thus the doctrine was as follows. God is neither one nor many, actual nor potential, in any sense which we can positively conceive and understand or illustrate from our experience of things. But there is in him something "more simple than the one," more unitary than unity in the ordinary sense, and more actual than actuality as men know actuality, some mysterious transcendent analogue to these.

The reader is asked to note that there are two principles here: first, the insufficiency of human conceptions to describe God; but, second, despite this general insufficiency, a favored status for one side of the ultimate conceptual contrasts, or a special disability for the other side. The contrasts are regarded as theologically invidious. For one side there is a transcendent analogue; for the other side, not. God is more simple than the one but not more complex than the many. Now this principle of the unequal competence of contrary categories does not follow from the principle of general incompetence. Nor does

the plausible idea of the "negative theology," that human conceptions must be denied rather than affirmed of deity, cover the case. Is "actual" more negative than "potential," knowledge than ignorance (God was said to be omniscient), voluntary than involuntary (one spoke of the divine will), cause than effect (he was cause of all things)? And what classical theologian avoided preferring the first members of these pairs to the second? Thus classical theism is far from a consistent doctrine of modesty with respect to human conceptions. Certain categories are favored over their contraries. And this is true of classical pantheism also, as we shall see (in chap. iv).

Is this favoritism justified? Of course many reasons for it were given. But at the last all reasons reduce in some sense to experience. Now experience does not, we submit, exhibit the implied essential inferiority of the theologically despised contraries (except those that are themselves genuinely negative, like "ignorant" and "involuntary"!). True enough, one often condemns things or persons as defective because their complexity is inadequately integrated into "unity" or simplicity; but then, equally, one often condemns them because their unity integrates inadequate variety or complexity. The good as we know it is unity-in-variety, or variety-in-unity; if the variety overbalances, we have chaos or discord; if the unity, we have monotony or triviality. The one defect is in principle as serious as the other, for infinite triviality would be as bad as infinite chaos, since neither would have any value whatever. Again, we view persons as defective because they are too exclusively "passive" to the influences of others; but no less may persons be depreciated for their wooden "inflexibility," their mulish stubbornness, their inadaptability, unresponsiveness, or insensitivity—all faults that imply insufficiently subtle and versatile passivity toward others. The conclusion of such considerations, which could be multiplied and varied on a vast scale, is that the contrast excellent-inferior, the truly invidious contrast, has no tendency to coincide with that between such polar contrasts as one-many, cause-effect, active-passive; but, rather, this invidious contrast breaks out indifferently on both sides of the categorical polarities. There is good or superior unity and bad or inferior unity; but, equally, good complexity and bad or inferior complexity; and so it is with active-passive and the others. Good passivity we are likely to call by special names, such as sensitivity, responsiveness, adaptability, sympathy—but they all mean that other beings are influencing us. Similarly, good plurality we may call richness, or variety of functions and constituents; but mere "simplicity" is radically excluded by these terms. The greatest beauty, indeed, obtains where the parts have the maximum individuality, despite their integration into a single reality. Thus drama is a greater art than mere decorative design, where the constituents are mere colors and shapes. According to such indications, one would think that the supreme excellence must somehow be able to integrate all the complexity there is into itself as one spiritual whole. Whatever is part of any whole would be even more completely integrated into this supreme whole, which could as well be called the least as the most "simple" reality.

So we arrive at a way of characterizing deity which is not that of either classical theism or classical pantheism. According to this other way, in order to indicate the supreme case—or, if you will, the inconceivable supercase—of the general conceptions, we must equally affirm both poles of each pair of ultimate contraries. But, to avoid contradiction, we must posit two main aspects in the essence of the supreme being, to one of which the one pole supremely applies (with only the limitation of the general inadequacy of all human ideas); to the other aspect, the other pole applies (with the same qualification). What we must strictly negate of both aspects is any nonsupreme form of either pole, any mediocre or merely ordinary unity or complexity, activity or passivity, self-sufficiency or dependence. True, these mediocre forms will also be contained in the supreme reality, which by virtue of its supreme complexity will include all things; but it will not include them in its essence, in either of the two aspects spoken of, but rather in its accidents. For, according to this doctrine (which may be called the "theory of dipolarity"), God will, like other individuals, but as a supreme case or supercase, have an individual essence, and he will have accidents as well, so that what is "in *him*" need not, for all that, be in *his essence*. To have accidents, some accidents or other, will be a requirement of the essence, by virtue of the pole of contingency, relativity, passivity; but the particular accidents which God has will be strictly outside his essence. "Essence" here means "the individual in abstraction from all in him that is accidental, or without which he would still be 'himself.'" As we said above, even mediocre forms of being will be contained in the supreme being by entering into his accidents; yet (*nota bene*) even these accidents will be characterized by mediocre predicates only in their parts, never as wholes—somewhat as a building need not be small merely because it has parts that are so, or as one who has the mediocre and more or less erroneous ideas of others as his own objects of contemplation, without believing in them, need not fall into error himself. The building, the contemplation, may be exalted above all smallness or mediocrity and in this sense be "transcendent" over all things. According to this account, everything—the supreme forms of both contraries and all mediocre forms as well—may be in God, without there being mediocrity, "defects" in any usual sense, in his essential character—and not even in the character of any of his accidental whole-states! In this way, may we not find an escape from the sterile dilemma of theism-pantheism by achieving a higher synthesis of the motifs of both?

To begin to see what all this means, one must observe that both poles of the categorical contraries do admit a supreme case, or supercase. If there may be a cause of which all else is effect, why not an effect of which all else is cause, a unitary or integral resultant not just of some but of all the productive factors in reality? And, again, if we can speak of an actuality which includes or surpasses all actuality, why not also of a potentiality which embraces all potentiality? A power-to-become-actual which as such includes or surpasses all such powers? Or why not a relativity consisting in this: that a being is made what it is not simply by relationship to some but to all other entities? If the exclusion of all relations is a unique characteristic, perhaps the inclusion of all is no less unique. To put it in other words: since to reflect changes in some other things by changes in one's self is a feature of ordinary beings, such as men, to reflect changes in any and all other things can only be a feature of something indeed extraordinary and even very different in principle from ordinary things and surely not by way of inferiority! Let us illustrate. A sleeping man disturbs a waking man with his snores, causing various changes in the consciousness of the other. These changes may effect no appreciable counterchange in the snorer. Yet sleeping is not, for all that, a superior state to waking. Quite the contrary! Or an obtuse person produces effects in his neighbors which escape his own notice and which thus leave him uninfluenced, in so far "impassible."

But an alert, subtle observer, the more he is such, tends to reflect by appropriate internal changes the changes around him. No being, however, unless God, could reflect in fullest measure all changes, no matter where. It is useless to reply that "matter" contains or reflects within itself all changes. For matter, whatever it be, is not an individual. We are speaking of an individual whose change is to be coextensive with all change, whose actuality is to be coextensive with all actuality, and whose power-to-become is to include all such power.

If each category and also its contrary thus admit a supreme case or supercase (whether in univocal or merely analogous application), then it seems that either we have the idea of two supreme beings or we have the idea of one supreme being with two really distinct aspects—to one of which the supreme case of a category, such as unity, applies, and to the other, its contrasting category, e.g., diversity. Either (for example) we must discuss the possibility of a supreme cause and, as another being, a supreme effect or we must discover reason for thinking that the very same being would, in one aspect, be supreme effect and, in another, supreme cause. Plato may be thought (in the *Timaeus*) to follow the first procedure, but some scholars (e.g., Cornford) find reason, admittedly inconclusive, for attributing to him rather the second, "mythically" presented as though it were the first, for the sake of vividness and to avoid the problems of a more exact analysis. (Plato, the first great philosophical theist of the West, was too wise to attempt to give "all the answers" in his pioneering studies.) After Plato, insight into the dipolarity of supremacy more and more waned until it became almost a blind automatism to identify God with "the absolute" or with the "purely," that is, sole-

*place of analogy*

*god like a man?*

ly, actual, active, immaterial, immutable, and the like.

Perhaps we can explain the prevalence, for long centuries, of this form—which we may call the "absolutistic"—of monopolar thinking in theology and metaphysics. First, as already observed, it is simpler to accept one and reject the other of contrasting categories than to show how each, in its own appropriate fashion, applies to an aspect of the divine nature. Monopolarity is simpler than dipolarity. But also, second, the absolutistic form of monopolarity is in a sense simpler than the contrary or relativistic form as a means of characterizing deity. For such expressions as "the eternal being," or "the necessary being," or "the independent being" do suffice to designate God as distinct from all other individuals, and that equally whether (as monopolarists hold) they describe him in all his reality or (as dipolarists think) only in one aspect. For, in either case, it may be maintained that other individuals than God are in no aspect eternal (they may in a certain sense be immortal), in no aspect strictly necessary or independent. God is the only individual who can, in any aspect, be designated by mere negation of a category (e.g., contingency, or becoming). Such negation is indeed the simplest verbal way to distinguish him. The reason is that this aspect of deity is the abstract, partly negative aspect, less rich in meaning, and hence more readily stated. Temporality, even in the ordinary form, is not to be stated as a partial abstraction from eternity—eternity with something left out. No mere omission of anything will give becoming. A mixture of being and nonbeing will not do it; for the mixture itself must change or become. Becoming (on our view) is something positive and ultimate. Similarly, possibility is no mere limitation of necessity; rather, necessity is what is left when we abstract from all alternatives of possibility. Thus, whereas, to

reach the extreme supercase of the more abstract poles, simple negatives will do—for instance, "the ungenerated and undying one" can only be God—to indicate in a word or two the supercase of contingency or becoming is more difficult. We must say something like this: God is a being whose versatility of becoming is unlimited, whose potentialities of content embrace all possibilities, whose sensitive responsiveness surpasses that of all other individuals, actual or possible. There are many ways of saying it; but none are quite so simple as those which suffice for the contrary and abstract poles. The advantages of the latter are patent, given our human tendency to try to make things easy for our understanding.

Third, there are emotional and volitional attitudes which favor stressing one polarity over the other. Thus the "will to power," certain feelings natural to brutal political conditions, and a preoccupation with external manipulation of things all favor the preference of cause over effect, of activity over passivity. Again, the longing for escape from the risks and uncertainties of life, under untoward circumstances, may induce a "failure of nerve," a lazy or despairing quest for mere security, which favors stress upon categories of permanence and being rather than novelty and becoming. However natural these and related attitudes may be, they are not necessarily altogether admirable, and their validity is scarcely self-evident, as compared to contrary extremes, such as the will to respond to others sympathetically—thus giving them in a very real sense a certain power over us—or the longing for adventure and the creation of otherwise nonexistent values. Are these simply inferior attitudes? We think not. A theology which treats them as such encourages a one-sided sense of values which may very well be one of the weaknesses in our religious tradition.

Every bias intrenches itself in a maze of argumentation that looks to its supporters like clear demonstration. To believers in the monopolar tradition, a God who in any aspect changes or is passive is scarcely better than a contradiction in terms. This raises the question: "What is to be meant by 'God'?" In other words, what is the subject matter of this book? Up to a certain point, we answer this question in agreement with the monopolarists. "God" is a name for the uniquely good, admirable, great, worship-eliciting being. Worship, moreover, is not just an unusually high degree of respect or admiration; and the excellence of deity is not just an unusually high degree of merit. There is a difference in kind. God is "perfect," and between the perfect and anything as little imperfect as you please is no merely finite, but an infinite, step. The superiority of deity to all others cannot (in accordance with established word usage) be expressed by indefinite descriptions, such as "immensely good," "very powerful," or even "best" or "most powerful," but must be a superiority of principle, a definite conceptual divergence from every other being, actual or so much as possible. We may call this divergence "categorical supremacy." Now our suggestion is that there is a monopolar and a dipolar way of conceiving such supremacy.

According to either way, the divine superiority is regarded as a matter of principle, not merely of degree. Let us elucidate this. One cannot say precisely, through principles or concepts alone, wherein the "nobility" of Lincoln, in contrast to that of all other humane men, actual or possible, consisted. Or what constituted the precise "wisdom" of Confucius, in contrast to that of other sages. Or the strength of Caesar, in contrast to other strong men. With nondivine individuals, one must always affix peculiar qualifications to general adjectives in order to reach the individ-

ual's form of the attributes in question; and this qualification cannot by any conceptual means be made exact enough to distinguish just the one individual from all others, actual or possible. But, with God, all that is necessary to rule out every other individual is simply to omit qualification of the general attributes. He is good—period. He is wise—period. He is powerful—period. Thus God alone is strictly or simply holy, omniscient, omnipotent; and this means that he alone is without arbitrary or peculiar limitation upon his righteousness, wisdom, or power (we shall see that this does not mean that he has a monopoly of power, that he determines all events); he and he alone has or is the conceptual ultimates in these attributes. Thus the essential meaning of certain basic value-concepts themselves must be exhausted if we are to "praise God" properly. (Does it really alter this to urge that God is superior to and beyond all our concepts—as though "superior" or "beyond" were not also our concept? To say that God is better than just good is to say that he is more good than good, and this is a doubtfully helpful play of words.) If God is the conceptual ultimate of various attributes, without arbitrary qualification, then his merit is not a mere matter of fact, for factuality always consists in introducing some qualification upon concepts. Wherever there are gradations, we can distinguish between these only on a factual basis by comparison, as when we say that this is larger than that or better than that. We cannot say, through mere concepts, *how* large or good. (A meter is a comparison with certain objects known to exist.) Where, however, there is no question of degree or quantity, but simply of the ultimate fulfilment of a concept, no factual comparisons are needed to complete our meaning.

From the foregoing we can see why theism is a central, or *the* central, philosophical issue. For the question of a conceptually ultimate form of basic attributes, since it is no question of fact, cannot fall within the province of natural science but must be assigned to that study which is concerned with fundamental meanings or principles, to which factual distinctions are neutral— that is, to philosophy. It is a question about knowledge as such, and in principle, whether there can—or must—be an all-inclusive knowing, an actual omniscience. Again, it affects the very concept of existence whether there can or must be a being who "exists necessarily," whose existence is so utterly secure that his nonexistence expresses neither a fact nor even so much as a possibility. And only such security would be the conceptual ultimate of security. Hence it is not surprising that theologians have generally agreed to regard God as the being who, in principle, exists, "whose essence it is to exist," rather than, as with all other beings, existing merely in fact and by accident or on sufferance of other things serving as causes, conditions, or favorable (but potentially unfavorable) environment. In some sense, then, God must coincide with Being as such; for he cannot be without existence, and therefore equally existence cannot be without him, so that the very meaning of "exist" must be theistic (or else theism is itself without cognitive meaning, as positivists say it is). God is thus the great "I am," the one whose existence is the expression of his own power and none other, who self-exists—rather than is caused, or happens, to exist—and by whose power of existence all other things exist.

From the foregoing we can see why it is not possible to conceive more than one God. If several "Gods" could exist, then this "existence" must be something distinguishable from any one of them; from this it follows that they do not self-exist and do not exist by being

identical with existence. Hence, by definition, they are not "Gods." Further, if self-existence were to be attributed to several beings, then for any one of them the others would constitute a sort of environment which it did not control; for, since all would enjoy self-existence, all would be essentially equals. In such a democracy of supreme beings it is only the democracy itself that could be genuinely self-existent, dependent for existence on nothing else; and thus the members of the democracy would not self-exist after all and would not be "Gods."

This inevitability of monotheism provides (again through ambiguity) one more source of the monopolar prejudice. There can be but one deity; there are many nondivine beings: hence the divine may legitimately and innocently be contrasted to other realities as the One versus the Many. This, however, ceases to be an innocent truism if one forgets that the oneness here concerns individuals, not internal aspects or parts. The class of "deities" can have but one member and therefore is "not a class" in the usual sense. But logically quite different is the question: "May there not be a genuine class of parts or factors or states of the one divine individual?" This question must be judged independently and on its merits.

Similarly, the "necessity" of deity which follows from categorical supremacy refers to his existence as an individual and ceases to be a truism if it is construed to mean that everything in God's total reality is necessary. Categorical supremacy is a comparison (or an incomparability) of God with respect to other individuals, not of the actuality of God in contrast to what he himself might have been. That God could not fail to exist as himself is not equivalent to saying that he could in no fashion be other than he is. A man is himself through a variety of states; we must consider objectively and fairly whether a categorically supreme form of this very distinction between individuality and state is not required. Nor need we accept the customary argument that the divine existence must be self-existence, hence must be involved in the very concept of being or existence; and therefore (it is thought) being must here have priority over becoming. On the contrary, any general concept or principle will express categorical supremacy, so long as arbitrary factual limitations are unnecessary in order to distinguish the divine individual from others. Becoming is not inferior to being in this regard. Perhaps, whereas other beings are accidental products of becoming, we should think of God as qualifying becoming essentially, so that he is always certain to become, his life being a process inherent in all process, in process as such, or within which all process must occur, therefore beginningless (for his beginning would be a process independent of him and with himself as accidental product) and for the same reason endless. If several gods become, then none of them could be the essence of process but must be its products or accidents.

True, you might suppose that one God is the essence of process or becoming and another of being. But being becomes, or becoming is—being and becoming must somehow form a single reality. Modern philosophy differs from most previous philosophy by the strength of its conviction that becoming is the more inclusive category. This does not mean that it is "more real." We can abstract from the stages of becoming various real common factors and call these "being." Redness "is" in diverse stages of process. But the process includes redness and more—even if all qualities common to diverse stages are taken as represented by "redness." Process is not the mere identities of "being"; it is the identities with the differences, or rather it is the diverse states

with abstract aspects of identity. Of course we can also say, "The present state of becoming is"; but this is no more than to say, "The present state of becoming." The "is" adds nothing. Questions about being arise in present experience and for present experience. "This experience" (as involving more than just "my," or just human, experience) is the final reference to concreteness. And this experience is always something that becomes.

The old Platonic objection (objections based on Scripture will be considered later) to the conception of the deity as changing is, of course, that all change implies previous or subsequent defect, and hence the supremely excellent or "perfect" being cannot change. Once more we have an ambiguity. "God is perfect" may mean various things. In any reasonable usage it means certainly not less than this: he has no possible rival (no equal or superior) among individuals. He could not be equaled or excelled by another. But could he be excelled by himself in another state? This is a question different in principle from the other question. It must be dealt with independently.

It may seem, however, that the conceptual ultimates of value must exclude even self-excelling. How can one go beyond what is already the uttermost possible? Of course, one could not. In those attributes of righteousness, wisdom, and power, with which we have so far been dealing in our account of categorical supremacy, God cannot be excelled even by himself. But this is on the assumption that these attributes do admit an ultimate form. It seems they do; for ultimate goodness is the adequate taking into account of all actual and possible interests, each given its due; ultimate wisdom is clear, certain, adequate knowledge, whose content is all that is, as it is, the actual as actual, the possible as possible; ultimate power is power adequate to control the uni-

*thesis of divine knowledge*

verse in the best possible way. But supposing for the moment all this to be granted, it does not follow that all categorical aspects of value admit ultimate forms. Take happiness, for instance. Who indeed wants wisdom or power except as it somehow contributes to or forms part of someone's happiness? What, then, is "ultimate happiness"? The theological treatment of this question seems to have been, for the most part, weak and fallacious. If happiness is contentment, then a satisfied oyster is as close to ultimate happiness as a man can ever get. Surely that is not the clue to divine happiness. Moreover, "knowing all things" would mean being aware of vast misery and much intense suffering in the world as well as of much joy and immense quantities of pleasure. Could "absolute happiness" accrue from or even coexist with this mixed knowledge of good things and evil things? To condense a long argument, our only clues to what happiness in principle is seem to be in conflict with the idea (or pseudo-idea) of "absolute" happiness. Such a state could not be the mere absence of discontent; for, as we have seen, to take that as the measure is an insult to all animals above the very lowest. The higher animals have correspondingly many ways of being discontented! Their desires are more complex, richer, more inclusive than others, so that their satisfaction, when they are satisfied, is indeed superior; but they are no more likely to be completely satisfied. Absolute happiness must then be the logical monstrosity: complete satisfaction of all possible desires—so to speak, infinite success of the advertisers in awakening desires, and infinite success of the producers in meeting them. But there are incompatible desires and values. Until one has made this truism central to one's thought about life, one has not the beginnings of practical wisdom. "You must renounce," said Goethe; and this

is true not merely because man is a limited, imperfect creature but because values are in principle subject to incompatibilities. A sonnet and a ballad exclude each other's merits. Try to put them together in a superpoem, and here too you will meet alternatives, mutually exclusive possibilities for the superpoem. Even if the whole universe is in question, it cannot be every possible kind of harmonious whole but must be one kind, excluding others that might have been. Since beauty and richness of experience vary not only as to harmony or unification of the factors but also as to variety and depth of the contrasts among them, absolute richness must be absolute unification of absolute variety. But absolute variety could only mean all possible variety. Here again we run into contradiction: there are mutually exclusive forms of variety.

So the old argumentation that runs, "God is eternally perfect; hence, of course, he cannot improve or in any sense increase in value," implicitly denies the all-inclusive value, happiness, to the supreme individual. Must we not proceed more cautiously and define "perfection" rather as the categorically ultimate form of all attributes that admit such form (it can be shown that they are abstract aspects of value) and the categorically superior form of all attributes that do not admit an ultimate form (they are all ways of expressing the concrete value, happiness)? By categorically superior we mean such that no other individual can rival it, thus leaving open the door to self-excelling. Through such self-excelling the most excellent being changes, not into a more excellent being, but into a more excellent state of the *same* being. God acquires, say, some new quality of enjoyment. He has not changed from "himself" into another person, another individual, any more than I do when I engage in a new conversation, perhaps with an old friend. This is no doubt

*logical absurdity of some*
*"absolute" combinations*

only an analogy, but the theologian cannot dispense with analogies. The question is: "Does he play fair with them; does he give every promising analogy its due consideration?" With respect to most theologians of the past, the answer (we suspect) is: "Far from it." God has (they held) consciousness analogous to a man's consciousness but not a body analogous to a man's body. He has will analogous to will in us, understanding analogous to our understanding, but nothing analogous to sensation or emotion; above all, nothing analogous to diversity of states with an enduring personal self-identity. Thus the asserted analogy is rendered problematic in the extreme by the negation of analogies logically inseparable from it.

What would it mean to say that God could have been "himself," though with other "experiences"? Any experience, to be that of God, the supremely excellent one, must be ideally clear and accurate as to its objects; it must be "omniscient," that is, infallible and adequate experience. But adequate experience or knowledge of *this* world is different from adequate knowledge of some alternative world. If another world was or is possible, then so was or is another divine knowledge, identical with the first in adequacy to its existent objects but with diverse objects existing and divinely known as existing.

The classical idea was rather this: God knows in eternity and in a wholly necessary way whatever at any time exists to be known. But this, to some of us at least, is meaningless, for we find that the notion of an eternally fixed total content of "all time" is a contradiction in terms. Time is "objective modality" (Peirce); it unites determinate, actual, past reality with indeterminate, potential, future reality. This union is perpetually enriched by new actualities, and there can, by the very meaning of time or process, be no ulti-

mate totality of actualities for anyone to know.

It must be admitted that contemporary science seems, prima facie, to imply the ultimate inclusion of all becoming within being. The simple way to interpret relativity physics is in terms of the Minkowski manifold of events in space-time, taken as a complete totality covering all time as well as all space. For, if we reject this view in favor of the theory of process as creation of new events whose totality is itself new each time it is referred to, we seem to imply a division between the settled past of the world, down to and including the present, and the open future; and this division looks very like the unique simultaneity which the new physics declares cannot be discerned. The difficulty seems grave. The philosophy of process must, it appears, contend either that the "looks very like" represents a mistaken identification or else that there is indeed a unique simultaneity, even though our method of physical observation through signal transmissions apparently fails to reveal it. Both contentions have been defended by philosophers and scientists. The task of evaluating them will not be attempted in this book. It is one of the most important philosophical tasks of our time.

We must also recognize that most logicians still maintain, with classical theists, that all truth, even truth of fact, is timeless or tenseless. If "rain in Chicago on March 30, 1953," is found true on that day, it would, according to this view, have been true had someone asserted it in 1900 or 900. Thus from the standpoint of truth there is no such thing as an open future, or indeed as "future," save in the sense of "later than some other event." There is no such qualitative difference between futurity and pastness as that between the determinate and the indeterminate. There is really no "becoming," for every event simply is what it is in its locus in the temporal series, as "viewed" by the timeless eye of "truth." The totality of events does not become but timelessly is. But, then, neither do single events become; for, if a single event became or came into being, there would to that extent be a new totality.

It may well be that this view has a convenient simplicity for purposes of logical analysis. It seems to us another question whether it is correct. In particular, it is an error to deduce the view in question from the Law of Excluded Middle if that is taken as a principle limiting propositions to the two values, true and false. Suppose that, in 1900, "It will rain in Chicago on March 30, 1953," was false; it does not follow that "It will *not* rain in Chicago on March 30, 1953," was true. What follows is only that one and only one of the two following propositions was true: (*a*) "[As of 1900] it will not rain in Chicago on March 30, 1953," or (*b*) "The relation of rain to Chicago on March 30, 1953, is [in 1900] still indeterminate, a matter of open possibility." (At any later time one may say, "As of 1900, the relation . . . was indeterminate.") We have, then, three propositions, two of which must be false and one true in each case: "It will," "It will not," "There is [when the statement is made] no settled will or will not concerning the predicate, place, and date in question." Thus, besides will and will not, we have may-or-may-not as modes of predication, not, however, as truth values. "May-or-may-not" must itself be true or false. A creationist denies that statements of the form, "Rain in Chicago, at time *T*," are complete propositions capable of being true or false. A proposition, he will contend, unless it concerns mere abstractions like those of pure mathematics, must describe some section of process from within some section of process. A tense is always involved, explicitly or implicitly. To admit the tenseless formulation

of propositions concerning matters of fact and yet to contest the tenseless theory of truth would indeed be foolish. But can we be fairly driven to the tenseless theory of propositions (save as at most a useful logical fiction)? It rather looks as though dipolar theism must stand or fall with the answer to this question, which we shall not further discuss in the present volume.[1]

However, even granting the possibility of an eternal knowledge of "all time," we may still argue that, if another totality of temporal things was possible (as theologians have generally held and as must be held if creation is regarded as a free act), then the divine knowledge of the existence of this other totality must also have been possible. Thus one still does not escape the implication of an alternativeness of divine states. This alternativeness, however, is intelligible only in temporal terms; for it is meaningless to say that eternity might have happened to be otherwise than it is.

It should already be apparent (though it was almost wholly overlooked in the best-known theological and philosophical writings of the past) that to admit change in God need not mean renouncing his prerogative of existing necessarily. If I can be myself, whether I do this—at a certain time—or that, experience this or experience that, am in this possible state or in that possible state, then God as necessarily existing may differ from me in principle thus: his possible states are co-ordinate with the

1. For a somewhat fuller treatment see Charles Hartshorne, *Man's Vision of God and the Logic of Theism* (New York: Harper & Bros., 1941), pp. 98–105. For the views of a logician who rejects the notion of timeless truths about temporal occurrences see Felix Kaufmann's essay in *Philosophic Thought in France and the United States*, ed. M. Farber (Buffalo, 1950). For the timeless view see Daniel D. Williams' essay in *Structure, Method, and Meaning*, ed. Henlé, Kallen, and Langer (New York, 1951).

possible states of existence in general, and so, whereas some possible states of existence in general would mean that I, for example, could not exist at all, by contrast, in any state of existence in general God can and will exist in some thereto appropriate state of himself. In other terms: according to the usual or monopolar view, necessity of existence means that there is no need to adjust to others; according to the dipolar view, it means unlimited capacity to adjust successfully—that is, with preservation of individual integrity—or it means ability to adjust to *all* others, whoever and whatever they may be. Given such capacity, the individual cannot fail to exist.

Nothing of all this will be understood by one who cannot detach himself at least a little from the inveterate habit of viewing polar contrasts as invidious; who thinks, for example, that "contingent" can only mean something bad by comparison with "necessary." Necessary and contingent are not rivals in merit but complementary poles of a unity in which is all meaning and all value. Only if we distinguish carefully, contrasting, not the necessary as such with the contingent as such, but the necessarily existing individual with contingently existing individuals, have we a question of comparative merit.

If everything in God were on the same level of necessity as the universal traits of existence as such, then how would God be anything more or less than just these traits themselves; that is, how would he be a concrete individual rather than an abstract universal or complex of universals? In monopolar terms an intelligible answer cannot, we think, be given to this question. Contingent facts are knowable not through concepts alone but always, in part at least, through direct intuitions. Moreover, only God himself can, with anything remotely like adequacy, intuit a whole-accident, a particular contingent

state, of the divine life. Here is the place for the negative theology. Here we must confess our incurable ignorance. Indeed, we cannot imagine how the actual contingent world looks to God, who sees it against the background of an immense if not an infinite past, and with no inhibitions of prejudice or apathy to dilute for his apprehension its wealth of qualities of life and feeling and sensation.

If the traditional view of God as exclusively and in all respects necessary violates the Law of Polarity, so does the opposite extreme, the view of him as exclusively contingent, implying that his very existence is a mere accident. This view (which is classical monopolarity in reverse) is somewhat favored by the prestige of empirical science in our age. Science concerns itself with facts and sees necessities only in mathematics or logic, viewing these as mere tools for the investigation of facts. It is plain that no mere fact could make anything exist necessarily. We mean by a "fact" something whose denial is conceivable though false; that is, a fact is the realization of a possibility. But absolute security or necessity of existence means an existence which is not to be contrasted to any contrary possibility; it means existence as a matter of principle and meaning, not merely of fact. Now the question, "Do first principles and meanings involve the existence of any being (who thus exists necessarily), or do they not?" is a question as to the content of the first principles or ultimate categories themselves. It is a purely philosophical question. For philosophy is the theory of first principles or ultimate categories. Unless, then, we know the necessary existence and essential nature of God, or his necessary nonexistence (for a merely factual nonexistence is meaningless here), we do not know what our fundamental concepts mean. Thus the solution of basic philosophical questions and of basic theological ones cannot be separated.

As another illustration of this, take omniscience. Could any being as a mere matter of fact know absolutely all there is? Such a conceptual ultimate could not just happen. Each of us happens to know certain things and happens not to know certain others. It depends on chance and circumstance, on mere facts, how our knowledge and ignorance are distributed. But could the ignorance, the cognitive maladjustment and inadequacy, simply by chance and circumstance reach zero? That we are partly ignorant and that we exist by chance and upon sufferance of favorable circumstances—are these not two aspects of the same limitation or deficiency? Our knowledge is restricted because it is not a pure matter of principle that we know but of fact; and facts may be favorable or unfavorable to knowledge of this or that given item. That all the facts should ever (for any factually existing knower) be favorable with respect to all the objects of knowledge seems infinitely unlikely in such a strict sense as to be downright impossible. Only a being who knows things on principle, without contrary possibility, could, it seems, be omniscient.

Similar remarks may be made about ultimate goodness or holiness or power. One conclusion from these considerations is that a merely "empirical theology" is a contradiction in terms. The study of mere facts, as such, yields only facts, more or less universal or particular; but God as a mere fact, however important or comprehensive or basic, is God as not God. Another consequence is that the distinction between a priori and a posteriori proof for God is invalid. The proofs are all a priori; proofs from principles or categories, not from facts; proofs from necessities, not from contingencies.

Traditional proofs were really of this a priori character, despite their seeming to rest upon some fact. The famous proof for an unmoved mover set out from a principle that actuality is (unconditionally) "prior to potentiality," that is, to any mode of reality other than actuality. In that case there are only the alternatives: (1) there is nothing, not even potentiality; or (2) there is an actuality which is not an actualization (of antecedent potentiality), which contains in itself the equivalent or superior of all that ever could be actualized, and from which all actualization (if such there be) derives. Now the first alternative is stark nonsense. If nothing is either actual or possible, then there is no thought and no object of thought and no meaning and no truth. That this is so plainly could not be true. For truth itself must be either actual or possible. So we are left with the second alternative, which posits the unmoved mover; and we reach this result without benefit of any particular facts, even the fact of motion.

The flaw in this proof is that both the premise and the conclusion embody the monopolar prejudice. Prior to both potentiality and actuality, according to the Law of Polarity, is the tension between them; their union in a process which is neither simply actual nor simply potential. In this process ever-new states of actuality, each with its own distinctive possibilities for further actualization, are reached. In accordance with this view, God is the union of supreme actuality and supreme potentiality, supreme activity and supreme passivity, supreme being and supreme becoming, the most strictly absolute and the most universally relative of all entities, actual or possible. We believe the cosmological proof can be reconstructed accordingly. (See our discussion of Aristotle in chap. ii.)

But is not such double predication contradictory? The answer is that there is no law of logic against attributing contrasting predicates to the same individual, provided they apply to diverse

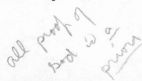

aspects of this individual. Thus a man may be "simple" in his fundamental intention but "complex" in the details of his actions and perceptions. Of course, if there be no diversity of aspects in deity—because of his oft-vaunted "simplicity"—then indeed he cannot be both absolute and relative. But the assumption of sheer simplicity is itself a monopolar one, and so it would beg the question to object to the dipolar view on this ground. In that aspect of deity to which "One" exclusively applies, of course, there is not a diversity of factors; but in the aspect to which "Many" applies, there is.

It may be asked if the dipolar view, which puts the ultimate contrasts within God, must not do the same with the contraries good and evil. The answer is that all contrasts, according to dipolarity, do fall within God (since, in one aspect of his reality, he is the most complex and inclusive of all beings), but each contrast is in God in its own appropriate way. Thus, for instance, only really ultimate or categorical contrasts can be used to describe the fixed character of God, that which is essential to his very existence or individuality. Now evil, in the sense of wickedness, is not a universal category. For example, the animals are incapable of it, because of their unconsciousness of principles. And God is incapable of it, as we shall see (e.g., in our "Comment" on al-Ghazzali). Thus wickedness is not in the divine "character" at all. True, the contrast between God's goodness and the wickedness of various individuals does fall within God (whose total reality is more than his mere character or essential individuality) but not in such fashion that he could be called wicked, even in his particular states. A round stone may be within a square building —to use a crude analogy. Evil in the sense of suffering, however, is indeed, we believe, a category. And, if so, the dipolar view must hold not only that

God contains suffering but that he suffers and that it is in his character to suffer, in accordance with the suffering in the world. Here the Christian idea of a suffering deity—symbolized by the Cross, together with the doctrine of the Incarnation—achieves technical metaphysical expression. In regard to this problem, Berdyaev is perhaps the most illuminating of all theologians or philosophers, though Schelling, Fechner, Whitehead, and many others could be mentioned here. (See also our "Comment" on von Hügel in chap. iii.)

## B. A CLASSIFICATION OF THEISTIC DOCTRINES

The dipolar view has two main consequences. First, it implies that to contrast God merely as the "eternal" with the world as "temporal" is question-begging. For we have to ask whether he has not both an eternal and a temporal aspect. (True, divine "time," like divine predicates in general, must be categorically supreme.) But, second, if God be conceived as in one aspect temporal, relative as well as absolute, "matter" as well as "form," there may be no longer any good reason to deny, but good reason to affirm, that through this relative, temporal, material aspect deity includes the world. Thus the motif of pantheism may, in a somewhat novel fashion, be given its due. The distinction from the classical form of pantheism remains; for the view is that in the absolute aspect of his dipolar nature the deity is not the actual world and does not even include it.

In addition to the questions just discussed concerning the relations of God to eternity, to time, and to the world or universe, there are two others that we wish to make crucial for our classification of types of theism. These are: "Is God conscious?" and "Does he know the universe? Is he omniscient?" One might query the exactitude of the terms used in these questions. Is the term "know" meant literally, it may be asked, or is it analogical rather than univocal? Must we not distinguish between "unconscious" and "superconscious," between what is below and what is above or beyond consciousness or knowledge? For the moment, let it be said simply that knowledge is meant in the sense appropriate to rigorously or categorically supreme excellence (this is our reply to the inevitable charge of anthropomorphism) and that such expressions as "beyond consciousness" are rather eulogistic or emotional than logical or cognitive. Since God is, by definition, categorically supreme, almost no one denies anything to his essential nature, save with the contention that he is better off without it. Similar remarks apply to the contention that, while God does not literally contain the universe, he does something much better, viz., enjoys a "more eminent" analogue of all its values, since he is cause of all its being and goodness, or since he is pure underived being and good. We are not asking, for the moment, "Does he do something better than this or that?" but only "Does he do this or that?" A girl who admits that her fiancé is not a professor is not thereby debarred from subsequently demonstrating that he is something even better (if this be possible), say, a great statesman.

Furthermore, a main purpose of this book is to present evidence to show that, when the questions above formulated are answered with any but one set of answers, the result is absurdity, and this whether there be "something better" to consider or no. There is also evidence that the "best" form of consciousness, or of knowing or inclusiveness, becomes conceivable only when the correct combination of them, along with the right relation to time, has been found. As this has seldom happened, it is not surprising that so many attempts have been made to give meaning to such expressions as "beyond consciousness" (or "beyond personality") or to the notion of a more eminent way of having or containing all things than literally having or containing them. Certainly the best consciousness or personality is beyond our mere human consciousness or personality in quality. But that is already said by affirming its "best" status, its unique excellence, thus implying that any other kind of consciousness must be inferior. Why affirm the uniqueness twice over, and that not as a mere matter of rhetorical emphasis but as an alleged doctrinal distinction? Similarly, if God is all-inclusive, of course this inclusiveness is not just ordinary inclusiveness, say, that of a man in relation to his cells, merely stretched to cover the universe. Most criticisms of "pantheism"—and many formulations by its defenders—are too crude on such matters to have much value.

The affirmative answers to our five questions—Is God eternal? Is he temporal? Is he conscious? Does he know the world? Does he include the world? —can be symbolized by the following letters:

E    Eternal—in some (or, if T is omitted, in all) aspects of his reality devoid of change, whether as birth, death, increase, or decrease

T    Temporal—in some (or, if E is omitted, in all) aspects capable of change, at least in the form of increase of some kind

C    Conscious, self-aware

K    Knowing the world or universe, omniscient

W    World-inclusive, having all things as constituents

If all the five factors are asserted together, ETCKW, they define the doctrine we call "panentheism" (also "surrelativism"). The joint affirmation of T and E (if consistently carried through) insures, as will we hope become apparent sooner or later to the reader, the conformity of a doctrine with the prin-

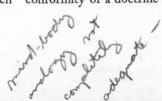

ciple of polarity discussed above. This means that there will be no favoritism as between ultimate contraries. (When E and T are thus both affirmed, it is to be understood that each is meant to apply to a different aspect of the divine being, so that no formal contradiction results.) By omission of one or more of the five factors, such omission being taken as implying denial, one can define various views which, by comparison with panentheism, may be termed "truncated" doctrines. Some of these combinations, however, may be dismissed as too obviously without plausible meaning. Thus it seems unmeaning to suppose that a being with full knowledge of all the universe will lack self-awareness or consciousness, and hence we omit combinations like EKW or EK, which affirm knowledge but not consciousness. Or, again, assuming that any being with (supreme) self-awareness will know what it includes, we need not consider such combinations as ETCW, which imply divine consciousness of a world-including self, without knowledge of the world which is included. Finally, it seems evident that every being has some status with respect to time as well as eternity, in that it must be one of the following: (1) in all aspects eternal; (2) in all aspects noneternal or temporal; (3) in some aspects the one and in some aspects the other. Accordingly, every admissible combination must begin with E or with T or with ET, and there can be no such truncated combinations as CWK, which would be silent as to temporal status.

Omitting a few remaining combinations as of little apparent importance, historical or otherwise, and in two cases admitting attenuated forms of one of the five factors—indicated by parentheses—we have as significant for our purposes the following:

| | |
|---|---|
| ETCKW | The Supreme as Eternal-Temporal Consciousness, Knowing and including the World. Panentheism. *Plato*, Sri Jiva, Schelling, Fechner, Whitehead, Iqbal, Radhakrishnan |
| EC | The Supreme as Eternal Consciousness, not knowing or including the world. *Aristotelian* theism |
| ECK | The Supreme as Eternal Consciousness, Knowing but not including the world. Classical theism. *Philo*, Augustine, Anselm, al-Ghazzali, Aquinas, Leibniz |
| E | The Supreme as the Eternal beyond consciousness and knowledge. Emanationism. *Plotinus* |
| ECKW | The Supreme as Eternal Consciousness, Knowing and including the World (so far as "real"). Classical pantheism. *Sankara*, Spinoza, Royce |
| ETCK | The Supreme as Eternal-Temporal Consciousness, Knowing but not including the world. Temporalistic theism. *Socinus*, Lequier |
| ETCK(W) | The Supreme as Eternal-Temporal Consciousness, partly exclusive of the World. Limited panentheism. *James*, Ehrenfels, Brightman |
| T(C)(K) | The Supreme as wholly Temporal or emerging Consciousness. *Alexander*, Ames, Cattell |
| T | The Supreme as Temporal and nonconscious: Wieman |

The above table, granted its (we hope) not grossly arbitrary choice of initial representatives or founders of the eight doctrines, follows a chronological order. (In our sequence of chapters we follow this order, save that we devote a separate chapter to modern panentheism and a separate main division—Part Three—to skeptics. Otherwise, both within chapters and in the succession of chapters, the order is chronological.) Our classification exhibits the history of theistic speculations as primarily a long experiment in omission. Leave out all characters save eternity and consciousness, and you have Aristotle's self-inclosed deity, whose entire being consists in "thinking of thinking," awareness concerned only with itself. Leave out temporality and world inclusiveness, and you have the standard doctrine of medieval and early modern theology, Jewish, Mohammedan, and Christian, which therefore seems eminently to deserve the title, "classical theism." Leave out all save eternality alone, and you have the One of Plotinus. Omit only the factor of temporality, and you have the God-totality, conscious and cognitive, of Spinoza, and (less equivocally affirmed) of Royce. Omit or attenuate the factor of world inclusiveness, and you have Brightman's temporalization of classical theism. Omit eternity, and you have the emergent theism of Alexander and others. Omit all but temporality, and you have Wieman's view of God as the mysterious creativity in life which, though not aware of self or world, produces ever-new values.

What is the lesson of this vast intellectual experiment? We hold that it is that none of the omissions succeed, that the "truncated" views really are mutilations, and that thought has been forced back, more and more imperatively, to the integral panentheistic conception adumbrated by Plato. We hold that eternity in total abstraction from time or becoming (EC, ECK, ECKW) is abstract—as why should it not be?—and deficient, for all that is said to the contrary, in fulness of actuality. It seems clear that eternity, in abstraction from consciousness and knowledge and from the actual universe (the One of Plotinus), is deficient in actuality (E). It is mere form without content, unity which unifies nothing—save unity itself. But, again, as to Aristotle's theism (EC), we must note that self-awareness is empty of content unless the self has some other mode of awareness than its awareness of its awareness of its awareness—of what? Every subject, even and especial-

ly the supreme subject, must have objects which are other than just itself. Finally, and least often realized concerning classical theism (ECK), it is to be observed that knowledge is deficient unless it fully and literally contains its objects. ECK is the paradox of a knowledge whose objects change, though the knowledge-of-these-objects does not change, and which is wholly necessary, though the objects are not. Thus we have a complex—knowledge-of-X—which is immutable, though a constituent of this complex is mutable, a complex which is wholly without contingency, though some of its constituents are contingent (could have been otherwise). To deny the applicability of this reasoning is to imply that what there is in the divine is only "knowledge of" rather than "knowledge of X." When we are told that it is the world that has relation to God, rather than God to the world, we are in effect informed that, while X is known by God, God does not know X, which seems senseless. It is useless to say that God knows directly his own essence and that, this being the cause of all, knowledge of it imparts knowledge of X. If God knows that by knowing his essence he knows X, then he knows X, and there we have the complex in question. If not, he is ignorant of something known to classical theists. Besides, we are told that God could conceivably have "decided" not to cause X. But, then, the essence must be neutral, as between the existence and nonexistence of X. For God cannot have been free to decide against something implicated in his very essence. If, then, the existence of X is not implicated in the essence, knowledge of the essence will not imply knowledge of that existence. ECK is thus even more manifestly inconsistent than EC.

There seem two sources for the common refusal to admit this. One is a failure to distinguish the truism that the thing known must be other than the knowing from the quite different stipulation that the known must be outside the knowing. A constituent of a whole is certainly other than the whole, yet obviously not outside it! But, we shall perhaps be told, the object must not only be other than—it must also be independent of—the knowledge. Suppose this too be granted, why may not parts be independent of the whole containing them? Must every whole be "organic" with respect to all its constituents? Most philosophers, at least, would reject such an extreme view. But then they must not argue, "independent of, therefore outside, the knowledge."

The second source of the denial that divine knowledge can literally include the world within itself is an unconscious piece of anthropomorphism. The very people who insist that divine knowledge is radically different from human knowledge, so that the term "know" is here analogical rather than univocal, are often the ones who argue (in effect) as follows: We as knowers do not literally include the known; therefore, God does not. This is to forget that human so-called "knowledge" of any concrete actuality is mostly ignorance and for the rest mostly guesswork and probability. In the highest sense of "knowledge," namely, direct, infallible, concrete, clearly conscious apprehension, we human subjects can scarcely be said to have any knowledge. Granted that we do not "include" mountains when we "know" them, unless in some very attenuated sense of include, equally we do not know mountains, except in a very attenuated sense of "know," by comparison with what the word means when we say that God knows mountains. What, then, is to demonstrate that the two attenuations are not identical? Furthermore, wherever our knowledge achieves something like infallibility, it also becomes evident that it includes the known within itself. Thus we know, in a sense infallibly, the aches and pains

we directly feel. Do we not also include these feelings? Are they not features of our consciousness at the moment?

Suppose that the divine knowing is indeed a self-inclosed reality, with the known entities outside it; we then have a total reality, God-and-World, which is more inclusive than either, and of which God is one constituent and World the other. If it is held an impiety that God have constituents, what about the more obvious impiety that he should be a mere constituent? The entire question alters its meaning according as one includes or omits the temporal factors, E or T. A purely eternal deity can have no constituents. Granted. Also, to have constituents in just the way in which purely temporal ("corruptible") beings have them is certainly unworthy of deity. But to have constituents in the manner appropriate to a being with an eternal aspect, but for the rest (in categorically supreme fashion) temporal, is something that neither classical theism nor classical pantheism, nor any other commonly held traditional doctrine, has adequately considered.

If the supreme lacks awareness of the world (EC, E), then he is not supreme in awareness. Besides, the adequate awareness-of-X is logically X plus something, and thus there is no sense to the notion of something superior to all possible awareness. But, on the other hand, if the supreme has awareness of the world, then, as we have seen, it cannot be without the contingency and change of the latter.

The only way, we suggest, consistently to relate the supreme to awareness and to the world is to admit a temporal aspect of deity. At once the foregoing difficulties vanish. For the temporal aspect of deity can very well include the temporal world, since a changing whole can certainly contain changing elements, and since the novel can certainly be known by knowledge similarly novel, or the contingent by knowledge like-

*unique nature of the knowledge of god — knowledge means direct feeling* wise contingent. There will then be nothing paradoxically superior to the supreme, no entirety of reality other than the supreme itself, no more concrete object of reference from which deity is abstracted. Rather deity will be the integrated totality, the ultimate concrete from which all abstract features are taken.

The beauty of this position is that, if a changing reality can include a changing world, it can equally well include an unchanging factor. For a whole, in order to change, has no need of altering all its components; indeed, it need not "alter" any, since it will suffice to acquire new components. There is obviously change in the passage from $abc$ to $abcd$. Yet no component has altered, unless the absence of $d$ be called a component—a strained use of language at best.

Precisely the same applies if, instead of change in components, we speak of contingency and necessity. If a whole is necessary, all its parts or members must be. But if a whole is accidental, not all its parts need be so. Suppose, in $Abcd$, $A$ has being by necessity, and $b, c, d$ are contingent items of existence. It will then be true that $Abcd$ exists contingently. For instance, suppose $A$ is the generic form "adequately knowing whatever exists, as existent, and whatever is merely possible as merely possible," and suppose that $b$ means "a certain thing adequately known as existent and as having a certain accidental character," and that $c$ means "something else known as having another accidental character." $A$ is then a necessary law of the divine knowing, with contingent application to each particular case, what is not contingent being only that there are some such applications or other.

The logical difficulties of ECK are not, contrary to common opinion, balanced by adequate religious values. A deity who cannot in any sense change or have contingent properties is a being for whom whatever happens in the contingent world is literally a matter of indifference. Such a being is totally "impassible" toward all things, utterly insensitive and unresponsive. This is the exact denial that "God is love." It means that nothing we can possibly do, enjoy, or suffer can in any way whatever contribute a satisfaction or value to the divine life greater or different from what this life would have possessed had we never existed or had our fortunes been radically other than they are. Strange that for so many centuries it was held legitimate to call such a deity a God of love, or purpose, or knowledge! What we really have is the idea of sheer power, sheer causation, by something wholly neutral as to what, if anything, may be its effects. The naked worship of power is with wonderful exactitude, although unwittingly, enshrined in this doctrine. Is it wholly an accident that a hierarchical view of ecclesiastical polity is historically connected therewith?

E, or the doctrine of Plotinus, is the paradox of a Something superior to all else but totally without internal contrast or diversity, even, apparently, such as is implied in self-awareness. However, as we shall see, Plotinus is wiser than he knows, and he almost gives us the two-aspect doctrine, ETCKW, but with a brave attempt to make it look like a one-aspect doctrine. After Plotinus, the T and W factors are lost for a thousand years. But indirectly these factors continue to qualify the dominant conception. For example, Jesus is a temporal being; yet, it was said, Jesus is God. Since identity is a transitive relation, it seems that God is a temporal being after all. (If it is but one of the "two natures" which is God, then God is a part of a man; or, if Jesus is not a man, but a God-man, then both "God" and "man" are constituents of a whole which is more than either and which, in one aspect, is temporal.)

The same sort of thing happened in India and China. The supreme—Brahma, Nirvana, Tao—is often described as timeless and wholly absolute; but, if the empty abstractness of the supreme so conceived is unsatisfying, then Vishnu or the Deified Buddha or an Avatar will serve better. Is it not time to face the issue at its center: Why not put concreteness, which means time as well as eternity, passivity as well as activity, sensitivity as well as power, into our concept of the supreme? (In what sense, if any, deity has been peculiarly "incarnate" in a man is a question that may then be discussed on its merits instead of being given a spurious meaning by assigning it the role of mitigating initial blunders in our concept of deity.)

Now we come to views which admit the T factor. They may do this either in combination with E or without it. In the latter case, the use of the word "God" is of dubious propriety. Only in mythology, not in any philosophy or systematic theology, can one speak of a merely created deity, a deity with no underived being whatever. Even apart from the terminological question, the basic point is that only a deity whose existence or essential individuality is eternal can have much philosophic relevance. The relevance lies just in the way in which deity alone among individuals is able to unite time and eternity, necessity and contingency, actuality and potency, and thus to explain the categories by exhibiting them as abstractions from its own actuality. But this function is equally jeopardized by the omission either of E or of T from the union ET.

Wittingly or unwittingly, all views other than ETCKW sacrifice categoriality. EC, ECK, E, and ECKW make the category of temporality (and with it contingency, relativity, diversity, complexity) extrinsic to God, inexpressible in terms of the divine nature. EC, in addition, makes knowledge, as having

contingent objects, similarly inexpressible, and (as we have seen) only by inconsistency does ECK, or classical theism, appear to escape this limitation. E makes even self-awareness inexpressible from the standpoint of deity. Thus ETCKW is the truly categorial conception of the supreme, the conception that reduces the categories to their proper status as essentially expressions of deity. Then anything you please is either God as knowing the world, or the world as known by God, or some aspect of these; but, since the subject includes its object, the form of the object is a form of the subject, on its "content" side. To describe the knowing-of-all-things is to describe all things known as well; so any category refers either to an aspect or to a member of the divine reality. Thus to be "actual" now is to be enjoyed by deity now (implying that there is a diversity of *now*'s in God); to be "possible" now is to be something God may come to enjoy. The divine is thus not pure actuality but the standard or definitive actuality, and by the same token he is the standard or definitive potentiality. The theory of pure actuality makes God neither the definitive actuality nor the definitive potentiality. For it implies that you cannot say what is actual and what is merely potential by saying what God is, because his actuality (according to the theory) has no alternatives and is wholly neutral as regards alternative possibilities. Thus the omniscient being cannot function, as he logically ought to, as the measure of all things, the actual as actual, the possible as possible. For he is not differential as between actualized and non-actualized potentialities in the world. This incurable neutrality, which is metaphysical incompetence, is the price of monopolarity. Pantheists seek to evade the problem by denying that there is a real distinction between actual and possible (even Royce finally did this). They thus make deity differential (in Pickwickian fashion) by abolishing all intelligible difference. Against all these difficulties, the T factor is our safeguard. It makes the W factor, the pantheistic motif, innocuous and thus opens the door of escape from the paradoxes of a supreme reality which yet cannot intelligibly contain the totality of the actual.

Since the W factor, as rendered innocuous by the T factor, is radically different in its implications from the W factor as otherwise interpreted, to call both ECKW and ETCKW by the one term "pantheism" is to open the door to numerous fallacies of ambiguity. ETCKW has been called, by several writers (who have not always clearly defined their view), "panentheism," and this term seems in every respect appropriate. God is not just the all of (other) things; but yet all other things are literally in him. He is not just the whole of ordinary individuals, since he has unity of experience, and all other individuals are objects of this experience, which is no mere sum of its objects; moreover, his identifying "personality traits" are entirely independent of any set of ordinary actual individuals whatever. To be himself he does not need *this* universe, but only *a* universe, and only contingently does he even contain this particular actual universe. The mere essence of God contains no universe. We are truly "outside" the divine essence, though inside God.

It will no doubt strike some as strange that, in listing the five factors that distinguish the various ideas of God, nothing is said as to "will" or "freedom" in God or as to "personality," and also nothing as to "power," "creation," or "goodness." Surely, it may be thought, these are vital for religion, and their omission a serious oversight. In brief, our defense is that the correct interrelation of our five factors will constitute a fairly adequate definition of divine will, freedom, personality, power, good-

ness; whereas, without these five factors, the traditional terms will have no sharp conceptual significance but will be merely honorific or emotional, mere epithets. Classical theists have often spoken of divine personality, or divine persons (as in the Trinity), and have derided the pantheists because of their "impersonal" deity; but what personality might be if entirely devoid of temporal process, potentiality, and passivity, they have as little told us as the pantheists. The same holds for "will" and "freedom." In the sheerly eternal, what is eternally is, and there is no meaning to the question, "What might it have been?" Hence, if God's will is that of a sheerly eternal being, it is meaningless to ask, "What might his volition have been (other than the actual one to create the world)?" And hence to speak of freedom, alternatives of possible volition, is here out of place. On the other hand, if God is an eternal-temporal being, eternal in essential individuality, temporal in the flux of his acts and experiences, if he is conscious and knows all things, how can he fail to be also a volitional personality? What is awareness, apart from all volitional response? Could one be aware, in the fullest degree, of the joys and sorrows of others and not share these sufficiently to wish to further the one and hinder the other? We think that only a verbal psychology could seem to justify such an abstraction of awareness from evaluation and response. Awareness is essentially a response, an adaptation to others. And what is "personality" but an enduring individual character or essence in a flux of such responses? As such is it known to psychology and common experience. What has made certain ideas of God impersonal has been the denial of alternativeness, of the distinction between character and act such that, of two mutually incompatible possible acts, either one would express the same individual or personal character. Now time is the order of alternativeness—the order which relates real and merely potential acts. Thus T in our symbolism might perhaps as well have been P, for potentiality. It is the denial of potentiality to deity, or the denial of temporality, that makes any genuine conception of divine personality impossible. (In thus equating nontemporal with nonpotential, we are in agreement with the great tradition of Western theism, which has almost always either denied both or affirmed both of deity and has assumed their equivalence.)

It is often thought that any two persons, even God and a man, must each be outside the other. But this seems a too narrow and ungeneralized use of anthropomorphic analogy. Human persons are indeed outside each other in space, since each is but a part of the whole actuality. But the whole of actuality, as content of the experience of one person, will be "outside" the other persons only as a whole is—partly—outside its parts (Fechner); they, however, will certainly not be outside it! Mutual externality here is not required. Mutual action and reaction, on the other hand, are indeed required. The whole-person and part-person interact. If they did not, then, since being is always (in one aspect) power, any part which, in relation to the whole, had no power to act but was merely passive would, in this relation, have no being, and hence, contradictorily, would not be a part. To have a self-deciding part is not to decide that part but rather to enjoy or suffer its self-decision. As Fechner has said, not all volitions in a mind need be *by* that mind. The sense in which evil is in God is thus explained. God suffers our evil acts, but his volition is always of good. It can be claimed that this does not limit the perfection of the divine power but makes it the ideal case of what all power essentially is—power over powers, partial determining of the finally self-determined actuality of others, participa-

tion in their self-creation (Whitehead). According to many of the greatest philosophers, experiences are the very actuality of all things, and they are always in one aspect *self*-created. No mere manipulation of pre-existent things can make a single new experience, nor can anything not the subject of that experience make it to be what it is. It must make, enact, itself.

What, then, becomes of the famous idea of *creation ex nihilo?* Whereas, it is commonly said, ordinary creative action presupposes "matter," divine creation does not. Admittedly, ordinary cases of creative power lack, in principle, something reserved for the categorically supreme case. But, still, "out of nothing" is a dubious way of formulating this categorically privileged way of creating. Does God create an adult out of nothing or out of a child? The creative functioning of deity involved in the production of Beethoven's music certainly did not treat as nothing the free self-decisions of Beethoven's predecessors in composition. Only in connection with an absolute first moment of time has even divine creation no antecedent data or conditions. (The contrary views of Augustine and Aquinas will be considered in chap. iii.)

Our classification of doctrines stresses consciousness and knowledge but not volition and power. There is an advantage in this. For only a conscious being with complete knowledge, or one "to whom all hearts are open," can be trusted to use power in ways appropriate to the state of these hearts. This is the goodness of God. (See our "Comment" on al-Ghazzali in chap. iii.)

It should be granted that any classification of doctrines is somewhat arbitrary and that other classifications remain not only possible but for some purposes superior. But there seems to be a real need to counteract the venerable tendency to put power or causality or eternity uppermost in theological speculation, leaving divine consciousness, awareness, and responsiveness to take their chances, often very poor chances at that. To impute responsiveness or love or even awareness or volition to a nontemporal being has always seemed at best a pious fiction. Words like "knowledge" or "personality" or "will" come cheaply enough; the task is to find a logical structure in our thinking about deity that makes room for the ideas thus labeled.

Since the monopolar doctrine assimilates the contrast between God and other individuals to that between being and becoming (or cause and effect, or simplicity and composition), one may say that in this doctrine the category of being is virtually the object of worship, and the contrary pole is degraded. So we may speak of "ontolatry," worship of being, or similarly "etiolatry," worship of cause. Now the remedy for these diseases is not to substitute the contrary pole, worshiping becoming and effect, and degrading being and cause. The remedy is to recognize that both poles under each category apply in one way to God and in another to other individuals. God is neither being as contrasted to becoming nor becoming as contrasted to being; but categorically supreme becoming in which there is a factor of categorically supreme being, as contrasted to inferior becoming, in which there is inferior being. Both poles have two levels, analogically but not simply comparable. The divine becoming is no more divine than the divine being; but both are incomparable (except analogically) to other being or becoming. For the line of categorical supremacy must always be crossed.

The divine becoming is more ultimate than the divine being only in the simple sense of being more inclusive, of being concrete while the other is abstract. So we maintain that our charges of cause-worship or being-worship or

power-worship cannot be countered by the simple expedient of accusing us of the contrary superstition, effect-worship, process-worship. We worship supreme-being-in-supreme-becoming, supreme-cause-in-supreme-effect; that is, we worship the supreme, not any polar category. If it be said that, after all, supreme-inferior is a polarity, we reply that even here we worship the supreme-as-containing-the-inferior and deriving enrichment from this containing. Even inferior being-becoming is not degraded in this doctrine but glorified by the recognition of its contribution to God himself. Nothing is debased to the status of irrelevance, whereas in the monopolar procedure all becoming and all effects are mere impertinences, since being just as being is held to have all value. God should least of all require the kind of praise that makes the better seem still better by saying that the inferior is even less than inferior, is nothing, merely evil, or wholly negligible. But that is the kind of praise he has generally received! We thus read our lack of imagination, or of generosity, or simply of love, into God himself.

Some of our selections present proofs or arguments for the reality of God. All such arguments amount to this: that the proposition, "There is a supremely excellent being, worthy of worship," expresses fundamental or categorical aspects of experience and thought, while the denial of this proposition contradicts such aspects. There can be as many arguments for God as one can distinguish fundamental aspects of experience and thought, and it seems unlikely that there is but one possible way of making such distinctions, or one fixed number of resulting arguments. The list we propose is as follows: there are three arguments corresponding, respectively, to aesthetics, ethics, and theory of knowledge, or beauty, goodness, and truth, and three arguments corresponding, respectively, to the ideas of

cosmic order, cosmic contingency (or change), and, finally, the very idea of God, or supremely excellent being, himself. In the order named, the six arguments are: the aesthetic argument, the ethical argument, the epistemological ("idealistic") argument, the design argument, the cosmological argument, and the ontological argument. All of these are found in some form from fairly early times but are usually so stated that they stand or fall by the tenability of classical theism, classical pantheism, or Aristotelian theism. Only in rather recent times have the arguments begun to shake off allegiance to one or other of these doctrines as their predestined conclusion. Since these doctrines are paradoxical, and any argument, however cogent, can be denied if one is willing to perpetrate paradox (contradiction), it is no wonder that the usual statements of arguments for God have been found less and less convincing. At best these statements pose a dilemma: accept the paradoxes of the conclusion of the argument or the paradoxes of the atheistic denial of the conclusion.

The cosmological argument, blended with the argument from order, seems to appear first in Plato (*Laws* x). Augustine gave a version, hardly a perspicuous or satisfactory one, of the argument from truth, which was almost correctly formulated by Royce in his *Conception of God*. Anselm, we believe, will yet be granted the glory of having achieved a nearly correct version (presented as supplement to an incorrect one which is all that most commentators seem to have noticed) of one step in the ontological argument. Plotinus seems sometimes to be groping toward an aesthetic argument (impeded by his failure to appreciate variety or contrast as no less essential to beauty than unity), but the possibilities of this form have not yet been properly evaluated. Kant offered an ethical argument, limited severely by his assumption of the absolute independence of deity, from which it followed that the union of righteousness and happiness which is indeed the "supreme good" to be served by our actions must be man's rather than God's, so that God becomes the means to our ethico-hedonic self-realization, instead of our self-realization being seen (Whitehead) as our enjoyment of the privilege of contributing to the self-realization of deity, which alone can possess the literal *summum bonum*.

Every one of these arguments for theism can, we believe, be given a more exact and perspicuous form than has hitherto been given them. But this is a subject for another occasion.

The reader is now invited to see how far the analysis presented in this introduction illuminates the intellectual history presented in samples through the following pages. It may be that he will find another interpretation more convincing. If so, good luck to him!

# PART ONE

## Classical Views

# Chapter I: *Ancient or Quasi-Panentheism*
## *An Enunciation of Themes*

## IKHNATON (*ca.* 1375–58 B.C.)

More than three thousand years ago there appeared "the first monotheist," Ikhnaton, pharaoh of Egypt. He or his supporters composed a number of astonishingly eloquent hymns of praise to the sun-god, sole deity and creator of all things. It is easy to dismiss this deification of the sun as naïve. But since, on the one hand, the use of light as symbol of divinity is continuous practice in theological history, and since, on the other, the ancient Egyptian had no definite knowledge of the real nature of the heavenly bodies or of light—even we are mystified enough in these matters—it seems reasonable to temper our criticisms of the "idolatry" or "materiality" of Ikhnaton's view. For him the sun with its light was supremely "living," intelligent and purposive (having "heart"), "wise," "loving," self-existent ("length of life of thyself"), "maker" of all, adored by all. The spiritual qualities here attributed to the sun-god are not only ethically exalted but are less primitive intellectually than the qualities attributed to deity in many later documents.

### *"The Earliest Monotheism"*

1. O sole God, beside whom there is no other.
Thou didst create the earth according to thy heart. . . .

For thou hast made them for thyself,
Thou lord of them all, who weariest thyself for them. . . .

Thou didst make the distant sky in order to rise therein,
In order to behold all that thou hast made. . . .

The world subsists in thy hand,
For thou art length of life of thyself,
Men live through thee. . . .

Thou risest beautifully, O living Aton,
Lord of eternity;

Thy glowing hue brings life to the hearts of men,
When thou hast filled the Two Lands with thy love.
O God, who himself fashioned himself,
Maker of every land. . . .

Thou makest the hearts of men to live by thy beauty. . . .

All flowers live and what grows in the **soil**
Is made to grow because thou dawnest.
They are drunken before thee.
All cattle skip upon their feet; the birds in the marsh fly with joy,
Their wings that were folded are spread,
Uplifted in adoration to the living Aton.

[Sec. 1, James Henry Breasted, *The Dawn of Conscience* (New York: Charles Scribner's Sons, 1933), verses from pp. 284, 284, 285, 286, 287, 288, 288, and 289, respectively.]

### COMMENT

It is manifest that such poetic outpourings are not doctrinal metaphysics and that no classification in precise metaphysical terms can unequivocally apply to them. However, there is an alternative to the usual procedure of either rejecting the ancient religious writings as mere crudity or idolatry or forcing them into the mold of classical theism (or pantheism). For if anything is clear it is that these spiritual ancestors of ours did not intend to sacrifice all

29

predicates implying dipolarity. It is reasonable to infer that the followers of Aton believed that the Supreme Reality was not temporal in the inferior sense of having been born or of being in danger of destruction. God lives, not provided this happens or that does not; but, rather, he is of himself length of life. And he is in some sense or aspect self-creative. But these men were not in love with abstract concepts like being, eternity, absoluteness, or infinity. They did not worship such thin abstractions, but rather love, consciousness, vision, and beauty. Indeed, the concreteness often regarded as mere crudity and primitive idolatry serves to some extent as a safeguard against the sophisticated idolatry of characterizing God solely by the abstract qualities of independence and self-sufficiency.

Perhaps the most serious objection to Ikhnaton is his failure to stress "righteousness" in God as well as love and beauty. Here, too, there are compensations. The wild abuse of the idea of divine justice, as seen in the cosmic extension of penal codes and rewards and the excessive moralization of reality, makes some of us feel kindly toward the God-intoxicated aesthete who was Ikhnaton.

## HINDU SCRIPTURES (*ca.* 1000 B.C.)

The oldest of surviving religions, Hinduism, goes back to the Vedic hymns, composed 1000 B.C. or earlier. These hymns, regarded as divine in origin, contain a strong element of pantheism, by which we mean the view that God, although devoid of temporality and spatiality, is neverthless the inclusive or sole reality. Such pantheism involves a monopolar emphasis, and this emphasis is found in most of the later commentators who constitute the chief figures in Hindu philosophy. Being is exalted over becoming, identity over difference, cause over effect, independence over dependence. In the *Bhagavad-Gita* this one-sidedness is, as it were, summed up and canonized. Action in this world of time and diversity is indeed a duty somehow included in devotion to the immutable One through which bliss is achieved; we are to act without valuing the results of action or the world in which they are brought about. But why there should be even an illusion of diversity, and a universal tendency to desire the fruits of diverse activity, is a mystery. The supreme unity is conceived for the most part as exclusive of the polarities of existence. It includes their unreality, not their re-

ality; it does not really include *them*. And how it can matter at all whether we achieve happiness or not is equally unclear. The One is not enhanced by our devotion (*Bakti*), and, since we are not really distinct from the One, neither are we really enhanced. No clear idea of divine love for the creatures is to be found, and in reality such love would be mere self-devotion.

In so far as these hymns represent pantheism, they will be discussed later (chap. iv). But we would deny that pantheism is the only conclusion which can be drawn from the Vedic hymns; indeed, the hymns are themselves far from being wholly consistent in their expressions. In some apparently atypical passages, such as those we here present, the panentheistic alternative is implied.

### Hymn to Time*

2. Time, the steed, runs with seven reins (rays), thousand-eyed, ageless, rich in seed.

The seers, thinking holy thoughts, mount him, all the beings (worlds) are his wheels.

With seven wheels does this Time ride, . . . immortality is his axle. . . .

He carries hither all these beings (worlds); . . . they call him Time in the highest heaven.

He surely did bring hither all the beings (worlds), he surely did encompass all the beings (worlds). Being their father, he became their son; there is, verily, no other force, higher than he.

Time begot yonder heaven, Time also (begot) these earths. That which was, and that which shall be, urged forth by Time, spreads out.

. . . in Time the sun burns. In Time are all beings, in Time the eye looks abroad.

In Time *tapas* (creative fervour) is fixed; in Time the highest (being is fixed); In time *brahma* (spiritual exaltation) is fixed; Time is the lord of everything, he was the father of Pragâpati.

By him this (universe) was urged forth, by him it was begotten, and upon him this (universe) was founded.

### The Universal Self

3. In the beginning this was Self alone, in the shape of a person. He looking round saw nothing but His Self. . . .

He feared, and therefore any one who is lonely fears. He thought, "As there is nothing but myself, why should I fear?" Thence his fear passed away. For what should he have feared? Verily fear arises from a second only.

But he felt no delight. Therefore a man who is lonely feels no delight. He wished for a second. He was so large as man and wife together. He then made this his Self to fall in two (*pat*), and thence arose husband (*pati*) and wife (*patnî*). . . .

Verily in the beginning this was Brahman, one only. That being one, was not strong enough. It created still further the most excellent Kshatra (power), viz. those Kshatras (powers) among the Devas—Indra, Varuṇa, Soma,

Rudra, Parganya, Yama, Mṛityu, Îsâna. . . .

He was not strong enough. He created the Viṣ (people), the classes of Devas. . . .

He was not strong enough. He created the Sûdra colour (caste), as Pûshan (as nourisher). This earth verily is Pûshan (the nourisher); for the earth nourishes all this whatsoever.

He was not strong enough. He created still further the most excellent Law (dharma). Law is the Kshatra (power) of the Kshatra, therefore there is nothing higher than the Law. Thenceforth even a weak man rules a stronger with the help of the Law, as with the help of a king.

[Sec. 2, *The Sacred Books of the East*, ed. F. Max Müller (Oxford: Clarendon Press, 1897), XLII, 224–25. Sec. 3, *ibid.*, XV, Part II, 85, 88–89.]

### COMMENT

Much of the Hindu emphasis on monopolarity seems to us a way of saying that the essence of God is absolute, immutable, independent, a glory which nothing can tarnish or enhance; also that this essence is in all of us, a universal point of identity in all differences. We shall argue later (in commenting upon Plato and Aristotle) for the great truth in this traditional affirmation. But missing from such traditional interpretations are the emphases present, for example, in the preceding passages, with their implication that it is also of the essence of God that there should be divine accidents which are in no sense less real, but are more concrete, than the mere essence, constituting a glory inclusive of the essential glory as the concrete includes the abstract.

We submit that it would be hard to imagine a clearer statement, in primitive mythical form, of the doctrine that becoming is the inclusive side of the duality, being-becoming, than the Atharva-Vedic "Hymn to Time." The striking figure of the wheel pictures immortality as deity's axle; by implication, then, the temporal world of becoming is the wheel's rim, revolving about the changeless axle. The conclusion would appear to follow that real temporal, as well as eternal, components make up the reality which is God. And how better convey the notion that the Supreme is both cause and effect, both creator and creature, both productive and receptive, than by describing the "lord of all" as both father and son of the worlds? Still, again, what better embodiment could there be of the principle that nonsocial reality is deficient reality (implying that relativity is somehow more than the merely "absolute") than the description from the Upanishads of the one Self which, finding itself without "delight," enriches its own life and "strengthens" itself by multiplying beings with which it can enjoy relationships? Even the mere presence of the concept of divine personality, which in the Vedas and the Upanishads vies with impersonal notions of the original One Thing, is enough to render the purely pantheistic account of this literature a debatable rendering. For personality as purely absolute is a mere jumble of words. A person knows, that is relates himself to, other beings; he has purposes with reference to them, etc. All of this is contradicted by a strict pantheism. To make personality supreme is to make dipolarity supreme, for a person intrinsically and irreducibly involves the contrast between dependence and independence, fixity and change, as both real. Herein lies part of the ground for our insistence that early expressions about God almost by necessity involve dipolar metaphysics and panentheistic motifs. If the main line of Hindu metaphysics developed only one side of an initial dipolar insight, the same is true of Christian and Mohammedan theology's main line, which we call classical theism. But, in all of them, some approximation to a dipolar view is to be found, as, for instance, in Sri Jiva and many others in India, including some contemporary Hindu thinkers.

## LAO-TSE (Fourth Century [?] B.C.)

Taoism is one of the oldest of the more subtle religious doctrines. The *Tao Tê Ching* seems to have been composed in the fourth century B.C. and to derive from sources somewhat earlier. Lao-tse is a legendary character whose very existence is disputed. The Taoist doctrine is primarily a design for living rather than a view of the cosmos, exalting such qualities as inaction (it is said to have been a time of "unemployment" among scholars), inconspicuousness, modesty, and noninterference. But more is involved; to praise inactivity seems to involve depreciating a certain human attitude of wishing to dominate, to rule tyrannically so that the ruled are essentially puppets. Also depreciated is a certain practicality that is forever wishing to be cause of effects envisaged definitely in advance. The Taoist attitude may yield something for the life of man and God, the view, namely, that rule should inspire rather than manipulate, that its role is to furnish an atmosphere or medium in which things freely grow of themselves rather than being made to be or become. Apart from this design for living, we find some fascinating but elusive metaphysical suggestions which deserve later comment.

### Double Nature of the Tao

*4.* The Tao that can be expressed is not the Unchanging Tao;

The name that can be named is not the Unchanging Name.

The Unnamable is that from which Heaven and earth derived, leaving itself unchanged.

Thinking of it as having a name, let it be called the Mother of all things.

He who is without earthly passions and without desire can perceive the profound mystery of that unmanifested existence.

He who has not rid himself of desire can perceive only the Manifest, with its differentiations.

Nevertheless, the Manifest and the Unmanifest are in origin the same.

This sameness is the Mystery of Mysteries, the deep within the deep, the Doorway into all Mystery. . . .

Because the world recognizes beauty as beauty, ugliness is known to be ugly.

Everyone knows goodness to be goodness, and to know this is to know what is not good.

Similarly, existence implies non-existence;

The hard and the easy complement each other; . . .

Before and after, earlier and later, back and front—

All these complement one another.

Therefore the Sage, the self-controlled man, dwells in actionless activity, poised between contraries. . . .

The highest good may be likened to water.

Water benefits all creatures yet does not strive or argue with them.

It rests content in those lowly places which others despise. . . .

He who while recognizing his manhood Yet holds also to his womanhood, Becomes a channel for all the world. . . .

All creatures, trees, and plants are soft and tender in their early growth,

And in dying become withered and dry.

Thus we may say that rigidity and hardness are related to death,

While weakness and tenderness are related to life. . . .

And truly, the Greatest Ruler interferes the least.

[Sec. 4, Hermon Ould, *The Way of Acceptance: A New Version of Lao Tse's Tao Tê Ching* (London: Andrew Dakers, Ltd., 1946), verses from pp. 15–16, 22, 42, 90, 42.]

#### COMMENT

The conceptual element is somewhat more heavily stressed here than in the hymns to Aton and the Vedic hymns. The assertion that there is an unchanging ultimate from which change proceeds is clear enough. In so far, the theory leans either toward classical theism or toward emanationism, especially the latter, since no attribution of consciousness to the Unchanging seems to be made. We are told that the unmanifested, undifferentiated, and unchanging Tao and the differentiated manifest changing principle are originally the same in a way that baffles explanation. The truth, we are reminded, is not in one side of the ultimate contraries but in the contrariety itself, the active with the passive, existence with nonexistence (actuality with potentiality? being with becoming?). Moreover, Taoism praises just that which unbridled classical theism ultimately dispraises, namely, the "passive," receptive, responsive, undominating, "yielding," "tender," pliant. In so far, it is a corrective to the all-too-unmistakable apotheosis of the masculine, managing, practical, causative, in our traditional theism. But, also, Taoism is hardly a pantheistic doctrine, for the characteristic denial of reality to the changing and diverse seems relatively absent. And nature is praised rather than depreciated. All this, plus Taoism's polemic against any principle of rigid causative control, is at least vaguely favorable to a nontruncated dipolar view of the Supreme. If we claim Lao-tse for this position, it is without wishing to strive with anyone who disputes the claim. Such strife would hardly be in the spirt of the Tao!

## THE JUDEO-CHRISTIAN SCRIPTURES
### (Fifth [?] Century B.C. to Second Century A.D.)

In contrast to the Egyptians, the Hebrews avoided selecting any one natural phenomenon, such as "light," as peculiarly divine. True, man himself was somehow an "image of God," and the views of the earliest biblical authors, which later writers struggled to refine, contained elements of anthropomorphism. Moreover, however far the refinement was carried, we can say—as we did of Ikhnaton—that the biblical authors certainly had no intention of giving up the spiritual or psychological predicates of deity, such as will, knowledge, and love, in order to exalt some mere monopolar category of Being or Infinity. Quarrel if you will with metaphorical expressions like "the wrath of God," or his "pity," as wholly nonliteral concessions to the weakness of the human understanding; still, it may be suggested that the minimum to be expressed by such metaphors is this: that God is not blankly neutral to the happenings in the world, not simply absolute with respect to them, but rather evaluatively sensitive to the differences in all things in a way analogous to "pleasure" and "displeasure" in us. The issue is not: Shall these terms have a simply identical or "univocal" meaning when used of God and of us? Theologians agree that the meaning is analogical. The issue is rather: Shall there be two levels of evaluative sensitivity or responsiveness, two forms of relativity, ordinary and divine, or shall we destroy the metaphor entirely by trying to maintain an analogue of "love" without any analogy to the sympathy, the responsiveness, the deriving of value from others, which is an essential dimension of love? Those who insist upon simply combining utter nonrelativity of deity with the assertion that, metaphorically speaking, God knows and loves the world are speaking, in our judgment, not analogically but equivocally.

For centuries certain biblical passages, samples of which are set forth hereinafter, have been interpreted by theologians who were convinced that their dogma of a purely absolute deity was supported thereby. We invite the reader to judge whether or not absolutistic dogmas are indeed present in the following lines.

### The Creator

5. When God began to create the heavens and the earth, the earth was a desolate waste, with darkness covering the abyss and a tempestuous wind raging over the surface of the waters. Then God said,

"Let there be light!"

And there was light; and God saw that the light was good. God then separated the light from the darkness. God called the light day, and the darkness night. Evening came, and morning, the first day.

Then God said,

"Let there be a firmament in the middle of the waters to divide the waters in two!"

And so it was. God made the firmament, dividing the waters that were below the firmament from those that were above it; and God called the firmament sky. Evening came, and morning, the second day.

Then God said,

"Let the waters below the sky be gathered into one place so that the dry land may appear!"

And so it was. God called the dry land earth, and the gathered waters seas. God saw that it was good.

Then God said,

"Let the earth produce vegetation, seed-bearing plants and the various kinds of fruit-trees that bear fruit containing their seed!"

And so it was. The earth brought forth vegetation, the various kinds of seed-bearing plants and the various kinds of trees that bear fruit containing their seed. God saw that it was good. Evening came, and morning, the third day.

Then God said,

"Let there be luminaries in the firmament of the sky to separate day from night; let them serve for signs, for fixed times, and for days and years; and let them serve as luminaries in the firmament of the sky to shed light on the earth!"

And so it was. God made the two great luminaries, the greater luminary to rule the day and the smaller one to rule the night—and the stars also. . . . God saw that it was good. Evening came, and morning, the fourth day.

Then God said,

"Let the waters teem with shoals of living creatures, and let birds fly over the earth across the firmament of the sky!"

And so it was. God created the great sea-monsters and all the various kinds of living, gliding creatures with which the waters teem, and all the various kinds of winged birds. God saw that it was good, and God blessed them, saying,

"Be fruitful, multiply, and fill the waters in the seas; and let the birds multiply on the earth!"

Evening came, and morning, the fifth day.

Then God said,

"Let the earth bring forth the various kinds of living creatures, the various kinds of domestic animals, reptiles, and wild beasts of the earth!"

And so it was. God made the various kinds of wild beasts of the earth, the various kinds of domestic animals, and all the various kinds of land reptiles; and God saw that it was good.

Then God said,

"Let us make man in our image, after our likeness, and let him have dominion over the fish of the sea, the birds of the air, the domestic animals, the wild beasts, and all the land reptiles!"

So God created man in his own image; in the image of God he created him; he created both male and female. Then God blessed them, and God said to them,

Be fruitful, multiply, fill the earth, and subdue it. . . .

Further, God said,

"See, I give you all the seed-bearing plants that are found all over the earth, and all the trees which have seed-bearing fruit; it shall be yours to eat. To all the wild beasts of the earth, to all the birds of the air, and to all the land reptiles, in which there is a living spirit, I give all the green plants for food."

And so it was. God saw that all that he had made was very good. Evening came, and morning, the sixth day.

Thus the heavens and the earth were finished, and all their host. On the seventh day God brought his work to an end . . . desisting on the seventh day from all his work in which he had been engaged. So God blessed the seventh day, and consecrated it, because on it he had desisted from all his work, in doing which God had brought about creation.

### The Character of God

6. The Lord is merciful and compassionate, slow to anger and abounding in kindness.

He will not always chide, nor hold his anger forever.

He has not treated us according to our sins, nor rewarded us according to our iniquities.

But high as the heavens are above the earth, so great is his kindness toward them that revere him;

Far as the east is from the west, so far has he removed our offenses from us.

As a father is kind to his children, so the Lord is kind to those who revere him.

7. ". . . I will draw near to you for judgment,

And I will be a swift witness against the sorcerers and adulterers, . . .

And against those who oppress the hireling in his wages,

The widow and the orphan . . . ," says the Lord of hosts.

"Though I, the Lord, change not, you, O sons of Jacob, are not destroyed.

From the days of your fathers you have revolted

From my statutes, and have not kept them. Return unto me, that I may return to you,"

Says the Lord of hosts.

8. The Kingdom of Heaven is like a man who sowed good seed in his field, but while people were asleep his enemy came and sowed weeds among the wheat, and went away. And when the wheat came up and ripened, the weeds appeared too. And when the owner's slaves came to him and said, "Was not the seed good that you sowed in your field, sir? So where did these weeds come from?" He said to them, "This is some enemy's doing." And they said to him, "Do you want us to go and gather them up?" But he said, "No, for in gathering up the weeds you may uproot the wheat. Let them both grow together until harvest time, and when we harvest I will direct the reapers to gather up the weeds first and tie them up in bundles to burn, but get the wheat into my barn."

9. Dear friends, let us love one another, for love comes from God, and everyone who loves is a child of God and knows God. Whoever does not love does not know God, for God is love. God's love for us has been revealed in this way—that God has sent his only Son into the world, to let us have life through him.

[Sec. 5, *The Bible: An American Translation*, trans. J. M. P. Smith and Edgar J. Goodspeed (Chicago: University of Chicago Press, 1935), Gen. 1:1—2:3. Sec. 6, *ibid.*, Ps. 103: 8–13. Sec. 7, *ibid.*, Mal. 3:5–7. Sec. 8, *ibid.*, Matt. 13:24–30. Sec. 9, *ibid.*, I John 4:7–9.]

### COMMENT

How far can panentheism be discerned in the foregoing passages? The Genesis account seems to suggest that the creative acts of deity begin with a situation, not with sheer nonentity; that they are successive, not all at once; and that the results produce effects in God (states of appreciation) as he beholds these results. If one objects that this is mere anthropomorphic imagery for transcendental truth which has nothing to do with temporal acts of modifying a given situation, or with registering of effects upon a beholder, the objector may be challenged to show what usable meaning, religious or philosophical, remains when one denies all such features to the divine action. It appears to us that the religious founders were trying to express not the absence of succession and of effect in deity but the transcendental or categorically supreme form of these. For instance, granting that it is merely foolish to think of God as needing to rest after "working" to create the world, what is not so obviously foolish is the idea that God does have two really different relations to his acts, first, while performing any such act, and, then, as contemplating its results, the creatures responding to God with their own spontaneity. This is not merely God responding to himself! The inference is then possible that we too should be contemplative of accomplished actualities, not merely immersed in production of new ones. So to view the matter does at least give meaning to the Sabbath idea that we should consciously imitate deity in two diverse functions, doing and beholding what has been done.

The seventh section, from Malachi, contains a typical case of scriptural affirmation apparently tending to confirm a monopolar metaphysical principle but in reality irrelevant to or even inconsistent with the principle. The Lord, we are told, persists in certain attitudes (devotion to Israel) and in certain principles of behavior (action against various forms of evil-doing), and in this constancy of basic attitude he changes not. But, so far from affirming or implying complete metaphysical immutability, the passage seems rather to support the idea of divine change. "Return to me, and I will return to you" amounts to this: change in a certain direction, and I will myself change in a thereto appropriate way. The principle of appropriateness is unchanging, but neither the worldly objects of divine attention nor the divine responses thereto are depicted as immutable.

The parable of the weeds may be given similar metaphysical import. God sows only good seed: he holds up before us a flawless ideal by which we are inspired. But we are not simply determined by this inspiration. We are also influenced by others, who are not divinely wise and good. And how can this be if they too are inspired by deity? Is not the answer that some at least of the creatures have a self-determining, self-creative power, so that the creature in its total reality is no mere inevitable consequence of the divine action? A second possible inference from the parable is that God is not just a sower but also and finally a harvester, not merely cause but enjoyer of effects, and in this enjoyment himself effect. The harvest is ultimately divine, not merely in its source but in itself, as achieved actuality. God utilizes what has value and so far as it has. The "burning" may be simply a vivid way of saying that only what is divinely utilizable is genuinely permanent or that only that which contributes to the divine self-realization, and only as it does so, is practicable.

There is little in the Bible to suggest directly that God genuinely shares in our sufferings. Indirectly, all descriptions of deity as conscious and perceptive imply this, if one agrees with our contention that only a deficient perception of suffering can remain merely serene and indifferent. The whole doctrine of the Incarnation and the sending of the Son of God seems an implicit expression of the divine passivity and passion. And the evasion that "love" means mere "outpouring" of benefits, not sympathetic sensitivity to the deeds and the joys and sorrows of others, is, we suggest, foreign to the spiritual atmosphere of the New Testament and not really in accord with the Old.

To the usual theory that the naïve concrete images of love, perception, will, pleasure, and displeasure are merely the best we can do to express the monopolar reality of the absolute independence and immutability, we propose the alternative view that these psychological predicates, which apply only to individuals, are essentially dipolar and in so far are ultimate conceptions, more complete than categories like "being" or "immutability." Only an individual loves, but an abstract essence may be immutable. On the principle that the individual is the ultimate inclusive reality, ideas which can apply only to individuals are more complete and inclusive than those which apply to universals as such. Thus, since an abstraction can, for example, be infinite ("time" or "space" as such are certainly without limits), infinity is not to be used as the distinguishing mark of deity. By this criterion it is the allegedly naïve conceptions of the Bible, such as will, pity, love, anger, which are really ultimate. An abstraction can be "immutable" or "nonrelative," but it cannot will or think or love or be angry; only an individual can do that. The great religious writings generally do by implication distinguish two levels of psychological individuality, on both of which dipolarity is essential: first, the ordinary becoming of individuals, whose successive decisions can be contradictory—this "becoming" is defective in that a present decision may be required which will negate past decisions; and, second, the becoming of God which has nothing to undo but only new creative decisions to add—this involves in God's nature a consciously flexible attitude which awaits the details of subsequent development so far as these details are not settled in advance.

It is curious that the clearest denial which Scriptures contain of the theory that we are contributory to God (who is thus not in every sense independent of us, and is effect and not merely cause) is put into the mouth of one of "Job's comforters," those pretentious persons who are rebuked at the close of the story, because "they have not spoken the truth concerning me [Jehovah]" (Job 35:7). Naturally this does not deter monopolarists from citing the verses in question! What is clear, however, is that in no simple objectively convincing way can Scriptures be shown to affirm monopolarity. And certainly they often seem to imply a dipolar conception.

## PLATO (*ca.* 427–*ca.* 347 B.C.)

Although the dialogue form employed by Plato suggests little intention of formal unity, and a denial of rigid system is implicit in the figure of Socrates, still there is enough unity of an informal type in Plato's writings so that one may be labeled "Platonist" or one may speak of "Platonism," and another will know in general what is meant. And yet a wholly satisfactory answer to the question, "Does one Platonic philosophy exist, or are there several philosophies to each of which Plato has given attention?" will doubtless continue to be impossible. If the changing concerns of successive dialogues are to be considered stages of development in Plato's thought—as Julius Stenzel and others insist—one must look to the works representing the final stages of that development for the most significant account of his position. If, rather than this, the dialogues present different aspects of a highly complex, yet essentially unified, system—as Schleiermacher, Raphael Demos, and others maintain—one must unite the important content of all the dialogues in the final systematic interpretation of Platonism. And if neither system nor tendency toward system is present, if the dialogues merely express a set of loosely related and, at times, conflicting themes, then, since philosophy appears to require system, one can at least hope to discover a manner of including the diverse themes in one relational whole. This would represent the most genuinely Platonic philosophy which could be derived from the dialogues.

The present writers incline to accept the first view in principle and to interpret the relation of earlier and later dialogues as asymmetrical, an irreversible transition in which the principles of early dialogues are retained in the later but utilized within a more profound system of concepts. The development has two phases: the *Republic* marking the end point of the first, the *Eleatic* dialogues serving as the vehicle of objections which may now be raised against the achieved system, and the final dialogues, primarily the *Timaeus* and the *Laws*, furnishing a mature restatement of these principles in such manner that the objections no longer apply with the same force. In these final dialogues God becomes a central concern, and Plato invests the concept with the greater clarity which follows as a natural consequence of his desire to conceive deity in such manner as to solve the problem of teleology. One might argue for an inverse correlation between the emphasis placed upon the concept of God and that placed upon the theory of ideas; at least Stenzel thinks he is able to discern a drastic shift of meaning in the system at the point where teleological explanation according to ideas is modified by teleological explanation in terms of God.[1]

Whether or not this position be accepted is of less concern than might be supposed. For in any case it must be granted that the final dialogues retain most of the emphases and, we would tend to insist, all of the basic categories of explanation which are to be found in earlier dialogues. And, if this is granted, the contention that Plato is presenting a complex but unified system of thought needs only a bit of qualification to become an adjunct of the first position.

But, further, this systematic unity is not such that, of two diverse principles of explanation, one must be un-Platonic. Alternate principles of explanation advanced by Plato lead to alternate conceptions of soul and, hence, of the divine being, which appear incompatible when brought together. Conflicts such as these, which may be taken to distinguish an earlier from a later dialogue, are likewise present in some form within the final dialogues themselves. For modern use there remains the need of deriving a consistent set of propositions from the Platonic writings in keeping with the basic principles of Plato's thought, if this is possible. Hence the third position is also virtually contained in the first. These qualifications, common to the three positions which may be taken with respect to system in Plato, suggest that, since the positions tend to envelop each other, all important Platonic concepts will be present in any adequate interpretation of the dialogues regardless of the initial systemic prejudice one attempts to impress upon the material.

If one will not grant two phases of Platonic development, doubtless there must at least be granted two facets in his thought. The first proceeds by a diaeresis of existence into the quantitative and the qualitative—more precisely, into the material and the formal or ideational; the one is given the property of mobility which is construed as mutability and hence destructibility, the other is given the property of immobility which is construed as immutability and hence eternality. The property of immobility is taken to be descriptive of the intellectual and hence descriptive of both soul and God. But in the second phase or facet of Plato's thought, while the ideational category retains its immutability and eternality, Plato grants motion to both souls and bodies. This destroys the exact opposition of the first phase. The real opposition of the second phase lies in the distinction of independent and dependent mobility, the soul having self-motion—a motion containing itself—and bodies having a received motion. The soul is still eternal

1. Cf. Julius Stenzel, *Plato's Method of Dialectic*, trans. D. J. Allen (Oxford: Clarendon Press, 1940), p. 58. "It may thus be said that there never was any 'general theory of Ideas'—that name is a relic of the one-sided 'systematic' interpretation of Plato. When the original theory had to be made general, it at once changed its nature."

and in a sense immutable; but this is now because of its superior type of mobility, which is comparable to circular as against the more common linear motion.

Plato has placed soul under two categories of explanation, one that of eternal fixture and the other that of self-initiating mobility. The opposition in the two interpretations of soul is roughly similar to the opposition of immutability and mutability. Three sets of contrasts are derived from the two approaches, as can be seen especially well in the *Timaeus*. A world soul has emerged containing all existence within itself and exemplifying the superiority of soul over body and its superior type of motion; yet the ideas are still looked to as a pattern for creation, and an eternal God exemplifies the principle of immutability which characterized soul in the first phase. This seems the most complete attempt made by Plato to interrelate his principles, since the oppositions mentioned elsewhere are restated: the opposition of immutable forms and mutable bodies, the opposition of self-motion and derived motion, the opposition of immutable God and mutable God.

Nor can the complex of opposed concepts be simplified by reducing God to the idea of the Good. Not even in the first phase has Plato ever made this equation. And it is evident in the *Parmenides* that the ideas—and the Good is mentioned directly—were subject to criticism for the reason that, as then understood by Plato, they did not allow the relation of knowing to obtain between God and the world. The nature of the Good, while having an important efficacy, must then be such that it is compatible with the rule of a supreme conscious being. In the *Philebus* (not here quoted) the Good is defined in a number of ways, not one of which equates it with God.

The conflict ·of opposing categories must, then, be viewed as inherent in the Platonic framework; and, if real contradictions were to be found, this would not give occasion for astonishment. Indeed, to find contradiction might be a sign that Plato once for all fulfilled the requirement of philosophic adequacy by having elaborated all the necessary themes, though leaving open the question how, if at all, the themes can exist together in meaningful consistency.

*The Category of Absolute Fixity*

10. . . . were we not saying long ago that the soul when using the body as an instrument of perception, that is to say, when using the sense of sight or hearing or some other sense (for the meaning of perceiving through the body is perceiving through the senses)—were we not saying that the soul too is then dragged by the body into the region of the changeable, and wanders and is confused; the world spins round her, and she is like a drunkard, when she touches change?

Very true.

But when returning into herself she reflects, then she passes into the other world, the region of purity, and eternity, and immortality, and unchangeableness, which are her kindred, and with them she ever lives, when she is by herself and is not let or hindered; then she ceases from her erring ways, and being in communion with the unchanging is unchanging. And this state of the soul is called wisdom.

That is well and truly said, Socrates, he replied.

And to which class is the soul more nearly alike and akin, as far as may be inferred from this argument . . . ?

I think, Socrates, that, in the opinion of everyone who follows the argument, the soul will be infinitely more like the unchangeable—even the most stupid person will not deny that.

And the body is more like the changing?

Yes.

Yet once more consider the matter in another light: When the soul and the body are united, then nature orders the soul to rule and govern, and the body to obey and serve. Now, which of these two functions is akin to the divine? and which to the mortal? Does not the divine appear to you to be that which naturally orders and rules, and the mortal to be that which is subject and servant?

True.

And which does the soul resemble?

The soul resembles the divine, and the body the mortal—there can be no doubt of that, Socrates.

Then reflect, Cebes: of all that which has been said is not this the conclusion?—that the soul is in the very likeness of the divine, and immortal, and intellectual, and uniform, and indissoluble, and unchangeable; and that the body is in the very likeness of the human, and mortal, and unintellectual, and multiform, and dissoluble, and changeable. Can this, my dear Cebes, be denied?

It cannot.

But if it be true, then is not the body liable to speedy dissolution? and is not the soul almost or altogether indissoluble?

Certainly.

*11*. And will not the bravest and wisest soul be least confused or deranged by any external influence?

True.

And the same principle, as I should suppose, applies to all composite things —furniture, houses, garments: when good and well made, they are least altered by time and circumstances.

Very true.

Then everything which is good, whether made by art or nature, or both, is least liable to suffer change from without?

True.

But surely God and the things of God are in every way perfect?

Of course they are.

Then he can hardly be compelled by external influence to take many shapes?

He cannot.

But may he not change and transform himself?

Clearly, he said, that must be the case if he is changed at all.

And will he then change himself for the better and fairer, or for the worse and more unsightly?

If he change at all he can only change for the worse, for we cannot suppose him to be deficient either in virtue or beauty.

Very true, Adeimantus; but then, would anyone, whether God or man, desire to make himself worse?

Impossible.

Then it is impossible that God should ever be willing to change; being, as is supposed, the fairest and best that is conceivable, every God remains absolutely and forever in his own form.

That necessarily follows, he said, in my judgment. . . .

And is he [God] not truly good? and must he not be represented as such?

Certainly.

And no good thing is hurtful?

No, indeed.

And that which is not hurtful hurts not?

Certainly not.

And that which hurts not does no evil?

No.

And can that which does no evil be a cause of evil?

Impossible.

And the good is advantageous?

Yes.

And therefore the cause of well-being?

Yes.

It follows therefore that the good is not the cause of all things, but of the good only?

Assuredly.

Then God, if he be good, is not the author of all things, as the many assert, but he is the cause of a few things only, and not of most things that occur to men. For few are the goods of human life, and many are the evils, and the good is to be attributed to God alone; of the evils the causes are to be sought elsewhere, and not in him.[2]

*12.* In the first place, I think, Socrates, that you, or anyone who maintains the existence of absolute essences, will admit that they cannot exist in us.

No, said Socrates; for then they would be no longer absolute.

True, he said; and therefore when ideas are what they are in relation to one another, their essence is determined by a relation among themselves, and has nothing to do with the resemblances, or whatever they are to be termed, which are in our sphere, and from which we receive this or that name when we partake of them. And the things which are within our sphere and have the same names with them, are likewise only relative to one another, and not to the ideas which have the same names with them, but belong to themselves and not to them.

What do you mean? said Socrates.

I may illustrate my meaning in this way, said Parmenides:—A master has a slave; now there is nothing absolute in the relation between them, which is simply a relation of one man to another. But there is also an idea of mastership in the abstract, which is relative to the idea of slavery in the abstract. These natures have nothing to do with us, nor we with them; they are concerned with themselves only, and we with ourselves. Do you see my meaning?

Yes, said Socrates, I quite see your meaning.

And will not knowledge—I mean absolute knowledge—answer to absolute truth?

Certainly.

And each kind of absolute knowledge will answer to each kind of absolute being?

Yes.

But the knowledge which we have will answer to the truth which we have; and again, each kind of knowledge which we have will be a knowledge of each kind of being which we have?

Certainly.

But the ideas themselves, as you admit, we have not, and cannot have?

No, we cannot.

And the absolute natures or kinds are known severally by the absolute idea of knowledge?

Yes.

And we have not got the idea of knowledge?

No.

Then none of the ideas are known to us, because we have no share in absolute knowledge?

I suppose not.

Then the nature of the beautiful in itself, and of the good in itself, and all other ideas which we suppose to exist absolutely, are unknown to us?

It would seem so.

I think that there is a stranger consequence still.

What is it?

Would you, or would you not say, that absolute knowledge, if there is such a thing, must be a far more exact knowledge than our knowledge; and the same of beauty and of the rest?

Yes.

And if there be such a thing as par-

---

2. Cf. Plato *Statesman* 270 for a similar view: ". . . we must not say that the world is either self-moved always, or all made to go round by God in two opposite courses; or that two Gods, having opposite purposes, make it move round. But as I have already said (and this is the only remaining alternative) the world is guided at one time by an external power which is divine and receives fresh life and immortality from the renewing hand of the Creator, and again, when let go, moves spontaneously, being set free at such a time as to have, during infinite cycles of years, a reverse movement: this is due to its perfect balance, to its vast size, and to the fact that it turns on the smallest pivot." (Cf. also below, sec. 14.)

ticipation in absolute knowledge, no one is more likely than God to have this most exact knowledge?[3]

Certainly.

But then, will God, having absolute knowledge, have a knowledge of human beings?

Why not?

Because, Socrates, said Parmenides, we have admitted that the ideas are not valid in relation to human things; nor human things in relation to them; the relations of either are limited to their respective spheres.

Yes, that has been admitted.

And if God has this perfect authority, and perfect knowledge, his authority cannot rule us, nor his knowledge know us, or any human thing; just as our authority does not extend to the gods,

3. Cf. P. E. More, *The Religion of Plato* (Princeton: Princeton University Press, 1921), p. 120, for a denial of the assertion that Plato identified God and the idea of the Good. Cf. *Republic* 508-9, the probable source of this identification: "Now, that which imparts truth to the known and the power of knowing to the knower is what I would have you term the idea of good, and this you will deem to be the cause of science, and of truth in so far as the latter becomes the subject of knowledge; beautiful too, as are both truth and knowledge, you will be right in esteeming this other nature as more beautiful than either; and, as in the previous instance, light and sight may be truly said to be like the sun, and yet not to be the sun, so in this other sphere, science and truth may be deemed to be like the good, but not the good; the good has a place of honour yet higher." "What a wonder of beauty that must be," he said, "which is the author of science and truth, yet surpasses them in beauty; for you surely cannot mean to say that pleasure is the good?" "God forbid," I replied; "but may I ask you to consider the image in another point of view?" "In what point of view?" "You would say, would you not, that the sun is not only the author of visibility in all visible things, but of generation and nourishment and growth, though he himself is not generation?" "Certainly." "In like manner the good may be said to be not only the author of knowledge to all things known, but of their being and essence, and yet the good is not essence, but far exceeds essence in dignity and power."

nor our knowledge know anything which is divine, so by parity of reason they, being gods, are not our masters, neither do they know the things of men.

Yet, surely, said Socrates, to deprive God of knowledge is monstrous.

These, Socrates, said Parmenides, are a few, and only a few of the difficulties in which we are involved if ideas really are and we determine each one of them to be an absolute unity. He who hears what may be said against them will deny the very existence of them—and even if they do exist, he will say that they must of necessity be unknown to man; and he will seem to have reason on his side, and as we were remarking just now, will be very difficult to convince; a man must be gifted with very considerable ability before he can learn that everything has a class and an absolute essence; and still more remarkable will be he who discovers all these things for himself, and having thoroughly investigated them is able to teach them to others.

I agree with you, Parmenides, said Socrates; and what you say is very much to my mind.

And yet, Socrates, said Parmenides, if a man, fixing his attention on these and the like difficulties, does away with ideas of things and will not admit that every individual thing has its own determinate idea which is always one and the same, he will have nothing on which his mind can rest; and so he will utterly destroy the power of reasoning, as you seem to me to have particularly noted.

Very true, he said.

But, then, what is to become of philosophy? Whither shall we turn, if the ideas are unknown?

I certainly do not see my way at present.

Yes, said Parmenides; and I think that this arises, Socrates, out of your attempting to define the beautiful, the just, the good, and the ideas generally, without sufficient previous training. I noticed your deficiency, when I heard you talking here with your friend Aristoteles, the day before yesterday. The impulse that carries you towards philosophy is assuredly noble and divine; but there is an art which is called by the vulgar idle talking, and which is often imagined to be useless; in that you must train and exercise yourself, now that you are young, or truth will elude your grasp.

### The Category of Absolute Mobility

13. The soul through all her being is immortal, for that which is ever in motion is immortal; but that which moves another and is moved by another, in ceasing to move ceases also to live. Only the self-moving, never leaving itself, never ceases to move, and is the fountain and beginning of motion to all that moves besides. Now, the beginning is unbegotten, for that which is begotten has a beginning; but the beginning is begotten of nothing, for if it were begotten of something, then the begotten would not come from a beginning. But if unbegotten, it must also be indestructible; for if beginning were destroyed, there could be no beginning out of anything, nor anything out of a beginning; and all things must have a beginning. And therefore the self-moving is the beginning of motion; and this can neither be destroyed nor begotten, else the whole heavens and all creation would collapse and stand still, and never again have motion or birth. But if the self-moving is proved to be immortal, he who affirms that self-motion is the very idea and essence of the soul will not be put to confusion. For the body which is moved from without is soulless; but that which is moved from within has a soul, such motion being inherent in the soul. But if this is true, must not the soul be the self-moving, and therefore of necessity unbegotten and immortal?

14. Ath. [An Athenian stranger] Let us assume that there is a motion able to move other things, but not to move itself;—that is one kind; and there is another kind which can move itself as well as other things, working in composition and decomposition, by increase and diminution and generation and destruction— that is also one of the many kinds of motion.

Cle. [Cleinias, a Cretan] Granted. . . .

Ath. . . . when one thing changes another, and that another, of such will there be any primary changing element? How can a thing which is moved by another ever be the beginning of change? Impossible. But when the self-moved changes other, and that again other, and thus thousands upon tens of thousands of bodies are set in motion, must not the beginning of all this motion be the change of the self-moving principle?

Cle. Very true, and I quite agree.

Ath. Or, to put the question in another way, making answer to ourselves: —If, as most of these philosophers have the audacity to affirm, all things were at rest in one mass, which of the above-mentioned principles of motion would first spring up among them?

Cle. Clearly the self-moving; for there could be no change in them arising out of any external cause; the change must first take place in themselves.

Ath. Then we must say that self-motion being the origin of all motions, and the first which arises among things at rest as well as among things in motion, is the eldest and mightiest principle of change, and that which is changed by another and yet moves other is second.

Cle. Quite true.

Ath. At this stage of the argument let us put a question.

Cle. What question?

Ath. If we were to see this power existing in any earthy, watery, or fiery substance, simple or compound—how should we describe it?

*Cle.* You mean to ask whether we should call such a self-moving power life?

*Ath.* I do.

*Cle.* Certainly we should.

*Ath.* And when we see soul in anything, must we not do the same—must we not admit that this is life?

*Cle.* We must.

*Ath.* And now, I beseech you, reflect; —you would admit that we have a threefold knowledge of things?

*Cle.* What do you mean?

*Ath.* I mean that we know the essence, and that we know the definition of the essence, and the name—these are the three; and there are two questions which may be raised about anything.

*Cle.* How two?

*Ath.* Sometimes a person may give the name and ask the definition; or he may give the definition and ask the name. . . .

*Cle.* Quite true.

*Ath.* And what is the definition of that which is named "soul"? Can we conceive of any other than that which has been already given—the motion which can move itself?

*Cle.* You mean to say that the essence which is defined as the self-moved is the same with that which has the name soul?

*Ath.* Yes; and if this is true, do we still maintain that there is anything wanting in the proof that the soul is the first origin and moving power of all that is, or has become, or will be, and their contraries, when she has been clearly shown to be the source of change and motion in all things?

*Cle.* Certainly not; the soul as being the source of motion has been most satisfactorily shown to be the oldest of all things.

*Ath.* And is not that motion which is produced in another by reason of another, but never has any self-moving

power at all, being in truth the change of an inanimate body, to be reckoned second, or by any lower number which you may prefer?

*Cle.* Exactly.

*Ath.* Then we are right, and speak the most perfect and absolute truth, when we say that the soul is prior to the body, and that the body is second and comes afterwards, and is born to obey the soul, which is the ruler?

*Cle.* Nothing can be more true.

*Ath.* Do you remember our old admission, that if the soul was prior to the body the things of the soul were also prior to those of the body?

*Cle.* Certainly.

*Ath.* Then characters and manners, and wishes and reasonings, and true opinions, and reflections, and recollections are prior to length and breadth and depth and strength of bodies, if the soul is prior to the body.

*Cle.* To be sure.

*Ath.* In the next place, must we not of necessity admit that the soul is the cause of good and evil, base and honourable, just and unjust, and of all other opposites, if we suppose her to be the cause of all things?

*Cle.* We must.

*Ath.* And as the soul orders and inhabits all things that move, however moving, must we not say that she orders also the heavens?

*Cle.* Of course.

*Ath.* One soul or more? More than one—I will answer for you; at any rate, we must not suppose that there are less than two—one the author of good, and the other of evil.

*Cle.* Very true.

*Ath.* Yes, very true; the soul then directs all things in heaven, and earth, and sea by her movements, and these are described by the terms—will, consideration, attention, deliberation, opinion true and false, joy and sorrow, confidence, fear, hatred, love, and other primary motions akin to these; which again

receive the secondary motions of corporeal substances, and guide all things
to growth and decay, to composition
and decomposition, and to the qualities
which accompany them, such as heat
and cold, heaviness and lightness, hardness and softness, blackness and whiteness, bitterness and sweetness, and all
those other qualities which the soul uses,
herself a goddess, when truly receiving
the divine mind she disciplines all things
rightly to their happiness; but when she
is the companion of folly, she does the
very contrary of all this. Shall we assume so much, or do we still entertain
doubts?

*Cle.* There is no room at all for doubt.

*Ath.* Shall we say then that it is the
soul which controls heaven and earth,
and the whole world?—that it is a principle of wisdom and virtue, or a principle which has neither wisdom nor virtue? Suppose that we make answer as
follows:—

*Cle.* How would you answer?

*Ath.* If, my friend, we say that the
whole path and movement of heaven,
and of all that is therein, is by nature
akin to the movement and revolution
and calculation of mind, and proceeds
by kindred laws, then, as is plain, we
must say that the best soul takes care of
the world and guides it along the good
path.

*Cle.* True.

*Ath.* But if the world moves wildly
and irregularly, then the evil soul guides
it.

*Cle.* True again.

*Ath.* Of what nature is the movement
of mind?—To this question it is not
easy to give an intelligent answer; and
therefore I ought to assist you in framing one.

*Cle.* Very good.

*Ath.* Then let us not answer as if we
would look straight at the sun, making
ourselves darkness at midday—I mean as
if we were under the impression that
we could see with mortal eyes, or know

adequately the nature of mind;—it will
be safer to look at the image only.

*Cle.* What do you mean?

*Ath.* Let us select of the ten motions
the one which mind chiefly resembles;
this I will bring to your recollection,
and will then make the answer on behalf of us all.

*Cle.* That will be excellent.

*Ath.* You will surely remember our
saying that all things were either at rest
or in motion?

*Cle.* I do.

*Ath.* And that of things in motion
some were moving in one place, and
others in more than one?

*Cle.* Yes.

*Ath.* Of these two kinds of motion,
that which moves in one place must
move about a centre like globes made
in a lathe, and is most entirely akin and
similar to the circular movement of
mind.

*Cle.* What do you mean?

*Ath.* In saying that both mind and
the motion which is in one place move
in the same and like manner, in and
about the same, and in relation to the
same, and according to one proportion
and order, and are like the motion of a
globe, we invented a fair image, which
does no discredit to our ingenuity.

*Cle.* It does us great credit.

*Ath.* And the motion of the other sort
which is not after the same manner, nor
in the same, nor about the same, nor in
relation to the same, nor in one place,
nor in order, nor according to any rule
or proportion, may be said to be akin to
senselessness and folly?

*Cle.* That is most true.

*Ath.* Then, after what has been said,
there is no difficulty in distinctly stating, that since soul carries all things
round, either the best soul or the contrary must of necessity carry round and
order and arrange the revolution of the
heaven.

*Cle.* And judging from what has been
said, Stranger, there would be impiety

in asserting that any but the most perfect soul or souls carries round the heavens.

*Ath*. You have understood my meaning right well, Cleinias, and now let me ask you another question.

*Cle*. What are you going to ask?

*Ath*. If the soul carries round the sun and moon, and the other stars, does she not carry round each individual of them?

*Cle*. Certainly.

*Ath*. Then of one of them let us speak, and the same argument will apply to all.

*Cle*. Which will you take?

*Ath*. Everyone sees the body of the sun, but no one sees his soul, nor the soul of any other body living or dead; and yet there is great reason to believe that this nature, unperceived by any of our senses, is circumfused around them all, but is perceived by mind; and therefore by mind and reflection only let us apprehend the following point.

*Cle*. What is that? . . .

*Ath*. . . . this soul of the sun, which is therefore better than the sun, whether taking the sun about in a chariot to give light to men, or acting from without, or in whatever way, ought by every man to be deemed a God.

*Cle*. Yes, by every man who has the least particle of sense.

*Ath*. And of the stars too, and of the moon, and of the years and months and seasons, must we not say in like manner, that since a soul or souls having every sort of excellence are the causes of all of them, those souls are Gods, whether they are living beings and reside in bodies, and in this way order the whole heaven, or whatever be the place and mode of their existence;—and will any one who admits all this venture to deny that all things are full of Gods?

*Cle*. No one, Stranger, would be such a madman.

*Ath*. And now, Megillus and Cleinias, let us offer terms to him who has hither-to denied the existence of the Gods, and leave him.

*Cle*. What terms?

*Ath*. Either he shall teach us that we were wrong in saying that the soul is the original of all things, and arguing accordingly; or, if he be not able to say anything better, then he must yield to us and live for the remainder of his life in the belief that there are Gods.—Let us see, then, whether we have said enough or not enough to those who deny that there are Gods.

*Cle*. Certainly—quite enough, Stranger.

*Ath*. Then to them we will say no more. And now we are to address him who, believing that there are Gods, believes also that they take no heed of human affairs: To him we say—O thou best of men, in believing that there are Gods you are led by some affinity to them, which attracts you toward your kindred and makes you honour and believe in them. But the fortunes of evil and unrighteous men in private as well as public life, which, though not really happy, are wrongly counted happy in the judgment of men, and are celebrated both by poets and prose writers—these draw you aside from your natural piety. Perhaps you have seen impious men growing old and leaving their children's children in high offices, and their prosperity shakes your faith—you have known or heard or been yourself an eyewitness of many monstrous impieties, and have beheld men by such criminal means from small beginnings attaining to sovereignty and the pinnacle of greatness; and considering all these things you do not like to accuse the Gods of them, because they are your relatives; and so from some want of reasoning power, and also from an unwillingness to find fault with them, you have come to believe that they exist indeed, but have no thought or care of human things. Now, that your present evil opinion may not grow to still greater impiety, and that we may if possible use arguments which may conjure away the evil before it arrives, we will add another argument to that originally addressed to him who utterly denied the existence of the Gods. And do you, Megillus and Cleinias, answer for the young man as you did before; and if any impediment comes in our way, I will take the word out of your mouths, and carry you over the river as I did just now.

*Cle.* Very good; do as you say, and we will help you as well as we can.

*Ath.* There will probably be no difficulty in proving to him that the Gods care about the small as well as about the great. For he was present and heard what was said, that they are perfectly good, and that the care of all things is most entirely natural to them.

*Cle.* No doubt he heard that.

*Ath.* Let us consider together in the next place what we mean by this virtue which we ascribe to them. Surely we should say that to be temperate and to possess mind belongs to virtue, and the contrary to vice?

*Cle.* Certainly.

*Ath.* Yes; and courage is a part of virtue, and cowardice of vice?

*Cle.* True.

*Ath.* And the one is honourable, and the other dishonourable?

*Cle.* To be sure.

*Ath.* And the one, like other meaner things, is a human quality, but the Gods have no part in anything of the sort?

*Cle.* That again is what everybody will admit.

*Ath.* But do we imagine carelessness and idleness and luxury to be virtues? What do you think?

*Cle.* Decidedly not.

*Ath.* They rank under the opposite class?

*Cle.* Yes.

*Ath.* And their opposites, therefore, would fall under the opposite class?

*Cle.* Yes.

*Ath.* But are we to suppose that one who possesses all these good qualities will be luxurious and heedless and idle, like those whom the poet compares to stingless drones?

*Cle.* And the comparison is a most just one.

*Ath.* Surely God must not be supposed to have a nature which He Himself hates?—he who dares to say this sort of thing must not be tolerated for a moment.

*Cle.* Of course not. How could He have?

*Ath.* Should we not on any principle be entirely mistaken in praising anyone who has some special business entrusted to him, if he have a mind which takes care of great matters and no care of small ones? Reflect; he who acts in this way, whether he be God or man, must act from one of two principles.

*Cle.* What are they?

*Ath.* Either he must think that the neglect of the small matters is of no consequence to the whole, or if he knows that they are of consequence, and he neglects them, his neglect must be attributed to carelessness and indolence. Is there any other way in which his neglect can be explained? For surely, when it is impossible for him to take care of all, he is not negligent if he fails to attend to those things great or small, which a God or some inferior being might be wanting in strength or capacity to manage?

*Cle.* Certainly not.

*Ath.* Now, then, let us examine the offenders, who both alike confess that there are Gods, but with a difference— the one saying that they may be appeased, and the other that they have no care of small matters: there are three of us and two of them, and we will say to them—In the first place, you both acknowledge that the Gods hear and see and know all things, and that nothing can escape them which is matter of sense and knowledge:—do you admit this?

*Cle.* Yes.

*Ath.* And do you admit also that they have all power which mortals and immortals can have?

*Cle.* They will, of course, admit this also.

*Ath.* And surely we three and they two—five in all—have acknowledged that they are good and perfect?

*Cle.* Assuredly.

*Ath.* But, if they are such as we conceive them to be, can we possibly suppose that they ever act in the spirit of carelessness and indolence? For in us inactivity is the child of cowardice, and carelessness of inactivity and indolence.

*Cle.* Most true.

*Ath.* Then not from inactivity and carelessness is any God ever negligent; for there is no cowardice in them.

*Cle.* That is very true.

*Ath.* Then the alternative which remains is, that if the Gods neglect the lighter and lesser concerns of the universe, they neglect them because they know that they ought not to care about such matters—what other alternative is there but the opposite of their knowing?

*Cle.* There is none.

*Ath.* And, O most excellent and best of men, do I understand you to mean that they are careless because they are ignorant, and do not know that they ought to take care, or that they know, and yet like the meanest sort of men, knowing the better, choose the worse because they are overcome by pleasures and pains?

*Cle.* Impossible.

*Ath.* Do not all human things partake of the nature of soul? And is not man the most religious of all animals?

*Cle.* That is not to be denied.

*Ath.* And we acknowledge that all mortal creatures are the property of the Gods, to whom also the whole of heaven belongs?

*Cle.* Certainly.

*Ath.* And, therefore, whether a person says that these things are to the Gods great or small—in either case it would not be natural for the Gods who own us, and who are the most careful and the best of owners, to neglect us.— There is also a further consideration.

*Cle.* What is it?

*Ath.* Sensation and power are in an inverse ratio to each other in respect to their ease and difficulty.

*Cle.* What do you mean?

*Ath.* I mean that there is greater difficulty in seeing and hearing the small than the great, but more facility in moving and controlling and taking care of small and unimportant things than of their opposites.

*Cle.* Far more.

*Ath.* Suppose the case of a physician who is willing and able to cure some living thing as a whole—how will the whole fare at his hands if he takes care only of the greater and neglects the parts which are lesser?

*Cle.* Decidedly not well.

*Ath.* No better would be the result with pilots or generals, or householders or statesmen, or any other such class, if they neglected the small and regarded only the great;—as the builders say, the larger stones do not lie well without the lesser.

*Cle.* Of course not.

*Ath.* Let us not, then, deem God inferior to human workmen, who, in proportion to their skill, finish and perfect their works, small as well as great, by one and the same art; or that God, the wisest of beings, who is both willing and able to take care, is like a lazy good-for-nothing, or a coward, who turns his back upon labour and gives no thought to smaller and easier matters, but to the greater only.

*Cle.* Never, Stranger, let us admit a supposition about the Gods which is both impious and false.

*Ath.* I think that we have now argued enough with him who delights to accuse the Gods of neglect.

*Cle.* Yes.

*Ath.* He has been forced to acknowledge that he is in error, but he still seems to me to need some words of consolation.

*Cle.* What consolation will you offer him?

*Ath.* Let us say to the youth:—The ruler of the universe has ordered all things with a view to the excellence and preservation of the whole, and each part, as far as may be, has an action and passion appropriate to it. Over these, down to the least fraction of them, ministers have been appointed to preside, who have wrought out their perfection with infinitesimal exactness. And one of these portions of the universe is thine own, unhappy man, which, however little, contributes to the whole; and you do not seem to be aware that this and every other creation is for the sake of the whole, and in order that the life of the whole may be blessed; and that you are created for the sake of the whole, and not the whole for the sake of you. For every physician and every skilled artist does all things for the sake of the whole, directing his effort toward the common good, executing the part for the sake of the whole, and not the whole for the sake of the part. And you are annoyed because you are ignorant how what is best for you happens to you and to the universe, as far as the laws of the common creation admit. Now, as the soul combining first with one body and then with another undergoes all sorts of changes, either of herself, or through the influence of another soul, all that remains to the player of the game is that he should shift the pieces; sending the better nature to the better place, and the worse to the worse, and so assigning to them their proper portion.

*Cle.* In what way do you mean?

*Ath.* In a way which may be supposed to make the care of all things easy to the Gods. If anyone were to form or fashion all things without any regard to the whole—if, for example, he formed a living element of water out of fire, instead of forming many things out of one or one out of many in regular order attaining to a first or second or third birth, the transmutation would have been infinite; but now the ruler of the world has a wonderfully easy task.

*Cle.* How so?

*Ath.* I will explain:—When the king saw that our actions had life, and that there was much virtue in them and much vice, and that the soul and body, although not, like the Gods of popular opinion, eternal, yet having once come into existence, were indestructible (for if either of them had been destroyed, there would have been no generation of living beings); and when he observed that the good of the soul was ever by nature designed to profit men, and the evil to harm them—he, seeing all this, contrived so to place each of the parts that their position might in the easiest and best manner procure the victory of good and the defeat of evil in the whole. And he contrived a general plan by which a thing of a certain nature found a certain seat and room. But the formation of qualities he left to the wills of individuals. For every one of us is made pretty much what he is by the bent of his desires and the nature of his soul.

*Cle.* Yes, that is probably true.

*Ath.* Then all things which have a soul change, and possess in themselves a principle of change, and in changing move according to law and to the order of destiny. . . .

### The Divine Duality: Eternal and Temporal Aspects

15. *Str.* [Stranger] Any power of doing or suffering in a degree however slight was held by us to be a sufficient definition of being?

*Theaet.* [Theaetetus] True.

*Str.* They deny this, and say that the power of doing or suffering is confined to becoming, and that neither power is applicable to being.[4]

*Theaet.* And is there not some truth in what they say?

*Str.* Yes; but our reply will be, that we want to ascertain from them more distinctly whether they further admit that the soul knows, and that being or essence is known.

*Theaet.* There can be no doubt that they say so.

*Str.* And is knowing and being known doing or suffering, or both, or is the one doing and the other suffering, or has neither any share in either?

*Theaet.* Clearly, neither has any share in either; for if they say anything else, they will contradict themselves.

*Str.* I understand; but they will allow that if to know is active, then, of course, to be known is passive. And on this view being, in so far as it is known, is acted upon by knowledge, and is therefore in motion; for that which is in a state of rest cannot be acted upon, as we affirm.

*Theaet.* True.

*Str.* And, O heavens, can we ever be made to believe that motion and life and soul and mind are not present with perfect being? Can we imagine that being is devoid of life and mind, and exists in awful unmeaningness an everlasting fixture?

*Theaet.* That would be a dreadful thing to admit, Stranger.

*Str.* But shall we say that being has mind and not life?

*Theaet.* How is that possible?

*Str.* Or shall we say that both inhere in perfect being, but that it has no soul which contains them?

*Theaet.* And in what other way can it contain them?

*Str.* Or that being has mind and life and soul, but although endowed with soul remains absolutely unmoved?

*Theaet.* All three suppositions appear to me to be irrational.

*Str.* Under being, then, we must include motion, and that which is moved.

*Theaet.* Certainly.

*Str.* Then, Theaetetus, our inference is, that if there is no motion, neither is there any mind anywhere, or about anything or belonging to anyone.

*Theaet.* Quite true.

*Str.* And yet this equally follows, if we grant that all things are in motion—upon this view too mind has no existence.

*Theaet.* How so?

*Str.* Do you think that sameness of condition and mode and subject could ever exist without a principle of rest?

*Theaet.* Certainly not.

*Str.* Can you see how without them mind could exist, or come into existence anywhere?

*Theaet.* No.

*Str.* And surely contend we must in every possible way against him who would annihilate knowledge and reason and mind, and yet ventures to speak confidently about anything.

*Theaet.* Yes, with all our might.

*Str.* Then the philosopher, who has the truest reverence for these qualities, cannot possibly accept the notion of those who say that the whole is at rest, either as unity or in many forms: and he will be utterly deaf to those who assert universal motion. As children say entreatingly "Give us both," so he will include both the movable and immovable in his definition of being and all.

*16.* Let me tell you then why the creator made this world of generation. He was good, and the good can never have any jealousy of anything. And being free from jealousy, he desired that all things should be as like himself as they could be. This is in the truest sense the origin of creation and

---

4. The reference is to the idealists or "friends of ideas," including perhaps Socrates, and so likewise perhaps including the early phase of Platonism.

of the world, as we shall do well in believing on the testimony of wise men: God desired that all things should be good and nothing bad, so far as this was attainable. Wherefore also finding the whole visible sphere not at rest, but moving in an irregular and disorderly fashion, out of disorder he brought order, considering that this was in every way better than the other. Now the deeds of the best could never be or have been other than the fairest; and the creator, reflecting on the things which are by nature visible, found that no unintelligent creature taken as a whole was fairer than the intelligent taken as a whole; and that intelligence could not be present in anything which was devoid of soul. For which reason, when he was framing the universe, he put intelligence in soul, and soul in body, that he might be the creator of a work which was by nature fairest and best. Wherefore, using the language of probability, we may say that the world became a living creature truly endowed with soul and intelligence by the providence of God.

This being supposed, let us proceed to the next stage: In the likeness of what animal did the Creator make the world? It would be an unworthy thing to liken it to any nature which exists as a part only; for nothing can be beautiful which is like any imperfect thing; but let us suppose the world to be the very image of that whole of which all other animals both individually and in their tribes are portions. For the original of the universe contains in itself all intelligible beings, just as this world comprehends us and all other visible creatures. For the Deity, intending to make this world like the fairest and most perfect of intelligible beings, framed one visible animal comprehending within itself all other animals of a kindred nature. Are we right in saying that there is one world, or that they are many and infinite? There must be one only, if the created copy is to accord with the original. For that which includes all other intelligible creatures cannot have a second or companion; in that case there would be need of another living being which would include both, and of which they would be parts, and the likeness would be more truly said to resemble not them, but that other which included them. In order then that the world might be solitary, like the perfect animal, the creator made not two worlds or an infinite number of them; but there is and ever will be one only-begotten and created heaven. . . .

Now the . . . Creator compounded the world out of all the fire and all the water and all the air and all the earth, leaving no part of any of them nor any power of them outside. His intention was, in the first place, that the animal should be as far as possible a perfect whole and of perfect parts: secondly, that it should be one, leaving no remnants out of which another such world might be created: and also that it should be free from old age and unaffected by disease. Considering that if heat and cold and other powerful forces which unite bodies surround and attack them from without when they are unprepared, they decompose them, and by bringing diseases and old age upon them, make them waste away—for this cause and on these grounds he made the world one whole, having every part entire, and being therefore perfect and not liable to old age and disease. And he gave to the world the figure which was suitable and also natural. Now to the animal which was to comprehend all animals, that figure was suitable which comprehends within itself all other figures. Wherefore he made the world in the form of a globe, round as from a lathe, having its extremes in every direction equidistant from the centre, the most perfect and the most like itself of all figures; for he considered that the like is infinitely fairer than the unlike. This he finished off, making the surface smooth all around for many reasons; in the first place, because the living being had no need of eyes when there was nothing remaining outside him to be seen; nor of ears when there was nothing to be heard; and there was no surrounding atmosphere to be breathed; nor would there have been any use of organs by the help of which he might receive his food or get rid of what he had already digested, since there was nothing which went from him or came into him: for there was nothing beside him. Of design he was created thus, his own waste providing his own food, and all that he did or suffered taking place in and by himself. For the Creator conceived that a being which was self-sufficient would be far more excellent than one which lacked anything; and, as he had no need to take anything or defend himself against any one, the Creator did not think it necessary to bestow upon him hands: nor had he any need of feet, nor of the whole apparatus of walking; but the movement suited to his spherical form was assigned to him, being of all the seven that which is most appropriate to mind and intelligence; and he was made to move in the same manner and on the same spot, within his own limits revolving in a circle. All the other six motions were taken away from him, and he was made not to partake of their deviations. And as this circular movement required no feet, the universe was created without legs and without feet.

Such was the whole plan of the eternal God about the god that was to be, to whom for this reason he gave a body, smooth and even, having a surface in every direction equidistant from the centre, a body entire and perfect, and formed out of perfect bodies. And in the centre he put the soul, which he diffused throughout the body, making it also to be the exterior environment of it; and he made the universe a circle moving in a circle, one and solitary, yet by reason of its excellence able to converse with itself, and needing no other friendship or acquaintance. Having these purposes in view he created the world a blessed god.

Now God did not make the soul after the body, although we are speaking of them in this order; for having brought them together he would never have allowed that the elder should be ruled by the younger; but this is a random manner of speaking which we have, because somehow we ourselves too are very much under the dominion of chance. Whereas he made the soul in origin and excellence prior to and older than the body, to be the ruler and mistress, of whom the body was to be the subject. . . .

Now when the Creator had framed the soul according to his will, he formed within her the corporeal universe, and brought the two together, and united them centre to centre. The soul, interfused everywhere from the centre to the circumference of heaven, of which also she is the external envelopment, herself turning in herself, began a divine beginning of never-ceasing and rational life enduring throughout all time. The body of heaven is visible, but the soul is invisible, and partakes of reason and harmony, and being made by the best of intellectual and everlasting natures, is the best of things created. And because she is composed of the same and of the other and of the essence, these three, and is divided and united in due proportion, and in her revolutions returns upon herself, the soul, when touching anything which has essence, whether dispersed in parts or undivided, is stirred through all her powers, to declare the sameness or difference of that thing and some other; and to what individuals are related, and by what affected, and in what way and how and when, both in the world of generation and in the world of immutable being. And when reason, which works with equal truth, whether she be in the circle of the diverse or of the same—in voiceless silence holding her onward course in the sphere of the self-moved—when reason, I say, is hovering around the sensible world and when the circle of the diverse also moving truly imparts the intimations of sense to the whole soul, then arise opinions and beliefs sure and certain. But when reason is concerned with the rational, and the circle of the same moving smoothly declares it, then intelligence and knowledge are necessarily perfected. And if any one affirms that in which these two are found to be other than the soul, he will say the very opposite of the truth.

When the father and creator saw the creature which he had made moving and living, the created image of the eternal gods, he rejoiced, and in his joy determined to make the copy still more like the original; and as this was eternal, he sought to make the universe eternal, so far as might be. Now the nature of the ideal being was everlasting, but to bestow this attribute in its fullness upon a creature was impossible. Wherefore he resolved to have a moving image of eternity, and when he set in order the heaven, he made this image eternal but moving according to number, while eternity itself rests in unity; and this image we call time. For there were no days and nights and months and years before the heaven was created, but when he constructed the heaven he created them also. They are all parts of time, and the past and future are created species of time, which we unconsciously but wrongly transfer to the eternal essence: for we say that he "was," he "is," he "will be," but the truth is that "is" alone is properly attributed to him, and that "was" and "will be" are only to be spoken of becoming in time, for they are motions,

but that which is immovably the same cannot become older or younger by time, nor ever did or has become, or hereafter will be, older or younger, nor is subject at all to any of those states which affect moving and sensible things and of which generation is the cause.

[Sec. 10, *The Dialogues of Plato*, trans. Benjamin Jowett (5 vols.; London: Oxford University Press, 1892), *Phaedo*, Pars. 78–80. Sec. 11, *ibid.*, *Republic*, Pars. 381, 379. Sec. 12, *ibid.*, *Parmenides*, Pars. 133–35. Sec. 13, *ibid.*, *Phaedrus*, Par. 245. Sec. 14, *ibid.*, *Laws*, Pars. 893, 894, 894–904. Sec. 15, *ibid.*, *Sophist*, Pars. 248–49. Sec. 16, *ibid.*, *Timaeus*, Pars. 29–31, 32–34, 36–38.]

### COMMENT

Plato's theology turns upon two principles: the pure being of the Forms and the supreme mobility or self-motion of soul. In the final dialogues both categories—absolute fixity and absolute mobility—find expression. That the divine is to be regarded as the supreme exemplar of each category may be inferred from the coincident predominance of the category of fixity where the divine is an immutable God and of the category of mobility where the divine is mutable in some respects. Where the opposed categories are affirmed with almost equal weight—in the *Timaeus*—the divine is dual, exemplifying the properties of both. Here the decision of the *Sophist*, referring to the achievement of interpretative adequacy, seems to be operative: "As children say entreatingly 'Give us both,' so he [the philosopher] will include both the movable and immovable in his definition of being and all."

The unchanging deity of the *Phaedo*, *Republic*, and *Parmenides* is the supreme instance of fixity; the self-moving deity of the *Phaedrus* and the *Laws* is the supreme instance of mobility; in the *Timaeus* the eternal God is the exemplar of fixity as principle and the world soul that of self-motion. The categories in turn claim for God eternality and temporality; so that, placing together the equivalent propositions suggested by each, Plato would seem to have affirmed opposing statements, such as: "The divine is an eternal creator and yet an everlasting creature"; "The divine is unchangeable, and yet the beginning of change is change of the self-changing principle"; "The supremacy of the divine requires that he be remote from ordinary existence, and yet, since soul contains its body, the supreme soul contains all existence within itself."

In the *Timaeus* such oppositions are exact and clearly stated. The properties of the opposed categories are fixed each in a different being so that the eternal God is unchangeable and remote; the world soul is everlasting, the beginning of change, and has the world as its internal environment. It is as though Plato's world soul were an answer to the criticism of the *Parmenides* that an absolute God could not know or be related to the world. But the same rigidity of structure which in the *Parmenides* separated God from the world would seem in the *Timaeus* to prevent any relation between the eternal God and the world soul. For the sake of consistency elsewhere, Plato has employed two radically different principles, apparently on the same level of concreteness, in order to describe the divine being. On the surface one might argue that this achievement succeeds only in transplanting a *non sequitur* from one portion of his system into the supreme instance treated by his categories.

The path of much later philosophy was to seek consistency by sacrificing either one or the other of these two types of propositions about God. Aristotle and the Middle Ages generally tended to remove from the scheme the propositions about the mutable and to retain those about the immutable. A modern attempt has tended to remove the propositions about the immutable and to retain those about the mutable. But, if consistency attained in this manner sacrifices adequacy, nothing has been gained. Finally—and we think rightly—Plato forced the problem of explaining the world process into a question about God's attributes; but the contradiction inhering in his apparent answer as given in the *Timaeus* is not wholly satisfactory.

Evidently the world soul and the eternal God cannot be related when both are concrete divine natures. But in fact it is the essence of Platonism to recognize—in the idea and its corresponding sense-object—distinct levels of ontological abstractness. Further, it is clear that the world soul contains the concrete aspects of reality—the object-realm with its spatial and temporal relations. Now for Plato "time is the image of eternity" as the world of sense is the image of the world of ideas. "Eternity," as a concept, is derived from the absence of qualifying temporal relations and means simply that: total absence of temporal relation.[5] And, since *abstractness* is among the ascriptions proper to the world of ideas, it would seem necessarily to serve as a partial *definiens* of eternity. An eternal God, then, could not be conceived Platonically as a concrete entity; hence, one infers that Plato did not conceive, or at least should not have conceived, the world soul and the eternal God to be on the same level of concreteness. The eternal God is the nonconcrete deity.

If Platonism leads us to this point, it appears doubtful that any difference in meaning can be found between Plato's assertion that the world soul and the eternal God are distinct divine natures and the assertion that deity possesses two aspects, one concrete and inclusive,

5. Cf. Harry Austryn Wolfson, *The Philosophy of Spinoza* (Cambridge: Harvard University Press, 1934), I, 358–60.

the other abstract and independent. And this is essentially the view of Whitehead. It cannot of course be said that Plato would have agreed to this modification; but we do claim (1) that these conclusions from the *Timaeus* follow from the basic Platonic distinctions and (2) that the above modification is in the direction of whatever logic led to the elaboration of the view of the *Timaeus* after the expression of the nonconsonant positions of the *Phaedo* and the *Republic*, on the one side, and of the *Phaedrus*, on the other. With this modification both types of propositions —those following from the category of absolute fixity and making up the attribute of eternality, along with those following from the category of absolute mobility and making up the attribute of temporality—are capable of belonging to God without contradiction.

Certain conceptions of deity contrary to those we have considered, such as the conception of a demiurge, or the occasional multiplication of gods into systems of astral spirits, are mythical expressions in a sense which does not apply to the world soul and the eternal God. Cornford has pointed this out. It is quite evident, for instance, that these latter can be inferred from Plato's categorial distinctions, while the former cannot be so derived. It is not myth but metaphor which halters the explanation of the *Laws;* deity is here described with admirable fullness in many respects, yet one cannot gain from the description as exact an understanding of God's categorial relations as is available in the *Timaeus.* The reason is that in the *Laws* the relation of self-motion to fixity is not stated but expressed in the figure of circular motion, a motion which has the property—like the fixed center of a circle—of remaining in one place.

The argument of the *Republic*, inferring God's immutability from his perfection (often repeated in later thought), is ambiguous and can be clarified from the perspective of the *Timaeus*. The reasoning mixes the two categories, for God is treated as a concrete being and yet as possessing a stated character of perfection and an implicit character of immutability which belong to ideas. The principle of fixity is ascendant in the *Republic*, and deity is hence being described by those considerations which pertain to the world of ideas. But only the God which is eternal can be so described. Plato recognizes this in the *Timaeus;* the world soul is not perfect but merely "the most perfect of created things." God as a concrete being is, it would seem, the nonsurpassable individual. Absolute perfection belongs only to God as eternal. Hence, one may say that no fault is to be found with the view of perfection in the *Republic*, but the category to which the property and the entity possessing that property belong has not yet been clearly defined.

Some see in Plato's apparent lapses into polytheism a failure to realize that deity is not merely *a* being (or set of beings) but *the* being, in a sense Being itself. The question is: "Has Plato found the principle by which to exclude polytheism?" Others see in Plato's description of God's dependence upon the forms, or, at least, the form of Good, a failure to achieve a true theism, wherein the forms would depend upon God or be created by him. The question is: "Have the forms supremacy over God?"

With respect to the latter question we suggest that the issue is secondary and largely verbal. The Good and God are alike eternal; now as between eternal things "independence" has no clear meaning. *A* is independent of *B* if, at some time or other, *A* occurs, or might occur, without *B*'s also occurring. But in things that do not occur but have eternal reality, the question does not arise. Moreover, for Plato the eternal God (or God so far as eternal) eternally contemplates the eternal Good or Pattern. So the Good is object of divine awareness and in that sense is an idea. Moreover, it is idle to ask whether or not the Good would exist if it were *not* a divine idea; the question has no clear meaning, for it suggests that the eternal God is a mere fact, something that perhaps comes to be, perhaps does not come to be. Of the eternal there is no "perhaps" to consider. Nor does it just happen that the eternal reason surveys the Good or that the Good is surveyed by it. To say that the Good is *essentially* something in the mind of God is only to say, more emphatically, that for all eternity there is no alternative to the contemplation of the Good by deity. But perhaps Plato can fairly be regarded as somewhat defective here; perhaps he should have raised the question explicitly.

With respect to monotheism the mere idea of a multiplicity of superhuman souls, astral or otherwise, is not incompatible with monotheistic intent. Even to call these "deities" or "gods" in a loose sense may be a passing concession to ordinary language where precision is not sought. Still, Plato's apparent separation of the divine into two natures makes it reasonable to suppose that he was something less than clear about the absolutely unique or categorical status of God among individuals. Perhaps Gilson is right that it was meditation on the biblical "I Am" which later led to this discovery. However, monotheism is close to the surface of the Platonic approach, for God is not posited as a mere fact to explain some observed facts. The eternal God comprehends the entire realm of ideas—of pattern—and the world soul comprehends the entire realm of things. The divine nature is, on the one hand, the very principle of order in change, that by which the totality of things is one cosmos, and, on the other hand, it is the all-inclusive soul. If there were several principles of order, they would have to be ordered among themselves; and there cannot be several all-inclusive beings or world souls containing all souls and bodies. No statement of more complete monotheistic intent is possible; indeed, the one critical weakness of Plato's theism we take to be his apparent failure to reach a definite and consistent unification of the categories, Being and Becoming, in terms of their supreme **exemplars.**

# Chapter II: *Aristotelian Theism*

## ARISTOTLE (384–322 B.C.)

The numerous trenchant distinctions drawn by Aristotle, and the care with which he patterned into a system the concepts gained from these distinctions, contributed greatly toward defining the role of philosophy in human affairs. Three of his basic doctrines are central to the present analysis, partly because of the light they throw upon his relation to Plato and partly because of the insight they give into Aristotle's position with respect to the principle of polarity. Among other basic results, Aristotle educes (1) a single categorial scheme which appears in some respects to reduce the polarity inherent in the Platonic division of reality into things and ideas; (2) a fourfold analysis of causation with which he thinks to correct certain inadequacies in the systems of his predecessors; and (3) an eternal and indeed necessary being (God, so far as Aristotle has a god) held to be essential to the explanation of process.

Aristotle contends that substance is the sole basic category, while the nine subcategories—quantity, quality, relation, place, time, position, state, action, and affection—are attributes of substance. As for the four causes: efficient cause denotes the manner in which substances act upon each other through locomotion and contact; final cause, when used in its most exalted sense, designates the eternal being, in its operation of inducing change through the attraction inherent in its own perfection, but in its ordinary sense final cause designates the end stage of a process which forms a natural unity, like the growth of an individual organism from seed to maturity, this end stage also apparently exercising a

sort of attraction because of its relative perfection compared to earlier stages of the process; while material and formal cause are the constituents—matter and form—within substance, and, in addition, as with final cause, there is the supreme example of the eternal or divine Form, the form of forms and final cause of final causes.

In substituting the single conception of substance for Plato's apparent dualism, Aristotle, we have said, seems to reduce the opposition within the Platonic scheme; in reality, a complex and perhaps not wholly consistent opposition remains. The polar contraries are to be discerned in the contrasting natures of temporal substances and unmoved mover, on the one hand, and in matter as opposed to form, within temporal substance, on the other. Aristotle has occasioned a shift in the major locus of duality such that it is now internal to the single category of substance, while the contrast of ordinary substance and the divine or unmoved being adds, as we shall see, a minor cluster of polar contraries to the list.

Perishable sensible substance, though somehow a unity, is also in some sense a composite of matter and form. The attributes of matter, so far as contrasted with form, are: potentiality, mutability, passivity, eternality (matter is neither created nor destroyed), and nonconcreteness (for to conceive matter we must, relatively at least, abstract from form). The attributes of form, which has its supreme instance in deity, are: actuality, immutability, activity, eternality (in the most strict sense of what is in no way generated, altered, or destroyed), and—it seems—nonconcreteness (for the concrete substance is

58

not merely the form but the form in the matter, so that form as such, like matter as such, is conceived by abstraction). In the contrast between these two lists of attributes, we meet with our dipolarities: potential-actual, mutable-immutable, and passive-active; but in neither list is it clear that concreteness, as one pole in the concrete-abstract polarity, is to be found, and in both lists we find eternality (though not perhaps in the same sense), which is one term of the eternal-temporal polarity.

Turning to our "minor cluster of contraries," as we have called them, those between deity and the world, we see that form is not only the factor in ordinary being which contrasts with matter but also the exalted being which contrasts with ordinary beings, or sensible and mutable substances; consequently, the same attributes making up one side of the form-and-matter duality will also make up one side of the duality of unmoved mover and movable things. The pure Form, which constitutes a substance or supersubstance without matter, is wholly actual, immutable, eternal, and thus stands in contrast to ordinary substance, which has the properties of actuality (always qualified more or less by potentiality), mutability (somewhat qualified by a formal immutability, since change of substance is restricted to movement from one form to the "contrary" which that form involves), activity (qualified by the passivity of matter), and an unqualified temporality or subjection to genesis and death. Here the eternal-temporal polarity makes its appearance. One term of the concrete-abstract polarity has likewise been gained; for do we not mean by concreteness that specification of an entity which results from determining its nature with respect to the subcategories of substance: quantity, quality, relation, place, time, etc.? But the other term, abstractness, is not present; for Aristotle's deity is not in-

tended to be a mere abstraction. Rather, he seems to believe that there are two kinds of concreteness, the physical and the spiritual. Deity is immaterial, but this negation is not to mean an abstraction from materiality. So some have supposed that Plato conceived his ideas as nonabstract although completely superior to the changing physical world, immune to becoming by their very fulness, not by deficiency. However, as we saw above, the corrective to this tendency is also in Plato. Aristotle is if anything more committed to such a dualism than Plato, for surely the unmoved mover is described as though it were a complete, self-sufficient actuality, yet it is conceived by abstracting from all change, potentiality, and multiplicity. Even the most extreme Platonic dualism could not go beyond this. The essence of such Platonism lies in refusing to employ the relation of abstract and concrete to explicate the contrast of eternity and time, or of the merely identical and unitary with the diverse and multiple. That Aristotle is here more extreme than Plato is shown also by his failure to include in his account of deity any Soul of the World, in which both being and becoming might be involved on the divine level, and thus a genuinely concrete deity attained; it is shown again in his description of the divine cause of motion as unmoved, whereas Plato, in the tenth book of the *Laws,* gives as proof for the divine existence the necessity of a supreme form of the "self-moving" principle which defines "soul." For Plato, soul is, on the one side, eternal with the eternal forms which it envisages; on the other side, and not by way of deficiency necessarily (though Plato at best seems to waver here), the soul is the very essence of becoming, the synthesis of actuality and potency, not mere actuality alone. In Aristotle the soul's becoming is identified with deficiency and denied of deity. True, one can attenuate this contrast between the two philosophers, but something remains when all has been said against it.

Ordinary substance is clearly dipolar, according to Aristotle: it is actual and potential, active and passive, mutable and immutable (in some aspects). But God is monopolar. Aristotle is not here guilty of any mere oversight; that no being save deity is unqualifiedly actual, active, and immutable serves, he thinks, to distinguish deity from the rest of reality. It appears that, while the massive oppositions internal to the system do illustrate the great polar contraries with which every philosophy must deal, such opposition does not apply to every type of being within that system. Ordinary substance is dipolar and illustrates the ultimate principles of thought in the duality inherent in these principles; but deity is monopolar, and this, as we have said, by design.

Aristotle does not argue that the series of past events must have had a first term, the world a beginning in time. On the contrary, he tries to prove that process can have neither beginning nor ending. A first or last moment is nonsense, for a moment is only a boundary between past and future. The reality of the unmoved mover is established not in order to account for a first moment but by way of accounting for the principle of necessity in process. If process cannot begin or end, then that there is process is no accident but a necessity. This implies an active agent whose existence realizes no mere potentiality but is purely necessary and eternal. If there were no agent whose existence was necessary, then all agents might fail to exist and therefore to act. But then there would be no process, which, we have seen, is impossible (sec. 17).

Though Aristotle does not deny an infinite regress of past events, he does deny such a regress of causes of the present event. For his theory is that what is causing a present event must be on hand now to effect this result. Past causes had past effects; present causes only can have present effects. If the man moves the stick, the man is real now with the stick. Thus God is not back of the series of past causal phenomena but back of any present series, its first term in the sense in which the man is first in the series whose final term is the object which is moved by the stick in the man's hand.

It is easiest perhaps to think of this in terms of final causes rather than efficient ones. One cannot, Aristotle argues, have an infinite regress of ends, of results for the sake of which an action occurs. One wants money, to take our own example, for the sake of buying a house; the house for the sake of protection from weather; and this for the sake of the feelings of well-being it makes possible, or for the freedom from distracting discomforts; and these results for their contribution to a happy life. But if one never in this way came to anything that had value for itself and not merely for something beyond itself, then the whole series of means to further means would lose its significance, and there would be neither means nor end. The ultimate end is the relation of each thing to deity. Our happiness or intrinsic value is our participation in or imitation of the sole perfect bliss which is enjoyed by deity. Thus all values have a point of identity or universality, and the unity and order of nature in some mysterious way express this convergence of all lines of valuation to a single point of intersection in the absoluteness of deity which points to no value beyond itself, being wholly self-satisfying.

### The Eternality of Motion

*17....* how can there be any "before" and "after" without the existence of time? Or how can there be any time without the existence of motion? If, then, time is the number of motion or itself a kind of motion, it follows that, if there is always time, motion must also be eternal. But so far as time is concerned we see that all with one exception are in agreement in saying that it is uncreated: in fact, it is just this that enables Democritus to show that all things cannot have had a becoming: for time, he says, is uncreated. Plato alone asserts the creation of time, saying that it had a becoming together with the universe, the universe according to him having had a becoming. Now since time cannot exist and is unthinkable apart from the moment, and the moment is a kind of middle-point, uniting as it does in itself both a beginning and an end, a beginning of future time and an end of past time, it follows that there must always be time: for the extremity of the last period of time that we take must be found in some moment, since time contains no point of contact for us except the moment. Therefore, since the moment is both a beginning and an end, there must always be time on both sides of it. But if this is true of time, it is evident that it must also be true of motion, time being a kind of affection of motion.

### The Unmoved Movent: Emphasis on Efficient Cause and Locomotion

*18.* . . . all things that are in motion must be moved by something.

Now this may come about in either of two ways. Either the movent is not itself responsible for the motion, which is to be referred to something else which moves the movent, or the movent is itself responsible for the motion. Further, in the latter case, either the movent immediately precedes the last thing in the series, or there may be one or more intermediate links: e.g., the stick moves the stone and is moved by the hand, which again is moved by the man: in the man, however, we have reached a movent that is not so in virtue of being

moved by something else. Now we say that the thing is moved both by the last and by the first movent in the series, but more strictly by the first, since the first movent moves the last, whereas the last does not move the first, and the first will move the thing without the last, but the last will not move it without the first: e.g., the stick will not move anything unless it is itself moved by the man. If then everything that is in motion must be moved by something, and the movent must either itself be moved by something else or not, and in the former case there must be some first movent that is not itself moved by anything else, while in the case of the immediate movent being of this kind there is no need of an intermediate movent that is also moved (for it is impossible that there should be an infinite series of movents, each of which is itself moved by something else, since in an infinite series there is no first term)—if then everything that is in motion is moved by something, and the first movent is moved but not by anything else, it must be moved by itself.

*19.* . . . there must be three things— the moved, the movent, and the instrument of motion. Now the moved must be in motion, but it need not move anything else: the instrument of motion must both move something else and be itself in motion (for it changes together with the moved, with which it is in contact and continuous, as is clear in the case of things that move other things locally, in which case the two things must up to a certain point be in contact): and the movent—that is to say, that which causes motion in such a manner that it is not merely the instrument of motion—must be unmoved. Now we have visual experience of the last term in this series, namely that which has the capacity of being in motion, but does not contain a motive principle, and also of that which is in motion but is moved by itself and not by anything else: it is reasonable, therefore, not to say necessary, to suppose the existence of the third term also, that which causes motion but is itself unmoved.

20. . . . if the whole moves itself we may distinguish in it that which imparts the motion and that which is moved: so while we say that $AB$ is moved by itself, we may also say that it is moved by $A$. And since that which imparts motion may be either a thing that is moved by something else or a thing that is unmoved, and that which is moved may be either a thing that imparts motion to something else or a thing that does not, that which moves itself must be composed of something that is unmoved but imparts motion and also of something that is moved but does not necessarily impart motion but may or may not do so. Thus let $A$ be something that imparts motion but is unmoved, $B$ something that is moved by $A$ and moves $C$, $C$ something that is moved by $B$ but moves nothing (granted that we eventually arrive at $C$ we may take it that there is only one intermediate term, though there may be more). Then the whole $ABC$ moves itself. But if I take away $C$, $AB$ will move itself, $A$ imparting motion and $B$ being moved, whereas $C$ will not move itself or in fact be moved at all. Nor again will $BC$ move itself apart from $A$: for $B$ imparts motion only through being moved by something else, not through being moved by any part of itself. So only $AB$ moves itself. That which moves itself, therefore, must comprise something that imparts motion but is unmoved and something that is moved but does not necessarily move anything else: and each of these two things, or at any rate one of them, must be in contact with the other. If, then, that which imparts motion is a continuous substance[1]—that which is moved must of course be so—it is clear that it is not through some part of the whole being of such nature as to be

capable of moving itself that the whole moves itself: it moves itself as a whole, both being moved and imparting motion through containing a part that imparts motion and a part that is moved. It does not impart motion as a whole nor is it moved as a whole: it is $A$ alone that imparts motion and $B$ alone that is moved.

21. From what has been said, then, it is evident that that which primarily imparts motion is unmoved: for, whether the series is closed at once by that which is in motion but moved by something else deriving its motion directly from the first unmoved, or whether the motion is derived from what is in motion but moves itself and stops its own motion, on both suppositions we have the result that in all cases of things being in motion that which primarily imparts motion is unmoved.

22. . . . the following considerations will make it clear that there must necessarily be some such thing, which, while it has the capacity of moving something else, is itself unmoved and exempt from all change, which can affect it neither in an unqualified nor in an accidental sense. Let us suppose, if anyone likes, that in the case of certain things it is possible for them at different times to be and not to be, without any process of becoming and perishing (in fact it would seem to be necessary, if a thing that has not parts at one time is and at another time is not, that any such thing should without undergoing any process of change at one time be and at another time not be). And let us further suppose it possible that some principles that are unmoved but capable of imparting motion at one time are and at another time are not. Even so, this cannot be true of *all* such principles, since there must clearly be something that *causes* things that move themselves at one time to be and at another not to be. . . . The eternity and continuity of the process cannot be caused either by any one of them singly or by the sum of them, because

1. I.e., an individual or single substance.

this causal relation must be eternal and necessary, whereas the sum of these movents is infinite and they do not all exist together. It is clear, then, that though there may be countless instances of the perishing of some principles that are unmoved but impart motion, and though many things that move themselves perish and are succeeded by others that come into being, and though one thing that is unmoved moves one thing while another moves another, nevertheless there is something that comprehends them all, and that as something apart from each one of them, and this it is that is the cause of the fact that some things are and others are not and of the continuous process of change: and this causes the motion of the other movents, while they are the causes of the motion of other things. Motion, then, being eternal, the first movent, if there is but one, will be eternal also: if there are more than one, there will be a plurality of such eternal movents. We ought, however, to suppose that there is one rather than many, and a finite rather than an infinite number. When the consequences of either assumption are the same, we should always assume that things are finite rather than infinite in number, since in things constituted by nature that which is finite and that which is better ought, if possible, to be present rather than the reverse: and here it is sufficient to assume only one movent, the first of unmoved things, which being eternal will be the principle of motion to everything else.

23. Now of the three kinds of motion that there are—motion in respect of magnitude, motion in respect of affection, and motion in respect of place[2]— it is this last, which we call locomotion, that must be primary. This may be shown as follows. . . . The fact that a thing is altered requires that there

should be something that alters it, something, e.g., that makes the potentially hot into the actually hot: so it is plain that the movent does not maintain a uniform relation to it but is at one time nearer to and at another farther from that which is altered:[3] and we cannot have this without locomotion. If, therefore, there must always be motion, there must also always be locomotion as the primary motion, and, if there is a primary as distinguished from a secondary form of locomotion, it must be the primary form. Again, all affections have their origin in condensation and rarefaction: thus heavy and light, soft and hard, hot and cold, are considered to be forms of density and rarity. But condensation and rarefaction are nothing more than combination and separation, processes in accordance with which substances are said to become and perish: and in being combined and separated things must change in respect of place. And further, when a thing is increased or decreased its magnitude changes in respect of place.

Again, there is another point of view from which it will be clearly seen that locomotion is primary. As in the case of other things so too in the case of motion the word "primary" may be used in several senses. A thing is said to be prior to other things when, if it does not exist, the others will not exist, whereas it can exist without the others: and there is also priority in time and priority in perfection of existence. Let us begin, then, with the first sense. Now there must be motion continuously, and there may be continuously either continuous motion or successive motion, the former, however, in a higher degree than the latter: moreover it is better that it should be continuous rather than successive motion, and we always as-

2. The more familiar designations of quantity, quality, and place are given to these respective motions in *Physics* 226a, 25.

3. "Alteration" is the second motion named above; in one omitted portion Aristotle has said that "increase," the first-named motion, requires alteration.

sume the presence in nature of the better, if it be possible:[4] since, then, continuous motion is possible . . . , and no other motion can be continuous except locomotion, locomotion must be primary. For there is no necessity for the subject of locomotion to be the subject either of increase or of alteration, nor need it become or perish: on the other hand there cannot be any one of these processes without the existence of the continuous motion imparted by the first movent.

Secondly, locomotion must be primary in time: for this is the only motion possible for eternal things. It is true indeed that, in the case of any individual thing that has a becoming, locomotion must be the last of its motions: for after its becoming it first experiences alteration and increase, and locomotion is a motion that belongs to such things only when they are perfected. But there must previously be something else that is in process of locomotion to be the cause even of the becoming of things that become, without itself being in process of becoming, as, e.g., the begotten is preceded by what begot it: otherwise becoming might be thought to be the primary motion on the ground that the thing must first become. But though this is so in the case of any individual thing that becomes, nevertheless before anything becomes, something else must be in motion, not itself becoming but being, and before this there must again be something else. And since becoming cannot be primary—for, if it were, everything that is in motion would be perishable—it is plain that no one of the motions next in order can be prior to locomotion. By the motions next in order I mean increase and then alteration, decrease, and perishing. All

4. The second sense of primary offers a stronger argument to contemporary minds; it is not only better that continuous motion be primary but necessary in order that the whole temporal series be not subject to perishing.

these are posterior to becoming: consequently, if not even becoming is prior to locomotion, then no one of the other processes of change is so either.

Thirdly, that which is in process of becoming appears universally as something imperfect and proceeding to a first principle: and so what is posterior in the order of becoming is prior in the order of nature. Now all things that go through the process of becoming acquire locomotion last. It is this that accounts for the fact that some living things, e.g., plants and many kinds of animals, owing to lack of the requisite organ, are entirely without motion, whereas others acquire it in the course of their being perfected. Therefore, if the degree in which things possess locomotion corresponds to the degree in which they have realized their natural development, then this motion must be prior to all others in respect of perfection of existence: and not only for this reason but also because a thing that is in motion loses its essential character less in the process of locomotion than in any other kind of motion: it is the only motion that does not involve a change of being in the sense in which there is a change in quality when a thing is altered and a change in quantity when a thing is increased or decreased.

*24.* In rectilinear motion we have a definite starting-point, finishing-point, and middle-point, which all have their place in it in such a way that there is a point from which that which is in motion can be said to start and a point at which it can be said to finish its course (for when anything is at the limits of its course, whether at the starting-point or at the finishing-point, it must be in a state of rest). On the other hand in circular motion there are no such definite points: for why should any one point on the line be a limit rather than any other? Any one point as much as any other is alike starting-point, middle-point, and finishing-point, so that we can say of certain things both that they are always and that they never are at a starting-point and at a finishing-point (so that a revolving sphere, while it is in motion, is also in a sense at rest, for it continues to occupy the same place). The reason of this is that in this case all these characteristics belong to the centre: that is to say, the centre is alike starting-point, middle-point, and finishing-point of the space traversed; consequently, since this point is not a point on the circular line, there is no point at which that which is in process of locomotion can be in a state of rest as having traversed its course, because in its locomotion it is proceeding always about a central point and not to an extreme point: therefore it remains still, and the whole is in a sense always at rest as well as continuously in motion.

25. Our present position, then, is this: We have argued that there always was motion and always will be motion throughout all time, and we have explained what is the first principle of this eternal motion: we have explained further which is the primary motion and which is the only motion that can be eternal: and we have pronounced the first movent to be unmoved.

26. . . . it is clear that the first unmoved movent cannot have any magnitude. For if it has magnitude, this must be either a finite or an infinite magnitude. Now we have already proved in our course on Physics that there cannot be an infinite magnitude: and we have now proved that it is impossible for a finite magnitude to have an infinite force, and also that it is impossible for a thing to be moved by a finite magnitude during an infinite time. But the first movent causes a motion that is eternal and does cause it during an infinite time. It is clear, therefore, that the first movent is indivisible and is without parts and without magnitude.

### The Unmoved Movent: Emphasis on Final Cause and Perfection

27. There is, then, something which is always moved with an unceasing motion, which is motion in a circle; and this is plain not in theory only but in fact. Therefore the first heaven must be eternal. There is therefore also something which moves it. And since that which is moved and moves is intermediate, there is something which moves without being moved, being eternal, substance, and actuality. And the object of desire and the object of thought move in this way; they move without being moved. The primary objects of desire and of thought are the same. For the apparent good is the object of appetite, and the real good is the primary object of rational wish. But desire is consequent on opinion rather than opinion on desire; for the thinking is the starting-point. And thought is moved by the object of thought, and one of the two columns of opposites is in itself the object of thought; and in this, substance is first, and in substance, that which is simple and exists actually. (The one and the simple are not the same; for "one" means a measure, but "simple" means that the thing itself has a certain nature.) But the beautiful, also, and that which is in itself desirable are in the same column; and the first in any class is always best, or analogous to the best.

That a final cause may exist among unchangeable entities is shown by the distinction of its meanings. For the final cause is (a) some being for whose good an action is done, and (b) something at which the action aims; and of these the latter exists among unchangeable entities though the former does not. The final cause, then, produces motion as being loved, but all other things move by being moved.

Now if something is moved it is capable of being otherwise than as it is. Therefore if its actuality is the primary form of spatial motion, then in so far as it is subject to change, in *this* respect it is capable of being otherwise—in place, even if not in substance. But since there is something which moves while itself unmoved, existing actually, this can in no way be otherwise than as it is. For motion in space is the first of the kinds of change, and motion in a circle the first kind of spatial motion; and this the first mover *produces*. The first mover, then, exists of necessity; and in so far as it exists by necessity, its mode of being is good, and it is in this sense a first principle. For the necessary has all these senses—that which is necessary perforce because it is contrary to the natural impulse, that without which the good is impossible, and that which cannot be otherwise but can exist only in a single way.

On such a principle, then, depend the heavens and the world of nature. And it is a life such as the best which we enjoy, and enjoy for but a short time (for it is ever in this state, which we cannot be), since its actuality is also pleasure. (And for this reason are waking, perception, and thinking most pleasant, and hopes and memories are so on account of these.) And thinking in itself deals with that which is best in itself, and that which is thinking in the fullest sense with that which is best in the fullest sense. And thought thinks on itself because it shares the nature of the object of thought; for it becomes an object of thought in coming into contact with and thinking its objects, so that thought and object of thought are the same. For that which is *capable* of receiving the object of thought, i.e., the essence, is thought. But it is *active* when it *possesses* this object. Therefore the possession rather than the receptivity is the divine element which thought seems to contain, and the act of contemplation is what is most pleasant and best. If, then, God is always in that good state in which we sometimes are, this compels

our wonder; and if in a better this compels it yet more. And God *is* in a better state. And life also belongs to God; for the actuality of thought is life, and God is that actuality; and God's self-dependent actuality is life most good and eternal. We say therefore that God is a living being, eternal, most good, so that life and duration continuous and eternal belong to God; for this *is* God.

Those who suppose, as the Pythagoreans and Speusippus do, that supreme beauty and goodness are not present in the beginning, because the beginnings both of plants and of animals are *causes*, but beauty and completeness are in the *effects* of these, are wrong in their opinion. For the seed comes from other individuals which are prior and complete, and the first thing is not seed but the complete being; e.g., we must say that before the seed there is a man—not the man produced from the seed, but another from whom the seed comes.

It is clear then from what has been said that there is a substance which is eternal and unmovable and separate from sensible things. It has been shown also that this substance cannot have any magnitude, but is without parts and indivisible (for it produces movement through infinite time, but nothing finite has infinite power; and, while every magnitude is either infinite or finite, it cannot, for the above reason, have finite magnitude, and it cannot have infinite magnitude because there is no infinite magnitude at all). But it has also been shown that it is impassive and unalterable; for all the other changes are posterior to change of place.

*28.* The nature of the divine thought involves certain problems; for while thought is held to be the most divine of things observed by us, the question how it must be situated in order to have that character involves difficulties. For if it thinks of nothing, what is there here of dignity? It is just like one who sleeps. And if it thinks, but this depends on something else, then (since that which is its substance is not the act of thinking, but a potency) it cannot be the best substance; for it is through thinking that its value belongs to it. Further, whether its substance is the faculty of thought or the act of thinking, what does it think of? Either of itself or of something else; and if of something else, either of the same thing always or of something different. Does it matter, then, or not, whether it thinks of the good or of any chance thing? Are there not some things about which it is incredible that it should think? Evidently, then, it thinks of that which is most divine and precious, and it does not change; for change would be change for the worse, and this would be already a movement. First, then, if "thought" is not the act of thinking but a potency, it would be reasonable to suppose that the continuity of its thinking is wearisome to it. Secondly, there would evidently be something else more precious than thought, viz., that which is thought of. For both thinking and the act of thought will belong even to one who thinks of the worst thing in the world, so that if this ought to be avoided (and it ought, for there are even some things which it is better not to see than to see), the act of thinking cannot be the best of things. Therefore it must be of itself that the divine thought thinks (since it is the most excellent of things), and its thinking is a thinking of thinking.

But evidently knowledge and perception and opinion and understanding have always something else as their object, and themselves only by the way. Further, if thinking and being thought of are different, in respect of which does goodness belong to thought? For to *be* an act of thinking and to *be* an object of thought are not the same thing. We answer that in some cases the knowledge is the object. In the productive sciences it is the substance or essence of the object, matter omitted,

and in the theoretical sciences the definition or the act of thinking is the object. Since, then, thought and the object of thought are not different in the case of things that have not matter, the divine thought and its object will be the same, i.e., the thinking will be one with the object of its thought.

A further question is left—whether the object of the divine thought is composite; for if it were, thought would change in passing from part to part of the whole. We answer that everything which has not matter is indivisible—as human thought, or rather the thought of composite beings, is in a certain period of time (for it does not possess the good at this moment or at that, but its best, being something *different* from it, is attained only in a whole period of time), so throughout eternity is the thought which has *itself* for its object.

We must consider also in which of two ways the nature of the universe contains the good and the highest good, whether as something separate and by itself, or as the order of the parts. Probably in both ways, as an army does; for its good is found both in its order and in its leader, and more in the latter; for he does not depend on the order but it depends on him. And all things are ordered together somehow, but not all alike—both fishes and fowls and plants; and the world is not such that one thing has nothing to do with another, but they are connected. For all are ordered together to one end, but it is as in a house, where the freemen are least at liberty to act at random, but all things or most things are already ordained for them, while the slaves and the animals do little for the common good, and for the most part live at random; for this is the sort of principle that constitutes the nature of each.

29. We must also consider about independence and friendship, and the relations they have to one another. For one might doubt whether, if a man be

in all respects independent, he will have a friend, if one seeks a friend from want and the good man is perfectly independent. If the possessor of virtue is happy, why should he need a friend? For the independent man neither needs useful people nor people to cheer him, nor society; his own society is enough for him. This is most plain in the case of a god; for it is clear that, needing nothing, he will not need a friend, nor have one, supposing that he does not need one.

30. For because God is not such as to need a friend, the argument claims the same of the man who resembles God. But by this reasoning the virtuous man will not even think; for the perfection of God is not in this, but in being superior to thinking of aught beside himself. The reason is, that with us welfare involves a something beyond us, but the deity is his own well-being.

31. There is no one thing that is always pleasant, because our nature is not simple but there is another element in us as well, inasmuch as we are perishable creatures, so that if the one element does something, this is unnatural to the other nature, and when the two elements are evenly balanced, what is done seems neither painful nor pleasant; for if the nature of anything were simple, the same action would always be most pleasant to it. This is why God always enjoys a single and simple pleasure; for there is not only an activity of movement but an activity of immobility, and pleasure is found more in rest than in movement. But "change in all things is sweet," as the poet says, because of some vice; for as it is the vicious man that is changeable, so the nature that needs change is vicious; for it is not simple nor good.

32. But that perfect happiness is a contemplative activity will appear from the following consideration as well. We assume the gods to be above all other beings blessed and happy; but what sort of actions must we assign to them? Acts

of justice? Will not the gods seem absurd if they make contracts and return deposits, and so on? Acts of a brave man, then, confronting dangers and running risks because it is noble to do so? Or liberal acts? To whom will they give? It will be strange if they are really to have money or anything of the kind. And what would their temperate acts be? Is not such praise tasteless, since they have no bad appetites? If we were to run through them all, the circumstances of action would be found trivial and unworthy of gods. Still, everyone supposes that they *live* and therefore that they are active; we cannot suppose them to sleep like Endymion. Now if you take away from a living being action, and still more production, what is left but contemplation? Therefore the activity of God, which surpasses all others in blessedness, must be contemplative; and of human activities, therefore, that which is most akin to this must be most of the nature of happiness.

[Sec. 17, *The Works of Aristotle*, trans. under editorship of J. A. Smith and W. D. Ross (Oxford: Clarendon Press, 1912), 251b, 10–28. Sec. 18, *ibid.*, 256a, 2–20. Sec. 19, *ibid.*, 256b, 14–25. Sec. 20, *ibid.*, 258a, 3–26. Sec. 21, *ibid.*, 258b, 5–9. Sec. 22, *ibid.*, 258b, 14–23; 258b, 28–259a, 14. Sec. 23, *ibid.*, 260a, 26–28; 260b, 1–261a, 23. Sec. 24, *ibid.*, 265a, 29–265b, 8. Sec. 25, *ibid.*, 266a, 5–10. Sec. 26, *ibid.*, 267b, 19–26. Sec. 27, *ibid.*, 1072a, 21–1073a, 11. Sec. 28, *ibid.*, 1074b, 15–1075a, 24. Sec. 29, *ibid.*, 1244b, 1–9. Sec. 30, *ibid.*, 1245b, 14–19. Sec. 31, *ibid.*, 1154b, 20–31. Sec. 32, *ibid.*, 1178b, 7–23.]

## COMMENT

Aristotle's extraordinarily careful and in some respects exact reasoning (only a part of it quoted) to show the necessity of a supreme cause of motion may be criticized from two aspects: (1) Does he establish the existence of an unmoved mover? (2) Does he correctly describe the character of this mover, apart from the mere absence of movement or change in it? Our position is that Aristotle does at least point to a possible valid argument for an unmoved causal factor in all motion, whether or not the details of his own argument can stand, but that there is no possibility of justifying his description of the nature of the Mover or of simply identifying it with God in a religious sense.

1. It is true that many details of the argument for an immutable Cause are rendered dubious by our present insights in science and metaphysics. Thus, for example, many leading logicians, scientists, and metaphysicians today regard the idea of a "changing thing" or "substance" as a confused one, whether in Aristotle's or any of the older formulations of it. The final actualities, they suggest, are events or occasions; change is the difference of each event from earlier events; "things" are more or less stable patterns or sequences in events. Again, Aristotle proves that circular motion is superior by showing that either straight lines must go on forever, which he asserts to be impossible, or there must be discontinuity to permit change of direction. But today there is the complication of relativity physics with its possibility of self-returning though "straight" lines. Again, the Stagirite argues that locomotion is prior to qualitative change because (for one reason) it involves the maximum of identity or being and the minimum of change or becoming. But the conclusion does not follow if one holds, as we do, that becoming is infinitely richer than mere being and is the concrete from which the latter is an abstraction. Aristotle's manner of argument here tends, wrongly, we think, to exalt mere motion above the qualitative changes involved in a progression of ideas or emotions.

2. However, these and other possible objections perhaps do not affect the main point of the argument, which is that the explanation of becoming is incomplete without reference to some factor that does not become but eternally and necessarily is: For, if all the factors ex-

planatory of becoming themselves become, then, since every becoming is contingent (what once was not does not exist necessarily), that anything at all occurs must, it seems, be contingent. Now this implies that an end or a beginning of time and process must be possible. Aristotle argues that it is not possible. A moment of time is in principle an end and a beginning; it is its nature to have a past and a future. A first moment would imply that reality has come out of nothing. To affirm that reality has its genesis in "nothing" and to deny the law of noncontradiction equally evince, in Aristotle's mind, utter irrationality. Rationality demands the impossibility of time's having a beginning or ending and thus requires the inclusion of an eternal and necessary factor in the explanation of process; the infinity of process implies an infinite, not a finite, power acting in it. The argument is not perhaps conclusive in this form, but it does suggest that Aristotle was not, in this instance, pursuing a mere phantom.

In any event our main objection to his reasoning concerns not the reality but the nature of the unmoved mover. Aristotle believes he has proved that (a) there is Something eternal and immutable and necessarily existent which is a causal factor in all change; (b) this Something is an actuality, not a mere abstract form, idea, ideal, or character; (c) it is an actual thinking whose object is simply itself. Now our position is that perhaps he has proved, or more or less clearly suggested ways in which one could prove, (a) but that (b) and (c) do not follow and are not proved; nor do we think them credible.

The eternal immutable cause, says Aristotle, is a final cause. It is an ideal, or an object of desire and love, which elicits change without changing. So far so good. But an ideal need not be an actuality. Indeed, it is arguable that a truly ultimate ideal could never be exhaustively actualized, for therein is its ultimacy. Thus, while Aristotle can very well conceive the ultimate ideal as an eternal immutable factor in actual change, he does not show that this very factor can be conceived to be also actual. It may be real, as an abstraction or idea is real, and yet not possess the actuality of a fully concrete entity. We insist that the concrete or actual is the determinate and that the ultimate ideal, being inexhaustible by actuality, is that which cannot be completely actualized and hence cannot be completely determinate; a universal purpose is then necessarily much less determinate than any manifestation thereof. Hence, the proper locus for the ultimate potentiality is in the final cause and not the actual world.

Thus, it could be maintained that Aristotle was really proving the need for an eternal purpose of extreme generality inspiring change, an ultimate or universal objective luring all things on to their several particular fulfilments as contributory to the universal objective. This purpose of course—Aristotle is here right—could not change if it is really the universal purpose, the common element of all possible purposes. Nor could it have any spatial magnitude. It could not be finite or in the usual theological sense infinite. But this common purposive element would not be any complete actual purpose or any actuality whatever.

An objection is here to be anticipated. If the ultimate ideal is indeterminate, a potentiality, not an actuality, what causally determines the realizations of this ideal? Surely the indeterminate cannot itself produce determinateness. We answer that this contention retains its point whether Aristotle's unmoved mover is regarded as an actual completion of value or an inactual but real ideal, such as "may there be ever more happiness, richness of experience, in the greatest variety, harmony, intensity,

possible at each moment." Particular decisions as to the happenings of the world can in neither case be deduced from the unmoved. But then no particular in its unique particularity can be deduced from anything antecedent. If it were logically contained in prior conditions, it would have existed before it existed. Events do not pre-exist and are not predefined exactly in any sense whatever. To the question, "What, then, is the efficient fully determining cause of an occurrence?" the answer is Whitehead's: "The actual event is self-determining, *causa sui*." Thus that it is impossible for the unmoved mover as an abstract ideal fully to determine any event in no way weakens our view that the unmoved mover must be abstract. This impossibility holds, be the unmoved mover abstract or not.

On the other hand, both Aristotle and his Christian disciples had a good reason for their assumption that there must be a supreme cause that is actual and concrete, not a mere abstract ideal or possibility. For how can a universally relevant and universally attractive ideal, inspiring all process, have its being solely in imperfect forms of process such as human or animal experiencing? Moreover, any one world order is arbitrary; there could have been others. Even supposing that all creatures are capable of entertaining the ideal for themselves, how could they operate to effect the collective decisions required to constitute a definite world order? Cosmic decisions seem to be required for local decisions to have mutual relevance. Only in a well-ruled country can citizens effectively arrange details of their lives by mutual concessions and joint decisions. And no mere general ideal can tell anyone which of the possible cosmic orders expressive of the ideal is to be adopted. Indeed, nothing purely eternal can do this. For no one cosmic order could be good for all eternity. Being arbitrary and only one possibility, any order has only a limited justification, a justification for a time, and then, its main values having been achieved, another cosmic order is requisite. Thus we need some manner of conceiving a perpetual re-creation of new cosmic order, an evolution of cosmic decisions. In short, we need a divine life, not merely a divine ideal. What we do not need is an identification of the two! To say that the ideal is entertained by the divine life is not equivalent to holding that it *is* the divine life, any more than a concept is the total reality of the experience in which it is thought.

Aristotle does not make this distinction. He identifies ideal and actual life, on the ground that the eternal cannot involve potentiality (since then it might fail to be at some time or other). What he overlooks is that the most general element in potentiality is not itself the realization of any anterior potency. The sort of being it has it could not fail to have: being the abstract common element in all possibility, it is itself no mere possibility or actualization of possibility. It is, as Whitehead puts it, not actual but "merely real." And there is no other status it *could* have. It can then very well be eternal. Indeed, it must be so. Aristotle, whose system is sometimes confused in regard to the contrary polarities, abstract-concrete, etc., felt that it was incumbent upon him to discover an immutable but yet actual or concrete process. He finds this process in an (evidently abstract) "thinking of thinking," the image for which process is the circle, since circularity has the property—figuratively speaking—of reissuing from itself without change; each point, serving equally as the end and the beginning, makes of the circle a form without beginning or end. It is evident that he must show thinking to be of this type. And the Stagirite does argue (appealing to Anaxagoras) that mind as ruler is impassive

and unmixed, hence ever-fixed and self-contained. But this seems contrary to experience. Intelligence is sensitive responsiveness to fact in the light of some purpose. It is not true that the commander of the army is *simpliciter* independent of the army while it *simpliciter* depends on him. The characteristics of the commander do impress themselves on the particular army; but also, if you change the commander's army, you will certainly not leave him unchanged. The more of a commander he is—certainly, the more of a man he is—the more sensitive he will be to differences in armies and the more flexible in adjusting himself to such differences so as to give each particular army the form of command suited to it. Sensitive reflection, in the mind, of alterations in the environment constitutes understanding in the concrete sense. A mathematician merely as such may be highly independent of environmental changes, but to exalt the mathematician over the statesman or psychologist or priest who understands individuals not only generically or collectively but individually or distributively is mere expression of the typical philosopher's bias for his own type of mental activity, which indeed tends toward the abstract and universal. It seems evident, then, that the range of Aristotle's affirmations demands an interpretation of deity capable of allowing opposed predicates to stand in contrast without conflict—demands, that is to say, an interpretation which provides for dipolarity.

An underlying reason for conceiving deity in monopolar terms was the belief that changelessness is implied in the very conception of a "necessary" being. In our general introduction we have seen that this is erroneous. One must distinguish between "existence" and "actuality." Things or persons exist, but events or experiences occur or are actual. Now, I shall exist tomorrow (if I am still alive) whether I actually get up at seven or at seven-thirty. But these would not be the same actual events. There are thus alternative possible actualities or occurrences which are equally compatible with my existing. This is involved in the idea of freedom: that the man does and experiences this but might have done and experienced that. And the contingency involved in the very idea of process, in part at least even as seen by Aristotle, implies that the existence of an individual is not identical with any fully determined actuality.

Now, if the premise, "John exists," allows alternative forms of actualization, provided only that *some* actuality expressive of John's personality and physical traits occurs, then to suppose "X exists" to be necessary does not remove the tolerance of alternatives but only implies that *some* actuality *or other* expressive of X's personality must occur. Suppose that any possible state of things would be related to a divine experience having that state of things as its object of awareness. Then, in any possible case, God would exist, that is, he exists necessarily. It follows that "necessary existent" is not the same as "necessary actuality," but rather means unlimited tolerance for alternative possibilities of actuality, so that the requirements of existence are certain to be fulfilled.

Aristotelianism is of course not unaware of the distinction between actual occurrences and existent individuals. But it so treats the distinction that its relevance is overlooked at critical points in the discussion. It contrasts substantial existence, the existence of an enduring individual, with its possibility; and it also contrasts the existence of an accident of a substance with its possibility. And it holds that the former distinction is "prior." But in this way, among numerous unfortunate results, it is overlooked that, whereas the actu-

ality of a particular event or occasion is completely decisive as between alternative possibilities, the existence of an individual in the sense here in question is not; and therefore the strict philosophical contrary of mere possibility is the actual, not the existent. It is actuality of accidents, not existence of substances, that is prior.

The assertion that change is due to inherent vice is suspect. If change here refers to basic principles of character, then the observation is somewhat more acceptable but irrelevant to the theistic issue. For the theistic question is not as to change in character or basic purpose, since this is, for nearly all theists, the unmoved element. The controversial question is as to change (growth) in detailed special purposes, along with additions of novel content. The value of these is aesthetic. There is growth in richness of experience but not in resolute goodness of intention.

If it be assumed that "absolute richness" is possible, then of course there is no point in ascribing increase to God. But if all actual beauty excludes something, if all experience must have some aspect of finitude, of limitation, of decision as among alternatives, if absolute beauty or richness is a contradiction in terms, then the only suitable state which can be ascribed to deity is endless increase, without possibility of termination of the process or loss of what is already acquired.

One reason for denying that absolute richness or absolute pleasure or happiness or bliss is possible is that to such bliss the whole world of limited, variable concrete particulars could contribute nothing of value, and this would mean that that world was a matter of sheer literal, absolute, strict, complete, unqualified indifference to the one lost in absolute bliss. Aristotle accepts this consequence. His deity is indifferent to nature and does not even trouble to contemplate it. This is simply logical, on the premises. But if we are irrelevant to God, then in what sense is he relevant to us? To talk of serving him is sheer nonsense. The most one can say is, "We admire him." But the only relevance of this to action would be that we might try to imitate him. This would mean that we would try to care less and less about other individuals! It is worthy of note that the religion which more than all others held that God cares about his creatures tried to adopt a philosophy which, logically carried out, implied that God is literally and rigorously indifferent to the world. The issue is clear. And we owe Aristotle an immense debt for having made it so clear. One may well prefer his clarity to the confusion which grew up later in the writings of those who could not agree with him and were also unable or unwilling to differ from him in logically clear fashion but spoiled his logic without furnishing another.

Our disagreement with certain Aristotelian premises is contained in the foregoing, but the axiom, "Actuality is prior to potentiality," calls for a more direct statement. The axiom is acceptable if it means that the possibility of a given actuality is always grounded in a prior actuality. We agree with Aristotle that there is no realm of mere essences or mere logical possibilities, independent of all actuality. One cannot go behind actuality to find mere potentiality. But it does not follow that one can go behind potentiality to find mere actuality. There is really nothing to talk about at all, we feel, save some aspect of the ultimate correlation of actual-and-potential which is process actually going on. Particular actualities become, and this implies a potentiality grounded in prior actualities. There is always both potentiality and actuality, in their unity-in-contrast which is process taken generically. Process itself is neither sim-

ply actual nor simply potential but always both. It is simply real (for it is no fiction). It is the principle of the contrast between actual and potential and hence is neither by itself. Actuality is indeed in one sense more inclusive than potentiality, for a potentiality, is, at least in part, some actuality viewed as ready to be succeeded by later actualities which will incorporate it as their past. Looking toward the past, we see actuality as the reality of process. Looking toward the future, we see potentiality. This contrast between past and future, taken generically, has nothing behind it but is eternal. Taking process as eternally both retrospective and prospective, we see that it is essentially actuality-and-potentiality. Adherence to the simple priority of either is one-sided. Hence the most general category becomes "process," not "substance" or "being."

That Aristotle failed correctly to relate abstract and concrete factors in his analysis of becoming, that he commits or does not clearly avoid the "fallacy of misplaced concreteness" (Whitehead), can be shown in many ways. Suppose a change of state in a substance from the absence ("privation") to the presence of quality $Q$. Now in what sense is that which lacks $Q$ the same entity as that which has $Q$? Is it because the *same matter*, first without $Q$, is later qualified by $Q$? But then it is the matter which contains the form as its possession, and thus the matter is the full actuality of the second state of the substance. But we are told that matter is potentiality. Now, a potentiality cannot contain its own realization. The realization of a potency does nothing to the potency. Only for the realization is there a relation to the potency. The potency is just potency and contains no realization of itself. So it cannot be the matter which comes to possess the form. No, the matter is an abstraction from the full actuality which is—what? Suppose it is the form. Then the form contains also the matter, for the realization of a potency is the realization-of-that-potency and is, in being itself, relative to and possessed of the potency as a relative term possesses its relatum. So now we see that the form is indeed the actuality and is the total reality of the substance as at a given time. But note what follows. The form as the present actuality comes into being only in the present moment and is not identical with any previous case of the form. For no previous case realized just *that* matter or potentiality. So form in the sense required to constitute the present actuality is a product of becoming. It is a Whiteheadian event, a new actuality. What becomes of identity through process? There is no identical matter first "not having," then "having," the quality Q; for, as we saw, the matter never has the form, as the potential never has its own actualization. (Aristotle says that the union of potency in actualization is familiar and cannot nor need be further analyzed. This means only that his analysis has not gone into the key question of process.) There is also no identical form, for, as we saw, the form (as capable of solving our problem as to what has the actualization of Q) is a novel actuality, which cannot have been there before in the state of privation with respect to Q. The third possible answer, if neither matter nor form will do, is to say that it is the substance which first lacks, then possesses, the form. But "substance" is, initially, a mere word. It is supposed to stand for the union of matter and form or the form in the matter or the matter in the form. But we have tried to construe such a union, and failed, on Aristotelian bases. The form cannot be in the matter, the actual in the potential. And, if the matter is in

the form, then we have a new actuality and not something identical in diverse events.

In any case, it is demonstrable in general terms that there can be no entity which both lacks and does not lack Q. The contradiction is not removed by remarking, "It lacks Q at one time and has it at another." For now we have to ask, "How can an identical entity have two successive events as its own property?" It can do so only by being something containing successive moments within an identity. This is to put becoming inside being. But no unity can be just the same at a second moment as at a first, if something it contains at the later moment is novel. The least addition or subtraction produces a new total reality. The converse is not true. Something partial may remain identical from one reality to another. An unfamiliar whole may contain familiar constituents or aspects, while a strictly familiar numerically identical whole can contain no novelty at all. It is the part or aspect only that remains fixed in change. Thus the concrete actuality must always be a novel becoming, and the identical aspects or portions in process must remain just that, aspects or portions, not the whole. They are predicates of actuality, not the final subjects of predication; they are abstractions, not concretes.

We can, in conclusion, agree with one of Aristotle's contentions that, if an individual "changes itself," then there is a part which is distinct from what is changed; there is a causal factor and a resultant. On our view, there is indeed an (abstract) unmoved mover, and there is divine actuality; but the two are not the same. God is more than the merely immutable. He is also the ever increasing process. He is greater than our facile distinctions, overflowing them in his unimaginably dipolar, all-inclusive, variably qualified actuality, or in his endless sequence of actualities forming a personal life.

Except for a few Mohammedan and Jewish philosophers (including al-Farabi, Avicenna, Gersonides), Aristotelian theism was in the Middle Ages displaced by classical theism. Eventually it died out completely and for hundreds of years has had no distinguished representative, so far as we are aware. It satisfied neither philosophical nor religious demands. But it constituted a most important step in the development of other doctrines.

# Chapter III: *Classical Theism*

## PHILO THE FOUNDER (*ca.* 20 B.C.—A.D. 54)

Whereas Aristotle wished merely to maintain the spiritual self-sufficiency of deity, the long line of Judeo-Christian orthodox thinkers, of whom Philo is the earliest known to us, added to this Aristotelian concept of spiritual independence the scriptural tenets of creation and providential concern with respect to the world. God must have full awareness not only of his own spirituality but of the concrete particulars of the universe. On the other hand, Philo is determined to relax nothing of the assertion of utter independence. In this double insistence upon divine absoluteness and omniscient providence, the one seeming to deny, the other to assert, a relatedness of God to all other beings, lies the logical tension of classical theism. We are glad to have the high authority of Wolfson for an opinion which we had already felt compelled to adopt—that Philo really is, more than any other man (according to the available evidence), the founder of this vast intellectual-religious movement, which, as Wolfson says, endured for well-nigh seventeen centuries as the almost unchallenged form of European theism.

That Philo, as faithful to his Jewish religion, had no choice but to accept the ideas of creation and of providence requires no elaboration. But something must be said as to his reasons for accepting also the Aristotelian denial of all relativity, temporality, dependence, passivity, inner complexity, to the divine. Several considerations seem to have merged here. The text, "The Lord our God is one," perhaps the most definitive of theological pronouncements for the Jews, was taken by him, and thereafter by countless others, Jewish and Christian, as the absolute denial of

any kind of complexity whatsoever in the divine actuality. "There is but one God" was converted into "God is but one entity"—in every possible sense "simple," single, unitary. Any distinction between internal complexity and external multiplicity was set aside in interpreting the biblical condemnations of polytheism.

Another factor was the text, "I am hath sent thee." Philo thought he discovered in this an assertion of the identity of essence and existence in God (see secs. 43–44). God is the one whose very nature it is to exist and whose actuality, therefore—so it is thought—must exhaust the possibilities of his nature. Hence the Aristotelian notion of an actuality unmixed with potentiality seemed to have biblical sanction.

A third consideration furthering a purely eternalistic or absolutistic conception was the biblical prohibition of idols or images of deity, which together with the denial that God can be seen, and the declaration that no creature is similar to him, were readily taken as excluding corporeal or spatial characteristics. Now, the Greeks had already inclined to the view that it is matter, not soul, which accounts for mutability. Even Plato seems at times to think in this fashion, although on the whole we believe he thought differently. But Aristotle had done all he could to minimize the aspect of change in connection with soul and to attribute our mutability to corporeality. If, then, God is incorporeal, it seems he will be immutable.

Fourth, there are scriptural texts which seem directly to affirm this immutability.

A fifth and perhaps minor source of

76

Philo's eternalism is the notion that the universe, in its general astronomical framework, is immutable or virtually so. This idea is of course also Aristotelian and, to a lesser degree, Platonic.

Sixth, Philo's sense of the majestic power of deity is stronger than his sense of the divine love. He feels that there is no danger of overstating the divine control of all things. Now it seems natural, perhaps, to suppose that the highest form of power will be a pure activity totally devoid of any passive aspect, totally immune to any counteraction or reaction coming from other things.

All these and doubtless other ideas and feelings fuse together in an ecstatic vision of a simple controlling actuality about which nothing further can really be said, save at most that all lesser and compound actualities derive from it. That God is utterly indescribable is frequently declared by our author. Thus he is founder of the negative theology, the *via negativa*.

### The Existence of God: Argument from Design

33. It has invariably happened that the works which they have made have been, in some degree, the proofs of the character of the workmen; for who is there who, when he looks upon statues or pictures, does not at once form an idea of the statuary or painter himself? And who, when he beholds a garment, or a ship, or a house, does not in a moment conceive a notion of the weaver, or shipbuilder, or architect, who has made them?

And if anyone comes into a well-ordered city, in which all parts of the constitution are exceedingly well arranged and regulated, what other idea will he entertain but that this city is governed by wise and virtuous rulers? He, therefore, who comes into that which is truly the greatest of cities, namely, this world, and who beholds all the land, both the mountain and the

champaign district full of animals, and plants, and the streams of rivers, both overflowing and depending on the wintry floods, and the steady flow of the sea, and the admirable temperature of the air, and the varieties and regular revolutions of the seasons of the year; and then too the sun and moon, the rulers of day and night, and the revolutions and regular motions of all the other planets and fixed stars, and of the whole heaven; would he not naturally, or I should rather say, of necessity, conceive a notion of the Father, and creator, and governor of all this system; for there is no artificial work whatever which exists of its own accord? And the world is the most artificial and skillfully made of all works, as if it had been put together by some one who was altogether accomplished and most perfect in knowledge.

It is in this way that we have received an idea of the existence of God.

### The Unknowability of God

34. Who can venture to affirm of him who is the cause of all things either that he is a body, or that he is incorporeal, or that he has such and such distinctive qualities, or that he has no such qualities? or who, in short, can venture to affirm anything positively about his essence, or his character, or his constitution, or his movements? But He alone can utter a positive assertion respecting himself, since he alone has an accurate knowledge of his own nature, without the possibility of mistake.

35. Are not those men then simple who speculate on the essence of God? For how can they who are ignorant of the nature of the essence of their own soul, have any accurate knowledge of the soul of the universe? For the soul of the universe is according to our definition—God.

36. Take this sun, which is perceptible by our outward senses, do we see it by any other means than by the aid

of the sun? And do we see the stars by any other light than that of the stars? And, in short, is not all light seen in consequence of light? And in the same manner God, being his own light, is perceived by himself alone, nothing and no other being co-operating with or assisting him, or being able at all to contribute to the pure comprehension of his existence; therefore those persons are mere guessers who are anxious to contemplate the uncreated God through the medium of the things which he created, acting like those persons who seek to ascertain the nature of the unit through the number two, when they ought, on the other hand, to employ the investigation of the unit itself to ascertain the nature of the number two; for the unit is the first principle.

But these men have arrived at the real truth, who form their ideas of God from God, of light from light.

### Via Negativa: What Must Be Denied of God

*37.* . . . the lover of self who being easily moved, and changeable, and fickle, both in his body and soul . . . did not consider that unchangeableness and steadiness belong to God alone, and to him who is dear to God. And the most evident proof of the unchangeable power which exists in him is this world, which is always in the same place and in the same condition. And if the world is immovable how can the Creator of it be anything but firm?

*38.* . . . God alone exists in a continual and unvarying existence. But those creatures which owe their existence to creation and generation, all are subject to changes in time.

*39.* God is alone: a single being: not a combination: a single nature: but each of us, and every other animal in the world, are compound beings: for instance, I myself am made up of many things, of soul and body. Again, the soul is made up of a rational part and

an irrational part: also of the body, there is one part hot, another cold; one heavy, another light; one dry, another moist. But God is not a compound being, nor one which is made up of many parts, but one which has no mixture with anything else; for whatever could be combined with God must be either superior to him, or inferior to him, or equal to him. But there is nothing equal to God, and nothing superior to him, and nothing is combined with him which is worse than himself; for if it were, he himself would be deteriorated; and if he were to suffer deterioration, he would also become perishable, which it is impious even to imagine. Therefore God exists according to oneness and unity; or we should rather say, that oneness exists according to the one God, for all number is more recent than the world, as is also time. But God is older than the world, and is its Creator.

*40.* But it is not right to be ignorant of this thing either, that the statement, "I am thy God," is made by a certain figurative misuse of language rather than with strict propriety; for the living God, inasmuch as he is living, does not consist in relation to anything; for he himself is full of himself, and he is sufficient for himself, and he existed before the creation of the world, and equally after the creation of the universe; for he is immovable and unchangeable, having no need of any other thing or being whatever, so that all things belong to him, but, properly speaking, he does not belong to anything.

### The Positive Way of Eminence

*41.* . . . He himself is to himself everything that is most honourable—relative, kinsman, friend, virtue, prosperity, happiness, knowledge, understanding, beginning, end, entirety, universality, judge, opinion, intention, law, action, supremacy.

*42.* . . . the living God . . . is superior to the good, and more simple than the one, and more ancient than the unity; with whom, however, who is there of those who profess piety that we can possibly compare?

*43.* . . . the virtues of God are founded in truth, existing according to his essence: since God alone exists in essence, on account of which fact, he speaks of necessity about himself, saying, "I am that I am," as if those who were with him did not exist according to essence, but only appeared to exist in opinion.

*44.* . . . the God who exists in essence, and who is duly thought of in respect of his existence. . . .

*45.* For all mortals, being compared with one another are looked upon as natives of the soil, and nobly born persons, all enjoying equal honours, and equal rank; but by God they are looked upon as strangers and sojourners; for each of us has come into this world as to a new city, in which he had no share before his birth, and having come into it he dwells here, until he has completed the period of life allotted him. At the same time, also, this doctrine of exceeding wisdom is introduced, that the Lord God is the only real citizen, and that every created being is but a stranger and a sojourner.

*46.* . . . he who serves is more worthy of credit than he who requires to be served. But it is impious to conceive that any thing can be better than the Cause of all things, since there is nothing equal to him, nothing that is even a little inferior to him; but every thing which exists in the world is found to be in its whole genus inferior to God.

*47.* . . . God, the creator of all living things, is thoroughly acquainted with all his works, and before he has completely finished them he comprehends the faculties with which they will hereafter be endowed, and altogether he foreknows all their actions and passions.

*48.* It is plain therefore that the creator of all created things, and the maker of all the things that have ever been made, and the governor of all the things which are subject to government, must of necessity be a being of universal knowledge; and he is in truth the father, the creator, and governor of all things in heaven and in the whole world; and indeed future events are overshadowed by the distance of future time, which is sometimes a short and sometimes a long interval. But God is the creator of time also . . . so that there is nothing future to God, who has the very boundaries of time subject to him; . . . and in eternity nothing is past and nothing is future, but everything is present only.

*49.* . . . you will perceive that there is a mind in you and in the universe; and that your mind, having asserted its authority and power over all the things in you, has brought each of the parts into subjection to himself. In like manner also, the mind of the universe being invested with the supremacy, governs the world by independent law and justice, having a providential regard not only for those things which are of more importance, but also for those which appear to be somewhat obscure.

## The Negative and Positive Ways Mixed

*50.* And the doctrine is this: God alone keeps festival in reality, for he alone rejoices, he alone is delighted, he alone feels cheerfulness, and to him alone is it given, to pass an existence of perfect peace unmixed with war. He is free from all pain, and free from all fear; he has no participation in any evils, he yields to no one, he suffers no sorrow, he knows no fatigue, he is full of unalloyed happiness; his nature is entirely perfect, or rather God is himself the perfection, and completion, and boundary of happiness, partaking of nothing else by which he can be rendered better, but giving to every individual thing a portion of what is suited to it, from the fountain of good, namely, from himself; for the beautiful things in this world would never have been such as they are, if they had not been made after an archetypal pattern, which was really beautiful, the uncreate, and blessed, and imperishable model of all things.

51. . . . the Deity is not benefited by any one, inasmuch as he is not in need of anything, nor is it in the power of any one to benefit a being who is in every particular superior to himself. But, on the contrary, God himself is continually and unceasingly benefitting all things.

52. . . . the great Cause of all things does not exist in time, nor at all in place, but he is superior to both time and place; for, having made all created things in subjection to himself, he is surrounded by nothing, but he is superior to everything. And being superior to, and being also external to the world that he has made, he nevertheless fills the whole world with himself; for, having by his own power extended it to its utmost limits, he has connected every portion with another portion according to the principles of harmony.

53. . . . all places are filled at once by God, who surrounds them all and is not surrounded by any of them, to whom alone it is possible to be everywhere and also nowhere. Nowhere, because he himself created place and space at the same time that he created bodies, and it is impious to say that the Creator is contained in anything that he has created.

Again, he is everywhere, because, having extended his powers so as to make them pervade earth, and water, and air, and heaven, he has left no portion of the world desolate, but, having collected everything together, he has bound them with chains which cannot be burst, so that they are never emancipated, on which account he is especially to be praised with hymns.

. . . no one of the words which implies a motion from place to place is appropriate to that God who exists only in essence; such expressions, I mean, as going upwards or downwards, to the right or to the left, forwards or backwards.

54. . . . as place is that which contains bodies, and that to which they flee for refuge, so also the divine reason contains the universe and is that which has completed it.

55. . . . the heaven . . . is indeed surrounded, but not, according to the account of Moses, by a vacuum, nor by any substance, nor by anything which is of equal magnitude with itself, nor by anything of unlimited size . . . but its boundary is God, and he also is its ruler and the director of its course.

### Creator and Creation

56. . . . it is indispensable that in all existing things there must be an active cause, and a passive subject; and that the active cause is the intellect of the universe, thoroughly unadulterated and thoroughly unmixed, superior to virtue and superior to science, superior even to abstract good or abstract beauty; while the passive subject is something inanimate and incapable of motion by any intrinsic power of its own, but having been set in motion, and fashioned, and endowed with life by the intellect, became transformed into that most perfect work, this world. And those who describe it as being uncreated, do, without being aware of it, cut off the most useful and necessary of all the qualities which tend to produce piety, namely, providence: for reason proves that the father and creator has a care for that which has been created; for a father is anxious for the life of his children.

57. . . . he is uncreated, and always acting not suffering.

58. He is also superior in power, for the agent is more glorious than the patient.

[Sec. 33, *Works of Philo Judaeus,* trans. C. D. Yonge (London: George Bell & Sons, 1890), III, 182–83. Sec. 34, *ibid.,* I, 162. Sec. 35, *ibid.,* p. 76. Sec. 36, *ibid.,* III, 466–77. Sec. 37, *ibid.,* II, 382. Sec. 38, *ibid.,* IV, 458. Sec. 39, *ibid.,* I, 80–81. Sec. 40, *ibid.,* II, 243. Sec. 41, *ibid.,* I, 162. Sec. 42, *ibid.,* IV, 1–2. Sec. 43, *ibid.,* I, 282. Sec. 44, *ibid.,* IV, 283. Sec. 45, *ibid.,* I, 204. Sec. 46, *ibid.,* p. 229. Sec. 47, *ibid.,* p. 131. Sec. 48, *ibid.,* pp. 348–49. Sec. 49, *ibid.,* II, 84. Sec. 50, *ibid.,* I, 196–97. Sec. 51, *ibid.,* p. 255. Sec. 52, *ibid.,* p. 289. Sec. 53, *ibid.,* II, 28–29. Sec. 54, *ibid.,* IV, 251. Sec. 55, *ibid.,* II, 138. Sec. 56, *ibid.,* I, 2. Sec. 57, *ibid.,* p. 338. Sec. 58, *ibid.,* III, 152.]

## COMMENT

The monopolar prejudice is pervasive in Philo. Thus he implies (echoing Plato) that the selfish man is typically the fickle and changeable one; as though the viciousness of egoistic rigidity, the self-seeking *idée fixe,* the stubborn refusal or inability to live creatively and expansively, with generous receptiveness to novelty, had been hidden from him by magic, the magic of the monopolar *idée fixe!* He asserts, as something obvious, that agent is superior to patient. On the contrary, one may object, the higher the being, the more versatile is its capacity for responding to influence. Perception and all knowledge of the concrete and actual is a kind of patience, a way of reflecting the forces and individuals around us. The less knowledge a thing has, the more limited is its role as patient. And what encouragement is unwittingly given to the lust for power by the monopolar doctrine! This lust is precisely the will to exist as agent rather than as patient; to push others around, to mold their thoughts and feelings at will, while their wishes and sufferings and efforts leave us unmoved, "impassible"!

Philo says that God is the soul of the universe, but how arbitrarily one-sided is his conception of soul! The truth that the soul is ruler over the parts of the body, as Philo interprets it, becomes a mere half-truth. For is not the soul also the most variously passive thing in the psychophysical system, the one that tends to echo most sensitively what is going on anywhere in that system? Indeed, even a "ruler," the better he is, tends to reflect in himself the main currents of the life over which he rules; and from this responsiveness, this unusually ample passivity, comes his responsibleness, his power to rule rightly. Unwittingly, by ruler Philo means tyrant and thus justifies the charge of Whitehead in this connection that the primitive oriental notion of a ruler was taken all too much to heart by early theology. Philo, we hold, misconceives both the political problem and the mind-body problem. The brain is the most sensitive portion of the organism, the *least* "impassible" of all (the bones being the most impassible). The brain, however, is not an individual but a city of tiny individuals. And the soul, the personality, is, as one individual, incomparably the least impassible of those in the bodily system. It is also the most complex, since it integrates into itself more of the diversity of that system than any other factor in it. Thus the famous unity of the soul is but one side of its privileged position, of which "multiplicity of contributing factors" is the other. Similarly, the famous activity of the soul, its power over the body, is but the other side of its unique passivity. The dominance of the soul over the trivial entities in the system is due to the greater richness which it derives through its perpetual reintegration of the diverse processes in the organism. If God is the categorically unique analogue of all this, then he is supremely passive and complex as well as supremely active and integrated. Similar remarks apply to "ruler"—the more so, the better he is.

(The dependence of the mind for existence upon the body, so often cited by materialists, proves simply that the ruler of *this* city cannot exist with no suitable city to rule or with too great a disruption of the orderly functioning of his city. If a ruler is, as said above, pre-eminent in power because pre-eminent in responsiveness, then of course his integrity cannot survive too great a loss of coherence in that to which he responds.)

At this point a defender of Philo might interrupt, saying that the incorruptibility of the categorically supreme being contradicts its being a soul in the above sense. Reply: This is again an instance of monopolarity or arbitrary one-sidedness in theology. An ordinary soul in an ordinary body is corruptible; but the question just raised concerns no such soul but rather a categorically supreme soul in a likewise categorically supreme body. Now, this categorical supremacy involves an incomparable superiority in that capacity to integrate the diverse activities of the body and, through the resulting superior richness of life, to dominate these activities and rule them, which constitutes soul in general. But the only way to give categorical uniqueness to the divine soul in such terms is to say that this soul can *always* integrate the activities of *its* body, which is the universe, in order to maintain its own coherence as reflection and guiding genius of these activities. *This* reign is one which cannot be overthrown, not because the ruler is impassive, but because his unique flexibility of response can deal with any situation which the ruled are capable of producing or ever could be capable of producing.

In our criticism so far we may seem to have forgotten Philo's contention that only God himself can show us his nature, that revelation through Scripture is crucial. But, even so, the man who quotes Scripture (like the man who wrote it) is still a man and not God. What tells him that his quotation is adequately in context? Or, if it is out of context, then almost anything can be "proved" by citing words. In Philo, as the earliest instance adequately known to history, begins the long tale of the metaphysical abuse of Scripture. Texts which were not written to answer abstruse philosophical questions (formulated usually in terms heavily loaded with monopolarity) are made to respond to such questions. To criticize Philo here it is not necessary to quarrel with his faith in the reliability of Scripture. For prior to the question of truth is the question of meaning. "The Lord our God is One" certainly meant that polytheism was to be rejected; but what is there to prove that it meant the denial of every form of internal complexity in the one divine Person? Again, the prohibition of idols or images of deity is not, of itself, a rejection of the view that God has a physical aspect. It implies only that, if there be such a physical aspect, it is, as such, unique and incomparable, so that no man-made construction or controllable object could represent it. Suppose the entire physical universe is the "body of deity"; does it follow that one could construct a statue of the Most High or that the form of an animal, say, could be even a caricature of the divine form? The universe is, among physical objects, utterly unique, and perhaps just as much so as is the divine "Will" or "Power" among wills or powers. Not even the saying, "None hath seen God," contradicts the identification of him, in physical aspect, with the universe. For it is at least highly problematic in what sense, if any, one can see the universe. If our bodily cells could see a few of the cells around them, they still might be incapable of seeing the physical man which these and multitudes of other cells compose or of having any notion of the form of a man. Now the difference between the universe and the things we definitely see is incomparably deeper than that between cells and a man. We see the stars but not that in them which binds them to each other and all other things as members of a cosmos.

Even the text, "I am hath sent thee" (in response to the request for the divine name), may be far enough from the metaphysical pronouncement Philo and his innumerable successors will have it to be. The Hebrew word originally, scholars tell us, meant "breathe" rather than "am." Thus it cannot decide the issue between being and becoming. Apparently it rather denotes the act of living. It may be legitimate (though certainly bold) to read into the passage an assertion that deity is the one who cannot fail to live, the one who primordially and immortally exists as living, the one to whose life there is no contrary possibility. But to go further and infer that the life of deity is simply timeless or immutable is to manipulate Scripture for ends that cannot be shown to have been even implicitly contained in the minds of its writers. Of course, if one is convinced that all change is corruption, or implies the possibility of corruption, then an immortally living being cannot change. But the axiom, "Change implies corruptibility," is itself nonbiblical, a foreign principle of metaphysics which must be evaluated on its own merits or demerits. Surrelativism denies the axiom, and therefore it cannot admit the use of Scripture as proof of divine immutability.

Of course, there are biblical texts which seem directly to assert the pure eternality of God. "I am the Lord, and I change not." But none of these texts occurs in a context in which the strict metaphysical question of a being in all aspects immutable is under discussion. On the contrary, the context is always that of the discussion of some specific sort of mutability, such as vacillation of purpose, or nonadherence to a resolution once formed. "I do not make and then unmake my mind on a given issue or alter my principles from righteous

to unrighteous ones," is what the passages seem to say, if viewed without metaphysical prejudice. It is of course an entirely unrealistic view of language to suppose that, every time we really mean "unchanging in the respect under discussion," we expressly formulate this qualification rather than simply say, "unchanging," leaving it to the context to fix the limits of what is meant. There is no reason to expect biblical writers not to avail themselves of this normal practice and every reason to think that they did so.

Let us turn to the basic metaphysical problems of Philo's system. Philo must relate the absolute or nonrelative God to the universe whose destinies he directs and minutely surveys. Our author is more or less aware of the difficulties this involves. His principal resource for dealing with them is in the concept of divine "powers," also termed "properties." These are plural only in terms of their effects. From the self-sufficient actuality of deity it follows that there is no limit to the effects he can produce. There is even a created reason (Logos) containing all the intelligible forms of things, or Platonic ideas—a thought which anticipates Plotinus and even, Wolfson holds, the Christian Trinity. That Philo does not in this way remove the difficulties of his position will probably be apparent. For example, the doctrine (sec. 39) denies complexity to deity, which means that he does not contain the complexity of the world within himself. But it is also denied that the world contains God. So it seems that the total reality is World-and-God, a whole of which both creator and creature are constituents. This whole is neither God nor world but a third entity of which no account is given in the system. Or does Philo mean it when he says, "God contains the world?" But then God is complex.

Again, we know of God only his power, and this only in terms of its effects. But "having" or "producing" effects seems to mean relation to these effects. Yet, it is held, God made the world in pure freedom and in such a way that it contributes nothing to his being, which is self-sufficing. Still, if God had not made the world, he would not have "had" it as his effect. How is God-having-a-certain-effect and God not having it simply and wholly the identical entity (as he must be if totally independent of the creation)? We seem driven to say that, while the world has God as its maker, God does not have the world which he has made. Likewise, the world is known by God, although it would be incorrect to say that he knows the world (for to know is to be in relation to). And how can there be a real passive relation (world to God) where there is no real active one?

Thus the attempt to combine the spiritual self-sufficiency of deity, which was Aristotle's sole theme in theology (at least, in the *Metaphysics*), with the notions of creation and providence seems to encounter downright logical contradictions. That for Philo, in contrast to Aristotle, God creates all things, even perhaps their "matter," does not remove the contradictions, since "God creates the world" asserts a relation of God to the world—all the more plainly so if the creation is held to be willed, intentional. We shall see if Philo's successors are any better able to deal with the problems of this type of doctrine.

Nothing in the foregoing criticisms is to be taken as directed against Philo's admirable contentions that God exists essentially, not accidentally; that he is no mere particular instance of the categories or general conceptions—for instance, of life or value—but is essentially, categorically existent, living, good, wise, etc. We merely hold that this is to be construed with polar fairness, as involving an essential, not merely accidental, passivity as well as activity, openness to novelty as well as capacity to retain

actualities once achieved, complexity as well as integrity, yes, and suffering as well as joy. If God is more simple than the one (in the ordinary sense of unity), he is also more complex than any nondivine composite thing, actual or possible. He is the eternal model of complexity, passivity, change—the individual whose individuality is inseparable from the principles of integration of diversity, responsiveness to others, passage to novel values—and he is this just as truly as he is the model of personal self-identity or singleness, activity, permanence, or steadfastness.

How this view contrasts with the Philonian will appear more and more fully in our discussions of later authors. It will also be clear how heartily we are able to admire Philo for his insistence upon the voluntary character of God, his freedom, of which, as Philo says, man has a spark. On the other hand, we fail to see any meaning whatever in the idea of volition if combined with the notion of absolute nonpotentiality. If something is willed freely, then something else might have been willed instead. But the divine volition is either essence or accident; if essence, then it could not have been otherwise, and is not free save in the Spinozistic sense, which is not Philo's and is not, we think, biblical; while, if the volition is accident, then there are accidents in God after all. (Or shall we say that the divine volition is not in but outside of deity?) Yet here too we cannot criticize Philo without wishing to praise him. For his notion of miracle as expressing the final superiority of creative fiat over mere law or order and his insistence that man as well as God has something of this supralegal creativity point in the direction of the doctrine which, in Whitehead, Berdyaev, and others, seems to us the highest pinnacle of philosophico-religious speculation. But only outside classical theism can this doctrine attain full clarity.

# AUGUSTINE (354–430): GOD AND TIME

Augustine is an outstanding example among Christians of a man who, like Philo, is at once saturated with Greek philosophy and persuaded of the trustworthiness of the vision of God proclaimed by the Jewish sacred writings—to which Augustine adds the New Testament and the creeds of the church. The problem of the following passage is how to understand the Genesis account of creation, on the assumption, which it never occurred to our author (any more than it did to Philo) to question seriously, that God is a wholly immutable or nontemporal actuality. The proposed key to the relations of eternity and the temporal world is the recognition that time is merely the order of the created, so that there can be no problem of what the eternal was doing "before creating." The eternal creates in his eternity, although the result is a temporal order with a beginning or first state. To establish firmly the view that time is merely a dimension of the created and does not apply to the creator, Augustine is not content merely to argue that time implies change and that only the created is changeable. To clinch the matter, he wishes to show just how, or in what sense, time is an order of the created, and he finds the familiar reference to moving bodies, as the essential and sufficient condition of time, unconvincing. This leads him to an analysis of temporality as essentially (at least, in one aspect) psychological, not merely physical, an analysis which to some extent anticipates the more fully generalized notions of Bergson, Whitehead, and Montague on the same subject. It is arguable that the Saint here makes a great discovery (though of course it has precedents, for instance, in Lucretius). True, this discovery is incidental to his chief purpose, which is merely to eliminate certain irrelevant

objections to the idea of "creation" as he understands it. Having disposed of these objections, the matter is closed, so far as Augustine is concerned. But not so far as the history of thought is concerned. Something momentous has been inaugurated, even though for more than a thousand years nothing comes of it.

## Eternity and Time

59. Lo are they not full of their old leaven, who say to us, "What was God doing before *He made heaven and earth?*" "For if (say they) He were unemployed and wrought not, why does He not also henceforth, and for ever, as He did heretofore? For did any new motion arise in God, and a new will to make a creature, which He had never before made, how then would that be a true eternity, where there ariseth a will, which was not? For the will of God is not a creature, but before the creature; seeing nothing could be created, unless the will of the Creator had preceded. The will of God then belongeth to His very Substance. And if aught have arisen in God's Substance, which before was not, that Substance cannot be truly called eternal. But if the will of God has been from eternity that the creature should be, why was not the creature also from eternity?"

Who speak thus, do not yet understand Thee, O Wisdom of God, Light of souls, understand not yet how the things be made, which by Thee, and in Thee are made: yet they strive to comprehend things eternal, whilst their heart fluttereth between the motions of things past and to come, and is still unstable. Who shall hold it, and fix it, that it be settled awhile, and awhile catch the glory of that ever-fixed Eternity, and compare it with the times which are never fixed, and see that it cannot be compared; and that a long time cannot become long, but out of many motions passing by, which cannot be prolonged altogether; but that in the Eternal nothing passeth, but the whole is present; whereas no time is all at once present: and that all time past, is driven on by time to come, and all to come followeth upon the past; and all past and to come, is created, and flows out of that which is ever present? Who shall hold the heart of man, that it may stand still, and see how eternity ever still-standing, neither past nor to come, uttereth the times past and to come?

60. Seeing then Thou are the Creator of all times, if any time was before Thou *madest heaven and earth*, why say they that Thou didst forego working? For that very time didst Thou make, nor could times pass by, before Thou madest those times. But if before *heaven and earth* there was no time, why is it demanded, what Thou then didst? For there was no "then," when there was no time.

Nor dost Thou by time, precede time: else shouldest Thou not precede all times. But Thou precedest all things past, by the sublimity of an everpresent eternity; and surpassest all [things] future because they are future, and when they come, they shall be past; *but Thou art the Same, and Thy years fail not.* Thy years neither come nor go; whereas ours both come and go, that they all may come. Thy years stand together, because they do stand; nor are departing thrust out by coming years, for they pass not away; but ours shall all be, when they shall no more be. Thy years are one day; and Thy day is not daily, but To-day, seeing Thy To-day gives not place unto to-morrow, for neither doth it replace yesterday. Thy To-day, is Eternity; therefore didst Thou beget The Coeternal, to whom Thou saidst, *This day have I begotten Thee.* Thou hast made all things; and before all times

Thou art: neither in any time was time not.

### The Paradoxical Nature of Time

At no time then hadst Thou not made any thing, because time itself Thou madest. And no times are coeternal with Thee, because Thou abidest; but if they abode, they should not be times. For what is time? Who can readily and briefly explain this? Who can even in thought comprehend it, so as to utter a word about it? But what in discourse do we mention more familiarly and knowingly, than time? And, we understand, when we speak of it; we understand also, when we hear it spoken of by another. What then is time? If no one asks me, I know: if I wish to explain it to one that asketh, I know not: yet I say boldly, that I know, that if nothing passed away, time past were not; and if nothing were coming, a time to come were not; and if nothing were, time present were not. Those two times then, past and to come, how are they, seeing the past now is not, and that to come is not yet? But the present, should it always be present, and never pass into time past, verily it should not be time, but eternity. If time present (if it is to be time) only cometh into existence, because it passeth into time past, how can we say that either this is, whose cause of being is, that it shall not be; so, namely, that we cannot truly say that time is, but because it is tending not to be?

And yet we say, "a long time" and "a short time"; still, only of time past or to come. A long time past (for example) we call an hundred years since; and a long time to come, an hundred years hence. But a short time past we call (suppose) ten days since; and a short time to come, ten days hence. But in what sense is that long or short, which is not? For the past, is not now; and the future, is not yet. Let us not then say, "it is long"; but of the past, "it hath been long"; and of the future, "it will be long." O my Lord, my Light, shall not here also Thy Truth mock at man? For that past time which was long, was it long when it was now past, or when it was yet present? For then might it be long, when there was, what could be long; but when past, it was no longer; wherefore neither could that be long, which was not at all. Let us not then say, "time past hath been long": for we shall not find, what hath been long, seeing that since it was past, it is no more; but let us say, "that present time was long"; because, when it was present, it was long. For it had not yet passed away, so as not to be; and therefore there was, what could be long; but after it was past, that ceased also to be long, which ceased to be.

Let us see then, thou soul of man, whether present time can be long: for to thee it is given to feel and to measure length of time. What wilt thou answer me? Are an hundred years, when present, a long time? See first, whether an hundred years can be present. For if the first of these years be now current, it is present, but the other ninety and nine are to come, and therefore are not yet, but if the second year be current, one is now past, another present, the rest to come. And so if we assume any middle year of this hundred to be present, all before it, are past; all after it, to come; wherefore an hundred years cannot be present. But see at least whether that one which is now current, itself is present; for if the current month be its first, the rest are to come; if the second, the first is already past, and the rest are not yet. Therefore, neither is the year now current present; and if not present as a whole, then is not the year present. For twelve months are a year; of which whatever be the current month is present; the rest past, or to come. Although neither is that current month present;

but one day only; the rest being to come, if it be the first; past, if the last; if any of the middle, then amid past and to come.

See how the present time, which alone we found could be called long, is abridged to the length scarce of one day. But let us examine that also; because neither is one day present as a whole. For it is made up of four and twenty hours of night and day: of which, the first hath the rest to come; the last hath them past; and any of the middle hath those before it past, those behind it to come. Yea, that one hour passeth away in flying particles. Whatsoever of it hath flown away, is past; whatsoever remaineth, is to come. If an instant of time be conceived, which cannot be divided into the smallest particles of moments, that alone is it, which may be called present. Which yet flies with such speed from future to past, as not to be lengthened out with the least stay. For if it be, it is divided into past and future. The present hath no space. Where then is the time, which we may call long? . . .

And yet, Lord, we perceive intervals of times, and compare them, and say, some are shorter, and others longer. . . .

*61.* I ask, Father, I affirm not: O my God, rule and guide me. "Who will tell me that there are not three times, (as we learned when boys, and taught boys,) past, present, and future; but present only, because those two are not? Or are they also; and when from future it becometh present, doth it come out of some secret place; and so, when retiring, from present it becometh past? For where did they, who foretold things to come, see them, if as yet they be not? For that which is not, cannot be seen. And they who relate things past, could not relate them, if in mind they did not discern them, and if they were not, they could no way be discerned. Things then past and to come are."

Permit me, Lord, to seek further. O my hope, let not my purpose be confounded. For if times past and to come be, I would know where they be. Which yet if I cannot, yet I know, wherever they be, they are not there as future, or past, but present. For if there also they be future, they are not yet there; if there also they be past, they are no longer there. Wheresoever then is whatsoever is, it is only as present. Although when past facts are related, there are drawn out of the memory, not the things themselves which are past, but words which, conceived by the images of the things, they, in passing, have through the senses left as traces in the mind. Thus my childhood, which now is not, is in time past, which now is not; but now when I recall its image, and tell of it, I behold it in the present, because it is still in my memory. Whether there be a like cause of foretelling things to come also; that of things which as yet are not, the images may be perceived before, already existing, I confess, O my God, I know not. This indeed I know, that we generally think before on our future actions, and that that forethinking is present, but the action whereof we forethink is not yet, because it is to come. Which, when we have set upon, and have begun to do what we were forethinking, then shall that action be; because then it is no longer future, but present.

Which way soever then this secret fore-perceiving of things to come be; that only can be seen, which is. But what now is, is not future, but present. When then things to come are said to be seen, it is not themselves which as yet are not, (that is, which are to be,) but their causes perchance or signs are seen, which already are. . . .

Thou then, Ruler of Thy creation, by what way dost Thou teach souls things to come? For Thou didst teach Thy Prophets. By what way dost Thou, to whom nothing is to come, teach things

to come; or rather of the future, dost teach things present? For, what is not, neither can it be taught. Too far is this way out of my ken: *it is too mighty for me, I cannot attain unto it;* but from Thee I can, when Thou shalt vouchsafe it, O sweet light of my hidden eyes.

What now is clear and plain is, that neither things to come nor past are. Nor is it properly said, "there be three times, past, present, and to come": yet perchance it might be properly said, "there be three times; a present of things past, a present of things present, and a present of things future." For these three do exist in some sort, in the soul, but otherwhere do I not see them; present of things past, memory; present of things present, sight; present of things future, expectation. If thus we be permitted to speak, I see three times, and I confess there are three. Let it be said too, "there be three times, past, present, and to come": in our incorrect way. See, I object not, nor gainsay, nor find fault, if what is so said be but understood, that neither what is to be, now is, nor what is past. For but few things are there, which we speak properly, most things improperly; still the things intended are understood.

I said then even now, we measure times as they pass, in order to be able to say, this time is twice so much as that one; or, this is just so much as that; and so of any other parts of time, which be measurable. Wherefore, as I said, we measure times as they pass. And if any should ask me, "How knowest thou?" I might answer, "I know, that we do measure, nor can we measure things that are not; and things past and to come, are not." But time present how do we measure, seeing it hath no space? . . .

My soul is on fire to know this most intricate enigma. Shut it not up, O Lord my God, good Father; through Christ I beseech Thee, do not shut up these usual, yet hidden things, from my desire, that it be hindered from piercing into them; but let them dawn through Thy enlightening mercy, O Lord.

62. I heard once from a learned man, that the motions of the sun, moon, and stars, constituted time, and I assented not. For why should not the motions of all bodies rather be times? Or, if the lights of heaven should cease, and a potter's wheel run round, should there be no time by which we might measure those whirlings, and say, that either it moved with equal pauses, or if it turned sometimes slower, otherwiles quicker, that some rounds were longer, other shorter? Or, while we were saying this, should we not also be speaking in time? Or, should there in our words be some syllables short, others long, but because those sounded in a shorter time, these in a longer? God, grant to men to see in a small thing notices common to things great and small.

63. Let no man then tell me, that the motions of the heavenly bodies constitute times, because, when at the prayer of one, the sun had stood still, till he could achieve his victorious battle, the sun stood still, but time went on. For in its own allotted space of time was that battle waged and ended. I perceive time then to be a certain extension. But do I perceive it, or seem to perceive it? Thou, Light and Truth, wilt shew me.

Dost Thou bid me assent, if any define time to be "motion of a body"? Thou dost not bid me.

64. For and if a body be sometimes moved, sometimes stands still, then we measure, not his motion only, but his standing still too by time; and we say, "it stood still, as much as it moved"; or "it stood still twice or thrice so long as it moved"; or any other space which our measuring hath either ascertained, or guessed; more or less, as we use to say. Time then is not the motion of a body.

And I confess to Thee, O Lord, that I yet know not what time is, and again I confess unto Thee, O Lord, that I know that I speak this in time, and that having long spoken of time, that very "long" is not long, but by the pause of time. How then know I this, seeing I know not what time is?

65. Do I then measure, O my God, and know not what I measure? I measure the motion of a body in time; and the time itself do I not measure? Or could I indeed measure the motion of a body how long it were, and in how long space it could come from this place to that, without measuring the time in which it is moved? This same time then, how do I measure? do we by a shorter time measure a longer, as by the space of a cubit, the space of a rood? for so indeed we seem by the space of a short syllable, to measure the space of a long syllable, and to say that this is double the other. Thus measure we the spaces of stanzas, by the spaces of the verses, and the spaces of the verses, by the spaces of the feet, and the spaces of the feet, by the spaces of the syllables, and the spaces of long, by the spaces of short syllables; not measuring by pages (for then we measure spaces, not times;) but when we utter the words and they pass by, and we say "it is a long stanza, because composed of so many verses; long verses, because consisting of so many feet; long feet, because prolonged by so many syllables; a long syllable because double to a short one." But neither do we this way obtain any certain measure of time; because it may be, that a shorter verse, pronounced more fully, may take up more time than a longer, pronounced hurriedly. And so for a verse, a foot, a syllable. Whence it seemed to me, that time is nothing else than protraction; but of what, I know not; and I marvel, if it be not of the mind itself? For what I beseech Thee, O my God, do I measure, when I say, either indefinitely "this is a longer time than that," or definitely "this is double that"? That I measure time, I know; and yet I meas-

ure not time to come, for it is not yet; nor present, because it is not protracted by any space; nor past, because it now is not. What then do I measure? Times passing, not past? for so I said.

Courage, my mind, and press on mightily. God is our helper, *He made us, and not we ourselves.* Press on where truth begins to dawn. Suppose, now, the voice of a body begins to sound, and does sound, and sounds on, and list, it ceases; it is silence now, and that voice is past, and is no more a voice. Before it sounded, it was to come, and could not be measured, because as yet it was not, and now it cannot, because it is no longer. Then therefore while it sounded, it might; because there then was what might be measured. But yet even then it was not at a stay; for it was passing on, and passing away. Could it be measured the rather, for that? For while passing, it was being extended into some space of time, so that it might be measured, since the present hath no space.

*66.* But when ended, it no longer is. How may it then be measured? And yet we measure times; but yet neither those which are not yet, nor those which no longer are, nor those which are not lengthened out by some pause, nor those which have no bounds. We measure neither times to come, nor past, nor present, nor passing; and yet we do measure times.

### Measured Time Is in Mind

*67.* It is in thee, my mind, that I measure times . . . the impression, which things as they pass by cause in thee, remains even when they are gone; this it is which still present, I measure, not the things which pass by to make this impression. This I measure, when I measure times. Either then this is time, or I do not measure times. What when we measure silence, and say that this silence hath held as long time as did that voice? do we not stretch out our

thought to the measure of a voice, as if it sounded, so that we may be able to report of the intervals of silence in a given space of time? For though both voice and tongue be still, yet in thought we go over poems, and verses, and any other discourse, or dimensions of motions, and report as to the spaces of times, how much this is in respect of that, no otherwise than if vocally we did pronounce them. If a man would utter a lengthened sound, and had settled in thought how long it should be, he hath in silence already gone through a space of time, and committing it to memory, begins to utter that speech, which sounds on, until it be brought unto the end proposed. Yea it hath sounded, and will sound; for so much of it as is finished, hath sounded already, and the rest will sound. And thus passeth it on, until the present intent conveys over the future into the past; the past increasing by the diminution of the future, until by the consumption of the future, all is past.

But how is that future diminished or consumed, which as yet is not? or how that past increased, which is now no longer, save that in the mind which enacteth this, there be three things done? For it expects, it considers, it remembers; that so that which it expecteth, through that which it considereth, passeth into that which it remembereth. Who therefore denieth, that things to come are not as yet? and yet, there is in the mind an expectation of things to come. And who denies past things to be now no longer? and yet is there still in the mind a memory of things past. And who denieth that the present time hath no space, because it passeth away in a moment? and yet our consideration continueth, through which that which shall be present proceedeth to become absent. It is not then future time, that is long, for as yet it is not: but a "long future," is "a long expectation of the future," nor is it time past, which now is not, that is long; but a long past, is "a long memory of the past."

I am about to repeat a Psalm that I know. Before I begin, my expectation is extended over the whole; but when I have begun, how much soever of it I shall separate off into the past, is extended along my memory; thus the life of this action of mine is divided between my memory as to what I have repeated, and expectation as to what I am about to repeat; but "consideration" is present with me, that through it what was future, may be conveyed over, so as to become past. Which the more it is done again and again, so much the more the expectation being shortened, is the memory enlarged; till the whole expectation be at length exhausted, when that whole action being ended, shall have passed into memory. And this which takes place in the whole Psalm, the same takes place in each several portion of it, and each several syllable; the same holds in that longer action, whereof this Psalm may be a part; the same holds in the whole life of man, whereof all the actions of man are parts; the same holds through the whole age of the sons of men, whereof all the lives of men are parts.

68. And now will I stand, and become firm in Thee, in my mould, Thy truth; nor will I endure the questions of men, who by a penal disease thirst for more than they can contain, and say, "what did God before He *made heaven and earth?*" . . . Let them see therefore, that time cannot be without created being, and cease to *speak* that *vanity.* . . . Certainly, if there be a mind gifted with such vast knowledge and foreknowledge, as to know all things past and to come, as I know one well-known Psalm, truly that mind is passing wonderful, and fearfully amazing; in that nothing past, nothing to come in after-ages, is any more hidden from him, than when I sung that Psalm, was hidden from me what, and how much

of it had passed away from the beginning, what, and how much there remained unto the end. But far be it that Thou the Creator of the Universe, the Creator of souls and bodies, far be it, that Thou shouldest in such wise know all things past and to come. Far, far more wonderfully, and far more mysteriously, dost thou know them. For not, as the feelings of one who singeth what he knoweth, or heareth some well-known song, are through expectation of the words to come, and the remembering of those that are past, varied, and his senses divided—not so doth any thing happen unto Thee, unchangeably eternal, that is, the eternal Creator of minds. Like then as Thou *in the Beginning* knewest *the heaven and the earth,* without any variety of Thy knowledge, so *madest* Thou *in the Beginning* heaven and earth, without any distraction of Thy action. Whoso understandeth, let him confess unto thee; and whoso understandeth not, let him confess unto Thee.

[Sec. 59, *The Confessions of St. Augustine,* trans. E. B. Pusey (New York: E. P. Dutton & Co., 1907), pp. 259–60. Sec. 60, *ibid.,* pp. 261–64. Sec. 61, *ibid.,* pp. 265–68. Sec. 62, *ibid.,* pp. 268–69. Sec. 63, *ibid.,* pp. 269–70. Sec. 64, *ibid.,* p. 270. Sec. 65, *ibid.,* pp. 271–72. Sec. 66, *ibid.,* p. 272. Sec. 67, *ibid.,* pp. 273–75. Sec. 68, *ibid.,* pp. 275–77.]

COMMENT

There must, Augustine seems to argue, be something capable of embracing past, present, and future within a unity. For only if there are different moments of time, all existing as parts of one whole, is there time as a knowable, measurable entity at all. But when and as what does such a whole exist? A whole of time cannot consist essentially in "motion"; for a body may remain at rest for a time. Moreover, how is a motion a whole? When the body is here, say, in Chicago, what is the reality of its "having been there," say, in Paris? Today many would answer that all events form portions of the space-time continuum and that a whole of motion is simply a portion of this continuum pervaded by certain characters, a "world-line." This solution, which is the final apotheosis of Eleaticism, reduces becoming entirely to being. The totality of happenings does not happen; it just is. But then nothing happens. Becoming is explained away.

Augustine apparently does not even think of this "solution." And yet in a sense it is finally his own. For to God's immutable vision of all time every fact is simply present. But Augustine leaves this conception as an obscure background of his thinking, while in the foreground he wrestles with the question, "How is time given *to us* as a whole?" In present experience, he answers, is the past found, as the remembered or retained, the still somehow possessed, and the future is found as the anticipated or in a fashion already possessed. Here is the unity sought for, in which a transition from moment $A$ to moment $B$, to be followed by moment $C$, is contained as a unit. We experience the present as following a certain past which in a fashion is still there for us, and consequently the present's relation to that past can be there also. And we experience the future as in a fashion already there for us, so that we *now* are in relation to that future. If $I$ am the moving body, then my having been in Paris is real for me here in Chicago. But mere empty matter cannot be positively conceived to contain in itself as here in Chicago a reference to a previous sojourn in Paris. (That from certain "laws" this might be inferred is merely the problem over again. How can a law be inscribed in a lump of stuff located somewhere in space? What is law to mere stuff?)

So far we are echoing Augustine or, at least, confirming his view that the motion of bodies does not explain time. But to us many questions arise which

his preoccupations inhibited. Memory and anticipation solve the problem of the unity of time only so far as, thanks to them, the past is not simply the no-longer, and the future the not-yet, existent. The parts of a whole must exist when the whole exists; and, if a collection of the moments of time never exists in any time, then time never exists. But, thanks to memory and anticipation, the past and future in a sense exist now. But, on the other hand, if they both exist now, what makes the one past and the other future? "No longer" and "not yet" must retain some meaning, if the unity of the no-longer and the not-yet is to have meaning. Augustine's solution seems to be to distinguish between the real past, which does not really now exist (and yet eternally it is there for God!), and the memory of it, which does; and so with future things and the anticipation of them. Is it then memories of the past and anticipations of the future which are long or short, not the past and future themselves? But this solution is too subjectivistic. It gives us a unitary image of temporal passage, which can be divided into hours or days, but not a unitary temporal passage itself. Moreover, if only the present has the mode of actual existence, then the past is either an inactual potency or has some third mode of being which is neither actuality nor potentiality. This third mode seems never to be elucidated in Greek or medieval philosophy. The present comes into being, our author says, by pushing the previous present out of being—into what, sheer nonentity? But this is characterless, and the past has very definite character. Into a mere possibility? This is nonsense. We do not say merely, "Washington could have crossed the Delaware, or could have lived." Washington is fact, not mere possibility. Indeed, nearly all the "facts" we refer to as such are past, not strictly present. The nature of process is not explained, then, merely by treating it as a combination of two forms of nonentity, past and future, plus the being of the present; nor is it explained by treating it as two forms of possibility, plus an actuality, the present. How then?

To bring in human memory, as Augustine does, seems insufficient. For we forget much more than we remember. Is the forgotten past nonentity?

The answer which seems suggested by Augustine's view of God is that only for our ignorance is the future or the past less real than the present. For the Absolute Mind, all events are equally facts. Perhaps they are not in the full sense realities, but, at least, what we call past and future are not less real than what we call present. There is a whole of events, or, at least, of "appearances" of events, and this whole is itself eternal. It does not become; it just is. The difficulty with this view is that a whole of events which never becomes but simply is cannot be a whole of events. For if the parts of a whole become, so does the whole, and if the whole does not, certainly the parts do not. Change is sheer illusion if there is an immutable final totality of changes. Classical theists, and Greek philosophers before them, did not unequivocally assert such a totality. But they offer no equally definite alternative view. And the nearest we can come to a definite conception of time in medieval theology is to suppose that implicitly it involves precisely the conception above considered and rejected. For to God's knowledge must appear, as known entity, every item of the temporal process. For an immutable omniscience, events, taken as timeless, each in its temporal place, just are. If the awareness-of-X is an immutable whole, then X is immutable too. A new part or constituent would mean a new whole. But classical theism seems not to accept this analysis. What, then, is time? Classical theologians do not quite tell us.

But Augustine has the clue, if only he were interested in following it up. Human memory is a partial retention of the being of the past in the being of the present, in spite of which retention the past is not effectively, with anything like its full actuality, contained in the present. Hence it is correct to distinguish between our memory and "the past itself." But then, after all, human awareness is not in any respect the adequate measure of things! Only divine awareness is that. The proper theistic procedure is to seek a conception of categorically superior knowledge able to have temporal passage as its content. If the purely eternalistic notion of deity does not meet this requirement, and we have just suggested that it does not, then another conception is to be sought for. The direction of the seeking is clear. We must generalize the idea of memory and anticipation so as to remove the defects of the human form of these functions. Memory in us is a pale, fluctuating, largely vague, essentially inadequate retention of the past. But could there not be a vivid, steady, distinct, and complete retention of past experiences? The objection arises: Would they then be past at all, if thus fully retained? The objection, however, is specious. Even the most complete preservation in memory of the past would not destroy the distinction between it and the present in which it is retained. That a part is in a whole does not make it identical with the whole. The past "when it was present" means the past when it was the totality of actuality. If a new totality contains this previous one as its retained past, this means that a richer synthesis of qualities embodies the other as an ingredient. Now between the more rich whole and the less rich ingredient, itself a whole with respect to constituent qualities less rich, a distinction is very well possible. Suppose I now remember the vague dreams with which I first entered college. Of course my fallible human memory is vaguer than the dreams were. But suppose the memory did accurately delineate the dreams; the latters' vagueness, by contrast with my present knowledge of what going to college meant and did for me, would only be made more obvious.

Process is in principle the addition of determinations, and only due to human defects does it seem to be also the loss of them. Time is "invention or nothing," as Bergson says; it is creation without any correlative decreation or annihilation. To understand this, we must note the difference between the past and the future as we experience them. Anticipation is in principle vague, for it does not intend to prejudice future decisions. We mean to leave some matters open for further consideration, and this is of the essence of anticipation, not an accidental defect. By contrast, memory refers to decisions already definite, and not even in principle or intention need it reserve for the past any indeterminacy, as a field for further decision. Therefore, that human beings do not remember all the detail of the past merely expresses the fact that human awareness is not the categorically supreme form. The basic difference between past and present is logically independent of such nonremembering. It is only anticipation that must have some indeterminateness as to details if temporal distinctions are to obtain. This "limitation" inheres in the intention and principle of anticipation and is no mere human failing. To anticipate future decisions in their full definition, one would have to make up one's mind now about future issues; whereas to recall just how one decided is not to have again to decide or redecide the same issues.

The upshot is that, in principle or ideally, memory is the absolute retention of definite actuality in all its qualities; while anticipation is the present delineation of an outline only of "future events," the range of possibilities within which further determination of details must take place. Does this impose limitations upon divine knowledge? Not if by "future events" one means those without complete definiteness. Then anticipation, as we have described it, can know the future as it is. Of course, when the future is present, it will be definite; but then it will no longer be future. And then the perfect knowledge will see it as definite. Thus Augustine's contrast between our imperfect memory and anticipation and the eternal, which knows things without memory or anticipation but as though all were for it simply present, is not the only possible way to formulate the contrast between imperfect and perfect knowledge of events. Nor, as we have argued, is it a tenable way. For it makes the temporality of time impossible to state without antinomies.

Augustine stopped in the midst of a promising investigation, or one which would have been promising had he not thought he knew beforehand most of the answers. The question of time in its full meaning was never so much as raised with freedom and persistence in all the philosophical tradition that Augustine knew. Human experience of time, on the one hand, and the alleged nontemporal intuitions of deity, were decisive for thought upon the subject, and the human experience (the only genuine datum with which thought had to work, since the eternalistic tenet was mere dogma) was not explored carefully with an eye to the distinction between specific accidental anthropomorphic limitations and ideal or generic and essential principles. Human loss of the past was taken as though it were evidence of the annihilation of the past, its deactualization; and yet, most paradoxically, it was held that both past and future events were fully determinate from the standpoint of eternity, which is divine and the very measure of reality! Thus, on the one hand, human memory, just in its specific character or defectiveness, was made the measure of reality (and yet this was also implicitly denied); but, on the other hand, human anticipation, just in its generic principle, was treated as merely anthropomorphic (this too not without inconsistency, for future events, it was said, are really nonexistent—though for God just as rich in definite qualities as an actuality could be). This complex of notions has, we suggest, no peculiar connection with piety but is a philosophical prejudice or maze of them.

The foregoing strictures may be illustrated by considering Augustine's example of the reciting of a psalm known by heart. Here it seems that anticipation aims to delineate just what is to come. But note that the mere words of the psalm do not even remotely describe future events in their particularity. The same words could occur in innumerable widely different events of speaking or hearing. Words are not events but characters that events may embody. In addition, the knowledge of what words are to come is rather potential than actual. The human attention span cannot contain the distinct images of very many words at once, whether in the form of memory or anticipation. It is also to be noted that, in so far as one resolves to recite a known poem, and in so far as one also decides in advance just how to recite it, the rest is mechanical, there could be no life of decision-making left to constitute the future. Of course, Augustine's view is that God decides, not in advance, but eternally, and he decides, or at any rate sees definitely and as something wholly determinate, not what he is to decide in future (there being for him no future) but what we are to decide at various times. Then how can it be our decision and responsibility? The decision being contained in eternal knowledge, any alternative is excluded by eternity itself and by the very essence of deity.

Must one not rather take the following position? The indeterminacy which is the essence of events, until they are present or past, is objectively involved in temporality itself, and this means that each portion of time must be seen in two ways, one of which is just as true as the other: first as partially indeterminate, then subsequently as determinate. This would be mere contradiction unless the "first" and "subsequently" are taken temporally or as genuinely successive. Unless omniscience successively goes through these two phases for each moment of time, either it contradicts itself or it fails to know what the moment is as temporal.

But the second phase, unlike the first, through memory includes both phases. To see as now determinate a moment whose content one previously saw as indeterminate is to experience the indeterminacy in the form of memory and the determinacy in the form of perception. One cannot have adequate knowledge of a richness one has lost, for then one would not have lost it. But one can very well know just what poverty has been transcended, for the more can contain the less as item of its total wealth. Thus process as enrichment of quality need not obliterate the previous phases. An outline of a picture and the detailed picture can be made into a total picture. But if process were a loss of richness, it is impossible that what had been lost should still be contained within the impoverished present as its richer past. Thus it is not optimism but logic that enforces the Bergsonian view that process is creation and only creation. "Destruction" is not a metaphysical category, for events, which are the concrete actualities, cannot be destroyed; they can only be created. "The moving finger writes; and, having writ, moves on: nor all your piety nor wit shall lure it back to cancel half a line. . . ." Such cancellation could not be a fact, for if the having-been-of-the-half-line is fact, then the half-line, which is constituent of this fact, is fact. Facts are, as the word implies, made, but they cannot be unmade, defactualized. To say that they can seems self-contradictory. Thus it is only the future that is inactual. But neither human experience nor a purely eternal divine experience can be the measure of the real actuality of the entire past and the real inactuality of the future. Only a divine experience which is in process toward novelty in such fashion that nothing is actual until it is content of this experience, and nothing which is thus actual can lose that status, can be the measure of temporal reality.

That destruction is not ultimate does not, however, prevent creatures from being mortal. Death is not destruction of events or experiences, which are the fully concrete actualities, but only the nonprolongation of a series of events. The series, so far as it has gone, is deathless, but death is the boundary of the last item. There is nothing in the nature of time, as we have analyzed it, to imply either that every series of events making up the life of a person or animal should have a final or last item or that none should have. On the contrary, the categorically supreme form of sequence is one which cannot have had and cannot ever have a first or a last item; but it is reasonable to think that every lesser sequence would have a last and a first item. Thus events would become but never lose their actuality, once acquired; sequences would in general have two temporal boundaries; yet one se-

quence would have neither commencement nor termination, would be primordial and deathless, and in every member would sum up adequately the entire past of the creation and its own previous members, and would thus be the absolute measure of determinate truth and actuality. This is the modern alternative to the classical theory of time and eternity. Since the supreme sequence would infinitely precede and temporally condition every event not a member of the sequence, it could, in a positive and significant sense, be called its creator.

But the question, "What was God doing previously?" must now be taken in good part and answered, as Origen answered it, "He was creating a previous universe or state of the universe." Our cosmic state of things looks to us like all reality, and its origin the origin; but who are we to measure the contents of the ultimate past? Much has been said about the mysteries of eternity, which "we cannot understand with our incurably temporal categories"; but, strangely, it is sometimes the very same people who tell us also that man cannot comprehend either a beginning of time or a beginningless past. Time itself is mysterious enough, and the categorically supreme form of temporality is not necessarily less sublime than a (verbally formulated) nontemporal actuality. Perhaps an absolute memory or retention of the once experienced is a suitable subject for meditation as ecstatic as Augustine's upon what he took to be a vision of all events in a moveless whole of awareness.

## ANSELM (1033–1109): GOD AS ABSOLUTE MAXIMUM AND THE ONTOLOGICAL ARGUMENT

Of all contributions to the arguments justifying belief in God, probably none is more original than Anselm's famous ontological proof. Unfortunately, An-

selm stated the proof in *two forms*, the first of which is probably untenable. Historians seem at this point to have allowed their excitement over the fallacy of Anselm's first formulation (sec. 70, fourth and fifth paragraphs) to distract their attention from the second formulation (last two paragraphs of sec. 70; also secs. 74–79), although it appears within a page of the first, is repeated a number of times (especially in the reply to the objections of Gaunilo), is evidently Anselm's preferred formulation, and cannot be invalid for the same reason as that which Kant has made canonical (that existence is unjustifiably taken as a predicate). Oddly enough, and again unfortunately, Descartes's revival of the argument also involves two similarly different formulations, appearing in the same order as Anselm's and equivalent to them, but, alas, separated not by a page but by the interval between the *Discourse* and the second edition of the *Meditations* (*Second Set of Replies to Objections*). Thus there was better excuse for the commentators' neglect of the second and more cogent form in Descartes's case than in Anselm's. As for Leibniz, he seems actually to have limited himself to the first and dubious form. And it is this form that Kant refutes in his slavishly accepted criticism.

The Anselmian-Cartesian point is this: Ordinary things may of course be conceived without conceiving them as existing, but this is because the existence of their natures is contingent, not necessary. However, this contingency as a mode of relationship to existence is itself necessary, inherent in the natures. We need not conceive them as actually existing, but nevertheless we must conceive them, if at all, as at least possibly existing, that is, as such that there could be such entities (if not in this world, then in some world itself at least possible). In that sense, relation to existence is always involved. (Only of the inconceivable can we say absolutely, "There cannot be such a thing.") If, then, we conceive God, or "perfect being," we suppose implicitly that the true view of

such being must be of it (1) as nonexistent but such that its existence is or was possible; or (2) as existent but such that its nonexistence was possible; or else (3) as existent and such that its nonexistence is and ever was impossible, inconceivable. (The fourth case, "nonexistent and incapable of existing," is excluded *if* it be admitted that perfection is not inconceivable—the most vulnerable point in Anselm's reasoning, as Leibniz correctly noted.)

Now we cannot conceive perfect being in either of the first two ways. For if perfection actually or even possibly fails to exist, then it is such that, "even should it exist," as Anselm says, it would exist only by accident, that is, on sufferance of some condition or chance, and this means precariously, dependently, derivatively (with a beginning, with parts, etc.)—in a word, as Descartes well says, imperfectly. But that whose manner-of-existence would, if it existed, be imperfect could not conceivably be unqualified perfection, or such that none greater can be conceived. For something greater is conceivable, namely, something which can be conceived only as self-existent, as incapable of nonexistence.

Who cannot see that our human imperfection is logically connected with our contingency, with the essential precariousness, dependence, derivativeness —hence as Anselm argues, the noneternity—of our existence? Men exist *if* the course of events favors it, otherwise not. Is this how perfect being would exist? Critics of the argument have yet to tell us what status, other than necessary existence, self-existence, nondependent and eternal existence, is compatible with perfection; or just what is fallacious about the argument if this be perfection's only conceivable status. However, we shall see in our "Comment" below that only a view of God which can distinguish his existence from his actuality can do justice either to the ontological proof or to its critics.

Kant's objection that we need affirm properties of a subject only if we affirm the subject is irrelevant to the argument, except on the assumption that perfection is inconceivable. What cannot be merely possible must either be bare nonentity or else exist. But if perfection is sheer nonentity, then "perfect" is a meaningless term. Anselm supposes that even "the fool" who "hath said in his heart, there is no God," admits that he has an idea of God, that the word is not meaningless. Before discussing this point further, we allow Anselm to speak for himself.

### The Sole and Sufficient Argument

69. . . . I began to ask myself whether there might be found a single argument which would require no other for its proof than itself alone; and alone would suffice to demonstrate that God truly exists, and that there is a supreme good requiring nothing else, which all other things require for their existence and well-being; and whatever we believe regarding the divine Being.

Although I often and earnestly directed my thought to this end, and at some times that which I sought seemed to be just within my reach, while again it wholly evaded my mental vision, at last in despair I was about to cease, as if from the search for a thing which could not be found. But when I wished to exclude this thought altogether, lest, by busying my mind to no purpose, it should be kept from other thoughts, in which I might be successful; then more and more, though I was unwilling and shunned it, it began to force itself upon me, with a kind of importunity. So, one day, when I was exceedingly wearied with resisting its importunity, in the very conflict of my thoughts, the proof of which I had despaired offered itself,

so that I eagerly embraced the thoughts which I was strenuously repelling.

70. I do not endeavor, O Lord, to penetrate thy sublimity, for in no wise do I compare my understanding with that; but I long to understand in some degree thy truth, which my heart believes and loves. For I do not seek to understand that I may believe, but I believe in order to understand. For this also I believe—that unless I believed, I should not understand. . . .

And so, Lord, do thou, who does give understanding to faith, give me, so far as thou knowest it to be profitable, to understand that thou art as we believe; and that thou art that which we believe. And, indeed, we believe that thou art a being than which nothing greater can be conceived. Or is there no such nature, since the fool hath said in his heart, there is no God? (Psalms xiv. I) But, at any rate, this very fool, when he hears of this being of which I speak—a being than which nothing greater can be conceived—understands what he hears, and what he understands is in his understanding; although he does not understand it to exist.

For, it is one thing for an object to be in the understanding, and another to understand that the object exists. When a painter first conceives of what he will afterwards perform, he has it in his understanding, but he does not yet understand it to be, because he has not yet performed it. But after he has made the painting, he both has it in his understanding, and he understands that it exists, because he has made it.

Hence, even the fool is convinced that something exists in the understanding, at least, than which nothing greater can be conceived. For, when he hears of this, he understands it. And whatever is understood, exists in the understanding. And assuredly that, than which nothing greater can be conceived, cannot exist in the understanding alone.

For, suppose it exists in the understanding alone: then it can be conceived to exist in reality; which is greater.

Therefore, if that, than which nothing greater can be conceived, exists in the understanding alone, the very being, than which nothing greater can be conceived, is one, than which a greater can be conceived. But obviously this is impossible. Hence, there is no doubt that there exists a being, than which nothing greater can be conceived, and it exists both in the understanding and in reality. . . .

And it assuredly exists so truly, that it cannot be conceived not to exist. For, it is possible to conceive of a being which cannot be conceived not to exist; and this is greater than one which can be conceived not to exist. Hence, if that, than which nothing greater can be conceived, can be conceived not to exist, it is not that, than which nothing greater can be conceived. But this is an irreconcilable contradiction. There is, then, so truly a being than which nothing greater can be conceived to exist, that it cannot even be conceived not to exist; and this being thou art, O Lord, our God.

So truly, therefore, dost thou exist, O Lord, my God, that thou canst not be conceived not to exist; and rightly. For, if a mind could conceive of a being better than thee, the creature would rise above the Creator; and this is most absurd. And, indeed, whatever else there is, except thee alone, can be conceived not to exist. To thee alone, therefore, it belongs to exist more truly than all other beings, and hence in a higher degree than all others. For, whatever else exists does not exist so truly, and hence in a less degree it belongs to it to exist. Why, then, has the fool said in his heart, there is no God (Psalms xiv. I), since it is so evident to a rational mind, that thou dost exist in the highest degree of all? Why, except that he is dull and a fool?

## Elucidation of Categorical Supremacy

71. What art thou, then, Lord God, than whom nothing greater can be conceived? But what art thou, except that which, as the highest of all beings, alone exists through itself, and creates all other things from nothing? For, whatever is not this is less than a thing which can be conceived of. But this cannot be conceived of thee. What good, therefore, does the supreme Good lack, through which every good is? Therefore, thou art just, truthful, blessed, and whatever it is better to be than not to be. For it is better to be just than not just; better to be blessed than not blessed.

But, although it is better for thee to be . . . compassionate, passionless, than not to be these things; how art thou . . . at once compassionate and passionless?

## Compassion Not Literally in God

72. For, if thou art passionless, thou dost not feel sympathy; and if thou dost not feel sympathy, thy heart is not wretched from sympathy for the wretched; but this it is to be compassionate. But if thou art not compassionate, whence cometh so great consolation to the wretched? How, then, art thou compassionate and not compassionate, O Lord, unless because thou art compassionate in terms of our experience, and not compassionate in terms of thy being.

Truly, thou art so in terms of our experience, but thou art not so in terms of thine own. For, when thou beholdest us in our wretchedness, we experience the effect of compassion, but thou dost not experience the feeling. Therefore, thou art both compassionate, because thou dost save the wretched, and spare those who sin against thee; and not compassionate, because thou art affected by no sympathy for wretchedness.

## Manner of God's Existence: His Eternal Wholeness

73. But if through thine eternity thou hast been, and art, and wilt be; and to have been is not to be destined to be; and to be is not to have been, or to be destined to be; how does thine eternity exist as a whole forever? Or is it true that nothing of thy eternity passes away, so that it is not now; and that nothing of it is destined to be, as if it were not yet?

. . . neither yesterday nor today nor tomorrow thou art; but simply, thou art, outside all time. For yesterday and today and tomorrow have no existence, except in time; but thou, although nothing exists without thee, nevertheless does not exist in space or time, but all things exist in thee. For nothing contains thee, but thou containest all.

Hence, thou dost permeate and embrace all things. Thou art before all, and dost transcend all. And, of a surety, thou art before all; for before they were made, thou art. But how dost thou transcend all? In what way dost thou transcend those beings which will have no end? Is it because they cannot exist at all without thee; while thou art in no wise less, if they should return to nothingness? For so, in a certain sense, thou dost transcend them. Or, is it also because they can be conceived to have an end; but thou by no means? For so they actually have an end, in a certain sense; but thou, in no sense. And certainly, what in no sense has an end transcends what is ended in any sense. Or, in this way also dost thou transcend all things, even the eternal, because thy eternity and theirs is present as a whole with thee; while they have not yet that part of their eternity which is to come, just as they no longer have that part which is past? For so thou dost ever transcend them, since thou art ever present with thyself, and since that to which they have not yet come is ever present with thee.

74. Therefore, thou alone, O Lord, art what thou art; and thou art he who thou art. For, what is one thing in the whole and another in the parts, and in which there is any mutable element, is not altogether what it is. And what begins from non-existence, and can be conceived not to exist, and unless it subsists through something else, returns to non-existence; and what has a past existence, which is no longer, or a future existence, which is not yet—this does not properly and absolutely exist.

But thou art what thou art, because, whatever thou art at any time, or in any way, thou art as a whole and forever. And thou art he who thou art, properly and simply; for thou hast neither a past existence nor a future, but only a present existence; nor canst thou be conceived as at any time non-existent. But thou art life, and light, and wisdom, and blessedness, and many goods of this nature. And yet thou art only one supreme good; thou art all-sufficient to thyself, and needest none; and thou art he whom all things need for their existence and well-being.

## Reply to Gaunilo's Defense of the Fool

75. You say—whosoever you may be, who say that a fool is capable of making these statements—that a being than which a greater cannot be conceived is not in the understanding in any other sense than that in which a being that is altogether inconceivable in terms of reality, is in the understanding. You say that the inference that this being exists in reality, from the fact that it is in the understanding, is no more just than the inference that a lost island most certainly exists, from the fact that when it is described the hearer does not doubt that it is in his understanding.

But I say: if a being than which a greater is inconceivable is not understood or conceived, and is not in the understanding or in concept, certainly either God is not a being than which a greater is inconceivable, or else he is not understood or conceived, and is not in the understanding or in concept. But I call on your faith and conscience to attest that this is most false. Hence, that than which a greater cannot be conceived is truly understood and conceived, and is in the understanding and in concept. Therefore either the grounds on which you try to controvert me are not true, or else the inference which you think to base logically on those grounds is not justified.

But you hold, moreover, that supposing that a being than which a greater cannot be conceived is understood, it does not follow that this being is in the understanding; nor, if it is in the understanding, does it therefore exist in reality.

In answer to this, I maintain positively: if that being can be even conceived to be, it must exist in reality. For that than which a greater is inconceivable cannot be conceived except as without beginning. . . .

Moreover, I will venture to make this assertion: without doubt, whatever at any place or at any time does not exist—even if it does exist at some place or at some time—can be conceived to exist nowhere and never, as at some place and at some time it does not exist. For what did not exist yesterday, and exists today, as it is understood not to have existed yesterday, so it can be apprehended by the intelligence that it never exists. And what is not here, and is elsewhere, can be conceived to be nowhere, just as it is not here. So with regard to an object of which the individual parts do not exist at the same places or times: all its parts and therefore its very whole can be conceived to exist nowhere or never. . . . Moreover, what is composed of parts can be dissolved in concept, and be non-existent. Therefore, whatever at any place or at any time does not exist

as a whole, even if it is existent, can be conceived not to exist.

But that than which a greater cannot be conceived, if it exists, cannot be conceived not to exist. Otherwise, it is not a being than which a greater cannot be conceived: which is inconsistent. By no means, then, does it at any place or at any time fail to exist as a whole: but it exists as a whole everywhere and always.

Do you believe that this being can in some way be conceived or understood, or that the being with regard to which these things are understood can be in concept or in the understanding? For if it cannot, these things cannot be understood with reference to it. But if you say that it is not understood and that it is not in the understanding, because it is not thoroughly understood; you should say that a man who cannot face the direct rays of the sun does not see the light of day, which is none other than the sunlight. Assuredly a being than which a greater cannot be conceived exists, and is in the understanding, at least to this extent—that these statements regarding it are understood.

### Perfect Island Not Perfect in the Relevant Sense

76. But, you say, it is as if one should suppose an island in the ocean, which surpasses all lands in its fertility, and which, because of the difficulty, or rather the impossibility, of discovering what does not exist, is called a lost island; and should say that there can be no doubt that this island truly exists in reality, for this reason, that one who hears it described easily understands what he hears.

Now I promise confidently that if any man shall devise anything existing either in reality or in concept alone (except that than which a greater cannot be conceived) to which he can adapt the sequence of my reasoning, I will discover that thing, and will give him his lost island, not to be lost again.

But it now appears that this being than which a greater is inconceivable cannot be conceived not to be, because it exists on so assured a ground of truth. . . .

Hence, if any one says that he conceives this being not to exist, I say that at the time when he conceives of this either he conceives of a being than which a greater is inconceivable, or he does not conceive at all. If he does not conceive, he does not conceive of the non-existence of that of which he does not conceive. But if he does conceive, he certainly conceives of a being which cannot be even conceived not to exist. For if it could be conceived not to exist, it could be conceived to have a beginning and an end. But this is impossible.

He, then, who conceives of this being conceives of a being which cannot be even conceived not to exist; but he who conceives of this being does not conceive that it does not exist; else he conceives what is inconceivable. The non-existence, then, of that than which a greater cannot be conceived is inconceivable.

## Why Ordinary Things, but Not God, Can Be Conceived Not To Exist

77. . . . all objects, except that which exists in the highest degree, can be conceived not to exist. For all those objects, and those alone, can be conceived not to exist, which have a beginning or end or composition of parts: also, as I have already said, whatever at any place or at any time does not exist as a whole.

That being alone, on the other hand, cannot be conceived not to exist, in which any conception discovers neither beginning nor end nor composition of parts, and which any conception finds always and everywhere as a whole.

Be assured, then, that you can conceive of your own non-existence, although you are most certain that you exist. I am surprised that you should

have admitted that you are ignorant of this. For we conceive of the non-existence of many objects which we know to exist, and of the existence of many which we know not to exist.

78. So, then, of God alone it can be said that it is impossible to conceive of his non-existence.

79. For the non-existence of what does not exist is possible, and that whose non-existence is possible can be conceived not to exist. But whatever can be conceived not to exist, if it exists, is not a being than which a greater cannot be conceived; but if it does not exist, it would not, even if it existed, be a being than which a greater cannot be conceived. But it cannot be said that a being than which a greater is inconceivable, if it exists, is not a being than which a greater is inconceivable; or that if it existed, it would not be a being than which a greater is inconceivable.

It is evident, then, that neither is it non-existent, nor is it possible that it does not exist, nor can it be conceived not to exist. For otherwise, if it exists, it is not that which it is said to be in the hypothesis; and if it existed, it would not be what it is said to be in the hypothesis.

## The Conceivability of That than Which None Greater Is Conceivable

80. . . . you say that when you hear of a being than which a greater is inconceivable, you cannot conceive of it in terms of any real object known to you either specifically or generally, nor have it in your understanding. . . .

But obviously this is not true. For everything that is less good, in so far as it is good, is like the greater good. It is therefore evident to any rational mind, that by ascending from the lesser good to the greater, we can form a considerable notion of a being than which a greater is inconceivable.

For instance, who (even if he does not believe that what he conceives of exists in reality) supposing that there is some good which has a beginning and an end, does not conceive that a good is much better, which, if it begins, does not cease to be? And that as the second good is better than the first, so that good which has neither beginning nor end, though it is ever passing from the past through the present to the future, is better than the second? And that far better than this is a being—whether any being of such a nature exists or not—which in no wise requires change or motion, nor is compelled to undergo change or motion?

Is this inconceivable, or is some being greater than this conceivable? Or is not this to form a notion from objects than which a greater is conceivable, of the being than which a greater cannot be conceived? There is, then, a means of forming a notion of a being than which a greater is inconceivable.

So easily, then, can the fool who does not accept sacred authority be refuted, if he denies that a notion may be formed from other objects of a being than which a greater is inconceivable. But if any Catholic would deny this, let him remember that the invisible things of God, from the creation of the world, are clearly seen, being understood by the things that are made, even his eternal power and Godhead. (Romans i. 20)

[Sec. 69, St. Anselm, *Proslogium; Monologium; An Appendix in Behalf of the Fool by Gaunilon; and Cur Deus Homo*, trans. S. N. Deane (La Salle, Ill.: Open Court Publishing Co., 1903, 1945), pp. 1–2. Sec. 70, *ibid.*, pp. 6–11. Sec. 71, *ibid.*, pp. 10–11. Sec. 72, *ibid.*, pp. 13–14. Sec. 73, *ibid.*, pp. 25–26. Sec. 74, *ibid.*, pp. 27–28. Sec. 75, *ibid.*, pp. 153–56. Sec. 76, *ibid.*, pp. 158–59. Sec. 77, *ibid.*, p. 160. Sec. 78, *ibid.*, p. 161. Sec. 79, *ibid.*, p. 162. Sec. 80, *ibid.*, pp. 167–68.]

## COMMENT

Anselm's most vulnerable assumption, so far as we see, is his belief that the idea of an absolute maximum of great-

ness is consistently meaningful; that positivism (which asserts the meaninglessness or the absurdity of all such ideas) is incorrect. How does he know "maximal greatness" is not similar to "a number than which none greater can be conceived"? (No such maximal number is conceivable.) Only a slight effort is made by the great Bishop to meet this difficulty, that is, to refute positivism (which Carneades had defended long before Comte or Carnap). In part Anselm here appeals to faith, but in so far he is suggesting that the argument is of no use to secular philosophy. However, he also proposes rational grounds for admitting the consistency of his concept (in the eighth reply to Gaunilo [sec. 80]). The grounds, as there presented, leave a good deal to be desired. Indeed, it is hard to see how classical theism, with its paradoxical view of deity, could ever establish the consistency of its basic conception. But a different form of theism, perhaps free from incurable paradox, might employ the argument without exposing itself to the same objection. Hence the present turn to a nonclassical form of theism gives the ancient argument of Anselm a new relevance.

Anselm wrestles valiantly with the difficulties of classical theism. God helps those in misery but does not pity them or suffer sympathetically with them. Why not? Because not to suffer is better than to suffer; and that than which none greater can be conceived must, by definition, always have the better of two possible predicates. So although the effect upon the wretched is as if God sympathized with them, really he does not. We have here an effect which analogy with our experience fails to illuminate. But, worse than that, Anselm has only shifted the difficulty. For he says that God beholds us in our wretchedness. Now this puts God in relation to us, makes him relative rather than merely absolute; and therewith classical the-

ism, which is Anselm's doctrine, is contradicted. Besides, how does one behold,
know, intuit—use what word you will—
the wretchedness of someone? How can
a being know what wretchedness is if
no shadow of suffering, disappointment,
unfulfilled desire or wish, has ever been
experienced by that being? Classical
theists have never, to our knowledge,
given us the least inkling of an answer
to this question. Could the adequate,
full, concrete knowledge of a particular
state of suffering be anything else than
a sympathetic participation in that suffering?

It is notable that a great Christian
predecessor of Anselm in one passage at
least adopted the opposite solution of
the same problem. The following, from
Origen, is one of the rare genuinely
dipolar utterances in all patristic theology:

When I speak to a man and entreat him
on some account to have pity on me, if
he is a man without pity, he is quite unaffected by the things I say. But if he is a
man of gentle spirit, and no callousness of
heart has grown within him, he hears me
and has pity upon me; his feelings are
softened at my prayer. Something of the
kind I pray you imagine with regard to the
Savior. He came down to earth in pity for
the race of men. By our affections He was
affected before He was affected by the sufferings of the cross and condescended to
take our flesh upon him. Had He not been
affected, He would not have entered into
association with the life of men. First He
is affected; then He comes down and is
seen. What is that affection whereby on
our account He is affected? It is the affection of love. The Father Himself too, the
God of the Universe, long suffering and
of great compassion, full of pity, is not He
in a manner liable to affection? Are you
unaware that, when He orders the affairs
of men, He is subject to the affections of
humanity? The very Father is not impassible, without affection. If we pray to him,
He feels pity and sympathy. He experiences an affection of love. He concerns
himself with things in which, by the

majesty of His nature, He can have no
concern, and for our selves He bears the
affections of men.[1]

The translator remarks: "As a rule
his position is that no $\pi\alpha\theta\sigma$ (affection)
must be attributed to the divine nature.
But his expressions are difficult to reconcile." And of course Origen could
not stem the torrent of etiolatry and
being-worship sufficiently to work out
a doctrine of divine Effect and Becoming. Nevertheless, in a moment of daring and great honesty, he did set down
the logic of the Christian view, undis-
torted for the moment by Greek philosophical prejudice and oriental or Roman despotism and legalism. True, he
guards himself with "in a manner" and
"in which, by the majesty of His nature,
He can have no concern." But these
scarcely spoil the picture. They can be
harmonized with the dipolar doctrine
that it is not the divine essence which
can be relativized with respect to particular things or events but only the
divine actual experiences, with their unimaginable fulness of accidents, of contingent concreteness.

The admission of a dipolar nature in
the supreme reality frees the connection
which Anselm discovered between perfection and necessity of existence from
a certain paradox which is probably the
chief cause of the prevalent failure to
appreciate the ontological argument.
The paradox is this: We intuitively feel
that full, concrete actuality is a surd
with respect to any abstract essence or
formula. The definition of perfection,
any definition, is clearly such a formula.
Therefore. . . . Now this reasoning is
valid and certainly quite as cogent as
Anselm's argument could possibly be.
But, if we shift to a dipolar view of

1. *Origines: Selections from the Commentaries and the Homilies,* trans. R. B. Tollinton
(London: Society for Promoting Christian
Knowledge; New York and Toronto: Macmillan Co., 1929), pp. 15–16.

deity, we can reconcile the two reasonings. For what is proved by the famous proof, thus reinterpreted, is not any actuality, even divine, but only an existence, and in dipolar thinking these are radically distinct. The existence to be proved necessary is just as abstract as the essence connoted by "perfect" or "categorically supreme." God exists if there is any divine actuality, any actual state, no matter which among possible ones, manifesting the divine essence.

Realization of a kind of possibility is what personal existence always means. I exist if some possible state of my life is actual, no matter which. In ordinary cases (and this includes that of any conceivable island, however "perfect") both actuality and existence are contingent, because it depends upon the rest of the universe (and upon God) whether the life or existence of the thing can go on at all, or whether it begins at all. In the divine form of the distinction existence-actuality, actuality is still contingent, since there are alternative possibilities for the divine life or experience. But here there is no possibility of a world state excluding any-and-all divine experiences of that state. On the contrary, it follows from the very meaning of "divinity" that, whatever happens, God can and will have experience of that happening and will accordingly exist. Thus the most cogent counterargument to the proof turns out to be irrelevant to the proof itself—taken as a discovery that categorical supremacy, exclusion of all possible rivalry with other individuals, necessarily exists. The counterargument is relevant (and fatal) only with respect to a proof favoring the monopolar interpretation of "categorical supremacy." For on that interpretation, a divine existent and a divine actuality cannot be distinguished, and thus our invincible intuition into the transcendence of actuality with respect to all essences bars the way to a proof of existence from essence. On the di-

polar interpretation, the objection falls; for here we assert as necessary no one divine actuality, but only that the class of divine actualities is not null. This "non-nullity of the class, actualities realizing divine potentialities for experiencing," is itself plainly something abstract and general, no concrete particular thing. Yet it requires that there be some such concrete thing. Which or just what, among the innumerable divine possibilities, is a question of fact and entirely beyond the reach of abstract proof. So the contentions of the two main parties to the dispute are reconciled. What a triumph for Anselm— even though one which might have surprised and troubled him!

The transition from Anselm's view of divine perfection to the dipolar alternative is easily made. "None greater can be conceived" is subtly ambiguous. It might mean that we conceive an entity such that no other entity could conceivably be greater; or it might mean that we conceive an individual such that *no other individual* could conceivably be greater. The difference is that the second formula allows the possibility that the same individual may be conceived as potentially in a greater state than its actual state, even though the formula excludes the possibility of any other individual (no matter in what state) being greater. Otherwise expressed, while the one formula posits a being unsurpassable by anything, the other formula posits a being unsurpassable save by itself. Now Anselm probably would have argued that a being which could be surpassed by itself would be surpassed even more by another being so complete that it could not be surpassed even by itself. This would reduce the second formula to a contradiction. But only on one assumption: that a being unsurpassable by anything, even itself, hence an absolute maximum of value in all respects, is genuinely conceivable. There are definite reasons for denying this. One of them is this: All possible value, a sheer maximum of value, is excluded by the law that values involve mutually incompatible alternatives, that potential value can therefore not be exhausted by any actual value. However this may be, it is remarkable how powerful Anselm's formulas are, in that but little change is required in them to embody the outcome of the chief criticisms of so many centuries.

## AL-GHAZZALI (1058–1111): MOHAMMEDAN THEISM

Contemporary with Anselm was the great Mohammedan orthodox theologian, al-Ghazzali. What was his theology? In some Mohammedan circles Aristotelian theism was able to flourish in a purer form than was possible among Jews or Christians. Thus we find the characteristic Aristotelian denial that God knows concrete particulars openly professed by several of the great Moslem philosophers, whereas no Christian and among Jews only Gerson (so far as we know) wished or dared to do this. But such a doctrine is as incompatible with Mohammedanism as with most other religions. So in al-Ghazzali we find the most emphatic possible defense of the doctrine of omniscience in the non-Aristotelian sense. Inasmuch as Mohammedan philosophy had become deeply implicated in so grave a heresy as the denial of omniscience and particular providence, the sense or illusion of harmony between theology (basing itself in part upon sacred writings) and philosophy tended to be less in evidence than in the Christian parallel. No doubt many causes contributed to this. And of course there were other issues than those of omniscience and providence which caused conflict between philosophers and theologians.

Al-Ghazzali went through a prolonged religious crisis of doubt and search, cultivated the mystic way with great personal sacrifices from a worldly standpoint, and finally achieved a dogmatic position which for him was satisfactory and which helped to crystallize the thinking and religious feeling of Islam. He was essentially a theologian rather than a philosopher; but he had wrestled mightily with certain philosophical systems, and his thought is given here as a specimen of religious doctrine which fuses monopolar metaphysics with certain obvious values of religion in a system which was coherent enough for practical purposes in an environment that somewhat discouraged criticism. The following passages are translated (we apologize for this) from a German rendering, which was as close as we could come to the original. We do not believe that the meaning is greatly in doubt, except so far as this type of philosophy is obscure in any language and to any man, whether he realizes it or not.

The passages are taken from the most important work of the author, his *Resuscitation of the Sciences of Religion.* They are part of an opening section of Book II containing a declaration of faith intended to be taught to children and therefore written in "rhyming prose."

It is to be borne in mind that numerous "liberal theologians" in Islam have defended views incompatible with some of al-Ghazzali's doctrines; for instance, his assertion that the immutable divine will determines all events, good or bad, to the last detail. Also, as we shall see, it is not easy to show that Aquinas, for example, held a different doctrine on this matter; and certainly the two agree that the divine knowledge in its eternal and immutable completeness envisages every event. We think that philosophically the main point is that this is a form of monopolar theism which insists upon omniscience and divine freedom deliberately to create or not to create the world. In short, it is classical theism, with minor Mohammedan variations. It has inspired the lives of countless millions and, if only for that reason, deserves respect.

It may be remarked that the first three sentences give a good statement of what we have called the categorical supremacy of deity. Only in the following passages is the definite monopolar version of this supremacy introduced.

## The Categorical Supremacy of God

*81.* Praise be to God, the creator.... He is one in essence, unequalled, unique, sole, incomparable, alone without opponent or rival. He exists from the beginning, without predecessor, from all eternity, beginningless; he endures, none follows him, he is everlasting without end.... He is no substance and there are no substances in him; he is not an accident and there are no accidents in him.... He is high above heaven and earth, and yet is "closer to a man than his own arteries" ... for his presence is not like that of a body ... he is not in things nor are things in him.... In his essence no other thing can exist, nor can his essence be in anything outside him. He is exalted above change and alteration; for him there are no happenings, no misfortune can befall him, but rather he possesses everlastingly the properties of his majesty, beyond the reach of decay, and for the attributes of his perfection he needs no growth or process of perfecting. The existence of his essence is rationally knowable.

*82.* He knows all things knowable... "he knows the very tread of the blackbird in the darkest night upon hard stone" and notices the movement of the motes in the sunbeams.... He knows the inward motives and impulses and the most secret thoughts, with an eternal knowledge which he has had before all time, not as though the knowledge were newly arisen in him or communicated to him.... He wills all that exists, and determines events. Thus all things ... good or bad ... acts of obedience or disobedience, they all occur solely according to his decision and determination, his wisdom and will. What he wills, takes place, and what he does not will, does not take place.... His will consists in his essence like his other properties and belongs to him always. From eternity he willed the existence of things in the times appointed for them, and they come into being at those times and no others, precisely in accordance with his knowledge and will.

*83.* He brought forth the creation to reveal his power ... not as though there were for him any necessity or need for the creation.... It is proof of his generosity, and not a necessity, that he showers mercy and good things upon his servants, a pure gift on his part, for he could have punished his servants with every possible affliction, suffering, and illness. And if he had done so, it would have been just of him, not bad and unjust. [For—the author has pointed out—we have received all things from him, and there is nothing which we possess in our own right of which he could rob us.]

*84.* Everywhere he could have done the opposite of what he has actually done ... or he could have done the same things earlier or later.

[Sec. 81, Hans Bauer, *Die Dogmatik al-Ghazzali's Nach dem II Buch seines Hauptwerkes* (Halle: Buchdrückerei des Waisenhauses, 1912), pp. 8–10. Sec. 82, *ibid.*, pp. 10–11. Sec. 83, *ibid.*, p. 13. Sec. 84, *ibid.*, p. 57.]

### COMMENT

One of the merits of al-Ghazzali is the daring honesty with which he reveals the basic logic of classical theism. This doctrine is essentially the identification of the good and worshipful with the powerful, supreme value with supreme cause as such. It is close to the naked worship of power. One grovels before the One who does whatever is done (good or bad). True, it is not a worship of automatic, blind, or unconscious power; the One knows what he is doing and freely decides upon it. But this agrees with the supposition that the worshiper of sheer power takes as his ideal the political form of power. The One is the absolute despot, who arbitrarily and as a matter of whim disposes of the activities and lives of his subjects, completely neutral or indifferent to their own feelings and decisions. Logically, all who assume as an axiom that Cause and Good coincide are in al-Ghazzali's camp, though they usually seek to disguise this somewhat.

What is the theory of value associated with the doctrine? Here too our author is admirably clear and forthright. Obligation is a matter of sanctions, of some anticipated good to the agent, either in this life or the next. (Bishop Paley said the same; did Aquinas offer a clear alternative?) God, being pure Cause, self-sufficient, unmodifiable, can receive no good or evil result from any action, hence for him there is no obligation and no right or wrong. The liberal Mohammedan theologians who, shocked at such transcendentalized despotism, declared that God must act justly and to promote the good of his creatures are easily refuted. Their "must" has no assignable meaning. God is not constrained by anything. And there is no divine purpose to effect which certain actions are indispensable means; for what purpose can a self-sufficient being pursue? He already has any good its success could involve.

In Jewish and Christian classical theology we find a somewhat different way of speaking. But do we find a definite logical alternative? One speaks, for instance, of the purpose of the world as serving or manifesting the glory of God, as though he would not be equally glorious without any such service or manifestation—according to the logic of the doctrine.

Even our present author does not wholly avoid such evasions. He too declares that God's dealings with us exhibit generosity on God's part, when what he really (if he is consistent) wishes to say is that God is simply indifferent to us and our fate, whether we suffer or not, and whether deservedly or not. Indifference is not generosity! And our author, in the heat of arguing God's lack of obligation to promote our good, declares that God is indifferent even to our obedience or disobedience of his will and is exalted above all purposes and all questions of advantage. God has no intentions, benevolent or otherwise, in regard to the world, since nothing in creation can make any difference to the good which he enjoys. The liberal notion that God would not cause anyone to suffer through no fault of his own, or without subsequent compensation, is held to be refuted by the example of the animals, who often suffer, always innocently, and who can hardly be thought to receive compensation in an afterlife.

It may be submitted that our author's basic trouble is not in the particular fashion with which he elaborates the classical or cause-worshiping doctrine but in the doctrine itself. A mere "cause" cannot have purposes, good or bad. To achieve a purpose is to enjoy an effect and, in this enjoyment, to *be* an effect. The basis of goodness, moreover, is a sense for the weal or woe of others, and this is essentially sympathy, taking their joy or sorrow into one's self. This means being effect of them as cause. So long as this is denied of God, there will be either sophistical evasions or worship of mere power.

The famous "fatalism" of the Moslems is in evidence also in our theologian. It tends to go with the exaltation of cause as such. If to be cause is the great thing, the greatest thing will be that of which, in every aspect, phenomena are simply effects, in no sense their own cause or self-determined. Only in rather recent times does a different view begin to make itself felt, the doctrine that all actuality involves a certain self-causation, genuine metaphysical freedom, so that the supreme Cause is merely a necessary but not, in the logical sense, a "sufficient" condition of things being what they are. The Cause is sufficient condition, indeed, of the possibility of phenomena but not of their actuality. This they must themselves enact, as "self-created creatures." If this is paradoxical, it cannot at worst be more so than the conceptions of classical theism.

For example, consider the logical consequences of saying: God's eternal essence contains knowledge and volition which exactly define all temporal process. Thus we have an eternally true premise from which logically follows the existence of this very world. (For God's knowing and willing the existence of this world surely implies that existence.) Now what a necessary premise implies is itself and in the same sense necessary (principle of modal logic). What is meant by saying that God might have made a different world? Surely in that case he would have known and willed a different one; that is, his knowledge and will would have been otherwise. This implies that his actual knowledge and will with respect to this world is an accident, not his necessary essence. So not all the candor and courage of our author in developing the shocking consequences of the doctrine for human conceptions of good and evil can enable him to avoid the incoherence of his fundamental exaltation of cause above effect. Etiolatry, cause-worship, is the unsuspected source of his troubles.

This comes out in a curious way in the thought of a Mohammedan philosopher of two and a half centuries earlier, Hisham. That strange man maintained that "God knows himself always but (other) things only after they come into being." "If God had known things from all eternity they must have been themselves eternal." But, nevertheless (and here is the strange part), God's knowledge is not something that comes into being in time, for knowing is a property, and one cannot speak of a property (such as, being temporal) of a property. By this ingenious dodge, Hisham seeks to avoid the problem of how change can be in the perfect being.[2]

As another example of what happens once classical theism is accepted, consider the debates over the "eternity of the Koran." Is it the very words that are eternal, or merely the divine ideas expressed in the words? How trivial the debate, once it is considered that all divine ideas are eternal, according to the doctrine, and so is God's knowledge of the least actions of the creatures, and thus, since "knowing and known are inseparable," the actions themselves only seem products of becoming to our ignorant and benighted mode of knowing. They are as eternally present to the eternal gaze as the most exalted entities. They may be said to come "into being," but they do not come into or before divine knowledge; they just are there. And this knowing measures the reality of things! What more absolute existence than to be divinely known to exist; if fixedly known, then so existent! Lequier was later to elaborate the argument into the finest and most exact detail.

Our German translator of al-Ghazzali suggests that this theologian was partly inspired by Christian ideals and offers the hypothesis that the inoculation of Mohammedanism in such ways with a minute dose of Christian idealism

2. See M. Horten, *Die philosophische Systeme der speculativen Theologen im Islam* (Bonn, 1912), pp. 172–73.

may furnish the reason for its comparative immunity to Christian proselytizing. Perhaps there is room for another or supplementary explanation. May not the existence in Christianity of the same obstacle to a consistent theology of love which operated in Mohammedanism, namely, the prejudice of monopolarity, and especially of cause-worship, have prevented Christianity from seeming a definite alternative with unequivocal superiority? A genuine acceptance of "God is love" is not easily learned, even from Christian—or Jewish—theologians. For few have had the courage, and the intellectual freedom and penetration, to work out a metaphysics on this basis.

Either we admit that love is always cause-effect, in principle dipolar, and then a liberal theology, or theology of love, not of mere power, of human freedom, not of servitude to an absolute despot, lies open before us, or we have no genuine alternative to the worship of power as power, the self-sufficient, aloof, and indifferent just *as* self-sufficient, aloof, and indifferent. We feel grateful to Mohammedanism for refusing to gloss over the issue, or at least for allowing it to come close to the surface, with brave candor and (within the limits of an intrinsically incoherent assumption) maximal consistency.

Furthermore, the denial that God is required to deal out pain and pleasure according to past deeds and fortunes in order to meet our demand for cosmic "justice" is, in our opinion, not nearly so shocking as the total context of our author makes it appear to be to our Christian sensibilities. We agree with al-Ghazzali that God is not a distributor of good and bad who is subject to a cosmically extended notion of appropriate rewards and punishments. But what is shocking is the alternative to this which is proposed, namely, that God is indifferent to the creatures. There is a radically distinct, third pos-

sibility, which is that God loves all creatures, well behaved or not; that his aim is to foster intense, varied, zestful, and therefore in a measure free and self-determined, creaturely living at each moment, so that the creatures may enjoy themselves and he may own this creaturely enjoyment as also his by sympathetic appropriation. This is not indifference, and it is equally remote from a cosmic bookkeeping of deserts with respect to reward or punishment. God need not have the legalistic complex. It is as though an orchestra leader were to assign instruments and indeed notes essentially in terms of reward and punishment rather than in terms of optimal chances of good performance. The present of the creatures is not for the sake of their past and its accumulated deserts but for its own sake and that of the future. Why assume an idea of divine righteousness which inverts this order and then debate about whether love or mercy can be brought in to mitigate the harsher implications of the assumption? Love alone is the essential principle. Only if reward or punishment contributes to present and future beauty of experience, creaturely and divine, made relevant to each other by love, have they any extra-legal significance whatever or any place in theology. So we may go part way with our ancient friend's seemingly so shocking denial of divine obligation to dispense good and evil "justly."

As to God's having no obligations at all, and being under no "must" to do good, we say that the must is simply the essence of God which is love. He cannot fail to love, and his actions are certain to express this love somehow. Why should we demand more? Are we to suppose that our feeble love can tell us how infinite love must or might express itself, save in the vaguest and most general way? But it seems a good guess that it could not express itself in terms intelligible to those afflicted with the legalistic *idée fixe* of desert and merit. It is impossible that the tragedies of existence should be essentially punishments or its good fortune essentially rewards. The freedom of other men and creatures, the interplay of our own freedom with the blind sway of natural laws (blind just so far as laws, in the sense of impersonal uniformities), the social unity of life and its interdependence (the best and most sensitive souls being far from the least dependent for their feelings)—these and other considerations make the notion of justice in this sense inapplicable. Unfortunately, our author, who sees that reason cannot justify the notion, yet holds to it in some form on the sole basis of the Koran.

The contrasting notion of divine justice is as follows. God is on our side in life's tragedy, in that he shares it with us, along with all our longing for happiness, so that this longing counts for all it is worth in the divine life, is just as real there as in us. We "have an advocate with the Father," who says for us the whole of what we say for ourselves, without the least omission. Only all other creatures have the same advocate; and the integrity of the divine life, which all enjoy and require, must be maintained. We are then denied nothing through divine indifference to

our feelings; but we cannot well ask that we be granted something through divine indifference to the feelings of others. We have exactly the rights that we can wish to lay claim to in so far as we love God and our neighbor. This is the divine justice, and it is absolute. To appreciate it, we must love; to that extent, there is reward and punishment. Need we any other? The beauty of love is its own argument; all others are degrading or irrelevant. Particularly degrading is the notion that the tragedies inherent in social and free existence must all be channeled away from the loving and dumped into the laps of the loveless. As though their lack of love were not almost tragedy enough! And as though the loving would enjoy the spectacle of their fate, would really escape feeling it themselves! Tragedy is inescapable, since it comes through freedom and sensitivity, not through the cunning manipulation of deity.

This is not the view of al-Ghazzali. But it may not be much farther from his than from that of many a Christian divine. The idea slowest to dawn is that there is nothing prior to love, to the cosmic divine principle of "shared [and free] experience" (Dewey), neither "power" nor "justice" nor "knowledge" nor "being" nor "cause."

## MAIMONIDES (1135–1204)

Maimonides (or Moses ben Maimon) faced the same task as Philo (and in part the same as Anselm) of reconciling Judaism with philosophical tenets derived from the Greeks. But the later author is more of an Aristotelian and less of a Platonist and, like Aristotle and most unlike Philo, is a highly systematic thinker who offers elaborate arguments, neatly set out in order, for his assertions—thus paving the way for the vast argumentation, on similar Aris-

totelian foundations, of Thomas Aquinas.

The Philonian paradoxes are readily recognized, above all, that of the indescribability of a deity who, nevertheless, for religious (yes and even for philosophical) purposes, inevitably must be described as "will," "ruler," etc. The proof that God is indescribable is admirably rigorous, seeming to leave no possible loophole. Especially notable is the demonstration of the impossibility (on the premises) that any positive predicates ascribable to deity could have anything in common with those accessible to our experience and thought.

The outstanding example is knowledge. If we say that God knows the world, we cannot mean by knowledge anything of what the word signifies in other cases. The demonstration has not, we think, ever been refuted within the framework of classical theism. One cannot know with infallible accuracy, that is, as the divine must know, an object capable of being otherwise, save with a knowledge that could have been or could be otherwise (which would contradict the pure necessity attributed to deity by this tradition). Knowledge and objects correspond, in true knowledge, and given an alternative object $O'$ instead of $O$, we must have knowledge of $O'$ instead of the knowledge of $O$. Mutability or nonnecessity of the known therefore means mutability or contingency in the knower. To support Maimonides on the impossibility of logical escape from this axiom, we have the admissions of Gersonides, Arnauld, and Leibniz (secs. 117–18). What, for Maimonides, results from this impossibility? That "knowledge" has no positive content when applied to deity. We use the same word, but no common meaning goes with it, for divine and human knowing. Later thinkers (especially Thomas Aquinas) endeavor to meet the difficulty by distinguishing univocal and analogical common meaning.

The basic assumption, as with Philo and Anselm, is the immutable perfection of the divine or—it is the same—his utter simplicity. As with the earlier thinkers, this assumption has a number of roots, biblical and Greek, and it is not supposed that either a clearly rational mind or a deeply religious one could question it. Maimonides stresses the Aristotelian argument for an unmoved mover as the clinching philosophical argument to establish the immutability, hence the nonpotentiality, hence the simplicity, of deity. Where there is composition, the elements put together to constitute deity might be otherwise arranged, so such a deity must be mutable. And, of course, "The Lord our God is One" stands ready to confound anyone who deviates in the slightest from the most extreme antipolytheism, from the most rigorous denial not only of many divine beings but even of many aspects or factors in one divine being. With such premises, shared by all classical theists of Europe, is it anything but logical consistency and candor to admit the complete indescribability of God? Yet, we must ask, was the prohibition on description really observed by its proponent, and, if he had observed it, could any religious or even philosophical values have survived such a pure negativism? To have sharpened this issue with such skill is a signal contribution of Maimonides.

### Attributes Either Essential or Accidental

85. . . . it is a self-evident truth that the attribute is not inherent in the object to which it is ascribed, but it is superadded to its essence, and is consequently an *accident;* if the attribute denoted the essence of the object, it would be either mere tautology, as if, *e.g.,* one would say "man is a man," or the explanation of a name, as *e.g.,* "man is a speaking animal"; for the phrase "speaking animal" includes the true essence of man, and there is no third element besides life and speech that constitutes man; when he, therefore, is described by the attributes of life and speech, these are nothing but an explanation of the name "man," that is to say, that the thing which is called man, consists of life and speech. It will now be clear that the attribute must be one

of two things, either the essence of the object described—in that case it is a mere explanation of a name, and on that account we might admit the attribute in reference to God, but we reject it from another cause as will be shown —or the attribute is something different from the object described, some extraneous superadded element; in that case the attribute would be an accident, and he who merely rejects the appellation "accidents" in reference to the attributes of God, does not thereby alter their character; for everything superadded to the essence of an object joins it without forming part of its essential properties, and that constitutes an accident. Add to this the logical consequence of admitting many attributes, viz., the existence of many eternal beings. There cannot be any belief in the unity of God except by admitting that He is one simple substance, without any composition or plurality of elements; one from whatever side you view it, and by whatever test you examine it; not divisible into two parts in any way and by any cause, nor capable of any form of plurality either objectively or subjectively.

### No Relation between God and Creatures

86. [The question is] . . . whether some real relation exists between God and any of the substances created by Him, by which He could be described? That there is no correlation between Him and any of His creatures can easily be seen; for the characteristic of two objects correlative to each other is the equality of their reciprocal relation. Now, as God has absolute existence, while all other beings have only possible existence, as we shall show, there consequently cannot be any correlation (between God and His creatures). That a certain kind of relation does exist between them is by some considered possible, but wrongly. It is impossible to

imagine a relation between intellect and sight, although, as we believe, the same kind of existence is common to both; how, then, could a relation be imagined between any creature and God, who has nothing in common with any other being; for even the term existence is applied to Him and other things, according to our opinion, only by way of pure homonymity. Consequently there is no relation whatever between Him and any other being. For whenever we speak of a relation between two things, these belong to the same species; but when two things belong to different species though of the same class, there is no relation between them. We therefore do not say, this red compared with that green, is more, or less, or equally intense, although both belong to the same class—colour; when they belong to two different classes, there does not appear to exist any relation between them, not even to a man of ordinary intellect, although the two things belong to the same category; e.g., between a hundred cubits and the heat of pepper there is no relation, the one being a quality, the other a quantity; or between wisdom and sweetness, between meekness and bitterness, although all these come under the head of quality in its more general signification. How, then, could there be any relation between God and His creatures, considering the important difference between them in respect to true existence, the greatest of all differences. Besides, if any relation existed between them, God would be subject to the accident of relation; and although that would not be an accident to the essence of God, it would still be, to some extent, a kind of accident. You would, therefore, be wrong if you applied affirmative attributes in their literal sense to God, though they contained only relations; these, however, are the most appropriate of all attributes, to be employed, in a less strict sense, in reference to God, because they do not imply that a plurality of eternal things exists, or that any change takes place in the essence of God, when those things change to which God is in relation.

## Describing God by His Actions

*87.* Fire melts certain things and makes others hard, it boils and consumes, it bleaches and blackens. If we described the fire as bleaching, blackening, consuming, boiling, hardening and melting, we should be correct, and yet he who does not know the nature of fire, would think it included six different elements, one by which it blackens, another by which it bleaches, a third by which it boils, a fourth by which it consumes, a fifth by which it melts, a sixth by which it hardens things —actions which are opposed to one another, and of which each has its peculiar property. He, however, who knows the nature of fire, will know that by virtue of one quality in action, namely, by heat, it produces all these effects. If this is the case with that which is done by nature, how much more is it the case with regard to those who act by free will, and still more with regard to God, who is above all description. If we, therefore, perceive in God certain relations of various characters—for wisdom in us is different from power, and power from will—it does by no means follow that different elements are really contained in Him, that He contains one element by which He knows, another by which He wills, and another by which He exercises power.

*88.* On the contrary, He is a simple essence, without any additional element whatever; He created the universe, and knows it, but not by any extraneous force. There is no difference whether these various attributes refer to His actions or to relations between Him and His works; in fact, these relations, as we have also shown, exist only in the thoughts of men. This is what we must

believe concerning the attributes occurring in the books of the Prophets; some may also be taken as expressions of the perfection of God by way of comparison with what we consider as perfections in us.

## God Is without Potentiality

*89.* We have already, on several occasions, shown in this treatise that everything that implies corporeality or passiveness, is to be negatived in reference to God, for all passiveness implies change; and the agent producing that state is undoubtedly different from the object affected by it; and if God could be affected in any way whatever, another being beside Him would act on Him and cause change in Him. All kinds of non-existence must likewise be negatived in reference to Him; no perfection whatever can therefore be imagined to be at one time absent from Him, and at another present in Him: for if this were the case, He would (at a certain time) only be potentially perfect. Potentiality always implies non-existence, and when anything has to pass from potentiality into reality, another thing that exists in reality is required to effect that transition. Hence it follows that all perfections must really exist in God, and none of them must in any way be a mere potentiality.

## God without Accidental Properties

*90.* It is known that existence is an accident appertaining to all things, and therefore an element superadded to their essence. This must evidently be the case as regards everything the existence of which is due to some cause. . . . But as regards a being whose existence is not due to any cause—God alone is that being, for His existence, as we have said, is absolute—existence and essence are perfectly identical; He is not a substance to which existence is joined as an accident, as an additional element. His existence is always absolute, and has never been a new element or an accident in Him. Consequently God exists without possessing the attribute of existence. Similarly He lives without possessing the attribute of life; knows, without possessing the attribute of knowledge; is omnipotent, without possessing the attribute of omnipotence; is wise, without possessing the attribute of wisdom; all this reduces itself to one and the same entity; there is no plurality in Him.

## Negative Attributes of God

*91.* Know that the negative attributes of God are the true attributes: they do not include any incorrect notions or any deficiency whatever in reference to God, while positive attributes imply polytheism, and are inadequate, as we have already shown.

*92.* The negative attributes, however, are those which are necessary to direct the mind to the truths which we must believe concerning God; . . . *e.g.,* it has been established by proof that some being must exist besides those things which can be perceived by the senses, or apprehended by the mind; when we say of this being, that it exists, we mean that its non-existence is impossible. We thus perceive that such a being is not, for instance, like the four elements, which are inanimate, and we therefore say it is living, expressing thereby that it is not dead. We call such a being incorporeal, because we notice that it is unlike the heavens, which are living, but material. Seeing that it is also different from the intellect, which, though incorporeal and living, owes its existence to some cause, we say it is the first, expressing thereby that its existence is not due to any cause. We further notice, that the existence, that is, the essence, of this being is not limited to its own existence; many existences emanate from it, and its influence is not like that of the fire in producing heat,

or that of the sun in sending forth light, but consists in constantly giving them stability and order by well-established rule, as we shall show: we say, on that account, it has power, wisdom, and will, *i.e.,* it is not feeble or ignorant, or hasty, and does not abandon its creatures; when we say that it is not feeble, we mean that its existence is capable of producing the existence of many other things; by saying it is not ignorant, we mean "it perceives" or "it lives,"—for everything that perceives is alive—by saying "it is not hasty, and does not abandon its creatures," we mean that all these creatures preserve a certain order and arrangement; they are not left to themselves, or produced aimlessly, but whatever condition they receive from that being is given them with design and intention. We thus learn that there is no other being like unto God, and we say that He is One, *i.e.,* there are not more Gods than one.

It has thus been shown that every attribute predicated of God either denotes the quality of an action, or—when the attribute is intended to convey some idea of the Divine Being itself, and not of His actions—the negation of the opposite.

*93.* All we understand, is the fact that He exists, that He is a Being to whom none of all His creatures is similar, who has nothing in common with them, who does not include plurality, who is never too feeble to produce other beings, and whose relation to the universe is that of a steersman to a boat; and even this is not a real relation, a real simile, but serves only to convey to us the idea that God rules the universe; that is, that He gives it duraton, and preserves its necessary arrangement. . . . In the contemplation of His essence, our comprehension and knowledge prove insufficient; in the examination of His works, how they necessarily result from His will, our knowledge proves to be ignorance, and in the endeavour to extol

Him in words, all our efforts in speech
are mere weakness and failure!

94. . . . every perfection we could
imagine, even if existing in God in accordance with the opinion of those
who assert the existence of attributes,
would in reality not be of the same kind
as that imagined by us, but would only
be called by the same name, according
to our explanation; it would in fact
amount to a negation. Suppose, e.g.,
you say He has knowledge, and this
knowledge, which admits of no change
and of no plurality, embraces many
changeable things; His knowledge remains unaltered, while new things are
constantly formed, and His knowledge
of a thing before it exists, while it exists, and when it has ceased to exist, is
the same without the least change: you
would thereby declare that His knowledge is not like ours; and similarly that
His existence is not like ours. You thus
necessarily arrive at some negation,
without obtaining a true conception of
an essential attribute.

[Sec. 85. *The Guide of the Perplexed of
Maimonides*, trans. M. Friedländer (London:
Trübner & Co. [Ludgate Hill], 1885), I, 174–
75. Sec. 86, *ibid.*, pp. 182–84. Sec. 87, *ibid.*, p.
187. Sec. 88, *ibid.*, pp. 190–91. Sec. 89, *ibid.*, p.
199. Sec. 90, *ibid.*, pp. 204–5. Sec. 91, *ibid.*, pp.
207–8. Sec. 92, *ibid.*, pp. 209–11. Sec. 93, *ibid.*,
p. 212. Sec. 94, *ibid.*, p. 222.]

### COMMENT

Let us begin with Maimonides' contention that the ascription of a plurality
of attributes to deity amounts to polytheism, the admission of a plurality of
eternal beings. This is a confusion of
logical levels. A mere property is not
a deity in any reasonable sense. Only if
the several properties could conflict
with each other, or interact as agent
and patient, or require a higher will to
compose their differences, or something
of that sort, does the question of polytheism arise. Monotheism means that all
wills are ordered by the will of one supreme individual, that all truth is

known by a supreme knower, etc. Of
course, supreme will and supreme
knowledge are inseparable and in this
sense one. Even in us plurality of psychic dimensions does not conflict with
the integrity of the individual; still less,
in the supreme or categorical instance.

What may be granted to Maimonides
is that an individual totally without accidents could not have positive attributes, even essential ones. Volitional or
cognitive individuality, personality, is
intelligible only as an essence capable
of an indefinite or infinite number of
embodiments in successive experiences
or acts. The acts are accidents, and the
essence is separable from, or independent of, any such act or set of them,
while the acts are not separable from
the essence. The acts are, however, not
eternal (though indestructible), and
hence no plurality of eternal beings results. Any possible such act will be related to any other as possible experiences of the one divine being, whose
diverse states are all interconnected in
categorically supreme fashion to constitute one personal Life. This Life indeed exists without possessing existence
as an accident, the accidental aspect being whether the life takes just this particular course or that, enjoys just this
particular content or that. And this life
is likewise good without possessing
goodness as an accident, that is to say,
the essential goodness of divinity is no
addition to it but eternally inherent.
And so on with essential perfection of
knowing and of power. Say, if one
wishes, that all these essential traits are
but one, diversely called goodness, life,
power. What we contend is that this
one essence cannot possibly be identical
with the God whose essence it is. For
it is abstract, and he is concrete; it excludes all particulars, and he includes
them; it is his personality trait, and he
is the person with actual experiences
(down to the given moment) characterized by the trait.

Following Philo, Maimonides faces the question: "Can God really have relations to the world?" Philo tried to have it both ways. Maimonides gives a flat negative, though not wholly without hesitation. His reasons are typically monopolar, assuming that God can in no aspect be physical, temporal, spatial, or contingent, whereas of course the question at issue just is as to whether this one-aspect view of deity is correct. We must also question a further but likewise monopolar assumption employed. This is that all relation must be correlation and imply that the two things belong in one class. Universals and particulars are related, or the notion of universal loses its function of furnishing predicates of particular things. But they are not correlative or equal for that which has the relation is more concrete than that which lacks it. Thus concrete particulars really have whiteness or roundness, but these universals are in themselves innocent of entanglement with this or that particular. In this freedom from entanglement consists their abstractness. Thus also an unrelated God must be abstract.

The denial of relations to God is a gigantic paradox. For then what becomes of the description of God in terms of "his" actions upon the world? Moreover, if God does not really possess his production of the world, then we are in a state of blank ignorance with respect to him. For it is denied that we know his absolute or nonrelative essence, what he is in independence of the world and would be were there no world. But it is also denied that he has accidents or relations to his effects. So the word God stands for the Unknowable purely and simply. And even negative descriptions posit relations, relations of otherness between God and what is denied of him. True, it may be held that these relations are in the other things, not in God; but then he becomes a constituent of the complex, X-other-than-God. This establishes his abstractness, and also it disproves the alleged unknowability of deity; for, since the things really are other than God, in knowing the things we know the relations they include and the constituents of the relational complexes. Therefore we know God.

It is perhaps worth noting that intellect and sight (supposing we were to grant that they are not in themselves related) are both contained in one experience, which possesses the relations between them. Thus they are abstractions from something more concrete. This, we affirm, is the rule where something is not in itself related.

Maimonides comes to the verge of a dipolar insight when he says that, if God really had relations, it would not require any change in his essence when he acquired new relations (as new things come into being in the world). This suggests that God has an unchanging essence but an ever changing actuality composed of essence and accidents. Naturally, Maimonides cannot accept such an idea. But in spite of himself he here suggests it. The very notion of essence suggests it, for all thought is by contrast, and What God is essentially is in implied contrast to What God is inessentially. Essence and accidents are correlative notions. It is a truism that, on the one hand, God, since he is perfect in wisdom, knows all reality, is omniscient, and is so essentially and without possibility of failing to be; but, on the other hand, it is mere fact that we men exist, and while we can infer that it is fact that God knows us as existent, yet, since we might not have existed, obviously God might have known us as nonexistent and would then not have known us to exist. Hence his knowing that we exist is not essential to him but merely factual, contingent.

The foregoing argument is in effect conceded by our author, who, however, says that the conclusion is that

"God knows the world" has no positive meaning, there being nothing identifiably common between divine knowledge and ordinary knowledge. And so with the other predicates applied to deity. They really have only negative meaning. God is not ignorant, in that neither ordinary nonknowledge nor ordinary knowledge can be applied to him.

This program of exclusively negative attributes of deity is not and it seems could not have been consistently carried through. Which is negative, "potential" or "actual"? The latter is affirmed, the former denied, of deity. Which is negative, cause or effect? The latter is denied, the former affirmed. Is it merely negative? Again, which is negative, acting with intention and design, or unintentionally? The former is affirmed. Is "giving" nothing positive? "Living?" "Perceiving?"

Suppose one says, "God is above, beyond, or superior to all our descriptions." Above is a relation! Is God then related? Or does the saying merely mean that our descriptions are beneath God, inadequate to him, but that he is not above or beyond or superior to what we affirm of him. Thus if we say, "Triangles consist of several lines," this description is inadequate and poor, but one cannot perhaps imagine how "superiority to this description" could be something in triangles. It is nothing to them how poorly we describe them, and precisely because they are unconscious and unknowing, mere objects not subjects. Is that how God escapes relations to us? Is he unconscious rather than conscious? ("Superconscious" would be a relation.)

In the very passage of our text where the impossibility of knowing the character of God is most emphatically pronounced, we find "will," "rule," "he gives," "he preserves." And well did Gersonides, a most acute thinker, reply to Maimonides that a completely nega-tive idea of God is worthless for any purpose. Gersonides himself sought to escape the difficulty by a return to Aristotelianism, to the view that deity is aware not of the concrete or particular aspects of the world but only of its spiritual plan or "providence," as embodied in the motions of the heavenly bodies and whatever is necessitated thereby. Our acts of free choice being not thus necessitated, God knows of them only what they may be, only their possibilities. Gerson argued that, if God eternally knew our free acts as definite, they would eternally be definite and so at no time open for determination or decision, at no time really free. This would be "error, not knowledge"; for the acts are really free, and true knowledge must be of things as they are, hence of the possible or unsettled as having this unsettled character. It is curious that Gerson did not see (obviously because of his monopolar or etiolatrous attitude) that since free acts are determinate after they have happened, yet are not determinate either beforehand or eternally, the only way God can know the whole truth is for him to have, besides his eternal knowledge of pure possibility, two forms of temporal knowledge with respect to each particular free act, *first* only the knowledge of what may-or-may-not take place, and *then* the additional knowledge of what does take place and has taken place. In short, as Socinus and Lequier cogently argue, the knowledge of temporal process must itself be a temporal process (with complete retrospective definiteness and with exactly so much indeterminacy of anticipation as there is real freedom in reality). Maimonides, Gerson, Socinus, and Spinoza agree that eternal knowledge, in any sense we can conceive it, can have no contingent objects. But the first concludes: Knowledge in God is not really knowledge, though it does embrace the contingent. The second concludes: The knowledge is knowledge, but it does not embrace the contingent. The third concludes: The knowledge is knowledge and does embrace the contingent, but it is temporal and contingent, not merely eternal and necessary knowledge. The fourth possible conclusion is Spinoza's: There is no contingency at all.

Maimonides's admission that "knowledge" is equivocal in theological usage is really of no avail, for an eternal whole, whether a whole of knowledge or of whatever you please, cannot be differential as between realized and unrealized possibilities, cannot either know or "know" that the world exists, and yet not prejudice the genuineness of the latter as contingent selection among the creative possibilities. Gerson's solution is at best the paradox that God knows less than the whole truth about reality, for the truth that certain contingent acts definitely occur is indisputable on his own admission. Spinoza's solution is not a solution; for the idea of contingency is ineradicable and indeed is presupposed by the contrary idea of necessity. Thus Socinus must be given the honor of being the first to draw the plain conclusion from the evidences in this matter, the first who asked, not how the problem could be solved without giving up the worship of independence and eternity (as though they were God himself), but simply how the problem could be solved without giving up God—and the irreducible concepts of eternity and time, necessity and contingency, which constitute the problem.

## AQUINAS (1225?–74?)

For no other philosopher have such claims been made as for this one. Indeed, non-Thomists cannot but see more than a trace of idolatry in the aura of virtual infallibility that Thomists often seem striving to impart to their master. But one claim which a Thomist has made is perhaps not open to this objection. Gilson once suggested that St. Thomas was "the greatest arranger of ideas that ever lived." As this implies, the ideas expounded in the famous *summae* are not to any great extent new, but how they are put through their paces, as it were, how skilfully set forth in orderly array! We must also bear in mind that this is the first or nearly the first of the great Christian theologians to whom the Aristotelian writings were in large part accessible. And how carefully he pondered them his commentaries show us. On the other hand, no man ever had a more exquisite sense of the line between orthodoxy and heresy, by which we need not mean between "right doctrine" and "wrong doctrine" but rather between accepted doctrines and those not accepted. True, the charge of heresy was actually made, but the ultimate judgment of the church on this point was reasonable enough; the doctrines of the Fathers, taken collectively, are scarcely departed from in the Thomistic system. Thus we have in this man the most Aristotelian Christian and the most Christian Aristotelian that one could well hope ever to find. So the prestige of Greek philosophy and the glory of the Gospels fuse to form the unique splendor that has fascinated so many.

The problems of Thomism are the problems of all classical (Philonian) theists, except for a special emphasis upon Aristotelian conceptions. One which Philo and Maimonides had already broached was that of the relations between God and the world and the difficulty these offer for the doctrine that God is wholly nonrelative and simple. Aquinas gives the classic text on this topic, in the course of which he makes a fine contribution to the theory of "external" and "internal" relations, to use language current recently. The Thomistic language is perhaps better: that relations are either "real" or merely "logical." Relations may be real so far as some terms are concerned, but, with respect to other terms, it may be only a way of viewing them to say that they are related thus and thus. They are then related for some mind but not for themselves. And the example of knowing and the thing known is persuasive: knowledge or science has to conform, and thus incur genuine relation, to its objects, not vice versa. Only with fictions, which are not cognitions, is the object conformed, related, to thought about it. Knowing is relative to the known, dependent upon it as one term of the cognitive relation. Of course the known as "known" involves the knower, but even then not any particular knower rather than another, since if anyone knows the thing it is known. On the other hand, the knowing is different with each alternative particular object. To know that "elephants exist" is different knowledge from that which could know that "elephants do not exist." To know is to hold for true upon adequate evidence, and one cannot thus hold for true contradictory propositions. Hence actual knowing is relative to what in particular happens to exist and therefore as existent can be known (knowledge of possibles merely as possibles is something else). But what in particular is known in a given knowledge is not in its existence relative to this knowledge. If, then, the known, or object, is the nonrelative, and knowing or subject the relative, factor, as we have just seen, must not God, as all-knowing, be supremely relative? On the contrary, says Thomas, the divine knowing is creative and hence not at all the same thing as human knowing. So we are back to Maimonides. "Knowing" has no literal common meaning in the two applica-

tions. Thomas thinks it has, however, an analogically common meaning. But it is an analogy which inverts the two terms, giving the "subject" the very role taken, in the ordinary case, by the object!

The issue can be focused, as we have repeatedly seen, on the question of divine knowledge as having *contingent* and mutable objects. What status can be assigned to the relations involved, without renouncing the basic tenet that God is devoid of contingency and change? Thomas seeks to deal with these problems. We are not aware of any important advance upon his treatment of them—within the confines of classical theism—in the seven centuries since he wrote.

## God's Relations to the World Not Real in God

*95. Reply Obj.* I. . . . Now a relation of God to creatures, is not a reality in God, but in the creature; for it is in God in our idea only: as, what is knowable is so called with relation to knowledge, not that it depends on knowledge, but because knowledge depends on it. Thus it is not necessary that there should be composition in the supreme good, but only that other things are deficient in comparison with it. . . .

*96. I answer that,* The names which import relation to creatures are applied to God temporally and not from eternity.

To see this we must learn that some have said that relation is not a reality, but only an idea. But this is plainly seen to be false from the very fact that things themselves have a mutual natural order and habitude. Nevertheless, it is necessary to know that since relation has two extremes, it happens in three ways that a relation is real or logical. Sometimes from both extremes it is an idea only, as when mutual order or habitude can only be between things in the apprehension of reason; as when we say a thing is *the same as itself*. For reason apprehending one thing twice regards it as two; thus it apprehends a certain habitude of a thing to itself. And the same applies to relations between *being* and *non-being* formed by reason, apprehending *non-being* as an extreme. The same is true of relations that follow upon an act of reason, as genus and species, and the like.

Now there are other relations which are realities as regards both extremes, as when for instance a habitude exists between two things according to some reality that belongs to both; as is clear of all relations consequent upon quantity; as great and small, double and half, and the like; for quantity exists in both extremes: and the same applies to relations consequent upon action and passion, as motive power and the movable thing, father and son, and the like.

Again, sometimes a relation in one extreme may be a reality, while in the other extreme it is an idea only: and this happens whenever two extremes are not of one order. . . . In science and in sense a real relation exists, because they are ordered either to the knowledge or to the sensible perception of things; whereas the things looked at in themselves are outside this order, and hence in them there is no real relation to science and sense, but only in idea, inasmuch as the intellect apprehends them as terms of the relations of science and sense. Hence, the Philosopher says (*Metaph*. V.) that they are called relative, not forasmuch as they are related to other things, but as others are related to them. Likewise for instance, *on the right* is not applied to a column, unless it stands as regards an animal on the right side; which relation is not really in the column, but in the animal.

Since therefore God is outside the whole order of creation, and all creatures are ordered to Him, and not conversely, it is manifest that creatures are really related to God Himself; whereas in God there is no real relation to creatures, but a relation only in idea, inasmuch as creatures are referred to Him. Thus there is nothing to prevent these names which import relation to the creature from being predicated of God temporally, not by reason of any change in Him, but by reason of the change of the creature; as a column is on the right of an animal, without change in itself, but by change in the animal.

*97. Reply Obj. 4.* Relations signified by these names which are applied to God temporally, are in God only in idea; but the opposite relations in creatures are real. Nor is it incongruous that God should be denominated from relations really existing in the thing, yet so that the opposite relations in God should also be understood by us at the same time; in the sense that God is spoken of relatively to the creature inasmuch as the creature is related to Him: thus the Philosopher says (*Metaph*. V.) that the object is said to be knowable relatively because knowledge relates to it.

*Reply Obj. 5.* Since God is related to the creature for the reason that the creature is related to Him: and since the relation of subjection is real in the creature, it follows that God is Lord not in idea only, but in reality; for He is called Lord according to the manner in which the creature is subject to Him.

*Whether This Name, HE WHO IS, Is the Most Proper Name of God?*

*98. I answer that,* This name, HE WHO IS, is most properly applied to God, for three reasons:—

First, because of its signification. For it does not signify form, but simply existence itself. Hence since the existence of God is His essence itself, which can be said of no other (Q. III, A, 4), it is clear that among other names this one specially denominates God, for everything is denominated by its form.

Secondly, on account of its universality. For all other names are either less universal, or if convertible with it, add something above it as least in idea; hence in a certain way they inform and determine it. Now our intellect cannot know the essence of God itself in this life, as it is in itself, but whatever mode it applies in determining what it understands about God, it falls short of the mode of what God is in Himself. Therefore the less determinate the names are, and the more universal and absolute they are, the more properly are they applied to God. Hence Damascene says (*De Fid. Orth.* i.) that, HE WHO IS, *is the principal of all names applied to God; for comprehending all in itself, it contains existence itself as an infinite and indeterminate sea of substance.* Now by any other name some mode of substance is determined, whereas this name HE WHO IS, determines no mode of being, but is indeterminate to all; and therefore it denominates the *infinite ocean of substance.*

Thirdly, from its consignification, for it signifies present existence; and this above all properly applies to God, whose existence knows not past or future, as Augustine says (*De Trin.* v.).

### Whether the Act of God's Intellect Is His Substance?*

99. *I answer that,* It must be said that the act of God's intellect is His substance. For if His act of understanding were other than His substance, then something else, as the Philosopher says (*Metaph.* xii.), would be the act and perfection of the divine substance, to which the divine substance would be related, as potentiality is to act, which is altogether impossible; because the act of understanding is the perfection and act of the one understanding. Let us now consider how this is. As was laid down above (A. 2), to understand is not an act passing to anything extrinsic; for it remains in the operator as his own act and perfection; as existence is the perfection of the one existing: just as ex-

istence follows on the form, so in like manner to understand follows on the intelligible species. Now in God there is no form which is something other than His existence, as shown above (Q. III.). Hence as His essence itself is also His intelligible species, it necessarily follows that His act of understanding must be His essence and His existence.

Thus it follows from all the foregoing that in God, intellect, and the object understood, and the intelligible species, and His act of understanding are entirely one and the same. Hence, when God is said to be understanding, no kind of multiplicity is attached to His substance.

### Whether God Knows Things Other than Himself?*

100. *We proceed thus to the Fifth Article:*—

*Objection* 1. It seems that God does not know things besides Himself. For all other things but God are outside of God. But Augustine says (*Octog. Tri. Quaest.*, qu. xlvi.) that *God does not behold anything out of Himself.* Therefore He does not know things other than Himself.

*Obj.* 2. Further, the object understood is the perfection of the one who understands. If therefore God understands other things besides Himself, something else will be the perfection of God, and will be nobler than He; which is impossible.

*Obj.* 3. Further, the act of understanding is specified by the intelligible object, as is every other act from its own object. Hence the intellectual act is so much the nobler, the nobler the object understood. But God is His own intellectual act. If therefore God understands anything other than Himself, then God Himself is specified by something else than Himself; which cannot be. Therefore He does not understand things other than Himself.

*On the contrary,* It is written: *All things are naked and open to His eyes* (Heb. iv. 13).

*I answer that,* God necessarily knows things other than Himself. For it is manifest that He perfectly understands Himself; otherwise His existence would not be perfect, since His existence is His act of understanding. Now if anything is perfectly known, it follows of necessity that its power is perfectly known. But the power of anything can be perfectly known only by knowing to what its power extends. Since therefore the divine power extends to other things by the very fact that it is the first effective cause of all things, as is clear from the aforesaid (Q. II., A. 3), God must necessarily know things other than Himself. And this appears still more plainly if we add that the very existence of the first efficient cause—viz., God—is His own act of understanding. Hence whatever effects pre-exist in God, as in the first cause, must be in His act of understanding, and all things must be in Him according to an intelligible mode: for everything which is in another, is in it according to the mode of that in which it is.

Now in order to know how God knows things other than Himself, we must consider that a thing is known in two ways: in itself, and in another. A thing is known in itself when it is known by the proper species adequate to the knowable object; as when the eye sees a man through the image of a man. A thing is seen in another through the image of that which contains it; as when a part is seen in the whole by the image of the whole; or when a man is seen in a mirror by the image in the mirror, or by any other mode by which one thing is seen in another.

So we say that God sees Himself in Himself, because He sees Himself through His essence; and He sees other things not in themselves, but in Himself; inasmuch as His essence contains the similitude of things other than Himself.

*Reply Obj.* 1. The passage of Augustine in which it is said that God *sees nothing outside Himself* is not to be taken in such a way, as if God saw nothing outside Himself, but in the sense that what is outside Himself He does not see except in Himself, as above explained.

*Reply Obj.* 2. The object understood is a perfection of the one understanding not by its substance, but by its image, according to which it is in the intellect, as its form and perfection, as is said in *De Anima* iii. For *a stone is not in the soul, but its image.* Now those things which are other than God are understood by God, inasmuch as the essence of God contains their images as above explained; hence it does not follow that there is any perfection in the divine intellect other than the divine essence.

*Reply Obj.* 3. The intellectual act is not specified by what is understood in another, but by the principal object understood in which other things are understood. For the intellectual act is specified by its object, inasmuch as the intelligible form is the principle of the intellectual operation: since every operation is specified by the form which is its principle of operation; as heating by heat. Hence the intellectual operation is specified by that intelligible form which makes the intellect in act. And this is the image of the principal thing understood, which in God is nothing but His own essence in which all images of things are comprehended. Hence it does not follow that the divine intellectual act, or rather God Himself, is specified by anything else than the divine essence itself.

*Whether God Knows Things Other than Himself by Proper Knowledge?**

*We proceed thus to the Sixth Article:—*

*Objection* 1. It seems that God does not know things other than Himself by proper knowledge. For, as was shown (A. 5), God knows things other than Himself, according as they are in Himself. But other things are in Him as in their common and universal cause, and are known by God as in their first and universal cause. This is to know them by general, and not by proper knowledge. Therefore God knows things besides Himself by general, and not by proper knowledge.

*Obj.* 2. Further, the created essence is as distant from the divine essence, as the divine essence is distant from the created essence. But the divine essence cannot be known by the created essence, as said above (Q. XII., A. 2). Therefore neither can the created essence be known by the divine essence. Thus as God knows only by His essence, it follows that He does not know what the creature is in its essence, so as to know *what it is,* which is to have proper knowledge of it.

*Obj.* 3. Further, proper knowledge of a thing can come only through its proper ratio. But as God knows all things by His essence, it seems that He does not know each thing by its proper ratio; for one thing cannot be the proper ratio of many and diverse things. Therefore God has not a proper knowledge of things, but a general knowledge; for to know things otherwise than by their proper ratio is to have only a common and general knowledge of them.

*On the contrary,* To have a proper knowledge of things is to know them not only in general, but as they are distinct from each other. Now God knows things in that manner. Hence it is written that He reaches *even to the division of the soul and the spirit, of the joints also and the marrow, and is a discerner of the thoughts and intents of the heart; neither is there any creature invisible in His sight.* (Heb. iv. 12, 13).

*I answer that,* Some have erred on this point, saying that God knows things other than Himself only in general, that is, only as beings. For as fire, if it knew itself as the principle of heat, would know the nature of heat, and all things else in so far as they are hot; so God, through knowing Himself as the principle of being, knows the nature of being, and all other things in so far as they are beings.

But this cannot be. For to know a thing in general and not in particular, is to have an imperfect knowledge of it. Hence our intellect, when it is reduced from potentiality to act, acquires first a universal and confused knowledge of things, before it knows them in particular; as proceeding from the imperfect to the perfect, as is clear from *Physic.* i. If therefore the knowledge of God regarding things other than Himself is only universal and not special, it would follow that His understanding would not be absolutely perfect; therefore neither would His being be perfect; and this is against what was said above (Q. IV., A. I). We must therefore hold that God knows things other than Himself with a proper knowledge; not only in so far as being is common to them, but in so far as one is distinguished from the other. In proof thereof we may observe that some wishing to show that God knows many things by one, bring forward some examples, as, for instance, that if the centre knew itself, it would know all lines that proceed from the centre; or if light knew itself, it would know all colours.

Now these examples although they are similar in part, namely, as regards universal causality, nevertheless they fail in this respect that multitude and diversity are caused by the one universal principle, not as regards that which is the principle of distinction, but only as regards that in which they communicate. For the diversity of colours is not caused by the light only, but by the different disposition of the diaphanous medium which receives it; and likewise, the diversity of the lines is caused by their different position. Hence it is that this kind of diversity and multitude cannot be known in its principle by proper knowledge, but only in a general way. In God, however, it is otherwise. For it was shown above (Q. IV., A. 2) that whatever perfection exists in any creature, wholly pre-exists and is contained in God in an excelling manner. Now not only what is common to creatures—viz., being—belongs to their perfection, but also what makes them distinguished from each other; as living and understanding, and the like, whereby living beings are distinguished from the non-living, and the intelligent from the non-intelligent. Likewise every form whereby each thing is constituted in its own species, is a perfection; and thus all things pre-exist in God, not only as regards what is common to all, but also as regards what distinguishes one thing from another. And therefore as God contains all perfections in Himself, the essence of God is compared to all other essences of things, not as the common to the proper, as unity is to numbers, or as the centre (of a circle) to the (radiating) lines; but as perfect acts to imperfect; as if I were to compare man to animal; or six, a perfect number, to the imperfect numbers contained under it. Now it is manifest that by a perfect act imperfect acts can be known not only in general, but also by proper knowledge; thus, for example, whoever knows a man, knows an animal by proper knowledge; and whoever knows the number six, knows the number three also by proper knowledge.

As therefore the essence of God contains in itself all the perfection contained in the essence of any other being, and far more, God can know in Himself all of them with proper knowledge. For the nature proper to each thing consists in some degree of participation in the divine perfection. Now God could not be said to know Himself perfectly unless He knew all the ways in which His own perfection can be shared by others. Neither could He know the very nature of being perfectly, unless He knew all modes of being. Hence it is manifest that God knows all things with proper knowledge, in their distinction from each other.

*Reply Obj.* 1. So to know a thing as it is in the knower, may be understood in two ways. In one way this adverb *so,* imports the mode of knowledge on the part of the thing known; and in that sense it is false. For the knower does not always know the object known according to the existence it has in the knower; since the eye does not know a stone according to the existence it has in the eye; but by the image of the stone which is in the eye, the eye knows the stone according to its existence outside the eye. And if any knower has a knowledge of the object known according to the (mode of) existence it has in the knower, the knower nevertheless knows it according to its (mode of) existence outside the knower; thus the intellect knows a stone according to the intelligible existence it has in the intellect, inasmuch as it knows that it understands; while nevertheless it knows what a stone is in its own nature. If however the adverb *so* be understood to import the mode (of knowledge) on the part of the knower, in that sense it is true that the knower has knowledge of the object known only as it is in the knower; for the more perfectly the thing known is in the knower, the more perfect is the mode of knowledge.

We must say therefore that God not only knows that things are in Himself; but by the fact that they are in Him, He knows them in their own nature and all the more perfectly, the more perfectly each one is in Him.

*Reply Obj.* 2. The created essence is compared to the essence of God, as the imperfect to the perfect act. Therefore the created essence cannot sufficiently lead us to the knowledge of the divine essence, but rather the converse.

*Reply Obj.* 3. The same thing cannot be taken in an equal manner as the ratio of different things. But the divine essence excels all creatures. Hence it can be taken as the proper ratio of each thing according to the diverse ways in which diverse creatures participate in, and imitate it.

### Whether God Knows Singular Things?*

*101.* . . . since God is the cause of things by His knowledge, as stated above (A. 8), His knowledge extends as far as His causality extends. Hence, as the active power of God extends not only to forms, which are the source of universality, but also to matter, as we shall prove further on (Q. XLIV., A. 2), the knowledge of God must extend to singular things, which are individualized by matter. For since He knows things other than Himself by His essence, as being the likeness of things, or as their active principle, His essence must be the sufficing principle of knowing all things made by Him, not only in the universal, but also in the singular. The same would apply to the knowledge of the artificer, if it were productive of the whole being, and not only of the form.

### Whether the Knowledge of God Is of Future Contingent Things?*

*102. We proceed thus to the Thirteenth Article:—*

*Objection* 1. It seems that the knowledge of God is not of future contingent things. For from a necessary cause proceeds a necessary effect. But the knowledge of God is the cause of things known, as said above (A. 8). Since therefore that knowledge is necessary, what He knows must also be necessary. Therefore the knowledge of God is not of contingent things.

*Obj.* 2. Further, every conditional proposition of which the antecedent is absolutely necessary, must have an absolutely necessary consequent. For the antecedent is to the consequent as principles are to the conclusion: and from necessary principles only a necessary conclusion can follow, as is proved in *Poster.* i. But this is a true conditional proposition, *If God knew that this thing will be, it will be,* for the knowledge of God is only of true things. Now, the antecedent conditional of this is absolutely necessary, because it is eternal, and because it is signified as past. Therefore, the consequent is also absolutely necessary. Therefore whatever God knows, is necessary; and so the knowledge of God is not of contingent things.

*Obj.* 3. Further, everything known by God must necessarily be, because even what we ourselves know, must necessarily be; and, of course, the knowledge of God is much more certain than ours. But no future contingent thing must necessarily be. Therefore no contingent future thing is known by God.

*On the contrary,* It is written (Ps. xxxii. 15), *He Who hath made the hearts of every one of them: Who understandeth all their works,* that is, of men. Now the works of men are contingent, being subject to free will. Therefore God knows future contingent things.

*I answer that,* Since as was shown above (A. 9), God knows all things; not only things actual but also things possible to Him and the creature; and since some of these are future contingent to us, it follows that God knows future contingent things.

In evidence of this, we must consider that a contingent thing can be considered in two ways; first, in itself, in so far as it is now in act: and in this sense it is not considered as future, but as present; neither is it considered as contingent (as having reference) to one of two terms but as determined to one; and on account of this it can be infallibly the object of certain knowledge, for instance to the sense of sight, as when I see that Socrates is sitting down. In another way a contingent thing can be considered as it is in its cause; and in this way it is considered as future, and as a contingent thing not yet determined to one; forasmuch as a contingent cause has relation to opposite things: and in this sense a contingent thing is not subject to any certain knowledge. Hence, whoever knows a contingent effect in its cause only, has merely a conjectural knowledge of it. Now God knows all contingent things not only as they are in their causes, but also as each one of them is actually in itself. And although contingent things become actual successively, nevertheless God knows contingent things not successively, as they are in their own being, as we do; but simultaneously. The reason is because His knowledge is measured by eternity, as is also His being; and eternity being simultaneously whole comprises all time, as was said above (Q. X., A. 2). Hence, all things that are in time are present to God from eternity, not only because He has the types of things present within Him, as some say; but because His glance is carried from eternity over all things as they are in their presentiality. Hence it is manifest that contingent things are infallibly known by God, inasmuch as they are subject to the divine sight in their presentiality; yet they are future contingent things in relation to their own causes.

*Reply Obj.* 1. Although the supreme cause is necessary, the effect may be contingent by reason of the proximate contingent cause; just as the germination of a plant is contingent by reason of the proximate contingent cause, although the movement of the sun which is the first cause, is necessary. So likewise things known by God are contingent on account of their proximate causes, while the knowledge of God, which is the first cause, is necessary.

*Reply Obj.* 2. . . . Therefore we must reply otherwise; that when the antecedent contains anything belonging to an act of the soul, the consequent must be taken not as it is in itself, but as it is in the soul: for the existence of a thing in itself is different from the existence of a thing in the soul. For example, when I say, *What the soul understands is immaterial;* this is to be understood [as meaning] that it is immaterial as it is in the intellect, not as it is in itself. Likewise if I say, *If God knew anything, it will be,* the consequent must be understood as it is subject to the divine knowledge, that is, as it is in its presentiality. And thus it is necessary, as also is the antecedent: *for everything that is, while it is, must necessarily be,* as the Philosopher says in *Periherm.* i.

*Reply Obj.* 3. Things reduced to act in time, are known by us successively in time, but by God (are known) in eternity, which is above time. Whence to us they cannot be certain, forasmuch as we know future contingent things as such; but (they are certain) to God alone, whose understanding is in eternity above time. Just as he who goes along the road, does not see those who come after him; whereas he who sees the whole road from a height, sees at once all travelling by the way. Hence what is known by us must be necessary, even as it is in itself; for what is future contingent in itself, cannot be known by us. Whereas what is known by God must be necessary according to the mode in which they are subject to the divine knowledge, as already stated, but not absolutely as considered in their own causes. Hence also the proposition, *Everything known by God must necessarily be,* is usually distinguished; for this may refer to the thing, or to the saying. If it refers to the thing, it is divided, and false; for the sense is, *Everything which God knows is necessary.* If understood of the saying it is composite and true; for the sense is,

*This proposition, 'that which is known by God is necessary.'*

Now some urge an objection and say that this distinction holds good with regard to forms that are separable from the subject; thus if I said, *It is possible for a white thing to be black*, it is false as applied to the saying, and true as applied to the thing: for a thing which is white, can become black; whereas this saying, *a white thing is black*, can never be true. But in forms that are inseparable from the subject, this distinction does not hold, for instance, if I said, *A black crow can be white*; for in both senses it is false. Now to be known by God is inseparable from the thing; for what is known by God cannot be not known. This objection, however, would hold if these words *that which is known* implied any disposition inherent to the subject; but since they import an act of the knower, something can be attributed to the thing known, in itself (even if it always be known), which is not attributed to it in so far as it stands under actual knowledge; thus material existence is attributed to a stone in itself, which is not attributed to it inasmuch as it is known.

### Whether the Knowledge of God Is Variable?*

*103. Obj.* 2. Further, whatever God can make, He can know. But God can make more than He does. Therefore He can know more than He knows. Thus His knowledge can vary according to increase and diminution.

*104. Reply Obj.* 2. God knows also what He can make, and does not make. Hence from the fact that He can make more than He makes, it does not follow that He can know more than He knows, unless this be referred to the knowledge of vision, according to which He is said to know those things which are in act in some period of time. But from the fact that He knows some things might be which are not, or that some things

might not be which are, it does not follow that His knowledge is variable, but rather that He knows the variability of things. If, however, anything existed which God did not previously know, and afterwards knew, then His knowledge would be variable. But this could not be; for whatever is, or can be in any period of time, is known by God in His eternity. Therefore from the fact that a thing exists in some period of time, it follows that it is known by God from eternity. Therefore it cannot be granted that God can know more than He knows; because such a proposition implies that first of all He did not know, and then afterwards knew.

### The Divine Will

#### Whether Whatever God Wills He Wills Necessarily?*

*105. We proceed thus to the Third Article:—*

*Objection* 1. It seems that whatever God wills He wills necessarily. For everything eternal is necessary. But whatever God wills, He wills from eternity, for otherwise His will would be mutable. Therefore whatever He wills, He wills necessarily.

*Obj.* 2. Further, God wills things apart from Himself inasmuch as He wills His own goodness. Now God wills His own goodness necessarily. Therefore He wills things apart from Himself necessarily.

*Obj.* 3. Further, whatever belongs to the nature of God is necessary, for God is of Himself necessary being, and the principle of all necessity, as above shown (Q. II., A. 3). But it belongs to His nature to will whatever He wills; since in God there can be nothing over and above His nature as stated in *Metaph.* v. 6. Therefore whatever He wills, He wills necessarily.

*Obj.* 4. Further, being that is not necessary, and being that is possible not to be, are one and the same thing. If, therefore, God does not necessarily will a thing that He wills, it is possible for Him not to will it, and therefore possible for Him to will what He does not will. And so the divine will is contingent upon one or the other of two things, and imperfect, since everything contingent is imperfect and mutable.

*Obj.* 5. Further, on the part of that which is indifferent to one or the other of two things, no action results unless it is inclined to one or the other by some other power, as the Commentator [Averroës] says on *Phys.* ii. If, then, the Will of God is indifferent with regard to anything, it follows that His determination to act comes from another; and thus He has some cause prior to Himself.

*Obj.* 6. Further, whatever God knows, He knows necessarily. But as the divine knowledge is His essence, so is the divine will. Therefore whatever God wills, He wills necessarily.

*On the contrary,* the Apostle says (Eph. i. II): *Who worketh all things according to the counsel of His will.* Now, what we work according to the counsel of the will, we do not will necessarily. Therefore God does not will necessarily whatever He wills.

*I answer that,* There are two ways in which a thing is said to be necessary, namely, absolutely, and by supposition. We judge a thing to be absolutely necessary from the relation of the terms, as when the predicate forms part of the definition of the subject: thus it is absolutely necessary that man is an animal. . . . In this way it is not necessary that Socrates sits: wherefore it is not necessary absolutely, though it may be so by supposition; for, granted that he is sitting, he must necessarily sit, as long as he is sitting. Accordingly as to things willed by God, we must observe that He wills something of absolute necessity: but this is not true of all that He wills. For the divine will has a necessary relation to the divine goodness, since

that is its proper object. Hence God wills His own goodness necessarily, even as we will our own happiness necessarily, and as any other faculty has necessary relation to its own proper and principal object, for instance the sight to colour, since it tends to it by its own nature. But God wills things apart from Himself in so far as they are ordered to His own goodness as their end. Now in willing an end we do not necessarily will things that conduce to it, unless they are such that the end cannot be attained without them; as, we will to take food to preserve life, or to take ship in order to cross the sea. But we do not necessarily will things without which the end is attainable, such as a horse for a journey which we can take on foot, for we can make the journey without one. The same applies to other means. Hence, since the goodness of God is perfect, and can exist without other things inasmuch as no perfection can accrue to Him from them, it follows that His willing things apart from Himself is not absolutely necessary. Yet it can be necessary by supposition, for supposing that He wills a thing, then He is unable not to will it, as His will cannot change.

*Reply Obj.* 1. From the fact that God wills from eternity whatever He wills, it does not follow that He wills it necessarily; except by supposition.

*Reply Obj.* 2. Although God necessarily wills His own goodness, He does not necessarily will things willed on account of His goodness; for it can exist without other things.

*Reply Obj.* 3. It is not natural to God to will any of those other things that He does not will necessarily; and yet it is not unnatural or contrary to His nature, but voluntary.

*Reply Obj.* 4. Sometimes a necessary cause has a non-necessary relation to an effect; owing to a deficiency in the effect, and not in the cause. Even so, the sun's power has a non-necessary relation to some contingent events on this earth, owing to a defect not in the solar power, but in the effect that proceeds not necessarily from the cause. In the same way, that God does not necessarily will some of the things that He wills, does not result from defect in the divine will, but from a defect belonging to the nature of the thing willed, namely, that the perfect goodness of God can be without it; and such defect accompanies all created good.

*Reply Obj. 5.* A naturally contingent cause must be determined to act by some external power. The divine will, which by its nature is necessary, determines itself to will things to which it has no necessary relation.

*Reply Obj. 6.* As the divine existence is necessary of itself, so is the divine will and the divine knowledge; but the divine knowledge has a necessary relation to the thing known; not the divine will to the thing willed. The reason for this is that knowledge is of things as they exist in the knower; but the will is directed to things as they exist in themselves. Since then all other things have necessary existence inasmuch as they exist in God; but no absolute necessity so as to be necessary in themselves, in so far as they exist in themselves; it follows that God knows necessarily whatever He knows, but does not will necessarily whatever He wills.

### Whether the Will of God Imposes Necessity on the Things Willed?*

*106. We proceed thus to the Eighth Article:—*

*Objection* 1. It seems that the will of God imposes necessity on the things willed. For Augustine says (*Enchir.* 103): *No one is saved, except whom God has willed to be saved. He must therefore be asked to will it; for if He wills it, it must necessarily be.*

*Obj.* 2. Further, every cause that cannot be hindered, produces its effect necessarily, because, as the Philosopher says (*Phys.* ii. 84): *Nature always works in the same way, if there is nothing to hinder it.* But the will of God cannot be hindered. For the Apostle says (Rom. ix. 19).: *Who resisteth His will?* Therefore the will of God imposes necessity on the things willed.

*Obj.* 3. Further, whatever is necessary by its antecedent cause is necessary absolutely; it is thus necessary that animals should die, being compounded of contrary elements. Now things created by God are related to the divine will as to an antecedent cause, whereby they have necessity. For the conditional statement is true that if God wills a thing, it comes to pass: and every true conditional statement is necessary. It follows therefore that all that God wills is necessary absolutely.

*On the contrary,* All good things that exist God wills to be. If therefore His will imposes necessity on things willed, it follows that all good happens of necessity; and thus there is an end of free will, counsel, and all other such things.

*I answer that,* The divine will imposes necessity on some things willed but not on all. The reason of this some have chosen to assign to intermediate causes, holding that what God produces by necessary causes is necessary; and what He produces by contingent causes contingent.

This does not seem to be a sufficient explanation, for two reasons. First, because the effect of a first cause is contingent on account of the secondary cause, from the fact that the effect of the first cause is hindered by deficiency in the second cause, as the sun's power is hindered by a defect in the plant. But no defect of a secondary cause can hinder God's will from producing its effect. Secondly, because if the distinction between the contingent and the necessary is to be referred only to secondary causes, this must be independent of the divine intention and will; which is inadmissible. It is better therefore to say that this happens on account of the efficacy of the divine will. For when a cause is efficacious to act, the effect follows upon the cause, not only as to the thing done, but also as to its manner of being done or of being. Thus from defect of active power in the seed it may happen that a child is born unlike its father in accidental points, that belong to its manner of being. Since then the divine will is perfectly efficacious, it follows not only that things are done, which God wills to be done, but also that they are done in the way that He wills. Now God wills some things to be done necessarily, some contingently, to the right ordering of things, for the building up of the universe. Therefore to some effects He has attached necessary causes, that cannot fail; but to others defectible and contingent causes, from which arise contingent effects. Hence it is not because the proximate causes are contingent that the effects willed by God happen contingently, but because God has prepared contingent causes for them, it being His will that they should happen contingently.

*Reply Obj.* 1. By the words of Augustine we must understand a necessity in things willed by God that is not absolute, but conditional. For the conditional statement that if God wills a thing, it must necessarily be, is necessarily true.

*Reply Obj.* 2. From the very fact that nothing resists the divine will, it follows that not only those things happen that God wills to happen, but that they happen necessarily or contingently according to His will.

*Reply Obj.* 3. Consequents have necessity from their antecedents according to the mode of the antecedents. Hence things effected by the divine will have that kind of necessity that God wills them to have, either absolute or conditional. Not all things, therefore, are absolute necessities.

[Sec. 95, Aquinas, *The Summa Theologica*, trans. Fathers of the English Dominican Province (London: Burns, Oates & Washbourne, Ltd., 1920), Part I, QQ. I–XXVI, p. 67. Sec. 96, *ibid.*, pp. 165–67. Sec. 97, *ibid.*, pp. 167–68. Sec. 98, *ibid.*, p. 176. Sec. 99, *ibid.*, pp. 187–88. Sec. 100, *ibid.*, pp. 188–94. Sec. 101, *ibid.*, p. 203. Sec. 102, *ibid.*, pp. 206–10. Sec. 103, *ibid.*, p. 212. Sec. 104, *ibid.*, p. 213. Sec. 105, *ibid.*, pp. 263–66. Sec. 106, *ibid.*, pp. 276–78.]

COMMENT

We have already noted the curiously inverted analogy which Thomism posits: as is the known to the knowing in the ordinary case of knowledge, so is the knowing to the known in the divine case. Does this not imply that God, so conceived, is a superobject rather than a supersubject? Every example which Thomas can give, every example that ever has been given, we think, confirms this supposition. Thus the animal has relation to the column, not the column to the animal; for nothing noticeable happens to the column by virtue of the relative positions of it and the animal, whereas something does happen to the animal, which guides its behavior with reference to such things, avoiding or approaching the column according as its purposes indicate. It is the animal, not the column, that takes account of relations. And this is because of its superior subjectivity, its awareness! But probably Thomas is thinking merely of the fact that the animal moves in relation to the column, not vice versa. Very well, which is superior, a self-moving organism, or a fixed inorganic aggregate of crystals? Which is God more like, a superstone or a superorganic individual?

Let us take another analogy. The abstract or universal is independent of any given concrete particular. There can be humanity without John Jones. No real relation of humanity to Jones is conceivable but only a relation of Jones to humanity. The concrete really embodies the abstract, but it is only a manner of speaking to say that the abstract "is embodied" in just this particular concrete or that. "The number *two*" is not a different entity because at a given moment someone embodies it by putting down two dots. But a set of dots must be different according as it does or does not embody the number two. This analogy suggests that the nonrelative (absolute) is the abstract rather than the concrete, as the former analogy suggested that it is object rather than subject.

If then God is supremely absolute, he must, it seems, be that which is most abstract and merely objective, or least concrete and least subjective or conscious. Yet God is to be the supremely rich and conscious being! Granted that we must think analogically in these matters, does it follow that we may arbitrarily invert the logical structure of all the analogies and still claim that to subject or concrete (rather than to object or abstract) in the ordinary or nondivine case corresponds the supersubjective or superconcrete in the divine case? By all the evidence, the correspondence must be wrecked by the inversion. The only defense is in terms of the monopolar axioms from which classical theism derives. But upon what valid analogy can these axioms themselves rest? Is not all experience thoroughly polar?

Concerning the key problem of classical theism, whether a wholly necessary being could know the contingent, we comment as follows on Thomas' argument as presented in the thirteenth article (sec. 102).

First, his reply to objection 1: that a cause which cannot fail to be can have effects which could have failed to occur, if the necessary cause is not the total cause, if subsidiary causes are also required for the thing; for these may fail, and the effect not take place. But (we rejoin) in this case the necessary cause (God's knowledge that $E$

takes place) would have been false knowledge, since $E$ would not have taken place. This is the supposition of possible falsity in the knowledge of an infallible intellect—a pure absurdity. That, the supposition of which involves intrinsic absurdity, is impossible, and its denial is unconditionally necessary. Hence "$E$ takes place" is, in spite of Thomas, on his own premises unconditionally necessary, and there can be no contingency in the world.

Again, take his reply to objection 2: that since things as in the mind can have properties they do not have in themselves—thus, for instance, material things as in the mind are immaterial—so things contingent in themselves can be necessary as present to the divine mind; further what is, while it is, must necessarily be, and what is presented to God, since it is presented to God, it necessarily is so presented. But (we rejoin) either it is or it is not a logical possibility that the thing might not have existed; if it is a possibility, then, if it had not existed, it would not have been present to God as existent, and then he would not have known that it existed. But this is (according to Thomism) impossible, since we are told that God's knowledge is wholly necessary. Now what implies the impossible is impossible. Hence the nonexistence of the thing is impossible, not merely "while it is presented," but absolutely; for it implies as possible what under no circumstances could be possible, namely, that something actually in God, his knowledge, might have been otherwise; that is, it implies that God has accidents.

The reply to objection 3—that all events, no matter whether those we call past or future, are determinate from the standpoint of eternity—seems adequately refuted by Socinus (sec. 287). It is a splendid illustration of what Bergson calls "spatializing time," that is, supposing all its parts determinate.

Concerning the nonnecessity of God's willing the world; it is held that, although he necessarily wills his own goodness, the world is not essential to this goodness, so he wills it nonnecessarily. But then there are two kinds of volitions in God: those that are there necessarily and those that are there nonnecessarily. Yet all the being of God is held to be purely necessary. Ergo, the nonnecessary acts are not in the being of God. Still they are either in God or not in him. If in him, then he has accidents, additional to what is necessary in him. If not in him, what is meant by calling them "his" acts, and why are we assured always that "God's will is his essence"?

We are told (sec. 105, reply to objection 4) that it is due to a defect in the world that God could have willed not to create it. Thus, supposing the sun is sure to shine, still the plant may not grow, owing to its defective ability to respond to the sun. But if the sun willed that the plant would grow but could instead have willed that it would not grow, we should then have to admit that such willing is a nonnecessary factor in the being of the sun. The sole relevance of what is here said would be if it were meant that God's willing to create the world and his willing not to create the world are identical willings in themselves; but in the one case the world manages to come into being, in the other it does not. But who would dare, on the basis of classical theism, to say this frankly as the meaning of divine "will"? Yet what other meaning fits the reasoning?

Concerning divine will and freedom (sec. 106), and the reply to objection 1, we argue: the phrase, "*if* God wills a thing," is self-contradictory, or simply meaningless, on the classical assumptions that God's will is his essence. There can then be no "if" about it, and the word is illegitimate. Concerning the reply to objection 2: since (not if) God wills (with his very essence, hence necessarily) that we do something, we must necessarily do it, for his will is said to be irresistible; and if he has willed that we nevertheless do it nonnecessarily, he has then willed a contradiction, and even he cannot actualize a contradiction! Reply to objection 3: as before, God is powerless to achieve a self-contradictory volition that we do something without possibility of not doing it, yet contingently, i.e., with possibility of not doing it!

Even if the reply to objection 1, with its meaningless "if" clause, were admissible, it would amount to saying that a sinner might not have sinned if God had willed that he should not. And on the reasoning offered, God could have willed: let him not sin, and let him nevertheless act freely in avoiding sin. Well, then, why did God not so will? It seems hard to see any excuse for his neglect to will the good in this instance, since on the principles offered there would be no sacrifice of human freedom.

Is this really the best that theism can do? If so, how strong indeed would be the position of positivism, holding that the idea of God is a mere confusion or absurdity!

# DESCARTES (1596–1650)

As every student of the history of philosophy knows, there is a famous "circle" in the reasoning of Descartes concerning God as the ground of the trustworthiness of our knowledge.

Doubting the reliability of human perception and memory, Descartes wonders whether even the self-evident principles of mathematics are wholly certain. Perhaps some powerful being is causing us in all our mental operations to deceive ourselves in some subtle way that we ourselves cannot detect. Then Descartes proves the existence of God as a perfect being; this being must have created us, and, since it is perfect, it would not be so unjust as to condemn us to invincible self-deception; rather, we must suppose that, as created, our faculties are excellent and designed to lead us to truth—provided only we employ them carefully and as best we can. But, protest the critics, it is by the very cognitive powers that we have affected to doubt that we have proved God. So how in this way can the doubt be disposed of?

Formally regarded, there is a vicious circle here. But it is possible to see dimly indicated in the reasoning a line of thought that would not be circular. If one puts the question, "On what supposition may we trust our cognitive faculties?" the answer can only be, "On any supposition." For to make suppositions, to think at all, is already to rely upon these faculties. But the proper question is rather, granting we are bound to suppose, in thinking, that we can think to some purpose: "How are we to understand this presupposed reliability of the human mind? What does it mean to say that we can find the truth? Indeed, what is meant by 'truth'?" Surely a mind that can think to any purpose is something with a certain amount of inner coherence and of harmony with its world. For a mind to exist at all already involves so much. But the question remains: Can the mutual co-ordination of things be merely their own affair, or does it necessarily express a common subordination to some supreme power? And what is meant by truth about events long past and not for us open to unequivocal evidence? What preserves intact the "having occurred" of such past events? All these matters become intelligible with the conception of God as the su-

preme ordering and all-knowing mind. And although we cannot prove with mathematical certainty that God would not wish us to be deceived, still the only way we can imagine of serving such a God is trustfully to use such faculties as he has given to us; and this trust seems more intelligible than trust in something we cannot imagine what, some community of forces which nothing orders in mutual relationships, or some wholly unimaginable ordering force other than will and mind.

So we submit that Descartes (and with him, Spinoza, Leibniz, Peirce, Whitehead, etc.) was on the right track in seeing the intelligibility of knowledge—not its guaranty, for we have no alternative but to trust it—in the possibility of our finding evidence for God, that is to say, in the intelligibility for us of his existence. Let us see what this evidence, or part of it, was. The reader will please note that, except in his reply to objections, Descartes, like Anselm in the first paragraph of his discussion of the ontological argument, speaks as though "existence" (in contrast to nonexistence) were a predicate or quality, to lack which would be to fall short of perfection; whereas, in the formulation to which objections drove him, he makes explicit that the contrast is not between existence and nonexistence but between necessary and contingent modes of existence. As Anselm had said, if God's existence were not necessary but accidental, then he would be imperfect, whether he existed or failed to exist. An accidental existent, or a candidate for contingent existence, be the existence granted or withheld, is a temporal, dependent entity, not an eternal, independent one. Contingency is limitation. On this point Anselm was clearer than Descartes on the whole. On the other hand, Descartes is a bit stronger in his dealing with the question, "How do I know that I have a genuine idea of perfection rather than a confused or self-contradictory pseudo-idea?" Here, we think, is the critical question.

## Descartes's Ontological Argument, Final Version

107. In the idea or concept of a thing existence is contained, because we are unable to conceive anything except under the form of an existent; that is, possible or contingent existence is contained in the concept of a limited thing, but necessary and perfect existence in the concept of a supremely perfect being.

### Proposition I*

The existence of God is known from the consideration of his nature alone.

### Demonstration*

To say that something is contained in the nature or in the concept of anything is the same as to say that this is true of that thing. . . . But necessary existence is contained in the nature or in the concept of God.

Hence it is true to say of God that necessary existence is in him, or that God exists.[3]

108. And I must not imagine that I do not apprehend the infinite by a true idea, but only by the negation of the finite, in the same way that I comprehend repose and darkness by the negation of motion and light: since, on the contrary, I clearly perceive that there is more reality in the infinite substance than in the finite, and therefore that in some way I possess the perception (notion) of the infinite before that of the finite, that is, the perception of God before that of myself, for how could

3. To retain the force of Descartes's emphasis on necessity (as a superior kind of existence) in his Second Replies to Objections, we have taken the liberty of adding the word in brackets wherever, in the following passages from the Meditations, it seemed to be implicit.

I know that I doubt, desire, or that something is wanting to me, and that I am not wholly perfect, if I possessed no idea of a being more perfect than myself, by comparison of which I knew the deficiencies of my nature?

109. But though, in truth, I cannot conceive a God unless as existing, any more than I can a mountain without a valley, yet, just as it does not follow that there is any mountain in the world merely because I conceive a mountain with a valley, so likewise, though I conceive God as existing, it does not seem to follow on that account that God exists; for my thought imposes no necessity on things; and as I may imagine a winged horse, though there be none such, so I could perhaps attribute existence to God, though no God existed. But the cases are not analogous, and a fallacy lurks under the semblance of this objection: for because I cannot conceive a mountain without a valley, it does not follow that there is any mountain or valley in existence, but simply that the mountain or valley, whether they do or do not exist, are inseparable from each other; whereas, on the other hand, because I cannot conceive God unless as [necessarily] existing, it follows that [the necessary or perfect mode of] existence is inseparable from him, and therefore that he really exists: not that this is brought about by my thought, or that it imposes any necessity on things, but, on the contrary, the necessity which lies in the thing itself, that is, the necessity of the existence of God, determines me to think in this way: for it is not in my power to conceive a God without [necessary] existence, that is, a being supremely perfect, and yet devoid of an absolute perfection, as I am free to imagine a horse with or without wings.

Nor must it be alleged here as an objection, that it is in truth necessary to admit that God exists, after having supposed him to possess all perfections, since [necessary] existence is one of them, but that my original supposition was not necessary; just as it is not necessary to think that all quadrilateral figures can be inscribed in the circle, since, if I supposed this, I should be constrained to admit that the rhombus, being a figure of four sides, can be therein inscribed, which, however, is manifestly false. This objection is, I say, incompetent; for although it may not be necessary that I shall at any time entertain the notion of Deity, yet each time I happen to think of a first and sovereign being, and to draw, so to speak, the idea of him from the storehouse of the mind, I am necessitated to attribute to him all kinds of perfections, though I may not then enumerate them all, nor think of each of them in particular. And this necessity is sufficient, as soon as I discover that [necessity of] existence is a perfection, to cause me to infer the existence of this first and sovereign being: just as it is not necessary that I should ever imagine any triangle, but whenever I am desirous of considering a rectilineal figure composed of only three angles, it is absolutely necessary to attribute those properties to it from which it is correctly inferred that its three angles are not greater than two right angles, although perhaps I may not then advert to this relation in particular. But when I consider what figures are capable of being inscribed in the circle, it is by no means necessary to hold that all quadrilateral figures are of this number; on the contrary, I cannot even imagine such to be the case, so long as I shall be unwilling to accept in thought aught that I do not clearly and distinctly conceive: and consequently there is a vast difference between false suppositions, as is the one in question, and the true ideas that were born with me, the first and chief of which is the idea of God. For indeed I discern on many grounds that this idea is not

factitious, depending simply on my thought, but that it is the representation of a true and immutable nature: in the first place, because I can conceive no other being, except God, to whose essence [the necessary mode of] existence pertains; in the second, because it is impossible to conceive two or more gods of this kind; and it being supposed that one such God exists, I clearly see that he must have existed from all eternity, and will exist to all eternity; and finally, because I apprehend many other properties in God, none of which I can either diminish or change.

[Sec. 107, René Descartes, *Second Replies to Objections*, trans. Marjorie Grene, quoted in T. V. Smith and Marjorie Grene, *From Descartes to Kant* (Chicago: University of Chicago Press, 1940), pp. 161–62. Sec. 108, *Descartes' Meditations and Selections from the Principles of Philosophy*, trans. John Veitch (Chicago: Open Court Publishing Co., 1913), pp. 54–55. Sec. 109, *ibid.*, pp. 78–80.]

## COMMENT

The greatest weakness of Descartes's argument (when we correct, as he himself learned to do, the initial error of treating simple universal existence as a predicate of a "perfection" and substitute the modality, necessity-with-respect-to-existence) lies in his failure to establish and clarify the initial thesis of the argument—"I have an idea of perfection." Has he such an idea? If our criticisms of classical theism are sound, Descartes's supposed idea of God is really incoherent and in the same class with those self-contradictory notions of whose "falsity" or "factitiousness" he speaks. What, then, of his argument purporting to show that he cannot be without a true idea of perfection, as the standard by which he becomes aware of his own imperfections? One may answer that consciously Descartes has the classical pseudo-idea of the divine nature but that unconsciously he has the genuine idea which all men (we think) intuitively have, the dipolar conception of perfection as having a temporal and relative and composite aspect as well as an eternal, absolute, and simple one. In this dipolar perfection all truth is contained, truth about the past and actual as past and actual, about the future and indeterminately potential as future and indeterminate, and how far indeterminate. It is by this as standard that our real defects and imperfections are judged. We, for our part, little know what is determinately actual and past, what is future and more or less indeterminate. The panentheistic concept fits the Cartesian situation—apart from its ecclesiastical factors—better than the classical one that alone was considered by Descartes.

# LEIBNIZ (1646–1716)

Leibniz rendered two great services in connection with theism. (1) He was the first not to propose (for Campanella and others had done that) but to work out the only coherent program, as it seems to us, of relating God and the world, by treating the universal properties of created things as inferior forms of that which, in supremely excellent form, constitutes the divine nature. Thus, if knowledge is perfect in God, then it is imperfect, but still present, in all other individuals. For the difference between the perfect and the imperfect is not that between something and nothing, or infinity and zero, but between the infinite and the finite (so far as infinity comes in properly at all).

Accordingly, to set up a threefold division—God, the perfectly knowing individual; men and the like, imperfectly knowing individuals; molecules, atoms, particles, individuals not knowing at all—is to destroy any logic in the theistic conception. The divine attributes cannot anywhere be present in merely zero degree, for God is in all his works positively reflected and imitated thereby. True, Campanella, Cardanus, and Telesius of the Renaissance period had set up this principle. But they did nothing cogent with it in detail. Despite all the mistakes in Leibniz's monadology, his systematic attribution of "perception" and "appetition," in however lowly forms, to all individual units of reality was a great contribution to theism of all varieties.

(2) Leibniz, by applying his power of exceptionally clear statement and analysis to certain traditional theistic conceptions, accomplished, in spite of himself, a *reductio ad absurdum* of these ideas which has materially aided in breaking their spell and thus in opening up fresh possibilities for thought. This is not a service he intended to perform, but its value is nonetheless real.

### Knowledge and Will in All Beings

*110.* In God are present: power, which is the source of everything; knowledge, which contains the details of the ideas; and, finally, will, which changes or produces things in accordance with the principle of the greatest good. To these correspond in the created monad, the subject or basis, the faculty of perception, and the faculty of appetition. In God these attributes are absolutely infinite or perfect, while in the created monads or in the entelechies they are imitations approaching him in proportion to their perfection.

### Perfection in God and the World

*111.* The conception of God which is the most common and the most full of meaning is expressed well enough in the words: God is an absolutely perfect being. The implications, however, of these words fail to receive sufficient consideration. For instance, there are many different kinds of perfection, all of which God possesses, and each one of them pertains to him in the highest degree.

We must also know what perfection is. One thing which can surely be affirmed about it is that those forms or natures which are not susceptible of it to the highest degree, say the nature of numbers or of figures, do not permit of perfection. This is because the number which is the greatest of all (that is, the sum of all the numbers), and likewise the greatest of all figures, imply contradictions. The greatest knowledge, however, and omnipotence contain no impossibility. Consequently power and knowledge do admit of perfection, and in so far as they pertain to God they have no limits.

Whence it follows that God who possesses supreme and infinite wisdom acts in the most perfect manner not only metaphysically but also from the moral standpoint.

*112.* Certain modern writers . . . boldly maintain that that which God has made is not perfect in the highest degree, and that he might have done better. . . . To show that an architect could have done better is to find fault with his work. Furthermore this opinion is contrary to the Holy Scriptures when they assure us of the goodness of God's work. For if comparative perfection were sufficient, then in whatever way God had accomplished his work, since there is an infinitude of possible imperfections, it would always have been good in comparison with the less perfect; but a thing is little praiseworthy when it can be praised only in this way.

*113.* A truth is necessary when the opposite implies contradiction; and when it is not necessary it is called contingent. That God exists, that all right angles are equal to each other, are necessary truths; but it is a contingent truth that I exist or that there are bodies which show an actual right angle.

*114.* But there must be also a sufficient reason for contingent truths or truths of fact; that is to say, for the sequence of the things which extend throughout the universe of created beings.

*115.* In my opinion, if there were no best possible series [of things in the world], God would certainly have created nothing, since he cannot act without a reason, or prefer the less perfect to the more perfect.

*116.* God, however, has chosen the most perfect [world], that is to say the one which is at the same time the simplest in hypotheses and richest in phenomena, as might be the case with a geometric line, whose construction was easy, but whose properties and effects were extremely remarkable and of great significance.

### The Antinomy of Necessary Knowledge and Will with Contingent Objects

*117.* [Arnauld:] . . . what do we know at present of God's knowledge? We know that he knows all things and that he knows them all by a single and very simple act, which is his essence. When I say that we know it I mean that we are sure that this must be so. But do we understand it? . . . Further, are we able to conceive that, although the knowledge of God is his very essence, wholly necessary and immutable, he has, nevertheless, knowledge of an infinity of things which he might not have had because those things might not have been? It is the same in the case of his will which is also his very essence where there is nothing except what is necessary; and still he wills and has willed, from all eternity, things which he would have been able not to will. I find therefore a great deal of uncertainty in the manner in which we usually represent to ourselves that God acts.

*118.* [Leibniz:] It is . . . very difficult to explain perfectly how God has knowledge which he was able not to have, that is, the knowledge of prevision, for, if future contingencies did not exist, God would have no vision of them. It is true that he might have simple knowledge of future contingencies which would become prevision when joined to his will so that the difficulty above would be reduced to the difficulties present in conceiving of the will of God. That is to say, the question how God is free to will. This, without doubt, passes our ken, but it is not essential to understand it in order to solve our question [concerning the nature of the individual].

### The Problem of Freedom

*119.* But does it not seem that in this way [since all human actions follow from God's choice of the best possible world] the difference between contingent and necessary truths will be destroyed, that there will be no place for human liberty, and that an absolute fatality will rule as well over our actions as over all the rest of the events of the world? To this I reply that a distinction must be made between that which is certain and that which is necessary. Every one grants that future contingencies are assured since God foresees them, but we do not say just because of that that they are necessary.

*120.* . . . the decrees of God do not change the possibilities of things and, . . . although God assuredly chooses the best, this does not prevent that which is less perfect from being possible in itself. Although it will never happen, it is not its impossibility but its imperfection which causes him to reject it. Now nothing is necessitated whose opposite is possible.

### How Bad Acts, Though Chosen by Divine Decree, Are Yet Contrary to Divine Commands

*121.* . . . God desires everything which is an object of his particular intention. When we consider the objects of his general intentions, however, such as are the modes of activities of created things and especially of the reasoning creatures with whom God wishes to cooperate, we must make a distinction; for if the action is good in itself, we may say that God wishes it and at times commands it, even though it does not take place; but if it is bad in itself and becomes good only by accident through the course of events and especially after chastisement and satisfaction have corrected its malignity and rewarded the ill with interest in such a way that more perfection results in the whole train of circumstances than would have come if that ill had not occurred—if all this takes place we must say that God permits the evil, and not that he desired it, although he has cooperated by means of the laws of nature which he has established. He knows how to produce the greatest good from them.

[Sec. 110, G. W. Leibniz, "Monadology," par. 48, quoted from *Discourse on Metaphysics, Correspondence with Arnauld and Monadology,* trans. George R. Montgomery (Chicago: Open Court Publishing Co., 1931), p. 261. Sec. 111, *ibid.,* p. 3. Sec. 112, *ibid.,* pp. 5–6. Sec. 113, *Die philosophischen Schriften von G. W. Leibniz,* herausgegeben von C. J. Gerhardt, III, 400, quoted in Bertrand Russell, *A Critical Exposition of the Philosophy of Leibniz* (London: George Allen & Unwin, Ltd., 1900, 1937), p. 208. Sec. 114, Leibniz, "Monadology," par. 36, *Discourse on Metaphysics,* p. 258. Sec. 115, Gerhardt, II, 424, Russell, *op. cit.,* p. 212. Sec. 116, Leibniz, *op. cit.,* p. 11. Sec. 117, *ibid.,* p. 96. Sec. 118, *ibid.,* pp. 114–15. Sec. 119, *ibid.,* p. 20. Sec. 120, *ibid.,* p. 22. Sec. 121, *ibid.,* p. 12.]

#### COMMENT

Leibniz, in distinguishing between merits which admit an absolute maximum, and thus can apply to the perfect being, and those which admit no maximum, such as numerical magnitude, overlooks, we think, the following. Excellences which involve an open infinity, with no upper limit, might yet be attributed to the being which no other being can rival or surpass, the supreme being, in terms of the formula: in any possible state of reality, the supreme being is sure to surpass all others with respect to the merit in question. Take Leibniz's example of figure: If the universe is, in any sense, the divine body, then we may say that its total shape or configuration belongs to God and to no other individual; and we may also say that, as the most complex configuration, which yet (we may hold) is no less well integrated, it inevitably surpasses, not indeed all other possible ones, but all others that are actualized, for this can only mean (on the hypothesis) all those that characterize the parts of the divine body rather than the whole. Take again Leibniz's view that the best world is the one most rich in results from the simplest basic principles or, more briefly, the most unified and at the same time the most diversified. Now what could be meant by such a greatest possible variety-in-unity? Variety has no maximum short of "all possibilities"; and these, according to Leibniz, cannot all be actualized and are not all actualized. The most reasonable view would seem to be that the world is always less various than it might be, even though with the same degree of integration. But the world is always the *de facto* greatest variety; and, if the world belongs to God as the content of his life, then his actual variety is necessarily and always supreme. This would be a law of actual superiority, and this law is itself an absolute maximum, even though variety has no possible absolute maximum. For the most excellent possible relation to variety as having no possible maximum is precisely to have guaranteed superiority over all actual variety (in unity).

This is the panentheistic or "surrelativistic" solution of the problem which Leibniz sought with such daring to solve. The solution was perhaps first formulated with any approach to clarity by Fechner.

Leibniz correctly saw that a world that God might have made better, or might have made worse, is hardly a convincing expression of divine perfection. But he overlooked three things.

1. God "could not have done better" does not imply that he could not have done equally well though differently. There may be problems with more than one equally good solution! Leibniz argues that to do this, rather than that, is rational only if this is better than that. Buridan's ass with two equally attractive bundles of hay must starve; and, even more, a rational deity cannot act without sufficient reason. But this is, we think, a sheer mistake. Even an ass should know that eating is better than starving, and to starve because one way of eating is equally good with another is the most irrational thing conceivable. Thus Leibniz's version of the principle of sufficient reason is itself without reason.

2. That God could not have done better (though he could, we hold, have done otherwise) does not imply that the resulting world could not have been better. For nothing is better than to create free beings, meaning beings whose exact use of their freedom is not predetermined by their mere creation. God's part in making the world is not the whole of its making; for free creatures are, in their lowly fashion, co-creators, making themselves and the world with the help of God. Each of us in a measure makes his own life, which is part of the world process. That God's part in the co-creation could not have been better is then compatible with our part's being less good than it might have been. Putting the two foregoing considerations together, we see that, though

it may be true that God's creative action is such that none better was possible, it follows neither that he had a "reason" for acting exactly as he did rather than any other way nor that the world is such that it could not have been better.

3. Leibniz assumes that the divine creative decision consisted in a single act which, once for all, selected the detail of the world throughout all time. But if there be, as dipolarists hold, relative and temporal aspects of deity, then creation must be not one act but an endless series of acts.

Each such act, except the first—if there was a first—has for its problem, not what is the best possible world, but what is the best possible succeeding state of a world already in being. And why must there have been a first state of the world? If not, then every divine act without exception had for its problem that of selecting a suitable successor for a world which, for *that* act, is given —though it was a result of a previous act—so that the problem of selecting the best world merely out of the realm of possibility never arises and never has arisen. This eliminates the embarrassing difficulty that we can form no conception of a character which would make a world better than any other possible one. The value of the world consisting, as Leibniz himself held, in its integrating of variety—the more variety the better— and there being no possibility of a maximal variety, the notion of a best possible world is not a possible conception.

Maximal variety could only be all possibilities actualized together. But since there are mutually contradictory possibilities, all cannot be actualized together. But, although no world can be the best possible, a state of the world might be at least as good as any alternative state as successor to a world state already in being. For here we have real restrictions upon possibility; we have a real, not merely an ideal, problem. And

here there is no need of maximal variety, for too great an increase in the world's variety would break the continuity or order of the world process. What is needed is the greatest assimilable increase; and for this we need not suppose an exhaustion of possibility in general—an impossibility.

Thus we escape the antinomy of necessity and freedom which Leibniz in vain seeks to resolve. To say that another world was possible is, on Leibniz's principles, simply to say that God might have created another. (For, according to him, God does all the creating. We are not and could not be co-determiners with him.) Further, to say that God might have created another world is to say, again on Leibniz's principles, that he might have acted imperfectly, by producing a work less good than was possible. But it is a contradiction to conceive a perfect being acting imperfectly. Moreover, the nonexistence of such a being would itself be a contradiction (Leibniz accepts the ontological argument in this sense). What becomes of the distinction between truths whose contrary involves contradiction and those of which this is not the case?

The paradox that the most wicked men are ingredients of the world precisely required by the most perfect world plan is dealt with by Leibniz in the same manner as, later, by Royce. The wicked do contribute, as surely as saints, to the world's perfection. But they do not intend thus to contribute; their contribution is in spite of themselves. And God does not like their act in and for itself but only for the consequences which he must go to the trouble, as it were, of eliciting from the act. The objection is that it really does not matter at all that the contribution of the wicked is thus roundabout or unintended. Nothing is at stake in the distinction; for everything is as perfection requires it to be. This solution will hardly do.

As for the problem of reconciling contingency in the world with sheer necessity in God's knowing and creating, Arnauld and Leibniz between them seem to succeed in refuting the theism they hold in common as plainly as an enemy could. Even Leibniz's suggestion that there is but the one difficulty, that of divine will, is untenable. For, if God wills, and might have willed otherwise, then not only does this contradict the asserted absence of contingency in his will and hence his being (for his will is his being and very essence) but there is the further contradiction that he must know that he wills thus, and that he might have willed otherwise; therefore he must have knowledge that he might not have had as to his own willing.

So both contradictions ("difficulties") pointed out by Arnauld with admirable naïveté, clarity, and directness remain completely unresolved and, by Leibniz's virtual admission, unresolvable on classical assumptions. True, as Leibniz says, the issue is not essential to his dispute with Arnauld, since it rather concerns tenets they hold in common. But this excuses Leibniz's failure on this occasion to answer the challenge only

if he elsewhere has given reason for thinking he could meet it. And where has he or anyone else shown that it can be met?

In a number of places Leibniz suggests that the perfection of the world is not static, consists not in its quality at any given time but rather in its endless progress. The cosmic law of development, he sometimes thinks, is the real merit of the universe. Owing to the infinite divisibility of space, there are always monads cramped in scope of action which may be expanded and thus enriched, and therewith the net value of the universe increased. But if only he had seen that the infinite divisibility of space is merely an aspect of the inexhaustibility of possibility, which permits no "richest compound" of actualities, then he might also have seen that the only way to relate this inexhaustibility intelligibly to God's care for the world is to suppose that his perfection too is something not wholly and once for all actual, but is rather, in one aspect, a law whereby his actual achievement is endlessly enriched by new achievement.

# KANT (1724–1804)

Of all criticisms of philosophical theology, probably none has been so influential as those of Kant. They are indeed so widely known to students of the philosophy of religion that we do not propose to quote them here. An additional reason is that much of the same ground is covered by Hume and others who are presented in this volume. Still another is that Kant's criticisms depend, more than is commonly noted, on certain features of his own system which are now usually rejected, even sometimes by those who urge the criticisms as conclusive. What we wish to do here is to present certain rather neglected as-

pects of Kant's treatment of theism which are at the same time, we feel, of considerable contemporary interest and which can be rather well understood without too much exposition of Kantianism.

Our text opens with what we believe to be an approach to an argument for God which Kant by implication outlines and then forbids us to follow, giving reasons for this prohibition which we shall consider later. The argument itself is the one also suggested by Spinoza in his doctrine that a true idea is its own standard. The argument is later elaborated by the post-Kantian idealists, notably by Royce. All these men judge that Kant's veto is misplaced. It is remarkable that Kant should have claimed, in his refutation of the theistic arguments, to have exhausted the possibilities, while yet the argument suggested by the first of the following selections scarcely seems covered at all in the classification utilized in the refutation.

It is to be understood that sensory intuition is for Kant the same as passive intuition, while intellectual intuition is active, creating its own objects.

### Kant's Implicit Argument for God: Phenomena and Noumena

122. Appearances, so far as they are thought as objects under the unity of the categories, are called phenomena. But if we assume entities which are objects of the understanding alone, and yet as such capable of being given to intuition, although a non-sensory, intellectual or active intuition, these would be called Noumena or Intelligibles.

Now it may seem that . . . the division of objects into phenomena and noumena is justified, in the sense that . . . things really fall into these two classes. For if the senses merely represent to us an entity as it appears, this entity must also be something in itself, and therefore an object of a non-sensory intuition, that is, an intuitive understanding. In other words, a form of knowledge must be possible, in which is no sensibility, and which has for its object the absolutely objective reality. For otherwise, it seems, we could not distinguish between things as they appear and things as they are.

123. . . . appearance is nothing in itself . . . the word "appearance" indicates a relation to something.

124. In this way arises the concept of a noumenon, but it is not a positive concept, giving knowledge of a definite object, but merely the thought of something in general, accompanied by abstraction from all the forms of sensory intuition. For a noumenon to be a genuine object, distinguished from all phenomena, it is not enough that I free myself from all conditions of sensory intuition, I must also have reason to suppose another kind of intuition than this; otherwise my conception is empty, although not contradictory.

125. . . . the very possibility of such a non-sensory intuition is entirely beyond our grasp . . . we are by no means justified in affirming this possibility.

### The Concept of God

126. The transcendental non-empirical concept of God as the most-real being is unavoidable in philosopohy, abstract as the idea is, since it is essential to the understanding, and to the interpretation of whatever concrete matter as may subsequently be introduced in applied theology and theory of religion. Now the question is, shall I think of God as the content (*complexus, aggregatum*) of all realities or as their highest ground? If I do the former, then I must furnish examples of the material out of which I construct the highest being, in order that the idea may not be wholly empty and without meaning. I will, then, attribute to him understanding, say, and even will, and other such realities. But all understanding with which I am acquainted is a capacity to *think*, that is, a discursive representing power which is possible only through properties common to various things (from whose differences thinking abstracts) and thus not without *limitation* in the subject thinking. Therefore a divine understanding cannot be regarded as a power of thinking. However, I have not the least notion of any other sort of understanding, such perhaps as one that should be a power of intuiting; accordingly, the concept of an understanding attributable to the highest being is empty of meaning.—Just so: if I at-

tribute a *will* to this being, whereby he is the cause of all things other than himself, I must suppose this will to be such that its satisfaction (*acquiescentia*) is totally independent of all things outside itself; for any such dependence would be limitation (*negatio*). But now once more, I have not the least conception, and can furnish no example, of a will whose subject would not derive satisfaction from the *success* of its volitions, and thus would not depend upon the existence of external things. The conception, then, of a will as inherent in the supreme being is, like that of an understanding, either empty or (what is still worse) anthropomorphic, such as must destroy religion and convert it into idolatry when, as is inevitable, it is practically applied.

But suppose I form the conception of the *ens realissimum* as the ground of all reality, then I say: God is the being who contains in himself the ground of everything in the world *which compels us human beings to posit an understanding* (for example all that is purposive in the world); he is the being, from whom all worldly existence originates, not from the necessity of his nature (*per emanationem*) but according to a relationship *which we human beings can understand only if we think of it as free will.* What the nature of the highest being may be in itself (objectively) we may regard as entirely beyond our comprehension, and yet (subjectively) these conceptions may have practical reality (as applied to the conduct of life); in which connection alone can an *analogy* of divine and human understanding, as both cognizant of the moral law, be admitted, whereas from the theoretical point of view there can be no such analogy. From the moral law, which authoritatively prescribes to our reason, not from the theory of the nature of things in themselves, proceeds the idea of God which the practical reason compels us to make for ourselves.

## Kant's Doctrine of Theistic Analogy

*127.* If I say that we are compelled to consider the world, as if it were the work of a Supreme Understanding, I really say nothing more, than that a watch, a ship, a regiment, bears the same relation to the watchmaker, the shipbuilder, the commanding officer, as the world of sense . . . does to the Unknown, which I do not hereby cognize as it is in itself, but as it is for me or in relation to the world.

Such a cognition is one of analogy, and does not signify (as is commonly understood) an imperfect similarity of two things, but a perfect similarity of relations between two quite dissimilar things.

*128.* There is, e.g., an analogy between the juridical relations of human actions and the mechanical relation of motive powers. I never can do anything to another man without giving him a right to do the same to me on the same conditions; just as no mass can act on another mass without thereby occasioning the other to react equally against it. Here right and motive power are quite dissimilar things, but in their relation there is complete similarity. By means of such an analogy I can obtain a notion of the relation of things which in their absolute characters are unknown to me. For instance, as the promotion of the welfare of children ($= a$) is to the love of parents ($= b$), so the welfare of the human species ($= c$) is to that unknown in God ($= x$), which we call love; not as if it had the least similarity to any human inclination, but because we can suppose its relation to the world to be similar to that which things of the world bear to one another. But the concept of relation in this case is a mere category, viz., the concept of cause, which has nothing to do with sensibility.

*129.* By means of this analogy, however, there remains a concept of the

Supreme Being sufficiently determined *for us*, though we have left out everything that could determine it absolutely or in itself; for we determine it as regards the world and as regards ourselves, and more we do not require. The attacks which Hume makes upon those who would determine this concept absolutely, by taking the materials for so doing from themselves and the world, do not affect us; and he cannot object to us, that we have nothing left if we give up the objective anthropomorphism of the concept of the Supreme Being.

### Kant's Explicit Argument for God as Ground of the Highest Good

*130.* . . . *virtue* (as worthiness to be happy) is the *supreme condition* of all that can appear to us desirable, and consequently of all our pursuit of happiness, and is therefore the *supreme* good. But it does not follow that it is the whole and perfect good as the object of the desires of rational finite beings; for this requires happiness also, and that not merely in the partial eyes of the person who makes himself an end, but even in the judgment of an impartial reason, which regards persons in general as ends in themselves. For to need happiness, to deserve it, and yet at the same time not to participate in it, cannot be consistent with the perfect volition of a rational being possessed at the same time of all power, if, for the sake of experiment, we conceive such a being.

*131. Happiness* is the condition of a rational being in the world with whom *everything goes according to his wish and will;* it rests, therefore, on the harmony of physical nature with his whole end, and likewise with the essential determining principle of his will. Now the moral law as a law of freedom commands by determining principles, which ought to be quite independent of nature and of its harmony with our faculty of desire (as springs). But the acting ra-

tional being in the world is not the cause of the world and of nature itself. There is not the least ground, therefore, in the moral law for a necessary connection between morality and proportionate happiness in a being that belongs to the world as part of it.

*132.* Nevertheless, in the practical problem of pure reason, i.e., the necessary pursuit of the *summum bonum*, such a connection is postulated as necessary: we ought to endeavor to promote the *summum bonum*, which, therefore, must be possible. Accordingly, the existence of a cause of all nature, distinct from nature itself, and containing the principle of this connection, namely, of the exact harmony of happiness with morality, is also *postulated*. Now, this supreme cause must contain the principle of the harmony of nature, not merely with . . . the will of rational beings, but . . . with their moral character.

*133.* Now a being that is capable of acting on the conception of laws is an *intelligence* (a rational being), and the causality of such a being according to this conception of laws is his *will;* therefore the supreme cause of nature, which must be presupposed as a condition of the *summum bonum*, is a being which is the cause of nature by *intelligence* and *will*, consequently its author, that is God. It follows that the postulate of the possibility of the *highest derived good* (the best world) is likewise the postulate of the reality of a *highest original good*, that is to say, of the existence of God. Now it was seen to be a duty for us to promote the *summum bonum;* consequently it is not merely allowable, but it is a necessity connected with deity as a requisite, that we should presuppose the possibility of this *summum bonum;* and as this is possible only on condition of the existence of God, it inseparably connects the supposition of this with duty; that is, it is morally necessary to assume the existence of God.

[Sec. 122, Immanuel Kant, *Kritik der Reinen Vernunft nach der ersten und zweiten Original-Ausgabe* ("Der Philosophischen Bibliothek," Band 37*a* [Leipzig: Verlag von Felix Meiner, 1930]), p. 298. Sec. 123, *ibid.*, p. 300. Sec. 124, *ibid.*, pp. 300–301. Sec. 125, *ibid.*, p. 304. Sec. 126, Immanuel Kant, *Zur Logik und Metaphysik* ("Philosophische Bibliothek," Band 46 [Leipzig, 1921]), III Abteilung, pp. 16–18 n. Sec. 127, *Kant's Prolegomena to Any Future Metaphysics*, ed. Paul Carus (Chicago: Open Court Publishing Co., 1933), p. 129. Sec. 128, *ibid.*, p. 129 n. Sec. 129, *ibid.*, pp. 129–30. Sec. 130, *Kant's Critique of Practical Reason*, trans. T. K. Abbott (New York: Longmans, Green & Co., 1898), p. 206. Sec. 131, *ibid.*, p. 221. Sec. 132, *ibid.* Sec. 133, *ibid.*, p. 222.]

## COMMENT

Nearly the whole of Kant's discussion of theology presupposes an identification, as old as Philo at least, between the supreme as absolute, eternal, independent, on the one hand, and the supreme as most concrete or rich in value, on the other. No logic compels us to regard the relation between the two as that of mere identity; indeed, logic implies that this cannot be the relation. But Kant always assumes such identity. Consequently, he sees no possibilities for theism beyond the purely absolutistic or eternalistic, and the purely relativistic or temporalistic ("anthropomorphic"), conceptions of deity. He is thus imprisoned in the half-truths in which the monopolar prejudice, the neglect of the principle of polarity, is bound to result. One must, he thinks, choose between divine inclusiveness of all knowable forms of reality and divine independence of all. He decides for the latter and infers that God cannot include even the most exalted conceivable forms of will or understanding. Surely not, if independence, without its polar contrast, is alone applicable to deity.

The dipolar synthesis here must distinguish between independence as to existence and essential individuality and independence as to total concrete content. The latter independence is, we

hold, to be rejected; the former to be retained. But the former, or essential independence, is quite compatible with understanding and will. Even divine knowledge must, according to the dipolar view, be passive to its objects—indeed, infinitely more exactly responsive to them than our knowledge—but this only means that, with a different world to know, God's knowledge would have been different; it does not mean that there would have been no divine knowledge or no God; and thus the essential independence of deity, independence as to his existence and divinity, is preserved. Again, even divine will must derive satisfaction from results attained by lesser beings and so must depend upon the latter for a certain accidental content. But this only means that, with other results, the divine satisfaction would be other, perhaps less or more; but in any possible case it would be and would be divine, incomparable to that of any other individual, actual or possible.

The dipolar view renders irrelevant Kant's most basic reason for denying that God can be positively conceived. This reason is that all our positive conceptions must be in terms of time, which furnishes the schema of all our ideas, whereas (Kant assumes) God must be wholly nontemporal. But suppose God is the categorically supreme example of temporal reality, the essential process in all process, hence without beginning or end of his life, in full possession in every present of all that is past to this present, and in this sense supertemporal or eternal, then the schema of time may serve after all to interpret him. Kant's reference to anthropomorphic errors by no means shows that he has considered the dipolar view. For he never distinguishes between a monopolar and a dipolar version of the temporalistic or relativistic conception of God. He just has not explored this region of thought, and it would have been sheer luck if nothing important had thereby been overlooked.

Kant's contention that we have no insight whatever into the possibility of an intuition which grasps things as they are rests on doubtful grounds and leads him into difficulties.

He thinks that our own intuition is merely passive and therefore gives us, not the object itself, but an effect on our sensibility, called the "appearance of the object." But this idea of sensibility as a stuff which takes on definite shape due to the unknown thing in itself is open to the following objection. Intuition, in the sense here in question, is direct grasp of an object, an entity intuited. Indirect awareness presupposes direct awareness, and we must have such.

Now, what Kant is really saying is that our direct awareness of something is only our direct awareness of our awareness of the something, or of our reaction to the something. But the reaction just is the direct awareness of the something. The passivity of our intuitive awareness does not mean that the datum grasped is only an effect on us of the intuited object; it means this: *that* I now intuit $x$ (rather than $y$, or nothing at all) is due to the existence of $x$. The object is the ground of the effect which is my awareness of the object. It does not follow that I am aware not of the object but only of its effect or appearance. For the effect is not what I am aware of, since my awareness itself is the effect, and it is not its own object! If an object appears to us, is given to us, then the object is given, not the appearance of the object. The object as given, and in so far as it is given, constitutes the appearance.

The real defect of our intuition is the one Leibniz indicated: its lack of clarity. Kant disputes this (rightly, insofar as Leibniz combined truth with error in his way of putting the point), but it is the only way out of the absurdity of an awareness which possesses no object and is aware only of itself, or the absurdity of an appearance which completely conceals what appears, and which latter therefore precisely does not appear but remains hidden, unintuited.

Part of the trouble lies in Kant's overlooking, along with a vast multitude of philosophers before and since, that the direct object of intuition is not necessarily what practical behavior, with its tendency to oversimplify, tends to suggest. It may be that I do not directly intuit the piece of chalk I look at. For here the object has indeed produced an effect upon what might be called my "sensibility," namely, my optical apparatus. There is in this case something between the thing we wish to know and our intuitive grasp; for there is an image on the retina, and a state of excitation in the nerves and brain. Now some philosophers and scientists hold that the direct datum of intuition here is this very process in the nervous system. True, one cannot learn the details of cell structure by mere consultation of such intuitions; but here the unclarity or indistinctness (Leibniz) to which we have referred is pertinent. Nevertheless, the data of vision are more definitely correlated with nervous activity (according to all our knowledge) than with anything outside the body. So far as their distinctness does go they are correct as to what is going on in the nerves, by any test we can apply. This theory, right or wrong, cannot simply be set aside by fiat in order to prove that we do not directly grasp *any* object as it is. Thus Kant's entire position concerning intuition is unestablished at best.

It is possible to conceive an intuition free from the defects of ours, not in that it reaches something wholly behind appearance—for there may be no such thing, as we have just seen, save so far as one object (nervous process) is taken as sign or map of another (piece of chalk)—but in that the intuition, unlike ours, clearly and distinctly depicts its objects. There are degrees of distinctness in our awareness, hence we are not wholly without clues as to what would constitute the ideal or perfect clarity of vision. We may also conceive the relation of a perfect intuition as that of a mind to a body completely transparent to the mind and consisting of the universe. Then for such intuition the main cause of the division between reality and its representation in a set of mere signs would be removed.

Of course along this path we should never arrive at Kant's classical theism. But that for us is no argument favoring Kant but one argument the more against classical theism.

But would not divine intuition, as Kant holds, create its objects? We incline to think that, as Whitehead seems to imply, God as creating us in a given state of our actuality is not God as knowing that state but as knowing the previous state. By his knowledge of what we have been we are now in part created; but in part also we are self-created.

Kant's doctrine of analogy is the old one. Has he rescued it from the objections of Hume and others? We think not. No "perfect similarity of relations" is possible for classical theism. An ordinary reason is related to its objects in such fashion that, if the latter are contingent, so is the state of the reason. Classical theism denies this of God. Then there is the fundamental question: "Is God related at all? Or is it merely that the world is related to God?" This would be the reverse of the relational principle that holds in general between mind and its objects. The cognitive reference is something real in and for mind, not in the things referred to. Besides, that which lacks relation lacks something real and so is less than "all realities." The notion that there is nothing in God similar to love, but yet the world is as if God loved it, is the famil-

iar doctrine of Anselm. It overlooks the fact that relations are not just outside the qualities of terms. The way a loving being is related is the way he loves. To shift to the mere concept of "cause" does not solve the problem. What is the causal relation? Is the divine causing of the world just one more case of cause, or is it merely analogous to ordinary causes? Do we have a regress of analogy here?

Further, if we have no conception of what purpose would be like in God, do we really have any idea of what we are looking for when we study the world (as Kant recommends) *as if* we knew it to be the object of divine purpose? What would a rational and purposive unity of the world be, standing to something unknown in God as rational and purposive creations of men stand to men? Kant's only way of conceiving a world purpose is that it would be the proportional union of goodness and happiness in finite rational beings. God is posited as the only cause which could thus proportion happiness to goodness. But is this an intelligible end for all creation? Supposing it to be such, we face a dilemma: either the achievement of this end does or does not enrich the totality of value actualized in God himself. If it does enrich it, then we have either panentheism or pantheism, neither of which seems to be Kant's position. If it does not, then creation was a futile act, productive of no value; or else there is a totality of value, that of the world and God, greater than that of God. This dilemma is not disposed of by Kant's position but merely ignored.

If we give up the idea that the creature (as other than God) is to be wholly its own end, and admit that creation is an enrichment of God's being, then suddenly we see that the *summum bonum* may indeed be defined as Kant defines it, the union of goodness and joy, and the definition literally applied, not directly to the creatures, but to God himself. The end we should serve, the only rational end, is indeed that there should be joyful goodness and that there should be more of it because of our efforts. Panentheism holds that God's enjoyment is enriched by our being, differentially according to our decisions, and that his goodness is eternal and unfailing. So the problem set by Kant is solved. Man's moral life is included in the solution; for relatively good and joyful creatures are more beautiful for divine sympathy to contemplate than relatively bad or joyless ones. Here is an exact solution of the very problem Kant poses: namely, what really ultimate end satisfying to reason can we promote? He replies: The union of goodness and happiness. He looks for this in man, with divine aid, and supernatural immortality. We say: It is more rational to look for it in God himself, who of course is immortal, and of course is good, but whose aesthetic richness of experience is not an absolute maximum (none such is conceivable) and in its degree is not a matter of course but subject to contribution from us.

It must be noted that we have departed from Kant's moral argument in another respect. He reasons: The rational end is moral perfection and complete happiness. Therefore this perfection and happiness must be attainable, at least in an infinite development. Apparently, what is meant is that we can approach indefinitely close to the goal. But the notion of perfect happiness is the old, old utopianism that has haunted most of human thought, the notion that somehow, somewhere, there must be a complete escape from evil, from the tragedy of life. This notion is not warranted, by Kant's argument or any other. Tragedy is inherent in the freedom of life, which makes conflict of individuals more or less inevitable. Besides, there are conflicting values, and no maximal realization of value is possible (Whitehead, Berdyaev). The rational end is the increase of actual value, that is, of joyful goodness. But any possible goodness will be tinged with tragedy, will *not* find that "everything goes according to his wish and will." Such absolute harmony contradicts the very notion of being as multiple or social creativity, freedom. One must find joy in tragedy, or one will not find it, and this is true of God himself. If the saved and happy do not know of the sufferings of the others, then at best they are ignorant. If they do know, then, since knowledge of good and evil is sympathetic in principle, they will not themselves wholly escape the tragedy. Least of all will God escape it.

The justice of God is his giving each feeling and thought its due place in the life of all things as within the life including all things.

Does this contradict the Kantian principle that we as rational beings are ends and never mere means? We are (one may reply) not unqualifiedly rational, so not unqualifiedly end; only God is unqualified rationality and end. However, the idea of *mere* means is inapplicable here. Our contribution to God is our very selves, our very acts and thoughts and feelings, which are all that we actually are. And as Whitehead puts it: "The function of being a means is not disjoined from the function of being an end. The sense of worth beyond itself is immediately enjoyed as an overpowering element in the individual self-attainment. It is in this way that the immediacy of sorrow and pain is transformed into an element of triumph."[4] This is the vision of life really motivated by love for the supreme reality (rather than for our own future utopia), a vision calling for no magic exorcizing of evil, such as nothing that we know about life suggests is possible.

4. Alfred N. Whitehead, *Process and Reality* (New York: Macmillan Co., 1941), p. 531.

All in all, Kant is a classical or mono-polar theist who emphasizes the theoretical difficulties in this position more than his predecessors but hopes to save it by appeal to a construction of the moral law which, particularly in this application, is open to no less grave objections. His God becomes a cosmic magistrate and policeman who sees to it that the good are given their deserts—an anthropomorphic conception, indeed, of the ultimate end of existence! What remains valid is Kant's insistence that we cannot rightly renounce the notion that there must be some supreme end to which in ethics we may adjust our purposes.

# CHANNING (1780–1842)

The emptiness of the merely simple and fixed deity of classical theism was for ages partly concealed by the doctrines of the Trinity and the Incarnation. God was wholly simple and immutable, yet after all there were in him no less than three personalities, with a sort of process or quasi-becoming connecting them. And one of these personalities was somehow identical with the human Jesus. Since, however, Jesus was finite, changeable, and embodied, and God is infinite, immutable, and wholly immaterial, there had to be two natures in Jesus, the first with one, and the second with the other, of these two sets of properties. Yet the two natures were one substance. Then, since Jesus suffered, and since the church is the mystical body of Jesus, the need that there be suffering in deity and that we, with our very being, may contribute to the divine is met, but only by an astonishing defiance of logic, according to what many of us think we see in this procedure. The case was stated with succinctness and boldness by Channing, a writer whose ethical and social insights seem fresh and inspiring after more than a century.

Channing also pointed to the inconsistency in speaking of a God of love, while yet attributing to him actions that seem to call for a very different motive.

## Objections to the Trinity

*134.* We object to the doctrine of the Trinity, that, whilst acknowledging in words, it subverts in effect, the unity of God. According to this doctrine, there are three infinite and equal persons, possessing supreme divinity, called the Father, Son, and Holy Ghost. Each of these persons, as described by theologians, has his own particular consciousness, will, and perceptions. They love each other, converse with each other, and delight in each other's society. They perform different parts in man's redemption, each having his appropriate office, and neither doing the work of the other. The Son is mediator, and not the Father. The Father sends the Son, and is not himself sent; nor is he conscious, like the Son, of taking flesh. Here, then, we have three intelligent agents, possessed of different consciousness, different wills, and different perceptions, performing different acts, and sustaining different relations; and if these things do not imply and constitute three minds or beings, we are utterly at a loss to know how three minds or beings are to be formed. It is difference of properties, and acts, and consciousness, which leads us to the belief of different intelligent beings, and, if this mark fails us, our whole knowledge falls; we have no proof that all the agents and persons in the universe are not one and the same mind.

*135.* We complain of the doctrine of the Trinity, that, not satisfied with making God three beings, it makes Jesus Christ two beings, and thus introduces infinite confusion into our conceptions of his character. . . .

According to this doctrine, Jesus Christ, instead of being one mind, one conscious, intelligent principle, whom we can understand, consists of two souls, two minds; the one divine, the other human; the one weak, the other almighty; the one ignorant, the other omniscient. . . . They have, in fact, no common properties. The divine mind feels none of the wants and sorrows of the human, and the human is infinitely removed from the perfection and happiness of the divine. Can you conceive of two beings in the universe more distinct?

*136.* Trinitarians profess to derive some important advantages from their mode of viewing Christ. It furnishes them, they tell us, with an infinite atonement, for it shows them an infinite being suffering for their sins. The confidence with which this fallacy is repeated astonishes us. When pressed with the question whether they really believe that the infinite and unchangeable God suffered and died on the cross, they acknowledge that this is not true, but that Christ's human mind alone sustained the pains of death. How have we then an infinite sufferer?

### The Character of God

*137.* We believe in the *moral perfection of God.* . . .

It may be said that in regard to this subject all Christians agree, that all ascribe to the Supreme Being infinite justice, goodness, and holiness. We reply, that it is very possible to speak of God magnificently, and to think of him meanly; to apply to his person high-sounding epithets, and to his government principles which make him odious.

*138.* We cannot bow before a being, however great and powerful, who governs tyrannically. We respect nothing but excellence, whether on earth or in heaven. We venerate not the loftiness of God's throne, but the equity and goodness in which it is established.

*139.* Now, we object to the systems of religion which prevail among us, that they are adverse, in a greater or less degree, to these purifying, comforting, and honorable views of God; that they take from us our Father in heaven, and substitute for him a being whom we cannot love if we would, and whom we ought not to love if we could.

*140.* By shocking, as it does, the fundamental principles of morality, and by exhibiting a severe and partial Deity, [this religious system] tends strongly to pervert the moral faculty, to form a gloomy, forbidding, and servile religion, and to lead men to substitute censoriousness, bitterness, and persecution, for a tender and impartial charity. We think, too, that this system, which begins with degrading human nature, may be expected to end in pride; for pride grows out of consciousness of high distinctions, however obtained, and no distinction is so great as that which is made between the elected and abandoned of God.

[Sec. 134, W. E. Channing, *A Sermon Delivered at the Ordination of the Rev. Jared Sparks* (Boston: Hews & Goss, 1819), p. 5. Sec. 135, *ibid.*, p. 12. Sec. 136, *ibid.*, p. 14. Sec. 137, *ibid.*, pp. 15–16. Sec. 138, *ibid.*, p. 16. Sec. 139, *ibid.*, p. 17. Sec. 140, *ibid.*, p. 18.]

### COMMENT

Channing (who was a great reformer and noble humanitarian rather than a metaphysician) understandably missed the locus of the problem which concerned him. That locus lay in classical theism itself with which, so far as we can discover, he did not break. The traditional procedure of first declaring the sheer simplicity of the divine and then introducing the decidedly complex machinery of the Trinity and the Incarnation was in effect a way of qualifying religiously inept monopolar principles in an age when they could not have been merely abandoned. Instead of admitting that there is a divine becoming or process toward novelty and enrichment, a higher kind of time in God, analogous to the lower kind in us, Trinitarians talked about a "begetting" of the Son which is not "making." Instead of admitting that there is a higher relativity, Trinitarians talked of relations between the divine persons, without conceding that this means any nonabsolute aspect of the divine actuality. We agree with Channing that it is uncandid for theologians to declare that God is immutable and simple—period—and then later announce (in effect) that this simplicity is not intended in any sense which would make impossible a complicated structure of social relations and derivations. But the whole of classical theism of necessity follows this pattern. God is without accidents—period. But, still, not in any sense in which this would make it impossible that he should know contingent things, things which might not have existed and which therefore he might not have known as existent! God is without relativity—period. But, still, not in any sense in which this prevents us from being loved by him, that is, to stand as terms to relations of which he is the subject.

While clearing away the trinitarian façade, Channing did not observe that what remained was a God whom we cannot love (if we try to take the doctrine consistently) for the reason that he cannot himself love, and on Channing's own showing only love is supremely lovely. The immutable, impassible God of classical theism has nothing in him conceivably analogous to love. Channing merely deprives classical theism of that saving garment of subtle "fallacies" by which its nakedness had previously been covered. True, he also clears away another and less admirable addition, the ascription of human-like hatred and vindictiveness to the bare simplicity of the merely eternal. Yet even here he weakens his case by himself speaking of "retributive justice" as essential to morality. Either love is the motive or it is not; if it is, what has punishment to do with the matter, save as a device of the police power to set limits to anarchy and social destructiveness? God as transcendental policeman is a suspicious character!

The Socinians, in accepting an aspect of temporality in deity, at least half-made the real change which was required in the orthodox view of God; Schelling and Fechner completed the change by taking this temporal aspect in an inclusive sense. It deserves to be remarked that, in Martineau, Unitarianism of the last century possessed a capable expositor of this view. Its emergence, as we shall more and more see, is pervasive and transcends most sectarian and other customary divisions.

## VON HÜGEL (1852–1925): GOD AND SUFFERING

Classical theism denies relativity, temporality, passivity, of God; so of course it denies suffering. God is the absolute case of joy or bliss, which in negative aspect means the total absence of suffering. On the other hand, those classical theists who were Christians have held that Jesus was both a suffering man and God. It might seem to follow that God suffers. The "Patripassionists" drew this conclusion. But the orthodox reply to this heresy was that only the manhood in Jesus included suffering, not the divine nature in him, and that these two natures were really distinct, even though they were natures of the one person. This raises the difficulties discussed by Channing above. Thus, according to orthodoxy, Jesus as suffering is not God and is not even a symbol of the nature of God, since the divine nature excludes all suffering. Only the love of Jesus symbolizes God, but love is in principle capable of escaping suffering no matter how the loved ones suffer.

The most eloquent statement of this point of view we have found is in the following selections from a distinguished Catholic writer. It should be explained that von Hügel felt it necessary to pay much attention to a now scarcely remembered author, James Hinton. This passionate thinker held that all the suffering in the world is included in the divine consciousness, although only as overcome in a joy that turns all, even pain, to account. Hinton thought pantheistically, not panentheistically. He was, for instance, a determinist. And God includes suffering, according to him, in such a way that he is nonetheless perfect in a wholly absolute sense. This is not the view of Whitehead, Berdyaev, and other panentheists, who hold that the happiness of God is tinged with tragedy in such a way that the regrettable remains regrettable, even as entering into deity. This view fits with the recognition of genuine freedom and a chance or chaotic element in process springing from creative freedom as universal category.

Von Hügel is also influenced by certain historical considerations: that, as he thinks, the great Greeks, Plato, Aristotle, Plotinus, the Old Testament, even the sayings of Jesus, imply on the whole a purely joyous deity, free from suffering; and that until modern times only the Patripassionists took exception to this prevailing view, and they only in terms of an impossible sheer identification of the man Jesus with God. Thus von Hügel thinks he is in accord with the entire weight of spiritual-philosophical authority in opposing the impu-

tation of suffering to God. Hinton's pantheism is no more possible than Patripassionism; and the remaining defenders of the tragic conception of divine blessedness have too little stature to give him pause. Schelling, Fechner, Berdyaev, Whitehead, Parker, Garvie, and other panentheists of genius or systematic ability were not, of course, in his mind as he wrote the following pages.

### Against the Exclusion of Suffering from God

*141.* The chief objections against the exclusion of Suffering from God appear to be three.

(i.) Real Sympathy means Real Suffering.

Here we first require a careful distinction between suffering precedent to the sympathy, suffering of our own as necessary to make us sufficiently understand the suffering of the other man, and suffering subsequent to the sympathy—the pain, even physical but chiefly psychical, which such sympathy produces and involves. Now this latter, the subsequent Suffering, cannot be pressed with regard to the Sympathy in God, unless we are prepared to hold that what is equivalent to our emotions in God works the effects, in Him the Bodiless Spirit of Spirits, which follow for us mortals, possessed of bodies, in and through our nervous and other physical systems and influences. And, as to the preceding Suffering, it is only partially true, even of us little men, that we can possess true sympathy only in the proportion that we have actually suffered sufferings identical or similar to those which now solicit our sympathy. Father Damien sympathised, he who had never suffered leprosy, with the sufferings of the lepers more, doubtless, than the average sufferer from leprosy sympathised; and this because his imaginative faculty, his altruistic emotions and the like were so much in excess of what that average leper possessed as to counterbalance, very largely, his, Father Damien's, lack of direct experience of leprosy. How much more must this be true of God, of Him Who is omniscient; of Him Who, according to most sound theology, alone can and does directly reach the human heart and will.

(ii.) Real Personality ultimately involves systems of Emotions which organize Feelings. We claim that God is Personalistic—consists of Persons. But where is such a system in God, if God is Joy alone? But there *are* other Emotions in God, besides Joy: there is also Love, this the primary Emotion, and Delectation; and these three Emotions are evoked in Him, and are applied by Him in countless degrees, ways and combinations—from the mutual love of the Three Persons in the Godhead for each other, then through a rich hierarchy of intelligent creatures, doubtless many realms of whom are more intelligent than man, on through mankind, the animal and the plant world, indeed to all extant things whatsoever. Also there are secondary, consequential attitudes of feeling and of will which we can, which indeed we apparently must, attribute to God, and these add to the articulation of the whole emotional life of God. . . .

(iii.) "Real Personality is an achievement, through Suffering at least as much as through Joy." Yes, certainly in man, and presumably so in every finite intelligent being. But it does not at all follow that Perfect Personality is thus intrinsically successive and discursive. Indeed, the deepest aspirations and implications, the most comprehensive and permanently fruitful experiences of religious souls all, in the last instance, require or indicate not Comingness but Givenness—the Realised Ideal.

## For the Exclusion of Suffering from God

142. The objections to the presence of Suffering in God appear, indeed, to be far more fundamental and far more widely and variously operative—the acceptance of Suffering in God leads to far more doubtful or definitely deleterious results or concomitances than can, I believe, be justly urged against the denial of such Suffering.

(i.) Suffering is intrinsically an Evil. It is impossible to read much of the literature which insists upon the presence of Suffering in God, without being struck with the trend—I believe the inevitable trend, once Suffering has been admitted into God—to treat that Suffering as but a seeming Evil. The reason of this transmutation of value is plain enough, viz. that no ingenuity can long reconcile the healthy religious instinct of an ethically developed soul to the conception of a God evil be it only in part. True, even Hinton, perhaps the most relentlessly consequential, certainly the boldest of these thinkers, does not make the Unincarnate God actually a sufferer; God Unincarnate—God Who, in both His conditions, is the supreme hero, the perfect Utiliser and Transfigurer of Suffering—is able, in the Unincarnate condition, to transform, without leaving a tell-tale fragment of suffering untransfigured, to turn all what, if left alone, would make Him suffer, would show Him to suffer, into utter Joy. Indeed, Joy everywhere and of necessity—by its very nature—is, according to Hinton, *overcome* Suffering—is Pain rightly met and transfigured; hence, since he admits that God Unincarnate is actually Consummate Joy, God must have worked up the utmost material of Suffering by the utmost heroism. Yet the overpowering trend towards the negation of all intrinsic reality in Suffering is shown by numerous utterances, especially in his, Hinton's, four volumes of *Manuscripts*, which declare outright that all Pain and Suffering are sheer misunderstandings on the part of the sufferer, are wrong volitional attitudes, etc.; as also in the complete exclusion, when he is in full swing, of any complementary movement, of any motives, towards the diminution of Pain and Suffering other than through this right conception of its nature. Nothing could be more marked than the contrast between this one movement of Hinton and the two movements of Jesus. Jesus cures pain and disease as though they could not be utilised, whilst Jesus also trains and empowers souls to utilise their sufferings, as though they were incurable; Hinton, on the contrary, when at the height of his peculiar enthusiasm, appears acutely alarmed lest you should, by any curative movement, diminish the material for the utilising movement —that is to say, lest you should reduce the conditions absolutely essential to heroism, which is the only true Joy, whether in heaven or on earth, in God or in man. There is thus in this outlook, in spite of its very large element of truth and of beauty, something strained and hectic, something that Matthew Arnold, at his fine best, would readily have scented out as wanting in *centrality*.

(ii.) Suffering and Sin are, indeed, not identical, yet they are sufficiently like to make the permanent treatment of Sin as intrinsically evil exceedingly difficult where Suffering is treated as not really evil at all. Here Hinton is again most tragically instructive.

*143.* Suffering and Sin must, neither of them, be sublimated into mere subjective false notions of our own. Love, even our love for God, must remain, and we must continue to desire it to remain, a *mutual* give and take. And Self-Love, Self-Regard, must be estimated an evil, not directly according as it is, or is not, a love of any Being for himself, but according as the self

of such a Being deserves, or does not deserve, such love. Hence, however little we may be able to picture God's love for Himself, in a humanly attractive way, we will not and cannot cease to hold that these our human words involve a profound, all-decisive truth. We will, thus at the very source, escape the feverish movement so all-pervasive of Hinton, and will not turn all Being into Becoming, nor measure all things by Process never by Product. Indeed, God will be apprehended, loved and served by us neither as Process nor as Product, but as overflowing Being, as Perfect Reality, as the Real Ideal. "In His Will"—in His Nature and Being as they already are, as they ever have been, not in any Becoming of Him, but in the Being of Him—"in His Will is our peace."

(iii.) Liberty exists in various kinds, and the Perfect kind—Perfect Liberty —excludes Choice. This is a position which practically all the most recent Broad High Church literature has, alongside of many a wise insight, most unhappily denied. William Temple, . . . Walter H. Moberley, and with these fine minds scores of lesser lights, have insisted that the possibility of Evil is involved in the very nature of all Freedom; and hence that our very nobility, as free willing beings, involves our possible baseness. The reasons for the prevalence of this view are, doubtless, apologetic; for, given this doctrine to be true, the problem of Evil is greatly simplified: Evil then becomes the reverse of the shield of Good according to the very nature of things—a nature which, Aquinas has already clearly taught us, cannot be contradicted even by God Himself. We can thus have Good and Evil (at least potential Evil), or we can have neither; but we cannot have one without the other. And, indeed, there certainly exist some clerics —not any that I have named—who do not shrink in conversation from finding, not only Suffering, but also Sin potentially in God, precisely because He is the Supreme Liberty and Supreme Goodness.

Yet we have here a very certainly erroneous doctrine. St. Augustine already finely formulates the real truth in this matter: "It is indeed a great liberty to be able not to sin; but the greatest liberty is to be unable to sin."

144. (iv.) The conviction of the Otherness of God is, in the long run, as essential to full, powerful religion as any and all conviction of the Likeness of God. Belief in Suffering in God is generally commended to us as necessary if we are really to feel God like unto us, if for our feeling He is truly to be our Father, indeed more or less our elder Brother. For not only our average toil and doing, but especially our highest ethical and spiritual achievements, appear to be essentially bound up with Suffering—Suffering heroically borne or heroically overcome, yet still Suffering. Is God, then, to be so different from man as to be less than man? God is Love, is He not? Is His Love, then, to be but nominal? At least, to be less costly, hence less heroic, hence again less sublimely good, than is our own? "He who did most, shall bear most": would not God thus alone be a worthy leader? Heroism would thus be overflowingly in God and be but poorly imitated by us mortals even at our best. Browning has, of course, magnificently presented the case for this view. And, indeed, this view cannot be all false if the Christian doctrine of the Incarnation be true, which insists upon genuine, indeed immense, Suffering within one of the two natures of the one Person, Christ, Himself the fullest revelation of God vouchsafed to man.

Nevertheless I find it impossible to believe, I will not say in the falsehood, but even in any permanent unattractiveness, of the doctrine that there is no Suffering in God, as such. Sympathy, yes, indeed, overflowing Sympathy—a Sympathy which we cannot succeed in picturing vividly without drawing upon our own experiences of ourselves, where sympathy and suffering are so closely intertwined; but no Suffering in God; and Suffering, indeed overflowing suffering in Christ, but as Man, not as God. Surely, poets, even the deepest poets, require not seldom some discounting of their more enthusiastic views, by philosophers and theologians; the correction of Browning here suggested would be a relatively small one.

With the two admissions—proclamations—of Sympathy in God and Suffering in Christ, we can, and I suggest we should, retain ample food for the other, I submit still more fundamental need and implication of the deepest religious thought and religious emotion, of Pure Joy, which would continue to attach to God as such.

(v.) And, finally, Religion itself requires the Transcendence of God in a form and a degree which exclude Suffering in Him. . . . The religious sense . . . must be allowed to press on to, to be moved and fully satisfied only by the Ultimate, the Absolute. This Absolute, however, is not conceived, or indirectly experienced by, such Religion, Plotinus-like, as without interiority—without richness or articulation, as above all Beauty, Truth and Goodness; but as overflowing with a life articulated within Itself—a life which, indeed, freely willed Creation, a Creation whose joy indeed adds to Its Joy, yet which in Itself, apart from such Creation, is full of Joy.

145. Let me then conclude with a statement, as inclusive, precise and yet short as I can make it, with regard to the problem of Suffering and God.

146. We experience things as contingent, as partial, as successive, as causes, as effects—especially as contingent. Yes: but we do so experience them, because the things directly ex-

perienced wake up in us the "ideas" of the Absolute, the Whole, the Simultaneous, the Uncaused, the Uneffected.

*147.* . . . against the foreground of our little frail and mixed love and joy and delectation, our small beginnings towards the fullness of spiritual being, their contrast, and by their contrast light up and give their poignant meaning to, this littleness, frailty and mixedness of our love, joy and delectation, Perfect Love, Unmixed Joy, Entire Delectation. It is quite plain and entirely certain that were man a purely changeful, transitory, contingent, rootless and accidental being, he could never know he was such, still less could he suffer, as he most certainly does suffer, from the very thought that he possibly may be only such. The Contrasting Other is real and certain—more real, richer far in reality, and quite as certain as the contingents felt to be such, since it is that Contrasting Other which gives them, for our mind and feeling, that pathetic and utterly unsatisfying character of contingency.

Now God is that Perfect Love, Unmixed Joy, Entire Delectation. He is all this, not as a bundle of separate qualities, however consummate each quality may be, but as a living, spiritual, Personalist Reality, Who Himself is all this overflowingly. I believe this to be a true account of the fundamental religious experience and apprehension. But if so, we will not admit the presence of any Evil, be it Sin or even only Sorrow, be they actual or even only potential, in Him Who thus dwarfs for us all our little human goodness and earthly joy by His utter Sanctity and sheer Beatitude. And all this Goodness and Joy God does not become, does not acquire: He simply *is* it. We will be watchful against the blurring over of the contrast between our self, as experienced by us, and other, contingent things, always experienced by us at the time: those

things and we are not identical, never were and never will be. How much more, then, will we be on our guard against any real blurring of the contrast between God and ourselves. His Otherness is as essential a part of the facts and of the power of religion as His Likeness can ever be. True, God is full of loving care for us, His creatures; He knows us each and singly in all our particularity, and can and does help us to become more like unto Himself. But this Sympathy is not Suffering; and, again, we never will, indeed never can, become really identical with Him. He has allowed real, direct Suffering to come as close to Him, in the humanity of Christ, as, in the nature of things, Suffering could come. Let us be wise and sober, and rest satisfied with that deep Sympathy in God and this deep Suffering in Christ.

*148.* We will, indeed, utilise all the suffering which may come to us in atonement for Sin and for the attainment of Joy; but we will not strain the facts of life into revealing, as the cause of all suffering, the provision of occasions for heroism and heroic joy. Still less will we find the possibility of Evil to spring directly from Liberty as such. On the contrary, we will adore in God the Perfect Liberty which spontaneously and joyously always wills alone its own Perfect Nature. We will thus rest content with an outlook, obscure and fragmentary in parts, but with tracts of glorious richness, variety, drama and tension, the whole lit up, sustained and vitalised by a continuously renewed conviction of the Perfect Goodness, the Pure Joy of God.

I began with a short anecdote from the life of the bee; let me end with a longer anecdote from my own personal experience. . . . I give this experience because it may help to light up the general position of this address with a homely, human radiance, and because it proves at least this much—that the vivid conviction of the Pure Joy of God is as capable now as in the days of Dante, of St. Francis, of St. Bernard, of St. Augustine, of St. Paul, and of Jesus Himself, to steady and subdue, to saturate and to satisfy our restless hearts and utterly exacting spirits.

It was on a Good Friday forenoon in Rome, I think in 1899, that I woke up with the sunshine streaming into my bedroom—I had somehow not been called by any of my people or of the domestics. Although I hurried through my toilet and through my breakfast, it was turned eleven o'clock when I reached the nearest church—all the service already over and the doors locked. I tried two other churches—the same result. Sad and lonely, empty-headed and dreary-hearted, I turned into the Villa Borghese, and there, in an ugly, newly-planted, still very shadeless tryst, with much sand about and an already baking sun, I sat down on the ground and relieved my aching back by leaning against one of the young trees. Many green lizards were soon frisking close around me—otherwise nothing living was to be seen or heard. I sat there thus—I suppose for half an hour or more—dull and dead, conscious of nothing but myself, so I felt; of that mass of failures, disappointments, pettinesses, with a dim background, though, of men at large hardly more inviting or inspiring than myself. And all this then articulated itself into special grievances and antipathies: Churchmen and Agnostics, Jews and Protestants, also such souls amongst them all as were dear to me at other times—all seemed empty, irritating, oppressive. And then—I know of no transition or connection—then—well, suddenly, ah, another, in very truth another outlook, an utterly other state wrapped me round. I felt—I seemed to see—now without any straining, without apparently any action of my own—one great, tender goodness and heroism pass before me after the

other—the souls which, in this "eternal" Rome, had meekly suffered and had manfully agonised for God; also thinkers, and men of action, seekers after God. There were Peter and Paul, Cæcilia and Agnes of the Catacombs, Rabbi Akiba dying a witness to God in the great Circus, Marcus Aurelius lonely on his throne, Plotinus uttering winged words to his students, Augustine now growing utterly weary and restless under his sins, so near to his utter renunciation of them, and so on and on, with many another figure long dear to me. And all of them were marked by Suffering—and more or less marred by Sin. But then, behind and above all these, appeared the Master of Masters, Suffering Love gently, pathetically triumphant—Jesus Christ, Our Lord, on this the day of His utter Passion. And yet, somehow, even this, especially this utter woe, this day of that woe, they seem best expressed just simply as Good —as "Good" Friday, better than in the Italian or French or German "Holy" and the like. For was it not *good*, supremely *good* for us? Wholesome, fruitful, renovating, all-transfiguring? The Suffering, even here, was certainly an evil, but then its utilisation, how good that was! And besides, here, no Sin! Somehow here the intense Suffering led on to Joy—to the infinite Good that had sprung from this infinite Sorrow. And, then, came the final state of soul and outlook: God, God in Himself. And here, in contrast with the first outlook, where fellow-creatures had appeared so largely suffering and so truly sinful, and even in contrast with the second outlook, where Jesus Christ had appeared, sinless indeed and Joy-bringing, yet also bowed down with suffering, appeared Joy, pure Joy, an Ocean of it, unplumbed, unplumbable, with not one drop of Evil within it—not one drop of Sin or Suffering or of the possibility of either. And I did not want it otherwise—far, far from it! God was too much our Friend, for us not to re-joice that He does not suffer; and this Joy of God is too much our sustenance, it too much shows us, contrastingly, our indigence, a sight of ourselves which constitutes our specific dignity, for me, for any of those great lovers of His, to wish His Joy mixed or limited or conditional. And yet this Pure Joy was utterly compassionate, utterly sympathetic; It bent down to, It entered into, the hearts of those great little ones; It was, indeed, at work all around me at that moment. What else, in the last resort, made those dear little emerald lizards so happy there, close to my feet? And then all ended with my receiving a happy impression that all the dreariness, which had preceded all this happiness, that that too, that it, especially for me just then, had already been an effect of that contrasting Joy of God, or rather of my very dim but real apprehension of that Joy.

For indeed dreary and petty, oppressive and imprisoning, is our poor little life, on its surface and apart from God and from His merciful condescensions towards us. But we would not know our misery, we would not feel it as such, were there not Saints and Heroes around us, and Christ our Lord above us, and, encompassing all and penetrating all, God—not a Sufferer, but indeed the Sympathiser, God Joy, the Ocean of Joy, our Home.

[Sec. 141, Baron Friedrich von Hügel, *Essays and Addresses on the Philosophy of Religion, Second Series* (New York: E. P. Dutton & Co., 1926), pp. 197–99. Sec. 142, *ibid.*, pp. 199–200. Sec. 143, *ibid.*, pp. 202–3. Sec. 144, *ibid.*, pp. 204–6. Sec. 145, *ibid.*, p. 207. Sec. 146, *ibid.*, pp. 207–8. Sec. 147, *ibid.*, pp. 208–9. Sec. 148, *ibid.*, pp. 210–13.]

### COMMENT

To deal critically with such noble eloquence is a forbidding task! Let us consider first the author's conception of the arguments for the inclusion of Suffering in deity. He admits (without including this in his list of arguments) that there is a human longing for a Fellow-Sufferer, one who shares our human sorrows, but he thinks this is furnished by Christ in his human aspect. However, we reply, Christ as human sufferer would only be one more of us; his sufferings might be nobler, more disinterested, but they could involve no *adequate* sympathy with *our* sorrows—for surely Christ as human is not omniscient! He knows our feelings, if at all, only in the radically inadequate way in which we know each other's feelings, by perception and inference and imagination, all based on a slender little round of experiences. This has nothing to do with the idea of an *adequate* or divine sharing of our sufferings.

What unwittingly results from von Hügel's historical remarks about Patripassionism, or the famous heresy which imputed suffering to God the Father, is that the issue of suffering in God was not discussed on its merits but only as bound up with the quite different issue of whether Jesus had one nature or two. The sufferings of Christ the man could not in any case have been divine sufferings, for they were not adequate or omnisciently sympathetic sufferings. Or, if they were, then there is no meaning in calling Christ "man."

1. Real sympathy means real suffering. But, says the author, not necessarily; even we men can possess true sympathy without having suffered the feelings which elicit our sympathy. Thus a nonsufferer from leprosy may sympathize with lepers more than the lepers with each other. Certainly. But the argument to be refuted is not that, if God is to share our sorrow over the loss of a limb, he must have arms and legs of his own. The argument is that sympathy, in its ideally concrete and adequate form, just is the full possession of the very feelings of the other. Father

Damien comes closer to this than a fellow-leper might, for the fellow-leper may be shut up in his own feelings. In imagination (the word is von Hügel's) Damien builds up in his mind something of a picture of how the other feels and reacts to this as to the feeling of another. But this is defective, indirect, inadequate, merely human sympathy; and obviously it depends upon Damien's having some images of suffering from his own past experiences. Adequate sympathy would go directly to the very sufferings of the other and feel them as sufferings. This would be sympathetic suffering. There seems nothing in the example that does not agree with the doctrine the author is combating.

2. God must have a system of emotions, including suffering, if he is a person. The author, however, feels that suffering may be omitted from such a system. But (we reply) there must be some way of realizing the contrast between good and evil. A being with only joy would be one to whom nothing would in any sense come amiss, who could not care what anyone did or endured. The divine "displeasure" would have not even a metaphorical meaning. And, again, we fail to see what the divine sympathy would be.

3. Personality is achieved through suffering no less than through joy. The author replies: The supreme personality would not be thus achieved. Personality, we should think, consists in part in a capacity to share the sorrows as well as the joys of others. Sympathetic suffering is no mere stepping stone; it is an element in the highest achievement or form of personality, most of all in God, who alone can be the adequate instance of such vicarious suffering. We human beings must protect ourselves from too much sharing in the sorrows of our fellows, lest we be depressed and overwhelmed. We cannot share, except slightly, in the joys of others; so naturally we cannot afford to get too much infected with their pains. Only God can balance full sharing in the one with full sharing in the other.

Let us consider the author's own arguments for the orthodox exclusion of suffering from deity.

1. Since God is supremely good, if there be suffering in God, it cannot really be an evil but must be good mistakenly taken for an evil. Answer: The supreme value need not be made supreme by the absence from it of all evil but by the incomparable way in which good overbalances evil. Absence of evil is a negative criterion of good, and positive criteria are alone ultimate. Mere insentience would be absolute guaranty of absence of suffering but would be no good at all. By the negative criterion a contented oyster can hardly be equaled by any man. It is the presence of joy, not the absence of pain, that measures value. (Of course, the pain must not be such as to exclude joy.) But, further, the perfection of deity, in its concrete aspect, is according to our view no absolute maximum that could not be increased and could not have been superior. The divine state is not the best possible state for deity, but rather it is incomparably better than any possible state of any nondivine being. According to this view, there is no necessity to "justify" suffering as needful to the maximum good in God. No such maximum is attainable, and the very idea of it is a confusion, the confusion or contradiction of an exhaustion of the inexhaustible potentialities of value. Thus the tragic element in God means that one can never say, even of him, that his joy could not have been greater. A maximal joy is nonsense. Hence tragic missing of opportunities is no mere illusion, in final perspective, and that is exactly why it is worth while to try not to miss opportunities. Even God has a stake in this; indeed, his stake measures the

real stake we all have in it, for omniscience is the measure of all things, and the divine valuation the measure of all value.

2. If, says the author, we admit suffering, a form of evil, in God, we open the way to the vicious notion that God is not immune to other forms of evil, say, of wickedness. And then we shall go on to say that wickedness, too, is not really an evil. Answer: All forms of evil are indeed in God, as is all reality; but to have wickedness "in" one is not the same as "being wicked." Properties of parts are not necessarily in the same sense properties of their wholes. And in no sense at all do they inhere in the essential "whole-quality" which dipolar theism distinguishes from accidental whole-states. But, further, wickedness is a partly negative quality, and it is negative in just the way in which the all-inclusive being cannot be negative, but only certain included beings. Wickedness is essentially exclusion, exclusion of the interests of others from our purview and responsive appreciation. Suffering, on the contrary, is not essentially exclusion; and the incomparable scope of the divine suffering is due entirely to the inclusiveness of the divine interest and feeling, to its absolutely all-embracing sympathy with creaturely sufferings. The love which cannot immunize itself to our sufferings equally cannot have any purpose which fails to give all interests their due place, and this means that it cannot be wicked.

3. In man there is freedom between good and bad acts; in God there is only the capacity for good acts; but those who posit suffering in God tend to impute to him also the capacity to sin. There seems here to be no argument save that *ad hominem*. And the chief expositors of panentheism are not touched by this reasoning, for they (thus Fechner, Whitehead, Montague, Parker) do not impute a liberty as between good and evil to God. The freedom of God according to panentheism (see our "Comment" on Leibniz) is as between good and good, not between good and evil, or even between better and worse. (It is worth mentioning again that Hinton was a determinist, which means he was a pantheist, not a panentheist. That he tended to "justify" evils as necessary to the good is due primarily, one suspects, to this determinism, this denial of acidents to reality and to God.) Liberty is the source of suffering because harmony between free beings is more or less at the mercy of chance, even if they are not wicked in their intentions. The liberty of creativeness, which is the source of all value, involves the inevitability of an element of chaos. This has nothing to do with a capacity of God to sin.

4. The otherness of God is as essential to religion as his likeness to man; and this otherness includes his inability to suffer, while the likeness is satisfied by a divine sympathy which is free from suffering. Answer: The suffering of God is just as unlike human suffering as is his joy unlike human joy. God enjoys and suffers through direct and adequate sympathy with all things; we enjoy and suffer through direct (but inadequate) sympathy with a few things, especially with constituents of our own bodies. Hence we can use most things as means, in terms of their effects upon the few things we really directly care about. But God can use nothing as mere means, and the least sorrows of the least creature are vividly felt by him. So are the least pleasures of the least creature. Not even with his best friend in his best moments has man any such relation. Divine sympathy whether with joy or with sorrow is then equally incomparable to human sympathy. In the second aspect, however, it tinges the divine experience with suffering.

5. The transcendence or absoluteness

of God excludes suffering. It is notable how vague and uncertain is the author's language here. He seems to compromise his classical theism by admitting (in passages not quoted) self-limitation in God, implying a relative as well as an absolute divine nature. And he has no intelligible doctrine of how the unlimited and the self-limited coexist in one being. The absolute deity (he implies) is the whole, the all-inclusive (yet it is exclusive of all suffering experience —quite a qualification!). At the same time, it is the uneffected, that is, it contains nothing that is an effect. Again, how then does it include everything? The limited God is in the unlimited God; but the world is not. So there is a greater being even than the unlimited God, namely, the limited world *and* the unlimited God together. Such confusions seem inevitable until we accept surrelativism, the insight that the ultimate relativity includes the absolute as an abstract aspect of itself. But then the "absolute" in the form of joy is not a complete concrete value but an element in all value. God primordially and forever enjoys the vision of his own necessary essence, the fixed and absolute element in his experience. This element is absolutely perfect, the contemplation of it yields a satisfaction that is untarnished, in the sense that it is all that the enjoyment of anything abstract could possibly be. The absolute adequacy of all God's relations, actual or possible, to creatures, is the "Real Ideal" of adequacy. This indeed is a divine value that does not become but simply is. But the author fails to show that an absolute value or joy in any more concrete sense is required or meaningful. True, a supreme joy, incomparably richer than ours, we do need to feel is in God, and, as the author says, it is our sense of this that makes our own lives seem by themselves insufficient. But a supreme joy, measured positively, need not be an absolute joy, measured negatively—in terms of nonsuffering. It is not an absolute at all but a surrelative.

The author's persuasive suggestion that God is too much our friend for us not to rejoice that he does not suffer seems his strongest argument. But is it not something positive we wish for our friends, richness of experience, not just contentedness, absence of all sorrow and sadness? If God *could* have all the richness of the world without its suffering—but this is a contradiction in terms. This world is not abstractable from its sufferings. And any possible world would have some sufferings or other. If God accepts relation to the creatures, then his actuality is qualified by them. And to wish freedom from suffering to God is to wish ignorance to him, as we have seen. We should then condescend to him as we do to an innocent child who does not know the misery of the world.

Concerning von Hügel's appeal (not included in our text) to Plato, the Prophets, and Jesus, we may observe that the way to think about God need not have been rightly grasped and clearly expressed by our ancestors. Moreover, it is reasonable to think that any tragic aspect of deity would be longest overlooked or wrongly denied. For men seek to escape tragedy, even the thought of it. By positing immunity to suffering in their God, they gain a sense of vicarious escape from it for themselves.

There is a way of interpreting Christianity that is not the historical form of Patripassionism at all, and is just as little Hinton's pantheism, which would make Christianity truly a religion of tragic divinity. This is the view that Jesus as loving and altruistically suffering human being is, not indeed God, but yet a supreme symbol of deity. Jesus made no effort to immunize himself to suffering. He tried to alleviate the suffering of others. But he put himself at the center of human suffering, opened himself to it in more ways than other men. This suggests that God is the being with absolute *non*immunity or openness, not absolute immunity, to suffering (save in the above-mentioned abstract element of his experience). Jesus is the man who deliberately and effectively embodies in his life the conviction that it is nobler and more Godlike to share the suffering of others (where these cannot be eliminated) than to escape into mere private joy. The Cross is thus the symbol of sympathetically suffering divinity, even though Jesus' sympathetic suffering is by no means the same as God's.

This more modest Christology, not a more extreme one, as was Patripassionism, seems the Christian way to

the theistic version of a "tragic view of life." With this modesty goes the recognition that we cannot tell a priori how much of what Jesus felt and embodied in his life, or of what can be learned by us from that life, or otherwise, must also have been uttered in his sayings, recorded or even not recorded. A philosophy which seeks for light everywhere, and especially in the Christian records, thus need not be deterred by the eloquence and learning of the author quoted in this section from worshiping God as the being who, infinitely more literally than any man, feels the sorrows and pains of other persons than himself, vicariously suffers them: for all that, preserving in himself always an enjoyment of an absolute, though not concrete perfection—his own contemplated essence.

## Appendix to Chapter III: *Mysticism and Classical Theism*

Associated with classical theism, Christian, Jewish, and Mohammedan, there have been numerous "mystical" doctrines. Perhaps on the whole these have been rather pantheistic than panentheistic, but often strong panentheistic motifs appear. The famous mystical saying, "Without me God cannot live an instant," is pantheistic, taken as it stands. For it says that the creatures are contained in the very essence of God, and panentheism denies this. If one supposes that the meaning is, "Creature as such, some creatures or other, are essential to God, but not just this or that creature," then the meaning is panentheistic or dipolar. Panentheism holds that we are accidents in God, and thus it is equally opposed to the classical, "there are no accidents in God but accidental realities outside him," and the pantheistic, "Nothing is accidental but all is in God as essential to him." Or, in other terms, panentheism conceives process, becoming, as real in God; classical theism as real outside God; and pantheism as somehow unreal but, in so far as real, in God. Now some mystics in their cloudy and often fantastically fan-

ciful language do seem closer to panentheism than to any other clearly defined doctrine.

Much Jewish mysticism comes under this head.[5] Often it is said that God is all-inclusive, the whole of things. Over and over it is indicated that there is real process and becoming, often dramatically conceived, in God and of God, a theogony, in some sense or other. Moreover, we contribute to this divine development by our own decisions. God is not just first cause but also supreme "effect." He is not merely active but passive. Symbolic of this is the idea that his highest emanation or Shekkina is feminine and that the goal of the divine-cosmic process is a sort of marriage of the Original Godhead (*En-sof*) with his Shekkina. Human marriage is a sacramental symbol of the divine union. In all this it is not very difficult, and not necessarily far fetched, to see a highly poetic, often highly fanciful, recognition of just

5. Gershom Scholem, *Major Trends in Jewish Mysticism* (New York: Schocken Books, 1941).

the factors in God which monopolarity refuses to allow, and for which dipolarity furnishes the logic. Lacking this logic, the mystics had no guide in their voyage through the deeps of intuition, just as their scholarly interpreter had no guide in his criticism of them. He gently queries their notions and suggests that they must have some aspect of truth which the professors of theology have missed and that what is required is to find this truth without departing from monotheism. If monotheism means classical theism and the rejection of panentheism, then the suggested search may as well be omitted. It is precisely monotheism, at least in this classical sense, that omits the religious values the mystics seek to express. Professor Scholem, in the course of his valuable work, says that the idea of a process in God has always involved those who have held it in the most complicated difficulties. He omits to mention the contradictions (perhaps simpler indeed than difficulties!) in which classical theism has always been involved! He mentions no alternative to classical theism but the sterile one of pantheism and thus perpetually seems to imply that the mystics are searching where there is nothing to find. He himself searches, one could scarcely say hopefully, among the superstitions of the mystics to find some wisdom or other, when the only wisdom that could well be there would be one that revealed an element of superstition in the seemingly so dry, orthodox, sober, and scholarly traditional theism! We refer to the superstition of etiolatry or ontolatry.

As Scholem well says, Jacob Boehme is close kin to the Jewish mystics. And certainly he goes a good way toward defining a dipolar theology. We have omitted him because of the obscurity of his language and because Schelling and Berdyaev seem to us to have appropriated what is of value in the earlier author. For example, Boehme in one passage speaks of God as changing or in time, and in another he seems to deny this. Berdyaev's doctrine of disintegrated or creaturely and integrated or divine time seems superior.

Where the mystic (for instance, one of the Sufis) says that he and God are the same, he falls into pantheism, not panentheism. For the latter, we are accidents of God but never his essence and never the whole of any of his accidental states; so in no sense, it seems, can a panentheist say that he is identical with God. Of course he is not outside God (but completely outside his essence); however, "not outside of" and "identical with" are far from synonymous.

A difficult question is how to classify the system of John the Scot. His notion of all things as existing in the medium of divine knowledge and of the reception or absorption of all things into God is either pantheism or panentheism, but which? There seems to be no clear recognition of genuine novelty and of contingency as such in deity. And does "God will be everything in everything when there is nothing but God alone" mean the preservation of our actual history in God or its relegation to unreality as such?

# Chapter IV: *Classical Pantheism*

## THE STOICS; ASVAGHOSHA (THIRD CENTURY B.C.; FIRST CENTURY A.D.)

It may with some plausiblity be maintained that the earliest philosophy which functioned as a religion was a form of pantheism. For Stoicism belongs on the whole under the pantheistic label. In the present book this label is the name of a paradox, the paradox that the unchanging and wholly necessary contains whatever is real in change and the contingent. This is a paradox—for how can the immutable have mutable beings as its constituents, the unmodifiable have "modes" or "modifications," the absolute yet contain all relations and relativity? Hence it is inevitable that every pantheist should seek in some way to soften the difficulty.

The softening takes one of three forms: one admits, more or less unclearly and implicitly, that deity or the supreme reality is not strictly unchanging and devoid of contingency; one admits, with similar vagueness or ambiguity, that the world of changing things is not strictly constituent of deity; or, finally, one denies, sometimes openly, that there *is* change and chance anywhere, whether in God or outside of him. All three ambiguities or equivocations are in Stoicism. God is the universal fire, warm fluid, or ether, which is also universal mind or reason; and this vaguely conceived Something both does and does not include all things. It is said to penetrate all things; at certain cosmic epochs it reabsorbs them all into itself. And, besides, things, so far as distinguished from it at all, are the body of which it is the soul, and if by God one means the soul-body, then God certainly includes all things. But the unity of soul and body is so vague in this doc-

trine that our charge of ambiguity is justified. Again, is God unchanging? Yes, no, and neither in a very clear sense. It seems that fire or a fluid or ether is not strictly immutable, to say the least. But the change thus implied is radically attenuated by the sharp denial of contingency, of novelty, except in the Pickwickian sense of something already defined in advance and a mere foregone conclusion. The famous determinism of the Stoics was perhaps the clearest and most emphatic of all their metaphysical tenets, and it meant that all events to the last detail are fixed in advance by the universal law, expressive of the reign of universal Reason; and to make this really plain we are told that all events precisely recur over and over forever through successive cosmic epochs. Thus change is admitted provisionally, only to be reduced to illusion from the final perspective. There is a detailed complete pattern of all events which does not become but eternally is. By this doctrine, one softens the clash between the change obvious in the world and the pantheistic tendency to deny change to the supreme, all-inclusive reality. The supreme changes but in trivial fashion (or self-contradictorily; for an exact recurrence is not a different event, is not a recurrence), and, by the same token, the world which is included in God (ambiguously, or via the unclarified soul-body duality of deity) is less mutable than it appears to be.

With so much ambiguity, it is not surprising that the Stoic ethic and religion was too formless to be really effective. The formlessness is distressingly manifest in the *Meditations* of Marcus Aurelius. Are we to be glad or sorry that all things are integral to God—yet not quite integral to him? Are we to be ascetics or live a full life, seeing that all things physical form the body of deity, which yet as mind or soul seems to derive no special value from this body, destroying it from time to time, and then futilely starting over again to build just the same body? Are we to think of the universal Law as providential, or as expressive of fondness for the creatures, or else rather as indifferent and neutral, seeing that it is unbending and rigid and that it produces vast sufferings as well as joys? And what does it mean to preach ethics to beings which, preached to or not, could not deviate in the slightest from the one eternal Plan? If it be said that the preaching itself, wherever it occurs, must be part of the Plan, the difficulty is that this only means that the idea of the Plan is useless to us. It only tells us afterward what was in accord with the divine will. If one neglects to preach, this too will prove to have been in accord with the Plan. This is the futility of all absolute determinisms. They become relevant only too late. Stoicism as a practiced philosophical religion was not likely to last many centuries with such handicaps.

Only in the Orient did pantheism become anything like the pervasive spiritual philosophy of a culture. Here it achieved a more definite and refined character, able to give more vivid guidance to aspiration. It did this by making still more one-sided the asceticism, the antinaturalism and abstractionism, common to all pantheisms. If all the physical world of striving and novel achievements is in God, but yet for God there is to be no novelty and (for nearly all pantheists except Parmenides and Spinoza) no spatial diversity, then one way to soften the conflict between the assertion and the denial is to attenuate the notion of the physical and temporal side of existence. What can this mean, if not asceticism, and that not simply in the sense of renouncing sensory pleasures but also in the sense of regarding as trivial all questions of social reform or of coming to the aid of other individuals? For only in space-time are there other individuals—at least, those we are able to assist—and yet the attenuation of physical diversity can be carried through rigorously (if at all) only by regarding all diversity of individuals and all change in their fortunes as somehow irrelevant, "unreal," or secondary. The word for this attenuation is "maya." It is not surprising that any account by an outsider of the meaning of this word is rejected. Of course it is, since it is the name for the solution of an insoluble problem. Besides, how can one who has not had the supreme realization of actualized attenuation, union with the wholly undiversified Brahman, know what the name for this union means?

It is sometimes said that "acosmism" is a better term for Brahmanism than pantheism. But acosmism, the denial of the cosmos, has its motivation in the two pantheistic tenets: God is all reality and God does not change or contain diversity. From this it follows that reality does not change or contain diversity. This is monopolarity in naked form. Whereas classical theists permit the categorical pole which is held inapplicable to deity to qualify a sphere of the real that is "outside" deity, the pantheists are in a sense even more extreme, since they refuse any application for the inferior pole; or, rather, they identify the contrast, superior-inferior, interpreted in monopolar fashion as invidious, with real-unreal.

There seems to be some difference between most European and most Indian pantheism in respect to the attitude toward space as distinguished from time. In one of the earliest pantheistic views, that of Parmenides, we find him describing his unchanging Being as a sphere.

It is spatial, though not temporal. (His argument: "being" cannot change, for it could only become "not-being"; and there can be no such thing as not being. The fallacy: to be, in general, means, to be something, this *or* that; real change or succession, and with succession time, requires only that first something should be this, and then a subsequent something should be that; both will be, in the generic sense, but they will not be the same specific beings.)

The Stoics, of course, do not deny the spatial character of reality, though their eternal recurrence is a somewhat equivocal denial of real process; and they are followed by Spinoza in this, inasmuch as he ascribes extension but not duration to deity. The Brahmans, however, with admirable rigor, set up the goal of transcending all diversity whatever and the entirety of natural things, that is to say, of finding them unreal, as not the Reality which alone is worth knowing. Now this may explain the apparent fact that determinism is less in evidence, at least in so sharp and clear a form. For if there is no real plurality of things, there is no great point in insisting upon their subjection to absolute causation. Yet here too a strong deterministic trend is present. The Law of Karma, less exact apparently than the Stoic network of divine causation, or more restricted to moral matters, having less to do with the course of "inorganic" nature, is one of the great dogmas of nearly all Hindu thought. This, too, is a symptom of the grand attenuation of time inherent in pantheism. It may have been ages ago that the individual committed his misdeed, but it still follows him and powerfully affects his life. He still is that individual; this illustrates the priority of being over becoming assumed throughout.

However, for the Brahman, the genuine Reality is entirely beyond Karma and all cycles. It does not become but is. For it is "nondifferent"; there is no this and that, now and then, you and I, but just Brahman in no way different from himself or from his worshiper either. Brahman is nothing physical, for that always posits spatiotemporal differences. It is the pure self, without differentiated objects or actions, consciousness not contrasted to any content of consciousness. Whatever is real in things is one with this Something; whatever is in any way different from it is unreal.

From the standpoint of value, what the view comes to is this. One sets aside the love of concrete individuals, and their ever varying differences and contrasts, in favor of the steady white light (or darkness) of eternal unity. This unity "includes" all things only by suppressing all their determinate qualities. Now the procedure is not without its use. For interest in the concrete and individual exposes us to innumerable anxieties and conflicts, to all the tragedy of life. There is real need to steady ourselves by some fixed love, by delight in some factor common to all changes and all differences, and hence indestructible. Then there is a limit set to our fluctuations and momentary sufferings, an inner citadel from which we cannot be driven, a light which always illumines our way.

An early expression of this manner of thinking is Asvaghosha's doctrine of "Suchness." Asvaghosha (*ca.* A.D. 100) was a follower of Buddha who, by his strong monistic and metaphysical bent, contributed (according to some authorities) to the rise of the form of Buddhism known as the Mahayana.

In the following statements our author appears almost to affirm a panentheistic position. There are two aspects of deity: a unitary, absolute immutable aspect and an aspect of multiformity, relativity, and change. But we are told that the second aspect is an illusion of ignorance or unenlightenment and that the world of changing and spatially extended phenomena is "without any reality." Thus Asvaghosha seems on the whole definitely to choose the pantheistic alternative and to anticipate the austere monism of Sankara.

### Suchness, or the Soul as All Things

149. In the one soul we may distinguish two aspects. The one is the soul as suchness, the other is the soul as birth-and-death. Each in itself constitutes all things, and both are so closely interrelated that one cannot be separated from the other.

What is meant by the soul as suchness, is the oneness of the totality of things, the great all-including whole, the quintessence of the Doctrine. For the essential nature of the soul is uncreate and eternal.

All things, simply on account of our confused subjectivity, appear under the forms of individuation. If we could overcome our confused subjectivity, the signs of individuation would disappear, and there would be no trace of a world of (individual and isolated) objects.

Therefore all things in their fundamental nature are not namable or explicable. They cannot be adequately expressed in any form of language. They are without the range of apperception. They (things in their fundamental nature) have no signs of distinction. They possess absolute sameness. They are subject neither to transformation, nor to destruction. They are nothing but the one soul, for which suchness is another designation. Therefore they cannot be (fully) explained by words or exhausted by reasoning.

150. The soul as birth-and-death comes forth (as the law of causation) from the Tathâgata's womb. But the immortal (i.e., suchness) and the mortal (i.e., birth-and-death) coincide with each other. Though they are not identical, they are not a duality. (Thus when the absolute soul assumes a relative aspect by its self-affirmation) it is called the all-conserving mind.

The same mind has a twofold significance as the organiser and the producer of all things.

Again it embraces two principles: (1) Enlightenment; (2) Nonenlightenment.

Enlightenment is the highest quality of the mind; it is free from all (the limiting) attributes of subjectivity. As it is free from all (limiting) attributes of subjectivity, it is like unto space, penetrating everywhere, as the unity of all.

151. The multitude of people are said to be lacking in enlightenment, because ignorance prevails there from all eternity, because there is a constant succession of confused subjective states from which they have never been emancipated.

But when they transcend their subjectivity, they can then recognise that all states of mentation, viz., their appearance, presence, change, and disappearance (in the field of consciousness) have no (genuine) reality. They are neither in a temporal nor in a spatial relation with the one soul, for they are not self-existent.

152. Though all modes of consciousness and mentation are mere products of ignorance, ignorance in its ultimate nature is identical and not-identical with enlightenment a priori; and therefore ignorance in one sense is destructible, while in the other sense it is indestructible.

This may be illustrated by (the simile of) the water and the waves which are stirred up in the ocean. Here the water can be said to be identical (in one sense) and not-identical (in the other sense) with the waves. The waves are stirred up by the wind, but the water remains the same. When the wind ceases, the motion of the waves subsides; but the water remains the same.

Likewise, when the mind of all creatures which in its own nature is pure and clean, is stirred up by the wind of ignorance, the waves of mentality make their appearance. These three (i.e., the mind, ignorance, and mentality), however, have no (absolute) existence, and they are neither unity nor plurality.

But the mind though pure in its essence is the source of the awakened (or disturbed) mentality. When ignorance is annihilated, the awakened mentality is tranquilised, whilst the essence of the wisdom remains unmolested.

*153.* While the essence of the mind is eternally clean and pure, the influence of ignorance makes possible the existence of a defiled mind. But in spite of the defiled mind, the mind (itself) is eternal, clear, pure, and not subject to transformation.

Further as its original nature is free from particularisation, it knows in itself no change whatever, though it produces everywhere the various modes of existence.

When the oneness of the totality of things is not recognised, then ignorance as well as particularisation arises, and all phases of the defiled mind are thus developed.

[Sec. 149, *Açvaghosha's Discourse on the Awakening of Faith in the Mahayana,* trans. Teitaro Suzuki (Chicago: Open Court Publishing Co., 1900), pp. 55–57. Sec. 150, *ibid.,* pp. 60–62. Sec. 151, *ibid.,* pp. 65–66. Sec. 152, *ibid.,* pp. 67–68. Sec. 153, *ibid.,* p. 79.]

COMMENT

In these passages, with marvelous conciseness, we seem to have the gist of Hindu monism. All things are in the one soul, but as unrealities, whose apparent diversity and change are due to our false view of existence. The pure mind, above ignorance, is, it seems, ignorant of one thing we all well know, namely, that we are ignorant, each of us in his own unique way. We are to rise to the height of pure knowledge; but, when we reach it, we are no longer to be aware of one of the most certain of all facts, the fact that ignorant states of mind occur in endless variety and succession! Is this really the secret of life? We reserve further comment until Sankara has been heard from—save for one remark. It is interesting to note how the two aspects of the one soul duplicate the divine soul-body duality of Stoicism in respect to the crucial matter of ambiguity or vagueness. The two are two, they are one, they are not two or one—the fundamental pantheistic paradox, either contradiction or sheer mystery, stares us in the face, as it always does in the pantheistic systems.

# SANKARA (*ca.* 788–820)

Sankara, writing early in the ninth century (thus just before Scotus Erigena in Europe, with whose views his own have some similarity), set the pattern for Hindu pantheism, somewhat as Philo, writing in the first century, had done for European classical theism. Sankara, however, had no strong independent philosophical tradition (comparable to Philo's inheritance from the Greeks) to combine with the teachings he found in the sacred writings of his people (the Vedanta Sutras, the *Bhagavad-Gita,* and the Upanishads). Hence the effect is simpler and the discords of motivation less obvious. In accord with Hindu traditions, Sankara Acharya was thought to be an incarnation of the divine Siva.

It is to be borne in mind that monism of Sankara's type, though seemingly the dominant, is far from the only important strand of Hindu philosophy. Ramanuja and many other thinkers also attain some prominence, and not all of them are so strongly monopolar as Sankara. Let us now allow the famous author to speak for himself.

### The Nature of Brahman

*154.* Brahman, which is all-knowing and endowed with all powers, whose essential nature is eternal purity, intelligence, and freedom, exists. For if we consider the derivation of the word "Brahman," from the root *brih* "to be great," we at once understand that eternal purity, and so on, belong to Brahman. Moreover the existence of Brahman is known on the ground of its being the Self of every one. For every one is conscious of the existence of (his) Self, and never thinks "I am not." If the existence of the Self were not known, every one would think "I am not." And this Self (of whose existence all are conscious) is Brahman. But if Brahman is generally known as the Self, there is no room for an enquiry into it! Not so, we reply; for there is a conflict of opinions as to its special nature. Unlearned people and the Lokâyatikas are of opinion that the mere body endowed with the quality of intelligence is the Self; others that the organs endowed with intelligence are the Self; others maintain that the internal organ is the Self; others, again, that the Self is a mere momentary idea; others, again, that it is the Void. Others, again (to proceed to the opinion of such as acknowledge the authority of the Veda), maintain that there is a transmigrating being different from the body, and so on, which is both agent and enjoyer (of the fruits of action); others teach that that being is enjoying only, not acting; others believe that in addition to the individual souls, there is an all-knowing, all-powerful Lord. Others, finally (i.e., the Vedântins), maintain that the Lord is the Self of the enjoyer (i.e., of the individual soul whose individual existence is apparent only, the product of Nescience).

*155.* . . . Brahman as the eternal subject (*pratyagâtman,* the inward Self) is never an object, and . . . the distinction of objects known, knowers, acts of knowledge, etc. . . . is fictitiously created by Nescience.

*156.* Of Brahman, . . . the two following passages declare that it is incapable of receiving any accretion and eternally pure, "He is the one God, hidden in all beings, all-pervading, the Self within all beings, watching over all works, dwelling in all beings, the witness, the perceiver, the only one; free from qualities" (Sv. Up. VI, 11); and "He pervaded all, bright, incorporeal, scatheless, without muscles, pure, untouched by evil" (Îs. Up. 8).

*157.* . . . Brahman, whose nature is eternal cognition—as the sun's nature is eternal luminousness—can impossibly stand in need of any instruments of knowledge.

*158.* . . . Brahman is apprehended under two forms; in the first place as qualified by limiting conditions owing to the multiformity of the evolutions of name and form (i.e., the multiformity of the created world); in the second place as being the opposite of this, i.e., free from all limiting conditions whatever.

*159.* With regard to this (unreal limitation of the one Self) the distinction of objects of activity and of agents may be practically assumed, as long as we have not learned—from the passage, "That art thou"—that the Self is one only. As soon, however, as we grasp the truth that there is only one universal Self, there is an end to the whole practical view of the world with its distinction of bondage, final release, and the like.

*160.* . . . between the embodied Self and the highest Self, there is the difference that the former acts and enjoys, acquires merit and demerit, and is affected by pleasure, pain, and so on; while the latter is of the opposite nature, i.e., characterized by being free from all evil and the like. On account of this difference of the two, the fruition of the one does not extend to the other.

To assume merely on the ground of the mutual proximity of the two, without considering their essentially different powers, that a connexion with effects exists (in Brahman's case also), would be no better than to suppose that space is on fire (when something in space is on fire). The same objection and refutation apply to the case of those also who teach the existence of more than one omnipresent Self.

*161.* In spite of their unity, fruition on the part of the soul does not involve fruition on the part of Brahman; because there is a difference. For there is a difference between false knowledge and perfect knowledge, fruition being the figment of false knowledge while the unity (of the Self) is revealed by perfect knowledge. Now, as the substance revealed by perfect knowledge cannot be affected by fruition which is nothing but the figment of false knowledge, it is impossible to assume even a shadow of fruition on Brahman's part.

*162.* . . . as the cause virtually contains all the states belonging to its effects, the heavenly world, and so on, may be spoken of as the members of the highest Self.

*163.* The Self is not to be known as manifold, qualified by the universe of effects; you are rather to dissolve by true knowledge the universe of effects, which is the mere product of Nescience, and to know that one Self, which is the general abode, as uniform.

### Brahman and the Individual Soul

*164.* That same highest Brahman constitutes—as we know from passages such as "that art thou"—the real nature of the individual soul, while its second nature, i.e., that aspect of it which depends on fictitious limiting conditions, is not its real nature. For as long as the individual soul does not free itself from Nescience in the form of duality—which Nescience may be compared to the mistake of him who in the twilight mistakes a

post for a man—and does not rise to the knowledge of the Self, whose nature is unchangeable, eternal Cognition—which expresses itself in the form "I am Brahman"—so long it remains the individual soul. But when, discarding the aggregate of body, sense-organs and mind, it arrives, by means of Scripture, at the knowledge that it is not itself that aggregate, that it does not form part of transmigratory existence, but is the True, the Real, the Self, whose nature is pure intelligence; then knowing itself to be of the nature of unchangeable, eternal Cognition, it lifts itself above the vain conceit of being one with this body, and itself becomes the Self, whose nature is unchanging, eternal Cognition. As is declared in such scriptural passages as "He who knows the highest Brahman becomes even Brahman" (Mu. Up. III, 2, 9). And this is the real nature of the individual soul by means of which it arises from the body and appears in its own form.

*165.* . . . . there is only one highest Lord ever unchanging, whose substance is cognition, and who, by means of Nescience, manifests himself in various ways, just as a thaumaturg appears in different shapes by means of his magical power. Besides that Lord there is no other substance of cognition.

*166.* To the highest Self which is eternally pure, intelligent and free, which is never changing, one only, not in contact with anything, devoid of form, the opposite characteristics of the individual soul are erroneously ascribed; just as ignorant men ascribe blue colour to the colourless ether.

*167.* A man may, in the dark, mistake a piece of rope lying on the ground for a snake, and run away from it, frightened and trembling; thereon another man may tell him, "Do not be afraid, it is only a rope, not a snake"; and he may then dismiss the fear caused by the imagined snake, and stop running. But all the while the presence and subsequent absence of his erroneous notion, as to the rope being a snake, make no difference whatever in the rope itself. Exactly analogous is the case of the individual soul which is in reality one with the highest soul, although Nescience makes it appear different.

*168.* . . . he only is absolutely independent.

*169.* As therefore the individual soul and the highest Self differ in name only, it being a settled matter that perfect knowledge has for its object the absolute oneness of the two; it is senseless to insist (as some do) on a plurality of Selfs, and to maintain that the individual soul is different from the highest Self, and the highest Self from the individual soul. For the Self is indeed called by many different names, but it is one only.

*170.* The Self is thus the operative cause, because there is no other ruling principle, and the material cause because there is no other substance from which the world could originate.

*171.* We therefore look on the relation of the highest Self and the soul as analogous to that of the snake and its coils. Viewed as a whole the snake is one, non-different, while an element of difference appears if we view it with regard to its coils, hood, erect posture and so on.

*172.* . . . when the absolute oneness, permanence, and purity of the Self have once been apprehended, we cognize that the highest aim of man has been attained, and therefore conceive no further desires.

### The Manifold World and Brahman

*173.* In the same way as those parts of ethereal space which are limited by jars and waterpots are not really different from the universal ethereal space, and as the water of a mirage is not really different from the surface of the salty steppe—for the nature of that water is that it is seen in one moment and has vanished in the next, and moreover,

it is not to be perceived by its own nature (i.e., apart from the surface of the desert)—; so this manifold world with its objects of enjoyment, enjoyers and so on has no existence apart from Brahman.

*174.* . . . the entire complex of phenomenal existence is considered as true as long as the knowledge of Brahman being the Self of all has not arisen; just as the phantoms of a dream are considered to be true until the sleeper wakes. For as long as a person has not reached the true knowledge of the unity of the Self, so long it does not enter his mind that the world of effects with its means and objects of right knowledge and its results of actions is untrue; he rather, in consequence of his ignorance, looks on mere effects (such as body, offspring, wealth, etc.) as forming part of and belonging to his Self, forgetful of Brahman being in reality the Self of all. Hence, as long as true knowledge does not present itself, there is no reason why the ordinary course of secular and religious activity should not hold on undisturbed. The case is analogous to that of a dreaming man who in his dream sees manifold things and, up to the moment of waking, is convinced that his ideas are produced by real perception without suspecting the perception to be a merely apparent one.

*175.* We maintain, therefore, . . . that milk and other substances are called effects when they are in the state of curds and so on, and that it is impossible, even within hundreds of years, ever to bring about an effect which is different from its cause. The fundamental cause of all appears in the form of this and that effect, up to the last effect of all, just as an actor appears in various robes and costumes, and thereby becomes the basis for all the current notions and terms concerning the phenomenal world.

*176.* . . . the effect exists already before its origination, and is non-different from its cause.

*177.* But—an objection will be raised—

your Self even if joined to a body is incapable of exercising moving power, for motion cannot be effected by that the nature of which is pure intelligence.—A thing, we reply, which is itself devoid of motion may nevertheless move other things. The magnet is itself devoid of motion, and yet it moves iron; and colours and the other objects of sense, although themselves devoid of motion, produce movements in the eyes and the other organs of sense. So the Lord also who is all-present, the Self of all, all-knowing and all-powerful may, although himself unmoving, move the universe.—If it finally be objected that (on the Vedânta doctrine) there is no room for a moving power as in consequence of the oneness (aduality) of Brahman no motion can take place; we reply that such objections have repeatedly been refuted by our pointing to the fact of the Lord being fictitiously connected with Mâyâ, which consists of name and form presented by Nescience.—Hence motion can be reconciled with the doctrine of an all-knowing first cause.

*178.* For unless there exists one continuous principle equally connected with the past, the present, and the future, or an absolutely unchangeable (Self) which cognises everything, we are unable to account for remembrance, recognition, and so on, which are subject to mental impressions dependent on place, time, and cause.

### Brahman and Pain

*179.* Just as the light of the sun or the moon which pervades the entire space becomes straight or bent as it were when the limiting adjuncts with which it is in contact, such as a finger, for instance, are straight or bent, but does not *really* become so; and just as the ether, although imagined to move as it were when jars are being moved, does not *really* move; and as the sun does not tremble, although its image

trembles when you shake the cup filled with water in which the sun's light is reflected; thus the Lord also is not affected by pain, although pain be felt by that part of him which is called the individual soul.

[Sec. 154, *The Sacred Books of the East,* trans. George Thibaut, ed. F. Max Müller (Oxford: Clarendon Press, 1890), XXXIV, 14–15. Sec. 155, *ibid.,* p. 32. Sec. 156, *ibid.,* p. 34. Sec. 157, *ibid.,* pp. 50–51. Sec. 158, *ibid.,* p. 61. Sec. 159, *ibid.,* p. 113. Sec. 160, *ibid.,* p. 115. Sec. 161, *ibid.,* p. 116. Sec. 162, *ibid.,* p. 145. Sec. 163, *ibid.,* p. 155. Sec. 164, *ibid.,* pp. 185–86. Sec. 165, *ibid.,* p. 190. Sec. 166, *ibid.* Sec. 167, *ibid.,* p. 251. Sec. 168, *ibid.,* p. 270. Sec. 169, *ibid.,* pp. 282–83. Sec. 170, *ibid.,* p. 286. Sec. 171, *ibid.,* XXXVIII, 174. Sec. 172, *ibid.,* p. 395. Sec. 173, *ibid.,* XXXIV, 321. Sec. 174, *ibid.,* p. 324. Sec. 175, *ibid.,* p. 341. Sec. 176, *ibid.* Sec. 177, *ibid.,* p. 369. Sec. 178, *ibid.,* p. 427. Sec. 179, *ibid.,* XXXVIII, 64–65.]

#### COMMENT

As Ramanuja later pointed out (Secs. 180–98 *passim*), the theory of nescience does not solve any problem. The seeing of disunity (we are told) is false seeing; but such false seeing actually occurs and is just as disunified as the world it is to explain away. And who is it who sees falsely? If you answer, "Brahman," then there is in Brahman a real diversity of false seeings and a real contrast between Brahman as subject knowing truly and Brahman as subject afflicted with ignorance. If it is not Brahman that is afflicted with nescience, then it is beings other than Brahman, but the theory is that other than Brahman there is nothing.

The technique of explaining things by calling them unreal is suspect. It appears to be a misuse of the term "reality." We distinguish between reality and fiction or fancy on the basis of a contrast between ideas perceptually vindicated and ideas not thus vindicated. But this very notion assumes that there are various ideas, perceptions, and things perceived; it assumes the contradictory of absolute monism. To use the term thus based in order to establish such monism is logical absurdity. If unreality were simply nothing, no one would ever have discussed it; if it is something, then there are at least two diverse factors, reality and unreality. In modern times (as in F. H. Bradley) resort is had to the formula, "degrees of reality." But here too we have a new diversity, that of degrees of reality, and we must ask, "Is this diversity of degrees itself real, and in what degree?" Or, again, we may reason: argument is a relating of ideas; why try to prove, self-contradictorily, by such a relating that there is no such thing as relation, since there is no such thing as a diversity of related terms?

Of course, monists will tell us that the idea of maya or nescience is subtler than such criticisms allow. But perhaps it is for them to show that this subtlety is anything better than extreme vagueness or ambiguity and to demonstrate that, when given a clear meaning, this meaning will turn out compatible with absolute monism, or nondiversity.

It should be repeated, however, that as was said in the introduction to this chapter, the monistic doctrine has an aspect of value. The world of change and extension is a world of agitation and uncertainty and tends to be one of anxiety, fretfulness, and futile suffering. To escape from such suffering, one must withdraw attachment from the ever changing and more or less inharmonious Many and concentrate upon the unchanging One. But it does not follow that, because suffering has been escaped, joy and bliss have been attained. Perhaps pure focusing upon oneness would only mean lapse of all consciousness. Moreover, the assumption that the goal of life is escape from suffering, that is to say, something negative, seems dubious at best. Why not accept as the goal the possible maximizing of joy and beauty and leave open the question whether the maximum of

joy is attainable apart from all tinge of suffering? Perhaps supreme beauty of experience is always more or less tragic. Perhaps the conditions of intense joy are also inevitably grounds for the possibility or probability of intense suffering. These conditions seem to be a rich development of individuality, of concrete diversity and plurality. We know that a composition is the more beautiful the more its parts have individuality of their own. Thus a drama, which weaves together individual personalities, is a richer experience than a mere musical chord, which combines impersonal tones, lacking in depth of individuality. Monism looks for the summit of value in the opposite direction to that which experience suggests, primarily because it seeks the negative value of painlessness rather than the positive value of intensity.

It remains true that the search for positive value must be safeguarded against the danger of futile anxieties, of overattachment to certain concrete forms, so that their loss leaves one helpless against despair. The safeguard is found in cultivation of a taste for the eternal principle pervading all things and changes, an object of cherishing that is ever fixed and immune to injury. But this principle, according to surrelativism, is abstract, and attachment to it has its full worth only if the common and the fixed is seen in, not apart from or in contradiction to, the diverse and the changing. Only because our grasp of the concrete is really abstract and partial can we seem to be missing the eternal while attending to the temporal. The Hindus have specialized in contemplation of the abstract unity; we Westerners have specialized in contemplation of rather abstract aspects of the particular and temporal (as in our science and technology). A balanced view will see in the really concrete one-many the final object of contemplation.

Granting that when we human beings attend to the particular affairs of daily living *we* miss something of the eternal and universal, it does not follow from this that the particular is not worth knowing or that supreme knowledge will scorn to attend to the particular and the changing. Rather, the supreme knowledge will be that which can see the common in the diverse, the everlasting in the temporal process, the universal in the individual. We may have at times to forget the creatures to see the creator; but the superiority of the creator is shown, in this connection, precisely in this—that he does not need to forget us in order to see himself. Just the contrary, he is himself through his unlimited power of attending to the universe in all its concreteness, thereby rendering it constituent of his own reality. Thus, in forsaking all to find God, we find the love for men and nature we have apparently renounced, only infinitely more rich and explicit. So we are sent back to life, where, one ventures to say, we belong. This is the panentheistic vision, in terms of its meaning in human living.

The natural suspicion that our objections to Sankara are due to our ignorance of Sanskrit or of Sankara's background may be met, first, by pointing out that Ramanuja did not suffer from these handicaps but was also unsatisfied by the doctrine and unconvinced by the arguments; second, by the observation that the numerous analogies employed are so concrete as to be independent of nuances of language; third, by the fact that only a certain number of logically possible solutions of the problem of the supreme reality or "highest lord" are available to any thinker, wherever and whenever he may live.

Let us consider some of the analogies. If space is not on fire when fire is in space, this can only mean (regardless of the Sanskrit for "space") that space is here taken (unwittingly no doubt) as abstract, for the concrete spatiotemporal reality is qualified by fire, even though it is not in the normal sense "on fire," when there is a fire. The concrete whole reality contains all the qualities that the burning stick has. Moreover, when a fire breaks out, either this is something new in the whole reality or else the whole of things embraces all the time process in a fixed totality to which nothing can ever be added. In the latter case, nothing really becomes but simply and eternally is. This is a denial of the patent fact of becoming, and the denial gains no support from the analogy. The "ether" is of course only space over again, if it is really completely independent of the jars and so on. That all causation is a case of a substance passing through diverse forms, like milk being curdled, presupposes that one accepts the idea of substantial identity in a particularly extreme form. Analysis seems to show that events are the final concretes, not things, and this means that there is a new actuality each moment. That Brahman is like an actor assuming diverse roles repeats the notion of substance and also implies spectators of the acting —or does Brahman watch itself perform? Even in that case, wherein consists the change of roles if there is no change at all?

If the sun does not tremble when its image in water does so, this is because the sun does not contain its effects and is not the concrete whole of things but a mere part. It is also because the sun is blind and does not know its effects. For if it did perceive the change in the images, it would then have a new perception to correspond with each new phase of the water. The only alternative is that all the phases are known eternally as a single fixed totality, and just this is the question at issue in another form. Is process a fixed totality, or is it a growing totality?

Take any example or analogy used by the monist, and it argues against him. He is not consulting experience for clues as to the basic dimensions or meanings; he is trying to force out of experience meanings nowhere given. It will be said that religious experience furnishes the meanings, and the sensory analogies are only efforts to express what is not literally expressible. But then why all the pretense of logic and argument and definition? Furthermore, it seems apparent that the author thinks the experiences he cites do support him. He really thinks the milk when curdled is essentially the same; he really thinks causes contain the value of their effects and yet are not qualified by them. This is not pure religion but rationalistic belief—in every case, we think, erroneous belief. Why should we trust his alleged religious experience to be infallible, when it seems highly likely that all sorts of philosophical prejudices entered into his interpretation of that experience? Some of us think there are other and better ways of being religious. Schweitzer, Buber, and Berdyaev are critical of this type of mysticism on religious and ethical grounds which are not easily refuted.

It is sometimes said that the Hindu doctrine is not "monism," for Brahman is as much beyond "one" as it is beyond "many" or any of our categories. This is hardly what our author says. But, in any case, either the doctrine is that no words at all apply to deity, or else it is that, as between contrary meanings, like one and many, absolute and relative, eternal and temporal, the one applies in some fashion but not the other, or, finally, both contraries in some fashion apply. That is, one either has an absolute ineffabilism, and then there is no need for elaborate exposition or any exposition, or one chooses between a monopolar and a dipolar doctrine. Now Sankara is hardly an absolute ineffabilist. And he certainly is not much of a dipolarist. He is without doubt a monopolarist, who thinks change, conflict, suffering, passivity, diversity, are unworthy to characterize the Highest Lord, and who hopes himself somehow to escape these things by identification with the Highest Lord. He is one of the innumerable company who think categorical contrasts are invidious rather than being at right angles with the contrast superior-inferior. When it is said that Brahman is without evil, suffering is even more in question than wickedness or ignorance. Yet sympathy is a positive power, and through it we extend the scope of our suffering to include those of others. The most excellent form of this power would mean a supreme openness to suffering, not a supreme immunity. No suspicion of this is observable in our author. He is by no means impartial as between the polar contraries.

How far the monopolar attitude is mistakenly read into the Upanishads, and other sacred writings of India, by its philosophers, as it is read into the Hebrew, Christian, and Mohammedan writings by Philo, Aquinas, and al-Ghazzali, is beyond our competence to judge. Ramanuja argues that the extreme nonduality of Sankara is not scriptural (Secs. 197 and 214); indeed, that the very idea of Scriptures contradicts it. But then the same question, in milder form, arises concerning his own interpretation, which is still not dipolar or panentheistic in a full or balanced form.

Although truth is always superior to error, as between two errors there is no necessity that one must be better or worse than the other. Thus to the question, "Which is superior, classical theism or pantheism?" there is perhaps no conclusive reason supporting a definite answer. Each of the two views has its merits, and each its defects. Classical theism has the great merit that, though its monopolar description cannot (if our criticisms are right) be correct of God in his total actuality, it can be correct, in large part, of something, and something really in God. There is, one may conceive, Something strictly immutable, with all mutable things real outside it. By contrast, there cannot (we think) be anything strictly immutable, but with nothing mutable and real outside it. Thus the status attributed to Brahman cannot belong to anything. So far, classical theism is superior. Nor is this all. An actual Self or Knower must have something really different from itself to know; this Brahman lacks, and yet it is described as knower, witness, self, etc. The classical deity does have a world to know and to act upon. The reality of this world is also required for the significance of our ethical ideals and actions. But, to look at the other side of the shield: it is impossible that the supreme actuality should have anything outside it, for then the supreme and the nonsupreme form a superreality of which the other two are mere constituents! Besides, to know something adequately is in the most absolute sense to possess it, and it is then meaningless to say that the known is outside the actual knowing. Thus after all it is Brahman who can know, not the classical deity. Further, the reality of the world is not enough to give our ethical life significance. For there is no possible general inclusive common good for the ethical will to serve short of the self-realization of the Inclusive Experience to which our experience can contribute. Once more the necessity is shown that we be inside, not outside, the supreme actuality.

Could anything be more hopeless than the attempt to adjudicate this issue without attaining a higher standpoint than either party has to offer? This higher standpoint can only be the dipolar one, for which it is no longer a scandal but an accomplishment to conceive categorically supreme accidents as well as categorically supreme essence, process toward novelty as well as fixity, responsiveness as well as independence.

# RAMANUJA (*ca.* 1016–1100)

That classical theism and pantheism have complementary merits and defects has as one of its results that each tends to produce the other by reaction. In Europe the dominant theism produces Stoicism, Spinozism, and Hegelianism (which is equivocal on the issue between pantheism and panentheism); in India the dominant pantheism produces in Ramanuja something rather like classical theism. The reality of the creatures is as sharply affirmed by this thinker as by his European counterparts. Change and diversity are ultimate facts. God has definite dealings with the world; he permits the acts of the human will; he rules over all things. God in his spiritual actuality as Soul or Highest Lord of the world is immutable.

What is all this but classical theism?

At first glance, however, there appears to be a decisive difference. Ramanuja affirms that the whole of created changing reality is within the total divinity as consisting of cosmic soul with its all-inclusive body. Here surely is pantheism! But look more closely. One man may say that the world is the body of deity and mean one thing; another man may say it and mean another thing; a third man may say that the world is certainly not the body of deity and yet mean about what the first or the second man means. What is a body in relation to a soul and a soul in relation to a body? Surely this relation is not so clear and unequivocal to all that a doctrine is adequately defined by the analogous extension of the relation to that between God and world. We invite the reader to notice what this relation is for Ramanuja and to consider how much contrast in strict logical content there really is between this doctrine and classical theism. There is, at least, agreement on two great issues: (1) the Highest Lord is to be conceived in monopolar fashion, as immutable, incapable of acquisition or suffering, etc.; and (2) the world is real and mutable and derivative from the Highest Lord.

Though in historical fact Ramanuja did not succeed in overthrowing the dominance of Sankara in Hindu thought, he did a vast service by lending encouragement through the ages to attempts to find a better way. The "official" version of this development is that, while the most strictly philosophical and true philosophy is that of Sankara, for more or less popular religious or semiphilosophical uses a more pluralistic notion like that of Ramanuja is valuable and permissible. This rather patronizing attitude has rationalized itself in recent times in the form of the claim that the six philosophical systems of India exhaust the major possibilities and that all are embraced in the Sankara system. However, the number six and the wide contrasts between the systems still do not guarantee that all important questions and answers are covered. Some of the obvious variants of European doctrine, such as materialism, atomism, empiricism, atheism, pantheism, and some forms of theism, may be found. But such a current Western metaphysics as Whitehead's is identical with none of these nor with a mere mélange of elements from them. Perhaps all the six systems are too vague or ambiguous or too limited by certain presuppositions to be anything like the best we are now in a position to construct. For example, either they are infected with the notion of substance in the sense

which exact analysis has more and more shown to be a logical confusion (whether the substance is plural and materialistic, or plural and spiritual, or not plural and spiritual) or they are skeptical, atheistic, and limited in speculative reach (or perhaps both in some cases). Does any of the systems (1) base itself on the notion that an actuality is an event or occasion, not a thing or person or a superior analogon to thing or person; (2) but yet take the form, not of a skeptical theory, or an atheistic theory, but of a well-developed cosmology, metaphysics, and theory of divinity; (3) make clear that the "absolute," "immutable" factor of "being" in actuality is an abstract element contained in the concrete which is process; (4) note the consequence that the Absolute is an abstract essence in the divine actuality, which as a whole is not absolute, or immutable, but growing, and is as truly effect as it is cause, in a mutual (though not equal) relation of creating and being created with the "creatures"? These are just some of the Whiteheadian ideas which possibly are not in Sankara or in any of the other ancient Indian systems. (It is of course another question whether they are tenable ideas.)

Returning to Ramanuja, what we claim for him is not a net superiority to Sankara. We do question the notion that the latter contains all the truth that is in his successor. Rather, it is as with classical theism and pantheism: they are complementary forms of monopolarity, each with its own defects and merits; and the grand issue of monopolarity versus dipolarity is scarcely covered at all in the main philosophical tradition of India. But, thanks in no small part to Ramanuja, a healthy instability does obtain and now and then results in approaches to dipolarism or panentheism, as in Sri Jiva of more recent times. Ramanuja thus had apparently something like the role of William James in our culture. With immense courage and penetration he attacked doctrines often supposed to be almost invulnerable and at least weakened the force of the pretensions with which they were hedged about.

### Mere Being, Devoid of Difference, Inadmissible

180. Those who maintain the doctrine of a substance devoid of all difference have no right to assert that this or that is a proof of such a substance; for all means of right knowledge have for their object things affected with difference.—Should any one, taking his stand on the received views of his sect, assert that the theory of a substance free from all difference . . . is immediately established by one's own consciousness; we reply that he also is refuted by the fact, warranted by the witness of the Self, that all consciousness implies difference: all states of consciousness have for their object something that is marked by some difference, as appears in the case of judgments like "I saw this."

181. To thought there at any rate belongs the quality of being thought and self-illuminatedness, for the knowing principle is observed to have for its essential nature the illumining (making to shine forth) of objects. And that also in the states of deep sleep, swoon, etc., consciousness is affected with difference we shall prove, in its proper place, in greater detail. Moreover you yourself admit that to consciousness there actually belong different attributes such as permanency (oneness, self-luminousness, etc.), and of these it cannot be shown that they are only Being in general. And even if the latter point were admitted, we observe that there takes place a discussion of different views, and you yourself attempt to prove your theory by means of the differences between those views and your own. It therefore must be admit-

ted that reality is affected with difference well established by valid means of proof.

182. Perception in the next place . . . also cannot be a means of knowledge for things devoid of difference. . . .

183. . . . if perception made us apprehend only pure Being, judgments clearly referring to different objects—such as "Here is a jar," "There is a piece of cloth"—would be devoid of all meaning. And if through perception we did not apprehend difference—as marked by generic character, etc., constituting the structure or make of a thing—why should a man searching for a horse not be satisfied with finding a buffalo?

184. Next as to the assertion that all difference presented in our cognition—as of jars, pieces of cloth and the like—is unreal because such difference does not persist. This view, we maintain, is altogether erroneous.

185. . . . jars, pieces of cloth and the like, do not contradict one another, since they are separate in place and time. If on the other hand the non-existence of a thing is cognised at the same time and the same place where and when its existence is cognised, we have a mutual contradiction of two cognitions, and then the stronger one sublates [cancels] the other cognition which thus comes to an end. But when of a thing that is perceived in connexion with some place and time, the non-existence is perceived in connexion with some other place and time, there arises no contradiction; how then should the one cognition sublate the other?

186. Hence mere Being [as devoid of differences] does not alone constitute reality. And as the distinction between consciousness and its objects—which rests just on this relation of object and that for which the object is—is proved by perception, the assertion that only consciousness has real existence is also disposed of.

*187.* Nor is there any consciousness devoid of objects; for nothing of this kind is ever known. Moreover, the self-luminousness of consciousness has, by our opponent himself, been proved on the ground that its essential nature consists in illumining (revealing) objects; the self-luminousness of consciousness not admitting of proof apart from its essential nature which consists in the lighting up of objects. And as moreover, according to our opponent, consciousness cannot be the object of another consciousness, it would follow that (having neither an object nor itself being an object) it is something altogether unreal, imaginary.

*188.* Against the assertion that the alleged non-origination of consciousness at the same time proves that consciousness is not capable of any other changes, we remark that the general proposition on which this conclusion rests is too wide: it would extend to antecedent non-existence itself, of which it is evident that it comes to an end, although it does not originate.

*189.* For according to your own view Nescience also (which is not "Being") does not originate, is the substrate of manifold changes, and comes to an end through the rise of knowledge! Perhaps you will say that the changes of Nescience are all unreal. But, do you then, we ask in reply, admit that any change is real? You do not; and yet it is only this admission which would give a sense to the distinction expressed by the word "Being."

Nor is it true that consciousness does not admit of any division within itself, because it has no beginning. For the non-originated Self is divided from the body, the senses, etc., and Nescience also, which is avowedly without a beginning, must needs be admitted to be divided from the Self.

*190.* . . . if the distinction of Nescience from the Self is not real, it follows that Nescience and the Self are essentially one.

*191.* To maintain that the consciousness of the "I" does not persist in the state of final release is again altogether inappropriate. It in fact amounts to the doctrine—only expressed in somewhat different words—that final release is the annihilation of the Self. The "I" is not a mere attribute of the Self so that even after its destruction the essential nature of the Self might persist—as it persists on the cessation of ignorance; but it constitutes the very nature of the Self. Such judgments as "I know," "Knowledge has arisen in me," show, on the other hand, that we are conscious of knowledge as a mere attribute of the Self. Moreover, a man who suffering pain, mental or of other kind—whether such pain be real or due to error only —puts himself in relation to pain—"I am suffering pain"—naturally begins to reflect how he may once for all free himself from all these manifold afflictions and enjoy a state of untroubled ease; the desire of final release thus having arisen in him he at once sets to work to accomplish it. If, on the other hand, he were to realise that the effect of such activity would be the loss of personal existence, he surely would turn away as soon as somebody began to tell him about "release."

*192.* No sensible person exerts himself under the influence of the idea that after he himself has perished there will remain some entity termed "pure light!" —What constitutes the "inward" Self thus is the "I," the knowing subject.

*193.* . . . whatever does not appear as an "I," does not appear to itself; as jars and the like. Now the emancipated Self *does* thus appear to itself, and therefore it appears as an "I." Nor does this appearance as an "I" imply in any way that the released Self is subject to Nescience . . . for this would contradict the nature of final release, and moreover the consciousness of the "I" cannot be the cause of Nescience and so on. Nescience (ignorance) is either ignorance as to essential nature, or the cognition of something under an aspect different from the real one (as when a person suffering from jaundice sees all things yellow); or cognition of what is altogether opposite in nature (as when mother o' pearl is mistaken for silver). Now the "I" constitutes the essential nature of the Self; how then can the consciousness of the "I," i.e., the consciousness of its own true nature, implicate the released Self in Nescience?

*194.* With reference to the assertion that Perception, which depends on the view of plurality, is based on some defect and hence admits of being otherwise accounted for—whence it follows that it is sublated by Scripture; we ask you to point out what defect it is on which Perception is based and may hence be accounted for otherwise.— "The beginningless imagination of difference" we expect you to reply.—But, we ask in return, have you then come to know by some other means that this beginningless imagination of difference, acting in a manner analogous to that of certain defects of vision, is really the cause of an altogether perverse view of things? If you reply that this is known just from the fact that Perception is in conflict with Scripture . . . we further ask, "By what means do you arrive at the conclusion that Scripture cannot possibly be assumed to be defective in any way, while defects may be ascribed to Perception?" It is certainly not Consciousness—self-proved and absolutely devoid of all difference—which enlightens you on this point; for such Consciousness is unrelated to any objects whatever, and incapable of partiality to Scripture. Nor can sense-perception be the source of your conviction; for as it is founded on what is defective it gives perverse information. Nor again the other sources of knowledge; for they are all based on sense-perception.

As thus there are no acknowledged means of knowledge to prove your view, you must give it up.

*195.* Now you will possibly argue as follows: "Scripture as well as Perception is founded on Nescience; but all the same Perception is sublated by Scripture. For as the object of Scripture, i.e., Brahman, which is one and without a second, is not seen to be sublated by any ulterior cognition, Brahman, i.e., pure non-differenced Consciousness, remains as the sole Reality." But here too you are wrong, since we must decide that something which rests on a defect is unreal, although it may remain unrefuted. We will illustrate this point by an analogous instance. Let us imagine a race of men afflicted with a certain special defect of vision, without being aware of this their defect, dwelling in some remote mountain caves inaccessible to all other men provided with sound eyes. As we assume all of these cave dwellers to be afflicted with the same defect of vision, they, all of them, will equally see and judge bright things, e.g., the moon, to be double. Now in the case of these people there never arises a subsequent cognition sublating their primitive cognition; but the latter is false all the same, and its object, viz., the doubleness of the moon, is false likewise; the defect of vision being the cause of a cognition not corresponding to reality. And so it is with the cognition of Brahman also. This cognition is based on Nescience, and therefore is false, together with its object, viz., Brahman, although no sublating cognition presents itself.

*196.* Nor can it be shown that (in the case of Brahman) there is no possibility of ulterior sublative cognition; for there may be such sublative cognition, viz., the one expressed in the judgment "the Reality is a Void." And if you say that this latter judgment rests on error, we point out that according to yourself the knowledge of Brahman is also based on error. And of our judgment (viz., "the Reality is a Void") it may truly be said that all further negation is impossible.—But there is no need to continue this demolition of an altogether baseless theory. . . .

### Brahman Includes Reality

197. [Scripture teaches] that the highest Brahman is essentially free from all imperfection whatsoever, comprises within itself all auspicious qualities, and finds its pastime in originating, preserving, reabsorbing, pervading, and ruling the universe; that the entire complex of intelligent and non-intelligent beings (souls and matter) in all their different estates is real, and constitutes the form, i.e., the body of the highest Brahman, as appears from those passages which co-ordinate it with Brahman by means of terms such as *sarîra* (body), *rûpa* (form), *tanu* (body), *amsa* (part), *sakti* (power), *vibhûti* (manifestation of power), and so on;—that the souls which are a manifestation of Brahman's power exist in their own essential nature, and also, through their connexion with matter, in the form of embodied souls;—and that the embodied souls, being engrossed by Nescience in the form of good and evil works, do not recognise their essential nature, which is knowledge, but view themselves as having the character of material things.—The outcome of all this is that we have to cognise Brahman as carrying plurality within itself, and the world, which is the manifestation of his power, as something real.

198. It . . . is impossible to ascribe to Brahman, whose nature is constituted by eternal free self-luminous intelligence, the consciousness of Nescience; for what constitutes its essence is consciousness of itself. If against this you urge that Brahman, although having consciousness of Self for its essential nature, yet is conscious of non-knowl-edge in so far as its (Brahman's) nature is hidden; we ask in return what we have to understand by Brahman's nature being hidden. You will perhaps say "the fact of its not being illumined." But how, we ask, can there be absence of illumination of the nature of that whose very nature consists in consciousness of Self, i.e., self-illumination?

199. To that substance which is pure light, free from all division and distinction, there cannot belong two modes of being, and hence obscuration and light cannot abide in it together.—Let us then say that Brahman, which is homogeneous being, intelligence, bliss, has its nature obscured by *avidyâ*, and hence is seen indistinctly as it were.—But how, we ask, are we to conceive the distinctness or indistinctness of that whose nature is pure light?

200. From all this it follows that the entire aggregate of things, intelligent and non-intelligent, has its Self in Brahman in so far as it constitutes Brahman's body. And as, thus, the whole world different from Brahman derives its substantial being only from constituting Brahman's body, any term denoting the world or something in it conveys a meaning which has its proper consummation in Brahman only: in other words all terms whatsoever denote Brahman in so far as distinguished by the different things which we associate with those terms.

201. Brahman, having for its modes intelligent and non-intelligent things in their gross and subtle states, thus constitutes effect and cause, and the world thus has Brahman for its material cause (*upâdâna*). Nor does this give rise to any confusion of the essential constituent elements of the great aggregate of things. Of some parti-coloured piece of cloth the material cause is threads white, red, black, etc.; all the same, each definite spot of the cloth is connected with one colour only—white, e.g., and thus there is no confusion of colours

even in the "effected" condition of the cloth. Analogously the combination of non-sentient matter, sentient beings, and the Lord constitutes the material cause of the world, but this does not imply any confusion of the essential characteristics of enjoying souls, objects of enjoyment, and the universal ruler, even in the world's "effected" state. There is indeed a difference between the two cases, in so far as the threads are capable of existing apart from one another, and are only occasionally combined according to the volition of men, so that the web sometimes exists in its causal, sometimes in its effected state; while non-sentient matter and sentient beings in all their states form the body of the highest Self, and thus have a being only as the modes of that—on which account the highest Self may, in all cases, be denoted by any term whatsoever. But the two cases are analogous, in so far as there persists a distinction and absence of all confusion, on the part of the constituent elements of the aggregate. This being thus, it follows that the highest Brahman, although entering into the "effected" condition, remains unchanged—for its essential nature does not become different.

## Brahman and Suffering

*202.* How . . . can Brahman, the cause of all, free from all shadow of imperfection, omniscient, omnipotent, etc., etc., be one with the individual soul, all whose activities—whether it be thinking, or winking of an eye, or anything else—depend on karman, which implies endless suffering of various kinds?

*203.* The individual soul being thus connected with the highest Self as its body, its attributes do not touch the highest Self, not any more than infancy, youth, and other attributes of the material body touch the individual soul. Hence, in the co-ordination, "Thou art that," the word "that" denotes the highest Brahman which is the cause of the

world, whose purposes come true, which comprises within itself all blessed qualities, which is free from all shadow of evil; while the word "thou" denotes the same highest Self in so far as having for its body the individual souls together with their bodies.

*204.* Nor must it be thought that the power of seeing and so on that belongs to the highest Self is dependent on sense-organs; it rather results immediately from its essential nature, since its omniscience and power to realise its purposes are due to its own being only.

## In What Sense the World Is Brahman's Body

*205.* Any substance which a sentient soul is capable of completely controlling and supporting for its own purposes, and which stands to the soul in an entirely subordinate relation, is the body of that soul. In the case of bodies injured, paralysed, etc., control and so on are not actually perceived because the power of control, although existing, is obstructed; in the same way as, owing to some obstruction, the powers of fire, heat, and so on may not be actually perceived. A dead body again begins to decay at the very moment in which the soul departs from it, and is actually dissolved shortly after; it (thus strictly speaking is not a body at all but) is spoken of as a body because it is a part of the aggregate of matter which previously constituted a body. In this sense, then, all sentient and non-sentient beings together constitute the body of the Supreme Person, for they are completely controlled and supported by him for his own ends, and are absolutely subordinate to him.

## Brahman and World Generation

*206.* Brahman—essentially antagonistic to all evil, of uniform goodness, differing in nature from all beings other than itself, all-knowing, endowed with the power of immediately realising all its purposes, in eternal possession of all it wishes for, supremely blessed—has for its body the entire universe, with all its sentient and non-sentient beings—the universe being for it a plaything as it were—and constitutes the Self of the Universe. Now, when this world which forms Brahman's body has been gradually reabsorbed into Brahman, each constituent element being refunded into its immediate cause, so that in the end there remains only the highly subtle, elementary matter which Scripture calls Darkness; and when this so-called Darkness itself, by assuming a form so extremely subtle that it hardly deserves to be called something separate from Brahman, of which it constitutes the body, has become one with Brahman; then Brahman invested with this ultra-subtle body forms the resolve, "May I again possess a world-body constituted by all sentient and non-sentient beings, distinguished by names and forms just as in the previous æon," and modifies (pariṇâma-yati) itself by gradually evolving the world-body in the inverse order in which reabsorption had taken place.

## Imperfection and Evil

207. While the highest Self thus undergoes a change—in the form of a world comprising the whole aggregate of sentient and non-sentient beings—all imperfection and suffering are limited to the sentient beings constituting part of its body, and all change is restricted to the non-sentient things which constitute another part. The highest Self is effected in that sense only that it is the ruling principle, and hence the Self, of matter and souls in their gross or evolved state; but just on account of being this, viz., their inner Ruler and Self, it is in no way touched by their imperfections and changes. Consisting of unlimited knowledge and bliss he for ever abides in his uniform nature, en-

gaged in the sport of making this world go round.

208. . . . a husband, wife, a son, etc., are not dear to us in consequence of a wish or purpose on their part, "may I, for my own end or advantage be dear to him," but they are dear to us for the wish of the Self, i.e., to the end that there may be accomplished the desire of the highest Self—which desire aims at the devotee obtaining what is dear to him. For the highest Self pleased with the works of his devotees imparts to different things such dearness, i.e., joy-giving quality as corresponds to those works, that "dearness" being bound in each case to a definite place, time, nature and degree.

209. The fact is, that not even non-sentient things are, essentially or intrinsically, bad; but in accordance with the nature of the works of those beings which are under the rule of karman, one thing, owing to the will of the Supreme Person, causes pain to one man at one time, and pleasure at another time, and causes pleasure or pain to one person and the opposite to another person. If the effects of things depended on their own nature only, everything would at all times be productive for all persons, either of pleasure only or of pain only. But this is not observed to be the case. . . . To the soul therefore which is subject to karman the connexion with different things is the source of imperfection and suffering, in agreement with the nature of its works; while to the highest Brahman, which is subject to itself only, the same connexion is the source of playful sport, consisting therein that he in various ways guides and rules those things.

## Individual Freedom

210. The inwardly ruling highest Self promotes action in so far as it regards in the case of any action the volitional effort made by the individual soul, and then aids that effort by granting its fa-

vour or permission (*anumati*); action is not possible without permission on the part of the highest Self. In this way (i.e., since the action primarily depends on the volitional effort of the soul) injunctions and prohibitions are not devoid of meaning. . . . The case is analogous to that of property of which two men are joint owners. If one of these wishes to transfer that property to a third person he cannot do so without the permission of his partner, but that that permission is given is after all his own doing, and hence the fruit of the action (reward or anything) properly belongs to him only.

### Brahman Substantially but Not Spatially or Temporally Limited

*211.* Now on the theory which holds that there is a plurality of separate existences, Brahman which is considered to differ in character from other existences cannot be said to be free from substantial limitation; for substantial limitation means nothing else than the existence of other substances.

*212.* Things substantially limited may be limited more or less with regard to time and place: there is no invariable rule on this point, and the measure of their connexion with space and time has hence to be determined in dependence on other means of knowledge. Now Brahman's connexion with *all* space and *all* time results from such other means of proof, and hence there is no contradiction (between this non-limitation with regard to space and time, and its limitation in point of substance—which is due to the existence of other souls).

*213.* The proof of infinity, we further remark, rests altogether on the absence of limitation of space and time, not on absence of substantial limitation; absence of such limitation is something very much akin to the "horn of a hare" and is perceived nowhere. On the view of difference, on the other hand, the whole world, as constituting Brahman's body, is its mode, and Brahman is thus limited neither through itself nor through other things.—We thus arrive at the conclusion that, as effects are real in so far as different from their cause, the effect of Brahman, i.e., the entire world, is different from Brahman.

### Identity and Difference of Self and Brahman

*214.* "He who dwelling within the Self is different from the Self, whom the Self does not know, of whom the Self is the body, who rules the Self from within; he is thy Self, the inner ruler, the immortal one"; "In the True all these beings have their root, they dwell in the True, they rest in the True; —in that all that exists has its Self"; "All this indeed is Brahman"—all these texts teach that all sentient and non-sentient beings spring from Brahman, are merged in him, breathe through him, are ruled by him, constitute his body; so that he is the Self of all of them. In the same way therefore as, on the basis of the fact that the individual soul occupies with regard to the body the position of a Self, we form such judgments of co-ordination as "I am a god—I am a man"; the fact of the individual Self being of the nature of Self justifies us in viewing our own Ego as belonging to the highest Self. On the presupposition of all ideas being finally based on Brahman and hence all words also finally denoting Brahman, the texts therefore make such statements of mutual implication as "I am thou, O holy divinity, and thou art me." On this view of the relation of individual soul and highest Self there is no real contradiction between two, apparently contradictory, sets of texts, viz., those on the one hand which negative the view of the soul being different from the highest Self, "Now if a man meditates upon another divinity, thinking 'the divinity is one and I another,' he does not know"; "He is incomplete, let him meditate upon Him as the Self";

. . . and on the other hand those texts which set forth the view of the soul and the highest Self being different entities, "Thinking of the (individual) Self and the Mover as different." For our view implies a denial of difference in so far as the individual "I" is of the nature of the Self; and it implies an acknowledgment of difference in so far as it allows the highest Self to differ from the individual soul in the same way as the latter differs from its body. The clause "he is incomplete" (in one of the texts quoted above) refers to the fact that Brahman which is different from the soul constitutes the Self of the soul, while the soul constitutes the body of Brahman.

[Sec. 180, *The Sacred Books of the East,* trans. George Thibaut, ed. F. Max Müller (Oxford: Clarendon Press, 1904), XLVIII, 39. Sec. 181, *ibid.,* p. 40. Sec. 182, *ibid.,* p. 41. Sec. 183, *ibid.,* p. 44. Sec. 184, *ibid.,* p. 46. Sec. 185, *ibid.,* p. 47. Sec. 186, *ibid.* Sec. 187, *ibid.,* p. 52. Sec. 188, *ibid.,* p. 54. Sec. 189, *ibid.* Sec. 190, *ibid.* Sec. 191, *ibid.,* pp. 69–70. Sec. 192, *ibid.,* p. 70. Sec. 193, *ibid.,* pp. 70–71. Sec. 194, *ibid.,* pp. 73–74. Sec. 195, *ibid.,* pp. 74–75. Sec. 196, *ibid.,* p. 78. Sec. 197, *ibid.,* pp. 88–89. Sec. 198, *ibid.,* p. 111. Sec. 199, *ibid.,* p. 113. Sec. 200, *ibid.,* p. 134. Sec. 201, *ibid.,* p. 142. Sec. 202, *ibid.,* p 215. Sec. 203, *ibid.,* pp. 228–29. Sec. 204, *ibid.,* p. 280. Sec. 205, *ibid.,* p. 424. Sec. 206, *ibid.,* p. 403. Sec. 207, *ibid.,* pp. 405–6. Sec. 208, *ibid.,* p. 390. Sec. 209, *ibid.,* pp. 609–10. Sec. 210, *ibid.,* p. 557. Sec. 211, *ibid.,* p. 444. Sec. 212, *ibid.,* pp. 452–53. Sec. 213, *ibid.,* p. 453. Sec. 214, *ibid.,* pp. 717–18.]

COMMENT

In the foregoing passages there are some apparent contradictions and some unclarity of language. The highest self undergoes a change, as a given world is brought into being, but the self "is in no way touched" by such changes. Brahman is "in eternal possession of all it wishes for," and yet, while in its causal state, forms the resolution, "May I again possess a world-body. . . ." But how does Brahman undergo a change without being touched by it, and what is the motive for calling a world into being if one has eternally all one wishes? Ramanuja's answer to the first part of the question is that the highest is "the ruling principle, and hence the self" of the changes; as ruler and self, Brahman is free from change, possessing the change only in his body. But the distinction leads only to further difficulties, for Brahman, as the being of unlimited intelligence, knows of any change within his world body (and indeed, according to some passages, must approve any prospective change by a part of his body), and the change must then itself become a possession of his conscious self. In answer to the latter part of the question, Ramanuja must apparently say that the motive in creation is sheer play, "sport," in order that the creation will not appear to contribute anything to Brahman's nature. But, even if this is the case, Brahman, it must be granted, has gained pleasure from his creation and in so far has been qualified thereby.

Ramanuja is perhaps closer to classical theism than to genuine pantheism. Change and multiplicity, though real, are in Brahman only in the sense in which Brahman is one with his body; while as distinguished therefrom and as the soul of this body, "having" rather than being it, he is changeless and unitary. And what does "having a body" mean in this system? With admirable explicitness the reply is given: The soul is the ruler of the body, disposing of it for its own purposes. This is a typical monopolar idea. (We have already encountered it in Philo.) Certainly the soul rules over the body. It is exactly as true that the soul, like any ruler, reflects changes in the "subjects," responds to them with appropriate reactions; the better the ruler, the more versatile his responsiveness. To possess a body, as to possess a kingdom, is to enjoy and suffer what goes on in it. Only an inhuman ruler could be entirely unmoved by the suffering of his people or undelighted by their joy. And the soul responds to injury of the bodily tissues with automatic and sometimes unbearable grief, as it likewise experiences intense delight in response to healthy bodily functioning. The arbitrary monopolar one-sidedness in Ramanuja's naïve account here is all the more striking in view of the subtlety of his thought where he is criticizing Sankara's monism.

Notable is the energy with which our author maintains the immunity of deity to all evil, including suffering. Brahman is not under Karma, the law that actions bring suitable results of joy and woe, reward and punishment. Only the divine body, not the highest self, is qualified by the world. Ramanuja is here tainted with the negativism which says, "Suffering must at all costs be avoided entirely." The highest good must be utterly nontragic. The redeemed may then participate in this nontragic bliss of Brahman. But bliss, as an ultimate goal, cannot be negative, the avoidance of suffering; for total insentience yields that. The ultimate goal must be somewhat like joy and beauty, and if, as there are good grounds for thinking, the soil in which these can grow is that in which an element of tragedy, of conflict and pain, is also sure to grow, then there is no reason for taking the attitude, "either joy without suffering, or neither joy nor suffering." (See Schelling, Royce, and Berdyaev for a very different attitude.) That deity participates in the tragedy of life with us, so that the world is not mere "sport" from the highest standpoint, is an insight not easily found outside of Christian circles (though it occurs in some forms of Buddhism) and not too easily within these circles. It does not appear that Ramanuja attained the insight, just as it is doubtful if ancient Judaism did so, or Mohammedanism. If there is no reason to try to prevent all change from touching the divine, then the contradictions which Ramanuja has left us may be resolved. Brahman may wish for a new world body in order that it may contribute to his experience; and change may indeed touch the conscious self of Brahman.

At one point in the argument one sees the influence of the Hindu belief that the individual soul is not produced by birth nor is its career in any sense terminated by death. Only so can one see force in his contention that it is the body, but not the soul, that is touched by infancy, youth, etc. This is an argument not from experience but from traditional dogma. No one *experiences* a soul that is mature when the body is infantile or adolescent! (And if the soul is neither mature nor immature, then it is abstract.) It is theory that is here trying to shape the evidence, not evidence that is shaping the theory. Thus in addition to the monopolar prejudice, or rather as one form which it takes, we have the doctrine of "substance" as not really changing, or not changing in any important qualities. This is the result of favoring being over becoming (unconsciously, the abstract over the concrete). The soul is above events, for it is a being, and they are merely becomings. Actually, it is being that is given as a mere aspect of becoming. The arbitrariness of the substance idea is illustrated by the ease with which it assumes contradictory forms. In the Orient it means: incapable of real beginning in birth or termination in death. In the West it means only: incapable of termination in death, and then only in the case of human beings or higher types of substance. Also, in the West it means: incapable of forming a constituent of a body, such as the body of God; but in Ramanuja this does not follow.

On this last point our author is a genuine panentheist. He grasps the principle, with which all our knowledge agrees, that a body is not essentially a single mass of stuff forming a single substance with a soul but is a plurality of items (cells, molecules) subject to the supreme influence or rule of one individual, which is the soul. But, as above remarked, this is only half of the truth, the other half being that the soul is ruler, not by virtue of a merely one-way influence between it and the ruled items, but by virtue of a mutual action and reaction in which the soul's influence upon any one item tends to be radically more decisive than that of this item alone upon the soul. There is a superiority of influence from the soul, but this is not a superiority in reference to zero, as though the items simply failed to influence the ruling item. A man can rule his dog without being simply uninfluenced by him. Merely to perceive what the dog is doing is to receive optical sensory influence from the dog. Much more must God perceive, that is, intuit, what we are doing and so much the more subtly and variously must he be influenced by us! In spite of himself our author admits this when he says that we have to get permission from the highest self to perform our acts. This means we influence the allegedly changeless to make a permissive decision which, according to the author, would not have taken place had *we* not decided as we do!

Perhaps the failure of Ramanuja to establish his position as against Sankara, save in the eyes of a minority of Hindu thinkers, even down to this day (as it appears), is due to his not having achieved a thoroughgoing and consistent panentheism. He is apparently the closest to such a doctrine that ancient India got, as Plato is the closest the ancient Western world got; but neither got close enough to make panentheism a live issue at any time in the next thousand years or more. In India only with Sri Jiva (see Prologue), and in Europe only with Boehme and Schelling, do we begin to get the full outlines of the view, ETCKW, set forth with any

clarity or cogency. (See also Radhakrishnan, secs. 441 ff.)

A simple way to arrive at panentheism from Ramanuja is to introduce into his doctrine the Platonic insight that body is in soul, not vice versa. For then bodily changes and sufferings are also in the soul. The Highest Lord is then inclusive of change and suffering. The immutable factor is not the actuality of the soul but only an abstract essence or personality form, the One of Plotinus. The tenet that body is in soul is no arbitrary assertion of Plato; it is a fact of experience. For just to the extent that the body is known and effectively possessed by soul do its changes and sufferings qualify the experiences which are the *de facto* actualities of soul. Merely to rule the body is not enough; the effects produced must be possessed. Now the Highest soul must completely know and possess its body; hence in this case the body must enter in categorically supreme fashion into that soul's experience or actuality. That "subject is more inclusive than object" is an insight running from Plato to Whitehead through Leibniz, Berkeley, and Hegel. In a way, it is also the doctrine of Sankara. Ramanuja's attempt to construe the Highest Lord as immutable soul-factor in the mutable totality of the divine body-soul is, it seems, the fatal error which made his protest against Sankara comparatively ineffective. The reality of the divine body cannot be anywhere save in the divine soul, the real totality; and if the body's changes are real, then the soul really changes, or, more accurately, its actuality is not immune to accretions but grows with each new phase of the world process.

On the other hand, there is no need to quarrel with the idea that there is something changeless in the divine body-soul. A soul has a character, a complex of personality traits, which is expressed or concretized in a variety of successive acts and experiences. In modern panentheism this factor is explicitly recognized; for example, by Whitehead in his concept of the primordial nature of deity. But this factor is not the highest self, if that means the highest spiritual actuality, but is rather the fixed trait or "essence" of this self in contrast to its changing accidents. To call the essence higher than the accidents is meaningless, since it is merely an abstract constituent of the divine actuality, which necessarily involves some accidents or other. Inasmuch as the concrete contains the abstract, not vice versa, any accidental state of the divine actuality contains all the value there then is, including all the value of the abstract. So the concrete may be said to surpass the abstract in value, so far as there can be comparison at all. The soul as possessing, enjoying-suffering-as-well-as-ruling, the body is the full supreme spiritual actuality, not the soul as it would be (or once was) without the particular body it has.

The contrast between the "causal" and the "effected" state of Brahman is subject to similar remarks. The merely causal aspect of the divine is the abstract factor just spoken of. In a relative or qualified sense, however, each actual phase of the divine soul-body is cause with respect to later phases. One may also attach some meaning to the rather obscure distinction between the subtle and the gross phases of items in the body and to their "reabsorption" into Brahman. A new nondivine individual is first an incompletely determinate anticipatory potentiality, next a determinate, self-active individual, then an immortally objectified possession of the divine consciousness (Whitehead, sec. 393), retaining forever the qualities of feeling and thought and volition actualized in the individual's life. For this immortalization "reabsorption" is a crude and misleading image, but the interpretation is perhaps not hopelessly far-fetched.

So near, and so far, was medieval India with respect to the nontruncated form of ETCKW! We admit that Europe scarcely came nearer until recently.

## SPINOZA (1632–77)

In Spinoza the classical theistic doctrine of the externality of the world to God finds its first great critic. And a devastating (though brief) criticism he gave to this doctrine! The contradictions inherent in the joint assertions of knowledge and will in God, contingency in the world, yet total noncontingency in God, are sharply pointed out. True, this had already been done by Gersonides. But the latter drew the conclusion that divine knowledge and providence must be limited to the noncontingent aspects of the world. From similar considerations, Maimonides had concluded that one cannot really speak of "knowledge" or "will" at all in respect to God. Spinoza was the first major thinker to say roundly that the way to resolve the contradiction is to give up the contingency of the world. If, however, the world is as necessary as God, there is no longer any reason to regard it as extrinsic to him. A necessary whole cannot have contingent parts, but may it not have necessary parts, or—as Spinoza says—modifications? From the essence of a triangle various properties, such as having three sides, follow, and we may say that these properties are all contained in the essence. If the triangle is necessary, so are the properties. Thus, thinks Spinoza, are all things contained in God as necessary qualifications of the necessary being. But then all notion of the world as a free creation, a choice of one possibility among others open to divine power, is excluded, and so is the notion of human freedom, if that means that more than one course is really open to a man at a given moment. What happens is always what must happen, in the strict sense of following from the immutable essence of God, which itself exists necessarily. And, since all events are thus inevitable, we should cease to fret over them and accept what in no case could have been otherwise.

We omit some of the proofs (and the references to previous propositions serving as premises therein), since the important concern is not how Spinoza proved his conclusions from his premises but the acceptability of the premises themselves. One who objects to the conclusions will surely quarrel with one or more of the premises ("Definitions," "Axioms"), and to such a one the proofs establish nothing save that certain objectionable assumptions have certain objectionable consequences. We no longer live in an age when educated men generally are willing to accept the possibility of axioms self-evident at a glance, so certain that their consequences must be believed no matter how unpalatable or incredible. Rather, we think that incredible consequences amount to the incredibility of the alleged axioms, and doubtful consequences to the doubtfulness of the axioms. We are prepared to allow difficulties in the outcome to cast a shadow back upon the starting point; and only a set of consequences that thoroughly satisfied us would reconcile us to a set of axioms or postulates. So we may be willing to accept Spinoza's propositions as correctly "proved" in his system, without in the least thereby committing ourselves to the system.

Historically the importance of Spinoza seems to have been, first, that he gave classical theism a wound from which, according to Wolfson, it has not recovered, and indeed cannot recover, by offering to it a challenge which cannot,

it seems, fairly be met; and, second, that he suggested to European thought the necessity of relating God and world by some more intelligible bond than that of "causation" so defined that the effect is simply external to the cause. No longer can it seem enough to say, "There is God, the cause, and there is the world, the effect." For it follows that there is God-and-World, Cause-and-Effect, and this is something not identical with the first factor, if that is independent of the second, while to make it identical with the second factor is to make the World include God, and hence to be greater than he, since he excludes the world. The least paradoxical solution is to say that God-and-World is identical with God, somewhat as a whole-and-its-parts is identical with the whole. The problem from this point on in European thought is to define more exactly the sense in which God is the total reality, literally inclusive of the world. From now on the issue is, as in India it had long been, that between pantheism and panentheism. But in the West, as in the East, in Spinoza as in Sankara, it is pantheism that first receives sharp formulation. The monopolar version, as the simpler, precedes the dipolar, in analytic (though not in intuitive, poetic) thought.

Particularly valuable is Spinoza's daring and comparatively novel insistence that "extension," or the physical aspect of reality, is a dimension of the divine. The objection that this would mean a particular quantity and shape of material extension for deity does not convince Spinoza; for he thinks the extension of deity is unique in being unlimited. Everything physical has size and shape, except the physical universe. Who can assess limits or assign a shape to that? We have here to do with categorically supreme extension, not with mere ordinary extension.

Similarly, to the objection that extension must make God composite, and hence corruptible, he cogently replies that the objection presupposes that physical reality is a mere composite—as though the world had been assembled from parts existing outside of the world. There is no proof that the physical universe ever was put together, and none that it could possibly fall apart. Dissolution or separation of bodies within the universe is not dissolution, but merely rearrangement, of the universe itself. There is, Spinoza believed, a much profounder unity in the material world than most people realize, and this unity is that of God himself, in one aspect. The universe is not just one more physical object, nor is it the mere sum of such objects. Moreover, he argues, if there is nothing physical in God, then we cannot explain the physical world by tracing it to him. We explain the imperfect thoughts of men by relating them to the perfect (categorically superior) thought of deity; we explain the imperfect bodies of men by relating them to the perfect body or extended reality of deity.

We wish only that Spinoza had dared further and had treated temporal extension according to the same logic. We endure through limited time, experience novelty and retention of the past, in an imperfect manner; God endures through unlimited time and experiences novelty and retention in a categorically supreme manner. But had Spinoza done this, he would have been a panentheist rather than a pantheist. We must take him as the pantheist which he is.

## Definitions*

215. I understand that to be *Cause of Itself* whose essence involves existence and whose nature cannot be conceived unless existing.

216. I understand *Substance* to be that which is in itself and is conceived through itself: I mean that, the conception of which does not depend on the conception of another thing from which it must be formed.

An *Attribute* I understand to be that which the intellect perceives as constituting the essence of a substance.

By *Mode* I understand the Modifications of a substance or that which is in something else through which it may be conceived.

God I understand to be a being absolutely infinite, that is, a substance consisting of infinite attributes, each of which expresses eternal and infinite essence.

. . . I say absolutely infinite, but not in its kind. For of whatever is infinite only in its kind, we may deny the attributes to be infinite; but what is absolutely infinite appertains to the essence of whatever expresses essence and involves no denial.

## Axioms*

217. All things which are, are in themselves or in other things.

That which cannot be conceived through another thing must be conceived through itself. . . .

## Propositions I, XIV, XV, XVI: The Identity of God and an Infinite World

218. A substance is prior in its nature to its modifications.

This is obvious from [the above definitions].

219. Except God no substance can be granted or conceived. . . .

It follows . . . that extension and thought are either attributes of God or modifications of attributes of God.

220. Whatever is, is in God, and nothing can exist or be conceived without God.

. . . Save God no substance is granted or can be conceived, that is, a thing which is in itself and through itself is conceived. But modifications cannot exist or be conceived without substance, wherefore these can only exist in divine nature, and through that alone be conceived. But nothing is granted save substances and their modifications. Therefore nothing can exist or be conceived without God.

*221.* All those who have considered divine nature in any manner have denied that God is corporeal; which they have excellently proved from the fact that by body we understand a certain quantity in length, breadth, and depth, with a certain shape, and what could be more absurd than to say this of God, a being absolutely infinite? And as they have clearly shown, among the other reasons, by means of which they have attempted to prove this, that corporeal or extended substance is very far removed from divine nature, they have said it is created by God. But they can in no wise tell from what divine nature [it] could be created; for this they say themselves they do not know. But I at least have proved with sufficient clearness, I think, that no substance can be produced or created from another. [Spinoza's argument, not quoted, is drawn at least in part from his definition of substance.] Moreover, we have shown that save God no substance can be granted or conceived. Hence we conclude that extended substance is one of the infinite attributes of God.

*222.* Infinite things in infinite modes (that is, all things which can fall under the heading of infinite intellect) must necessarily follow from the necessity of divine nature.

This proposition must be manifest to every one who will but consider this, that from a given definition of everything the intellect gathers certain properties, which in truth necessarily follow from the definition (that is, the very essence of the thing), and so the more reality the definition of a thing expresses, *i.e.,* the more reality the essence of a definite thing involves, the more properties the intellect will gather. But as divine nature has absolutely infinite attributes, each of which expresses infinite essence in its kind, infinite things

in infinite modes (that is, all things that fall under the heading of infinite intellect) must necessarily follow [from] its necessity.

### *Propositions XXIX, XXXIII: The Absence of Contingency in God and World*

*223.* In the nature of things nothing contingent is granted, but all things are determined by the necessity of divine nature for existing and working in a certain way.

Whatever is, is in God. But God cannot be called a contingent thing: for he exists of necessity and not contingently. Again, the modes of divine nature do not follow from it contingently, but of necessity, and that either in so far as divine nature be considerered absolutely or as determined for certain action. Now God is the cause of these modes, not only in so far as they simply exist, but also in so far as they are considered as determined for the working of anything. For if they are not determined by God, it is impossible, not contingent indeed, that they should determine themselves; and on the other hand, if they are determined by God, it is impossible and in no wise contingent for them to render themselves undetermined. Wherefore all things are determined by the necessity of divine nature, not only for existing, but also for existing and working after a certain manner, and nothing contingent is granted.

Before proceeding, I would wish to explain, or rather remind you, what we must understand by active and passive nature (*natura naturans* and *natura naturata*), for I think that from the past propositions we shall be agreed that by nature active we must understand that which is in itself and through itself is conceived, or such attributes of substance as express eternal and infinite essence, that is, God, in so far as he is considered as a free cause. But by nature passive I understand all that follows from the necessity of the nature of God, or of any one of his attributes, that is, all the modes of the attributes of God, in so far as they are considered as things which are in God, and which cannot exist or be conceived without God.

*224.* Things could not have been produced by God in any other manner or order than that in which they were produced. . . .

All things must have followed of necessity from a given nature of God, and they were determined for existence or action in a certain way by the necessity of divine nature. And so if things could have been of another nature or determined in another manner for action so that the order of nature were different, therefore, also, the nature of God could be different than it is now: then another nature of God must exist, and consequently two or more Gods could be granted, and this is absurd. Wherefore things could not have been produced in any other way or order, etc. . . . I make no doubt, however, but that many will deride this opinion as absurd, nor will they agree to give up their minds to the contemplation of it: and on no other account than that they are wont to ascribe to God a freedom far different to that which has been propounded by us. They attribute to him absolute will.

*225.* . . . although it be conceded that will appertains to the essence of God, yet it nevertheless follows that things could not have been created in any other manner or order than that in which they were created; and this will be easy to show if first we consider the very thing which they themselves grant, namely, that it depends solely on the decree and will of God that each thing is what it is, for otherwise God would not be the cause of all things. They grant further, that all the decrees of God have been appointed by him through and from all eternity: for otherwise it would argue mutability

and imperfection in God. But as in eternity there are no such things given as *when, before,* or *after,* hence it follows merely from the perfection of God that he never can or could decree anything else than what is decreed, or that God did not exist before his decrees, nor without them could he exist. But they say that although we suppose that God had made the nature of things different or had decreed otherwise concerning nature and her order from all eternity, it would not thence follow that God was imperfect. Now if they say this, they must also admit that God can change his decrees. For had God decreed otherwise than he has concerning nature and her order, that is, had he willed and conceived anything else concerning nature, he must necessarily have some other intellect and will than those which he now has. And if it is permitted to attribute to God another will and intellect than those which he now has, without any change in his essence or perfection, what would there be to prevent him from changing his decrees concerning things created, and yet remaining perfect? For his intellect and will concerning things created and their order is the same in respect to his essence and perfection, in whatever manner they may be conceived. Furthermore, all the philosophers, I have seen, concede that no such thing as potential intellect in God can be granted, but only actual. But as they make no distinction between his intellect and will and his essence, being all agreed in this, it follows then that if God had another actual intellect and will, he must necessarily also have another essence; and thence, as I concluded in the beginning, that, were things produced in any other way than that in which they were, God's intellect and will, that is, as has been granted, his essence, also must have been other than it is, which is absurd.

Now since things could not have been

produced in any other manner or order than that in which they were, and since this follows from the consummate perfection of God, there is no rational argument to persuade us to believe that God did not wish to create all the things which are in his intellect, and that in the same perfection in which his intellect conceived them. But they say that in things there is no such a thing as perfection or imperfection, but that which causes us to call a thing perfect or imperfect, good or bad, depends solely on the will of God; moreover that if God had willed it, he could have brought to pass that what is now perfection might have been the greatest imperfection, and *vice versa*. But what else is this than to openly assert that God who necessarily understands what he wishes, could bring to pass by his own will that his intelligence should conceive things in another manner than they now do? This (as I have just shown) is the height of absurdity. Wherefore I can turn their argument against them in the following manner. All things depend on the power of God. That things should be different from what they are would involve a change in the will of God, and the will of God cannot change (as we have most clearly shown from the perfection of God): therefore things could not be otherwise than as they are. I confess that the theory which subjects all things to the will of an indifferent God and makes them dependent on his good will is far nearer the truth than that which states that God acts in all things for the furthering of good. For these seem to place something beyond God which does not depend on God, and to which God looks in his actions as to an example or strives after as an ultimate end. Now this is nothing else than subjecting God to fate, a greater absurdity than which it is difficult to assert of God, whom we have shown to be the

first and only free cause of the essence of all things and their existence.

[Sec. 215, Spinoza, *Ethics and De intellectus emendatione*, trans. A. Boyle (London: J. M. Dent & Sons, Ltd., 1913), p. 1. Sec. 216, *ibid.*, pp. 1–2. Sec. 217, *ibid.*, p. 2. Sec. 218, *ibid.*, p. 3. Sec. 219, *ibid.*, p. 11. Sec. 220, *ibid.* Sec. 221, *ibid.*, pp. 11–12. Sec. 222, *ibid.*, p. 15. Sec. 223, *ibid.*, pp. 23–24. Sec. 224, *ibid.*, pp. 26–27. Sec. 225, *ibid.*, pp. 27–29.]

### COMMENT

Spinoza assumes that there is an absolute distinction between the self-explanatory (conceived through itself alone) and that which must be explained through something else and that this is the same as the distinction between what exists in itself and what exists in something else. The self-explanatory, existing in itself alone, he calls "substance." What is excluded by this way of thinking? For one thing, the idea of a regress of inherence, such that *A* is in *B*, *B* in *C*, and so on without final end. Now, it may be held that temporal process is just such an endless regress of inherence, since each event becomes inherent in a new event having the first as its past. And, except other events, nothing is given in which an event can inhere. We do not find occurrences in things or substances, but certain stabilities of relationship and sequence among experiences, which are occurrences, and these stabilities we call "things" (or, in some cases, "persons"). The final subjects of predication are the occurrences, and each such occurrence is only provisionally final. It becomes predicate for new events as part of their past. An event is independent of, self-explanatory with respect to, the new events, not because it does not come to inhere in them, but because it will be equally well suited by whatever new events may occur to house it. Spinoza excludes all this by fiat. In that way nothing is really proved.

Again, in his remarks about infinity, Spinoza assumes that all possibility can be actualized and defines God as the substance in which this "absolutely infinite" actualization inheres. Of course it is then easy to "prove" that such a God exists and that all things follow necessarily from his essence. The place to quarrel with this reasoning is right at the beginning, with the concept of an exhaustive actualization of possibility. For us, it is axiomatic that infinity is the character of the possible as such, while actuality is by definition in some sense finite. To do everything possible is to do nothing. To act is to choose among incompatible alternatives. There is a definite or actual world because not everything possible is in it.

Spinoza's denial of all contingency, all possibilities alternative to actuality, involves him in typical paradoxes of monopolar thinking. Necessity itself has no meaning save in terms of possibility, as something irreducible to actuality. A thing is necessary if no alternative to it is possible; but this presupposes a meaning and a referent for "possible" and for "alternative" which the doctrine that all things are necessary cannot provide. As monopolarists always do, Spinoza is continually availing himself unofficially of the pole he denies. Thus he speaks of "modifications" or "affections" or "determinations" of substance, which he contrasts with its essence. Now, either these are contingent (accidental) or they are necessary (essential) modifications. Spinoza denies the former. But what is an essential or necessary qualification of a thing? Surely essential qualities are just the essence over again. You may say they are parts of the essence. And Spinoza once compared modes to the waves of the sea. But he denies that substance is a mere aggregate of the modes and insists that the parts are in this case conceived through the whole, not the whole through the parts.

This means that the essence of substance is or contains a single infinitely complex quality, a superparticular embracing and also pervading all particulars, a *gestalt* quality of the whole of things. Now, no matter how complex a particular quality is, it remains perfectly arbitrary, and its nonexistence cannot be inconceivable. For only that which is involved in existence as such, taken generically, exists necessarily; but no complex of particulars, even though all-inclusive, can be contained in existence-as-such, for this means just existence taken in abstraction from particulars. No doubt Spinoza would quarrel with this abstractability of existence as such. But then he renders the notion of necessary existence unintelligible. And, moreover, unless the essence of substance can be abstracted from the modes, it is meaningless to say that they are conceived by reference to it, and not vice versa.

Where everything is necessary, what does it mean to speak of priority or logical independence? If "God exists" could and would be true whether or not "men at some time exist" were true (that is, if the existence of men does not follow from the existence and essence of God), then God's existence is logically independent of that of men, and if, further, the truth of the second proposition quoted involves the truth of the first proposition, then the idea of God is necessary to the conception of men but not vice versa. Spinoza denies this meaning of the distinction between conceptions which are self-explanatory and those which are not, but he fails, it seems, to furnish any other meaning. He tries to escape what appears logically inescapable—that a thing is not independent of what it necessarily involves but dependent upon it. And if modes require God and God necessitates the modes, if neither can be unless the other is, then where is there any priority or any relation of independence? And is not the most trivial thing as valuable as deity? For greater importance than absolute indispensability there cannot be.

Thus Spinozism faces a dilemma: either it denies the reality of finite things, like Sankara, or it cannot explain in what sense they constitute necessary qualifications of the one substance. The mathematical analogy comparing the modes of substance to properties deducible from the definition of "triangle" is no help. For all such properties are universals on the same level of universality as triangle itself, and the problem of modes is the relation of particulars to substance or being as such, in its eternal or generic essence. According to Wolfson's interpretation of Spinoza,

all things are in God as the less universal is in the more universal. . . .

He is their internal cause as the genus is the internal cause of the species or the species of the particulars and as the whole is the internal cause of its parts. Now the universal, even though it does not exist separately from the particulars, is not logically identical with the sum of the particulars.[1]

Spinoza seems here to be guilty of a vicious confusion between class property and class taken in extension. Only of an extensional class is it true that the more universal contains the less universal. Humanity as a property does *not* contain Socrates and *is* separable from Socrates. So Wolfson's analysis only makes it more sharply clear that Spinoza's doctrine of divine causation of the modes or finite things is devoid of any definite and coherent meaning. God as inseparable from the world cannot have the necessity of the universal, of being as such. God as universal, necessary, or inherent in being as such must be God as abstract and exclusive

1. H. A. Wolfson, *The Philosophy of Spinoza* (Cambridge: Harvard University Press, 1948), I, 323, 324.

of particulars; God as inclusive of particulars can only be God as nonuniversal, accidentally particularized, contingent. The essence of God cannot include particularity. The divine inclusion of particularity must be extraessential, must consist of divine accidents. The unmodifiable cannot have modifications.

Spinoza's famous saying, "If we love God, we cannot desire him to return our love, for then he would lose his perfection by becoming passively affected by our joys and sorrows," is another consequence of monopolarity. And it leads to the following paradox: in God there is a clear idea corresponding to every true proposition and every real fact, for all true ideas are in God; but it is true that we enjoy and suffer, hence in God there is a clear idea of this enjoyment and suffering. Now the only way to intuit a feeling is to feel it. One cannot have a merely intellectual awareness of a concrete suffering or pleasure, for intellect as such is merely the tracing of relations, and a feeling is no mere relational pattern like a mathematical form. If our feelings are real facts in God, then God feels.

Let us consider, finally, the doctrine that there is but one substance. If by substance is meant the categorically supreme form of individuality, then of course God is the sole substance, just as he is the sole categorically supreme intellect or consciousness. But, then, just as we are nevertheless real though not supreme intellects or consciousnesses, so are we real individuals. If God is supremely self-active, we (and this Spinoza himself says) are in our own measure and degree self-active. But Spinoza seems to think we act only on one another, not on God, who thus escapes all passivity, since there is no one who can act upon him. But why cannot we act upon God? Our relation to God's knowledge is the measure of our reality, and, if we are self-active, we cannot be solely passive in relation to God.

In summary: Spinoza, in conceiving the world as in God, is by implication saying that all categorical contrasts fall in some appropriate sense within God, not merely between God and something else. In part, Spinoza adheres to this: he admits that the contrast between infinite and finite, universal and particular, is at both ends descriptive of deity, for the finite particular things are modes of God's reality. Similarly, with the contrast between quality and quantity, or immaterial and material, thought and extension. Similarly, with the contrast between cause and effect, or *natura naturans* and *natura naturata:* the effects too are God in his aspect as "determined to a particular mode." But Spinoza fails to see that exactly as good reasons obtain for conceiving God in terms of the contrast between eternal and temporal, necessary and contingent, and that, indeed, only through the concept of contingency as polar contrary of necessity can the contrast between cause and effect, or independent and dependent, or universal and particular, have any meaning. And he fails to see that God must be passive as well as active, suffering as well as joyous, loving as well as knowing. Thus Spinoza, like every pantheist, is merely a half-hearted panentheist. We may nonetheless be grateful to him for going part of the way from classical theism to surrelativistic panentheism.

# ROYCE (1855–1916)

The old idea that truth and reality must be defined in terms of ideally perfect knowledge, which one finds in Augustine, Spinoza, and Malebranche, is developed by Royce into an argument for the existence of God of striking cogency. Unfortunately, Royce largely ruined his effectiveness in this matter by striving, in his best-known and major work, *The World and the Individual,* to give the argument a technical form which not only did not help matters but which actually introduced a fallacy.

The fallacy was this: Royce defined realism as the doctrine that being is independent of our ideas; but from this he inferred that our ideas must be wholly independent of being, from which, again, it would follow that they had no tendency to be true. This of course is fallacious; independence need not be a symmetrical relation. Royce's entire argument, apart from this fallacy, had already been stated in the work from which we quote below. There is nothing in it of the fallacy in question.

The argument might be put succinctly thus: we cannot measure knowledge by its agreement with a reality simply outside knowledge, for the unknown is not available as a standard. On the other hand, human knowledge cannot regard itself as the measure of reality: what we know is not, even for us, the same as what is real. What, then, do we mean by the reality which we partly know and partly do not know? The answer is that knowledge has certain internal criteria which human knowledge only partly fulfils but which an ideal form of knowledge, which we can conceive of, would entirely fulfil. This ideal knowledge then serves to define reality, which is simply: what the internally perfect knowledge would have, or does have, as its presented content. Finally, we cannot say "would have," for that is to turn reality, as the actual, into something merely potential, which is contradictory. Hence we must say: "does have." That is, the ideal knowledge must exist. It is not that, since "reality" is unknown to us, our knowledge is defective. For how could we know a reality which is unknown to us and thus know our defects? Rather, we know, without needing to use the idea of reality, that our knowledge is defective. For example, it is not clear or fully definite and is infected with doubt and inconsistency. Hence we infer that the known is by us not *adequately* known, and we express this by saying that things as real and as known to us are not identical. This amounts to defining reality as the adequately known. It also follows that the real is within knowledge and consists in its relation to the adequate knower. Thus we have a theism which admits divine world inclusiveness.

### Definition of Omniscience

226. An omniscient being would be one who simply found presented to him . . . by virtue of an all-embracing, direct, and transparent insight . . . the complete, the fulfilled answer to every genuinely rational question. Observe the terms used. . . . To question means to have ideas of what is not now present, and to ask whether these ideas do express, or could express, what some experience could verify. I question, on the country road, "Is it four miles to the railway station, or more, or less?" In this case I have ideas or thoughts about possible experiences not now present to me. I question in so far as I wonder whether these possible experiences, if I got them—that is, if I walked or rode to yonder railway station and measured my way—would fulfill or verify one or another of these my various thoughts or ideas about the distance. . . .

On the other hand, to answer to the full, and with direct insight, any question, means to get your ideas, just in so far as they turn out to be true ideas, fulfilled, confirmed, verified by your experiences. When with full and complete insight you answer a question, then you get into the direct presence of facts, of experiences, which you behold as the confirmation or fulfillment of certain ideas, as the verification of certain thoughts. Take your mere ideas, as such, alone by themselves, and you have to question whether or no they are true accounts of facts. Answer your questions, wholly for yourself, without intermediation, and then you have got your ideas, your thoughts, somehow into the presence of experienced facts. There are thus two factors or elements in completed and genuine knowing, namely: fact, or something experienced on the one hand; and mere idea, or pure thought about actual or possible experience, on the other hand. . . .

Very well, then, an omniscient being is defined as one in whom these two factors of knowledge, so often divorced in us, are supposed to be fully and universally joined.

227. The two factors of his knowledge would, however, still remain distinguishable. He would think, or have ideas—richer ideas than our present fragments of thought, I need not say; but he would think. And he would experience. That is, he would have, in perfect fulness, what we call feeling—a world of immediate data of consciousness, presented as facts. This his world of feeling, of presented fact, would be richer than our fragments of scattered sensation, as I also need not say; but he would experience. Only—herein lies the essence of his conceived omniscience—in him and for him these facts would not be, as they often are in us, merely felt, but they would be seen as fulfilling his ideas; as answering what, were he not omniscient, would be his mere questions.

228. An omniscient being could answer your bitter *Why?* when you mourn, with an experience that would not simply ignore your passion. For your passion, too, is a fact. It is experienced. The experience of the omniscient being would therefore include it.

Only his insight, unlike yours, would comprehend it, and so would answer whatever is rational about your present question.

### Absolute Experience and Reality Correlative

*229.* To conceive any human belief as false—say the belief of a lunatic, a fanatic, a philosopher, or of a theologian —is to conceive this opinion as either possibly or actually corrected from some higher point of view, to which a larger whole of experience is considered as present.

Passing to the limit in this direction, we can accordingly say that by the absolute reality we can only mean either that which is present to an absolutely organized experience inclusive of all possible experience, or that which would be presented as the content of such an experience if there were one. If there concretely is such an absolute experience, then there concretely is such a reality present to it. If the absolute experience, however, remains to the end barely possible, then the concept of reality must be tainted by the same bare possibility. But the two concepts are strictly correlated. To conceive, for instance, absolute reality as containing no God, means simply that an absolutely all-embracing experience, if there were one, would find nothing Divine in the world. To assert that all human experience is illusory, is to say that an absolutely inclusive experience, if there were one, would have present, as part of its content, something involving the utter failure of our experience to attain that absolute content as such. To conceive that absolute reality consists of material atoms and ether, is to say that a complete experience of the universe would find presented to it nothing but experiences analogous to those that we have when we talk of matter in motion. In short, one must be serious with this concept of experience. Real-

ity, as opposed to illusion, means simply an actual or possible content of experience, not in so far as this experience is supposed to be transient and fleeting, but in so far as it is conceived to be somehow inclusive and organized, the fulfillment of a system of ideas, the answer to a scheme of rational questions. . . .

The conception of organized experience, in the limited and relative form in which the special sciences possess it, is unquestionably through and through a conception that, for us men, as we are, has a social origin. . . . Man begins his intelligent life by imitatively appealing to his fellow's experience. The life-blood of science is distrust of individual belief as such. A common definition of a relatively organized experience is, the consensus of the competent observers. Deeper than our belief in any physical truth is our common-sense assurance that the experience of our fellows is as genuine as our own, is in actual relation to our own, has present to it objects identical with those that we ourselves experience, and consequently supplements our own. . . .

My fellow's experience, however, thus supplements my own in two senses; namely, as actual and as possible experience.

*230.* The experience to which, as a social being, I first appeal when I learn to talk of truth, is the live actual experience of other men, which I, as an imitative being, primarily long to share, and which I therefore naturally regard as in many respects the norm for my experience.

*231.* But, in the course of more thoughtful mental growth, we have come to appeal from what the various men do experience to what they all ought to experience, or would experience if their experience were in unity; that is, if all their moments were linked expressions of one universal meaning which was present to one Universal

Subject, of whose insight their own experiences were but fragments. Such an ideally united experience, if it could absolutely define its own contents, would know reality. And by reality we mean merely the contents that would be present to such an ideal unity of experience. But now, on this side, the conception of the ideally organized experience does indeed at first look like a mere ideal of a barely possible unity. The problem still is: Is this unity more than a bare possibility? Has it any such concrete genuineness as the life of our fellows is believed to possess?

### Absolute Experience Must Be Real

232. The question: Is there an absolutely organized experience? is equivalent to the question: Is there an absolute reality? You cannot first say: There is a reality now unknown to us mortals, and then go on to ask whether there is an experience to which such reality is presented. The terms Reality and Organized Experience are correlative terms. The one can only be defined as the object, the content of the other. Drop either, and the other vanishes. Make one a bare ideal, and the other becomes equally such. If the organized experience is a bare and ideal possibility, then the reality is a mere seeming. . . .

But now there can be no such thing as a *merely* possible *truth*, definable apart from some actual experience. To say: So and so is possible, is to say: There is, somewhere in experience, an actuality some aspect of which can be defined in terms of this possibility. A possibility is a truth expressed in terms of a proposition beginning with *if,* or a hypothetical proposition—an *is* expressed in terms of an *if*. But every hypothetical proposition involves a categorical proposition. Every *if* implies an *is*. . . . The suitor asks for the daughter. The father replies: "I will give thee my daughter *if* thou canst touch heaven." Here the father expresses his

actually experienced intention in the form of a hypothetical proposition each member of which he believes to be false. The suitor cannot touch heaven, and is not to get the gift of the daughter. Yet the hypothetical proposition is to be true. Why? Because it expresses in terms of an *if* what the father experiences in terms of an *is,* namely, the obdurate inner will of the forbidding parent himself. Just so with any *if* proposition. Its members, antecedent and consequent, may be false. But it is true only in case there corresponds to its fashion of assertion some real experience.

And now, to apply this thought to our central problem, you and I, whenever we talk of reality as opposed to mere seeming, assert of necessity, as has just been shown, that *if* there were an organized unity of experience, this organized experience *would have* present to it as part of its content the fact whose reality we assert. This proposition cannot, as a merely hypothetical proposition, have any real truth, unless, to its asserted possibility, there corresponds some actual experience, present somewhere in the world, not of barely possible, but of concretely actual experience.

233. . . . one who thinks, who aims at truth, who means to know anything, is regarding his experience as suggesting truth. Now to regard our experience as suggesting truth is, as we have seen, to mean that our experience indicates what a higher or inclusive, *i.e.,* a more organized experience would find presented thus or thus to itself. It is this meaning, this intent, this aim, this will to find in the moment the indication of what a higher experience directly grasps —it is this that embodies for us the fact of which our hypothetical proposition aforesaid is the expression. But you may here say: "This aim, this will, is all. As a fact, you and I aim at the absolute experience; that is what we mean by

wanting to know absolute truth; but the absolute experience," so you may insist, "is just a mere ideal. There need be no such experience as a concrete actuality. The aim, the intent, is the known fact. The rest is silence—perhaps error. Perhaps there is no absolute truth, no ideally united and unfragmentary experience."

But hereupon one turns upon you with the inevitable dialectic of our problem itself. Grant hypothetically, if you choose, for a moment, that there is no universal experience as a concrete fact, but only the hope of it, the definition of it, the will to win it, the groaning and travail of the whole of finite experience in the search for it, in the error of believing that it is. Well, what will that mean? This ultimate limitation, this finally imprisoned finitude, this absolute fragmentariness and error of the actual experience that aims at the absolute experience when there is no absolute experience at which to aim—this absolute finiteness and erroneousness of the real experience, I say, will itself be a fact, a truth, a reality, and, as such, just the absolute truth. But this supposed ultimate truth will exist for whose experience? For the finite experience? No, for although our finite experience knows itself to be limited, still, just in so far as it is finite, it cannot know that there is no unity beyond its fragmentariness. For if any experience actually knew (that is, actually experienced) itself to be the whole of experience, it would have to experience how and why it were so. And if it knew this, it would be *ipso facto* an absolute *i.e.* a completely self-possessed experience, for which there was no truth that was not, as such, a datum—no ideal of a beyond that was not, as such, judged by the facts to be meaningless—no thought to which a presentation did not correspond, no presentation whose reality was not luminous to its comprehending thought. Only such an absolute experience could say with assurance: "Beyond my world there is no further experience actual." But if, by hypothesis, there is to be no such an experience, but only a limited collection of finite experiences, the question returns:—The reality of this final limitation, the existence of no experience beyond the broken mass of finite fragments—this is to be a truth—but for whose experience is it to be a truth? Plainly, in the supposed case, it will be a truth nowhere presented—a truth for nobody. But, as we saw before, to assert any absolute reality as real is simply to assert an experience—and, in fact, just in so far as the reality is absolute, an absolute experience—for which this reality exists. To assert a truth as more than possible, is to assert the concrete reality of an experience that knows this truth. Hence —and here, indeed, is the conclusion of the whole matter—the very effort hypothetically to assert that the whole world of experience is a world of fragmentary and finite experience is an effort involving a contradiction. Experience must constitute, in its entirety, one self-determined and consequently absolute and organized whole.

*234.* This absolute experience is related to our experience as an organic whole to its own fragments. It is an experience which finds fulfilled all that the completest thought can rationally conceive as genuinely possible.

### God and Suffering

*235.* . . . Job's problem is, upon Job's presuppositions, simply and absolutely insoluble. Grant Job's own presupposition that God is a being other than this world, that he is its external creator and ruler, and then all solutions fail. God is then either cruel or helpless, as regards all real finite ill of the sort that Job endures. Job, moreover, is right in demanding a reasonable answer to his question. The only possible answer is, however, one that undertakes to develop what I hold to be the immortal soul of the doctrine of the divine atonement. The answer to Job is: God is not in ultimate essence another being than yourself. He is the Absolute Being. You truly are one with God, part of his life. He is the very soul of your soul. And so, here is the first truth: When you suffer, *your sufferings are God's sufferings*, not his external work, not his external penalty, not the fruit of his neglect, but identically his own personal woe. In you God himself suffers, precisely as you do, and has all your concern in overcoming this grief.

The true question then is: Why does God thus suffer? The sole possible, necessary, and sufficient answer is, Because without suffering, without ill, without woe, evil, tragedy, God's life could not be perfected. This grief is not a physical means to an external end. It is a logically necessary and eternal constituent of the divine life. It is logically necessary that the Captain of your salvation should be perfect through suffering. No outer nature compels him. He chooses this because he chooses his own perfect selfhood. He is perfect. His world is the best possible world. Yet all its finite regions know not only of joy but of defeat and sorrow, for thus alone, in the completeness of his eternity, can God in his wholeness be triumphantly perfect.

*236.* In endeavoring to grapple with the theoretical problem of the place of evil in a world that, on the whole, is to be conceived, not only as good, but as perfect, there is happily one essentially decisive consideration concerning good and evil which falls directly within the scope of our own human experience, and which concerns matters at once familiar and momentous as well as too much neglected in philosophy. When we use such words as good, evil, perfect, we easily deceive ourselves by the merely abstract meanings which we associate with each of the terms taken apart from the other. We forget the experiences from which the words have been abstracted. To these experiences we must return whenever we want really to comprehend the words. If we take the mere words, in their abstraction, it is easy to say, for instance, that if life has any evil in it at all, it must needs not be so perfect as life would be were there no evil in it whatever. Just so, speaking abstractly, it is easy to say that, in estimating life, one has to set the good over against the evil, and to compare their respective sums. It is easy to declare that, since we hate evil, wherever and just so far as we recognize it, our sole human interest in the world must be furthered by the removal of evil from the world. And thus viewing the case, one readily comes to say that if God views as not only good but perfect a world in which we find so much evil, the divine point of view must be very foreign to ours, so that Job's rebellious pessimism seems well in order and Prometheus appears to defy the world-ruler in a genuinely humane spirit.

*237.* Now . . . I hold that God's point of view is not foreign to ours. I hold that God willingly, freely, and consciously suffers in us when we suffer, and that our grief is his. And despite all this I maintain that the world from God's point of view fulfills the divine ideal and is perfect. And I hold that when we abandon the onesided abstract ideas which the words good, evil, and perfect suggest, and when we go back to the concrete experiences upon which these very words are founded, we can see, even within the limits of our own experience, facts which make these very paradoxes perfectly intelligible, and even commonplace.

### Evil Necessary to the Good Experience

*238.* . . . man is a very complex creature. He has many organs. He performs many acts at once, and he experiences his performance of these acts in one highly complex life of consciousness. As the next feature of his life we all observe that he can at the same time shun one object and grasp at another. In this way he can have at once present to him a consciousness of good and a consciousness of ill.

239. But this is by no means an adequate notion of the complexity of man's life, even as an animal. If every conscious act of hindrance, of thwarting, of repugnance, means just in so far an awareness of some evil, it is noteworthy that men can have and can show just such tendencies, not only towards external experiences, but towards their own acts. That is, men can be seen trying to thwart and to hinder even their own acts themselves, at the very moment when they note the occurrence of these acts. One can consciously have an impulse to do something, and at that very moment a conscious disposition to hinder or to thwart as an evil that very impulse.

240. Now it is easy to say that such states of inner tension, where our conscious lives are full of a warfare of the self with itself, are contradictory or absurd states. But it is easy to say this only when you dwell on the words and fail to observe the facts of experience. As a fact, not only our lowest but our highest states of activity are the ones which are fullest of this crossing, conflict, and complex interrelation of loves and hates, of attractions and repugnances. As a merely physiological fact, we begin no muscular act without at the same time initiating acts which involve the innervation of opposing sets of muscles and these opposing sets of muscles hinder each other's freedom. Every sort of control of movement means the conflicting play of opposed muscular impulses. We do nothing simple, and we will no complex act without willing what involves a certain measure of opposition between the impulses or partial acts which go to make up the whole act. If one passes from single acts to long series of acts, one finds only the more obviously this interweaving of repugnance and of acceptance, of pursuit and of flight, upon which every complex type of conduct depends.

One could easily at this point spend time by dwelling upon numerous and relatively trivial instances of this interweaving of conflicting motives as it appears in all our life. I prefer to pass such instances over with a mere mention. There is, for instance, the whole marvelous consciousness of play, in its benign and in its evil forms. In any game that fascinates, one loves victory and shuns defeat, and yet as a loyal supporter of the game scorns anything that makes victory certain in advance; thus as a lover of fair play preferring to risk the defeat that he all the while shuns, and partly thwarting the very love of victory that from moment to moment fires his hopes. There are, again, the numerous cases in which we prefer to go to places where we are sure to be in a considerable measure dissatisfied; to engage, for instance, in social functions that absorbingly fascinate us despite or even in view of the very fact that, as long as they continue, they keep us in a state of tension which makes us, amongst other things, long to have the whole occasion over. Taking a wider view, one may observe that the greater part of the freest products of the activity of civilization, in ceremonies, in formalities, in the long social drama of flight, of pursuit, of repartee, of contest and of courtesy, involve an elaborate and systematic delaying and hindering of elemental human desires, which we continually outwit, postpone and thwart, even while we nourish them. When students of human nature assert that hunger and love rule the social world, they recognize that the elemental in human nature is trained by civilization into the service of the highest demands of the Spirit. But such students have to recognize that the elemental rules the higher world only in so far as the elemental is not only cultivated, but endlessly thwarted, delayed, outwitted, like a constitutional monarch, who is said to be a sovereign, but who, while he rules, must not govern.

But I pass from such instances, which in all their universality are still, I admit, philosophically speaking, trivial, because they depend upon the accidents of human nature. I pass from these instances to point out what must be the law, not only of human nature, but of every broader form of life as well. I maintain that this organization of life by virtue of the tension of manifold impulses and interests is not a mere accident of our imperfect human nature, but must be a type of the organization of every rational life. There are good and bad states of tension, there are conflicts that can only be justified when resolved into some higher form of harmony. But I insist that, in general, the only harmony that can exist in the realm of the spirit is the harmony that we possess when we thwart the present but more elemental impulse for the sake of the higher unity of experience; as when we rejoice in the endurance of the tragedies of life, because they show us the depth of life, or when we know that it is better to have loved and lost than never to have loved at all, or when we possess a virtue in the moment of victory over the tempter. And the reason why this is true lies in the fact that the more one's experience fulfills ideals, the more that experience presents to one, not of ignorance, but of triumphantly wealthy acquaintance with the facts of manifold, varied and tragic life, full of tension and thereby of unity. Now this is an universal and not merely human law. It is not those innocent of evil who are

fullest of the life of God, but those who in their own case have experienced the triumph over evil. It is not those naturally ignorant of fear, or those who, like Siegfried, have never shivered, who possess the genuine experience of courage; but the brave are those who have fears, but control their fears. Such know the genuine virtues of the hero. Were it otherwise, only the stupid could be perfect heroes.

241. Generalizing the lesson of experience we may then say: It is logically impossible that a complete knower of truth should fail to know, to experience, to have present to his insight, the fact of actually existing evil. On the other hand, it is equally impossible for one to know a higher good than comes from the subordination of evil to good in a total experience. When one first loving, in an elemental way, whatever you please, himself hinders, delays, thwarts his elemental interest in the interest of some larger whole of experience, he not only knows more fact, but he possesses a higher good than would or could be present to one who was aware neither of the elemental impulse, nor of the thwarting of it in the tension of a richer life. The knowing of the good, in the higher sense, depends upon contemplating the overcoming and subordination of a less significant impulse, which survives even in order that it should be subordinated.

242. Now if the love of God is more inclusive than the love of man, even as the divine world of experience is richer than the human world, we can simply set no human limit to the intensity of conflict, to the tragedies of existence, to the pangs of finitude, to the degree of moral ill, which in the end is included in the life that God not only loves, but finds the fulfillment of the perfect ideal.

243. . . . and if even we, in our weakness, can frequently find rest in the very presence of conflict and of ten-

sion, in the very endurance of ill in a good cause, in the hero's triumph over temptation, or in the mourner's tearless refusal to accept the lower comforts of forgetfulness, or to wish that the lost one's preciousness had been less painfully revealed by death—well, if even we know our little share of this harmony in the midst of the wrecks and disorders of life, what limit shall we set to the divine power to face this world of his own sorrows, and to find peace in the victory over all its ills?

*244.* Job's rebellion came from the thought that God, as a sovereign, is far off, and that, for his pleasure, his creature suffers. Our own theory comes to the mourner with the assurance: "Your suffering, just as it is in you, is God's suffering. No chasm divides you from God. He is not remote from you even in his eternity. He is here. His eternity means merely the completeness of his experience. But that completeness is inclusive. Your sorrow is one of the included facts." I do not say: "God sympathizes with you from without, would spare you if he could, pities you . . . as a Father pities his children." I say: "God here sorrows, not *with* but *in* your sorrow. Your grief is identically his grief, and what you know as your loss, God knows as his loss, just in and through the very moment when you grieve."

But hereupon the sufferer perchance responds: "If this is God's loss, could he not have prevented it? To him are present in unity all the worlds; and yet he must lack just this for which I grieve." I respond: "He suffers here that he may triumph. For the triumph of the wise is no easy thing. Their lives are not light, but sorrowful. Yet they rejoice in their sorrow. . . . They wander and find their home even in wandering. They long, and attain through their very love of longing. Peace they find in triumphant warfare. . . ."

Yet the mourner may still insist: "If my sorrow is God's, his triumph is not mine. Mine is the woe. His is the peace." But my theory is a philosophy. It proposes to be coherent. I must persist: "It is your fault that you are thus sundered from God's triumph. His experience in its wholeness cannot now be yours, for you just as you—this individual—are now but a fragment, and see his truth as through a glass darkly. But if you see his truth at all, through even the dimmest light of a glimmering reason, remember, that truth is in fact your own truth, your own fulfillment, the whole from which your life cannot be divorced, the reality that you mean even when you most doubt, the desire of your heart even when you are most blind, the perfection that you unconsciously strove for even when you were an infant, the complete Self apart from whom you mean nothing, the very life that gives your life the only value which it can have. In thought, if not in the fulfillment of thought, in aim if not in attainment of aim, in aspiration if not in the presence of the revealed fact, you can view God's triumph and peace as your triumph and peace.

*245.* What if the sinner now triumphantly retorts: "Aha! So my will is God's will. All then is well with me." I reply: What I have said disposes of moral ill precisely as definitely as of physical ill. What the evil will is to the good man, whose goodness depends upon its existence, but also upon the thwarting and the condemnation of its aim, just such is the sinner's will to the divine plan. God's will, we say to the sinner, is your will. Yes, but it is your will thwarted, scorned, overcome, defeated.

*246.* God wills you not to triumph. And that is the use of you in the world —the use of evil generally—to be hated but endured, to be triumphed over through the very fact of your presence, to be willed down even in the very life of which you are a part.

But to the serious moral agent we say: What you mean when you say that evil in this temporal world ought not to exist, and ought to be suppressed, is simply what God means by seeing that evil ought to be and is endlessly thwarted, endured, but subordinated. In the natural world you are the minister of God's triumph. Your deed is his.

247. The justification of the presence in the world of the morally evil becomes apparent to us mortals only in so far as this evil is overcome and condemned. It exists only that it may be cast down. Courage, then, for God works in you. In the order of time you embody in outer acts what is for him the truth of his eternity.

[Sec. 226, Josiah Royce, *The Conception of God* (Berkeley: Executive Council of the Philosophical Union of the University of California, 1895; New York: Macmillan Co., 1898), pp. 9–11. Sec. 227, *ibid.*, p. 11. Sec. 228, *ibid.*, p. 12. Sec. 229, *ibid.*, pp. 24–25. Sec. 230, *ibid.*, p. 26. Sec. 231, *ibid.* Sec. 232, *ibid.*, pp. 27–28. Sec. 233, *ibid.*, pp. 29–30. Sec. 234, *ibid.*, p. 32. Sec. 235, Josiah Royce, *Studies of Good and Evil* (New York: D. Appleton & Co., 1915), pp. 13–14. Sec. 236, *ibid.*, pp. 15–16. Sec. 237, *ibid.*, pp. 16–17. Sec. 238, *ibid.*, p. 19. Sec. 239, *ibid.* Sec. 240, *ibid.*, pp. 21–23. Sec. 241, *ibid.*, p. 24. Sec. 242, *ibid.*, p. 25. Sec. 243, *ibid.*, pp. 25–26. Sec. 244, *ibid.*, pp. 26–27. Sec. 245, *ibid.*, pp. 27–28. Sec. 246, *ibid.*, p. 28. Sec. 247, *ibid.*]

## COMMENT

An ambiguity is to be noted in Royce's conception of the ideal experience. Such an experience must indeed see that there cannot now be anything beyond itself, for reality is defined as the content of the ideal experience. But "cannot now be" is not the same as "could not now have been" or as "can never be." If the divine experience is ideally temporal, a process, not just eternal, or a being, then each moment of divine experience defines what *then* is real. This reality, however, does not exhaust possibility, even "genuine possibility" (sec. 234), for the future remains open for further experience and

therefore for further reality; and, also, to the previous moment of divine experience and its reality there might have succeeded a different present experience. The divine perception sees the completeness of its given world in the sense that it sees the identity of "what I now experience" and "what now is." (Indeed, the latter phrase would be totally superfluous.) But this identity is compatible with another: that of "what might now have been" with "what I might now have experienced"; also of "what may eventually be" and "what I may eventually experience." Divine actuality (of experience with its content) and actuality as such, and also divine potentiality and potentiality as such, may coincide; but it would not follow that divine actuality and potentiality, or actuality as such and potentiality as such, must or could coincide.

We grant to Royce that the truth, "further experience is possible," must itself be divinely experienced. All truth that now is, is now experienced. But we hold—admittedly against the views of many logicians—that new truths are created every moment. The ideal experience, then, is not one for which all "questions" have an answer fixed once for all, for the whole of time; but, rather, an experience which entertains determinate questions of particular detail only about the past and present, and with regard to the concrete details of the future considers only what is possible or probable, recognizing that the future (in its most concrete aspects) really consists of possibility and probability. Royce offers an argument or two (not included in our selections) for viewing the future as determinate no less than the past; but the reasoning is weak. Like Leibniz and so many others, he simply did not take the issue seriously. Thus Royce concludes that the ideal or definitive experience must be "complete" in the sense of answering all questions and fulfilling all desires that ever shall or may be entertained. This is the familiar monopolar procedure of treating potentiality as not real at all. God is all possible perfections—as if possibility could be collapsed into actuality in this fashion!

The ideal measure of knowledge which we need is not of this character. That we are ignorant means that we do not know what is past, settled, and actual, nor yet what is future, open for determination, and potential. Of course, we wish to predict, so far as the world is causally settled, so far as there are determining tendencies now in being, so far as the creativity from which alone the future can issue into the present is already channeled in advance. The ideal experience knows this advance channeling but knows it for what it is, the dead part of the living creativity, the already crystallized and precipitated aspect of the otherwise unpredictable process of living. Royce never sees this and brushes potentiality aside as either all sheer actuality or a "merely logical," that is, not real, possibility. But the indeterminate determinableness of life is not merely logical but is inseparable from its actuality. It is one pole of the dipolar affair, actual-potential, past-and-future, which is reality itself.

We ask the reader to note that the force of the argument for the existence of a definitive or adequate knowledge, an omniscience, is not weakened by this oversight of Royce. On the contrary, the paradoxes which Royce had on his hands as soon as he had committed himself to the notion of God as eternally complete and beyond possibility of further growth or enrichment constituted (together with the fallacy in The World and the Individual version of the argument mentioned in our opening discussion of this philosopher) a main cause of Royce's failure to carry conviction to his generation. He was then compelled to argue that even the worst things are necessary parts of the one perfect whole. The bad man is bad only in intention—actually he is required for the supreme goodness, even though in spite of himself. And this is the Theodicy over again. Once more, it is no solution; for what of the fact that the bad man's usefulness is unintentional? This fact itself has no bad consequences ultimately, for ultimately the consequence of all things is sheer maximal perfection. So it matters not at all whether one is bad or good. Like a giant, as Santayana said, Royce wrestled with this problem and did not solve it. The problem is unnecessary, since we can conceive the standard experience as able to grow, and then it can make a difference to the rate of this growth what acts we perform. It will adequately grasp all that we are and do, but its satisfaction in this will depend in part upon the quality of the acts and experiences we contribute. Here cognitive adequacy is not the sole criterion of beauty; richness and harmony of content known are also involved.

What we welcome in Royce, aside from his easily correctible argument, is his insistence upon the inclusion in God of all the suffering in reality. One needs only to add that this ought to carry with it a genuine duality of past and future. For suffering is evil, is really suffering, only if it was once more or less avoidable, or, if something similar may yet be avoided, only if something is undecided and open to decision. In eternity is no decision and no suffering; things merely are as they are. Spinoza is the more plausible interpreter of a deity for whom there is no open future and no indeterminacy. On the other hand, is not Royce exceedingly cogent in his contentions that (1) the particular actual goods of life are inseparable from certain elements of conflict and evil, so that sheer escape from evil as such would mean the loss of all concrete good; and (2) only the ignorant could escape suffering, since to know suffering concretely and adequately can only mean to have it within one's own experience; hence (3) an all-knowing being must contain within its own life all the suffering of the world? What does

not follow, we contend, is that the particular sufferings must have been divinely chosen once for all, eternally without "really possible" alternative. To this issue we shall frequently return, for instance, in our "Comment" upon the author next to be quoted.

# JEFFERS (1887——): TRAGIC PANTHEISM

A vivid expression of pantheistic motifs is a striking feature of the work of a leading poet of our time, Robinson Jeffers. Here we see a typical result of combining the all-inclusiveness of deity with a one-sided or monopolar conception of the nature of deity thanks to which the full reality of the world is rendered homeless, since it can neither qualify God nor have its being outside him. True, our poet says that time is in God, and there is no direct attempt to deny the reality of time. But any such admission of time is equivocal until the status of associated categories, such as contingency and freedom, is clarified.

Notable is the full recognition that pain and conflict are in God. Here Jeffers associates himself, unknowingly very likely, with numerous modern thinkers. God undergoes our sufferings. But, since all is his doing, his torture is self-inflicted. On the whole he enjoys this infliction, as mere peace and pleasantness could not be enjoyed. Intensity of experience requires evil. This recalls Royce, though there is a much less moralistic flavor in the poet. It is not that God must be noble, heroic, and therefore endure suffering but just that the alternative is lack of all intensity of experience or even of any experience. This is scarcely more than a difference of accent. Logically the positions seem the same.

*The Divine Self-torture, from "At the Birth of an Age"*

248. The Hanged God: Pain and their endless cries. How they cry to me:

but they are I: let them ask themselves.

I am they and there is nothing beside. I am alone and time passes, time also is in me, the long

Beat of this unquiet heart, the quick drip of this blood, the whirl and returning of these stars. . . .

. . . without strain there is nothing. Without pressure, without conditions, without pain,

Is peace; that's nothing, not-being; the pure night, the perfect freedom, the black crystal. I have chosen

Being; therefore wounds, bonds, limits and pain. . . .

Whatever electron or atom or flesh or star or universe cries to me,

Or endures in shut silence: it is my cry, my silence;

I am the nerve, I am the agony,

I am the endurance. I torture myself to discover myself. . . .

Discovery is deep and endless,

Each moment of being is new: therefore I still refrain my burning thirst from the crystal-black

Water of an end.

*The Divine Cruelty, from "Apology for Bad Dreams"*

249. He brays humanity in a mortar to bring the savor

From the bruised root: a man having bad dreams, who invents victims, is only the ape of that God.

*Determinism: Pantheism's Denial of
Freedom, from "Meditation
on Saviors"*

250. How should one caught in the
stone of his own person dare tell
the people anything. . . ?
And what could his words change?
The mountain ahead of the world is not
forming but fixed. But the man's
words would be fixed also,
Part of that mountain, under equal compulsion; under the same present compulsion in the iron consistency.

*How God Is To Be Loved, from
"Going to Horse Flats," "Still
the Mind Smiles," and
"Triad"*

251. Man's world is a tragic music and
is not played for man's happiness,
Its discords are not resolved but by
other discords.
     But for each man
There is real solution, let him turn from
himself and man to love God.
He is out of the trap then. He will remain
Part of the music, but will hear it as
the player hears it.
. . . he will still suffer and still die, but
like a God, not a tortured animal.

252. From here for normal one sees
both ways,
And listens to the splendor of God, the
exact poet, the sonorous
Antistrophe of desolation to the strophe
multitude.

253. . . . God, who is very beautiful,
but hardly a friend of humanity.

[Sec. 248, *The Selected Poetry of Robinson
Jeffers* (New York: Random House, 1937),
pp. 558–59. Sec. 249, *ibid.,* p. 176. Sec. 250,
*ibid.,* p. 202. Sec. 251, *ibid.,* pp. 583–84. Sec. 252,
*ibid.,* p. 460. Sec. 253, *ibid.,* p. 459.]

COMMENT

In his denial of freedom, or assertion
of strict determinism, and in his denial
that the Inclusive One can be related to

the included individuals, this grand poet
is a typical pantheist. Here once more
we have the implicitly terrible consequences of monopolarity. God in relation to us is sheer cause; we, mere effects. Only in relation to each other are
we mutually active and passive, but in
relation to God purely passive or unreal.
We do nothing to the divine. Our sufferings are God's, but this means that
God causes himself to suffer. Is it not
clear that the one-sided denial of receptivity, contingency, relativity to
others, rather than merely the assertion
that God includes others, is responsible
for the sense of desperation and cruelty
which haunts this doctrine? Apparently,
Jeffers somehow inherited nineteenth-
century determinism and never thought
to question it. Deterministic pantheism
is always cruelly paradoxical, as one can
see in the Stoics and in Spinoza, though
the latter was unusually skilful in con-
cealing this aspect.

The perpetual battle in Jeffers between his ethical nobility and his amor-
alistic naturalism is mostly tragic,
though sometimes tedious. It belongs
with just those features which distinguish pantheism from panentheism.

On the other hand, what the two doctrines just mentioned have in common—
the sense that we by our very being
enrich the life of God—is sometimes
wonderfully exploited by this author.
And the explanation of why deity is not
mere peace and quiet and immobility is
in part that which panentheism gives.
But only in part. True, God apart from
all conditions, conflicts, pressures, ac-
tion-reaction, would be empty potentiality and no actual experience or consciousness. But Jeffers' one oversight,
simple and gigantic, is in not seeing that
the conditions, conflicts, cannot be simply self-imposed. God cannot fight with
himself to enjoy a battle. It is not the
divine freedom or decision that limits
the divine freedom but freedom in general—ours, all creatures'. Berdyaev and
Whitehead almost alone seem clear

here: God does not create our free acts, nor does he create some faculty of freedom from which our acts flow. "He induces us to create ourselves" is a more nearly correct way of putting it. (Those who see depth in paradox ought not to balk at this one!) God fosters and cherishes the flow of free creaturely acts that enter into his life; but they are not his acts or decisions but ours. Only in general and in principle is evil the predetermined, inevitable partial outcome (the total outcome is always essentially good); in detail, the evils are unforeseen, unintended, in no sense deliberate choices. Thus God has a destiny, things happen to him—not indeed from without but from within. He is tortured, not by himself, but by the creatures who, in injuring each other, in some degree and manner crucify deity itself. But then we need not reject the idea that the divine loves us. He shares and contains our suffering because he loves us, or this containing and this sharing are one. The divine unity is the divine sympathy, accepting our free acts and their results for each other as also of divine import.

What a difference this makes! True, Jeffers might still perhaps hold that what most men mean by God's "love" for them is something more naïve and less worthy of belief. He might perhaps still have said, to the self-imposed query why he has not written about the divine love: "I can tell lies in prose." But, no, he must then have felt obliged to set forth the higher conception of divine sympathy. His whole spiritual development must have been otherwise. Some weird beauty would have been lost, but also some spiritual ugliness, and much other beauty would have been possible.

# Chapter V: *Emanationism or Exclusive Monism*

## PLOTINUS (*ca.* 205–70)

The importance of this thinker is due to the fact that he is the only great intellect—or at least the greatest intellect—living after Aristotle and before Spinoza who was free from ecclesiastical or creedal commitments. Put in other words, he was the one great European mind in all that long period who was not a Christian, a Jew, or a Mohammedan. Yet he had some acquaintance with the religious doctrines of his time. Thus he enjoyed a unique range of speculative possibilities. No doubt his personal convictions limited him severely, but such limitation had at least a partly different incidence from that of the others.

In a sense Plotinus, the "Neo-Platonist," really does substantially reaffirm the Platonic view. The three aspects of the ultimate in the *Timaeus*—the form of Good (with the other forms), the eternal demiurge, and the created divinity or world soul—reappear as the One, the Intelligence or *Nous*, and the World Soul of Plotinus. However, whereas Plato resorts to frankly mythical language in regard to the status of the intermediary factor, the *Nous* or eternal Consciousness, and its relations to the World Soul, Plotinus seems to think he has a logical principle for the progression from One to World Soul. The One is what is left when we transcend all duality, even that of subject and object; the *Nous* contains this minimal duality, but its objects are limited to pure forms, including the One; the Soul contains in addition the entire physical world. Thus the order is from simplicity and stability to complexity and, finally, change. On the assumption that unity is superior to multiplicity, the progression is a sort of descent—though not a degeneration, since the One is not changed or infected by the multiplicity it somehow produces or which emanates from it.

Is this view Platonic? Plato in the *Republic* does indeed talk like Plotinus in exalting the good, apparently taken in its sheer unity as a form, above all things. And one may argue that the Demiurge in the *Timaeus* is depicted as superior to the world soul and as wholly timeless. And this too would agree with the view of Plotinus that the *Nous* is above the world soul. But in the *Laws* the very argument for the existence of deity depends upon the nature of soul as self-moving; and, as we saw (and much more could be said—see, for example, Raphael Demos), Plato is by no means unequivocally on the side of the view that the immutable, nonrelative, or unitary is superior to the moving, relational, and multiform. Plato's interest in deity is bound up with his idea that the divine takes an interest in the affairs of men and that the divine power produces only the good in the world, the evil having another cause. Now, interest in the world is relativity to what happens in the world; and, if the success of the divine intent is qualified by evils introduced from other sources, this, too, implies that Plato's worship is of a being whose life is not without its relativities and complexities.

In Plotinus there is something of the Platonic wavering or ambiguity. He, too, does not always seem content to say flatly that the One is simply above soul and intelligence and purpose. In spite of himself he keeps employing the language of consciousness and will to describe the highest Good. But still his main intent is wonderfully clear. Consciousness is smitten with the duality of knower and known. Volition is smitten with that of goal and effort to reach the goal. Unity is superior to all multiplicity and duality; ergo, our supreme reverence must be for something held to be wholly superconscious, supercognitive, and supervolitional. And for the Platonic self-motion of soul we have a more Aristotelian notion (not, we admit, wholly lacking in Plato) of the merely accidental and superficial motility of soul, derived from body rather than from the soul's own nature.

The aesthetic argument for God, hinted at in Plato, is given some development in Plotinus. In beauty the soul recognizes its affinity to things or their affinity to soul. Beauty is Oneness, and, since the corporeal is always divisible and mutiple, this Oneness is spiritual, of the nature of soul rather than body. Even soul, however, is not wholly and absolutely one, as we saw above; hence, that Oneness in things which is beauty must be something in them which is even more diverse from matter than soul is diverse, it must be that spirituality beyond spirit which is the One or Good.

In a sense Plotinus' form of theism has almost everything. If you wish a divinity beyond all change and multiplicity, worship the One. If you wish a divine intelligence, worship the *Nous*, the eternal reason enjoying all universal forms. If you wish a deity concretely experiencing the details of all existence and providentially caring for all things, worship the World Soul. This soul cannot fail to care for our souls, for they are integral to its being.

We now let Plotinus speak for himself in his own eloquent language.

### Unity Instinctively Present to Us

254. It is a common conception of human thought that a principle single in number and identical is everywhere present in its entirety; for it is an instinctive and universal truism that the divinity which dwells within each of us is single and identical in all.

255. That is the most solid principle of all, a principle that our souls whisper instinctively, and which is not deduced from the observation of particular things, but which claims our attention far before them, even before the maxim that everything aspires to the Good. Now this principle is true if all the beings aspire to unity, form an unity, and tend towards unity. This unity, advancing towards all other things, so far as it can advance, seems to be manifold, and indeed becomes so, in certain respects, but the ancient nature which is the desire of the Good, that belongs to itself, really leads to unity; and every nature aspires to possess this unity by turning towards itself; for the good of the nature which is One, is to belong to oneself; that is, to unify oneself.

256. All beings, both primary, as well as those who are so called on any pretext soever, are beings only because of their unity. What, indeed, would they be without it? . . . No army can exist unless it be *one*. So with a choric ballet or a flock. Neither a house nor a ship can exist without unity; by losing it they would cease to be what they are. So also with continuous quantities which would not exist without unity. On being divided, by losing their unity they simultaneously lose their nature. Consider further the bodies of plants and animals. . . . On losing their unity by being broken up into several parts, they simultaneously lose their nature. They are no more what they were, they have become new beings, which themselves exist only so long as they are one. What effects health in us, is that the parts of our bodies are co-ordinated in unity. Beauty is formed by the unity of our members. Virtue is our soul's tendency to unity, her becoming one through the harmony of her faculties.

257. If unity be no more than a numbering device invented by the soul, then

unity would possess no real existence. But we have above observed that each object, on losing unity, loses existence also.

258. . . . it is unreasonable to insist that the notion of the subject one comes to us from the subject itself (which is one), from the visible man, for instance, or from some other animal, or even some stone. Evidently the visible man and the One are things entirely different, which could not be identified; otherwise, our judgment would not be able (as it is) to predicate unity of the non-man. . . . It cannot be believed that the judgment says that an object is one because it sees that it is alone, and that there is no other; for, while saying that there is no other, the judgment implicitly asserts that the other is one. Further, the notions of "other" and "different" are notions posterior to that of unity; if the judgment did not rise to unity, it would not assert either the "other" or the "different"; when it affirms that an object is alone, it says, "there is one only object"; and therefore predicates unity before "only." Besides, the judgment which affirms is itself a substantial (being) before affirming unity of some other (being); and the (being) of which it speaks is one likewise before the judgment either asserts or conceives anything about it. Thus (being) must be one or many; if it be many, the one is necessarily anterior, since, when the judgment asserts that plurality is present, it evidently asserts that there is more than one; likewise, when it says that an army is a multitude, it conceives of the soldiers as arranged in one single corps. By this last example, it is plain that the judgment (in saying one body), does not let the multitude remain multitude, and that it thus reveals the existence of unity; for, whether by giving to the multitude a unity which it does not possess, or by rapidly revealing unity in the arrangement (which makes the body of the multitude), the judg-ment reduces multitude to unity. It does not err here about unity, any more than when it says of a building formed by a multitude of stones that it is a unity; for, besides, a building is more unified than an army. If, further, unity inhere in a still higher degree in that which is continuous, and in a degree still higher in what is not divisible, evidently that occurs only because the unity has a real nature, and possesses existence; for there is no greater or less in that which does not exist.

259. We cannot indeed deny existence to the thing (the One) without whose existence we could not assert or conceive anything. Now that which it is everywhere necessary to speak and to conceive must be anterior to speech and conception, so as to contribute to their production. If, besides, this thing be necessary to the hypostatic existence of every essence—for there is no essence that lacks unity—it must be anterior to being, and being must be begotten by it. That is why we say "an essence" instead of first positing "essence" and "a" only thereafter, for there must be "one" in essence, to make "several" possible; but (the converse is not true; for) unity does not contain essence, unless unity itself produce it by applying itself to the begetting of it.

### The Complex Requires a Principle of Simplicity

260. Above all beings there must be Something simple and different from all the rest which would exist in itself, and which, without ever mingling with anything else, might nevertheless preside over everything, which might really be the One, and not that deceptive unity which is only the attribute of essence, and which would be a principle superior even to being, unreachable by speech, reason, or science. For if it be not completely simple, foreign to all complexity and composition, and be not really one, it could not be a principle.

It is sovereignly absolute only because it is simple and first. For what is not first, is in need of superior things; what is not simple has need of being constituted by simple things. . . . we do not say that . . . the One and First is a body; for every body is composite and begotten, and consequently is not a principle; for a principle cannot be begotten.

261. What is most shocking in the Stoics' doctrine, is that they assign the first rank to what is only a potentiality, matter, instead of placing actualization before potentiality. It is impossible for the potential to pass to actualization if the potential occupy the first rank among beings. Indeed, the potential could never improve itself; and it implies the necessary anteriority of actualization; in which case potentiality is no longer a principle.

## Unity through Complete Abstraction

262. . . . there is for everything a unity to which it may be reduced. . . . Therefore, considering what is unitary in an animal, in a soul, or in the universe, you will everywhere have that which is most powerful and precious. If, at last, you consider that unity of the things that really exist, that is, their principle, their source, their (productive) power, can you doubt its reality, and believe that this principle amounts to nothing? Certainly this principle is none of the things of which it is the principle; it is such that nothing could be predicated of it, neither essence, nor being, nor life, because it is superior to them all. If you grasp it, by abstracting from it even being, you will be in ecstasy. By directing your glance towards it, by reaching it, and resting in it, you will get a unitary and simple intuition thereof; you will conceive of its greatness by both itself and its derivatives.

263. Thus, whenever you wish to speak of (the Divinity), or to gain a conception of Him, put aside all the rest. When you will have made abstraction of all the rest, and when you will thus have isolated (the Divinity), do not seek to add anything to Him; rather examine whether, in your thought, you have not omitted to abstract something from Him. Thus you can rise to a Principle of whom you could not later either assert or conceive anything else. Classify in the supreme rank, therefore, none but He who really is free, because He is not even in dependence on Himself; and because he merely is Himself, essentially Himself, while each of the other beings is itself, and something else besides.

## Unity Is Formless and Ineffable

264. As Unity is the nature that begets all things, Unity cannot be any of them. It is therefore neither any particular thing, nor quantity, nor quality, nor intelligence, nor soul, nor what is movable, nor what is stable; it is neither in place nor time; but it is the uniform in itself, or rather it is formless, as it is above all form, above movement and stability.

265. Indeed, the mere statement that the One is above essence, does not imply any determinateness on His part, affirms nothing concerning Him and does not even undertake to give Him a name. It merely states that He is not this or that. It does not pretend to embrace Him, for it would be absurd to attempt to embrace an infinite nature. The mere attempt to do so would amount to withdrawing from Him, and losing the slight trace of Him thereby implied. To see intelligible Being, and to contemplate that which is above the images of the sense-objects, none of these must remain present to the mind. Likewise, to contemplate Him who is above the intelligible, even intelligible entities must all be left aside to contemplate the One. In this manner we may attain knowledge of His existence, without attempting to determine what He is. Besides, when we speak of the One, it is not

possible to indicate His nature without expressing its opposite. It would indeed be impossible to describe a principle of which it is impossible to say that it is this or that. All that we human beings can do is to have doubts poignant enough to resemble pangs of childbirth. We do not know how to name this Principle. We merely speak of the unspeakable, and the name we give Him is merely (for the convenience of) referring to Him as best we can. The name "One" expresses no more than negation of the manifold. That is why the Pythagoreans were accustomed, among each other, to refer to this principle in a symbolic manner, calling him Apollo, which name means denial of manifoldness. An attempt to carry out the name of "One" in a positive manner would only result in a greater obscuration of the name and object, than if we abstained from considering the name of "One" as the proper name of the first Principle.

266. For, in order to express something, discursive reason is obliged to go from one thing to another, and successively to run through every element of its object. Now what can be successively scrutinized in that which is absolutely simple? It is, therefore, sufficient to reach Him by a sort of intellectual contact. Now at the moment of touching the One, we should neither be able to say anything about Him, nor have the leisure to speak of Him; only later is it possible to argue about Him.

### The One as Good

267. Let us now determine the nature of the Good, at least so far as is demanded by the present discussion. The Good is the principle on which all depends, to which everything aspires, from which everything issues, and of which everything has need. As to Him, He suffices to himself, being complete, so He stands in need of nothing; He is the measure and the end of all things;

and from Him spring intelligence, being, soul, life, and intellectual contemplation.

268. The subsistence of the Good implies that of choice and will, because He could not exist without these two. But (in the Divinity) (these three, choice, being and will) do not form a multiplicity; they must be considered as having fused. Since He is the author of will He must evidently also be the author of what is called self-direction ("being for oneself"). This leads us to say that He made Himself; for, since He is the author of will, and as this will is more or less His work, and as it is identical with His essence, (we may say that) He gave Himself the form of (hypostatic) existence. Not by chance therefore is He what He is; He is what He is because He wished to be such.

### The One as above Thought

269. What thinks must have its good outside of itself. The Good, therefore, is not active; for what need to actualize would actualization have? To say that actualization actualizes is tautology. Even if we may be allowed to attribute something to actualizations which relate to some principle other than themselves, at least the first actualization to which all other actualizations refer, must be simply what it is. This actualization is not thought; it has nothing to think as it is the First. Besides, that which thinks is not thought, but what possesses thought. Thus there is duality in what thinks; but there is no duality in the First.

270. Consequently, the Good does not think itself either as good, nor as anything else; for it possesses nothing different from itself. It only has "a simple perception of itself in respect to itself"; but as there is no distance or difference in this perception it has of itself, what could this perception be but itself?

271. There is indeed no reasoning in the divinity. When we speak of it, in connection with the divinity, it is only

to explain that He has regulated every-thing as might have been done by some wise man, who would have reasoned about results. Attributing foresight to the divinity indicates merely that He has disposed everything as might have been done by some wise man who had foreseen results. . . . Prevision proposes to effect some one thing instead of an-other, and seems to fear that that which it desires might not occur. But, for a (being) which can do but one thing, both foresight and the reasoning that decides between contraries, are useless; for there is no need of reasoning when, of two contrary courses of action, one only is possible.

### No Temporal Succession in the One

272. Thus as, to the divinity, the fu-ture is already present, there could not be anything posterior to Him; but what is already present in Him becomes pos-terior in some other (being). Now if the future be already present in the divinity, it must be present in Him as if what will happen were already known; that is, it must be so disposed as to find itself sufficiently provided for, so as not to stand in need of anything. Therefore, as all things existed already within the divinity (when living beings were created), that had been there from all eternity; and that in a manner such that it would later be possible to say, "this occurred after that." Indeed, when the things that are in the divinity later de-velop and reveal themselves, then one sees that the one is after the other; but, so far as they exist all together, they constitute the universal (Being), that is, the principle which includes its own cause.

### Contingency and Necessity in the One

273. If, in ascending towards greater simplicity, contingency decreases, so much the more impossible is it that contingency could extend to the Nature that is the simplest (namely, the Good).

274. As the principle of all things must be better than they, He must be determinate; and by this is here meant that He exists in an unique matter. This, however, not by necessity; for necessity did not exist before Him. Necessity ex-ists only in the beings that follow the first Principle, though the latter im-poses no constraint upon them. It is by Himself that the First exists uniquely. He could not be anything but what He is; He is what He ought to have been; and not by accident. He is that; He had to be what He was. So "He who is what He ought to have been" is the principle of the things that ought to exist. Not by accident, nor contingently, therefore, is He what He is; He is what He had to be; though here the term "had to be" is improper.

### The One Is and Contains All Things

275. . . . the principle that we seek must be considered as the "Self-suffi-cient supremely independent of all things." . . . Which then is this principle in which all participate, which makes Intelligence exist, and is all things? Since it makes Intelligence exist, and since it is all things, since it makes its contained manifoldness self-sufficient by the pres-ence of unity, and since it is thus the creative principle of "being" and self-sufficiency, it must, instead of being "being," be super-"being" and super-existence.

276. But as . . . it is true that the divinity is nowhere, and false that He is anywhere, because He could not be contained in any other divinity, the re-sult is that the divinity is not distant from anything. If then He, being no-where, be not distant from anything, then He will in himself be everywhere. One of his parts will not be here, while another is there; the whole of Him will not be only in one or another place. The whole of Him will therefore be everywhere; for there is no one thing which exclusively possesses Him, or

does not possess Him; everything is therefore possessed by Him.

277. The Soul is not contained in the world; on the contrary, it is the Soul that contains the world; for the locus of the Soul is not the body, but Intelligence. The body of the world is therefore in the Soul, the Soul in Intelligence, and Intelligence itself in some other Principle. But this Principle Himself could not be (contained) in any other principle, upon which He would depend; He is therefore not within anything, and consequently He is nowhere. Where then are the other things? They are in the first Principle.

### The One as Source of Intelligence and Soul

278. What conception are we then to form of this generation of Intelligence by this immovable Cause? It is a radiation of light which escapes without disturbing its quietness, like the splendor which emanates perpetually from the sun, without affecting its quietness, which surrounds it without leaving it. . . . Thus does fire radiate heat; thus snow spreads cold. Perfumes also furnish a striking example of this process; so long as they last, they emit exhalations in which everything that surrounds them participates. Everything that has arrived at its point of perfection begets something. That which is eternally perfect begets eternally; and that which it begets is eternal though inferior to the generating principle. What then should we think of Him who is supremely perfect? Does He fail to beget? On the contrary, He begets that which, after Him, is the greatest. Now that which, after Him, is the most perfect, is the second rank principle, Intelligence. Intelligence contemplates Unity, and needs none but Him; but the Unity has no need of Intelligence. That which is begotten by the Principle superior to Intelligence can be nothing if not Intelligence; for Intelligence is the best after the One, since it is superior to all other beings. The Soul, indeed, is the expression and actualization of Intelligence, just as Intelligence is the expression and actualization of the One. But the Soul is an obscure expression. Being an image of Intelligence, she must contemplate Intelligence, just as the latter, to subsist, must contemplate the One. Intelligence contemplates the One, not because of any separation therefrom, but only because it is after the One. There is no intermediary between the One and Intelligence, any more than between Intelligence and the Soul. Every begotten being desires to unite with the principle that begets it. . . . Now when the begetter is supremely perfect, the begotten must be so intimately united to Him as to be separated from Him only in that it is distinct from Him.

279. He is superior to reason, to intelligence, and to the senses, because He gives these things without being what they are.

How does he give them? Is it because He possesses them, or because He does not possess them? If it be because He does not possess them, how does He give what He does not possess? If it be because He does possess them, He is no longer simple. If He give what He does not possess, how is multiplicity born of Him? It would seem as if only one single thing could proceed from Him, unity; and even so one might wonder how anything whatever could be born of that which is absolutely one. We answer, in the same way as from a light radiates a luminous sphere (or, fulguration). But how can the manifold be born from the One? Because the thing that proceeds from Him must not be equal to Him, and so much the less, superior; for what is superior to unity, or better than Him? It must, therefore, be inferior to Him, and, consequently, be less perfect. Now it cannot be less perfect, except on condition of being less unitary, that is, more manifold. But as it must aspire to unity, it will be the "manifold one."

*280.* It is not necessary that a principle should itself possess what it gives; in intelligible things, it suffices to consider the giver superior, and the receiver inferior; that (giving and receiving) is the content of generation in the order of veritable beings. What occupies the front rank must be in actualization; posterior things must be in potentiality of what precedes them. What occupies the front rank is superior to what occupies the second rank; the giver, likewise is superior to the gift, because he is better. If then there be a Principle anterior to actualization, it must be superior both to actualization and to life; and because it gave life to Intelligence it is more beautiful, still more venerable than Life. Thus Intelligence received life, without necessity for the principle from which it received life having had to contain any variety. Life is the impress of Him who gave it, but it is not his life. When Intelligence glanced towards Him, it was indeterminate; as soon as it fixed its glance on Him, it was determined by Him, although He Himself had no determination.

## The World Soul

*281.* The nature and power of the Soul reveal themselves still more gloriously in the way she embraces and governs the world at will. She is present in every point of this immense body, she animates all its parts, great and small. Though these may be located in different places, she does not divide as they do, she does not split up to vivify each individual. She vivifies all things simultaneously, ever remaining whole and indivisible, resembling the intelligence from which she was begotten by her unity and universality. It is her power which contains this world of infinite magnitude and variety within the bonds of unity.

*282.* The unity of the universal Soul does not hinder the multitude of the individual souls contained within her; the multitude of the individual souls does not hinder the unity of the universal Soul. They are distinct without being separated by any interval; they are present to each other instead of being foreign to each other; for they are not separated from each other by any limits, any more than different sciences are within a single soul. The Soul is such that in her unity she contains all the souls. Such a nature is, therefore, infinite.

*283.* On the other hand, if the soul were absolutely one, essentially indivisible and one within herself, if her nature were incompatible with manifoldness and division, she could not, when penetrating into the body, animate it in its entirety; she would place herself in its centre, leaving the rest of the mass of the animal lifeless. The soul, therefore, must be simultaneously one and manifold, divided and undivided, and we must not deny, as something impossible, that the soul, though one and identical, can be in several parts of the body simultaneously. If this truth be denied, this will destroy the "nature that contains and administers the universe" (as said the Stoics); which embraces everything at once, and directs everything with wisdom; a nature that is both manifold, because all beings are manifold; and single, because the principle that contains everything must be one. It is by her manifold unity that she vivifies all parts of the universe, while it is her indivisible unity that directs everything with wisdom. In the very things that have no wisdom, the unity that in them plays the predominating "part," imitates the unity of the universal Soul. That is what Plato wished to indicate allegorically by these divine words: "From the 'Being' that is indivisible and ever unchanging; and from the 'being' which becomes divisible in the bodies, the divinity formed a mixture, a third kind of 'being.' " The (universal) Soul, therefore, is (as we have just said) simultaneously one and manifold; the forms of the bodies are both manifold and one; the bodies are only manifold; while the supreme Principle (the One), is exclusively an unity.

*284.* Indeed, the soul's action is successive, and divided by the different objects that attract its attention. Now it thinks Socrates, and then it thinks a horse; never does it grasp but one part of reality, while intelligence always embraces all things simultaneously. Intelligence, therefore, possesses all things immovable in identity. It is; it never has anything but the present; it has no future, for it already is all it could ever later become; it has no past, for no intelligible entity ever passes away; all of them subsist in an eternal present, all remain identical, satisfied with their present condition. Each one is both intelligence and existence; all together, they are universal Intelligence, universal Existence.

### The Soul and Time

*285.* We still have to solve one question. . . . If eternity relate to Intelligence, and time to the Soul—for we have stated that the existence of time is related to the actualization of the Soul, and depends thereupon—how can time be divided, and have a past, without the Soul's action itself being divided, without her reflection on the past constituting memory in her? Indeed, eternity implies identity, and time implies diversity; otherwise, if we suppose there is no change in the actualizations of the Soul, time will have nothing to distinguish it from eternity. Shall we say that our souls, being subject to change and imperfection, are in time, while the universal Soul begets time without herself being in it?

Let us admit that the universal Soul

is not in time; why should she beget time rather than eternity?

*286.* Neither are the other souls within time; nothing of them except their "actions and reactions" (Stoic terms). Indeed, the souls themselves are eternal; and therefore time is subsequent to them.

[Sec. 254, Plotinus, *Complete Works,* trans. Kenneth S. Guthrie (London: George Bell & Sons, 1918), II, 314. Sec. 255, *ibid.,* pp. 314–15. Sec. 256, *ibid.,* I, 147. Sec. 257, *ibid.,* p. 149. Sec. 258, *ibid.,* III, 663–64. Sec. 259, *ibid.,* p. 665. Sec. 260, *ibid.,* I, 134–35. Sec. 261, *ibid.,* III, 879–80. Sec. 262, *ibid.,* II, 547–48. Sec. 263, *ibid.,* III, 811. Sec. 264, *ibid.,* I, 153. Sec. 265, *ibid.,* II, 584–85. Sec. 266, *ibid.,* IV, 1120. Sec. 267, *ibid.,* p. 1143. Sec. 268, *ibid.,* III, 797–98. Sec. 269, *ibid.,* II, 338–39. Sec. 270, *ibid.,* III, 764–65. Sec. 271, *ibid.,* pp. 699–700. Sec. 272, *ibid.,* p. 700. Sec. 273, *ibid.,* p. 798. Sec. 274, *ibid.,* pp. 787–88. Sec. 275, *ibid.,* IV, 1119. Sec. 276, *ibid.,* II, 590. Sec. 277, *ibid.,* p. 590. Sec. 278, *ibid.,* I, 182–83. Sec. 279, *ibid.,* IV, 1115. Sec. 280, *ibid.,* III, 729–30. Sec. 281, *ibid.,* I, 176. Sec. 282, *ibid.,* II, 292. Sec. 283, *ibid.,* I, 281–82. Sec. 284, *ibid.,* p. 179. Sec. 285, *ibid.,* II, 460. Sec. 286, *ibid.,* pp. 460–61.]

### COMMENT

Although Plotinus, with his three great hypostases or emanations of deity, offers several elements of a complete theism, still there are serious difficulties. The *Nous,* exalted as it is, and even more the Soul, with the material world within itself, are treated as lesser deities, not on the highest level. Now, in the matter of values, such accents of preference are important. In practical application Plotinus is saying: We should make ourselves as unitary and changeless and immaterial as possible. We should devaluate the world of multiplicity and action and exalt that form of contemplation which most closely approaches the *Nous* in its freedom from particularity and mutability. This would mean (it seems) exalting mathematical truth over historical truth, science above friendship, intellect above emotion, celibacy above marriage, etc.

Although Plotinus was a most wonderful character, still the narrowness of the ascetic and the hater of the flesh is not absent from him. "He was ashamed that he had a body." He preached philosophical salvation, not human salvation.

This dubious emphasis purports to rest upon logic, the superiority of unity to multiplicity. Now the logic is specious, we think. "Without unity, what could things amount to?" asks Plotinus, and answers, "Nothing." We agree; but we put another question: "Without multiplicity, what could things amount to?" and we answer, "Nothing." Unity is always unity of something which is not itself just unity (Plotinus admits this of all but the supreme case); likeness is significant only because there is contrast; identity, only because there is difference. In his theory of beauty, Plotinus seems not to be aware that it consists not just of unity but of unity in or of variety. (Or, if he does anywhere admit this, he says the word "variety" [or some equivalent word] under his breath and the word "unity" out loud.)

Furthermore, when Plotinus tells us in so many words that we arrive at the thought of the One by persistent abstraction, we may object that a thought arrived at by the extreme exercise of abstraction must be an extremely abstract thought and that its object must be a mere factor in something more concrete. Also, why suppose that the abstract is better than the concrete? Its whole value, for all we can see, is that it is or may be embodied in something concrete—for instance, in some concrete state of mind or soul in which it is enjoyed. Abstractions are useful in exploring the concrete—that is apparent to all—but Plotinus seems to be saying that abstractions are essentially useful for exploring abstractions, ultimately, the emptiest abstraction of all, bare entity or being or something. The

brutal truth seems to be that certain types of minds like the abstract as such, and they may yield to the usual human temptation to glorify their own type of individuality by claiming that its products or activities are pre-eminent. The contrast, good and not-good, cannot on objective grounds be identified with that between abstract and concrete. Some abstractions are superior to others if both compete for the same function. But this they can only do if they are on the same level of abstractness. But abstract and concrete cannot compete with each other, since they are complementary and complete each other. The same with intellect and emotion, or intellect and perceptive experience, or contemplation and action.

Plotinus of course would deny that the One is to be evaluated in terms of function or as an instrument. He argues that the source of all good must itself be good in supreme measure. But that out of which good has come is thereby proved to be good only in the sense of utility. An instrument is something which issues in good rather than is good. And the nonutilitarian or intrinsic good we can identify only as a state of satisfaction, of feeling or consciousness. But then it would not be the One but a state of soul, with distinctions of subject and object and the like.

There is another objection. By denying essential temporality to Soul, Plotinus is debarred from conceiving it as possessing free or creative choice. The eternal is without open alternatives (secs. 268–71); it simply is what it is, and it is meaningless to ask if it might have been otherwise. And nowhere does Plotinus unequivocally affirm freedom of deity or perhaps even of men. Thus his world is a world of things, not really of persons or souls properly understood. It is all essence with no genuine existence. It is all eternity with no genuine duration or action.

In contrast, but as we argued in our

"Comment" on Plato not necessarily in contradiction, to the doctrine of Plato, Plotinus views the forms as essentially objects-for-*Nous*. The *Nous* is also essentially contemplator of the forms and of the supreme form or the One. And Plotinus appears not to realize that, since the subject in its full actuality includes what it is aware of, in so far as it is aware of it, a subject whose awareness of its object is ideally adequate can in no way be less than its object. What, then, becomes of the alleged inferiority of the *Nous* to the One? We think it vanishes as illusory.

In what sense or fashion does reality proceed or "emanate" from the One? Plotinus gives us no clear answer. We may confront him with a dilemma. Is emanation simply a brute fact, or was its nonoccurrence impossible; in other words, does the world result from the supreme Cause contingently or necessarily? If we say (as our author seems to do) that the world issues necessarily from the One, we are implying that the One just in being itself involves the coming-to-be of the many, and thus we render the One complex after all.

Suppose we take the other horn of the dilemma and try to view emanation as contingent. This could mean one of two things: (1) not alone the details but also the generic principles of the world are accidental, since there was no need that any world at all should exist; (2) the details only are contingent, since it was necessary that the One produce *a* world, some world or other, though not necessarily just this one.

The first view would make Plotinus' conception of creation the same in its logical pattern as that of classical theism and would largely destroy the distinctiveness of his doctrine. The second view seems best to fit his requirements. For it permits us to say that the actual many, or complexity of the world, is extrinsic to the One, which thus preserves its vaunted simplicity; while

only the bare principle of manyness, "*some* many or other," is involved in the One. And this principle is not itself any actual many. So far, emanationism, thus construed, and panentheism might agree.

But now the issue arises, "What is the supreme reality?" Our contention is that it cannot be the mere One, the mere source of Emanation, or Cause of all. To say that causation must always, like water, go toward the inferior (really, water goes toward the center of gravity of the earth) is to make pessimism the norm of logic!

The only conceivable point of causative action is to produce something better than reality as constituted by the mere cause. Plotinus argues that the actual must be the ground of the possible and that the One must be "anterior" to all actualization from potentiality and must thus possess everything in the form of sheer actuality. But even if we grant that any specific potentiality involves some antecedent actuality, it does not follow that actualization produces no new or additional actuality but only something differing from its cause solely as the potential differs from the actual. For, in that case, causation or begetting is meaningless. The meaning of causation is that, where there was previously only the potentiality of a certain value, there is now the actuality of this value. (Of course there was previously the actuality of certain other values.) Actuality begets new and additional actuality rather than sheer potentiality actuality or sheer actuality potentiality. In any case, emanationism, in its treatment of contingency or necessity, is not a distinctive position with respect to Spinozistic pantheism, classical theism, or panentheism. It can only coincide with one of these or else dissolve into mere ambiguity.

The lack of any consistent logic in Plotinus' theory is seen if we compare sections 277 and 279–80. In section 277 he says that, as the world is in Soul, so Soul is in Intelligence, and Intelligence in the One or First Principle. As it stands, this imputes complexity to the One. This consequence of a literal construction is explicitly recognized in section 279, and in 280 we learn that it is not really the world or the Soul, but only something "better" than they, which is in the One. The principle of the hierarchy of beings is thus not literal inclusiveness but rather exclusiveness, compensated for by some superior analogue of what is excluded. Yet this does not work for the step from world to soul. Soul as awareness really does contain the world, in that awareness-of-$X$ is awareness of $X$ itself, not of something else, however better.

But, even apart from the question of awareness, inclusiveness is one of our best-established principles of value. "$A$ and $B$" must have at least the value of $A$ and that of $B$. (That artistic value, for instance, involves exclusion does not contradict this; for the artistic point is that certain elements cannot in their full vividness and clarity be included in one experience, and the attempt to include them results in failure, in the exclusion of one or both.) If we do not know this, we can still less know the sort of value principles Plotinus and those who think with him seem to be assuming. For instance, it is argued that infinity-plus-one is still only infinity, and so is infinity-minus-one. Thus it may seem no loss to the Supreme if the world is not literally within it. However, adding or subtracting one with respect to infinity is not a real operation but a mere technical device, like multiplying by zero. Is the creation of the world similarly unreal? Are the One and the Cosmos mere abstract quantities? If not, then we must, to avoid the difficulties discussed above, conceive each world that comes into being as an enrichment of the Supreme. "God and world" is then simply God

in an enriched state. Any such state is contingent, in that neither the essence of deity nor any antecedent divine state wholly determines it. In this way, freedom both of God and of creatures is preserved (cf. chap. vii).

It is easy to detect one reason for the oscillation between the assertion and the denial of the inclusiveness of the supreme. Plotinus assumes as an axiom that the supreme as such is the wholly independent (sec. 277) or noncontingent (sec. 273). Now, as he realizes, to include an actual complexity is to depend upon it. So he denies inclusiveness. But if the higher does not include the lower, then must not the higher be included in the lower? For, if neither includes the other, would there not be a third something or total reality, not accounted for as either higher or lower? But Plotinus thinks that to be in a whole is to depend upon it, to require it as "locus." Hence, the higher, which is independent, cannot be in the lower. So Plotinus faces a problem to him incapable of solution.

If, however, one accepts the dipolar principle that there are both a supreme independence and a supreme dependence, one may reason as follows: Unless all wholes are completely "organic" and all relations internal to all terms (and most logicians dispute this), the independent may be in the dependent by relations of whole-to-part which are internal to the whole, as they clearly must be, but external to the "part," which in itself is not a part. It is the whole in such a case which has the things called its parts, not the parts which have the whole. (It may be that the part must be in some whole or other, but its being is neutral at least as between alternative possible wholes which might include it.) Only in this way can we make sense out of independence. For, as Plotinus sees, nothing can be independent of what it contains, since, were the least constituent different, there would be a numerically different totality. Unwittingly, Plotinus is reacting to the law of the noninclusiveness or abstractness of the independent or necessary, as contrasted to the dependent or contingent. The concrete total reality can only be dependent and contingent. But then the dilemma, for all our author's wavering, is rigorous: the supreme is inclusive, and therefore complex, or it is simple, and therefore not the total reality.

Plotinus elects the latter position but strives to soften its paradoxicality through ambiguity. Yet note that the dilemma is rigorous only in the sense that a monopolar supremacy must be limited either to independent simplicity at the price of noninclusiveness or to inclusiveness at the price of dependent complexity. If, however, there are two really diverse aspects of the supreme, the one aspect may be independent and simple, the other dependent and complex. The latter, since it is inclusive, will contain the former. A complex total reality may very well contain a simple constituent. This simple constituent is abstract and cannot contain the actuality of all value, but it may for all that have a strictly unique excellence among abstractions. It may be the one essence that, though an essence not an actuality, is worthy of worshipful adoration—the essence of God.

It is notable how Plotinus, just at the point where he should state the logic of his theory, if it has one, takes refuge in vague analogies, such as the mere sensory image of the sun, to illustrate his notion of a cause whose effects, even the greatest of them, are inferior to the cause itself and contribute nothing to the cause nor yet diminish it. The light and heat given off by the sun are of lesser intensity than the light and heat in the sun itself, and the sun (it is thought) continues to retain its own intensity, neither increased nor decreased by its shining. One weakness of such

physical analogies is that no one knows what they amount to unless he is privy to the most difficult secrets of physical science. What is light? What is the sun? The theologians of the past have not known much about this, and what they did not know may, for all that they could tell, be just what is important for their analogy. The sun is a process, and this process includes certain phenomena of radiation out into all space. The total reality here is more than just the sun itself. Indeed, can we form any conception of what a sun merely in itself would be like? According to contemporary theories, the sun is wasting away its own matter. Above all, if the sun receives nothing in return from its effects, this is precisely because it is blind and unconscious; otherwise, the spectacle of life on earth would mean an immense aesthetic content streaming back to the sun!

One of the striking features about much Western theology is its combination of emphatic scorn for the physical, the "corporeal," which must, it holds, be absolutely and in every sense denied of God, who is pure spirit, together with a scarcely less decided preference for analogies drawn from our perception of physical things, inanimate objects, rather than from our observations of spiritual things (love, hate, memory, etc.) as vehicles of theological meaning and reasoning. It could be shown that a rather crass materialism often, if not always, accompanies such extreme spiritualism.

Plotinus' system, one may say, is mostly upside down and needs little more than to be inverted again. The Soul as essentially in process toward novelty is supreme. *Nous* is merely an abstract element in Soul, Soul so far as aware of what is common to all its actual or possible objects, the primordial and fixed essence of the correlation Soul-World. As for the One, it is merely that essence just spoken of and is the *Nous* over again, with a change of emphasis. But we must add a word concerning "matter." The sequence, One, Intelligible Forms, *Nous*, Soul, Material World, is not, as perhaps some suppose, a single progression in one direction. If it were, then the material world would be even more complex or rich in its actuality than Soul. On the contrary, Soul is the inclusive entity, inclusive in both directions, of the abstract forms and of determinate physical things. What, then, is "matter"? Either it is an abstract form or, as Plotinus hints (in a passage not quoted) and as Leibniz, Whitehead, and many other gifted interpreters of modern science have held, it is a great number of more or less rudimentary souls, embraced of course in the World Soul.

Whatever its faults, Plotinus' is a great system, with its elaborate deductions from unity or eternity and its rich structure of levels of deity.

# Chapter VI: *Temporalistic Theism*

## SOCINUS (1539–1604)

Since classical theism is the affirmation of God's eternity, consciousness, and world knowledge, with the denial of his temporality and world inclusiveness, someone was bound to try the experiment of affirming temporality but otherwise making no change in the theistic tradition. The clearest early instance of such a temporal theism we have found is Fausto Socinus and his immediate followers in the Socinian movement. It is admirable how well the program is carried through. If God is really temporal, then for him there must be past and future as well as present. It follows that his "eternity" means, not absence of change, but only absence of birth or death or possibility of destruction. He exists without having ever begun to exist and without possibility of failing to exist. It follows also that his wisdom cannot consist in a survey of all time in a single moment and that for him, too, there must be such a thing as new knowledge—knowledge of events which until they happened were unknown to him.

As Gersonides had already done, the Socinians give clear reasons for holding that this possibility of new knowledge does not imply any defect in the divine omniscience. Moreover, not content with meeting possible objections from the vast camp of classical theists, that is to say, nearly all of Europe, the Socinians subjected classical doctrine to sharper, more penetrating criticism than it had perhaps ever before received. We need scarcely add that they were unpopular! The following passages are somewhat condensed translations of the account of Socinian doctrine (which closely follows the Latin texts, not accessible to us, of Fausto Socinus and Johannes Crell) to be found in Otto Fock's *Der Socinianismus.* (In the second clause of the first sentence below, use has been made of a Latin passage quoted by Fock in his footnote to p. 428.)

### Eternity as Beginningless and Endless Duration

287. The eternity of God is his being without commencement or termination; he is eternal inasmuch as he exists and cannot not exist. . . . Our opponents appeal to the definition of Boethius: eternity is the wholly simultaneous and complete possession of an unlimited life. But how, we ask, can the possession of an unlimited life be simultaneous, that is, complete in a moment? An unlimited life can only be one that everlastingly endures, how can it be confined to a moment? Further, how can the indivisible contain in a point or moment all the stretches of time, which are infinitely divisible? For the eternity of God embraces all times, as well past as future. Still further, if the eternity of God exists entire in every moment, then everything must be eternal. For all the moments of eternity must exist in and with the whole. Therewith all distinctions of time must be obliterated.

### Omniscience Is Temporal

288. What is the object of the divine knowledge? The immediate answer is, Everything, including everything past, present, and future. . . . But in order to render this answer more precise, we must above all remember the axiom that, just as God's power consists in the ability to do all that is possible, so

his knowledge consists in his knowing all that is knowable. The knowable is what has reality in some form, whether as past, present, or future. . . . Also, God must know the real as that which it is, the past as past, the present as present, the future as future. . . . The future, however, consists either of what necessarily will occur, or of what only possibly, or under certain conditions and contingently may occur. Under the latter come all acts of human freedom. Since God knows all things as they are, accordingly he knows the necessary future as such and the contingent future also as such. If it were otherwise, God would not know things as they are, for truth is the congruence of knowledge with its object. . . . So far, then, from implying a restriction upon the divine knowledge, the recognition that future possibles are known by it only as possible, as uncertain, is the only way to preserve the absolute truth of this knowledge.

## Criticism of the Classical View of Omniscience

289. If it were correct that God knows the future as determinate, there would be nothing accidental or contingent. Nor is the distinction here of avail, that the contingent is such only in relation to secondary causes, whereas all is necessary in relation to the primary cause [God]. For ultimately the relation to the primary cause is decisive, and if here everything is necessary, then there is nothing truly contingent. Everything must then be necessary and determined from all eternity, since from all eternity known by God. But then there is no human freedom. There is also [according to the hypothesis] no divine freedom, since from all eternity God could act only as he actually does act. . . . Nor can one escape this consequence by contending that things are necessary only as a result of the divine decision, while the

decision itself is free. If this is taken to imply that there was a time when God had not yet decided, this would mean, a time when he did not yet know determinately what the decision was to be; . . . and if it implies that the decision is eternal, then nothing is won for contingency, since God would from all eternity have given up his freedom. . . . Furthermore, it would follow that from all eternity God knew that his will [that men should not sin] was to be frustrated.

The usual view appeals to two arguments. The first is . . . that future events will not happen because God knows them, but rather he knows them because they are to happen. . . . The objection is that knowledge of the future can be determinate only if the future is determinate, if there is some cause implying the happening; but then the thing is necessary. . . . The other argument is that for God's eternity there is neither past nor future, but rather everything is present. Hence God sees events not in their causes, but from all eternity he beholds them in themselves. Very well then, from all eternity the events must have being; for only what *is* can be known by God.

[Sec. 287, Otto Fock, *Der Socinianismus* (Kiel: Carl Schröder & Co., 1847), passages from pp. 427–31. Sec. 288, *ibid.*, pp. 438–39. Sec. 289, *ibid.*, pp. 439–42.]

### COMMENT

Had Socinus, who affirmed both change and contingency (acts of will that might have been otherwise) of God, added only that *all* changes and contingent things are in God, he would have been a panentheist. It seems that he did not take this step. His freedom from tradition was not unnaturally exhausted in the twofold daring shown in his denial of the classical conception of eternity and divine foresight and in his, to his contemporaries even more shocking, denial of the Trinity—which presumably was the main cause for the cruel persecution which decimated the Socinian movement.

We need not concern ourselves with the difficulties which certain biblical texts (especially those describing Christ's prediction of Peter's denial) occasioned the Socinians, since these are not philosophical difficulties. We wish only to remark that, in our opinion, no one has refuted the position that knowledge of all that is must be a changing knowledge, if the totality changes by addition of new items. And if the totality of being does not thus change by addition, then there is no change, nothing ever comes into existence, but all reality is from all eternity. We agree with Socinus as to the absurdity of this consequence of the classical doctrine.

It may be noted, however, that it is a caricature to speak of this doctrine as making the divine life simply parallel to the temporal process of the world, except without beginning or ending. For since the past is determinately actual, God will know it thus, and hence his knowledge at any moment contains all the past in a single present. Thus eternity, even in this doctrine, might be described as "all of time in a single now," but it is a different totality of time, of actualized events, and a different now, each time we refer to it.

The essential weakness of temporal theism, as contrasted to panentheism, is that outside God there is the world, and thus (to mention only one objection) implicitly God is less than "God and World," which is the supreme reality. The obvious escape from this difficulty is in the panentheistic direction.

Although modern Unitarianism acknowledges a debt to Socinus, this has to do with the trinitarian question specifically. No heed seems to have been given in Unitarian circles (except by the English theologian, Martineau) to the metaphysics of time and freedom for which the sixteenth-century movement is interesting.

Those who have broken with pure eternalism today usually also reject the extreme antipantheism of classical theology, and more or less completely and explicitly adopt panentheism (e.g., Brightman and James, chap. viii). In this, they move some distance back toward trinitarianism. For, once real novelty in God is admitted, one might begin to speak with some meaning of a plurality of persons in him. At each moment there is a new state of experience with its novel subjective pole, in a sense a new person. This however would give an infinity of persons, not a trinity.

In their own century the furor over the Socinians' stand on the Trinity largely nullified what otherwise might have been recognized as their contributions to theistic metaphysics. Spinoza and Leibniz indeed both refer, scornfully enough, to these contributions. These thinkers were too utterly committed to eternalism—and Leibniz, in addition, was too orthodox in temper —to take the Socinians seriously. The present age is less dogmatic (in some parts of the world and of culture), and to a greater extent theistic temporalism can now be considered on its merits.

# LEQUIER (1814–62)

About one hundred years ago the reasoning of Socinus concerning omniscience and time reappeared in the French philosopher Lequier. There is in Lequier the same recognition that an eternal knowledge of all events would render these events themselves eternal, since they would be items in a whole (the knowledge of the events) which never becomes but eternally is, and since a whole which does not become can have no parts which do; also the same recognition that nonnecessary events cannot enter into a wholly necessary "knowing" as its objects. There is the same argument that knowing the indeterminate or potential as indeterminate is true knowledge, not ignorance in the proper sense.

How far Lequier was actually influenced by Socinianism we shall not attempt to decide. He had at least some acquaintance with the movement. In any case, his originality is sufficiently remarkable. In his great dialogues on the idea of freedom, Lequier shows himself a superlative master of this form of writing. The standard theological view of eternity and time, divine knowledge and human freedom, is expounded and defended with neglect of no scholastic nicety of logic—or what scholastics take to be logic, that is to say (all too often), verbal distinctions invented to remove the appearance of contradiction, while leaving, as Lequier's spokesman in the dialogue says, the two contradictory assertions intact. All the devices, the resources, the evasions of classical theism are adduced. But the defense of freedom shows itself superior on the score of consistency and the responsible use of terms. And this man was a fervent Catholic, according to his friends. It is fitting that an adequate commentary on the excruciating declaration—God determines exactly what we shall do, but he also determines that we shall do it freely, that is, in such fashion that we shall have been free not to do it—should have come from a loyal son of the Roman church.

Lequier considers, from almost every angle, the question, "Can an eternal knowing have noneternal objects?" He shows how vain are the attempts to make sense out of the affirmative answer or to hold that God makes our decisions eternally, this making—so far as his at all

—being one with his necessary essence; but, yet, part of what is decided is that the decision shall be noneternal, really ours, and not necessary but contingent. The customary explanation, "God knows our future acts not in advance but eternally," as Lequier sees, only makes the matter worse. What is fixed from the standpoint of eternity and omniscience is absolutely fixed. Omniscience measures reality; if for it nothing is unsettled, indeterminate, then all notion of indeterminate potentiality for free determination is sheer illusion. But this summary is crude and inaccurate. Lequier is exact, subtle, witty, ardent, masterful. He is the first man in history to see clearly and comprehensively what freedom means from the metaphysical standpoint. In addition, he embodies this perception, or a good part of it, in a literary masterpiece.

It is Lequier's idea that freedom is *the* philosophical principle. This is a long stride toward Whitehead's "category of the ultimate, creativity" or Berdyaev's "freedom is not created by God." Lequier distinctly anticipates the Bergsonian sensitivity to the contrast between time and space. And he also anticipates the Bergsonian-Whiteheadian-Berdyaevian awareness that human freedom means genuine creation—means, indeed, creation of something of the actuality of God himself.

Our classification of Lequier and Socinus merely as temporalistic theists is not made wholly without hesitation. Perhaps they could be shown to have been panentheists as well. True, the denial that God is "all-being" seems to exclude this. Yet the meaning might have been that there is no final totality of the real but only a growing totality, and this growing totality might be in God. This would be the doctrine we call panentheism, as defined by ETCKW.

In all the Western world, who else in the middle of the last century had the equivalent of the ideas expressed in the texts which follow? (Fechner comes closest perhaps. Hints might have been derived from l'Abbé Bautain.) Such was the remarkable originality and prophetic power of Lequier.

### Free Will a Self-creation

290. I now possess and shall always cherish the most certain of truths and the one which should come first: I am free; beyond my dependence I am independent, and beyond my independence I am dependent; I am a dependent independence; I am a person responsible for myself who am my work, to God who has created me creator of myself.

Behold man: he thinks, he rules over his thought. God retires, God leaves man to his solitary reflections . . . this august creature not being able to endure tutelage, for such is the nature and necessity of things, that the human person must determine himself by himself in his uncertainties; he requires to be treated with respect, and to come to his aid would be to commit assault against his nature. The human person: a being who can do something without God! who can, if it pleases him, prefer himself to God, who can will something which God does not will, and refrain from willing what God wills, that is to say, a new God who can offend the other! What a terrifying marvel: man deliberates and God awaits his decision. Homage truly worthy of God, if the man is not rebellious; but what an insult, if he is not submissive!

### Free Will Implies Change in God

291. The relation of God to the creature [is] as real as the relation of the creature to God.

Suddenly, O surprise, O excess of wonder, I have been witness of a change in the bosom of the absolute permanence. The world exists henceforth, they are two, the Creator and the creature. The act of the man makes a spot in the absolute which destroys the absolute. God, who sees things change, changes also in beholding them, or else he does not perceive that they change.

A change in God! It is an idea which disturbs, a phrase which one does not pronounce without terror. Nevertheless, it is necessary to recognize that either God in his relationship to the world contracts a new mode of existence which participates in the nature of the world, or else this world is before God as though it did not exist. Indeed, to say that the world is before God as though it did not exist is not enough; inasmuch as the world is anything but a pure non-entity, the supreme intelligence cannot confuse it with non-entity, and just so far as it is not, it suffices to deprive God of the totality of all-being. It makes a spot in the absolute, which destroys the absolute. This universe compared to immensity is, I agree, but a grain of sand; but this grain of sand has its form of existence, and the changes which go on in it being as real as the things in which they occur, God, who sees these things change, changes also in beholding them.

### Omniscience and Future Events

292. There is contradiction in saying that a thing will be, and that it might well not be. One must choose: either the reality of free will with the ambiguity of future events, or the appearance of free will with the certainty of the future.

293. I believe that God has only a conjectural knowledge of the acts determined by human activity, so long as these acts are only potential; and it is only after they are realized that he knows them as realized.

294. *Probus.* Since God can do all things, God can make a square circle? Otherwise something would be impossible for him.

*Caliste.* A square circle is not anything.

*Probus.* Correct. But . . . can a man resist the will of God?

*Caliste.* Only the wicked resists God, but God punishes the wicked.

*Probus.* And does the wicked do something in doing evil?

*Caliste.* He does what he ought not to do, and he does not what he ought to do.

*Probus.* Just as one says, without restricting the power of God, that he cannot cause contradictories to exist together, and that his will, without ceasing to be supreme, does not will all that occurs, should one not similarly say: the infinite knowledge of God cannot apply itself to that which by its very nature is not an object of this knowledge?

*Caliste.* I do not understand you very well.

*Probus.* A square circle cannot be the object of the divine power; the evil will of the wicked is not intended by the will of God; similarly a volition which I am free to effect or not to effect is not known in advance by God.

*Caliste.* What language! God then is ignorant of something.

*Probus.* That which he does not know is not a thing: as you said just now that a square circle is not a thing.

Listen. You are free to do something. God does not know that you will do it, since you are able not to do it, and God does not know that you will not do it, since you can do it. God knows only that you are free, and just as in making man free he has freely restrained the exercise of his power in the government of the world, just so he has restrained his knowledge in relation to our acts.

[Sec. 290, Jules Lequier, *La Recherche d'une première vérité,* fragments ed. Ch. Renouvier (Paris: Librairie Armand Colin, 1924), passages from pp. 141–42. Sec. 291, *ibid.,* pp. 145–47. Sec. 292, *ibid.,* p. 147. Sec. 293, Jean Wahl, *Jules Lequier* (Geneva and Paris: Éditions des Trois Collines, 1948), p. 78. Sec. 294, Lequier, *La Recherche,* passages from pp. 250–53.]

## COMMENT

There seems little need for criticism of the foregoing texts. The evidence is that Lequier possessed genius of a high order and that dismally unfortunate circumstances and an early mysterious death by drowning (called a suicide which was not a suicide) alone stood between him and a position among the great names of philosophy. The romantic style of the writing of Lequier need not prevent us from admiring the concentrated intellectual perceptions which are embodied in it. Lequier was one of the not large number of those who, up to his time, had dared to face without evasion the implications of the conception of a deity freely and knowingly creating beings themselves also free. Relations of God to the world, he insists, cannot be less real than the world itself; and just to that extent must God be relative, not absolute. But, moreover, if the creatures are self-determining to any extent, then God is relativized, not simply by his own self-limitation, as is often ambiguously said, but by the creatures through their decisions. True, as Lequier was aware, it is God's will that he shall be *somehow* relativized by the creatures, but just how, just what particular "marks" or "spots" in his actuality shall relate him to the creatures, depends upon what these creatures determine themselves to be. Thus the creatures make their own "fame before God" in the august sense, emphasized also by Berdyaev and Whitehead, of creating something of the divine actuality or experience itself.

Lequier's "audacity," which, he said, was his essential merit, was allied to a power of incisive penetration into unfamiliar but logical relationships of familiar ideas that entitles him to fame, even in the eyes of forgetful man, not alone in the undying memory of deity.

# PART TWO

## Modern Views

# Chapter VII: *Modern Panentheism*

## SCHELLING (1775–1854)

Schelling's contention is that the concept of God is not to be expressed in one word, like "first" or "oldest" or "necessary" but rather in pairs of contrasting terms, such as "necessity and freedom," "eternity and time," "self-sufficiency and relativity to others," "joy and suffering," "infinity and finitude," "subject and object." This, if consistently and clearly carried out, is the dipolar or panentheistic doctrine. Schelling is usually somewhat obscure. But he does give some good reasons for preferring the dipolar view, and he points out with some clarity the absurdities entailed by monopolarism: for instance, the absurdity of supposing all reality to result from a purely necessary being and yet asserting the nonnecessity of the world and of the creative act which in the purely necessary being produces that world and is conscious of it.

Schelling not only distinguishes between what is necessary and what is not necessary in God; he also posits a contrast "even in what is necessary in God." This every panentheist must somehow do, for that there be something nonnecessary in God is itself necessary (since the alternative is, as we have often seen, absurd). Thus contingency as such necessarily applies to God as well as necessity as such. Nor is this contradictory. "It is necessary that accidents happen [in God], though not necessary just which accidents," is entirely free from contradiction.

Schelling also points out that to predicate P and not-P (necessity and nonnecessity) of one individual being is no contradiction provided that opposed predicates apply to diverse aspects of that being. The relevance of this humble truism of logic had been largely overlooked in theology prior to this time, partly because "simplicity," or the absence of a diversity of aspects, was also taken to be a predicate of God. But there was a begging of the question here, since simplicity too might apply to only one aspect (the necessary aspect) of God. Even with regard to that aspect, one might have to distinguish between plurality of abstract aspects and a real plurality of concrete parts or members. In effect trinitarian theists had taken to themselves the right to employ such a distinction in holding (no matter if on the basis of revelation alone) that in the one simple essence of deity there were three personalities. That these formed but one "substance" points precisely (if it has any meaning) to the distinction between abstract and concrete diversity above referred to.

Waiving here the question whether Schelling is always clear and consistent in carrying through the above distinctions, we wish to praise especially his recognition that the problem of tragedy is honestly or realistically treated only if tragedy be given a place within the divine Life, the measure and receptable of all things. Various mystics had asserted their own internality to deity, but who (unless Boehme in his cloudy fashion and some of the Jewish mystics) had ventured to carry this through by including the tragic aspects of our existence? If we in our reality are "in" God, as even St. Paul appears to say, then so is our suffering. Our wickedness? Yes, it too is within the divine actuality; but, as we explain elsewhere, wickedness of a member is not wickedness of the including Life, although suffering of the member is suffering of the including Life. Suffering is a universal category; but wickedness is something specific, the animals being below, and deity above, its scope. Schelling seems at least close to this view. His lonely wrestling with this great problem, though not we admit entirely without parallel in Hegel, seems to have been little regarded in his time. It may, however, have had some effect upon Fechner and other later panentheists.

A signal achievement of Schelling is his insight that the freedom of the creatures is not a result of divine choice, or of some special motive, like the Platonic generosity or "freedom from envy," if this is supposed to involve a real alternative. God has no choice whatever between there being free creatures and there being no free creatures. The divine life is essentially a transaction with free creatures, some free creatures or other. As Berdyaev later came to put it, freedom as such is uncreated, a primordial principle of reality inherent in deity as such and in all concrete actualities. The recognition that God requires the freedom of the creatures for his own life is the best way to insure against a false conception of omnipotence as suppressing that freedom. Divine power is an ability to deal with free beings, not an ability to suppress or avoid their existence or to manipulate them so thoroughly that they would not be free. They would then (to argue from an inconceivable hypothesis) not be at all, and neither would God be; for he would be an empty power without actual operations. Schelling's insight here is the most radical to be met in all philosophy prior to Whitehead, so far as we know.

(NOTE.—The translator has frequently inserted explanatory phrases, or the German terms which he is translating, in brackets. These insertions we have in most cases omitted in the interest of readability.)

## The Antithesis in God

295. God is the oldest of beings. This judgment is said to be as ancient as Thales of Miletus. But the concept of God is of great, indeed, of the very greatest compass, and not thus to be expressed in one word. Freedom and necessity are in God. The latter is already acknowledged in that a necessary existence is ascribed to him. To speak naturally, necessity is in God before freedom, inasmuch as a being must first be in order to be able to act freely. Necessity lies at the basis of freedom and, as far as there can be such a distinction in God, is the first and oldest thing in God himself, which is only to be clarified by further consideration. Now, even though the God who is the necessary is also he who is the free, the two are not the same. What a being is by nature and what it is by freedom are two quite different things. If it were already everything by necessity, then it would be nothing by freedom. And yet, by common consent, God is the most spontaneous being.

Everyone recognizes that God created beings besides himself, not by virtue of a blind necessity of his nature, but by the highest spontaneity. Indeed, to be more exact, by virtue of God's mere necessity there would be no creature, since that necessity only refers to *God's* being as his own.

296. What is necessary in God we call God's nature.

297. But even this nature of God is living, is indeed the greatest vitality, and not to be expressed at once. Only by progress from the simple to the compound, by gradual generation, may we hope to attain the entire concept of this vitality.

All agree that the deity is a being of all beings, the purest love, infinite communicativeness and emanation. Yet they wish at the same time that it exist as such. By itself, however, love does not come to be. To be is se-ity ["seinheit"], own-ness, seclusion. Love, however, is the nought of own-ness; it does not seek what is its own, and therefore also by itself cannot have being. Hence a being of all beings is by itself without support and supported by nothing; it is in itself the antithesis of personality. Thus another power making for personality must first give it a ground. An equally eternal power of selfhood, of egoity, is demanded so that the being which is love may subsist as independent and be for itself.

There are thus two principles even in what is necessary in God: the outflowing, outspreading, self-giving essence, and an equally eternal power of selfhood, of return unto self, of being-in-self. Without his further deed, God is in himself both of these, that essence and this power.

It is not enough to see the antithesis; it must also be recognized that these contraries are equally essential and original. The power by which the essence confines itself, denies itself, is in its kind as real as the contrary principle; each has its own root, and neither is to be derived from the other. For if this were to be the case, then the antithesis would again immediately cease. But it is in itself impossible that exact opposites be derived from each other.

To be sure, men show a natural preference for the affirmative, as, on the other hand, they turn away from the negative. Everything expanding and ongoing is intelligible to them; they cannot so immediately comprehend what is self-confined and withdrawing, although it is just as essential, and meets them everywhere in many forms. Most people would find nothing more natural than if everything in the world consisted purely of meekness and kindness, though they very soon become aware that the reverse is the case. Something hindering, resisting, obtrudes itself everywhere: this other thing which, so to speak, should not be and yet is, indeed must be, this No which is opposed to the Yes, this darkening opposed to the light, this crooked opposed to the straight, this left opposed to the right, and however else one has sought to express in images this eternal contrast. But it is not easy to reach the point of expressing it or understanding it scientifically.

The presence of such an eternal antithesis could not escape the first man who felt and perceived intimately. Already finding this duality in the primordial beginnings of nature, but nowhere finding its sources in the visible, he would soon have to say to himself that the basis of the antithesis is as old as, indeed even older than, the world; that, as in all that is living, so already in the primal life there is indeed a doubleness which, descended through many steps, has determined itself as that which appears to us as light and darkness, the male and the female, the spiritual and the corporeal. Therefore precisely the most ancient doctrines represented the first nature as an essence with two modes of action which clash with each other.

But in the later ages, which were more and more estranged from that original feeling, the attempt was often made to destroy the antithesis at its very source, that is, to annul the antithesis right at the outset, by seeking to reduce one of the opponents to the other and to derive the other from it. In our times this has applied chiefly to the power opposing the spiritual. The contrast finally received the most abstract expression, that of thought and being. Being always stood opposite thought in this sense as something unconquerable, so that philosophy, which would explain everything, found nothing more difficult than to give an explanation of just this being. It had to accept as explanation precisely this incomprehensibility, this active opposition toward all thought, this dynamic darkness, this positive inclination to obscurity. But it would have preferred to do away altogether with the inconvenient, to dissolve the unintelligible entirely into reason or (like Leibniz) into representation.

Idealism, which really consists in the denial or nonrecognition of that primordial negating power, is the general system of our times. Without this power, God is that empty infinite which the new philosophy has put in his place. This philosophy calls God the most unlimited being (*ens illimitatissimum*), without considering that the impossibility of any limit outside of him cannot undo the possibility of something in him whereby he limits himself from within, renders himself, to a certain degree, finite (as an object) for himself. To be infinite is by itself no perfection; rather it is the token of the imperfect. What is perfected is just what is in itself rounded, completed, finished.

Yet it is not enough merely to discern the antithesis, if the unity of the essence is not recognized at the same time, or if it is not seen that it is indeed *one and the same* which is the affirmation and the negation, the outspreading and the restraining. The concept of coherence or anything like it is much too weak for the thought which is to be expressed here. Even the merely different can cohere; the directly opposed has the power to be one only intrinsically, and, so to speak, personally, as only the individual nature of man is capable of uniting opposites. But if one wanted to call coherence everything which is not identity, then one would have to say even of a man who appears now gentle, now angry: the gentle man coheres in him with the angry man, whereas, in truth, they are one and the same man.

## The Essential Contradiction

298. Perhaps some already find a contradiction here. But the principle of contradiction, correctly understood, really only says this much, that one and the same *as such* cannot be something and its opposite—which, however, does not preclude what is *A* from being able to be something else not *A* (*contradictio debet esse ad idem*). The same man may be called, for example, "good" with respect to his disposition or in action; thus, *as such*, that is with respect to his disposition or in action, he cannot be evil. This does not preclude, however, that he may be evil with respect to what is not disposition, or what is inactive in him, and that in this way two completely opposed predicates can quite well be ascribed to him.

299. Thus we find that the first nature is of itself in contradiction—not in an accidental contradiction, or one in which it would be placed from without (for there is nothing outside of it), but in a necessary contradiction, posited together with its nature, and which therefore, strictly speaking, is its nature.

Men appear no more disinclined from anything in life than from contradiction, which compels them to act and drives them from their comfortable rest; if contradiction cannot be covered up any longer, they try at least to hide it from themselves, and to postpone the moment when action becomes a matter of life and death. A similar comfort was sought in science by an interpretation of the law of contradiction, according to which there was to be not even any possibility of contradiction. Yet how is a law to be established for something which can never be in any way? In knowing that there can be no contradiction, it must nevertheless be known that in a certain way there is one. How else should its inability to be become manifest, how should the law hold good, that is, prove itself true?

All else allows activity to be in some sense optional; that which absolutely does not permit inactivity, which urges, indeed forces, to activity is solely contradiction. Without contradiction there would thus be no motion, no life, no progress, but eternal immobility, a deathly slumber of all powers.

If primal nature were in harmony with itself, it would remain; there would be an abiding one and never a two, an eternal immobility without progress. As certainly as there is life, there is contradiction in primal nature. As surely as the nature of science consists in progress, the positing of contradiction is necessarily its first postulate.

A transition from unity to contradiction is unintelligible. For how should what is in itself one, complete, and perfect, be tempted, charmed, and lured to step out of this peace? On the other hand, the transition from contradiction to unity is natural, for, because nothing can tolerate contradiction, nothing which finds itself in contradiction will rest until the unity which reconciles or overcomes it has been found.

### The Eternal Beginning

*300.* The current doctrine of God is that he is without any beginning. Scripture, on the other hand, says that God is the beginning and the end. We would have to conceive of an essence without beginning in any respect, as eternal immobility, purest inefficacy. For no action is without a point from which and a point to which it goes. An action which had nothing firm for a ground, and no definite goal and end which it desires, would be an action completely undetermined, not actual and distinguishable as an action. A nonactual eternal without beginning may indeed be conceived, but never an actual one. Now, however, we are discussing the necessary actuality of God. God then has no beginning only in so far as there is no beginning of his beginning. The beginning in God is eternal beginning, that is, such a one as was beginning from all eternity, and still is, and also

never ceases to be beginning. The beginning which a being has outside itself and that which it has within itself are different; and different is the beginning from which a being can be separated and from which it can withdraw, and the beginning in which it remains eternally because it is the beginning of itself.

*301.* Metaphysicians, indeed, act as if there were a concept of eternity completely free of all admixture of concepts of time. They may be right, if they speak of the eternity which is completely ineffectual toward all outside it, which is, as we have shown, like a nothing in relation to all else. From this kind of eternity the concept of the present, as well as that of the past and the future, is excluded. But as soon as they would talk about a real, living eternity, they do not know better than that this eternity is a continual "now," an eternal present. . . .

But if a present cannot be conceived which does not rest on a past, then also no eternal present can be conceived which is not grounded in an eternal past.

True eternity is not that which excludes all time, but that which contains time (eternal time) subjected to itself. Real eternity is the overcoming of time, as the significant Hebrew language expresses victory (which it places among the first attributes of God) and eternity by one word (*naezach*).

There is no life without simultaneous death. In the very act whereby being . . . is posited, one [being] must die in order that the other may live. For that which is can only rise as such above something which is not. At the moment when an organic body is to come to be, matter must lose its independence and become mere form for the real essence.

Every kind of life is a succession and concatenation of states, since each preceding is the ground, the mother, the bearing potency of the succeeding.

*302.* There is movement, progress, even in the divine life, as in all others. The question is only how this divine life again distinguishes itself in that respect from every other, particularly human life.

First by this, that that succession and concatenation, dissoluble in human life, is indissoluble in the divine life. God is in continual exaltation ["Erhebung"]; the ways of the Lord are just, as Scripture expresses itself, that is, the ways are straight, everything retrograde is against God's nature. Therefore he can have that life which rotates in a continual circle only as an eternal past within him.

The dissolubility of life, or the possibility that the continuity of transition from the lower into the higher potency may be annulled, is the cause of sickness and of natural as well as spiritual death. Therefore God alone is called the imperishable, who alone has immortality.

A second difference is that that succession in God is a real one, and yet not therefore one which has occurred in time. In one and the same act (the act of the great decision), 1 (the first potency) is posited as what has preceded 2, 2 as what has preceded 3, and so again the whole (1, 2, 3) as what has preceded 4, that is, even *in* eternity a succession, a time, is included. It is not an empty (abstract) eternity, but one which contains time conquered in itself.

### The Voluntariness of Nature

*303.* But as eternal spirit, free and bound to nothing, keeps above nature, so also nature is not coercively but voluntarily subject to the eternal spirit. The sight and presence of that essential purity have no other effect on nature than to liberate it, so that it can yield to the separation, or resist it and fall anew into the life of passion and desire. By this voluntariness of submission, however, nature truly proves itself as divine nature, as nature which already in itself, outside of that relation to the pure godhead, was divine. Nature itself, when liberated, gains a victory over itself by the power of the highest, and posits its own life as past in so far as it is something peculiar, different from God.

Thus nothing should rest on mere necessity, and the highest voluntariness, even in the first beginnings of life, should witness to the unlimited freedom of God.

*304.* But just because nature is only voluntarily subjected, it always contains in itself the possibility of deviating again from that order, and of returning into a life of its own which is turned away from God. In submission it has not renounced being, but only its own life independent from God, and it has given this up not with respect to its root or possibility, but only with respect to reality. Therefore even in this submission it preserves its own ground of self-movement, a source of freedom which does not come to effect (to actuality) but always stays in mere possibility (potentiality).

Even if the godhead were not unenvious, as Plato says, it still could not annul the powers of this life, because it would thereby have to annul its own vitality.

Indeed, if that relation, whereby alone God is the living God, is itself not a dead but an eternally live relation, we must even conceive that life, now subject to the godhead, in continual readiness to proceed on its own account, in order that there may be not a blind submission but an eternal rapture, an alleviation of seeking (of passion), an eternal joy of finding and of being found, of conquering and of being conquered.

In the sound body there is a feeling of health only in that the unity presiding over the body continually suppresses the false life, which is always prepared to step forth, suppresses the movement deviating from harmony and opposing it. Similarly there would be no life or joy of life in God, if the powers now subordinated did not have the continual possibility of arousing the contradiction against the unity, and were not also incessantly quieted and reconciled again by the feeling of that beneficent unity by which the powers are suppressed.

*305.* If an organic being falls ill, those powers appear which previously lay hidden in it. Or if the bond of unity is totally dissolved, and the powers of life, previously subject to something higher, forsaken by the ruling spirit, can freely follow their own inclinations and ways of operation, then it becomes clear what a terrible thing, about which we had no perception during life, was suppressed by this magic spell of life. And what was but now the object of reverence or love, becomes an object of fear and the most terrible horror. When the abysses of the human heart open up in evil, and those terrible thoughts come forth which should be eternally buried in night and darkness, only then do we know what lies in man with reference to possibility, and how his nature in itself or left to itself is really constituted.

If we consider all that is terrible in nature and the spirit world, and all the rest which a benevolent hand seems to hide from us, then we cannot doubt that the godhead sits enthroned over a world of horrors, and, with reference to what is in him and is hidden by him, God could be called the awful, the terrible, not in a figurative but in a literal sense.

### Duality and Succession in God

*306.* Everything depends upon comprehending that unity in God which is at the same time duality, or, conversely, the duality which is at the same time unity. If God were identical with his eternal nature or bound to it, then there would only be unity. If both were completely external to each other and separated, then there would only be duality. But the concept of that unity, which, because it is a voluntary one, just on that account encloses a duality, is completely foreign to our era. This era wants only unity and wants to know of nothing but spirit and purest simplicity in God.

*307.* . . . God as Yes and God as No cannot be *in the same time.* We express ourselves thus intentionally, for the relation surely cannot be of the kind that when what follows, perhaps *A*, is, then what precedes, therefore *B*, is annulled or absolutely ceases being what is. Rather does that which is, necessarily and always, remain this *at its time;* and if *A* is posited, then *B* must still subsist only *as something preceding,* therefore in such a manner that they nevertheless are, at once, *in different times.* For different times as such (a concept which, like many others, has been completely lost from modern philosophy) can well be at once; indeed, to speak precisely, they must necessarily be at once. Past time is not annulled time. What has passed can, to be sure, not be as present, but must be as something past at the same time with the present. What is future is, to be sure, not as something that now is, but is simultaneously with the present, as something that is in the future. And it is equally absurd to consider being past as well as being future as a complete nonbeing.

Thus it is only the contradiction at its climax which breaks eternity, and, instead of one eternity, posits a succession of eternities (æons) or times. But just this succession of eternities is what we commonly call time. Therefore eternity opens out into time in this decision.

*308.* Everywhere, what is necessary has proved itself to us as the first (*prius*), freedom as what follows; or, to say the same thing, freedom appears everywhere conquering necessity.

*309.* We must conceive the course of events thus, and yet this may not be considered as having actually happened. For God as Yes, as No, and as the unity of both, is only one; there are no separate personalities. Therefore the whole thing can only be considered as having happened in a flash, since it is conceived as something which happened without having really (*explicite*) happened. This resolution, coming from the innermost unity, is comparable only to that incomprehensible primordial act in which the freedom of a man for the first time becomes decisive. Of the man who hesitates to be completely one thing or another, we say that he is without character. Of the resolute person in whom a definite expression of [his] entire being manifests itself, we say that he has character. And yet it acknowledged that no one has chosen his character according to reasons or deliberation. He did not take counsel of himself. Yet each person judges this character as a work of freedom, as an eternal (never ceasing, continual) act, as it were. Consequently, general moral judgment discerns in each man a freedom which is ground, fate, and necessity unto itself. But most people are afraid of this abysmal freedom, just as they are afraid of the necessity of being completely one thing or another. And where they see a ray of freedom, they turn away as before an all-consuming lightning flash, and feel cast down as by a phenomenon which comes from the inexpressible, from eternal freedom, from where there is no ground at all.

That is unconditioned freedom, which is not for the single act, but which is an ability to be completely the one or the other of contradictories. It had to be recognized in one and the same indivisible act that, if God wanted to reveal himself, he could do so only as eternal No, as eternal Yes, and as the unity of both. It was recognized in the same act that this revelation could only happen in different times, or in succession, and that just that would have to be posited as beginning which had just been overcome, the necessary [character] of God's freedom, the No of all external being and thus far of all revelation (for without an overcoming there is no beginning). All this was contained in one and the same resolution, at once the freest and most irresistible, by a miracle of eternal freedom which is sole ground unto itself and is therefore its own necessity.

This much may be said about the process of that great decision in which God, as eternal No, as eternal rigor and necessity, was placed at the beginning of his own revelation.

From now on the history of the realization, or of the real revelations of God, begins.

*310.* . . . if the godhead is an eternal freedom to be, to realize, reveal itself, then actual being or self-realization can surely not already be posited with the eternal ability to be or realize oneself. Between possibility and act there must be something, if the act is to be a free one; this even the most ordinary intellect comprehends. But in the pure eternity in which these people conceive God, there is no interval, no before and after, no earlier and no later. Therefore, even the mere idea that there must be something between possibility and actuality, loses meaning for those who want to recognize nothing but the pure godhead.

*311.* In science, as in life, men are governed everywhere more by words than by clear concepts. Thus, on the one hand, they explain God in an indefinite way as a necessary being, and, on the other hand, they become angry at a nature being ascribed to God. They would like thus to give the appearance of saving God's freedom. But how little they understand—or, rather, that they understand nothing at all concerning this, is clear from the preceding, since, without a nature, freedom in God could not be separated from act, and would therefore not be real freedom. Thus they reject, as is reasonable, the system of a universal necessity, and yet appear just as eager [to do the same] with respect to any sequence in God, although, if there is no sequence, only one system remains, namely, that everything is simultaneous, everything necessary with the divine being.

### Why God Spatializes Himself

312. This is the ultimate design, that everything as much as possible take shape and be brought into visible, corporeal form. Corporeality is, as the ancients expressed themselves, the aim of the ways of God (*finis viarum Dei*), who wants to reveal himself spatially or in a particular place as well as time.

Conclusiveness, outward finitude not only of visible nature but of the universe, already follows from this alone, that there is a power drawing the universe together from the outside inward, by which the universe became spatial for the first time. This power, therefore, since it surrounds and encloses the whole, is also the power that really posits bounds and limits, as it is expressed in the passage . . . : "When he circumscribed the deep with his circle"; and, also, the expression, heaven and earth are the expanse of divine strength, surely does not merely refer to the attracting power lying in nature, but to the power of negation integrating the whole. But the eternal can only be finite unto himself, only he himself can comprehend and circumscribe his own being. Therefore the finiteness of the world on the outside includes a perfect infinitude within.

The whole spatially extended universe is nothing but the swelling heart of the godhead. Held by invisible powers, it persists in a continual pulsation, or alternation of expansion and contraction.

### Suffering in God

313. Pain is something universal and necessary in all life, the inevitable point of transition to freedom. We recall the pains of development in human life in the physical as well as in the moral sense. We shall not shun representing even that primordial essence (the first possibility of the externally manifest God) in a state of suffering of the kind involved in development. Suffering is generally the way to glory, not only with regard to man, but also in respect to the creator. God leads human nature through no other course than that through which his own nature must pass. Participation in everything blind, dark, and suffering of God's nature is necessary in order to raise him to highest consciousness. Each being must learn to know its own depths; this is impossible without suffering. Pain comes only from being, and because everything living must first enclose itself in being, and break through from the darkness of being to transfiguration, so the being which in itself is divine must also, in its revelation, first assume nature and thus far suffer, before it celebrates the triumph of its liberation.

[Sec. 295, Schelling, *The Ages of the World*, trans. F. de Wolfe Bolman, Jr. (New York: Columbia University Press, 1942), pp. 95–96. Sec. 296, *ibid.*, p. 96. Sec. 297, *ibid.*, pp. 96–99. Sec. 298, *ibid.*, pp. 100–101. Sec. 299, *ibid.*, pp. 105–6. Sec. 300, *ibid.*, pp. 111–12. Sec. 301, *ibid.*, pp. 147–48. Sec. 302, *ibid.*, pp. 149–50. Sec. 303, *ibid.*, pp. 153–54. Sec. 304, *ibid.*, pp. 154–55. Sec. 305, *ibid.*, p. 156. Sec. 306, *ibid.*, p. 157. Sec. 307, *ibid.*, pp. 190–91. Sec. 308, *ibid.*, p. 192. Sec. 309, *ibid.*, pp. 192–93. Sec. 310, *ibid.*, pp. 194–95. Sec. 311, *ibid.*, p. 197. Sec. 312, *ibid.*, p. 215. Sec. 313, *ibid.*, p. 225.]

### COMMENT

We have two questions concerning Schelling's analysis. These concern his ascription of a positive role to contradiction as ground of process and his particular way of relating time and eternity, taken as aspects of deity. Schelling rightly holds that opposed predicates can without inconsistency be applied to God, provided they apply to different aspects of his nature. This is the surrelativist or dipolar view of theological predication.

But then Schelling maintains that nevertheless there is contradiction in the divine life, issuing in an endless unrest through which the divine potentialities achieve their actualization. His argument is that were there sheer harmony in the divine essence no development or process could ensue. Peace remains content with itself and is static; only conflict leads to development. Perhaps the issue is verbal here. If the meaning is that there are incompatible possibilities (cf. Whitehead, secs. 380 and 384) for realization confronting God, so that an exhaustive actualization or achievement of value is excluded, and hence deity reaches or possesses no final sum of perfections but goes on endlessly to enrich itself with new values, then one may say, with Whitehead, that such contradiction among possibilities necessitates or grounds process in the divine life. But contradictory possibilities are not actual contradictions; there is no contradiction in "P is possible and not-P is possible"; though there is in "P-and-not-P is possible." But only a confused mind would assert the latter proposition. People do often contradict themselves or each other by asserting the actualization of two incompatible possibilities, but the incompatibility of the possibilities for joint realization is no contradiction, so long as they are taken as mere possibilities. And only as possibilities do they both have reality. So it remains true, in spite of Schelling (or Hegel or Marx), that contradiction (as distinguished from incompatibility) is not objective.

How, then, do we answer Schelling's argument that the self-consistent is static? By pointing out that deity is ever conscious (and lesser beings have ever at least the dim feeling) of an inexhaustible potentiality of further realization and that this potentiality acts as a lure for perpetual further acts of realization. The actual is always incommensurate with the possible. This is no contradiction, but it is a sort of ground of unrest, if you will. It also issues in conflict, since each individual is striving to realize further value in his own way, freely; and hence no exact harmony of intentions can be guaranteed. Perfect peace is not a danger, in any case. But, again, conflict of intentions is not contradiction. "I wish for the truth of P and you wish for the truth of not-P" is a consistent statement; even though it is logically impossible that both of us be satisfied in our wish by the outcome. This logical consistency of existing wishes whose joint satisfaction is logically excluded is a sufficient source of activity.

But, really, one should not seek a ground or cause of process; for this is to make becoming secondary to being, whereas the surrelativist insight is that concrete reality is process or becoming, with an abstract aspect of being. Becoming never issued from mere being, consistent or contradictory; but rather "being" connotes a mere abstraction from a beginningless and endless becoming. There is no ground of the concretization of the abstract; the abstract is a mere aspect of concrete process, which is the absolute presupposition of all thought, its ultimate datum and medium. "Mere being," not an aspect of any becoming, is indeed contradictory; but process does not go on driven by the fear of this contradiction's becoming actual. It could not be actual, and only confused thinking even raises the question of its actuality. Becoming goes on to realize ever more value, but not as if there were the alternative of resting content with actual value. The very idea of resting is absurd, taken absolutely. Absolute rest is the mere negation of activity, not a positive alternative.

Our other query is as to whether Schelling is always clear and coherent in his statements about the eternal temporality of the divine life. That there is an eternal past and an eternal future in God as well as an eternal present is capable of intelligible interpretation. Always God as he actually is contains within himself an actual past and a potential future. But in each phase of his actuality it is a partly new and different past and a partly new and different future that is involved. Is this Schelling's opinion? We find him rather puzzling on this point.

The somewhat pictorial language shown in expressions like "outflowing," "return unto self," seem to belong rather to poetry than to rational metaphysics. The "independence" of God needs to be given a sharp analytic meaning, in terms of necessity and contingency, essence and accident, abstract and concrete.

All in all, however, we wish to commend Schelling as having gone perhaps furthest, prior to Fechner (who certainly read some of his writings), toward an adequate surrelativism.

## FECHNER (1801–87)

Gustav Theodor Fechner was not another Plato; yet no one between Plato and Fechner was able to affirm of God with such clarity and forcefulness the full range of themes common to the writings of these two philosophers. Indeed, Fechner at his best advanced the view of an inclusive eternal-temporal deity far beyond the point which Plato at his best had reached. The reader may note Fechner's appreciation of the complexity of the God concept; seeing its many levels, he could understand opposing views as partial truths, requiring only reinterpretation or completion to be brought into harmony with his more general conception. He understood the relationship between novelty and freedom, between freedom and law, between our exercise of freedom and the quality of self-determination in the universe. He saw that consciousness is essentially an activity and that a mere quibble is involved in terming ourselves "conscious" and withholding the term from cosmic activity. He agreed with Plato that God's environment was internal and that change occurs through change of the self-changing principle.

He saw that laws evolve. He understood that God has to be a self-surpassing being with unlimited progress as his goal, that God feels all tragedy, that not everything happens according to God's will any more than all our inner experiences are willed by us, and that the possibility of evil may be intrinsic to the possibility of existence.

Indeed, he saw so much and wrote with such feeling that one is amazed that he has been subject to such neglect. If the reader has been a party to this state of affairs, we now urge him to correct it by turning to Fechner's own words.

### Abstract and Concrete Ideas of God

314. When one speaks of God, it can be with more than one meaning. We may understand by God merely the spiritual principle ruling over nature, or over the world as the totality of externally appearing things. This is the conventional conception, and our religion recognizes no other. And—since this religion deals solely with relations of spirit to spirit—why should it not in-

terpret God as pure spirit, indeed must it not so interpret him?

However, that does not contradict—rather it makes but the more significant—our sense of the inner relationship between God as spirit and his world of material appearances. We become aware of this relationship when, instead of contrasting the world with God, we rather treat it as the other side of the divine existence, as something belonging to God, in the same manner as we view a man's body, which we contrast with the real inner or spiritual man—taken in the narrow sense—as nevertheless belonging to the man himself—in the wider sense—as his external aspect. This is not to say, however, that nature and the divine spirit, the body and the soul, are of equal excellence and dignity, nor is anything yet decided in general in regard to the manner of their reciprocal relations. One can regard a pedestal with its statue as one structure, since they do, in a certain respect, form a whole, or one can consider separately the higher element in this whole, the statue, as the essential thing, which nevertheless without the pedestal would be incomplete—only, one must not confuse the pedestal with the statue and take it for the dominant factor.

Such will be our practice in this work, in that it is necessary to emphasize, not only the relation of the finite spirit to the divine spirit and the antithesis of the divine spirit to nature—which always in one respect obtains—but likewise, in another respect, the equally real inner relation of the divine spirit to nature, which indeed deserves still greater emphasis. So we employ the name of God, according to the context, now in a narrow, now in a wide sense, in that we think of God, either as the statue above the pedestal of the material world, or as the whole of the statue and the pedestal. The comparison, to be sure, though in certain respects striking and enlightening, is in other respects as inappropriate as possible; for the spirit of God stands not, any more than the human soul, in a dead, external fashion above the bodily world, but manifests itself, rather, as a living essence immanent in it, or else (we shall explain both ways of putting it) nature itself is an expression of God which remains immanent in him. Yet, in abstraction it always remains separable from its penetration by God, or its suspension in God, and has then always the character of the lower compared with a higher, which, in the narrower sense, is to be taken as God. It is, however, natural that the necessity of also employing, in its place, the wider idea of God, in which no such separation through abstraction is involved, should be more fully admitted in our treatment than elsewhere, since elsewhere the separation of God and nature is regarded as more or less real.

Having, then, abstracted nature from God and contrasted it to him, viewed as a spiritual being, one can, abstracting yet more completely, thereby introduce distinctions even within the spiritual being itself, by means of which still more precise interpretations of the idea of God are formed.

So God may be viewed as a unitary inclusive spirit, as absolute, universal spirit, superior to and contrasted with the individual created spirits which are its members, in the same way that the spirit of man as a whole is known to include under it separately intelligible and distinguishable ideas as its constituent members. But it would be just as erroneous to think of the individual spirits created by God as outside of him as to think of the ideas, created by our spirits, as outside of ourselves. It is a purely internal or abstract contrast with which we are here concerned, that between the unitary whole and its members—the very opposite of a real or external contrast. However, the individual member always remains disposed to confuse the two; for, since he sees the constituents of the whole, other than himself, as outside himself, or does not see them at all, he supposes himself in general to have an outward contrast with the whole, while he nevertheless forms an essential ingredient of it. Only his *complement* in the whole can the member properly contrast with himself; but this complement is certainly not the whole, to whose fulfilment the member must himself contribute. How many wholes there would be if each part were able to regard his complement as the whole; for each complement is a different one, and all these wholes would, so to speak, be pierced, each in a different place.

*315.* As the divine, universal spirit, taken as a unitary whole, may be contrasted to our individual spirits, so nature also, or the divine body as a unitary whole, may be contrasted to our individual bodies, and our body, as a unitary whole, to its individual organs; and, yet, nature participates in our body, and our body participates in its organs. Here too the confusion of the abstract, inner contrast with a genuinely external one very frequently occurs. Man is ever disposed, not to attribute his body to nature, but to regard the two as in a real, external contrast, in spite of the fact that nature is contrasted to his body only as its completion in an inclusive whole.

*316.* It may indeed seem that the narrowest meaning, according to which one contrasts God as universal spirit to the particulars of the world, best meets our practical interest, since this interest requires that we see in God, on the one hand, the omnipresent, omnipotent, omniscient being, and, on the other hand, a being who does not share in the limitedness, imperfection, sinfulness, and evil which are in the realm of the particulars. And indeed we are not opposed to this; but it must not mislead us, as too easily happens, to overlook or deny the truth of those relationships which are explicitly included in the widest meaning; for then the apparent advantage of the narrower conception would not hold. The latter may indeed most directly meet the practical interest; but, if held in essential contradiction to the widest meaning, it can least fully satisfy that interest; rather, the widest meaning, which abstracts nothing from God, promises the most satisfaction, according to the pertinent consideration that the standpoint, measure, foundation, and fruition of perfection, goodness, and wisdom consist everywhere not in the particular, the separate, but in the whole which includes the particular.

## The Highest Universal Law and Its Relations to Freedom; Reasons for the Existence of God*

*317.* Probably there are many who can with difficulty imagine that an omnipresent and everlastingly self-identical being rules over and binds the whole into one. For what do they see in this world? Matter everywhere scattered and snarled in thousand-fold forms; the most stable, to a keen eye and reason, still decomposable into parts . . . ; forces go out this way and that, from body to body . . . ; motions cross each other in diverse paths; there are centers enough, yet where is a common center? There are laws enough, yet they differ for each different realm. And as in the realm of bodies, so it is in the realm of spirits. Each spirit stands over against the others; . . . they assemble, disperse, press each other and drive each other; there are principles enough, yet even more controversy about the principles; there are purposes enough; where is there a purpose of the purposes? No hour, no day, no place is sure of any other. The new always produces the new. From the elsewhere also depends an otherwise. The whole always seems to be merely built up from the particulars; the particulars seem not to derive from any whole.

Yet we have only the superficiality of our view to blame, not the depth of the matter, if nothing actually appears to us as one and in harmony in the world. If we only deepen our view somewhat, then we shall at last recognize that in the realm of the physical, whether here or a trillion miles from here, whether today or a trillion years before or after today, in short everywhere and at all times, two bodies will always work in the same way upon each other, will counteract each other in the same way, when they meet under the same circumstances, i.e., with the same masses, at the same distance, with the same initial speed and direction; also, the further course of their movement remains everywhere and at all times the same. Here we have at least one case where something remains identically the same between the farthest spaces and times; the same law is in effect here and everywhere, today and always, and in this manner unites the farthest spaces and times—to be sure only in reference to material events, yet as though with spiritual power. And quite as sure is it that whenever and wherever two bodies meet under different conditions in their masses, distance, speed, and direction, they nowhere and at no time affect each other and act toward each other in the same manner; they guard against that as if it were the subject of a divine prohibition.

*318.* The same law which extends between bodies also extends into them, indeed it reaches through them down into their deepest depth, down into their center; it even first gives them the center, around which everything they have in and through themselves is bound together and set apart from other things, as though the bodies were only the hardest knots of all the heavenly twisting and entwining bonds. According to the same laws by which the sun draws the earth, and the earth draws the moon, the earth also draws the stone; all parts of the earth strive against one another, and are first given their center by these laws, and by them every earthly body is given its special center. According to the same law by which the course of the earth is held in its orbit, the earth itself has been formed into the globe, the ocean billows circle around the globe, and the rivers are hurled into these billows. In spite of the fact that it is one law which governs all these effects at every place and at every time in heaven and on earth, things everywhere behave differently according to gravity itself, to which all these effects belong. But it is still not contrary to law; it is rather a manifestation of it, because, given the most diverse conditions, it governs also the most diverse results. For bodies do not forget the prohibition of ever acting the same when they meet under different conditions. As, however, at any place and any time the conditions become again the same, the result also becomes the same.

*319.* As it is with bodies and the operations of gravity, so, upon closer examination, we see it to be with all things, all happenings and effects in the world in general, the physical and the spiritual. We follow it in the realm of the mechanical, physical, chemical, organic, in water, fire, air, earth, under the earth, in the sun, moon, the farthest fixed stars, in or outside of human beings, animals, plants, stones, in consciousness or in unconsciousness.

*Whenever and wherever the same conditions are repeated, and whatever these conditions may be, the same results are also repeated, and under other conditions other results arise.*

*320.* While our law is the most universal which can be conceived, it bears at the same time in itself the principle of its individuation, down to the last detail. For each and every conjunction of things, be it ever so special, brings with itself its special law, which is always confirmed anew whenever and wherever the same structure is repeated, and only for this same kind of structure is it confirmed. Take 2 masses of 2 pounds at a 2-foot distance, take 2 masses of 3 pounds at a 3-foot distance; in a vacuum they attract each other in both cases by a special law, valid only for the particular type of conjunction; but this law remains valid for all space and all time, and so it always remains a law. Because, however, nothing in the world is so particular that it is not subordinated in this or that aspect to some general principle, likewise all particular combinations of conditions, and the laws of happening and acting valid for them, universalize themselves and finally subordinate themselves to the most universal, which is itself bound by no special determination, but binds everything.

*321.* Therefore, there is also, far above gravitation, something possessing the attributes which we admired in that—something single, eternal, omnipresent, omnipotent, omni-governing, ever-acting, . . . binding nature and the spirit world into one, and yet not into a bondage of servitude; for the same results recur only so far, according to the law, as the same conditions recur; but they never and nowhere recur completely, and the law does not require it. So the world develops itself, progressing to something new, and this is everywhere different; the old, the native, can never be wholly suitable for the new, the foreign, because the law merely demands the repetition of the same results for the same conditions, which remain continually the same in certain respects only.

*322.* One cannot give a reason for the new, the different, so far as it is new and different. If, however, the world is thought of as entirely new, then everything remains, according to the law, entirely free. The law determines neither what the first conditions had to be nor what the first effects had to be; it does not even determine what it itself had to be in the beginning, and if we conceive for ourselves a highest being, creating and ordering the world, according to our law, from the beginning on, this being was able to create and regulate as it wished, without being bound in any way; indeed, it found in the law, in the beginning, scarcely any support according to which it could direct itself; it was directed purely by its free, undetermined self-determination. Only, what it once fixed, had to be binding for all future effects. So it was able to create the very law of all things with freedom; indeed, the supreme law could itself be thought of as created in freedom, since in the idea of it there is nothing whatever which guarantees to us its reality, while it guarantees to us all reality. Every primary thing in the world, everything, which cannot be made to depend upon circumstances which arise also at other times and places . . . is to be regarded as formed with a free beginning; and in so far as the world, in the whole and in individual regions, constantly develops something new and in this or that respect incomparable with everything previous, there is also a principle of free change in the world as a whole and in ourselves, our consciousness and actions; we ourselves are assistants in the free changing of the whole. Our freedom is included in the supreme freedom itself, in such a way that it receives no rule or pre-determination from the supreme freedom, and can give it no rule or pre-determination, but as a co-determination entering into it, helps it to give rules and determinations for the future, the different.

*323.* What indeed do we demand of lawfulness in human affairs?

That the laws should derive from

the nature of men and things, that . . . once definitely established they should also be definitely and inviolably maintained and obeyed . . . that the lawful order should leave room for the play of freedom, and permit development of new relations in the whole, as in the individual; indeed, that it should furnish the basis for this. Its fixedness should be only the firm support of freer movement; its inflexibility, only the heart of living, continued development; . . . this development is to appear only as further construction, not as destruction of what was earlier developed and established. The ultimate legislative power must have the capacity to be further determinative, as the circle of conditions for which it is valid is further determined . . . for the same conditions, the same requirements must be everywhere valid, and dissimilar for the dissimilar; every one shall be bound by them, as each is bound through what it has in common with the others, and is free in that which is peculiar to it. Each shall be equal before them as he appears before them under the same conditions.

*324.* Now, at last, the very existence of God, his reality and truth in respect to all the attributes which we require him to have, are guaranteed to us through the reality and the sway of the highest law, to the extent that there is lacking only our being God himself, and having his consciousness of himself, in order to have, together with the highest law, all evidence for his existence as conscious being.

*325.* For did we not discover, in the rule of the supreme law, an intrinsically unitary, eternal, omnipresent, omniruling, omnipotent, reality, not only working through all causes but first producing the causes, primarily conditioning all the flux from ground to consequence, encompassing and binding time and space, nature and spirit, into one, and yet in the process leaving room for

the play of independent and individual freedom . . . ? And are these not the very things we desire from God; indeed the marks by which we exalt him above all other beings? Therefore, what do we still lack, concerning God? Only his consciousness, and whatever is perfected only through consciousness. That, indeed, we cannot know directly and completely in the rule of law beyond ourselves; however, we must not insist on this impossibility . . . since no one is able to know consciousness beyond himself, directly; for, in order to do so, he himself must first be beyond himself. It is enough, however, if we recognize, in the rule of that law, enough of the attributes of God so that only that is lacking which, in the nature of the case, is not discernible by us, but only by itself.

*326.* And the supreme law clearly proves to us all the attributes of God . . . even all essential attributes of a being conscious in the highest degree, though only in so far as they can be known by beings themselves without consciousness in the highest degree.

For if we observe our own consciousness, in which alone we can measure what consciousness is, is not consciousness in its essence an active, constant relationship of what has been to what now is, and what is to come; does it not bind the far and the near, the past and the future, into one; does it not include under itself a thousand diversities in unbreakable unity; has it not its aspect of free, creative development, and its aspect of being bound to the previous and the other; does it not govern soul and body in unity; indeed, does it not contain all these integrating attributes themselves, joined in a unity? The world law is a unity of the very same attributes, except that they appear in unlimited measure, while our consciousness appears merely in limited measure. But if this unity of attributes is still not yet the full consciousness, but rather only, as it were, the barren form-giving skeleton in the living flesh of consciousness, then the same unity of attributes, like the world law which is recognized by us in everything, will be also only an abstraction from a world consciousness. . . . Indeed, we shall certainly be able to conclude that, just as to the world, so to the barren skeleton of consciousness, its living flesh is not lacking. Our consciousness itself with its unity of attributes is to be regarded as flesh of this flesh with bone of this bone. It has indeed that unity of attributes only in so far as the world law penetrates therein, and governs our thinking, willing, feeling, behaving, according to the aspects of both freedom and necessity.

## God as Supreme Being in Relation to the Beings of the World*

327. In the hierarchy of beings, as we have presented it, God, taken in the widest meaning as ground and fulness and completion of all, radically surpasses all, and, since everything is only a step leading up to him, while he is not a step to anything higher, he is not to be considered in terms of degrees. Rather, as something above all degrees, he is a being unique of his kind, in a certain respect entirely different from all the stages under him, and in a certain respect corresponding to all of them, as father, creator, archetype, standard, and measure for them all, in spiritual as in corporeal aspects; a supratemporal, supraspatial, indeed a suprareal being—not however that time, space, and reality lie far beneath him, no, but that all space and all time and all reality are included within him, and in him find their basis, truth, and essence.

328. Man measures space according to lines, inches, feet, yards, miles; and time according to seconds, minutes, hours, days, weeks, months; but the basic standard of all this is not the small, but the large; how large the earth, and how long the time in which it completes a revolution around itself, is the basic standard, the single standard firmly established on earth for man, and every smaller standard is only a fragment of this. Therefore—the final basic standard of all reality and existence in the world is not the small, but the great, indeed the greatest of all, God himself, or God's own measure. Do you ask: Who is able to use the basic standard that surpasses everything, who is able to find the fraction of the infinite which applies to the finite? However, though going beyond everything, the standard also goes through everything; it is by nature related to everything and measures everything, not in relation to one thing alone, but rather to every other thing. Everyone uses it every moment and simply does not think about it; and without it one is unable to find the standard of his own progress, whether with his feet or in his thoughts; and, thus, one is unable to find the proper step and does not take it. The bond is also the standard. It is the same law which goes through God's entire being, according to which each thing, wherever and whenever it occurs, is a standard for any other, whenever and wherever it may occur, both the like and the unlike, and yet the law, while it enables everything to be measured by everything else, cannot measure the unique freedom of God.

329. However high any being stands, it still has an external world; other beings, similar to it, limit it; only as it rises higher does it contain more within itself, exist more purely within itself, possess more self-determination, because it includes more of the determining grounds of existence within itself.

But God, as the totality of being and acting, has no external environment, no beings outside himself; he is one and unique; all spirits move in the inner world of his spirit; all bodies in the inner world of his body; he exists purely within himself, he is determined by nothing external to him, his is a purely inner, self-determination, because he includes the determining grounds of all existence.

330. Each thing, indeed, the more excellent it is, the more does it include of the creative power, the more does it originate out of itself and contain within and under itself . . . and the less does it have outside of and superior to itself, by which its existence is supplemented.

But God and only God is self-identically creator and creation; wholly his own creator, wholly his own creation proceeding from nothing, for he is wholly himself and out of himself, and is supplemented by nothing else . . . ; yet everything is produced out of him, is completed within him, and by him.

331. How is it with the tension of a violin string? Each small part of the string lies in a different place, but it does not gain the power which stretches it from the particular place in which it lies; it gains it from the whole string and can gain it only from that source. The tension of the whole string acts directly and equally in each part of the string. Now each small part may vibrate in a different arc, according to whether it is nearer to the center or to the end, or to a knot; but that it is able to vibrate in any way, and that the vibrations all conform to one basic tone, is due solely to the tension of the whole string overlapping every single part.

It is not otherwise with the divine tension which reaches through the whole world, and through the entire scale of existence in the world, conditioning and uniting every single motion, feeling, and thought therein in the most universal manner.

### The Universal Union of All Consciousness in God

332. In the consciousness of God everything is finally united and flows together into a unity, so that the very same things which in his world are seen, felt, thought, willed, and experienced by inferior and superior beings are equally seen, felt, thought, willed, and experienced by him, even though the beings are a trillion miles from one another; the spatial distance is of no importance whatever, and likewise the temporal, in so far as God, even after endlessly many years, will continue to preserve, to feel, and to know within himself, the same object of experience, the same concept, the same idea, which only in respect to space and time had been succeeded by something else.

But one should not represent this to himself as though what we, the inferior beings, perceive, think, feel, would be perceived, thought, and felt over again by a superior being, such as the world soul, and then by God. Rather, while we think a thought, the higher being thinks it through us, and in us, and God in and through the higher soul. It is a single thought. Just as when circles are within one another, the largest circle contains every smaller circle just as it is in the intermediate circles.

333. Driven by God we proceed as a flock upon a broad, long path. Each one in the flock has freedom to go as he desires, up to certain limits. And so we move about confusedly; one turns to the right; another to the left; . . . here one capers and springs around; there another creeps slowly; one is far ahead of the rest, another far behind. And nevertheless on the whole it always remains a flock, and on the whole it always holds to the precise direction in which God is urging it. And no one can and is able, with all his freedom, to wander so far from the way, or go backward, or stay so long behind that he would get lost; God draws him safe again, and again urges him forward; no one is given the power, through his wandering within the flock or around the flock, to disturb the path of the flock itself. . . . A storm arises; the

whole flock is in terror; they flee from one another; yet when the storm is over, all are again together. Even in the storm the shepherd was still there. . . . You do not see the shepherd; you do not see him out in front or behind, as some earthly shepherds lead or follow the sheep. Is he then a fiction? You do not see him from without, because you have him within you, not to be sure within you alone, rather, within the entire flock, and not merely within the human flock, but the whole flock of heaven, and not within the flock alone, but also within the course along which the flock moves. Only that makes it possible for the shepherd to lose not a single one from the whole flock on so broad a path; indeed, if he were to lose anything, he would be losing a part of himself. That is the difference of the divine from all earthly shepherds; they . . . are there only because God himself places them in front of the rest; . . . whoever, feeling the impulse from God more strongly, goes first in the procession, will also experience joyousness and strength more intensely, for he possesses God in a more primary sense than the others. . . .

Then in what direction and with what purpose does God drive his flock? Is it to go always upon a barren road to a barren pasture? It is not to go thereon, but to rise above it, from the pasture which has become barren, to the more beautiful, greener pasture; for this pleases the good shepherd. And because the shepherd does not move outside his flock but rather within, the movement of the flock is his own movement; therefore, he also feels the thirst, the hunger of the most isolated one within the flock, and wills to gratify and must gratify it in his own time, in order to gratify himself.

*334. To find one's satisfaction in satisfying God, as that one who finds his greatest satisfaction in the utmost possible satisfaction of all—higher than this no feeling of satisfaction can go.*

## The Progress of the Divine or World Consciousness[*]

335. If we see how man emerged so late on the earth . . . how so many creatures of lower degrees of consciousness preceded him, how the consciousness of man himself is always advancing higher, is always learning better how to reflect upon itself, God, and the nature of things, finally how each individual man develops himself in the same sense, then we shall, it seems, have to recognize in this an indication of the general direction in which the world consciousness develops itself; for from what could we know it other than from so much of it as is knowable by us?

Yet will not God begin then from the beginning, comparable to a child, wholly in folly and in sense-experience? For does not every man's formation begin thus? Therefore, can it be otherwise with God, if we wish to reason to God from man?

And yet it must be otherwise, in so far as the child in respect to his source and human essence is different from God as he has always been.

336. The child is part of a whole world and has a whole world behind his origin; this it is which makes all the difference between him and God. It is provided that he should receive his rearing from the whole prior and present world, and for this is he born in order to receive his training from his parents, other men, and the surrounding world, and without this he would never be able to develop himself spiritually; and the men who reared him had in turn a teacher in their prior and environing world. The world along with God had however to rear itself from the beginning on, wholly out of its own means alone: its constitution included from the first the ability to do so; not only to develop itself generally, but in particular to rear within itself the many children of men, whose education belongs to its self-education. It is wholly its own teacher and wholly its own pupil. God

has indeed no parents around him or prior to him; but the earlier God is so to speak himself at the same time father, teacher, and educator of the later God; what God in his youth thought, did within himself, experienced within himself, that it is which teaches God as he grows older. If the earlier God is to be considered as a child, then he is one such as was the boy Christ who taught the wise elders; God is however also the mature wise one himself, and as such develops the teaching which he receives from the boy; only further than the boy was able to, so that it becomes the teaching of a still more mature wise Being. Therefore, each later time looks down upon the earlier time, yet the whole height on which it stands is established only through the whole earlier time. The same applies to the children of men, yet the height to which man brings his wisdom is not established in the same way as is the height of God, through his own earlier time, but only through God's earlier time. And while in one sense God is growing into old age, in another sense he is growing back again into youth; for as he becomes older in time there are always new individual beings within him which become young; they (in turn) learn primarily from the old God, and therefore man begins with folly. The child is so inexperienced and foolish because it must open itself like a new gate through which old wisdom is to move in a new direction and with renewed impetus. While the child learns the old from the old God, the old God learns of the new through the new beings; in and through them he is aware of novelty, and lifts up into the whole every treasure of the new which he collects in and through individuals, brings it to a higher application and a higher development in human intercourse and human affairs than could be possible through the individuals alone, and out of this treasure everyone receives this and that through education and rearing, and develops further by means of the received fund.

Should we say now that because the later God develops beyond the earlier, there was a defect in the earlier? But it was no other defect than that which progress to the higher itself determines, and each earlier time stands in this relation to a later time, and each later time stands in this relation to the one following; in *this* respect the world never advances, because this is the ground of its whole progress, to will something transcending the present; herein lies the impulse of the eternal, progressive development. In the earliest time, however, as in the latest, God with equally flawless wisdom fulfils the task of properly leading the world, in the condition in which it is, out beyond this condition; and the perfection of God generally is not in reaching a limited maximum but in seeking an unlimited progress. In such a progress, however, that the whole God in each time is the maximum not only of all the present, but also of all the past; he alone can surpass himself, and does it continually, in the progress of time.

Therefore, if we desired to call the earlier condition of God lowly, then our lowly concept of lowliness would be unsuitable. We call that lowly which is small in relation to a higher, or which is not equal to a difficult task. But in every time everything is small compared to God, and in every time God satisfies the most difficult task, compared to which all finite tasks disappear. The later God looks down only upon himself—perceiving, however, at the same time, in that same earlier God the one who has elevated him to his present height. The earlier God is not lowly compared to the later, as the root is more lowly than the blossom; but rather as the plant willing to bloom someday is more lowly than the plant really blooming, and the blooming plant is more lowly than the plant blooming more beautifully. But this image also goes only halfway. For the world does not grow from small to large as the plant, and does not nourish itself from outside; it was large and powerful from the beginning, as today, and has also probably flourished from the beginning as today, only in a different manner than it does today.

337. So we should not believe God's earlier existence to have been like that of the child or of the primitive savage, controlled by the sensual faculty. Rather, God's primordial reason governed his physical nature from the beginning as today.

### The Goodness of God and the Evil in the World*

338. If the supreme being is self-conscious, then he would hurt only himself by an evil will; for against what can he turn this will except against himself, since everything is in him? His will can only be good; and because he perceives and surveys everything in unity, the knowledge for the enlightenment of this will is not lacking to him. Yet there is evil in the world, according to our conceptions of evil. . . . How can this be reconciled with what we require of God?

339. There is much here that I cannot understand and that I leave undecided. What however I do understand, I understand and view as follows:

Does everything which happens in *our* souls happen by means of our will? Does not an infinity of things emerge involuntarily in the will from unconscious or conscious lowly instincts? Is not my self-conscious will merely the supreme ruler in my soul which strives to lead everything to the common goal which appears to be the best for me; which seeks harmony and peace between my knowing and believing, sensing and striving, even when things resist, and strives to gain salutary progress over every obstruction; and whatever does not harmonize with this striving the will persistently twists and turns and changes and mortifies until it submits thereto; and what at last harmonizes wholly therewith, it summons into the stream of its general advance, and uses as a wave of that advance? Will it be otherwise in God of whose soul our soul too is a part and a symbol? Should God's soul consist of nothing save a supreme will? Should there be nothing involuntary (though for itself perhaps voluntary) in relation to this highest will in his consciousness? Then indeed there could be no individual beings in God; for this alone makes them particular creatures in Him, that his higher will can be stimulated in particular ways through their inferior will and impulse. Were all inferior wills lost—through lack of independence—in his supreme will, what would we be? Should not the supreme will even in God be only the supreme, the ruler, the guide who strives to lead the universe to the universally best goal—best in and for God—who seeks harmony and peace between all knowing and believing, all sensing and striving, however individuals may resist, and who strives to gain salutary progress over every obstruction; and what will not harmonize with this striving he twists and turns and changes and mortifies until it submits thereto, and what finally entirely conforms with it he summons into the stream of his universal advance and utilizes as a wave of this advance?

340. Now man is judged good and evil not . . . according to what emerges in him on the lower level of his consciousness, but rather, according to the direction which his higher will takes in the ordering and directing of the particular factors within his total being. If the bad which enters his consciousness becomes simply a motive for him to better and heal it, and to further and continually develop the good, then he is good. And we must therefore call God good, in spite of all the evil which appears in his world in the guise of individual be-

ings, if his supreme will is not the creator of this evil but its healer and reformer.

*341.* In our opinion, we do not restrict the omnipotence of God, if we thus interpret it, not as a concept void of foundation, but rather in a manner compatible with the concept of the divine goodness. God would fall short of omnipotence only if he could not do what he wanted to do, or wanted to do what he could not do, or if evil limited his highest will rather than furnished its occasion; or if in general anything arose not through and in him. But according to our account, even the evil arises through and in him, only not through his will; rather his will is directed solely to the ordering and guiding to a higher level of that which has arisen involuntarily on a lower level. But if you, in order to avoid tampering with God's omnipotence, wish to hold that whatever happens happens through God's supreme will, then do you see to it how you rescue your holy and good God from responsibility for the evil. I for my part prefer to conceive his all-power as meaning that he can do all that he wants to do, and that what he wants to do is always good . . . ; for what is not good in the world I seek the origin outside of God's will, although not outside God, since I see in it the occasioning obstacle against which the power and action of his supreme will is directed, analogously to the same situation on the human level.

Is the ultimate origin of evil explained in this manner? No, as little as the origin of the world and God. . . . To be sure, I do not know how there could be a superior will if there were not something beneath it to make its activity possible; but what I cannot explain is why those inferior to the highest will must carry in themselves the possibility of pain and sin. . . . Yet the possibility of individual creatures themselves may depend upon the possibility of evil, and their reality upon its reality.

*342.* And is that not the best God for us who bears within himself our good fortune and misfortune, and whose own untroubled happiness depends upon his leaving no misfortune without a remedy? What would he be if he looked upon our misery merely from the outside, as we look upon the misery of a beggar in rags to whom we throw a penny? In truth, however, he feels all our grief just as do we, only with the difference that he also at the same time feels in advance the turning and redeeming and overcoming through pleasure.

*343.* He into whose mind these considerations have rightly gone will in the bitterest suffering find a comfort above all comfort in thinking upon God.

[Sec. 314, Gustav Theodor Fechner, *Zend-Avesta: Oder ueber die Dinge des Himmels und des Jenseits, vom Standpunkt der Naturbeschreibung* (5th [identical with the 4th] ed.; Leipzig: Leopold Voss, 1922), I, 200–202. Sec. 315, *ibid.*, p. 202. Sec. 316, *ibid.*, pp. 205–6. Sec. 317, *ibid.*, pp. 207–8. Sec. 318, *ibid.*, pp. 208–9. Sec. 319, *ibid.*, p. 210. Sec. 320, *ibid.*, p. 212. Sec. 321, *ibid.*, pp. 212–13. Sec. 322, *ibid.*, p. 213. Sec. 323, *ibid.*, p. 215. Sec. 324, *ibid.*, p. 217. Sec. 325, *ibid.* Sec. 326, *ibid.*, pp. 217–18. Sec. 327, *ibid.*, pp. 222–23. Sec. 328, *ibid.*, p. 224. Sec. 329, *ibid.*, pp. 224–25. Sec. 330, *ibid.*, p. 225. Sec. 331, *ibid.*, pp. 226–27. Sec. 332, *ibid.*, p. 228. Sec. 333, *ibid.*, pp. 231–32. Sec. 334, *ibid.*, p. 232. Sec. 335, *ibid.*, pp. 239–40. Sec. 336, *ibid.*, pp. 240–42. Sec. 337, *ibid.*, p. 242. Sec. 338, *ibid.*, p. 243. Sec. 339, *ibid.*, pp. 244–45. Sec. 340, *ibid.*, p. 245. Sec. 341, *ibid.*, pp. 247–48. Sec. 342, *ibid.*, p. 249. Sec. 343, *ibid.*]

COMMENT

Of Fechner's pioneer contributions to theism, one may say that they have been not so much forgotten as from the outset unnoticed. Even William James, with all his enthusiasm, only half-realized what Fechner had accomplished in philosophical theology. The trouble lay partly with Fechner himself, in that he failed to discriminate between different levels, including levels of importance, in his own doctrine. He presented it as a system, to be taken or left as a whole. It could scarcely be accepted as a whole; so it was set aside.

The chief stumbling block for most readers, though James rather liked it, was Fechner's decidedly original version of panpsychism, his theory of plant souls and planetary souls. If a case can be made for the view that plants, planets, and stars are conscious individuals, Fechner made that case. The human soul is within the earth soul as the human body belongs to the physical earth mass, the earth soul is within some higher soul, and ultimately all are within an all-inclusive soul, God. Thus the inclusion of souls within God is only the supreme instance of a general principle according to which all souls, save those on the lowest levels, include inferior souls within themselves. The greatest weakness of the theory, in the form which Fechner gave it, is that plants—and heavenly bodies even more—seem insufficiently integrated to possess unitary consciousness of themselves. A plant seems to be a cell colony with rather less integration, taken as a whole, than its constituent cells; and, even more obviously, the earth is a mere mass of adjacent molecules. Yet the theory of plant souls and an earth soul is so attractive, poetically, and such a striking departure from common sense in a scientific era that it was bound to receive a certain amount of attention, even notoriety—all the more so, as Fechner puts great stress upon this aspect of his doctrine.

William James even drew the conclusion that for Fechner the idea of God itself was little more than an afterthought in the system, a mere concession to tradition or the "monistic prejudice," and that Fechner's chief concern was elsewhere. But one cannot read the chapter from which the foregoing passages are taken and retain this view. It seems that James must have contented himself with at most a hasty and partial perusal of the hundred pages of the chapter, which seem to us to show that if ever any man took the idea of God seriously, and entertained it with enthusiasm, it was Fechner. They also show that his version of the idea, while it seems compatible with the plant-planet-soul hypothesis, does not require it. Finally, it reveals Fechner not as simply adopting a traditional theism but as creatively exploring partly new possibilities for conceiving deity.

Since Fechner has sometimes been called the founder of experimental psychology, it is not surprising that his chief contribution should have consisted in a kind of psychology of deity. He knows, as well as classical theists perhaps, that God is not to be conceived as a mere human being with magnified powers. But he also knows, even better than classical theists, that save for some sort of analogy between God and man there can be no rational theism. And his proposal is that, when we speak of "will" or "consciousness" in theology, we pay careful attention to what these words mean in their human instance. For this is one end of the analogy, and the end from which theory has to start.

It is a basic fact in psychology that will is nothing if taken simply in and of itself—in complete abstraction from the involuntary, from impulses and feelings with which the will deals but which are not themselves acts of will and are as much its data or preconditions as its consequences. The will is simply a *control* of such nonvoluntary factors, which are as essential to human experience as the will itself. To posit in God, then, a pure will which has no impulses to control, which operates either in a vacuum or upon something merely outside the divine personality, is to destroy any genuine analogy whatever and to use words with no identifiable meaning, according to Fechner's analysis. Add one more point, and we have Fechner's stroke of genius in this matter. That in

God which is not his will, but the set of "impulses" over which this will is the "supreme ruler," may in itself consist, at least in part, of volitions, acts of will, but not acts of the supreme will. It may be our willing, what we (in part) voluntarily think and feel, which for God is the matter upon which his will formatively acts to control and guide, to inhibit or encourage. Thus our wills are outside the will of God, though not outside God. For God is more than just bare will—by itself an empty abstraction. He does not will our volitions; he suffers them. He finds them going on in his life or experience and decides in each case how far to encourage or check them. Thus the sufficiently orthodox notion of divine guidance of partly free human beings is given a psychological basis, perhaps for the first time.

Another point of interest is Fechner's discovery of the dynamic or temporal concept of perfection as the status of surpassing all individuals other than self but also surpassing self from moment to moment, so that, although later phases of divine experience are richer than earlier, this is a transcendence of God only by God. So far as other beings are concerned, God is exactly as unrivaled and unapproachable as classical theism wished to hold. Fechner seems also to have hit upon the most intelligible way of relating novelty in the world to divine purpose. For each child the whole world is something new, unprecedented; for his parents, and for God, such things as animals, trees, sun, water, etc., are no novelties. But it does not follow that childish enjoyment of novelty contributes nothing new to the parent, human or divine. No previous child quite duplicated just this way of enjoying the freshness of incipient existence. Thus God can experience in himself the vividness of the child's feelings (which could not be possible if the child had already perceived the same objects over and over again) despite the fact that he has himself experienced some at least of

these objects for ages. But this is only on condition that, even for God, the child himself (and the parent enjoying the child) is a new quality of individual, valued as such.

Fechner's discussion of the "law of laws," the principle of order in the world which reveals God as supreme orderer, is at least an eloquent version of the argument from design, divested of its eternalism and given an evolutionary or genuinely creative character. Yet the Fechnerian formula for the divine law (every difference in conditions means a difference, and every similarity a similarity, in the resulting occurrences, to put it in slightly other words than those used by him) is to us of doubtful validity as it stands. Our author insists that this formula leaves ample room for freedom; but we incline to agree with William James that Fechner leans toward the error of determinism. As James says, the feeling, "I *should* have acted otherwise," implies that, under the very conditions under which I did act, another outcome was possible; and Fechner's formula seems to deny this or, at least, fails to give clear logical expression to what Fechner perhaps really wants to affirm, namely, that, while results register completely the nature of their conditions, conditions are to some extent innocent of the nature of their results. In psychological terms memory is ideally and in principle the absolutely faithful record of the details of the past, but anticipation is, even in ideal, only a more or less indefinite outline of the future, which as future consists in somewhat indeterminate potencies, not in determinate actualities. That every difference in conditions occasions a difference in outcome may be accepted by an indeterminist, but that every similarity in conditions means an equal similarity in outcome is scarcely acceptable as a basis for freedom.

Perhaps, however, there is a way of interpreting the formula that renders it acceptable. If two poems in English are to be translated into various languages, ideally every difference and every similarity between the two poems will reappear in their translations into a given foreign language. But suppose the translators are left free to choose into just what languages they will translate the two poems. Suppose even that they have some power actually to create languages for their purpose. Then from a perusal of the original poem one could not foresee the outcome of their operations. The analogy is not adequate, in that, given the translations (the results), one would not be able to tell from what language (the conditions) the translations had been made. The question is whether the synthesis of order and freedom which Fechner intuits as required can be imprisoned in such a simple, albeit neat, formula as he offers us.

Fechner's theory of mind and matter as two aspects of reality, the latter being the aspect in which minds or souls appear to each other externally (that is, excluding cases where one soul includes another), is not wholly clear, and his hypothesis of plant and star souls is dubious. More important, his great principle that the inclusion of all souls in God has analogy to the way in which one imperfect soul (e.g., man) is included in another imperfect soul (e.g., the earth soul) is capable of more forceful illustration in a somewhat different form of panpsychic idealism than his. We have no definite way of conceiving the feelings of the earth soul; for (despite our author's arguments) the earth is not a living being recognizably analogous to an animal organism. But the cells of the human body do appear, even to ordinary scientists, as living organisms. They respond to the environment as constituted by neighbor cells and to inorganic stimuli also; and, where there is "response," there may also be "sensitivity" in the psychological sense. Why not suppose, then, that our feelings embrace within themselves, without clear discrimination of details to be sure, the pooled feelings of many cells? Then we have a basis of theological analogy which is at least much closer to definite scientific results than Fechner's. Fechner rather holds that the animal soul is the lowest level of the soul within soul series. This means that the world of microörganisms and "inorganic" suborganisms is left unilluminated by his theory of the individual. (Leibniz seems more helpful at this point, and the Leibnizian approach is resumed in revised form by Peirce, Whitehead, Montague, Parker, and others of our time.)

Fechner's famous treatment of "life after death" is a mixture of philosophically cogent considerations of striking originality with conventional religious feelings and attitudes whose rationale is to us at least less clear. That God, as Fechner's philosophy requires him, would endow our every experience with a kind of immortality through its perfect retention in the divine memory is easily deduced. For the very being of the past can only, on Fechner's panentheistic principles, consist in its inclusion in the present divine consciousness. But to this minimal immortality—which be it noted is not "impersonal," inasmuch as nothing is more personal than human experiences in their concrete particularity, and inasmuch as it is just such experiences of ours that are immortalized in God—Fechner adds notions about our awaking to new experiences, apart from the use of our present bodies; and here his reasons are harder to see, apart from mere religious tradition. Worse still, we think, he indulges in conventional notions about divine justice in the anthropomorphic sense of rewards and punishments, as though God kept everlasting account books of our deserts and the like. Here we, at least, feel the deadening influence of tradition upon an otherwise marvelously fresh and courageous pioneer.

# PEIRCE (1839–1914)

It is perhaps not out of place to mark a certain similarity between Charles Peirce and Plato. Both were astonishingly inventive; both had the faculty of coaxing insights from many different grounds and on many different subjects; and the work of neither yields easily to a single structure of thought. As with Plato, so with Peirce, scholars disagree as to the unity implicit or explicit in the sum of his philosophic production. Justus Buchler and T. A. Goudge feel there is no final unity of system capable of binding together all the themes which Peirce developed. Others, as James Feibleman, believe a highly complex structure can be discerned. Still others feel that such a structure is foreshadowed in his writings, although not completely elaborated by Peirce. At least one cannot possibly hold that Peirce is just a naturalist; his metaphysical intent is much too obvious for this to represent a final evaluation of his work.

The following selections do not present a unified doctrine; Peirce's reflections about God are fragmentary. The whole of his thought with its vigor and freshness seems to strain against arrangement into a single coherent system. It is very likely too much for us to expect a great germinal thinker to be likewise a great system-builder; and, if one should insist that Peirce was both a germinal thinker and a system-builder, then it is surely too much to expect of such a one that he also be adept in the processes of finishing and polishing the structure. But the case is more critical with respect to his concept of God; in addition to the general difficulty of system, other reasons must be mentioned to explain the fragmentary nature of his writings on this topic.

Peirce was primarily concerned with logic and cosmology; these required much of his lifelong energy. Again, Peirce deeply believed that the path of future philosophy demanded of one a consuming interest in research, particularly of the laboratory variety, and Peirce was interested in marking out that path. Once again, partly as a consequence of the foregoing, Peirce greatly distrusted the reasoning of theologians and the philosophy of the seminary which was very likely, he felt, to be armchair philosophy. But perhaps the most important consideration bearing upon the idea of God was his belief that practical matters must rest upon instinct and that close reasoning about such matters was finally inappropriate.

All of this being so, Peirce's thinking about God could not well have resulted in a single, consistent doctrine. For the most part his insights here are reflections from the consideration of other problems; and in this connection it is highly instructive that the argument for God which Peirce advances, where his thinking is not just a consequence of some other line of thought, rises not through reasoning but through "musing." The operation is highly appropriate for the class into which Peirce most often fitted the idea of God; namely, that of practical matters concerning the conduct of life.

The reason that we claim him for this chapter is primarily that he is one of the chief exponents of the supporting conceptions which in other thinkers have led to an unequivocally dipolar conception of God. These are his recognition of potentiality as a real feature of the universe, the primacy of becoming over being, growth as a feature of the universe, and his thesis of panpsychism. This cluster of ideas supports no consistent view which might be an alternate to surrelativism.

In the selections which follow those

familiar with Peirce's writings will recognize that the "three universes" so often mentioned are Peirce's final disposition of his categories, firstness, secondness, and thirdness. For readers not yet acquainted with Peirce some further explanation is proper. Under firstness, Peirce comprehended quality, feeling, spontaneity, originality, and the like (secs. 361–65), all of which became the mode of potentiality; by secondness, Peirce intended such items as "fact" with its particularity, self-assertiveness, and resistance (sec. 361)—this became the mode of actuality; by thirdness, Peirce intended the element of generality which is to be found in the operation of law and in thinking, as discernible, for example, in the general nature of symbols (sec. 364)—thus also a mode of generality was recognized. The description is here very much compressed, but the three universes are just these categories converted into modes of being.

"Synechism" (sec. 355) is Peirce's doctrine of continuity, derived from the categories and applied to the universe. "Retroduction" is Peirce's term for the process by which a hypothesis is constructed; where used (sec. 354), the term is virtually explained by its context.

The most valuable features in the selections which follow are, first, the somewhat novel manner in which the idea of God is justified by appeal to experience and to the pragmatic doctrine of meaning and, second, the vivid way in which the logic of freedom, or of creation from general potentiality to general actuality, is set forth. This account is to be compared with those of Berdyaev (secs. 389, 393) and Whitehead (secs. 397, 398, 401, 405).

### A Neglected Argument for God's Reality*

344. The word "God," so "capitalized" (as we Americans say), is *the* definable proper name, signifying *Ens necessarium;* in my belief Really creator of all three Universes of Experience.

345. If God Really be, and be benign, then, in view of the generally conceded truth that religion, were it but proved, would be a good outweighing all others, we should naturally expect that there would be some Argument for His Reality that should be obvious to all minds, high and low alike, that should earnestly strive to find the truth of the matter; and further, that this Argument should present its conclusion, not as a proposition of metaphysical theology, but in a form directly applicable to the conduct of life, and full of nutrition for man's highest growth. What I shall refer to as the N.A.—the Neglected Argument—seems to me best to fulfill this condition, and I should not wonder if the majority of those whose own reflections have harvested belief in God must bless the radiance of the N.A. for that wealth. Its persuasiveness is no less than extraordinary; while it is not unknown to anybody. Nevertheless, of all those theologians (within my little range of reading) who, with commendable assiduity, scrape together all the sound reasons they can find or concoct to prove the first proposition of theology, few mention this one, and they most briefly. They probably share those current notions of logic which recognize no other Arguments than Argumentations.

### Musement

There is a certain agreeable occupation of mind which, from its having no distinctive name, I infer is not as commonly practiced as it deserves to be; for indulged in moderately—say through some five to six per cent of one's waking time, perhaps during a stroll—it is refreshing enough more than to repay the expenditure. Because it involves no purpose save that of casting aside all serious purpose, I have sometimes been half-inclined to call it reverie with some qualification; but for a frame of mind so antipodal to vacancy and dreaminess such a designation would be too excruciating a misfit. In fact, it is Pure Play. Now, Play, we all know, is a lively exercise of one's powers. Pure Play has no rules, except this very law of liberty. It bloweth where it listeth. It has no purpose, unless recreation. The particular occupation I mean—a *petite bouchée* with the Universes—may take either the form of aesthetic contemplation, or that of distant castle-building (whether in Spain or within one's own moral training), or that of considering some wonder in one of the Universes, or some connection between two of the three, with speculation concerning its cause. It is this last kind—I will call it "Musement" on the whole—that I particularly recommend, because it will in time flower into the N.A. One who sits down with the purpose of becoming convinced of the truth of religion is plainly not inquiring in scientific singleness of heart, and must always suspect himself of reasoning unfairly. So he can never attain the entirety even of a physicist's belief in electrons, although this is avowedly but provisional. But let religious meditation be allowed to grow up spontaneously out of Pure Play without any breach of continuity, and the Muser will retain the perfect candour proper to Musement.

*346.* Different people have such wonderfully different ways of thinking that it would be far beyond my competence to say what courses Musements might not take; but a brain endowed with automatic control, as man's indirectly is, is so naturally and rightly interested in its own faculties that some psychological and semi-psychological questions would doubtless get touched; such, in the latter class, as this: Darwinians, with truly surprising ingenuity, have concocted, and with still more astonishing confidence have accepted as proved, one explanation for the diverse and delicate beauties of flowers, another for those of butterflies, and so on; but why is all nature—the forms of trees, the compositions of sunsets—suffused with such beauties throughout, and not nature only, but the other two Universes as well?

*347.* Psychological speculations will naturally lead on to musings upon metaphysical problems proper, good exercise for a mind with a turn for exact thought.

*348.* Let the Muser, for example, after well appreciating, in its breadth and depth, the unspeakable variety of each Universe, turn to those phenomena that are of the nature of homogeneities of connectedness in each; and what a spectacle will unroll itself! As a mere hint of them I may point out that every small part of space, however remote, is bounded by just such neighbouring parts as every other, without a single exception throughout immensity. The matter of Nature is in every star of the same elementary kinds, and (except for variations of circumstance), what is more wonderful still, throughout the whole visible universe, about the same proportions of the different chemical elements prevail. Though the mere catalogue of known carbon-compounds alone would fill an unwieldy volume, and perhaps, if the truth were known, the number of amino-acids alone is greater, yet it is unlikely that there are in all more than about 600 elements, of which 500 dart through space too swiftly to be held down by the earth's gravitation, coronium being the slowest-moving of these. This small number bespeaks comparative simplicity of structure. Yet no mathematician but will confess the present hopelessness of attempting to comprehend the constitution of the hydrogen-atom, the simplest of the elements that can be held to earth.

From speculations on the homogeneities of each Universe, the Muser will naturally pass to the consideration of homogeneities and connections between two different Universes, or all three.

*349.* In growth, too, we find that the three Universes conspire; and a universal feature of it is provision for later stages in earlier ones. This is a specimen of certain lines of reflection which will inevitably suggest the hypothesis of God's Reality. It is not that such phenomena might not be capable of being accounted for, in one sense, by the action of chance with the smallest conceivable dose of a higher element; for if by God be meant the *Ens necessarium*, that very hypothesis requires that such should be the case. But the point is that that sort of explanation leaves a mental explanation just as needful as before. Tell me, upon sufficient authority, that all cerebration depends upon movements of neurites that strictly obey certain physical laws, and that thus all expressions of thought, both external and internal, receive a physical explanation, and I shall be ready to believe you. But if you go on to say that this explodes the theory that my neighbour and myself are governed by reason, and are thinking beings, I must frankly say that it will not give me a high opinion of your intelligence. But however that may be, in the Pure Play of Musement the idea of God's Reality will be sure sooner or later to be found an attractive fancy, which the Muser will develop in various ways. The more he ponders it, the more it will find response in every part of his mind, for its beauty, for its supplying an ideal of life, and for its thoroughly satisfactory explanation of his whole threefold environment.

## Growth and Purpose Ineradicable from the Idea of God

The hypothesis of God is a peculiar one, in that it supposes an infinitely incomprehensible object, although every hypothesis, as such, supposes its object to be truly conceived in the hypothesis. This leaves the hypothesis but one way of understanding itself; namely, as vague yet as true so far as it is definite, and as continually tending to define itself more and more, and without limit. The hypothesis, being thus itself inevitably subject to the law of growth, appears in its vagueness to represent God as so, albeit this is directly contradicted in the hypothesis from its very first phase. But this apparent attribution of growth to God, since it is ineradicable from the hypothesis, cannot, according to the hypothesis, be flatly false. Its implications concerning the Universes will be maintained in the hypothesis, while its implications concerning God will be partly disavowed, and yet held to be less false than their denial would be. Thus the hypothesis will lead to our thinking of features of each Universe as purposed; and this will stand or fall with the hypothesis. Yet a purpose essentially involves growth, and so cannot be attributed to God. Still it will, according to the hypothesis, be less false to speak so than to represent God as purposeless.

*350.* . . . reference to the future is an essential element of personality. Were the ends of a person already explicit, there would be no room for development, for growth, for life; and consequently there would be no personality. The mere carrying out of predetermined purposes is mechanical. This remark has an application to the philosophy of religion. It is that a genuine evolutionary philosophy, that is, one that makes the principle of growth a primordial element of the universe, is so far from being antagonistic to the idea of a personal creator that it is really inseparable from that idea; while a necessitarian religion is in an altogether false position and is destined to become disintegrated. But a pseudo-evolution-ism which enthrones mechanical law above the principle of growth is at once scientifically unsatisfactory, as giving no possible hint of how the universe has come about, and hostile to all hopes of personal relations to God.

### The Neglected Argument and Pragmatism

*351.* . . . [I am] assured, from what I know of the effects of Musement on myself and others, that any normal man who considers the three Universes in the light of the hypothesis of God's Reality, and pursues that line of reflection in scientific singleness of heart, will come to be stirred to the depths of his nature by the beauty of the idea and by its august practicality, even to the point of earnestly loving and adoring his strictly hypothetical God, and to that of desiring above all things to shape the whole conduct of life and all the springs of action into conformity with that hypothesis. Now to be deliberately and thoroughly prepared to shape one's conduct into conformity with a proposition is neither more nor less than the state of mind called Believing that proposition, however long the conscious classification of it under that head be postponed.

*352.* If a pragmaticist is asked what he means by the word "God," he can only say that just as long acquaintance with a man of great character may deeply influence one's whole manner of conduct, so that a glance at his portrait may make a difference, just as almost living with Dr. Johnson enabled poor Boswell to write an immortal book and a really sublime book, just as long study of the works of Aristotle may make him an acquaintance, so if contemplation and a study of the physico-psychical universe can imbue a man with principles of conduct analogous to the influence of a great man's works or conversation, then that analogue of a mind—for it is impossible

to say that *any* human attribute is *literally* applicable—is what he means by "God." Of course, various great theologians explain that one cannot attribute *reason* to God, nor perception (which always involves an element of surprise and of learning what one did not know), and, in short, that his "mind" is necessarily so unlike ours, that some—though wrongly—high in the church say that it is only negatively, as being entirely different from everything else, that we can attach any meaning to the Name. This is not so; because the discoveries of science, their enabling us to *predict* what will be the course of nature, is proof conclusive that, though we cannot think any thought of God's, we can catch a fragment of His Thought, as it were.

Now such being the pragmaticist's answer to the question what he means by the word "God," the question whether there really *is* such a being is the question whether all physical science is merely the figment—the arbitrary figment—of the students of nature, and further whether the *one* lesson [of] the Gautama Boodha, Confucius, Socrates, and all who from any point of view have had their ways of conduct determined by meditation upon the physico-psychical universe, be only their arbitrary notion or be the Truth behind the appearances which the frivolous man does not think of; and whether the superhuman courage which such contemplation has conferred upon priests who go to pass their lives with lepers and refuse all offers of rescue is mere silly fanaticism, the passion of a baby, or whether it is strength derived from the power of the truth. Now the only guide to the answer to this question lies in the power of the passion of love which more or less overmasters every agnostic scientist and everybody who seriously and deeply considers the universe. But whatever there may be of *argument* in all this is as nothing, the merest nothing, in comparison to its force as an appeal to one's own instinct, which is to argument what substance is to shadow, what bed-rock is to the built foundations of a cathedral.

## Appeal of the Neglected Argument to the Normal Mind

353. The theologians could not have *presented* the N.A.; because that is a living course of thought of very various forms. But they might and ought to have *described* it, and should have defended it, too, as far as they could. . . . They are accustomed to make use of the principle that that which convinces a normal man must be presumed to be sound reasoning; and therefore they ought to say whatever can truly be advanced to show that the N.A., if sufficiently developed, will convince any normal man. Unfortunately, it happens that there is very little established fact to show that this is the case. I have not pretended to have any other ground for my belief that it is so than my assumption, which each one of us makes, that my own intellectual disposition is normal. I am forced to confess that no pessimist will agree with me. I do not admit that pessimists are, at the same time, thoroughly sane, and in addition are endowed in normal measure with intellectual vigour; and my reasons for thinking so are two. The first is, that the difference between a pessimistic and an optimistic mind is of such controlling importance in regard to every intellectual function, and especially for the conduct of life, that it is out of the question to admit that both are normal, and the great majority of mankind are naturally optimistic. Now, the majority of every race depart but little from the norm of that race.

354. The student, applying to his own trained habits of research the art of logical analysis—an art as elaborate and methodical as that of the chemical analyst, compares the process of thought of the Muser upon the Three Universes with certain parts of the work of scientific discovery, and finds that the "Humble Argument" is nothing but an instance of the first stage of all such work, the stage of observing the facts, or variously rearranging them, and of pondering them until, by their reactions with the results of previous scientific experience, there is "evolved" (as the chemists word it) an explanatory hypothesis. He will note, however, that this instance of Retroduction, undeniable as this character is, departs widely from the ordinary run of instances, especially in three respects. In the first place, the Plausibility of the hypothesis reaches an almost unparalleled height among deliberately formed hypotheses. So hard is it to doubt God's Reality, when the Idea has sprung from Musements, that there is great danger that the investigation will stop at this first stage, owing to the indifference of the Muser to any further proof of it. At the same time, this very Plausibility is undoubtedly an argument of no small weight in favor of the truth of the hypothesis.

In the second place, although it is a chief function of an explanatory hypothesis (and some philosophers say the only one) to excite a clear image in the mind by means of which experiential consequences of ascertainable conditions may be predicted, yet in this instance the hypothesis can only be apprehended so very obscurely that in exceptional cases alone can any definite and direct deduction from its ordinary abstract interpretation be made. How, for example, can we ever expect to be able to predict what the conduct would be, even of [an] omniscient being, governing no more than one poor solar system for only a million years or so? How much less if, being also omnipotent, he be thereby freed from all experience, all desire, all intention! Since God, in His essential character of *Ens necessarium*, is a disembodied spirit, and since there is strong reason to hold that what we call consciousness is either merely the general sensation of the brain or some part of it, or at all events some visceral or bodily sensation, God probably has no consciousness. Most of us are in the habit of thinking that consciousness and psychic life are the same thing and otherwise greatly to overrate the functions of consciousness.

The effects of the second peculiarity of the hypothesis are counteracted by a third, which consists in its commanding influence over the whole conduct of life of its believers. According to that logical doctrine which the present writer first formulated in 1873 and named Pragmatism, the true meaning of any product of the intellect lies in whatever unitary determination it would impart to practical conduct under any and every conceivable circumstance, supposing such conduct to be guided by reflexion carried to an ultimate limit.

### Direct Experience of God

355. A difficulty which confronts the synechistic philosophy is this. In considering personality, that philosophy is forced to accept the doctrine of a personal God; but in considering communication, it cannot but admit that if there is a personal God, we must have a direct perception of that person and indeed be in personal communication with him. Now, if that be the case, the question arises how it is possible that the existence of this being should ever have been doubted by anybody. The only answer that I can at present make is that facts that stand before our face and eyes and stare us in the face are far from being, in all cases, the ones most easily discerned. That has been remarked from time immemorial. [We] can know nothing except what

we *directly* experience. So all that we can anyway know relates to experience. All the creations of our mind are but patchworks from experience. So that all our ideas are but ideas of real or transposed experiences. A word can mean nothing except the idea it calls up. So that we cannot even *talk* about anything but a knowable object.

356. The Unknowable is a nominalistic heresy. The nominalists in giving their adherence to that doctrine which is really held by all philosophers of all stripes, namely, that experience is all we know, understand experience in their nominalistic sense as the mere first impressions of sense. These "first impressions of sense" are hypothetical creations of nominalistic metaphysics: I for one deny their existence. But anyway even if they exist, it is not in them that experience consists. By experience must be understood the entire mental product. Some psychologists whom I hold in respect will stop me here to say that, while they admit that experience is more than mere sensation, they cannot extend it to the whole mental product, since that would include hallucinations, delusions, superstitious imaginations, and fallacies of all kinds; and that they would limit experience to sense-perceptions. But I reply that my statement is the logical one. Hallucinations, delusions, superstitious imaginations, and fallacies of all kinds are experiences, but experiences misunderstood; while to say that all our knowledge relates merely to sense perception is to say that we can know nothing—not even mistakenly—about higher matters, as honor, aspirations, and love.

Where would such an idea, say as that of God, come from, if not from direct experience? Would you make it a result of some kind of reasoning, good or bad? Why, reasoning can supply the mind with nothing in the world except an estimate of the value of a statistical ratio, that is, how often certain kinds of things are found in certain combinations in the ordinary course of experience. And scepticism, in the sense of doubt of the validity of elementary ideas—which is really a proposal to turn an idea out of court and permit no inquiry into its applicability—is doubly condemned by the fundamental principle of scientific method—condemned first as obstructing inquiry, and condemned second because it is treating some other than a statistical ratio as a thing to be argued about. No: as to God, open your eyes —and your heart, which is also a perceptive organ—and you see him. But you may ask, Don't you admit there are any delusions? Yes: I may think a thing is black, and on close examination it may turn out to be bottle-green. But I cannot think a thing is black if there is no such thing to be seen as black. Neither can I think that a certain action is self-sacrificing, if no such thing as self-sacrifice exists, although it may be very rare. It is the nominalists, and the nominalists alone, who indulge in such scepticism, which the scientific method utterly condemns.

### God and Time

357. A disembodied spirit, or pure mind, has its being out of time, since all that it is destined to think is fully in its being at any and every previous time. But in endless time it is destined to think all that it is capable of thinking.

358. "Do you believe Him to be omniscient?" Yes, in a vague sense. Of course, God's knowledge is something so utterly unlike our own that it is more like willing than knowing. I do not see why we may not assume that He refrains from knowing much. For this thought is creative. But perhaps the wisest way is to say that we do not know how God's thought is performed and that [it] is simply vain to

attempt it. We cannot so much as frame any notion of what the phrase "the performance of God's mind" *means*. Not the faintest! The question is gabble.

"Do you believe Him to be Omnipotent?" Undoubtedly He is so, vaguely speaking; but there are many questions that might be put of no profit except to the student of logic. Some of the scholastic commentaries consider them. Leibnitz thought that this was the best of "all possible" worlds. That seems to imply some limitation upon Omnipotence. Unless the others were created too, it would seem that, all things considered, this universe was the only possible one. Perhaps others do exist. But we only wildly gabble about such things.

359. Metaphysics has to account for the whole universe of being. It has, therefore, to do something like supposing a state of things in which that universe did not exist, and consider how it could have arisen. However, this statement needs amendment. For time is itself an organized something, having its law or regularity; so that time itself is a part of that universe whose origin is to be considered. We have therefore to suppose a state of things before time was organized. Accordingly, when we speak of the universe as "arising" we do not mean that literally. We mean to speak of some kind of sequence, say an objective logical sequence; but we do not mean, in speaking of the first stages of creation before time was organized, to use "before," "after," "arising," and such words in the temporal sense.

### The Logic of Freedom

360. If we are to proceed in a logical and scientific manner, we must, in order to account for the whole universe, suppose an initial condition in which the whole universe was nonexistent, and therefore a state of absolute nothing.

*361.* We start, then, with nothing, pure zero. But this is not the nothing of negation. For *not* means *other than*, and *other* is merely a synonym of the ordinal numeral *second*. As such it implies a first; while the present pure zero is prior to every first. The nothing of negation is the nothing of death, which comes *second* to, or after, everything. But this pure zero is the nothing of not having been born. There is no individual thing, no compulsion, outward nor inward, no law. It is the germinal nothing, in which the whole universe is involved or foreshadowed. As such, it is absolutely undefined and unlimited possibility—boundless possibility. There is no compulsion and no law. It is boundless freedom.

So of *potential* being there was in that initial state no lack.

Now the question arises, what necessarily resulted from that state of things? But the only sane answer is that where freedom was boundless nothing in particular necessarily resulted.

In this proposition lies the prime difference between my objective logic and that of Hegel. He says, . . . the whole universe and every feature of it, however minute, is rational, and was constrained to be as it is by the logic of events, so that there is no principle of action in the universe but reason. But I reply, this line of thought, though it begins rightly, is not exact. A logical slip is committed; and the conclusion reached is manifestly at variance with observation. It is true that the whole universe and every feature of it must be regarded as rational, that is as brought about by the logic of events. But it does not follow that it is *constrained* to be as it is by the logic of events; for the logic of evolution and of life need not be supposed to be of that wooden kind that absolutely constrains a given conclusion. The logic may be that of the inductive or hypothetic inference.

This may-be is at once converted into must-be when we reflect that among the facts to be accounted for are such as that, for example, red things look red and not blue and *vice versa*. It is obvious that that cannot be a necessary consequence of abstract being.

*362.* I say that nothing *necessarily* resulted from the Nothing of boundless freedom. That is, nothing according to deductive logic. But such is not the logic of freedom or possibility. The logic of freedom, or potentiality, is that it shall annul itself. For if it does not annul itself, it remains a completely idle and do-nothing potentiality; and completely idle potentiality is annulled by its complete idleness.

I do not mean that potentiality immediately results in actuality. Mediately perhaps it does; but what immediately resulted was that unbounded potentiality became potentiality of this or that sort—that is, of some *quality*.

Thus the zero of bare possibility, by evolutionary logic, leapt into the *unit* of some quality. This was hypothetic inference. Its form was:

> Something is possible,
> Red is something;
> ∴ Red is possible.

Now a *quality* is a consciousness. I do not say a *waking* consciousness—but still, something of the nature of consciousness. A *sleeping* consciousness, perhaps.

### The Continuum of Potentiality

*363.* Every attempt to understand anything—every research—supposes, or at least *hopes*, that the very objects of study themselves are subject to a logic more or less identical with that which we employ.

*364.* Now continuity is shown by the logic of relations to be nothing but a higher type of that which we know as generality. It is relational generality. How then can a continuum have been derived? Has it for example been put together? Have the separated points become welded, or what?

Looking upon the course of logic as a whole we see that it proceeds from the question to the answer—from the vague to the definite. And so likewise all the evolution we know of proceeds from the vague to the definite. The indeterminate future becomes the irrevocable past. In Spencer's phrase the undifferentiated differentiates itself. The homogeneous puts on heterogeneity. However it may be in special cases, then, we must suppose that as a rule the continuum has been derived from a more general continuum, a continuum of higher generality.

From this point of view we must suppose that the existing universe, with all its arbitrary secondness, is an offshoot from, or an arbitrary determination of, a world of ideas, a Platonic world; not that our superior logic has enabled us to reach up to a world of forms to which the real universe, with its feebler logic, was inadequate.

If this be correct, we cannot suppose the process of derivation, a process which extends from before time and from before logic, we cannot suppose that it began elsewhere than in the utter vagueness of completely undetermined and dimensionless potentiality.

The evolutionary process is, therefore, not a mere evolution of the *existing universe*, but rather a process by which the very Platonic forms themselves have become or are becoming developed.

*365*. The evolution of forms begins or, at any rate, has for an early stage of it, a vague potentiality; and that either is or is followed by a continuum of forms having a multitude of dimensions too great for the individual dimensions to be distinct. It must be by a contraction of the vagueness of that potentiality of everything in general,

but of nothing in particular, that the world of forms comes about.

We can hardly but suppose that those sense-qualities that we now experience, colors, odors, sounds, feelings of every description, loves, griefs, surprise, are but the relics of an ancient ruined continuum of qualities, like a few columns standing here and there in testimony that here some old-world forum with its basilica and temples had once made a magnificent *ensemble*. And just as that forum, before it was actually built, had had a vague underexistence in the mind of him who planned its construction, so too the cosmos of sense-qualities, which I would have you to suppose in some early stage of being was as real as your personal life is this minute, had in an antecedent stage of development a vaguer being, before the relations of its dimensions became definite and contracted.

The sense-quality is a feeling. Even if you say it is a *slumbering* feeling, that does not make it less intense; perhaps the reverse. For it is the absence of *reaction*—of feeling *another*—that constitutes slumber, not the absence of the immediate feeling that is all that it is in its immediacy. Imagine a magenta color. Now imagine that all the rest of your consciousness—memory, thought, everything except this feeling of magenta—is utterly wiped out, and with that is erased all possibility of comparing the magenta with anything else or of estimating it as more or less bright. That is what you must think the pure sense-quality to be. Such a definite potentiality can emerge from the indefinite potentiality only by its own vital Firstness and spontaneity. Here is this magenta color. What originally made such a quality of feeling possible? Evidently nothing but itself. It is a First.

Yet we must not assume that the qualities arose separate and came into relation afterward. It was just the reverse. The general indefinite potentiality became limited and heterogeneous. Those who express the idea to themselves by saying that the Divine Creator determined so and so may be incautiously clothing the idea in a *garb* that is open to criticism, but it is, after all, substantially the only philosophical answer to the problem. Namely, they represent the ideas as springing into a preliminary stage of being by their own inherent firstness. But so springing up, they do not spring up isolated; for if they did, nothing could unite them. They spring up in reaction upon one another, and thus into a kind of existence. This reaction and this existence these persons call the mind of God. I really think there is no objection to this except that it is wrapped up in figures of speech, instead of having the explicitness that we desire in science. For all you know of "minds" is from the actions of animals with brains or ganglia like yourselves, or at furthest like a cockroach. To apply such a word to *God* is precisely like the old pictures which show him like an aged man leaning over to look out from above a cloud. Considering the *vague intention* of it, as conceived by the *non-theological* artist, it cannot be called false, but rather ludicrously figurative.

[Sec. 344, Peirce, *Collected Papers of Charles Sanders Peirce*, ed. Charles Hartshorne and Paul Weiss (6 vols.; Cambridge: Harvard University Press, 1935), Vol. VI, par. 452. Sec. 345, *ibid.*, pars. 457–59. Sec. 346, *ibid.*, par. 462. Sec. 347, *ibid.*, par. 463. Sec. 348, *ibid.*, pars. 464–65. Sec. 349, *ibid.*, pars. 465–66. Sec. 350, *ibid.*, par. 157. Sec. 351, *ibid.*, par. 467. Sec. 352, *ibid.*, pars. 502–3. Sec. 353, *ibid.*, par. 484. Sec. 354, *ibid.*, pars. 488–90. Sec. 355, *ibid.*, pars. 162 and 492. Sec. 356, *ibid.*, pars. 492–93. Sec. 357, *ibid.*, par. 490. Sec. 358, *ibid.*, pars. 508–9. Sec. 359, *ibid.*, par. 214. Sec. 360, *ibid.*, par. 215. Sec. 361, *ibid.*, pars. 217–18. Sec. 362, *ibid.*, pars. 219–21. Sec. 363, *ibid.*, par. 189. Sec. 364, *ibid.*, pars. 190–94. Sec. 365, *ibid.*, pars. 196–99.]

## COMMENT

One cannot properly render definite what are essentially indefinite themes concerning God; but Peirce's categories did, after all, become the three universes; and we are tempted to suggest that a definite concept could have been reached through relating the idea of God to the modes of being. The suggestion is not wholly arbitrary. Peirce's neglected argument derives the hypothesis of God from meditation upon the three universes. And in 1890 Peirce indicated that application of the three categories to the idea of God would do much to explain this primeval mystery. And, further, it was one of Peirce's chief convictions that man's success in advancing scientific thought required recognition of a similarity between the operation of the human mind and the processes of nature. Taken together, these attitudes do suggest that God's nature should exemplify the basic categories of the emerging system. This would be treating the idea of God categorically, yet it seems that Peirce never did quite this, even though he, of all men, one would expect, might have done so.

While certain of God's reality, he is remarkably hesitant with respect to decisions about God's nature. Note the peculiar quality of his uncertainty. Growth or development is essential in God (secs. 349, 350); yet this must be "partly disavowed," since it is not in keeping with the idea of a changeless being. The remainder of the paragraph is a masterpiece of indecision, supporting on the whole, however, the notion of growth in the details of God's being. Peirce is obviously fighting the fixed tradition of classical theism without discerning that on different levels both growth and changelessness can be affirmed.

Once again, Peirce states that God is "the only philosophical answer" capable of explaining the development of potentiality in the universe and that the universe—at least in this respect—may be termed "the mind of God." Thereafter he remarks that this "only philosophical answer" is to be regarded as highly figurative; hesitancy once more colors his discussion. Here the issue is God's inclusiveness; and to view the universe as the mind of God is scarcely in keeping with the idea of a "disembodied spirit."

With respect to the other attributes of God, Peirce's views, quoted and unquoted, reveal the same wavering. It would appear that God cannot be omniscient in the traditional sense because of the need for an open future (sec. 350); yet elsewhere (sec. 358) the whole question of God's knowledge becomes an impenetrable problem.

The performance suggests this: Whenever Peirce began to frame his concept of God from the principles of his system, insights relevant to his position in this chapter tended to emerge. But in mid-course of such speculation he often seems to veer toward his methodological decision that this is, after all, a practical and not a logical concern. Thereupon Peirce's view becomes indefinite, and part of what had been asserted is withdrawn. At such times, too, he incorporates segments of classical theism, borrowing from the very seminary philosophers and theologians of whom he had voiced his disapproval.

His stress on becoming rather than being separates him from classical theists; his stress on indeterminancy separates him from classical pantheists. The panentheistic elements, more or less clearly asserted, are these: that the universe exists in the mind of God (sec. 365); that the freedom of original potentiality was bound to manifest itself in some universe or other but not bound to do so in just *this* universe (in other words, creation as such, but not any particular creation rather than another, is an inevitable consequence of the divine reality) (secs. 360–62); that the divine purpose is not in its details antecedently explicit but is gradually "developed" in the process of its fulfilment; and that the divine thought, as thus creative of novel determinations, is not necessarily omniscient in the old sense of seeing all events in an eternal now (secs. 350, 358).

He did not put these ideas together in this manner or even, as we have seen, assert all of them with confidence. Had he only seen fit to apply the views of Schelling, whom he had studied, to this problem his doctrine might have been more definite; but then about such matters we only wildly gabble.

# PFLEIDERER (1839–1908)

Among German theologians, Pfleiderer was perhaps the first to adopt the surrelativist position. (Schleiermacher had indeed turned decisively away from classical theism toward pantheism, but he failed to safeguard the full reality of the Many, as free and temporal, within the One.) Pfleiderer's views agree essentially with those of the later Schelling and of Fechner, though derived, it seems, primarily from Hegel. In the following passages we find incisive criticism of the classical theistic conceptions of the eternity of God, his omnipresence and omniscience, and of creation. This criticism, it should be noted, is on religious grounds as well as philosophical. The panentheistic distinction between the eternal and the temporal (also physical) aspects of deity is held to be necessary in order to avoid the dilemma: deistic separation of God and world *or* monistic denial of the world's reality, either of which alternatives is religiously unacceptable. If God genuinely cares for the world, if it is real as content of his love and consciousness, then it is manifestly within, not outside, his actuality; but then temporality and physicality are genuine realities and, in their own fashion, divine realities. God faces a real future and has a real physical body.

The example of Pfleiderer, like that of Garvie and many others who could be cited, suggests that Christianity as such has no necessary ties with classical theism and no essential antagonism with panentheism. Note that Pfleiderer agrees with Schelling and Fechner (also with Whitehead) that the merely eternal aspect of deity is "abstract." This we hold to be the basic discovery of modern philosophical theism: the abstractness of the absolute as such, or (what is the same thing) the necessary relativity of the concrete, even the divine concrete.

We do not think these brief selections call for any "Comment." We regret only that Pfleiderer was not of sufficient stature to produce more than a moderate effect upon the development of religion or philosophy.

### Eternity

366. The eternity of God is presented in the Holy Scriptures as freedom from the limitations of temporality (beginning, end, alteration) and as self-determined control of all happenings in the world; in this respect it is the basis of our trust in the divine dependability as unalterable through all earthly alterations.

The dogmatic conception of eternity as the simple negation of time, by which any real relationship of the consciousness and activity of God to worldly events is made impossible, rests upon an abstract conception of the idea of God, and would have as consequence either the deistic separation of God from the real world or the monistic re-duction of the world process to a mere appearance in our imagination. Rather does the idea of God as living and self-conscious spirit absolutely require the admission of a temporal alterability in the content of the divine knowing and acting, despite the eternal immutability characterizing his essence and the form (of the laws and purposes) of his thinking and willing.

### Omnipresence

367. The omnipresence of God involves his incorporeality or immateriality, which, however does not prevent us from thinking of the relation of God to the entire physical world as analogous to that of the human mind to its physical organism.

### Omniscience

368. . . . The dogmatic conception of the divine omniscience as both immediate, and also eternal and immutable, awareness of all temporal occurrences not only destroys the analogy with human consciousness, which is not thinkable without succession of states, but also renders questionable either the real relation of God to the temporal process or else the reality of this process (deistic or monistic consequence). If the temporal structure of successive development is essential to the existence of the world, this structure must also be reflected in the divine consciousness of the world, and only in distinguishing successive states of consciousness can God be aware of the eternity of his essence. It follows that foresight of the future must be distinguished from knowledge of the present and must be thought to refer not to the accidents of the particular but rather to the essential features of the universal, so that it coincides with the purposive ideas of the world-ordering wisdom.

### Creation

369. For the dogmatic conception of

a creation out of nothing, with a temporal beginning, and concluded in six days, we would do well to substitute the generic idea of the beginningless and endless activity of the creative and preservative omnipotence and wisdom, which fully satisfies religious faith and leaves to science full freedom to explore the development and laws of the universe and of life on the earth.

[Sec. 366, Otto Pfleiderer, *Grundriss der Christlichen Glaubens und Sittenlehre* (Berlin: Druck & Verlag von Georg Reimer, 1888), pp. 69–70. Sec. 367, *ibid.*, p. 71. Sec. 368, *ibid.*, pp. 71–72. Sec. 369, *ibid.*, p. 88.]

# VARISCO (1850–1933)

A central problem in theism is that of the relation of divine knowing to its objects. A striking discussion of this matter is given by the recent Italian thinker Varisco. His main point, in the following passages, is that to know a thing is to include it. Our human knowing may seem indeed not to include its objects; thus we know the mountain, although it is apparently wholly without us, etc. But Varisco (like Whitehead and Leibniz) points out that most of our awareness of the almost infinite complexity of objects is subconscious intuitive feeling without clarity as to detail. (Or that there is mere imagination of detail not actually given or surely known at all.) But in the clearest case of direct and certain knowing—thus, to take his example, when we know a color, a sensory quality—it is likewise clear that this quality becomes a determination of our own actuality, our own experience. In the divine instance we must suppose absent those features of vagueness, indirectness, and uncertainty which in us are responsible for the sense that the object is outside us; we must suppose explicit direct consciousness of the object in its fulness. Hence to think that the world which God knows is entirely outside his knowing and indeed even less constitutive of his actuality than what we know is of ours (and this is implied by the classical theistic notion of God as absolutely unaffected by the world) is the opposite of logical. Let Varisco now put this matter in his own way.

*The World Is a Determination of God*

370. The stone over which I stumble is a resistance opposing me. I am aware of it. My being aware consists in an act on my part, partially obstructed and partially determined by the obstruction to which it is correlative and which is a constituent of it; in a suffering on my part; further in a knowledge on my part, that is to say in a system of concepts and judgments belonging to me. No one of these distinguishable elements exists or can exist separately from the rest. The thought on my part, to which my phenomenon can be reduced is my vital action in its intrinsic fullness and in the complexity of its intrinsic relations. We do not pretend to reduce the matter of the phenomenon to that form of it which is abstract thought (we are not idealists, in the sense in which many, perhaps most people, understand idealism).

371. To imagine that the consciousness of the universal Subject is less rich, less energetic, less vivid, than the consciousness of the particular subject, would be an extravagance. . . . We can and must say that the world is one and the same with the . . . cognition, which God possesses of it. . . . We mean, not that a divine thought, as adequate as we like, but different or other than reality, corresponds to reality, but that reality is precisely the [intrinsic content of the] divine thought of such reality. The distinction between thought and phenomenon, since the two, in their fullness, in

their actuality are coincident, has not an absolute value even with regard to the particular subject; it has, as we have recognized, a certain value with regard to it, but a value correlative to its particular limited being, as a compound of consciousness and subconsciousness; with regard to the universal Subject it becomes an absurdity pure and simple.

372. No doubt, God knows my subjective thought; indeed, it would not exist if God did not know it. My subjective thought, too, is included in the divine consciousness, and exists in so far as it is included in that consciousness.

## God Is Not the World

373. We have still to discover whether Being has, or has not, only those determinations by which the phenomenal universe is constituted. Under the second hypothesis, the determinations just mentioned are not essential to Being; Being, in the fullness of its essential determinations, is God: This is Theism.

374. God, whom we suppose to be personal, is not simply the world. He is Being, but Being endowed with other determinations than concretes; and in this sense He is certainly distinct from the world. So, for instance, I see blue. Blue, in so far as it is seen, is a determination of myself; it is not however my only determination; whence it follows that I am not only the blue; I am distinct from the blue, because I am both the blue and more (much more). That my doctrine is irreconcilable with a distinction between God and the world, even more radical than that which exists between each subject and the world, is not to be thought.

But God is the creator of the world. ... The operation of God on the world does not presuppose the existence of the world; it creates the existence of the world.

375. The disagreement between the two conceptions is, I believe, only verbal; but time, and not a short time, is required in order that all may perceive its intrinsic emptiness. Theologians now understand that the heliocentric structure of the solar system is not irreconcilable with the faith; they will understand some day that divine immanence also—that immanence which cannot absolutely be denied, and is not irreconcilable with divine personality—is not irreconcilable with the faith. But that day must be prepared for; it is impossible meanwhile to solve completely and in a comprehensible way, the dilemma which I have left unsolved (but which is not unsolved for me: I am a theist). My wishes hasten to meet that day; and I work as best I can to prepare it.

[Sec. 370, Bernardino Varisco, *Know Thyself*, trans. Guglielmo Salvadori (London: George Allen & Unwin, Ltd., 1915), pp. 224–25. Sec. 371, *ibid.*, pp. 225–26. Sec. 372, *ibid.*, p. 309. Sec. 373, *ibid.*, p. 319. Sec. 374, *ibid.*, p. 323. Sec. 375, *ibid.*, pp. 323–24.]

### COMMENT

Varisco does not make very clear whether he is what we have called a "pantheist" (he uses the term somewhat differently) or a "panentheist." If all determinations are determinations of God, then novel determinations are novelties in God, and the divine is not immutable. Would Varisco have conceded this? It seems difficult to be sure.

The phrase seeming to identify God with the essential determinations of Being, as contrasted with the inessential, apparently contradicts the implication of the second paragraph asserting that God is Being with *all* its determinations, since he is a subject knowing the world; and, according to our author, a subject has what it knows as its own determinations. The panentheistic solution is to admit both an essence of God—the one eternal and necessary factor in existence, which yet defines an individual being—and a multiplicity of accidental determinations of God. The essential determinations are what make God always himself, even though not always in the same state of experience.

## WHITEHEAD (1861–1947)

The varied reactions with which Whitehead's contribution to theism has been received are due in part to the fact that so few philosophers or theologians have learned to see the development of thought about God in anything like its full range and with anything like adequate balance and freedom. Whatever difficulties we have with his system, we regard him as the supreme example that has yet appeared of the complete application of the polar contrasts, without partiality or favor, to deity. He is the outstanding surrelativist or panentheist.

Why did Whitehead accept theism? We suggest that his entire system requires the theistic principle. One of the lines of reasoning is that "the general potentiality of the universe must be somewhere" and can only be in a primordial mind. Since his doctrine is that experience is the principle of all being, potential being must also be expressed in terms of experience; further, the potential can only be in the bosom of the actual (the "ontological principle"), so that, if general or undifferentiated potentiality is presupposed by all differentiated potentiality, then there is some primordial persistence of actual experience in which this general potency resides. The argument, thus briefly stated, is doubtless not entirely clear. Easier to see is the argument for God as ground of order. All actualities are units of experience, each of which is partly self-determined and partly influenced by other such units. But no such unit can exist unless it is furnished with a world of units already in being, to offer it data of experience. And there must be some measure of harmony among the data. Units influence one another, but

this influence is expressed partly in frustrations, in mutual incompatibilities.

Why should not the "cross currents of incompatibility" be so great as to render existence intolerable? What keeps the world going, if nothing opposes the alternative of frustration, issuing in cessation of all experience? Whitehead's answer is the one which the situation suggests: There is at any moment *one* unit of experience whose influence upon all is supreme; and, since all thus undergo a common influence to which they subordinate themselves, there is bound to be a measure of agreement among them.

Only in this context can we see the meaning of the famous but rather misunderstood and not wholly happy phrase, "principle of limitation," as descriptive of God. When Whitehead introduced this expression (in *Science and the Modern World*), he perhaps had not yet achieved clarity as to the panentheistic structure of his theism. Certainly the God of his later writings is no mere "principle," that is, mere abstraction, but a concrete stream of "experience" containing at each moment the unity of the whole of reality, as actual at that moment. Whitehead's point is not that selection among abstractly possible alternatives can be made only by deity; for, according to the Whiteheadian philosophy, every actual entity is an agent of such selection. The "self-created creature" (synonymous with "actual entity") is the partly self-determining act of experience, for instance, a human experience. But the point is that a multitude of agents could not select a common world and must indeed simply nullify one another's efforts, unless some common limitation or bias pervades their acts. This common limitation to the selections must itself be selected, for there is no one world order which alone is possible. Who or what can select the *universal* limitation or direction of the secondary, local selections? Obviously, only a being with universal influence. But supreme qualities alone could endow a being with such influence, could make it universally irresistible, within such limits of possible resistance as would not nullify cosmic order. So we come to God as the supreme self-determining act, or perpetual series of such acts (for Whitehead holds that no one order is valid for all time), a series which never began and can never cease and which has in supreme form that highest mode of unity through development which constitutes personality.

God is, as Whitehead agreed in a carefully noted conversation with A. H. Johnson, a linear sequence (which Whitehead terms "a personally ordered society") of occasions—with the difference, as contrasted to ordinary personal sequences, that in God there is no lapse of memory, no loss of immediacy, as to occasions already achieved. However, no theologian of the past who is credited with conceiving God as personal ever failed to make at least *this* difference between human and divine personality—that God is not, like man, separated from a past which he has largely forgotten!

It may indeed be said that this is one of the first philosophies which has any intellectual right to speak of divine personality. For personality, as any psychologist knows, is a sort of cluster of habits and purposes and ideas, and it therefore has a certain abstractness, in that it expresses itself now in this particular experience and now in that, whether one looks out the window and sees rain or sunshine or opens a book and sees words. Thus personality is, in Whitehead's language, a "defining characteristic" of a sequence of experiences, and the characteristic does not fully determine the sequence; for, if it did, we should never know any persons until they were dead, since we certainly never anticipate their experiences in their concreteness, even our own. All concepts of personality seem to imply this partial independence of particular experiences from the determining influence of the personality. We shall not here pursue the argument, but we doubt if anyone can really, or other than verbally, mean by a "person" more than what Whitehead means by a "personally ordered" sequence of experiences with certain defining characteristics or personality traits. This is also how he conceives God, with the appropriate qualification that in God the imperfection involved in forgetting is denied. God, indeed, in this philosophy as in that of Royce, is the home of all truth; and for God to forget would mean that it could not be true that what he forgets really occurred, and so it would not be forgetting after all.

It is to be noted how Whitehead, unlike so many others, is able to introduce God into his system in terms of concepts universally operative in it. When he says that God exerts providential influence upon the world, he means by influencing something identifiable in experience as he describes it. We are influenced by God because we "prehend" him, as we do other actualities, for example, our past experiences. God's influence is supreme because he is the supreme actuality, supremely beautiful and attractive. Thus one need not resort to some wholly mysterious "power" to create *ex nihilo*, analogous to nothing known or imaginable, and in no imaginable relation to our freedom of self-determination.

There is no "power" anywhere, on earth or in heaven, except the direct and indirect workings of attractiveness ("persuasion"). We have power over other men's minds through the value they find in our thoughts and feelings; we have power over our bodies because the sentient units composing them derive such inspiration as their lowly natures can receive from these same thoughts and feelings; and through controlling our own bodies we can indirectly influence other men's bodies and minds. But the direct influence of God is analogous only to the direct power of thought over thought, and of feeling over feeling, and this is the power of inspiration or suggestion. It could not possibly suppress all freedom in the recipient, since a minimum of response on his part is presupposed. It is not that God "makes" us to be what we are—these are mere words with vague or inconsistent meanings—it is rather that we make ourselves, utilizing his beauty as inspiration.

Even Fechner perhaps did not quite reach this insight. That our volitions are God's impulses (Fechner's great discovery), however, is valid for Whitehead, though he does not use this language. For the language he does use comes to the same. God influences us, and we in our turn influence God, "react" upon his prehensive nature, give him data for new "physical feelings"; the communication back and forth is on both sides partly receptive or "passive" (ending the long sad tradition of unreasoning intellectual hatred for passivity) and on both sides partly creative and active. This does not make God merely a greater man. For God, but not man, is the general ground of possibility who *cannot* not exist, who cannot be generated as a new personality, or ever reach an end of his personal development, or fail to do for all beings as much as can be done for them (fail in perfect fidelity to the ultimate "ideals" inherent in his primordial nature). These are infinite differences.

It is also to be noted that Whitehead steers a middle course between those who make the world without qualification necessary to God, required by his very essence, and those who make God so independent of the world that it is literally nothing to him, and might exactly as well, so far as his entire reality is concerned, never have been. Our philosopher says: "The world's nature is a primordial datum for God; and God's nature is a primordial datum for the World" (*Process and Reality*, p. 529). Observe that it is not said that the world is a primordial datum, or that God is, but reference is in each case to the nature of world and of God. This means that there can never have failed to be *some* world *or other* and likewise that some state of (the consequent nature of) God is always given to entities in the world. But *what* world and *what* state of God is not primordially or eternally or necessarily determined. Thus while God is not free as between world and no world, and the world is not free as between God and no God, yet God could have existed without ever having been presented with just this world, and there could have been a world though God had never been just as he actually is. The difference between deity and world in this correlation is that God is always the same personal sequence, the same individual (though not the same particular actuality), while the world is not any single individual but a mere form-of-collection of individuals as presented to one individual (God). So God is the only individual who exists necessarily and independently of what other individuals exist or fail to exist. Though he requires *some* such other individuals, he has power always to elicit or entice some such into being. If this unconditional power to entice something into being is a mystery, then mystery there is in this philosophy. Yet we all experience something analogous to it. Each of us has a sense of actively affirming his own aliveness at each moment; and he also senses that he would scarcely be inspired to go on with this affirmation if no one cared about him, and if there were none about whom he could care. God's power to keep existence going is the "eminent" case of this social nature of the act of existing.

Another phrase upon which we wish to comment is this: "Either of them, God and the World, is the instrument of novelty for the other" (sec. 389). In this passage Whitehead is expressing partial agreement with the ancient idea that, if an individual changes, something other than himself must have changed it. But Whitehead follows experience in taking the typical case to be a mutual rather than a one-way affair. Take a conversation: *A* says something, *B* makes a comment thereon, *A* replies to the comment, *B* comments upon the reply, etc. Here each individual changes in a certain way because the other has changed in a certain way. There is no need that any individual involved in the process should be unchanging. True, there must be something fixed throughout, but this need not be an individual in its concreteness but may be an abstract ideal. This for Whitehead is furnished by the primordial nature of God, which is Aristotle's unmoved mover or Plato's demiurge or Plotinus' *nous*. But it is only a nature of God, not God himself in his total being. The primordial nature is devoid of change, but it changes the concrete God in his consequent nature, and all other concrete individuals ("societies," in our author's phrase) also—in such fashion, however, that their change is a social affair in which each occasion "decides" or enacts itself upon the basis of data furnished by the others. All this contradicts the axiom that the antecedent cause must be at least equal in dignity to the effect; rather, the inclusive effect is always a new and richer phase of the divine life as including all life. For process philosophy the axiom is merely the

arbitrary denial of creative interaction—indeed, of any creation—since it is meaningless or contradictory that creating something should leave the antecedent total reality unenriched.

Much perplexity in interpreting Whitehead has been due to his concept of "creativity," which is expressly distinguished from God, and is once almost equated with Spinoza's substance and once with Aristotle's matter. And we are told that both God and the world are in the grip of the creative ground, driving them on to ever new states (sec. 389). Now, the most coherent interpretation of the various statements seems to be attained if we view creativity as simply the common generic abstraction or form of forms (we are on occasion told it is just that, and we are also warned that it is not a concrete actuality). But whereas in Thomism, for example, the generic abstraction is "being," in the philosophy of process it is "becoming" or, rather, self-creation. (Even in Thomism, being is said to be an act, but we are never allowed to see, in any experiential sense, how it is an act.) Again, the generic abstraction in Thomism is said to be analogical, not univocal; and to this also there is something corresponding in Whitehead. The divine becoming or creation is not just another case of the "process" which other things illustrate. For the divine becoming has properties whose uniqueness can be stated in categorical terms; it alone is able adequately to embrace all actuality as its data; it alone goes on primordially and everlastingly in the same individual way, embodying the same individual personality traits; etc. These are not just differences; they are categorical differences, statable in purely general terms (as the "self-existence" of God in contrast to "existence through another" was statable in Thomism). So there is no simply univocal concept here. But, on the other hand, there is a unity lacking to the Thomistic "being" (a lack which has bothered many a Thomist and occasioned controversy). For the advance of reality from achieved actuality to additional achieved actuality is *one* advance both for us and for God in the sense that each addition is fully taken account of by him as well as (or infinitely better than) by us. There is a "solidarity" of becoming, so that, as all things qualify the Spinozistic substance, so each actuality is once for all added to the common stock of "real potentials" (adequately contained only in the *de facto* state of the Consequent Nature) for further creation. This is the panentheistic principle, with stress upon the temporalistic aspect of process, divine as well as worldly.

The metaphor "in the grip of" may mislead some into thinking that God must be under some constraint to go on creatively. But there is no constraint, any more than his "necessary existence" in classical theism was something constrained. The Deity could not fail to exist, but he also does not, and could not, even wish not to exist. Similarly, in Whitehead's view, God could not wish not to go on experiencing novel content, since his ideals are incapable of final exhaustive realization. This inexhaustibility of the ideal is again no alien power over God but the intrinsic nature of his own primordial essence, yet embracing the general principles of all value, including the principle of incompatibility which makes exhaustive realization nonsense. A temporalistic theism has no trouble with the ancient problem, signalized by Carneades, that if God is to be judged by an ideal of goodness he is relativized to something not himself. The ideal is not good because God arbitrarily wills it, nor are his acts good because they express goodness as something nondivine; they are good, as our acts (in their categorically inferior way) are good, because of an abstract ideal antecedent to each

such act; however, this ideal is not antecedent to God but his eternal and unchangeable purpose (to be contrasted with his special purposes, new for each occasion). We and God serve the same ideal; but in us it is our glimpse of God's essence, and in God it is his clear intuition into that same essence. The old dilemma thus proves to be sophistical.

We wish to warn the reader that Whitehead must be read rather slowly. One must expect a good many ideas in each dozen lines and must expect these ideas to qualify each other backward and forward, to some extent. This is particularly true of the score or so of pages which are all that Whitehead has written directly dealing with God.

## God as the Valuation of the World

376. The depths of his [God's] existence lie beyond the vulgarities of praise or of power. He gives to suffering its swift insight into values which can issue from it. He is the ideal companion who transmutes what has been lost into a living fact within his own nature. He is the mirror which discloses to every creature its own greatness.

The kingdom of heaven is not the isolation of good from evil. It is the overcoming of evil by good. This transmutation of evil into good enters into the actual world by reason of the inclusion of the nature of God, which includes the ideal vision of each actual evil so met with a novel consequent as to issue in the restoration of goodness.

God has in his nature the knowledge of evil, of pain, and of degradation, but it is there as overcome with what is good. Every fact is what it is, a fact of pleasure, of joy, of pain, or of suffering. In its union with God that fact is not a total loss, but on its finer side is an element to be woven immortally into the rhythm of mortal things. Its very evil becomes a stepping stone in the all-embracing ideals of God.

377. The power by which God sustains the world is the power of himself as the ideal. He adds himself to the actual ground from which every creative act takes its rise. The world lives by its incarnation of God in itself.

378. He is the binding element in the world. The consciousness which is individual in us, is universal in him: the love which is partial in us is all-embracing in him. Apart from him there could be no world, because there could be no adjustment of individuality. His purpose in the world is quality of attainment. His purpose is always embodied in the particular ideals relevant to the actual state of the world. Thus all attainment is immortal in that it fashions the actual ideals which are God in the world as it is now.

379. He is not the world, but the valuation of the world.

### Evil as Loss and Incompatibility

380. The ultimate evil in the temporal world is deeper than any specific evil. It lies in the fact that the past fades, that time is a "perpetual perishing." Objectification involves elimination. The present fact has not the past fact with it in any full immediacy. The process of time veils the past below distinctive feeling. There is a unison of becoming among things in the present. Why should there not be novelty without loss of this direct unison of immediacy among things? In the temporal world, it is the empirical fact that process entails loss: the past is present under an abstraction. But there is no reason, of any ultimate metaphysical generality, why this should be the whole story. The nature of evil is that the characters of things are mutually obstructive. Thus the depths of life require a process of selection. But the selection is elimination as the first step towards another temporal order seeking to minimize obstructive modes. Selection is at once the measure of evil, and the process of

its evasion. It means the discarding the element of obstructiveness in fact. No element in fact is ineffectual: thus the struggle with evil is a process of building up a mode of utilization by the provision of intermediate elements introducing a complex structure of harmony. The triviality in some initial reconstruction of order expresses the fact that actualities are being produced, which, trivial in their own proper character of immediate "ends," are proper "means" for the emergence of a world at once lucid, and intrinsically of immediate worth.

The evil of the world is that those elements which are translucent so far as transmission is concerned, in themselves are of slight weight; and that those elements with individual weight, by their discord, impose upon vivid immediacy the obligation that it fade into night.

381. So long as the temporal world is conceived as a self-sufficient completion of the creative act, explicable by its derivation from an ultimate principle which is at once eminently real and the unmoved mover, from this conclusion there is no escape: the best that we can say of the turmoil is, "For so he giveth his beloved—sleep."

### Dipolarity in God: His Primordial and Consequent Natures

382. . . . God is not to be treated as an exception to all metaphysical principles, invoked to save their collapse. He is their chief exemplification.

Viewed as primordial, he is the unlimited conceptual realization of the absolute wealth of potentiality. In this aspect, he is not *before* all creation, but *with* all creation. But, as primordial, so far is he from "eminent reality," that in this abstraction he is "deficiently actual"—and this in two ways. His feelings are only conceptual and so lack the fulness of actuality. Secondly, conceptual feelings, apart from complex integration with physical feelings, are devoid of consciousness in their subjective forms.

Thus, when we make a distinction of reason, and consider God in the abstraction of a primordial actuality, we must ascribe to him neither fulness of feeling, nor consciousness.

*383.* But God, as well as being primordial, is also consequent. He is the beginning and the end. . . . Thus by reason of the relativity of all things, there is a reaction of the world on God. The completion of God's nature into a fulness of physical feeling is derived from the objectification of the world in God. He shares with every new creation its actual world; and the concrescent creature is objectified in God as a novel element in God's objectification of that actual world. . . . God's conceptual nature is unchanged, by reason of its final completeness. But his derivative nature is consequent upon the creative advance of the world.

Thus, analogously to all actual entities, the nature of God is dipolar. He has a primordial nature and a consequent nature. The consequent nature of God is conscious; and it is the realization of the actual world in the unity of his nature, and through the transformation of his wisdom. The primordial nature is conceptual, the consequent nature is the weaving of God's physical feelings upon his primordial concepts.

One side of God's nature is constituted by his conceptual experience. This experience is the primordial fact in the world, limited by no actuality which it presupposes. It is therefore infinite, devoid of all negative prehensions. This side of his nature is free, complete, primordial, eternal, actually deficient, and unconscious. The other side originates with physical experience derived from the temporal world, and then acquires integration with the primordial side. It is determined, incomplete, consequent, "everlasting," fully actual, and conscious. His necessary goodness expresses the determination of his consequent nature.

Conceptual experience can be infinite, but it belongs to the nature of physical experience that it is finite.

*384.* . . . every occasion of actuality is in its own nature finite. There is no totality which is the harmony of all perfections. Whatever is realized in any one occasion of experience necessarily excludes the unbounded welter of contrary possibilities. There are always "others," which might have been and are not. This finiteness is not the result of evil, or of imperfection. It results from the fact that there are possibilities of harmony which either produce evil in joint realization, or are incapable of such conjunction. This doctrine is a commonplace in the fine arts. It also is—or should be—a commonplace of political philosophy. History can only be understood by seeing it as the theatre of diverse groups of idealists respectively urging ideals incompatible for conjoint realization. You cannot form any historical judgment of right or wrong by considering each group separately. The evil lies in the attempted conjunction.

This principle of intrinsic incompatibility has an important bearing upon our conception of the nature of God. The concept of impossibility such that God himself cannot surmount it, has been for centuries quite familiar to theologians. Indeed, apart from it there would be difficulty in conceiving any determinate divine nature. But curiously enough, so far as I know, this notion of incompatibility has never been applied to ideals in the Divine realization. We must conceive the Divine Eros as the active entertainment of all ideals, with the urge to their finite realization, each in its due season. Thus a process must be inherent in God's nature, whereby his infinity is acquiring realization.

*385.* The perfection of God's subjective aim, derived from the completeness of his primordial nature, issues into the character of his consequent nature. In it there is no loss, no obstruction. The world is felt in a unison of immediacy. The property of combining creative advance with the retention of mutual immediacy is what . . . is meant by the term "everlasting."

The wisdom of subjective aim prehends every actuality for what it can be in such a perfected system—its sufferings, its sorrows, its failures, its triumphs, its immediacies of joy—woven by rightness of feeling into the harmony of the universal feeling, which is always immediate, always many, always one, always with novel advance, moving onward and never perishing. The revolts of destructive evil, purely self-regarding, are dismissed into their triviality of merely individual facts; and yet the good they did achieve in individual joy, in individual sorrow, in the introduction of needed contrast, is yet saved by its relation to the completed whole. The image—and it is but an image—the image under which this operative growth of God's nature is best conceived, is that of a tender care that nothing be lost.

The consequent nature of God is his judgment on the world. He saves the world as it passes into the immediacy of his own life. It is the judgment of a tenderness which loses nothing that can be saved. It is also the judgment of a wisdom which uses what in the temporal world is mere wreckage.

Another image which is also required to understand his consequent nature, is that of his infinite patience. The universe includes a threefold creative act composed of (i) the one infinite conceptual realization, (ii) the multiple solidarity of free physical realizations in the temporal world, (iii) the ultimate unity of the multiplicity of actual fact with the primordial conceptual fact. If we conceive the first term and the last term in their unity over against the intermediate multiple freedom of physical realizations in the temporal world, we conceive of the patience of God, tenderly saving the turmoil of the intermediate world by the completion of his own nature.

*386.* . . . he is the poet of the world, with tender patience leading it by his vision of truth, beauty, and goodness.

The vicious separation of the flux from the permanence leads to the concept of an entirely static God, with eminent reality, in relation to an entirely fluent world, with deficient reality. But if the opposites, static and fluent, have once been so explained as separately to characterize diverse actualities, the interplay between the thing which is static and the things which are fluent involves contradiction at every step in its explanation.

*387.* But civilized intuition has always, although obscurely, grasped the problem as double and not as single. There is not the mere problem of fluency *and* permanence. There is the double problem: actuality with permanence, requiring fluency as its completion; and actuality with fluency, requiring permanence as its completion. The first half of the problem concerns the completion of God's primordial nature by the derivation of his consequent nature from the temporal world. The second half of the problem concerns the completion of each fluent actual occasion by its function of objective immortality, devoid of "perpetual perishing," that is to say, "everlasting."

*388.* The final summary can only be expressed in terms of a group of antitheses, whose apparent self-contradiction depend on neglect of the diverse categories of existence. In each antithesis there is a shift of meaning which converts the opposition into a contrast.

It is as true to say that God is permanent and the World fluent, as that the World is permanent and God is fluent.

It is as true to say that God is one and the World many, as that the World is one and God many.

It is as true to say that, in comparison with the World, God is actual eminently, as that, in comparison with God, the World is actual eminently.

It is as true to say that the World is immanent in God, as that God is immanent in the World.

It is as true to say that God transcends the World, as that the World transcends God.

It is as true to say that God creates the World, as that the World creates God.

389. Opposed elements stand to each other in mutual requirement. In their unity, they inhibit or contrast. God and the World stand to each other in this opposed requirement. God is the infinite ground of all mentality, the unity of vision seeking physical multiplicity. The World is the multiplicity of finites, actualities seeking a perfected unity. Neither God, nor the World, reaches static completion. Both are in the grip of the ultimate metaphysical ground, the creative advance into novelty. Either of them, God and the World, is the instrument of novelty for the other.

## Creation and Immortality

390. The theme of Cosmology, which is the basis of all religions, is the story of the dynamic effort of the World passing into everlasting unity, and of the static majesty of God's vision, accomplishing its purpose of completion by absorption of the World's multiplicity of effort.

The consequent nature of God is the fulfillment of his experience by his reception of the multiple freedom of actuality into the harmony of his own actualization. It is God as really actual, completing the deficiency of his mere conceptual actuality.

391. This final phase of passage in God's nature is ever enlarging itself. In it the complete adjustment of the immediacy of joy and suffering reaches the final end of creation. This end is existence in the perfect unity of adjustment as means, and in the perfect multiplicity of the attainment of individual types of self-existence. The function of being a means is not disjoined from the function of being an end. The sense of worth beyond itself is immediately enjoyed as an overpowering element in the individual self-attainment. It is in this way that the immediacy of sorrow and pain is transformed into an element of triumph. This is the notion of redemption through suffering, which haunts the world. It is the generalization of its very minor exemplification as the aesthetic value of discords in art.

392. Thus the consequent nature of God is composed of a multiplicity of elements with individual self-realization. It is just as much a multiplicity as it is a unity; it is just as much one immediate fact as it is an unresting advance beyond itself. Thus the actuality of God must also be understood as a multiplicity of actual components in process of creation. This is God in his function of the kingdom of heaven.

Each actuality in the temporal world has its reception into God's nature. The corresponding element in God's nature is not temporal actuality, but is the transformation of that temporal actuality into a living, ever-present fact. An enduring personality in the temporal world is a route of occasions in which the successors with some peculiar completeness sum up their predecessors. The correlate fact in God's nature is an even more complete unity of life in a chain of elements for which succession does not mean loss of immediate unison.

*393.* But the principle of universal relativity is not to be stopped at the consequent nature of God. This nature itself passes into the temporal world according to its gradation of relevance to the various concrescent occasions. There are thus four creative phases in which the universe accomplishes its actuality. There is first the phase of conceptual origination, deficient in actuality, but infinite in its adjustment of valuation. Secondly, there is the temporal phase of physical origination, with its multiplicity of actualities. In this phase full actuality is attained; but there is deficiency in the solidarity of individuals with each other. This phase derives its determinate conditions from the first phase. Thirdly, there is the phase of perfected actuality, in which the many are one everlastingly, without the qualification of any loss either of individual identity or of completeness of unity. In everlastingness, immediacy is reconciled with objective immortality. This phase derives the conditions of its being from the two antecedent phases. In the fourth phase, the creative action completes itself. For the perfected actuality passes back into the temporal world, and qualifies this world so that each temporal actuality includes it as an immediate fact of relevant experience. For the kingdom of heaven is with us today. The action of the fourth phase is the love of God for the world. It is the particular providence for particular occasions. What is done in the world is transformed into a reality in heaven, and the reality in heaven passes back into the world. By reason of this reciprocal relation, the love in the world passes into the love in heaven, and floods back again into the world. In this sense, God is the great companion—the fellow-sufferer who understands.

We find here the final application of the doctrine of objective immortality. Throughout the perishing occasions in the life of each temporal Creature, the inward source of distaste or of refreshment, the judge arising out of the very nature of things, redeemer or goddess of mischief, is the transformation of Itself, everlasting in the Being of God. In this way, the insistent craving is justified—the insistent craving that zest for existence be refreshed by the ever-present, unfading importance of our immediate actions, which perish and yet live for evermore.

[Sec. 376, Alfred North Whitehead, *Religion in the Making* (New York: Macmillan Co., 1926), pp. 154–55. Sec. 377, *ibid.*, p. 156. Sec. 378, *ibid.*, pp. 158–59. Sec. 379, *ibid.*, p. 159. Sec. 380, Whitehead, *Process and Reality* (New York: Macmillan Co., 1929), pp. 517–18. Sec. 381, *ibid.*, p. 519. Sec. 382, *ibid.*, pp. 521–22. Sec. 383, *ibid.*, pp. 523–24. Sec. 384, Whitehead, *Adventures of Ideas* (New York: Macmillan Co., 1933), pp. 356–57. Sec. 385, Whitehead, *Process and Reality*, pp. 524–25. Sec. 386, *ibid.*, p. 526. Sec. 387, *ibid.*, p. 527. Sec. 388, *ibid.*, pp. 527–28. Sec. 389, *ibid.*, p. 529. Sec. 390, *ibid.*, pp. 529–30. Sec. 391, *ibid.*, pp. 530–31. Sec. 392, *ibid.*, p. 531. Sec. 393, *ibid.*, pp. 532–33.]

## COMMENT

It is impossible to avoid a feeling of impertinence in attempting to comment on thinking so great as this. Not in many centuries, perhaps, has such a contribution been made to philosophical theism.

We wish to remind the reader of the passage quoted on the frontispiece from *Adventures of Ideas*.

The foregoing passages seem to make it very clear that Whitehead fully accepts the five factors which we have specified as essential to the divine nature: eternity, temporality, consciousness, world knowledge, and world inclusion. God as primordial is strictly eternal in the sense of being immutable and ungenerated. (As ground of all possibility, how could he be generated?) God as consequent is "fluent," reaches no final completion, contains succession, and is ever in "process" of further creation. And the passage (not quoted) which says that God is "in one sense temporal" must refer to God in this aspect. Hence the contrast drawn between God and temporal world does not mean that God is simply above time or immutable but rather that he is beginningless and that process in him has a unique perfection of mnemonic retention of past experiences. This does not imply that all is merely "present" or nonsuccessive for God. For the part is always distinguished from the whole, and the remembered is only the content of the memory, while the memory is the memory-of-the-content, i.e., the content and something more. The past is present in the sense of given but not in the sense of being the whole experience in which there is this givenness. *The* present is always this whole.

That God is conscious is explicitly stated and never denied. To quote (as is sometimes done) the denial of consciousness to the primordial nature in this connection is as irrelevant as it would be to say, "Socrates is not a conscious being, because the innate character of Socrates is not aware of itself" (rather, "Socrates is aware of his character").

That God knows the entire actual world is also clear; for the physical experience of all actual occasions as they occur, integrated with conceptual experience, and fully conscious of itself, is just what complete and perfect knowledge would be in this philosophy. It also renders better justice to the old idea of the divine knowledge as intuitive or concrete and direct, rather than discursive or essentially abstract and indirect, than classical theists were effectively able to do—since they really denied any concrete union of God with the world such as an intuition of it must be. Finally, we are told by Whitehead, over and over again, that God is the unity of all things—that he contains all actuality. And, thanks to the admission of fluency or temporality in God, there is no need and no tendency to deny the full individual reality of the creatures in God. The consequent nature is just as much multiple as one—this is one aspect of the panentheistic principle.

What is said about particular providence and suffering love is meant literally enough. God perceives the concrete particularity of actual experiences, say, of men. He reacts to these in the light of his primordial wisdom as he receives them into his experience, giving them the best place they are capable of in the total synthesis of this experience. Then, in the next phase, persons in the world in the depths of their largely unconscious feelings take account of this divine reaction to them. In this way they tend to find the place which divine love has made for them. That God's physical experience is not "mere happiness" but involves tragedy or suffering is not sentimentalism but logic. How can the quality of suffering be concretely perceived by one in whose experience there is only joy? We think the answer is, "In no way."

The use of the word "transformation," or "transmutation," in connection with the consequent nature has led to discussion as to whether the "immortality" affirmed in this philosophy is in any sense personal or individual. Are we not absorbed into the divine experience in such fashion as to lose what is unique and individual in us? It is somewhat doubtful if Whitehead is always fully consistent on this point. Not that there is a contradiction in his position but that he wavers between two positions. On the one hand, we are told many times that it is the individualities of the world in their actual uniqueness and multiplicity that are received into and immortalized in deity. And the reason is given: The beauty of a whole with intensely individual components is greater than that of one whose elements lack intense individuality.

On the other hand, we are also told that all objectification, or physical perception, "abstracts," it prehends its object under a limitation; and in conversation A. H. Johnson was told by Whitehead that this applies also to God —which agrees with one possible meaning of "he saves whatever can be saved." Is this the "transformation"? But then it is not true that "there is no loss." And then also it cannot be that "the truth itself is only the way all things are together in the consequent nature"; for how can it be true that something is left out if the truth is just what is retained? And then, too, if abstractness or limitation affects even divine prehensions, in what is their "supreme" quality? Nor is there any ground for such limitation in the principle that all realization is finite or limited; for, granted unlimited retention of all occasions, this would still limit God (in his actual data) to the actual occasions, in contrast to all that might have, but, in fact, have not, been achieved in the past of the world. And while not all possible values can be realized together, the problem here is only whether all actual ones can be so realized. Their coactuality already implies, it seems, a kind of compatibility. As for the meaning of "transformation," we suggest that the data perceived are not altered but that an emergent synthesis is effected which as a whole or unity is more than the world taken collectively and, in this sense only, is a transformation of the world.

The word "transformed" occurs in the following passage, among others: "The sense of worth beyond itself is immediately enjoyed as an overpowering element in the individual self-attainment. It is in this way that the immediacy of sorrow and pain is transformed into an element of triumph. This is the notion of redemption through suffering, which haunts the world. It is the generalization of its very minor exemplification as the aesthetic value of discords in art" (sec. 391). This will be viewed by some as showing that Whitehead's God sadistically exploits our sorrows for his own enjoyment. But we must avoid errors due to anthropomorphism. When *we* enjoy the spectacle of the suffering of others, we do so from outside, without full realization of that suffering as such. But God fully internalizes the suffering into himself. Any good he can derive from it is not sadistic but tragic. It is the very sort of good we ourselves derive from our own suffering when and if we achieve perspective upon it, as in tragic drama and moments of heroic joy. And, Whitehead reminds us, we can always to some degree participate—through cultivating the religious imagination—in God's sublime experience of all the world's joy and sorrow.

The one thing that one must not do, according to Whitehead, is to hold that all evil is required just as it is for the perfection of the whole. There is no finally perfect whole and no reason to suppose that a more harmonious whole would not have been possible at this very moment than actually exists.

We must also remember Whitehead's doctrine that pain is a halfway house between full harmony and the zero value of utter indifference or boredom. Both for us and for God our sorrows are better than mere indifference. We, as well as he, have a stake in the intensity of existence. Nietzsche's insistence that dramatic tragedy is an assertion of power and vitality is correct and has theological relevance. Not that tragedy is simply good but that for God to exclude it through the only possible method, that of eliminating all dangerous freedom, would reduce, not enhance, the total value.

The common notion of immortality,

that after death we begin a new series of adventures bound together by a prolongation of our present personality, is apparently ignored by Whitehead. But are we in a position to say that there ought to be such prolongation? The argument that only thus, through transcendental rewards and punishments, can the injustices of the present life be overcome, and only by the expectation of such future consequences to "ourselves," can our acts be adequately motivated, leaves a Whiteheadian unconvinced, to say the least. For consider: The present occasion enjoys itself; this occasion has already all the reward *it* can ever have. The same human personality may be re-embodied in future occasions falling into the same personal sequence; but our interest in *these* future occasions is only one of our interests, with no absolute metaphysical priority. Whether future joys belong to the series constituting my personal life, or even to any human series now existing, is a secondary, not a primary, question, from the ethical, and from any imaginative or generous, point of view. We should love our children and in principle their children's children as ourselves. This does not mean that there is no truth in the deep feeling that there must be a thread of personal identity connecting our present act and any future good with which it can be concerned. Indeed, there must be, for truth itself depends on this thread, and so do the coherence and order of the world. But not *our* personality is this necessary, this primary, personal unity, but only God's. It is a hard lesson to learn—that God is more important than we are.

It remains true that the Whiteheadian immortality is "personal" in a literal sense. For all that is known to be actual of any human personality is the life of that person while on earth. And all this actuality, as actuality of experience—and what is value beyond all experience?—is just what, according to Whitehead, is immortalized in the all-receptive unity of God. Nothing is more personal about a man than his concrete experiences—which "perish, and yet live for evermore"—in the divine, supremely personal life!

## BERDYAEV (1874–1948)

The Eastern Orthodox church has had a strikingly different intellectual history from the churches of western Europe and the United States. Instead of the flat rejection of anything that seemed to incline toward "pantheism," the Russians (for example, Soloviev) have actually taught that the divine somehow literally contains the world. But they have had less interest than the Scholastics in sharp definitions and logical devices, and the divine inclusiveness was treated more as a mystical than as a philosophical truth. Partly because they were less intellectualistic, and because their theory of church government was somewhat more demo- cratic and less centralized, the ecclesiastical restrictions upon freedom of speculation have apparently been less rigid. Still, prior to Berdyaev, and even today in such a representative as Lossky, we find the Russian theologians agreeing with classical theism in the monopolar doctrine that the highest Being is immutable and impassive.

Berdyaev marks a rather new departure, to an extent that one may plausibly ascribe to genius, even though he admittedly got the stimulus for his view from Boehme and Schelling. Here at last is an out-and-out dipolar theology! Berdyaev speaks frankly of a divine history, a divine becoming, divine need, and, above all, divine suffering. These views are not merely held; they are immensely alive and rich in consequences in his writings. The divine history is the key to human history, since only if something accrues to God from our tragedy can there be a meaning to our lives from the final perspective. What we accomplish merely for ourselves and other men can never furnish the meaning of history. From the merely human point of view, the last word is always failure and tragedy. But we are creatively responsive to God and enrich the divine life itself. On his side, God shares our pain, and thus we can be reconciled to him in spite of our trials and disappointments. This theodicy is scarcely like any that went before it. Here is something on a more sublime level than the usual cold-blooded justifications of evil. Evil springs from the indeterminacy which providence itself cannot banish; indeed, providential action on God's part presupposes indeterminacy in God himself (action being the resolution of an indeterminacy), and it must allow such indeterminacy in the creatures if they are to exist as real or active. This (our enthusiasm may perhaps be pardoned) is really a metaphysics of love! To be sure, it is held to be irrational, mystical, but why? To us it seems the most rational of any, save that of Whitehead, to which it has profound similarities.

In a work not quoted here (*The Meaning of History*) Berdyaev sets forth a doctrine of two kinds of time: false, disintegrated time and true, integral, or divine time which is also eternity. The divine life is "not in time" if that means that its process is free from the disintegration of our mode of temporality. The integrity of time is through memory, but we are too much absorbed in the present, and often too fearful about the future, to enjoy much of such integrity. For us each moment "murders" the preceding moment, in our author's strong phrase. In divine time, it seems at least to be the implication, the present and future would not frustrate memory in this fashion. This of course recalls Whitehead's doctrine of "everlastingness." Although little is said about it, one infers that even in divine time the future is genuinely open, indeterminate, so that anticipation is not a mere reversed counterpart of memory. The sting of "disintegration" is that qualities of experience actually achieved and determinate (which is what is meant by past experience) are forgotten, not in our possession; but since future experience, simply as such, is the indeterminate which is to-be-determined, there are no fully definite qualities belonging to it. Hence it is no shame that anticipatory knowledge does not refer to such qualities. This must, it seems, be Berdyaev's view, since he expresses horror at the notion of God seeing from all eternity the outcome of human history. And, besides, to reject immutability, impassivity, and so on, and yet retain the idea that God can never experience anything he does not already know would be too weak a compromise to be ascribed to a mind of this order. Also he speaks of the "creation of new images." It seems fair to conclude that what we have here to do with is a thoroughgoing dipolarist, one of the most thoroughgoing who have yet appeared.

Although Berdyaev and Whitehead appear to have had no influence whatever upon each other (both may have derived something from a common ancestor, Schelling), there are remarkable parallels of doctrine between them. (1) Whitehead says that the ultimate principle of reality is Creativity, which is neither identical with God nor created by him (how could creativity be created?). Berdyaev uses another word, "freedom," but also "creativeness," "creation," and "spontaneous activity." There seems to be no essential difference. And Berdyaev emphasizes the ultimacy of "freedom" which is "prior to being," whether the being of God or of man. In this freedom, which is no mere quality of man as a moral being but is a universal or metaphysical category of all reality, is the origin of evil. (2) Evil, for Berdyaev, as for Whitehead, is not merely or most essentially a conflict of good with not-good but of good with good. This is the tragedy inherent in value as such—that values conflict with values, not merely with disvalues. (3) Since this tragedy is in principle metaphysically ultimate, it applies to God also. The divine joy is tinged with tragedy. Here, too, our thinkers are at one. (4) The consolation for suffering is that it issues in a tragic joy shared with deity and is thereby given everlasting significance. (5) The meaning of life is to be creative, to produce new realities which contribute to the actuality of God himself. We are not mere creatures but are in part self-creative and in this self-creation part-creators of deity. These doctrines of Berdyaev are thoroughly Whiteheadian. In the Russian thinker they are expressed with a more intense religious fervor.

It is to be understood that the primacy of freedom over even divine being does not mean that, first, there was creativity and then there was God. The relation between freedom and God is "from all eternity." Whitehead's way of putting it is that reality has two forms, that of the actual and that of the "merely real" or the "potential." Further, God himself has never been merely real or merely potential; for he has a primordial individual essence which has always been actualized somehow, in some actual experience or other. But any particular phase of this actuality was once merely potential. Berdyaev for some reason seems to avoid the words "potential" and "possible." But he contrasts two forms of not-being, mere nothing, and something between this nothing and determinate actuality, and thus the priority of freedom even to divine being means that each phase of divine actuality is a resultant of creative action. There is a beginningless process of divine actualization.

## The Moral Source of Atheism

*394.* The good as well as the wicked rebel against God, for they cannot reconcile themselves to the existence of evil. Atheism may spring from good motives and not solely from evil ones. The wicked hate God because He prevents them from doing evil, and the good are ready to hate Him for not preventing the wicked from doing evil and for allowing the existence of evil.

*395.* It is precisely the traditional theology that leads good men, inspired by moral motives, to atheism. The ordinary theological conception of freedom in no way saves the Creator from the responsibility for pain and evil. Freedom itself is created by God and penetrable to Him down to its very depths. In His omniscience, ascribed to Him by positive theology, God foresaw from all eternity the fatal consequences of freedom with which He endowed man. He foresaw the evil and suffering of the world which has been called into being by His will and is wholly in His power; He foresaw everything, down to the perdition and everlasting torments of many. And yet He consented to create man and the world under those terrible conditions. This is the profound moral source of atheism. In expecting an answer to His call from man whom He endowed with freedom, God is expecting an answer from Himself. He knows the answer beforehand and is only playing with Himself. When in difficulties, positive theology falls back upon mystery and finds refuge in negative theology. But the mystery has already been over-rationalized. The logical conclusion is that God has from all eternity predetermined some to eternal salvation and others to eternal damnation.

*396.* True, predetermination itself is an impenetrable mystery, terrifying to reason and conscience, but we are led to it by rational theology. Positive theology goes too far in rationalizing the mystery and at the same time it does not go far enough, for it puts limits to knowledge and lays down prohibitions. When we pass to negative theology, we begin to breathe more freely as though coming out of a prison-house. Mystery, *docta ignorantia*, have a profound significance. The whole meaning, importance and value of life are determined by the mystery behind it, by an infinity which cannot be rationalized but can only be expressed in myths and symbols. God is the infinite mystery that underlies existence—and this alone makes the pain and evil of life endurable.

*397.* . . . all systems of positive theology are exoteric and do not touch upon the last things. Mystical negative theology brings us closer to the final depths. The limit to rational thought is set by a mystery and not by a taboo.

## The Absolute Not the Creator

The Divine Nothing or the Absolute of the negative theology cannot be the Creator of the world. This has been made clear by German speculative mysticism. It is the burden of Eckehardt's doctrine of the *Gottheit* and of Boehme's conception of the *Ungrund*. Out of the Divine Nothing, the *Gottheit* or the *Ungrund*, the Holy Trinity, God the Creator is born. The creation of the world by God the Creator is a secondary act. From this point of view it may be said that freedom is not created by God: it is rooted in the Nothing, in the *Ungrund* from all eter-

nity. Freedom is not determined by God; it is part of the nothing out of which God created the world. The opposition between God the Creator and freedom is secondary: in the primeval mystery of the Divine Nothing this opposition is transcended, for both God and freedom are manifested out of the *Ungrund*. God the Creator cannot be held responsible for freedom which gave rise to evil. Man is the child of God and the child of freedom—of nothing, of non-being, το μηον. Meonic freedom consented to God's act of creation; non-being freely accepted being. But through it man fell away from the work of God, evil and pain came into the world, and being was mixed with non-being. This is the real tragedy both of the world and of God. God longs for His "other," His friend; He wants him to answer the call to enter the fullness of the divine life and participate in God's creative work of conquering non-being. God does not answer His own call: the answer is from freedom which is independent of Him. God the Creator is all-powerful over being, over the created world, but He has no power over non-being, over the uncreated freedom which is impenetrable to Him. In the first act of creation God appears as the Maker of the world. But that act cannot avert the possibility of evil contained in meonic freedom. The myth of the Fall tells of this powerlessness of the creator to avert the evil resulting from freedom which He has not created. Then comes God's second act in relation to the world and to man. God appears not in the aspect of Creator but of Redeemer and Savior, in the aspect of the suffering God who takes upon Himself the sins of the world. God in the aspect of God-the-Son descends into the abyss, into the *Ungrund*, into the depths of freedom out of which springs evil as well as every kind of good. This is the only possible interpretation of the mystery of the Incarnation—if we are not to interpret it in the juridical sense. Out of the abyss, out of the Divine Nothing is born the Trinitary God and He is confronted with meonic freedom. He creates out of nothing the world and man and expects from them an answer to His call—an answer from the depths of freedom. At first the answer was consent to creation, then it was rebellion and hostility towards God, a return to original non-being. All rebellion against God is a return to non-being which assumes the form of false, illusory being, and is a victory of non-being over the divine light. And it is only then that the nothing which is not evil becomes evil. Then comes God's second act: He descends into non-being, into the abyss of freedom that has degenerated into evil; He manifests Himself not in power but in sacrifice. The Divine sacrifice, the Divine self-crucifixion must conquer evil meonic freedom by enlightening it from within without forcing it, without depriving the created world of freedom.

## The Inner Life of God

*398.* It is strange that human thought and especially theological thought has never concerned itself with God's inner life. Probably this was considered impious. The most incomprehensible part of traditional theological theories is the psychology of the Deity. These theories were always framed from the human point of view. Theology has been anthropocentric rather than theocentric, and this is particularly true with regard to the monarchic conception of God. Can God be said to have no inner life, no emotional and affective states? The static conception of God as *actus purus* having no potentiality and completely self-sufficient is a philosophical, Aristotelian, and not a biblical conception. The God of the Bible, the God of the revelation, is by no means an *actus purus:* He has affective and

emotional states, dramatic developments in His inner life, inward movement—but all this is revealed exoterically. It is extraordinary how limited is the human conception of God. Men are afraid to ascribe to Him inner conflict and tragedy characteristic of all life, the longing for His "other," for the birth of man, but have no hesitation in ascribing to Him anger, jealousy, vengeance and other affective states which, in man, are regarded as reprehensible. There is a profound gulf between the idea of perfection in man and in God. Self-satisfaction, self-sufficiency, stony immobility, pride, the demand for continual submission are qualities which the Christian religion considers vicious and sinful, though it calmly ascribes them to God. It becomes impossible to follow the Gospel injunction, "Be ye perfect as your Father in Heaven is perfect." That which in God is regarded as a sign of perfection, in man is considered an imperfection, a sin. In accordance with the principles of negative theology God, of course, cannot be described as good or perfect, for He is above goodness or perfection, just as He is above being. He is not something but no-thing, and none of our determinations are applicable to Him. We can only think of God symbolically and mythologically. And a symbolic psychology of God is possible—not in relation to the Divine Nothing of negative theology, but in relation to God-the-Creator of positive theology. And it is utterly unthinkable to ascribe to God the Creator self-sufficiency, self-satisfaction and despotism as characteristics of His inner life. It is more worthy of God to ascribe to Him a longing for the loved one, a need for sacrificial self-surrender. People are afraid to ascribe movement to God, because movement indicates the lack of something, or the need for something which is not there. But it may equally well be said that immobility is an imperfection, for it implies a lack of the dynamic quality of life. Tragic conflict in the life of the Deity is a sign of the perfection, and not of the imperfection, of the divine life. The Christian revelation shows us God in the aspect of sacrificial love, but sacrificial love, far from suggesting self-sufficiency, implies the need for passing into its "other." It is impossible to deny that the Christian God is, first and foremost, the God of sacrificial love, and sacrifice always indicates tragedy. Dramatic movement and tragedy are born of the fullness, and not of the poverty of life. To deny tragedy in the Divine life is only possible at the cost of denying Christ, His cross and crucifixion, the sacrifice of the Son of God. This is the theology of abstract monotheism. Abstract monarchic monotheism which refuses to recognize the inner dramatism of the Divine life is a clear instance of the confusion between negative and positive theology. Creation of the world cannot be deduced from the Absolute which is perfectly self-sufficient. Creation of the world implies movement in God, it is a dramatic event in the Divine life. It is unthinkable that there should be movement in the Absolute, creating an order of being external to It. In the Absolute nothing can be thought positively, it admits of negative characteristics only. If the Absolute of negative theology be identified with the Creator of positive theology, the world proves to be accidental, unnecessary, insignificant, having no relation to the inner life of the Deity and therefore, in the last resort, meaningless. Creature has meaning and dignity only if the creation of the world be understood as the realization of the Divine Trinity within the inner life of the Absolute, as a mystery of love and freedom. For an exoteric theology the inner life of the Deity does not exist, but an esoteric theology is bound to recognize the presence of tragic conflict in God. It is

what Jacob Boehme calls the theogonic process. It takes place in eternity and signifies not the birth of a previously non-existent God, but a divine mystery-play going on in the eternal hidden life of the Deity, the perpetual birth of God out of the *Ungrund....*

The world and the center of the world—man, is the creation of God through Wisdom, through Divine Ideas, and at the same time it is the child of meonic uncreated freedom, the child of fathomless non-being. The element of freedom does not come from God the Father, for it is prior to being. The tragedy in God is connected with freedom: God the Creator has absolute power over being, but not over freedom. Fathomless freedom springing from non-being entered the created world, consenting to the act of creation. God the Creator has done everything to bring light into that freedom, in harmony with His great conception of creation. But without destroying freedom He could not conquer the potency of evil contained in it. This is why there is tragedy and evil in the world; all tragedy is connected with freedom.

399. Christianity reveals tragedy in the Divine life itself. God Himself, the Only Begotten Son, suffers and is crucified, an innocent sufferer. The tragedy of freedom shows that there is a struggle between the conflicting principles which lie deeper than the distinction between good and evil.

400. The Golgotha is the supreme tragedy just because the Crucified is absolutely sinless and innocent. It is impossible to moralize about tragedy, for it lies beyond good and evil. The tragedy of freedom is overcome by the tragedy of the cross. Death is conquered by death.

### Man as Free Creator

401. God created man in His own image and likeness, i.e., made him a

creator too, calling him to free spontaneous activity and not to formal obedience to His power. Free creativeness is the creature's answer to the great call of its Creator. Man's creative work is the fulfillment of the Creator's secret will. But creativeness by its very nature is creation out of nothing, i.e., out of meonic freedom which is prior to the world itself.

*402. Creation means transition from non-being to being through a free act.*

*403.* Pantheism is false if only because it is bound to deny freedom. But dualistic theism denies it, too, or admits it solely for the sake of man's moral responsibility. . . . It must be admitted that in the antinomies of the Creator and the creature freedom appears as a paradox which cannot be subsumed under any category. A monistic or a dualistic interpretation of the relation between the Creator and the creature equally lead to a denial of freedom. Man is not free if he is merely a manifestation of God, a part of the Deity; he is not free if he has been endowed with freedom by God the Creator, but has nothing divine in himself.

*404.* If grace acts upon man independently of his freedom we get the doctrine of predestination. The only possible way out is to admit that freedom is uncreated and has its roots in non-being.

*405.* Through creation there always arises something perfectly new that has never existed before, i.e., the "nothing" becomes "something." Hegel discovered in his own way the truth that dynamism, becoming, the appearance of the new, presuppose non-being. . . . Man's creativeness is similar to God's, but God does not need any material for His creation, while man does. A sculptor makes a statue out of marble. Without marble, without material, he cannot create. In the same way, man needs cosmic matter for all his creation. A philosopher's creative thought needs the world for its matter and without it would hang in the void.

All this leads people to believe that human creation never is out of nothing. But the creative conception itself, the original creative act, does not depend upon any material. It presupposes freedom and arises out of freedom. It is not marble that gives rise to the sculptor's conception, nor is that conception entirely determined by the statues or human bodies which the sculptor has observed and studied. An original creative work always includes an element of freedom and that is the "nothing" out of which the new, the not yet existent, is created.

*406.* A creative act is therefore a continuation of world-creation and means participation in the work of God, man's answer to God's call. And this presupposes freedom which is prior to being.

*407.* The faculty of imagination is the source of all creativeness. God created the world through imagination. In Him imagination is an absolute ontological power. Imagination plays an enormous part in the moral and spiritual life of man. There is such a thing as the magic of imagination. Imagination magically creates realities. Without it there can be no works of art, no scientific or technical discoveries, no plans for ordering the economic or the political life of nations. Imagination springs from the depths of the unconscious, from fathomless freedom. Imagination is not only imitation of timelessly existent patterns, as Platonism in all its forms interprets it, but creation out of the depths of non-being of images that had never existed before.

### Christianity and Suffering

*408.* Christianity alone accepts suffering and takes up a manly attitude to it throughout. It teaches us not to fear suffering, for God Himself, the Son of God, has suffered. All other doctrines are afraid of suffering and try to escape it. Buddhism and Stoicism—lofty examples of non-Christian moral theories—are afraid of suffering and teach how to avoid it, how to become insensible to it and dispassionate. Buddhism recognizes compassion but denies love, for compassion may be a way of escaping from the pain of existence while love affirms existence and, consequently, the pain of it. Love increases sorrow and suffering. Strictly speaking, Buddhism is concerned with physical and not with moral evil. It is bound to be so if freedom be denied. Evil is pain and suffering. All existence is pain and suffering. Christianity has the courage to accept the pain and the suffering, Buddhism has not and therefore it renounces existence and seeks refuge in non-being. Buddhism does not know how life can be endurable if suffering be accepted; it does not know the mystery of the Cross.

*409.* From what has been said it follows that [the] Christian attitude to compassion is not the same as the Buddhist. In Buddhism compassion means a desire that the sufferer should attain non-being and is a refusal to bear suffering on behalf of others as well as of oneself. In Christianity compassion means a desire for a new and better life for the sufferer and a willingness to share his pain.

### Personality Not Self-contained

*410.* . . . Scheler is wrong in saying that personality is self-contained. He maintains this in order to defend the faith in God as a Person, but he is mistaken. Personality from its very nature presupposes another—not the "not self" which is a negative limit, but another person. Personality is impossible without love and sacrifice, without passing over to the other, to the friend, to the loved one. A self-contained personality becomes disintegrated. Personality is not the absolute, and God as the Absolute is not a Person. God as a Person presupposes His other, another Person, and is love and sacrifice. The Person of the Father presupposes the Persons of the Son and of the Holy Spirit. The Holy Trinity is a Trinity of Persons just because they presuppose one another and imply mutual love and intercommunion.

On another plane the personality of God and of man presuppose each other. Personality exists in the relation of love and sacrifice. It is impossible to conceive of a personal God in an abstract monotheistic way. A person cannot exist as a self-contained and self-sufficient Absolute. Personalistic metaphysics and ethics are based upon the Christian doctrine of the Holy Trinity. The moral life of every individual person must be interpreted after the image of the Divine Tri-unity, reversed and reflected in the world. A person presupposes the existence of other persons and communion between them. Personality is the highest hierarchical value and never is merely a means. But it does not exist as a value apart from its relation to God, to other persons and to human society.

*411.* . . . Love is, as it were, the universal vital energy capable of converting evil passions into creative forces. Thus the thirst for knowledge is love directed in a certain way, and the same is true of philosophy, which means love of truth; and there may be love of beauty and love of justice. Evil passions become creative through Eros. Hence the ethics of creativeness, in contradistinction to the ethics of law, is erotic.

But love can only transform evil passions into creative ones if it is regarded as a value in itself and not as a means of salvation. Love in the sense of good works useful for the salvation of the soul cannot give rise to a creative attitude to life and be a source of a life-giving energy. Love is not merely a fount of creativeness but is itself creativeness, radiation of creative energy.

Love is like radium in the spiritual world. The ethics of creativeness calls for actual, concrete realization of truth, goodness, spirituality, for a real transfiguration of life and not for a symbolic and conventional realization of the good through ascetic practices, good works and so on. It demands that we should love every man in his creative aspect, which is the image and likeness of God in him, i.e., that we should love that which is good, true, superhuman and divine in him.

[Sec. 394, Nicolas Berdyaev, *The Destiny of Man*, trans. Natalie Duddington (New York: Charles Sribner's Sons, 1937), p. 31. Sec. 395, *ibid.*, p. 32. Sec. 396, *ibid.*, p. 33, Sec. 397, *ibid.*, pp. 33–35. Sec. 398, *ibid.*, pp. 37–40. Sec. 399, *ibid.*, p. 41. Sec. 400, *ibid.*, p. 42. Sec. 401, *ibid.*, p. 43. Sec. 402, *ibid.*, p. 44. Sec. 403, *ibid.*, p. 45. Sec. 404, *ibid.* Sec. 405, *ibid.*, p. 85, Sec. 406, *ibid.*, p. 86. Sec. 407, *ibid.*, p. 97. Sec. 408, *ibid.*, p. 151. Sec. 409, *ibid.*, pp. 153–54. Sec. 410, *ibid.*, p. 74. Sec. 411, *ibid.*, p. 178.]

## COMMENT

Berdyaev offers as a mystical suprarational doctrine concerning God approximately what Whitehead proposes as sober metaphysics. Whereas Whitehead maintains that the monopolar doctrine of deity leads to incoherence, irrationality, and contradiction, Berdyaev actually suggests that the monopolar or purely absolutistic view is, in purely rational terms, more intelligible and consistent than his own doctrine and implies—like William James in a famous passage—so much the worse for human logic and rationality. It is not necessary for us to elaborate the conviction we have already expressed many times that monopolar doctrines are always irrational, that the law of polarity to which dipolar theism appeals is a supreme law of rational understanding, and that freedom is no less rational than necessity, which is entirely incomprehensible without it. Assume possibility, and necessity is an abstract identity common to all possibilities; assume free creativeness,

and causality can be understood as the relevance of an act of creating to the already created, as preserved and valued in memory; assume relativity, and the absolute can be deduced as an aspect thereof. But if we start with the absolute, necessary, and merely unitary, then no relations, potentialities, process, can ever be deduced or derived. The monopolar prejudice is partly an attempted oversimplification to make our task easier, partly it has emotional (escapist) origins, partly origins in primitive and slavish ideas of political power. Nothing of this is rational in any commendable sense, and the challenge to it need not be a resort to the suprarational. True, freedom implies that the outcome of a situation could not be altogether conceived beforehand or deduced from the causal conditions, but this does not mean that "freedom" itself cannot be conceived. The mathematician understands just as positively when he sees that being square is not deducible from being rectangular as when he sees that being rectangular is deducible from being square. Relations of nonimplication are as much the subject of reason as relations of implication, and neither would be understood if the other were not. To know what is meant by old is to know what is meant by new; to understand "predictable" is to understand "unpredictable." It is out of the question that we could conceive necessity but not freedom, for all such concepts are correlative. Those who have difficulty with one pole of the contrast but think they are masters of the other deceive themselves. They are merely more in the habit of putting the one pole into words, but, if they go into the matter of explaining these words, they will soon find that an understanding of the other pole is presupposed even though on a less verbal level.

We shall meet in Schweitzer the same problem, the same gratuitous granting of the claims of monistic, one-sided doctrines to philosophical superiority or merit. But none of this detracts from the value of Berdyaev's insistence upon the spiritual, religious, ethical superiority of the dipolar view. This it has, we believe, not in compensation for its inferior rationality, but in keeping with and one aspect of its superior rationality.

# IQBAL (1877–1938): A MOSLEM PANENTHEIST

It is a pleasure to be able to include a modern Mohammedan among our panentheists. True, there is a strong and fully acknowledged influence of Bergson and other western European authors upon this writer; but the eloquence and sincerity of the numerous references to Moslem sources are no less striking. Since it has been our view throughout that no concrete religion is correctly expressed by classical theism, there is for us no absurdity or paradox in a panentheistic version of Islam. Really the older theological orthodoxy of Mohammedanism is the greater paradox, as Sir Mohammad Iqbal suggests.

The following are taken from lectures given before Moslem audiences.

## Ultimate Reality as Pure Duration

412. A critical interpretation of the sequence of time as revealed in ourselves has led us to a notion of the ultimate Reality as pure duration in which thought, life, and purpose inter-penetrate to form an organic unity. We cannot conceive this unity except as the unity of a self—an all-embracing concrete self—the ultimate source of all individual life and thought. . . . It is the appreciative act of an enduring self only which can seize the multiplicity of duration—broken up into an infinity of instants—and transform it to the organic wholeness of a synthesis. To exist in pure duration is to be a self, and to be a self is to be able to say "I am." Only that truly exists which can say "I am." It is the degree of the intuition of "I-amness" that determines the place of a thing in the scale of being. We too say "I am." But our "I-amness" is dependent and arises out of the distinction between the self and the not-self. The ultimate Self, in the words of the Quran, "can afford to dispense with all the worlds." To Him the not-self does not present itself as a confronting "other," or else it would have to be, like our finite self, in spatial relation with the confronting "other." What we call Nature or the not-self is only a fleeting moment in the life of God. His "I-amness" is independent, elemental, absolute. Of such a self it is impossible for us to form an adequate conception. As the Quran says, "Naught" is like Him; yet "He hears and sees." Now a self is unthinkable without a character, i.e., a uniform mode of behaviour. Nature, as we have seen, is not a mass of pure materiality occupying a void. It is a structure of events, a systematic mode of behaviour, and as such organic to the ultimate Self. Nature is to the Divine Self as character is to the human self. In the picturesque phrase of the Quran it is the habit of Allah. From the human point of view it is an interpretation which, in our present situation, we put on the creative activity of the Absolute Ego. At a particular moment in its forward movement it is finite; but since the self to which it is organic is creative, it is liable to increase, and is consequently boundless in the sense that no limit to its extension is final. Its boundlessness is potential, not actual. Nature, then, must be understood as a living, ever-growing organism whose growth has no final external limits. Its only limit is internal, i.e., the immanent self which animates and sustains the whole. As the Quran says: "And verily unto thy Lord is the

limit" (53:14). Thus the view that we have taken gives a fresh spiritual meaning to physical science. The knowledge of Nature is the knowledge of God's behaviour. In our observation of Nature we are virtually seeking a kind of intimacy with the Absolute Ego; and this is only another form of worship.

The above discussion takes time as an essential element in the ultimate Reality.

*413.* If we regard past, present, and future as essential to time, then we picture time as a straight line, part of which we have travelled and left behind, and part lies yet untravelled before us. This is taking time, not as a living creative moment, but as a static absolute, holding the ordered multiplicity of fully-shaped cosmic events, revealed serially, like the pictures of a film, to the outside observer. We can indeed say that Queen Anne's death was future to William III, if this event is regarded as already fully shaped, and lying in the future, waiting for its happening. But a future event, as Broad justly points out, cannot be characterized as an event. Before the death of Anne the event of her death did not exist at all. During Anne's life the event of her death existed only as an unrealized possibility in the nature of Reality which included it as an event only when, in the course of its becoming, it reached the point of the actual happening of that event.

## Ultimate Reality and Change

*414.* But the question you are likely to ask is—"Can change be predicated of the Ultimate Ego?" We, as human beings, are functionally related to an independent world-process. The conditions of our life are mainly external to us. The only kind of life known to us is desire, pursuit, failure, or attainment—a continuous change from one situation to another. From our point of view life is change, and change is essentially imperfection. At the same time, since our conscious experience is the only point

of departure for all knowledge, we cannot avoid the limitation of interpreting facts in the light of our own inner experience.

*415.* Serial change is obviously a mark of imperfection; and, if we confine ourselves to this view of change, the difficulty of reconciling Divine perfection with Divine life becomes insuperable.

*416.* There is, however, a way out of the difficulty. The Absolute Ego, as we have seen, is the whole of Reality. He is not so situated as to take a perspective view of an alien universe; consequently, the phases of His life are wholly determined from within. Change, therefore, in the sense of a movement from an imperfect to a relatively perfect state, or vice versa, is obviously inapplicable to His life. But change in this sense is not the only possible form of life. A deeper insight into our conscious experience shows that beneath the appearance of serial duration there is true duration. The Ultimate Ego exists in pure duration wherein change ceases to be a succession of varying attitudes, and reveals its true character as continuous creation, "untouched by weariness" and unseizable "by slumber or sleep." To conceive the Ultimate Ego as changeless in this sense of change is to conceive Him as utter inaction, a motiveless, stagnant neutrality, an absolute nothing. To the Creative Self change cannot mean imperfection. The perfection of the creative self consists, not in a mechanistically conceived immobility. . . . It consists in the vaster basis of His creative activity and the infinite scope of His creative vision. God's life is self-revelation, not the pursuit of an ideal to be reached. . . . The "not-yet" of God means unfailing realization of the infinite creative possibilities of His being which retains its wholeness throughout the entire process.

*417.* There is, however, one question which will be raised in this connexion.

Does not individuality imply finitude? If God is an ego and as such an individual, how can we conceive Him as infinite?

*418.* The infinity of the Ultimate Ego consists in the infinite inner possibilities of His creative activity of which the universe, as known to us, is only a partial expression. In one word God's infinity is intensive, not extensive. It involves an infinite series, but is not that series.

*419.* I have conceived the Ultimate Reality as an Ego; and I must add now that from the Ultimate Ego only egos proceed. The creative energy of the Ultimate Ego, in whom deed and thought are identical, functions as ego-unities. The world, in all its details, from the mechanical movement of what we call the atom of matter to the free movement of thought in the human ego, is the self-revelation of the "Great I am." Every atom of Divine energy, however low in the scale of existence, is an ego. But there are degrees in the expression of egohood. Throughout the entire gamut of being runs the gradually rising note of egohood until it reaches its perfection in man.

*420.* It is now time to pass on to the Divine attributes of Knowledge and Omnipotence.

The word knowledge, as applied to the finite ego, always means discursive knowledge—a temporal process which moves round a veritable "other," supposed to exist *per se* and confronting the knowing ego.

*421.* From the standpoint of the all-inclusive Ego there is no "other." In Him thought and deed, the act of knowing and the act of creating, are identical.

*422.* Unfortunately, language does not help us here. We possess no word to express the kind of knowledge which is also creative of its object. The alternative concept of Divine knowledge is omniscience in the sense of a single in-

divisible act of perception which makes God immediately aware of the entire sweep of history, regarded as an order of specific events, in an eternal "now." This is how Jalaluddin Dawani, Iraqi, and Professor Royce in our own times conceived God's knowledge. There is an element of truth in this conception. But it suggests a closed universe, a fixed futurity, a predetermined, unalterable order of specific events which, like a superior fate, has once for all determined the directions of God's creative activity.

## God and the Future

*423.* The future certainly pre-exists in the organic whole of God's creative life, but it pre-exists as an open possibility, not as a fixed order of events with definite outlines.

*424.* If history is regarded merely as a gradually revealed photo of a pre-determined order of events, then there is no room in it for novelty and initiation. Consequently, we can attach no meaning to the word creation, which has a meaning for us only in view of our own capacity for original action. The truth is that the whole theological controversy relating to pre-destination is due to pure speculation with no eye on the spontaneity of life, which is a fact of actual experience. No doubt, the emergence of egos endowed with the power of spontaneous and hence unforeseeable action is, in a sense, a limitation on the freedom of the all-inclusive Ego. But this limitation is not externally imposed. It is born out of His own creative freedom whereby He has chosen finite egos to be participators of His life, power, and freedom.

But how, it may be asked, is it possible to reconcile limitation with Omnipotence? The word limitation need not frighten us. The Quran has no liking for abstract universals. It always fixes its gaze on the concrete. . . . All activity, creational or otherwise, is **a** kind of limitation without which it is impossible to conceive God as a concrete operative Ego. Omnipotence, abstractly conceived, is merely a blind, capricious power without limits. The Quran has a clear and definite conception of Nature as a cosmos of mutually related forces.

### Soul and Body

425. . . . the body is . . . a system of events or acts. The system of experiences we call soul or ego is also a system of acts. This does not obliterate the distinction of soul and body; it only brings them closer to each other. The characteristic of the ego is spontaneity; the acts composing the body repeat themselves. The body is accumulated action or habit of the soul; and as such undetachable from it. . . . What then is matter? A colony of egos of a low order out of which emerges the ego of a higher order, when their association and inter-action reach a certain degree of co-ordination. It is the world reaching the point of self-guidance wherein the ultimate Reality, perhaps, reveals its secret, and furnishes a clue to its ultimate nature.

[Sec. 412, Sir Mohammad Iqbal (Muhammad Ikbal), *The Reconstruction of Religious Thought in Islam* (London: Oxford University Press, 1934), pp. 53–54. Sec. 413, *ibid.*, pp. 54–55. Sec. 414, *ibid.*, p. 56. Sec. 415, *ibid.* Sec. 416, *ibid.* Sec. 417, *ibid.*, p. 61. Sec. 418, *ibid.* Sec. 419, *ibid.*, p. 68. Sec. 420, *ibid.*, p. 73. Sec. 421, *ibid.* Sec. 422, *ibid.*, p. 74. Sec. 423, *ibid.*, p. 75. Sec. 424, *ibid.*, pp. 75–76. Sec. 425, *ibid.*, p. 100.]

### COMMENT

We limit our critical discussion to a few points. Although Iqbal's book contains a treatment of the question of how the existence of evil is to be reconciled with divine goodness and an indication that the self-determination essential to the creature is the source of evil, there is apparently no mention of the idea that God himself contains the suffering of the world within his life (this of course is implied by the author's doctrine), and hence there is a divine and not merely a human or animal tragedy. But scarcely any non-Christians and only a few Christians (among philosophers) seem to have dared to view the matter in this light. If there is any unique value in Christianity, this is surely close to the heart of it. Perhaps another aspect of this unique value is the notion of a social character of deity, not only in relation to his creatures, but as between God and God (the Trinity). Iqbal follows Bergson in so stressing the unity of duration that the plurality of experiences, each with its own immanent subject pole, and its social relations of love or antipathy toward its predecessors or its (without full detail) anticipated successors, is not fully realized. (He discusses, only to reject it, the theory of the atomic or discontinuous nature of the divine creative process as developed in the Ashari school.) Here the exaggeration of "unity" in "monotheism" makes itself felt. (The influence of Bergson was also involved.) Nor does our author quite come to the point of saying that man contributes to the divine life, though that seems to follow from his view.

In any case, it is inspiring to see the motifs of dipolarity emerging so vividly in this tradition, as they have in so many others. The long reign of monopolarity and being-worship or etiolatry need not last forever. The past of man is short compared to his possible future!

# SCHWEITZER (1875——)

The human greatness of Albert Schweitzer is widely acknowledged. His purely intellectual stature is perhaps not yet adequately seen. What is his doctrine? We know God within ourselves as supreme ethical will and love with which we are united in so far as we accept our ethical calling and in so far as we ourselves live from love or reverence for life and for the will to life. But we also dimly glimpse God in nature, as the supreme power or powers, and here we do not find love or anything ethical but forces which are now creative and now destructive and which seem to pursue no purpose to which we can contribute.

Nature alternately fosters life and then destroys it, in the most casual fashion, for all we can see. Thus man's very life on this planet is ultimately at the mercy of cosmic forces which may one day put an end to terrestrial life by rendering the earth uninhabitable. Here and there is purposiveness; but no inclusive purpose appears. It follows that we must either give up our inner vision of God, and with it any sense of purposive relation to the eternal and the cosmic, or else give up the hope of understanding nature and ourselves in terms of a common principle. Either a soul-destroying monism or a dualism which defies understanding! The first is theoretically more rational, but practically it is irrational, since it sets the will to live (which is basic to our thought also) at variance with itself. The dualism is not to be taken as objective, but it is ultimate as far as our understanding goes. Somehow God is all-in-all, but the God of love is for our understanding only an aspect of this All.

Such a doctrine is not strictly subject to our classificatory scheme, for it refuses to commit itself as among theism, pantheism, and panentheism. The failure even to see the last-mentioned alternative, and the implied conviction that the mysterious truth beyond our grasp must be some sort of combination or higher synthesis of theistic and pantheistic principles, which is just what panentheism claims to be, suggests that, if Schweitzer could be induced to accept any metaphysical doctrine, it could only be this one, and that his certainty that no solution is possible may be partly due to the fact that he apparently was unfamiliar, for all his extraordinarily wide learning, with any clear statement of the ETCKW doctrine.

In our opinion, Schweitzer is well justified in refusing to subordinate the ethical will to any of the monisms which he has in mind as well as in rejecting classical theism. It may well be better to have no metaphysics than any of these. They have all proved inadequate for the spiritual and intellectual needs of man. And since the taste for metaphysics is a variable factor in men, while the ethical task is there for all, it may be that many would do well indeed to follow Schweitzer in accepting the combination of a subjectively ultimate dualism and an incurably mysterious objective pantheism. The position is not so far from that of Berdyaev but is less explicit in its metaphysical implications.

## God as Ethical Will and Impersonal Force

426. All problems of religion, ultimately, go back to this one—the experience I have of God within myself differs from the knowledge concerning Him which I derive from the world. In the world He appears to me as the mysterious, marvellous creative Force; within me He reveals Himself as ethical Will. In the world He is impersonal Force, within me He reveals Himself as

Personality. The God who is known through philosophy and the God whom I experience as ethical Will do not coincide. They are one; but how they are one, I do not understand.

Now, which is the more vital knowledge of God? The knowledge derived from my experience of Him as ethical Will. The knowledge concerning God which is derived from nature is always imperfect and inadequate, because we perceive the things in the world from without only. I see the tree grow and I see it cover itself with leaves and blossoms; but I do not understand the forces which effect this; their generative power remains a mystery to me. In myself, on the other hand, I know things from within. The creative force which produces and sustains all that is, reveals itself in me in a way in which I do not get to know it elsewhere, namely, as ethical Will, as something which desires to be creative within me. . . . My life is completely and unmistakably determined by the experience of God revealing Himself within me as ethical Will and desiring to take hold of my life. . . .

There is an ocean—cold water without motion. In this ocean, however, is the Gulf Stream, hot water flowing from the equator towards the pole. . . . Similarly, there is the God of love within the God of the forces of the universe —one with Him, and yet so totally different. We let ourselves be seized and carried away by that vital stream.

*427.* All profound religion is mystical. To be freed from the world by being in God: that is the longing we have within us, so long as we do not numb ourselves in thoughtlessness. A union with God, however, which is realized through the intellectual act of "knowing," as conceived in the Eastern religions, must always remain a dead spirituality. It does not effect a rebirth, in God, into living spirituality. Living spirituality, real redemption from the world, cannot come but from that union with God which is ethically de-

termined. The religions of the East are logical mysticism, Christianity alone is ethical mysticism.

Thus we go on our way through the world, not troubled about knowledge, but committing to God what we hope for, for ourselves and the world, and possessing all in all through being apprehended by the living, ethical God.

*428.* Again and again, in the course of the centuries, Christianity has sought to harmonize the philosophical and the ethical conceptions of God, but it has never succeeded. It carries within itself, unresolved, the antinomy between monism and dualism, between logical and ethical religion.

*429.* Every form of living Christianity is pantheistic in that it is bound to envisage everything that exists as having its being in the great First Cause of all being. But at the same time all ethical piety is higher than any pantheistic mysticism, in that it does not find the God of Love in Nature, but knows about Him only from the fact that He announces Himself in us as Will-to-Love. The First Cause of Being, as He manifests Himself in Nature, is to us always something impersonal. But to the First Cause of Being, who becomes revealed to us as Will-to-Love, we relate ourselves as to an ethical Personality. Theism does not stand in opposition to pantheism, but emerges from it as the ethically determined out of what is natural and undetermined.

[Sec. 426, Albert Schweitzer, *Christianity and the Religions of the World*, trans. Johanna Powers (New York: George H. Doran Co., 1923), pp. 83–85. Sec. 427, *ibid.*, p. 87. Sec. 428, *ibid.*, p. 82. Sec. 429, Albert Schweitzer, *Out of My Life and Thought*, trans. C. T. Campion (New York: Henry Holt & Co., 1933), p. 278. These selections were originally chosen from *Albert Schweitzer: An Anthology* (Boston: Beacon Press, 1947).]

## COMMENT

If by a rational or logical philosophy were meant a system of knowledge embracing all important facts, or if by understanding God were meant seeing through his specific intentions for the world, standing in the perspective of Providence with respect to the course of nature, then Schweitzer's renunciation of the hope of such philosophy or such understanding would be very well justified. One cannot quarrel with it as a (delayed) reaction to Hegel or as a reaction to many oriental systems which profess either to understand what nature is up to or to arrive at something more ultimate which makes nature a matter of indifference. These are all attitudes which endanger the ethical life of man, and, in our opinion, none is "logical" save by lax and loose criteria. But it may not be the same with a metaphysics which distinguishes itself from factual knowledge, not by relegating the latter to a realm of unreality or unimportance, but by trying to exhibit the completely general principles of concrete factual existence. These principles, since they are the most general, must indeed be illustrated in any actual but equally in any possible facts, and therefore they cannot tell us what are the actual facts. Such a metaphysics makes no claim to explain the actual course of nature but only to say what is common to that and any possible course. This is something utterly general and abstract, nothing so definite as a specific purposive pattern calling for the events which occur.

Still, we must, if our metaphysics is valid, be able to see in a very general way how actual nature *could* contribute to a divine purpose. Schweitzer himself thinks we can at least know that life is universal in reality, that nothing is merely dead. Now it is in principle intelligible how all life can contribute to the divine life. For sympathy is participation, and God is love. The variety and intensity of life enriches the all-participating life. So far there is no difficulty. But, Schweitzer says, in na-

ture we find destruction and creation of life interwoven without any rationale that we can see. In the first place, one may reply, the creation is absolute, the introduction of new experiences, while the destruction is not a contrary, equally absolute wiping-out of previous experiences but merely the nonfulfilment of a potentiality for further creation in a particular direction. An avalanche or forest fire obliterates no actuality of life, for actuality is experience, and every experience, once it is past, is out of the reach of damage. What a catastrophe of this kind does is to prevent many experiences that otherwise *would* have become actual from being ever achieved. But the previous experiences are not affected. Thus to contrast destruction with creation, as though both were on the same level, is, we hold, a metaphysical error.

However, we still confront the question, "Why does providence allow so many wonderful potentialities to be frustrated by blind forces, as in earthquakes and the like?" Suppose humanity is one day wiped out, as (Schweitzer reminds us) seems likely, if not inevitable, by some planetary upheaval or change. How could we see any reasonable purpose in such an ending of the human development by the blind forces of gravity and the like? Let us grant that we could not know why God would permit such a termination of the human story. We know virtually nothing of the alternatives, in their cosmic implications. For one thing, we can hardly grasp the values involved for various beings in the sway of somewhat rigorous patterns of law, as compared with less rigorous patterns. Yet we can see in principle that rigorous laws cannot possibly impinge on partly free beings without sometimes conflicting with their desires and potentialities. No law can be perfectly adjusted to the unforeseeable acts and needs of free individuals. Either the development of the race must take its chances with "blind" forces or the forces must be modified from time to time. But, then, to that extent no laws will be valid, except at most over very short periods of time.

One supposes that God would wish the race to last long enough to realize its main potentialities of development. This need not be forever, for why suppose that the potentialities are unlimited (apart from trivial variations)? How long it will take cannot be foreknown, for it depends upon a vast multitude of acts, every one of which is to some extent free. Thus no law valid throughout human history can be adjusted exactly to the duration required to bring to flower the principal capacities of man.

Schweitzer's ethics of "reverence for life" is not perhaps free from a slightly superstitious aspect. Since all animals die, death must be a part of the meaning of life, not its contradiction. It is one thing to wish to diminish animal suffering; it is another to wish indefinitely to prolong the life of this or that individual. The value inheres not in the person or individual who goes on from experience to experience; the actual value is in the experiences themselves, with their individual or personal qualities. "Individuality" is not a whole containing all experiences but a quality which experiences contain. Each animal has a natural round during which, on the average, its main forms of experience can come to fruition. In a world of free action no providence could prevent the normal round from being interrupted and terminated prematurely in numerous cases. Is this so shocking?

Is it so shocking even that animals prey on each other? If they are not to live forever, and if their death is to be partly a matter of chance and freedom, it is no worse for them that the agents are other animals than that they should be forms of life on a still lower (or a much higher) level. True, given conscious realization of the situation, such

as man comes to have, and given the indefinite extension of sympathy which this consciousness brings with it, there results a certain participation in the tragedy which our actions produce in the lives of other species. But it is not clear what other system would enable creatures to live interesting, zestful lives, therefore partly free lives, in relation to one another, all being supported in their freedom by certain basic uniformities which, so far as they are rigorous and universal, must be blind and pitiless in their effects upon individuals but which yet are perhaps required to enable so much freedom in such variety to form a mutually compatible system of natural forms.

There is something else to be said. It is not merely loyalty to our ethical will that justifies conceiving God as love. It is a principle of rationality to judge the unknown by the known. As Schweitzer suggests indeed, the only individuals a man knows with much intimacy are himself and a few other humans. In inanimate nature we have conceptual abstract outline knowledge of individuals (atoms and the like) only. We do not know what it is qualitively like to be an atom but only what it is like to be a man doing things with atoms. There is then a perfectly "logical" reason for looking to human experience, as such, to furnish a model of reality rather than to "matter." And if love is the central reality of human experience, as science itself now testifies, then the idea that love, rather than stuff or bare spatiotemporal process, is the key to the universe is simply good epistemology. Also biology is finding that the social principle pervades all life, and this means that there is no anthropomorphism in taking love to be central, to life at least. (Schweitzer does not seem always to remember his own contention that the world is living.)

True, there is hostility, but is a man

hostile to his own cells? We are something like cells in the universe. The cosmic power cannot, then, be hostile to us, and the only other relation our experi-

ence exhibits is love. Are not Schweitzer's arguments against a more positive doctrine less conclusive than their author seems to think?

## BUBER (1878——)

Although he is hardly a metaphysician but rather a phenomenologist—and one of the very greatest—of the religious life in its primary form of direct dealing with God, Martin Buber seems to furnish unmistakable support to some of the main theses of panentheism, which is all the more valuable because not intended. The primary reality is relation; the only absolute is the absolute relation (which is mutual) of the *I* to the eternal *Thou;* the world is in God, who is self-related to all things, deriving value from them, so that there is real becoming of the God who is, though not a God who becomes. Here in outline is practically the whole of panentheism. Once more we see that this doctrine is not an eccentricity but something very like the central message of modern reflection upon the ancient question.

We also see in Buber that the distinctions between panentheism and mere theism, on the one hand, and mere pantheism, on the other, are not solely theoretical matters but have practical religious bearings. For Buber is able to avoid that isolation of the religious self from concern for the human community which is so striking, and so painful, in Kierkegaard and also to avoid the ultimate denial of both self and community, the flight from all life, personal or social, which is at the heart of Buddhism and to some extent of Brahmanism; and he avoids them by one and the same perception of the Thou as in mutual relation, "absolute relation," to all members of the cosmic community. When we encounter God, we encounter the world as contributory to the

life of God, which is social, receptive, very far from "impassible," or exclusive of finite things. To find God, we do not leave the world or deny its reality; we "hallow" it; we see it as integral to the actuality of him who is Thou for each of us and who alone is individually the same Thou for all.

We cannot refrain from expressing gratitude for Buber's eloquent and healing rebuke to the slavish notion that we are merely "dependent," merely effect, in relation to God, and he merely cause in relation (though, according to classical theism, somehow not in relation) to us. This notion, of course, implies that sensitivity is a weakness, and the most glorious form of power that which works exclusively downward toward that which is beneath it and permits no form of reciprocal action. Yet all our political life is an effort to find forms of power which permit the ruled to influence the ruler, and that not simply because the ruler is fallible and does not "have all the answers" but because to a certain extent there are no "answers" if the question be, "What shall be done with self-determining (i.e., conscious) beings?" save such answers as these beings themselves decide upon and transmit to the ruler for execution (with suitable modifications or amplification). The democratic ideal that power should go with sensitivity, with receptiveness to the decisions of others, not only has theological application but furnishes a more literal description of deity than of any possible earthly ruler, who never can have unlimited sensitivity or receptiveness.

The value of humility, great as it is,

can be prevented from turning into a vice only if it is inspired with the sense of high calling involved in the belief that God responds differentially to our decisions, so that, as Buber says, we participate with him in the creation, not just of the world, but of something in God himself—for there is no world, save in God. It is too seldom considered that, if we do less than decide something as to God himself, we decide nothing at all. God's appreciation measures reality. Therefore to decide anything is to decide something as to that which alone can adequately register the result of our decision. If we do not write in the book of the divine life itself, we do not write at all. And, if we do not write at all, we should be not merely humble; we should admit our total inanity. Or, if we say that we write but that the divine registers nothing as a result, then we declare in effect that God is not the measure of the real. Thus we are at once abject rather than humble—and blasphemers into the bargain.

These are some of the distortions of the religious life from which Buber, with Berdyaev and Whitehead, should save us.

### The "I—Thou" Relation

*430.* Primary words do not signify things, but they intimate relations.

*431.* Let no attempt be made to sap the strength from the meaning of the relation: relation is mutual.

*432.* The extended lines of relations meet in the eternal *Thou*. Every particular *Thou* is a glimpse through to the eternal *Thou*.

*433.* . . . the inborn *Thou* is realized in each relation and consummated in none. It is consummated only in the direct relation with the *Thou* that by its nature cannot become *It*.

Men have addressed their eternal *Thou* with many names. In singing of Him who was thus named they always had the *Thou* in mind: the first myths were hymns of praise. Then the names took refuge in the language of *It;* men were more and more strongly moved to think of and to address their eternal *Thou* as an *It*. But all God's names are hallowed, for in them He is not merely spoken about, but also spoken to.

*434.* For he who speaks the word God and really has *Thou* in mind (whatever the illusion by which he is held) addresses the true *Thou* of his life, which cannot be limited by another *Thou*, and to which he stands in a relation that gathers up and includes all others.

*435.* Every real relation with a being or life in the world is exclusive. Its *Thou* is freed, steps forth, is single, and confronts you. It fills the heavens. This does not mean that nothing else exists; but all else lives in *its* light. As long as the presence of the relation continues, this its cosmic range is inviolable. But as soon as a *Thou* becomes *It*, the cosmic range of the relation appears as an offence to the world, its exclusiveness as an exclusion of the universe.

In the relation with God unconditional exclusiveness and unconditional inclusiveness are one. He who enters on the absolute relation is concerned with nothing isolated any more, neither things nor beings, neither earth nor heaven; but everything is gathered up in the relation. For to step into the relation is not to disregard everything but to see everything in the *Thou*, not to renounce the world but to establish it on its true basis. To look away from the world, or to stare at it, does not help a man to reach God; but he who sees the world in Him stands in His presence. "Here world, there God" is the language of *It;* "God in the world" is another language of *It;* but to eliminate nothing or leave behind nothing at all, to include the whole world in the *Thou*, to give the world its due and its truth, to include nothing beside God but everything in Him—this is full and complete relation.

Men do not find God if they stay in the world. They do not find Him if they leave the world. He who goes out with his whole being to meet his *Thou* and carries to it all being that is in the world, finds Him who cannot be sought.

Of course God is the "wholly Other"; but He is also the wholly Same, the wholly Present. Of course He is the *Mysterium Tremendum* that appears and overthrows; but He is also the mystery of the self-evident, nearer to me than my *I*.

If you explore the life of things and of conditioned being you come to the unfathomable, if you deny the life of things and of conditioned being you stand before nothingness, if you hallow this life you meet the living God.

Man's sense of *Thou*, which experiences in the relations with every particular *Thou* the disappointment of the change to *It*, strives out but not away from them all to its eternal *Thou*; but not as something is sought: actually there is no such thing as seeking God, for there is nothing in which He could not be found. How foolish and hopeless would be the man who turned aside from the course of his life in order to seek God: even though he won all the wisdom of solitude and all the power of concentrated being he would miss God. Rather it is as when a man goes his way and simply wishes that it might be the way: in the strength of his wish his striving is expressed. Every relational event is a stage that affords him a glimpse into the consummating event. So in each event he does not partake, but also (for he is waiting) does partake, of the one event. Waiting, not seeking, he goes his way; hence he is composed before all things, and makes contact with them which helps them. But when he has *found*, his heart is not turned from them, though everything now meets in the one event. He blesses every cell that sheltered him, and every cell into which he will yet turn. For this finding is not the end, but only the eternal middle, of the way.

### Man Not Merely Dependent

436. God cannot be inferred in anything—in nature, say, as its author. . . . Something else is not "given" and God then inferred from it; but God is the Being that is directly, most nearly, and lastingly, over against us, that may properly only be addressed, not expressed.

Men wish to regard a feeling (called feeling of dependence, and recently, more precisely, creaturely feeling) as the real element in the relation with God. In proportion as the isolation and definition of this element is accurate, its unbalanced emphasis only makes the character of complete relation the more misunderstood.

437. If the soul is the starting point of our consideration, complete relation can be understood only in a bi-polar way, only as the *coincidentia oppositorum*, as the coincidence of oppositions of feeling.

438. Yes; in pure relation you have felt yourself to be simply dependent, as you are able to feel in no other relation—and simply free, too, as in no other time or place: you have felt yourself to be both creaturely and creative. You had the one feeling no longer limited by the other, but you had both of them limitlessly and together.

You know always in your heart that you need God more than everything; but do you not know too that God needs you—in the fullness of His eternity needs you? How would man be, how would you be, if God did not need him, did not need you? You need God in order to be—and God needs you, for the very meaning of your life. In instruction and in poems men are at pains to say more, and they say too much—what turgid and presumptuous talk that is about the "God who becomes"; but we know unshakably in our hearts that there is a becoming of the God that is. The world is not divine sport, it is divine destiny. There is divine meaning in the life of the world, of man, of human persons, of you and of me.

Creation happens to us, burns itself into us, recasts us in burning—we tremble and are faint, we submit. We take part in creation, meet the Creator, reach out to Him, helpers and companions.

Two great servants pace through the ages, prayer and sacrifice. The man who prays pours himself out in unrestrained dependence, and knows that he has—in an incomprehensible way—an effect upon God, even though he obtains nothing from God; for when he no longer desires anything for himself he sees the flame of his effect burning at its highest.—And the man who makes sacrifice? I cannot despise him, this upright servant of former times, who believed that God yearned for the scent of his burnt-offering. In a foolish but powerful way he knew that we can and ought to give to God. This is known by him, too, who offers up his little will to God and meets Him in the grand will. "Thy will be done," he says, and says no more: but truth adds for him "through me whom Thou needest."

What distinguishes sacrifice and prayer from all magic?—Magic desires to obtain its effects without entering into relation, and practices its tricks in the void. But sacrifice and prayer are set "before the Face," in the consummation of the holy primary word that means mutual action: they speak the *Thou*, and then they hear.

## Concerning Mysticism

To wish to understand pure relation as dependence is to wish to empty one of the bearers of the relation, and hence the relation itself, of reality.

The same thing happens if we be-

gin from the opposite side and look on absorption, or entering, into the Self (whether by means of the Self's deliverance from all being that is conditioned by *I*, or by its being understood as the One thinking Essence) as the essential element in the religious act.

*439.* . . . by the first way, in a supreme moment the saying of the *Thou* ceases, for there is no more twofold being, and by the second the saying of the *Thou* does not in truth exist at all, for there is in truth no twofold being: the first way believes in the unification, the second in the identification of the human with the divine. Both assert a state that is beyond *I* and *Thou*, the first—as in ecstasy—one that becomes, the second—as in the self-observation of the thinking subject—one that is and that reveals itself. Both abolish relation, the first as it were dynamically, through the swallowing up of the *I* by the *Thou*—which is, however, no longer *Thou*, but that which alone is —and the second, as it were, statically through the self-recognition of the *I*, which has been freed and has become the Self, as that which alone is. If the doctrine of dependence considers the *I* that bears the span of pure relation in the world to be so weak and empty that its ability to bear it is no longer credible, the one doctrine of absorption causes the span of relation to disappear at its consummation, the other treats it as a delusion to be overcome.

[Sec. 430, Martin Buber, *I and Thou*, trans. R. G. Smith (Edinburgh: T. & T. Clark, 1937), p. 3. Sec. 431, *ibid.*, p. 8. Sec. 432, *ibid.*, p. 75. Sec. 433, *ibid.* Sec. 434, *ibid.*, pp. 75–76. Sec. 435, *ibid.*, pp. 78–80. Sec. 436, *ibid.*, pp. 80–81. Sec. 437, *ibid.*, pp. 81–82. Sec. 438, *ibid.*, pp. 82–83. Sec. 439, *ibid.*, p. 84.]

### COMMENT

Buber seems to us least clear in his account of the dipolarity of time and eternity, or permanence and flux. Sometimes he has ascribed temporal process to deity, sometimes denied it, and nowhere is there much clarification of the issue. Note, too, that he speaks of God as "in the fullness of his eternity" needing us; whereas the dipolar logic of the matter is that God in his eternal aspect needs only some creatures or other but in his actual *de facto* present reality needs us in particular. However, Buber is not seeking a formal metaphysics and doubtless would distrust any such doctrine. For it turns God into an *It* or *Object*.

Yet the contention that God can only be *Thou*, never *It*, calls perhaps for some qualification. Every abstraction is an *It;* if there is process in God, one may abstract what is common to every possible stage of this process. This will be the essence of God but not God as actual, now or at any other moment. It will not be *Thou*, if that means, as it seems to in Buber, the other term of the dual relation of which I am one term. For the act of abstraction spoken of is precisely that of excluding from the term referred to any such concrete relation with its concrete terms. However, in another sense, even the essence of God is *Thou*, in that only the one individual, God, has such an essence. Still, if the abstraction is permissible—and once becoming and receptivity in God are granted, it seems

impossible to forbid it—then in spite of what Barth, Brunner, and Buber seem to say, theoretical dealing with deity, as well as personal "encounter" with him, must be possible. True, the theoretical theologian himself is also a man in encounter with God, but his doctrine deals not with the God whom he encounters but with an abstract individuality in the encountered one.

Buber's discussion of the word "God" as synonym for the supreme form of Thou is notable, for it is the answer to those who wish us to employ a new word. The word by overwhelming usage is the proper name for which each man is to substitute Thou, and this universal substitutability of Thou is the sense of "God." Theologies are merely theories about how this is possible.

We also think with our author that theorists who in effect reduce God to a mere It, as Wieman, for example, seems to do, by denying consciousness to deity, are indulging in marginal usage of the word, which may be excused but not wholly condoned. In the end, the theologian must be allowed by his theory to address God and say, as Augustine does (but did *his* theory of the immutability and nonrelativity of the divine allow this?), "Thy nature, Lord, is thus and thus."

## RADHAKRISHNAN (1888——)

Strong as the influence of Sankara's monism still is in India, the spirit of Ramanuja is also much in evidence. Perhaps this is especially true of those Hindu thinkers who are deeply versed in European as well as in Indian systems. Of these, none is more distinguished than the author about to be presented. We think that the ease with which Radhakrishnan interprets European authors is not only no disproof of his representativeness as modern

product of Hinduism but is rather one reason the more for accepting such representativeness. For only those who can face the international community of philosophers, who can speak to philosophical humanity at large, can in our shrinking world be regarded as philosophically competent. The rest are spokesmen of the remnants of primitive tribalism.

It will be clear from the following selections that our author affirms the real temporality of deity as well as his eternity; that for him God includes the world without prejudice to its reality or the freedom of its members; and that God is conscious of himself and of the world. Furthermore, even the reality of suffering in God is indicated, although not quite explicitly stated. Thus panentheism is carried far toward its complete expression. The religious tone of the discussion will also be apparent.

### Three Aspects of God

*440.* The conception of God as wisdom, love and goodness is not a mere abstract demand of thought but is the concrete reality which satisfies the religious demand. If we combine the ideas we are led to posit from the different directions of metaphysics, morals and religion, we obtain the character of God as the primordial mind, the loving redeemer and the holy judge of the universe. The Hindu conception of God as Brahmā, Viṣṇu and Śiva illustrates the triple character. Brahmā is the primordial nature of God. He is the "home" of the conditions of the possibility of the world, or of the "eternal objects" in Whitehead's phrase. If the rational order of the universe reflects the mind of God, that mind is prior to the world. But the thoughts of Brahmā, or the primordial mind, should become the things of the world. This process of transformation of ideas into the plane of space-time is a gradual one which God assists by his power of productive and self-communicating life. In the world process all things yearn towards their ideal forms. They struggle to throw off their imperfections and reflect the patterns in the divine mind. As immanent in the process, God becomes the guide and the ground of the progress. He is not a mere spectator, but a sharer in the travail of the world. God as Viṣṇu is sacrifice. He is continuously engaged in opposing every tendency in the universe which makes for error, ugliness and evil, which are not mere abstract possibilities, but concrete forces giving reality to the cosmic strife. God pours forth the whole wealth of his love to actualize his intentions for us. He takes up the burden of helping us to resist the forces of evil, error and ugliness, and transmute them into truth, beauty and goodness.

*441.* While there is no risk that the world will tumble off into ruin so long as God's love is operative, yet the realization of the end of the world depends on our co-operation. As we are free beings, our co-operation is a free gift which we may withhold. This possibility introduces an element of contingency into the universe. The creative process, though orderly and progressive, is unpredictable. There is real indetermination, and God himself is in the make.

*442.* So far as the world is concerned, God is organic with it. It is impossible to detach God from the world. The Hindu theologian Rāmanuja regards the relation of God to the world as one of soul to body. He brings out the organic and complete dependence of the world on God. God is the sustainer of the body as well as its inner guide. Struggle and growth are real in the life of God. Time is the essential form of the cosmic process, including the moral life, and it has a meaning to God also. Life eternal which carries us beyond the limits of temporal growth may take us to the Absolute, but God is essentially bound up with the life in time. Progress may be derogatory to the Absolute, but not to God, who is intensely interested in it.

*443.* The process of the world is creative synthesis, where the formative energy, local situation and cosmic control are all efficient factors. The final end is not contained in the beginning. The interest and attractiveness of the end cannot be divorced from the process which leads up to it. A God who has arranged everything at the beginning of the world and can change nothing, create nothing new is not a God at all. If the universe is truly creative, God works as a creative genius does. The end grows with the process and assumes a definite shape through the characteristics of the parts of the process. There is thus an element of indetermination throughout the process, though it diminishes in degree as the amount of actuality increases. God the planner acts with real genius when confronted by actual situations.

God, though immanent, is not identical with the world until the very end. Throughout the process there is an unrealized residuum in God, but it vanishes when we reach the end; when the reign is absolute the kingdom comes. God who is organic with it recedes into the background of the Absolute. The beginning and the end are limiting conceptions, and the great interest of the world centers in the intermediate process from the beginning to the end. God is more the saviour and redeemer than creator and judge.

*444.* The love of God is more central than either his wisdom or his sovereignty. These latter may lead to predestination theories which reduce the world process to a sham, where the freedom of man and the love of God are both illusory. If predestination is true, then the creation of novelties, the loving trust and surrender of man to God and the grace of God are illusions.

*445.* While the character of God as personal love meets certain religious needs, there are others which are not fulfilled by it. In the highest spiritual experience we have the sense of rest and fulfillment, of eternity and completeness. These needs provoked from the beginning of human reflection conceptions of the Absolute as pure and passionless being which transcends the restless turmoil of the cosmic life. If

God is bound up with the world, subject to the category of time, if his work is limited by the freedom of man and the conditions of existence, however infinite he may be in the quality of his life, in power, knowledge and righteousness, he is but an expression of the Absolute. But man wants to know the truth of things in itself, in the beginning—nay, before time and before plurality, the one "breathing breathless," as the Rg Veda has it, the pure, alone and unmanifest, nothing and all things, that which transcends any definite form of expression, and yet is the basis of all expression, the one in whom all is found and yet all is lost. The great problem of the philosophy of religion has been the reconciliation of the character of the Absolute as in a sense eternally complete with the character of God as a self-determining principle manifested in a temporal development which includes nature and man. The identification of the absolute life with the course of human history suggested by the Italian idealists may be true of the supreme as God of the world, but not of the Absolute, the lord of all worlds. Creation neither adds to nor takes away from the reality of the Absolute. Evolution may be a part of our cosmic process, but the Absolute is not subject to it. The Absolute is incapable of increase.

While the Absolute is pure consciousness and pure freedom and infinite possibility, it appears to be God from the point of view of the one specific possibility which has become actualized. While God is organically bound up with the universe, the Absolute is not. The world of pure being is not exhausted by the cosmic process which is only one of the ways in which the Absolute reality which transcends the series reveals itself. The Absolute is the foundation and *prius* of all actuality and possibility. This universe is for the Absolute only one possibility.

Its existence is an act of free creation. Out of the infinite possibilities open to it, this one is chosen. When we analyze our sense of freedom we find that it consists in accepting or rejecting any one of a number of possibilities presented to us. The Absolute has an infinite number of possibilities to choose from, which are all determined by its nature. It has the power of saying yes or no to any of them. While the possible is determined by the nature of the Absolute, the actual is selected from out of the total amount of the possible, by the free activity of the Absolute without any determination whatsoever. It could have created a world different in every detail from that which is actual. If one drama is enacted and other possible ones postponed, it is due to the freedom of the Absolute.

It is not necessary for this universe to be an infinite and endless process. The character of a finite universe is not incompatible with an infinite Absolute. We can have an infinite series of terms which are finite. The Absolute has so much more in it than is brought out by this world.

As to why there is realization of this possibility, we can only say that it is much too difficult for us in the pit to know what is happening behind the screens. It is *maya*, or a mystery which we have to accept reverently.

Sometimes it is argued that it is of the very nature of the Absolute to overflow and realize possibilities. The great symbol of the sun which is used in Hindu thought, Plato's system and Persian mythology signifies the generous self-giving and ecstasy of the Absolute, which overflows, and gives itself freely and generously to all.

*446.* The Indian figure of *lila* makes the creation of the universe an act of playfulness. Play is generally the expression of ideal possibilities. It is its own end and its own continuous reward. The Absolute mind has a perfect realm of ideal being, and is free creativity as well. Though the creation of the world is an incident in the never-ending activity of the Absolute, it satisfies a deep want in God. The world is as indispensable to God as God is to the world.

God, who is the creator, sustainer, and judge of this world, is not totally unrelated to the Absolute. God is the Absolute from the human end. When we limit down the Absolute to its relation with the actual possibility, the Absolute appears as supreme Wisdom, Love and Goodness. The eternal becomes the first and the last. The abiding "I am," the changeless center and the cause of all change is envisaged as the first term and the last in the sequence of nature. He is the creative mind of the world, with a consciousness of the general plan and direction of the cosmos, even before it is actualized in space and time. He holds the successive details in proper perspective and draws all things together in bonds of love and harmony. He is the loving saviour of the world. As creator and saviour, God is transcendent to the true process, even as realization is transcendent to progress. This internal transcendence of God to the true process gives meaning to the distinctions of value, and makes struggle and effort real. We call the supreme the Absolute, when we view it apart from the cosmos, God in relation to the cosmos. The Absolute is the pre-cosmic nature of God, and God is the Absolute from the cosmic point of view.

[Sec. 440, S. Radhakrishnan, *An Idealist View of Life* (London: George Allen & Unwin, Ltd., 1932), pp. 334–35. Sec. 441, *ibid.*, pp. 335–36. Sec. 442, *ibid.*, p. 338. Sec. 443, *ibid.*, pp. 339–40. Sec. 444, *ibid.*, p. 340. Sec. 445, *ibid.*, pp. 342–44. Sec. 446, *ibid.*, pp. 344–45.]

#### COMMENT

Criticism of these passages on our part may be little more than quibbling.

Perhaps essentially we agree with the author. We fear only that in certain phrases the door is half-open to monopolar misinterpretations. To speak of "limiting down the Absolute to its relation with the actual" suggests that the absolute as such is *more* than the supreme as relative to the world. But the logical construction is rather that the absolute as such is an empty abstraction, a mere ingredient in the richness of actuality, worldly or divine. And we think it somewhat objectionable to use "the Absolute" as expression for the supreme in its totality of aspects, or to speak of the Absolute "selecting" among possibilities for actualization. The subject which really owns such an act of selection is relative if anything is, and this act owns the absolute as its abstract essence, while the absolute as such can own nothing relative. In this sense we can accept the saying that the Absolute is the precosmic nature of God, for this correctly makes "God" the subject of all the divine properties, including absoluteness. ("Precosmic" indeed is open to the objection that it may seem to imply a beginning of the temporal process.)

The one word we miss in Radhakrishnan's book (it may occur somewhere else in his writings with this sense) is the word "abstract" as applied to the absolute or nontemporal and immaterial aspect of deity. Here Pfleiderer, Fechner, and Whitehead seem a degree clearer.

It should be noted that the Absolute is indeed the home of the unbounded possibilities and that any actual world or state of deity is never the actualization of all, or of any finite fraction, of these possibilities. In this sense actuality limits down the absolute. But the point is that the absolute no more realizes the other possibilities than the actual relative world does; the Absolute has or is such possibility, but not its actualization. Actuality thus never exhausts the Absolute, not because it is less than the Absolute; rather because, although always more than the merely abstract absolute essence, it is never as much more as it is possible for an actuality to be. And again it must be remembered that the relative, according to surrelativism, includes the absolute, as the concrete the abstract, so that to say that the absolute is in any sense more than the relative is to say that $x$ is more than $xy$. This could be so only if $y$ were a negative quantity, or if, when $x$ were combined with $y$, it lost something of its nature so that in reality $xy$, taken literally, is an impossibility. But if the abstract could not preserve its identity in the concrete it would be inconceivable (for any conception is itself a concrete act) and would qualify nothing in any true propositions, and so would be useless. So we conclude that God, as relative to the world, though not exhausting the possibilities inherent in the Absolute as his own abstract essence, is in no sense less than this essence but in every sense in which it is distinguished at all from it simply more than its deficient reality.

# WEISS (1901——)

In the article from which the following pages are taken, Paul Weiss argues for God's existence. The system in terms of which his argument is made reflects the modern metaphysics which has emerged through Bergson, Peirce, and Whitehead; but it is qualified in this instance by the more geometric philosophizing of the less recent past. The initial problem of his essay is to show that the ontological, cosmological, and teleological arguments "presuppose" and "specialize" one another. In this he has advanced beyond Kant, who considered the ontological argument as the ground for the others; Weiss argues that, in a different respect, each argument serves in turn as basis for the other two. These paragraphs, although valuable, have been omitted, since it is Weiss's belief that the prime function of the traditional arguments is to clarify distinctions. The richer basis, necessary in his view for the argument's success, concerns the affective, valuational, questing nature of man which becomes the burden of the essay.

It is striking that Weiss agrees so often, but for somewhat different reasons, with the views advanced by the central figures of this chapter and perplexing that on occasion Weiss, advancing the same reasons, reaches seemingly contrary conclusions. Certain of these differences may be semantic. Others may be largely a matter of emphasis; the view we favor places a greater stress on time in such manner as to clarify, in our opinion, the proper meaning of omniscience and omnipotence; our view stresses human self-identity much less than the view of Weiss, which seems to us an overstress. Our more realistic view of tragedy as affecting God may represent only a difference of emphasis from Weiss's view of a nonsuffering God; but it is more likely that this is a real opposition.

The reader will find the essay original and stimulating; and we have the feeling that, could meanings but he clarified with sufficient precision, Weiss's doctrine would be in agreement with the others illustrated in this chapter.

## A New Proof for God*

447. It does seem peculiar that, after all these years, a new proof of God must be or could be given. This would be true were the proof offered, one which was new to religion, for the religious conscience certainly has not waited until now for justification. Justification, in fact, goes the other way. All arguments must look to religion for certification that they are talking of a God, rich beyond expression. The new proof I am offering is new not to religion but to philosophy and theology, and is new because it is framed, on the one hand, in the light of a new approach to the universe, and on the other, in terms of a fuller acceptance of the meaning and validity of religious experience.

The essence of all discourse regarding God, no matter what its being and no matter what its form or end is: *Seek and you shall find.* To be religious is to seek God with all one's being; to be blessed is to find him; to be theological is to make the search and its object evident in discourse. To every request, to every criticism, to every objection and to every doubt raised in connection with God there can be but one answer: Seek again and you will be answered. Everything else is exegesis, the function of which is to show that the search is inescapable and universal and that the finding is unavoidable. The difference in the various kinds of proof that are offered in theology and the various kinds of discourse offered in philosophy and in sermons is a difference in content and surety. Some begin well, others poorly, some make a strong effort, others are anemic; some end with rich content, others with a deity impoverished and dispirited. In different ways they tell us when, why, where and how we are to seek, what we are to find and what the finding means. Each of these must now be examined. . . .

*When do we seek God.* It is rare indeed that men seek God when they are joyous. It is tragedy, sorrow and pain that provide the initial stimulus for their search. It is because of this that the Hebraic tradition which stresses the fact that God is a troubled, anxious being retains a vital religious spark often forgotten by Christians in their stress on God as the source of all perfection and joy.

*448.* To achieve perfect stability and be most a man we must control and be controlled by everything that exists in nature. It is of our essence to be concerned with them for our sake and theirs. But every thing has its day, suffering the onslaught of others and the passage of time. It is when we see that which we cherish pass away that we turn to God as the warrant that they still remain, and as the source of acts which can minimize such tragedies in the future.

*Why we look for God.* The *occasion* for our search for God is our concern for whatever is actually good in this world of ours. The *reason* we look to Him is because we are aware of the fact that He does preserve what nature cannot retain. We do not look to Him so that we may have a higher regard for what is good in man and nature, but in order that we may still have it and it have us. It is thus a false bit of dogma to affirm that because we know God we love our fellowman; the reverse is the truth. It is because we love man that we can know God. But if we love only man, the God we will know, will be a God only of the family, the state or society. That God is rich in value but limited in the range of his concerns and activities. We can know God as unlimited in power and interest only so far as we turn to Him in the light of our concern for the value and being of every thing there may be. Since we never attain the state of having a full grasp of every value, we cannot grasp anything near the depth of his being....

*The formal proof of God's existence:* These observations can be congealed within a formal proof that God exists.

Man is a part of nature, excluding and excluded by other natural things. These define him as finite and limited, without which he would cease to be the specific determinate thing that he is. Both they and he change at every moment. Yet he is responsible for what he formerly did. As a responsible being he remains identical despite all change within or without. No matter how his appearance differs today and tomorrow he still is responsible for what he did yesterday. But since his nature is interlocked with the natures of other things, if he persist they must too. They must be outside nature as well as within, and he can know that he is the self-same being he was, only so far as he refers to them as they stand apart from the changing world. As outside nature they are eternal, and he as their counterpart must therefore be immortal. My search for God is a search for the being of the passing things I need in order to remain myself. I know that the search has a terminus so far as I know I am myself, two moments together.

The formal proof of the existence of God can be summarized: I persist, therefore God exists. From this follows the corollary: God exists, therefore I am immortal.

Other things depend on me as surely as I depend on them. I too must be preserved within God and they too must have an immortal core. Every thing is closed within nature at the same time that it is part of the eternal essence of God. As a part of nature it has a supernatural longing for the eternal being of all the others, and this eternal being it finds only in God. Each in adjusting itself to the others as a part of nature must, at the same time, adjust itself to them as a part of God. But then the eternal essence of God must become adjusted to the changes which the world undergoes. Each thing, in short, persists because it acts with respect to the eternal as well as the temporal natures of other things, and the eternal nature is abreast of the changes the things undergo because it shifts its stress to correspond. God is the eternal memory to which all natural things refer for a constant reference appropriate to their identities. As the things change, the memory grows in content without losing any of the details that went before.

*Where do we seek for God.* We cannot find God unless we are active participants in the affairs of others. But if we immerse ourselves in the world, we are sure to lose God. To find God we must retreat from the world, but in such a way that that world is still with us. We can look for Him, in other words, only so far as we have allowed the other things to submit themselves to us and have made their natures and values, a part of ourselves. The search for God is thus rooted in a double submission—a submission to their being, which leads to a search for Him, and a submission to their natures which makes possible an acknowledgment of His presence as the external counterpart of ourselves as including all nature within us. It is because we are a part of the others that we know that God exists; it is because they are a part of us that we know what He is. To find Him we must look within ourselves. There we will find a longing for Him which alone is an adequate guide as to where we must then go. We search for God wherever our longing for him directs us.

*How do we seek God:* There is no one unique way in which the search for God is to be conducted. He can be sought through prayer and reveries, in mystic contemplation and in active good works, in fear and trembling and in jubilation. But the most effective perhaps is through sorrow mixed with confidence. The more concerned we are with tragedy and the more confident we are that it is truly and deeply

tragic, the more acutely do we become aware of God. To attain this end we must be actively sympathetic towards everything of value, human and sub-human, and yet strong enough to overcome the natural weakness which ensues when we see them pass. The search for God is a moral search; we carry it through only so far as we avoid the excess of submission without assertion, or assertion without submission.

## The Nature of God*

*449.* The search for God can never come to an end. We never actually reach Him as He exists on His own, an eternal being, suffused with value, conserving all the good there may be. But we can anticipate the end of the search by reflecting on what it means to be a self-sufficient being. In this way we outrun religion and obtain results of primarily theological value. But if we get somewhere near the truth, our pale result should nevertheless be of some value to religion, when the longing for God becomes too tense for man to bear or when it is on the verge of being confounded with other desires and needs.

Every thing, whether persistent or changing, infinite or finite, divine or profane, is self-identical. It is what it is. But the self-identity of God is different from the self-identity of other things. To say that Jones is self-identical, i.e., that "Jones is Jones" is to say that here, where Jones is, the law of identity holds. That law holds also where Smith is, and it is equally true to say that "Smith is Smith." It is the same law that holds in both cases, the tautologies, "Jones is Jones" and "Smith is Smith" differing only in the kind of filling they provide for the bare law of identity, "$x$ is $x$." These tautologies express the fact that the law of identity is embodied in foreign substances, and that these substances, by virtue of their very disparity, are not altogether appropriate to the meaning of that law. When we say, "God is God," however, we do not root the law of identity in an alien substance, but locate it in the only being which is adequate to its meaning. In God, the being of the law is as intelligible as the law; in other things, the being is not as wide or as lucid as the law itself. God offers the law of identity a locus where its being is completely appropriate to its meaning; His being is therefore perfectly expressed in the assertion that He is the self-identical.

God's own reported name for Himself is "I am that I am"—i.e., "God is God" or "God is *the* self-identical." This is but another way of saying that He is through and through intelligible, and that the grasp of the law of identity as existing on its own and in its purity is a grasp of His very nature.

*450.* "God" expresses the full meaning of the law of identity as a substantial self-contained thing, and that law expresses the full meaning of God as a perfectly intelligible being. "Jones is Jones" is, on the other hand, a tautology after the fact. It is an analytic result of the synthesis of the being of Jones with the meaning of identity. "Jones" tells us nothing about the law of identity, nor does the law of identity tell us anything about "Jones." To be able to affirm "Jones is Jones" we must get outside "Jones" to the law of identity, and outside the law of identity to "Jones." To affirm "God is God," on the other hand, is to remain within God and the law of identity, affirming both fully and at once.

It follows from this that there is a sense in which God is closed off from nature as surely as nature is closed off from God. Each thing, as self-identical, roots the law of identity in a concrete substance. That substance must, itself, however, be self-identical. Instead then of being something opposed to the law of identity it is something that already

exhibits it. When we separate off the law of identity from a thing we are left with a remainder in which we must be able to find the law once again; if we separate it off there, we must be able to find it in that which is left over, and so on without end. But then it must be true that each thing, instead of being describable as the law of identity in an alien substance will be that law endlessly repeated. But a law of identity in an appropriate substance is nothing other than God. The more we look at things in the light of the essence of God, the more surely do we see them disappear into that essence.

This conclusion, paradoxical though it sound to modern ears, was long ago seen to be legitimate and inescapable. It expresses exactly what is required by the contention that God is omniscient. God knows only Himself, for nothing else, as Aristotle long ago acutely observed, is worthy of his attention. Aristotle, however, failed to see that in thus knowing Himself God thereby knows the nature of every particular thing, and that in knowing all things He knows Himself. From the standpoint of God, a thing is nothing more than the nature of God repeated in multiple ways, one thing differing from another only in the manner in which the repetitions occur; i.e., in the different kinds of dissections required to obtain layer on layer of identities. Now, God knows Himself in infinite ways, for despite His simplicity He is infinitely rich, and all these different ways of knowing have the same result, for despite His infinitude He affirms nothing but His identity. Since each thing is analyzable into an endless series of identities, and since it is nevertheless finite and limited, it is nothing other than part of God's infinite essence and being. When then God knows a thing He knows nothing alien to Himself, and in knowing Himself He knows all things.

Since each thing repeats the nature of God, one can differ from another only in the sense that it combines these repetitions in a unique way. Now, if God knows only identities, He can know nothing of the way in which those identities are combined in special ways, unless His act of knowledge is also an act of combining these identities, and thus of reproducing the very being of actual things. The act of omniscience is thus also the act of omnipotent creation. God creates all things as and while He knows them; His affirmation of Himself is the creation of things so far as that affirmation falls short of complete self-affirmation.

God is thus completely self-enclosed, in no way dependent on things. He knows them without going outside Himself, and He makes them where and as He knows them. But this in no way affects the fact that the things exist apart from Him, within a self-contained nature. God reproduces, rather than produces them, knows them within Himself rather than within nature. There is thus no conflict between the Aristotelian contention that the universe is not created, and the Platonic thesis that He makes all things, any more than there is a conflict between the thesis of the naturalists, that nature is self-sufficing, and the view of the super-naturalists, that each thing in nature makes a necessary reference to the eternal. Though from the standpoint of God, a thing is nothing more than a tissue of repetitions of the law of identity, from the standpoint of nature, it is a being whose essence is to exclude and be excluded by other things. The assertion, "Jones is Jones" is recognized to be trivial by all of us because it fails to reveal anything about Jones as a being in nature. We get no further information, but we are at least back on solid ground when we assert instead that Jones is in fact other than Smith, and that his nature is what it is because

he has taken account of the nature of that other in at least an act of natural submission to it. Discourse in terms of identity comes nowhere near the being or meaning of any natural thing, just as discourse in terms of exclusions fails to come near to the being or meaning of God. The one makes things divine, the other makes God finite.

Evil, defect and imperfection mar the nature of every existent thing. But God cannot contain anything which is evil. What God knows and reproduces can thus be only the goodness of things— the things of nature so far as they are harmonized in themselves and with one another. It is the evil that is interred in men's bones and the good that lives on after them. The punishment for evil is divine forgetfulness, for only a tincture of the man who devotes himself to bad is left within the eternal being of God. To be evil is so far to fail to attain the status of an eternal being for which everything else has a longing, and is to spend one's energy in perverting one's own longing and immortality so that it assumes the shape of a passing desire and a transient soul. . . .

The fact that evil is precluded from God does not detract from His omniscience. His knowledge is a knowledge of the best in things. When they are predominantly evil His knowledge is abstract; when they are predominantly good His knowledge is concrete, more intimate. He knows the evil in things by knowing the kind of knowledge He has of them, by knowing that the good in them is not concrete enough to be entirely good.

God is omnipotent, omniscient and the great conserver of values. His omnipotence does not involve the creation of a world streaked with evil, but the reproduction of things so far as they are good. His omniscience is not a knowledge, cold and bloodless, but a knowledge which is dynamic, the incidental product of an act of sweeping across the infinite extent of His being and noting the details of Himself in the process. His conservation of values is not an act tearing them out of the matrix of the world, but of affirming His own nature. He is eternal but internally dynamic, simple but infinite, omnipotent but uncreating, omniscient but without a direct knowledge of evil. Were this all, however, he would not be a God for us and our world, but a God for Himself alone. God is less than divine, if He is not concerned with the affairs of the world, responsive to our appeals, just and merciful in His estimates—a force for good as well as a guarantee of its eternality. God must not only affirm Himself, but be receptive of the assertions of actual things; He must not only be one of whom others take account but one who actually submits Himself to them to use as they can. But then there must be a natural appetite in God for things, just as there is a supernatural longing in things for God. It is the interplay of these two which constitutes that theological space in which the drama of the conquest of the evil by the good takes place.

### Theological Space*

451. The quest for God terminates in a perfect, self-identical being. Such a being lacks nothing real and must, accordingly, preclude the possibility of the existence of anything else. So far as nature and God are completely other, the existence of the one cancels the possibility of the existence of the other. But no thing, as we saw before, is altogether other than God; each is a part of Him as well, the object of the longing of whatever else there may be in nature. But then neither can God be altogether other than the things in nature; otherwise He would be unable to know just what new goods were appearing in the world, and would be

unable to do anything to make them better.

God's goodness is not entirely good until it is endlessly multiplied in all possible ways, and it can be multiplied only if there are things which exist independently of Him, at once receptive of His goodness and sufficiently self-assertive to be able to make use of it. He knows that it is possible for things to exist independently of Him because He has a need for them; He knows they must be in time, because He knows that He alone is infinitely rich, able to be Himself, completely and exhaustively, at an instant. He proves their possibility in the act of desiring independent constantly changing objects where His goodness can be continuously multiplied, just as we prove the possibility of God in the act of longing for Him as the place where our finite goods are fixed and preserved. He proves the existence of things by noting how the details of his self-knowledge change from moment to moment, just as we prove He exists by noting that we remain ourselves though we live in time.

The existence of God precludes the existence of the world only so far as God contemplates Himself with a fixed and glassy stare. But in fact He becomes aware of other things because He sweeps over the infinite range of His being in new ways at every moment to conform with the changes in the actual world. He knows the details of Himself, reconstructing each of the objects in the world, not according to His own interests or desires, but in accordance with their natures and development. His omnipotence and omniscience are thus perfect after the fact. He produces everything because it is already in existence; He knows everything by introspection because He allows that act to be guided by things beyond. He acts in terms of the nature of the objects in which His goodness has found a resting place. He can know nothing of evil because He knows only what is contained within Himself and that is wholly good; but He is aware of evil, because He can feel the resistance His gift of Himself meets in the world, and thus that it is not there in its full concreteness.

We know that we long for God and that that longing attains its end more or less adequately. If we did not, however, also know that God was searching for and finding us, we would have no direct knowledge that He was in any way concerned with us. A God who was the mere object of a longing would be all-receptive, all merciful, but as fluid as water. But God, as the Hebrews were acutely aware, insists on Himself, and that insistence we feel in the very act of longing for Him. It is this feeling which reveals to us that our longing is accurately directed and sincere, and which provides the religious with the sense of having communicated with one who has heard and sympathetically received one's requests.

Conversely, God must feel the longing of natural things for Him if His projection of His goodness is to conform to the structure of the world and the need things have of Him. A God who insists on Himself would be righteous and as hard as iron, callous to our desires but just according to His own lights, did He not supplement His insistence with a receptiveness of the longing which searches for Him. It is His feeling of the longing which things have for Him which dictates the direction in which His own acts of knowledge and production are to follow, and which reveals to Him that His gift of Himself has found some root. He knows when He has communicated with us just as we know when we have communicated with Him.

We long for God and feel the effect of His desire for us. He desires us and feels the effect of our longing for Him. We are to Him as a body is to its soul.

Because our longing is infected by His desire for us, our search for Him is joyous, a sublime version of that bodily delight which arises when the body adjusts itself to an independently acting soul. Because His desire for us is infected by our longing for Him, He can have that providential concern for us which is a divine version of that prudence which arises when a good soul adjusts itself to an independent and appropriate body.

His desire for us and our longing for Him cross the infinite vasts which separate us. So far as they complement one another, they together constitute a "theological space" in which they "move" with respect to one another. Since both a joyous search and a providential concern are the products of the union of divine desire and finite longing, theological space has, as its termini, the religious, on the one hand, and their God on the other. Or more accurately, since everything longs and is answered to some degree, and since God needs all things and feels the effect of every longing, theological space is the region which unites nature and God so that they together form a single cosmos.

This is a conclusion against which most theologians would rebel, though it follows out of the premises they themselves would acknowledge. They admit that the universe has its own laws and man a free-will, that God is perfect and self-contained, that man longs for and reaches to God and that God is concerned with and infects the nature of things. But how could there be two independent beings which have anything to do with one another if there were not a common "space" in which they were related? The theologians shy away from the idea of a theological space because they think that, on the one hand, nothing could encompass both God and the world without God being reduced to the status of a being dependent on and subsumed under it as an inferior being, and on the other, that no one could bridge the gap between Him and us but God Himself. But space is not more real than the things in space; space in fact is a product of the interplay of the things said to be within it. Nor does the space include God within it; it terminates in God, but God also lives outside it. That is why he can be said to have an independent, immutable being. Nor is it true that the only way of bridging the gap which exists between God and the world is by God coming down to that world. After all, we do voluntarily reach towards God and get to Him with more or less success. Our experience of our longing for Him and our joy in Him contains no evidence that He has helped us. Reflection shows that God reaches towards us; experience shows that we reach towards Him as well.

It is by virtue of this double fact that it is still possible to speak significantly of that mean between time and eternity which classical theologians called the "aeon" and which they falsely characterized as the "time" of the heavenly bodies. The heavenly bodies are part of nature and are caught in the passage of ordinary mundane time. If the aeon is to have any application it must characterize theological space, the medium between the eternal God and the changing universe. The aeon like time allows for a distinction between the earlier and the later, but like eternity allows what is earlier to exist together with what comes later. Theological space is the body of that living and accumulated history of the adventures of God and the world in their everlasting struggle to become perfectly adjusted. The past is retained in it now in the form of tendencies to become moulded in this way or that, which is one of the most conspicuous ways in which it differs from ordinary space.

Theological space is the region through which Satan was

Hurld headlong flaming from th' Ethereal Skie
With hideous ruine and combustion down
To bottomless perdition,

for Satan is the name for that limiting kind of religious being whose longing for God is so misdirected that it is countered by a minimum divine desire and a maximum divine and merciless insistence. Satan lives at the furthest distance from God in a theological space whose measure is not inches or miles but the degree of communication and mutual concern achieved. In the very sense in which the kingdom of God is within us, so is Satan and the nether regions.

452. Hell on earth is a longing misdirected and unanswered, heaven is that longing satisfied. Hell after death is to be forgotten, heaven to be remembered.

The theological space which stretches between an independently acting God and an independently acting nature is flat, without any properties of its own except that of relating the termini. As longing becomes more intense and better directed, and is met by an equally effective divine desire, that space becomes contorted. The more that space becomes contorted the more new properties, the product of the overlapping of longing and desire, become manifest, just as new properties, characteristic of water and stones, appear when independent atoms come close together. We have only a faint glimmer of the nature of contorted theological space—but to judge from the accounts of careful students of religious experience, it has sharp dips and surprising bends, easing the progress towards God for a time only to slow it up at another, or sometimes even bringing it to a sudden and momentary halt.

453. It would, however, be absurd to suppose that an omniscient God could have no knowledge of the theological space which separates Him from things.

He must somehow not only be one of the termini of that space, but must actually make that space a part of Himself and thereby know it in the course of knowing Himself. The space between God and the world must belong to God in somewhat the same way that the space between a soul and its body belongs to that soul. The space which the soul owns is a space which terminates in the organic unity of the living body. That unity is to be sharply distinguished but not separated from the unity that results from the conjunction of the parts of the body, contrasting with the latter as the living from the dead, the biological from the physiological, the concrete from the abstract. It is because the living organic unity belongs to the soul that the soul can possess the space which lies between itself and that unity. The soul knows the nature of that space because it is able to feel the difference between itself as mere soul and itself as the organic unity of a body. A similar kind of knowledge must be characteristic of a truly omniscient God. But if that God is to possess a space outside Himself, He must lay hold of something beyond that space, acquiring thereby a boundary to His extended being. Now, what lies beyond that space, to pursue the analogy, must be a living unity of the whole of nature, a unity which is to be distinguished from the unity determined by the co-presence of the things in nature, as the living from the dead. God knows the theological space between Himself and the universe because He is not merely a being who dwells in isolation, but one who lives throughout the space, and possesses the "soul" of the universe.

From this it follows that the more or less neglected contentions of Spinoza and Plato are amply justified, once the pantheism of the one and the organicism of the other are put aside. Spinoza said that God was extended; Plato said that the world had a soul. These are two sides of the same fact. God's omniscience requires that He be extended, and that extension demands a termination in a nature divinely unified and within which the occurrences of nature take place with more or less freedom. The extension which characterizes God pertains to Him, however, not as He is in Himself, but as He is for a universe beyond; the soul or life which embraces the whole of nature is not a soul within the universe but a soul which lies outside it. Spinoza unfortunately defined extension as a part of God's very essence, while Plato took the soul of the universe to infect the content of nature. The one ignored the theological extension which separates God from the extended unified whole of nature which He makes possible, though that theological extension is a more intimate part of God than the unity of nature; the other ignored the unity which natural things themselves determine and failed to see therefore that the soul of the universe was not a part of its being. Only by supplementing the one by the other can we avoid the pantheism offered by the one and the organic theory of nature presented by the other, without giving up the insights they attained.

Our theologies have moved so far in a different channel that these conclusions will sound perversely paradoxical if not absurd and unintelligible. No accumulation of argument could perhaps ever dislodge this distrust. But perhaps the points could be shown to be more acceptable if we approach the matter from another side. Part of the difficulty of the previous discussion hinges on the fact that we have tried to grasp theoretically how the nature of theological space can be understood from the standpoint of God. We could say, with some assurance, what it meant for God to exhibit Himself in the guise of an organic unity of the universe, for we were capable of doing something similar ourselves, with respect to our bodies. But this told us little of what God was like and what His mastery meant.

454. The defects of our account can be partly redeemed if we look to the reports of genuine mystical experiences. The mystic submits himself to God across the vasts of theological space. His object is . . . to obtain the prophetic gift of knowing what the highest good of nature is. He tries, and to some degree succeeds, in emptying his finite natural self into the longing which stretches towards and terminates in God. His act enables him to grasp, as no one else can, something of that unity of goods which God's omnipotence forged out of the finite and defective materials of nature.

The mystic can reach his goal only because God finds his presence acceptable. The mystic offers God direct evidence of a kind beyond His actual, unaided reach—the evidence of the nature of those particular limited beings which live beneath the organic unity of nature that God determines. They are to Him what an atom would be to us, if it could reach through the organic unity of our living bodies and tell us what it was like. . . .

The mystic in offering himself offers to God the whole stretch of the longing which separates them. God thereby knows theological space, not as before, by having reached out beyond Himself, but by having the mystic carry the meaning of it into Him. But the mystic must then know the nature of that space as well, contemplating it as he contemplates the rest of God. More important, and more directly relevant to the question of what the finding of God means, is the fact that a mystical experience is a way of infecting oneself with goods otherwise beyond one's reach. The mystic becomes transformed, in attaining his goal, into a

medium by which the goodness that is in God can be introduced within nature. The mystic who returns on earth in the same spirit in which he left it, is a dreamer of fancies, not a being divinely illuminated. The true mystic returns filled with a sense of the possibility of making the universe better. He leaves the universe as a representative of all finitude and comes back again with a knowledge of what it might be were it purged of evil. But if his knowledge be a truly inspired knowledge it would be too rich and valuable for him to be able to enjoy by himself and he must be inevitably driven to put it in practice. His unavoidable duty is to return to the world with his vision intact and make it apply to the world in fact.

455. Only through longing can we find God as he is in Himself, only through reflection can we find Him in the form of the unity of nature.

456. God knows what occurs in nature in a three-fold way. He knows Himself, He knows the things which present themselves to Him, and He knows the way some of them disturb the organic unity He imposes. As the first He is omniscient—our self-knowledge is the counterpart. As the second He is the merciful judge—mystical experience is its reciprocal. As the third He is the great recorder—the feeling of pain and pleasure we obtain from the disturbance produced by the cells within our bodies providing an analogue of the kind of thing He reports. Because of the latter two He makes a difference to what happens in nature, changing the course of history through the agency of beings which act as the media through which Divine goodness can have some force on earth, and changing the direction of the whole of nature through the agency of a providential care which dictates the course of the whole of nature without disturbing the independent existence of the things within

it. God directs the whole of nature to higher ends, not by forcing natural things to submit to an edict, but by allowing His meaning to be conveyed within it, and by limiting the direction in which the whole of things can move of itself.

Providence is Divine prudence constraining nature as a whole. . . . It contains more than the harmony of all the things that now exist, since it includes as well the end which is appropriate to that particular state of affairs. The mystic has a grasp of the kind of goods which may be realized; the philosopher has a grasp of the kind of ends which are now most relevant.

457. For providence to be at its most effective, the mystic must submit himself to the discipline of philosophy and thereby become ready to use his knowledge of a higher good as a means by which a present, appropriate, cosmic end is to be attained, and the philosopher must listen to the mystic and thereby recognize that what is now the highest and best end falls far short of the end which nature could attain. But neither of them could work with greatest effect through and within nature unless they supported their insight with a scientific knowledge of what nature's independent being meant and was. Science is *the* instrument for the attainment of divine goods in and for nature.

## Conclusion*

The preceding account is undoubtedly streaked with error, overrun with confusions, marred by dogmatism, and perhaps even a contradiction here and there. But it does attempt to approach the problem of God and the world in such a way that the diverse claims of theology, religion, ethics, philosophy and science, are revealed to be compatible, independent aspects of a truth which is flexible enough to accept much of classical thought and allow some

place for truths beyond the vision of today. It finds room to acknowledge the scientific ideals of an independently existing nature and a universe governed by a single set of laws. It acknowledges the insights of the orient in its stress on the occurrence and validity of natural mysticism and the rights and values of subhuman things. It tries to interweave the Hebraic emphasis on sorrow and God's concern with the affairs of the world, with the Christian emphasis on the golden rule and the peace that is God's to overflowing. It affirms with Plato that the universe is overarched by a soul, with Aristotle that God contemplates Himself, with Spinoza that He is extended, and with Whitehead that He works together with the world in His production of new goods. It attempts to reconcile God's omniscience and omnipotence with the fact of evil, His eternity with His concern for a changing world, His justice with His mercy, and the passage of time with the fact that values are preserved. It holds that the soul has a natural origin and yet is immortal, that force is a good and yet must be restrained, that nature goes its own way and yet is divinely restricted. It puts its greatest emphasis on the continuity of natural desire, religious experience and mystical ecstasy, and takes most seriously the three biblical statements: Seek and you shall find, I am that I am, and Man is made in God's image. The first provides a new proof of God's existence, the second a fresh account of His nature, and the third a clue to His relation to the world beyond.

One way of summarizing the foregoing is to accept wholeheartedly the statement that man is made in God's image. Man is not a mere soul nor a mere body. He is a soul which expresses itself as the organic unity of a body within which multiple subsidiary atoms, molecules and cells go their own way. These subsidiary elements are the analogue of the things in nature; the organic unity of those elements is the analogue of God's providential hold on the whole universe, and the soul is the analogue of God as He dwells alone. Just as the bodily elements are constrained by the organic unity and yet reach to the self-contained soul, so the things in nature are constrained within God's providentially designed order, and reach to Him in fact. And just as the soul possesses the entire region which stretches from itself, as it exists on its own, to itself as the living unity of the body, so God possesses the entire region which stretches from Himself to the organic unity of the world. And, finally, just as the distance between the soul by itself and the soul for the body is a function of the independent but complementary extended references which the soul and the bodily elements make to one another, so the region between God and the world is a function of the expressed and extended concerns they have for one another.

The relation of God to nature is like that of the soul to the body. They are independent, they interact, they move in parallel paths, they reflect occurrences in one another and they form together a single organic whole. They are never perfectly adjusted to one another and neither can make the adjustment alone. God's task can be described as being like ours, or as the complement of it, though in both cases His is of a different order and value. Just as we must struggle to attain a stable state where soul and body are independent, at their maximum and yet perfectly attuned, so God must strive to attain that state where He and nature are independent, most fully active and yet perfectly stabilized with respect to one another. His effort, which involves an adjustment of His demands to our needs and which introduces into the universe as much goodness as it is ready to absorb, has its reciprocal in our effort to find a stable place in nature, and in reference to Him.

A good deal of the foregoing can be discarded while leaving a number of important consequences intact.

A true concern for God is a concern for a being who is a God of all there is. To recognize the intrinsic worth of men, animals, plants and inanimate things is a way of making oneself worthy of knowing and loving God.

A respect for the self-sufficiency of nature is a respect for the limits of God's responsibility. To recognize that nature goes its own way is to avoid the callousness of denying the existence of evil, the mistake of attributing its occurrence to God, or the folly of doing nothing about it.

A grasp of the nature of God's omniscience, omnipotence and providence is a grasp of the existence of goods, open to, but not yet possessed by us, or not yet resident in nature. To know God and His inclinations is to become prepared to battle for ideals never before realized.

An approach to the problems of religion, theology, philosophy and ethics in terms which have a direct relevance to science, makes it possible to avoid that radical pluralism in theoretical enterprises which drives these subjects into opposition and mutual denial. Science thereby becomes not merely the best instrument for the understanding of the details of nature, but the most effective means for attaining the good; philosophy supplements its speculations with an appreciation of the values involved in providence; theology frees itself from the arbitrary restrictions of the classical tradition, adjusting itself to the truths of science and the dynamics of religious inquiry; while mysticism and ethics become related branches of a single whole.

It is some such view as this which I take to express the essence of democracy. Democracy, as I see it, is expressed in a double faith—the scientific faith in the existence of an independent, self-contained world of valuable things where a man comes to be, acts and dies without aid from without, and a religious faith in the existence of a God who is forever on the side of the right. A democrat, whether he belongs to a church or not, is a religious man. His God is not altogether accurately portrayed in the extant religions, which after all blossomed in and sustained another day. His God is not a finite God, not a God of miracles, of angry passion, of dogmatic commands and demands, or a God of indifferent and bloodless perfection. He is a God who cannot alone make the good prevail on earth.

His God is troubled and concerned, not merely for one man—Messiah or saint, for one race, Jew or Christian, or even for the whole of mankind, but for whatever is good in this world of ours.

The democrat recognizes no privileged classes and makes no distinction between men on the basis of position, race, creed, money or color, for he judges all in religious, not social terms. He views men as characters, as moral agents who vary in the degree of their longing, and who in different degrees, therefore, make possible an unlimited community of free and happy men in a perfected world.

The democrat is seared with the Hebraic sense of the full tragedy of existence and sustained by the Christian's confidence in the power of love as he struggles together with his fellows to mould a community where all men are and can continue to be human. Science and sympathy are his means; God and the good his guide.

[Sec. 447, Paul Weiss, "God and the World," in *Science, Philosophy and Religion: A Symposium* (New York: Conference on Science, Philosophy and Religion in Their Relation to the Democratic Way of Life, Inc., 1941), I, 412–13. Sec. 448, *ibid.,* pp. 413–16. Sec. 449, *ibid.,* pp. 416–18. Sec. 450, *ibid.,* pp. 418–22. Sec. 451, *ibid.,* pp. 422–26. Sec. 452, *ibid.,* pp. 426–27. Sec. 453, *ibid.,* pp. 427–29. Sec. 454, *ibid.,* pp. 429–31. Sec. 455, *ibid.,* p. 431. Sec. 456, *ibid.,* pp. 431–32. Sec. 457, *ibid.,* pp. 432–36.]

## COMMENT

Though Professor Weiss often seems to lean toward classical theism, certain of his statements appear rather extreme in a contrary sense, some pointing toward classical pantheism, some toward limited panentheism (see below, chap. viii). Thus he says, on the one hand, that God is not finite, that he cannot contain anything which is evil, apparently not even suffering, that he is "in no way dependent on things." On the other hand, things are also independent of God, who "needs" them, who reflects occurrences in and interacts with nature, to which he must strive to "adjust" himself. Such language would, to a classical theist, mean that God was in very truth finite, imperfect, dependent, limited in power and excellence. And we find such expressions as that the "eternal essence" of God becomes adjusted to the changes in the world.

Our total impression is that the author has the essential dipolar insights (the second and third paragraphs of the admirable "Conclusion" are especially indicative of this) but that he cannot resist the fascination of bits of traditional monopolar rhetoric and that, in general, he chooses to let his statements limit each other rather than to put into each statement, so far as possible, the dipolar tension which would allow for the contrasting aspect without contradiction. Thus there ought, it seems, to be a plain statement of the difference between the eternal and absolute essence of deity and that in deity which is not simply eternal and absolute and essential but temporal and relative and accidental, though with a richness of temporal novelty and contingent relativity unparalleled in ordinary cases of change and dependence. It may be that Weiss really holds that everything in God is absolute and necessary and essential. But will he be able to make us understand how this can be while his other assertions are allowed to stand?

It is noteworthy that our author thinks it a valid Jewish insight, shared in some measure by Christianity, that God is a troubled anxious being. This seems to mean that there is in some sense such a thing as divine suffering. And yet this our author denies. And one may add that neither Jews nor Christians have been very clear or consistent in this direction but that the Cross is, potentially at least, a superlative symbol of what is involved.

That the arguments for God must start from a rich base of spiritual insight if they are to reach the spiritual richness of God is undeniable. The author's proof does this to some extent. But all the proofs can do it, in so far as we illustrate the meaning of the categories employed by examples from spiritual experiences, as we well may. The whole of experience is always relevant to philosophical questions. Weiss's proof stresses the experience of self-identity in change, involving memory as essential. But any philosophical discussion of change should stress these things also. For self-identity and memory are the initial, clear-cut experiential examples we have to work with of enduring individuality and relation of present to past. To neglect them is to make it problematic what such concepts refer to.

In the world today there are few philosophers who, while not functioning as "theologians," can so vividly and eloquently and with such penetration expound a positive doctrine of theism.

# WATTS (1915——)

The writings of Alan Watts may be taken as furnishing evidence for the thesis propounded by William James (secs. 479–517) that appropriateness of feeling must be added to a disciplined intellect in order satisfactorily to resolve the problem of God's nature. Watts urges that the philosophies of feeling, those disciplines of the Orient which surpass our philosophies aesthetically quite to the extent that ours surpass their philosophies intellectually, can strengthen our conceptual constructions. The theological, philosophical, and aesthetic difficulties of both pantheistic monism and theistic dualism can be overcome, and the insights of the two views can be made consonant. He proposes to achieve this grand resolution through substituting a logic of identity-in-diversity for the Western logic of strict identity. In those philoso-phies whose proponents have cultivated feeling extensively, Watts finds that unity is affirmed without excluding diversity, freedom without excluding necessity, the identity of God and universe without accepting the pantheistic correlatives; further, mystic experience has at its center the joint assertion of unity with God and of the mystic's particular individuality. Unity in diversity, then—an aesthetic principle—should be utilized to gain both logical and aesthetic strength for traditional theistic views. The reader will recognize that Watts is drawing out of the resources of mystic experience and aesthetic feeling a dipolar concept of deity in which traditional oppositions are considered to be contrasting aspects of his nature. This author represents an approach through feeling which in a measure yields the conclusions agreed upon by the other members of this chapter.

## Dualism and Union with God

*458.* The human mind is profoundly dissatisfied with any form of absolute dualism, with a religion or a metaphysic for which ultimate Reality is not one and undivided. The dissatisfaction is not only felt with such crude dualisms as the Zoroastrian contrast of ultimate light and ultimate darkness, Ormuzd and Ahriman, or the Manichaean dualism of Spirit and Matter; as we have seen, it is even felt with the monotheistic "dualism" of Creator and creature *ex nihilo.* On the other hand, reason and the moral sense rebel at pantheistic monism which must reduce all things to a flat uniformity and assert that even the most diabolical things are precisely God, thus destroying all values.

*459.* On the whole, traditional theology has leaned principally to the theology of transcendence, of God's holiness and otherness. After the Renaissance, to meet the rise of Humanism, it combined the stress on transcendence with an increased emphasis on the personality of God as this was revealed in the divine humanity of Jesus. Theology and spirituality became more and more Christocentric, and at the same time quite alien to the traditions of Christian mysticism! Contemplation, as understood by the mediaeval mystics, was replaced by affective and imaginative devotion to the humanity of Jesus. From the standpoint of mysticism this was a disaster based on a misunderstanding of the Incarnation, for it made the divine humanity transcendent and humanized the mystery of God. It frustrated the very purpose of the Incarnation because, in practice, it did not raise humanity to union with God; it raised only the historic Jesus. . . .

Mediaeval mysticism as we find it in the *Cloud of Unknowing,* in Eckhart, Tauler, the Victorines, Ruysbroeck, and even as late as Denis the Carthusian, St. John of the Cross and Augustine Baker is little concerned with devotions to the humanity of Jesus. Yet the intensity and intimacy of the union with God which it experiences can only be justified in a Christian context by the doctrine of the Incarnation. For, in the words of St. Athanasius, "God became man that man might become God." . . .

When, however, theology tries to achieve a compromise between immanence and transcendence, both are deprived of their effect. God is not quite immanent and not quite transcendent; the world conceals his omnipresent Being like a veil; he is "in" all things, but not thoroughly united with them, just as water is not fully united with the jar which contains it because the substance of the water and the substance of the jar are mutually exclusive. In this sense God and the world are simply mixed. They may even interpenetrate to some degree like air and dust, but still they are mutually exclusive. But if God and the world are mutually exclusive, God does not actually transcend the world, because mutually exclusive entities must belong to the same order of being. For example, different shapes are mutually exclusive, and although a square can be put inside a circle, it cannot be fully united with it. A square can in no sense *be* a circle. But color is wholly other than shape, and there is no mutual exclusiveness between a circle and redness. Color can no more be described in terms of shape than God can be described in terms of created things. Yet although the color red is quite other than the shape circle, there is a sense in which a circle can *be* red.

*460.* For practical purposes mystical religion has always tended to insist that man and the world must be utterly united with God, must in some sense *be* God.

*461.* Upon the certainty of this union with God depends the entire joy, power, and world-transfiguring character of the mystical experience. Here, too, is the source of the mystic's vivid sense of spiritual freedom: he is one with God, and "neither height nor depth, neither principalities nor powers" can break this union. The mystic knows that he has it in spite of himself; that it is God's gift, and that it is given quite irrespective of his merits.

*462.* The attractive feature of pantheism is just that it imparts this sense of certain and unbreakable union with God. But its danger and falsity is that it excludes any basis for worship and gratitude, for in pantheism union with God is an automatic necessity; it is not a gift. On the other hand, the extreme of transcendental theism reduces the divine gift to mere "justification"—that is, the chance for a new start after the remission of past sins—coupled with the "grace" to imitate the divine life more perfectly.

*463.* This extreme immanentism or quasi-pantheism of the mystics only becomes a problem when we try to consider the mystical experience from the strictly logical standpoint of theology. In practice the mystic does not find any conflict in his experience of God; nor, save in comparatively rare instances, does his sense of being one with God destroy his sense of values. This remains true even when mysticism is related to such an extremely immanentist theology as Hindu Vedanta or Mohammedan Sufiism. He may say to himself with the *Upanishads,* "Thou art Brahman!" but he does not then proceed to claim omnipotence and omiscience. . . . the moral blindness which most theologians attribute to the pantheist is largely theoretical. It might well arise if the pantheist were not a mystic; but a mystical pantheist is scarcely ever a consistent and logical pantheist, because he is trying to describe a relationship to God which is not in fact pantheism although it seems to be when he uses theological terms.

## God and Nonduality

*464.* Unless, therefore, we can find some terms other than pantheistic monism or theistic dualism there can be no vital relationship between mysticism and Christian theology. The highly desirable goal of a presentation of Christian doctrine interpreted by mystical religion will be impossible.

*465.* Language and intellectual thought . . . can never so embrace and describe the mystical experience that it may be communicated from one soul to another by mere words and ideas. But theology can adopt a principle of thought which will in great measure resolve the antinomy of transcendence and immanence, monism and dualism, without resort to compromise.

*466.* The root of the difficulty is that Western theology and philosophy, grounded as it is in Greek thought, has an inadequate conception of the unity of God. Our logic, our method of reasoning, is entirely dualistic, and therefore cannot without contradictions treat of a Being who surpasses duality. The unity of God is therefore seen as *opposed* to multiplicity in God. God has no opposite, and yet we apply to him the term unity in a sense which has an opposite, for unity as we conceive it is unthinkable without the contrast of multiplicity. But we find in Indian thought a method which surpasses dualism in so far as the intellect is capable of so doing. This method is developed in Sankara's *Advaita Vedanta* and in Mahayana Buddhism.

Neither of these two systems carry the method to a conclusion which would satisfy the Christian, because they are working with basic material (i.e., revelation) which he would deem inadequate. But this need not concern us, for what is important is the method itself, and not the use which Vedantists and Buddhists have made of it. To some extent the quest of Vedanta is the same as that of Christianity, namely, the transcending of dualism, the realization of union with God. Both are agreed that God is the one supreme Reality, and that no second reality stands over against him on an equal footing, imposing any limitation upon him. God has no opposite. This is a sufficient basis of agreement for the Indian method to have relevance for Christianity. . . .

God is That which has no opposite; he is One-without-a-second. All created things have opposites whereby they are conditioned and limited; all creatures are of a mutually exclusive character in their relations to each other, for *this* is not *that*, I am not *thou*, *light* is not *darkness*, *red* is not *blue*. But God transcends creatures in the sense that nothing has power to exclude him, to set any boundaries to his being and power. He is absolutely free of every external restraint. In a peculiar and profound sense God is all-inclusive; there is nothing "outside" him, for had he any "outside" he would have limitations and would not be infinite. It may be shown, then, that God has a power which no creature, as such, possesses—the power to be what he is not, to "other" himself.

If this can be shown, it will, on the one hand, entirely fulfill the mystic's intuition that God is "all in all" and that the universe is one with him. On the other hand, it will also account for the other aspect of his intuition, which is that individual things are not lost and obliterated in the unity of God but transfigured, seen as more perfectly and uniquely themselves. For if the unity of God is truly all-inclusive and non-dual, it must include diversity and distinction as well as one-ness; otherwise the principle of diversity would stand over against God as something opposite to and outside him. This inclusion of

diversity is impossible for the God of pantheism, who cannot comprehend *real* diversity. The universe of the pantheist is *un*real.

Thus the logic of non-duality makes short work of pantheism. If all things are in reality one thing, God, such one-ness is exclusive, dual and limited, because it excludes real multiplicity. . . .

On the other hand, the statement that all things are *not* God is, by itself, as dualistic as the statement that they are God. The God so conceived still fails to transcend the creaturely realm of duality. Orthodox theology, and especially theology in the tradition of St. Thomas, failed to see that God could include and even be many as well as one, *because it regarded multiplicity and diversity as a privation and not a perfection of being*. It saw diversity as the subjection of unity to division and disintegration. Particular things—men, trees, stones and stars—were particular just because they *lacked* the fullness of being, and expressed only a fragment of the divine Being. But this was a wholly negative idea of particularity. It did not realize that particularity was a great and positive good, that God's expression of himself in particular things neither added to his being nor disintegrated it. It expressed the splendor of the divine unity in the splendor of variety, which, as the proverb says, is the spice of life. But the Neo-Platonic background of mediaeval thought, tinged as it was with Manichaeism, held a prejudice against variety and multiplicity. It was the old story of world-hatred, so inconsistent with the religion of the Incarnation.

Thus God's "othering" of himself in the creation is not, as in pantheism, a *maya*, an illusion. The multiplicity is as real as the unity, since the creature is one with God in the very act of being other than God. Thus we must change the meaning of the statement that God made the world out of nothing, and understand the nothing as the no-thing (*sunyata*), the unutterable mystery, the divine darkness, which is God himself as he appears to human sense and thought and feeling. . . . God as he is absolutely in himself, beyond all duality —neither one nor many, nor both one and many, and yet with equal reality one and many, and both one and many. Human speech cannot surpass its own inherent duality!

The attempt to conceive a Being beyond all duality swiftly brings thought to the limits of its power and reduces philosophy and theology to silence before the mystery of God. But it does leave us with some positive concepts, as true as any idea of God, any formulation of the infinite, can be.

Firstly, it lays greater stress than ever upon the divine *freedom*. For every form of pantheism God's manifestation of himself in the universe is necessary, because the universe, if simply identical with God, must be as eternal as God. But to say that God is non-dual is another way of saying that he is free— absolutely. He is free to be One, not bound to be One. He is free to include diversity in his unity, free to "other" himself. This "othering" of himself is the free gift of his Being to creatures who otherwise might not have existed. . . . Thus non-duality means that God is entirely free from the essential limitation of finite existence, which is that a creature cannot at once be itself and another. More than ever, the creature may thank God for the free gift of life and being, not only because it might not have been given, but also because the gift is God.

Secondly, the idea of God's non-duality is a new way of understanding his *love*. For love is not simply, as St. Thomas suggests, the willing of another's good; it is giving oneself entirely to another being. . . . Thus a creature fulfills God's love and will for itself not by being, or trying to be, God—but by being itself.

*467.* This corrects one of the most usual perversions of mysticism—the attempt to become one with God by mere flight from everyday life and experience. It is a perversion because it is a half truth. Certainly mysticism begins with the contemplation of God as transcendent. Because God is the maker of all sensible and intelligible things, he himself can neither be sensed nor known. As transcendent, he can never be an object of experience or knowledge, and, conversely, no particular experience or state of mind can be the immediate knowledge of God. For all experiences and states of mind belong to the realm of duality, and are mutually exclusive. Thus the mystical experience is neither a particular state of mind nor (for this, too, has an opposite) mere blankness of mind. Like the mirror which reflects all images yet is not itself an image, the mystical experience underlies and is one with all experience, as is God himself.

*468.* The state of union, like God himself, has no opposite; it is all-inclusive, for which reason any experience may participate in it.

Therefore we discover the union of ourselves and of the creation with God through the very realization that they are themselves and not God. His very transcendence effects his perfect immanence, for "he ascended up far above all heavens, that he might fill all things." The distinct, individual reality of things is the very measure of their union with God, of their fulfillment and expression of his freedom to include diversity, to love and be what is other than himself. . . .

Any view which stresses the unity of the universe with God will in some quarters be termed pantheistic, and any formal denial of pantheism will be called "merely verbal." But, strictly speaking, pantheism is the very definite doctrine that God and the universe are coterminous; that God is solely immanent, and that God minus the universe equals nothing. Such a doctrine is not only inconsistent with Christian dogma, but also with the theology of the Vedanta and Mahayana Buddhism, all of which insist that the ultimate Reality is infinite, free from all necessity and limitation, and that its existence would in no way be affected by the dissolution of the universe.

*469.* Since by definition the infinite cannot be subject to any constraint, the existence as well as the union of finite beings with it must be entirely gratuitous. Thus the essential distinction between the doctrines of non-duality and pantheism is that the former, conceiving God as infinite, regards his union with the universe as a free act of grace, whereas the latter, conceiving him to be no more than a universe of finite and composite beings, regards it as necessary.

### Aesthetic Aspects of the Idea of God

*470.* Western man has attained a far greater degree of culture and discipline in his thinking than in his feeling—so much so that the idea of evaluating religion from an aesthetic as well as from an intellectual standpoint seems to him quite frivolous. He considers the beauty or ugliness of religious symbols and concepts quite irrelevant to their truth, and, of course, it is truth which matters. Yet however much their truth may matter, their power lies more than we care to admit in their effect upon our feelings. Mature and disciplined feelings have as much right to evaluate the worth of a religion as the intellect, since they reflect upon an aspect of reality which is hidden from pure thought—a fact almost incomprehensible to the overdeveloped intellectualism of Western philosophy. But if our feeling were as highly developed an instrument as our intellect, the acceptance of certain ideas would depend both upon their being thought true and felt true. Only because of the disproportionate growth of our thinking do we consider it a more reliable judge of spiritual values than feeling, which, for us, is as unreliable as primitive man's intellect. Our feelings mislead us just as the primitive's thinking misleads him—simply because it has never been developed. There is no inherent deficiency in the faculty itself.

It is otherwise with a people such as the Chinese. From our standpoint their strictly intellectual development leaves much to be desired, for we find their philosophical reasoning, for instance, lacking in coherence. But in feeling and aesthetic judgment they are so far beyond us that we cannot really translate much of their philosophic literature into any occidental language. They have, for example, more than a hundred words expressing nuances of aesthetic experience for which we have absolutely no equivalents. While we may regard this as a decadent overrefinement of culture, we must not forget that our own high degree of intellectual subtlety could give them a similar impression. But the Chinese "aesthete" is not at all decadent, for he has what the occidental aesthete usually lacks—strength of character and amazing emotional control. He is a philosopher of feeling as distinct from a philosopher of thinking. . . . His standards of judgment are aesthetic rather than intellectual. This has seldom been taken into account in presenting the Christian religion to the Chinese. The best minds of China find it unconvincing and repellent because of an entirely unnecessary ugliness which we have had neither the wisdom nor the imagination to avoid.

*471.* In the last thousand years Western man has undergone a development which has made certain primitive notions of God unacceptable to him. Christian thought has kept pace with this development, constantly deepening and purifying the intellectual conception of God so that no one is asked to think of him as an old man with a white beard sitting upon a cloud-borne throne among the stars. But so far from there having been any parallel deepening of our aesthetic conception, most theologians consider such sensitivity to the beauty of an idea a sign of a womanish softening of the brain, thinking that when confronted with a logically sound truth the duty of the feelings is simply to "take it," as if there were some salutary medicine in the very pain of the feelings. This attitude denies the divine intention of the union of the *whole* man with God, wherein man contemplates him perfectly with *all* the faculties of the soul. Those, therefore, who neglect the aesthetic contemplation of God are remaining insensitive to him, and even at discord with him, in an important part of their souls.

There is a reciprocal relation between the aesthetic image of God and the response of our feelings towards him. And since, whether we like it or not, the quality of feeling dictates the whole atmosphere of piety, generations of immature feeling build up a collective image which, although it has many slight variations, permeates Christian piety as a crude perfume will linger in the draperies of a house. . . .

The spell of this bad atmosphere is tremendous and, to a great degree, unconscious. Undeveloped as our feelings are, they are none the less powerful, and in practice they mold our religion to a far greater degree than our thinking. Saturated in this atmosphere, otherwise mature souls are retarded in their growth and remain content with a piety which, lacking the genuine naïveté and unaffected simplicity of the child, has rather the bad infantilism and maudlin emotionalism of prolonged adolescence.

This problem is particularly acute for Christianity because it knows God as a person and not as a principle. A person,

a living being, affects the feelings much more violently than an impersonal Absolute. In Christianity the personality of God is more strongly emphasized even than in Judaism and Mohammedanism because of its central belief that the highest symbol of God is the human character of Jesus. Intellectually, we know that while God is a person he is not a man, or even an infinitely glorified, cosmically proportioned superman. He transcends entirely the hierarchy of created forms and natures. But this lofty intellectual discernment of God, having no parallel in the realm of feeling, has little effect upon piety, which still responds to God as to a man, often as crude in conception as vast in proportion.

Our collective image of God is frequently inferior to accepted human standards of perfection. Such inferiority would be understandable if it were caused by unavoidable limitations of vision. But the limitations of our image of God are by no means unavoidable. There is no reason at all why we should not recognize in God the beauty which we perceive in nature and create in art. . . .

## Masculine and Feminine Traits in God

472. Despite the fact that while God is living he is not a man, and that while he is called "he" (for "it" would indicate something lifeless), God has no sex, the image of God which determines so great a part of our relations with him is that of an immeasurably great man and of a male. This is true not only of popular notions of God, but also of that important type of Catholic mysticism in which the soul plays the female role of the Beloved, while God the Lover is the male who "ravishes" the soul. For the history of the Christian idea of God begins in the patriarchal culture of the Hebrews where the supremacy of the male was unquestioned. Yahweh was the King of kings

and Lord of lords, titles of those oriental tyrants of whom he became the heightened image.

Philosophically, we do not think of God as having the peculiar personal characteristics of a tribal patriarch, nor yet of an oriental despot of uncertain temper and undoubted power, whose every whim is law and before whom all must grovel in the dust. Even when this awesome creature is endowed with a sense of perfect justice and mercy, he does not fit our philosophic conception, because he is still very much of a man—ridiculous in that he takes himself too seriously. Nearer to our intellectual idea of God is the type of emperor envisaged by Lao-tzu, who advised the would-be ruler to be like the Tao, governing his subjects without letting them know that they were being governed.

473. In our spiritual tradition this sublime idea of the greatness of God consisting in his humility appears first in Deutero-Isaiah's conception of the "suffering Servant," and finds its highest expression in the humility of Christ, for "whosoever will be chief among you, let him be your servant."

But in our working image of God the masculine element of the oriental tyrant and the "feminine" element of the mysterious and self-effacing servant of the universe have not been quite happily combined. However incomplete and crude it may be, there is something gloriously robust and splendid in the figure of the wise and all-merciful King of kings, enthroned on high in infinite majesty, whose gaze is so terrible that none may look upon it and live. This conception lives on in the Mohammedan picture of Allah, and, for all its limitations, is aesthetically sound.

The problem is to synthesize the feminine qualities of cherishing love, self-effacement, compassion and graciousness with a figure so positively and aggressively male, and to achieve a result which is not mere effeminate masculinity, a "wishy-washy" compromise. With this symbolically feminine element go also the qualities of beauty and playfulness, which have, as we have seen, to be included in an image of God almost exclusively righteous and purposeful. Lacking the feminine element this righteousness is stiff and solemn, and incompatible with all forms of beauty excepting the sculptural and architectural. Purely masculine righteousness is rigidity and tension, unbending self-control and fixity of principle. Here, projected upon God, is all that fear and distrust of suppleness and charm which man on the defensive associates with "women's wiles."

474. The root of the matter is this: that an image of God in which the rigid qualities predominate, which excludes the beautiful, the fluid, the playful and the feminine, simply mirrors that fear of life and Reality which we saw as the chief obstacle to our realization of union with God. The rigid, male God embodies the ideal of the possessive will—to grasp and hold the mystery of life, to freeze the desired form of the living moment into an eternal and immobile possession. And so frozen, the thing is quite dead. The moment, the movement, the life has passed on and gone free. The feminine element is lacking in our image of God because we fear it in life as the beauty which burns our fingers when we try to hold it. . . . Here is the origin of all the Manichaean and Gnostic horror of the earth and of woman which has so infected the Christian Church.

This fear, too, was responsible for involving our theology so deeply with Neo-Platonic and Aristotelian conceptions of the divine nature as the impassive and unmoving One, as if the suppleness of movement implied some imperfection, perfection being identified with the finished, the complete and the symmetrical, which is again the dead. Bound up with this particular idea of perfection, theology has never been able to explain how or why this inert Unity should have produced such an active multiplicity as the created universe. . . .

With all his robust masculinity, the God of the Hebrews is a long way from this frozen rigidity. He is the embodiment of *true* manliness, however crudely conceived, because his nature contains a subordinate feminine element, for he is above all a creative artist, and the great symbol of his presence is not rock but fire—the burning bush of Horeb. Passage after passage in the Old Testamant dwells on his delight in beauty, for there is not a trace of Manichaeism in the Hebrew religion. The woman is subordinate, but not despised. But for those who conceived God as the impassive, primal Unity, the creation was always problematic; the process whereby the One produced the many amounted to a "progressive disintegration" through a hierarchy of intermediary principles or aeons, the number of which was multiplied in proportion to the horror in which the physical world was held. But this device solved and explained nothing. . . . With a similar view of the divine Unity, Christian theology has, as we have seen, been unable to bridge the gulf between the Creator and creation. . . .

But the living God of the Hebrews is an infinity of inexhaustible life and being—not a mathematical and abstract infinity—and, as the mythos makes plain, he transcends the dualism of activity and rest. The merely one God, in the Greek sense of unity, is *bound* to rest, but the non-dual God is free both to rest and to move, for he worked for six days and rested the seventh. Thus there is nothing in the *truly* Biblical image of God hostile to the feminine principle . . . but when, in Christianity, this God was explained according to Neo-Platonic and Aristotelian princi-

ples, the feminine was wholly abstracted and the remaining masculinity became rigid and dead. For man is not truly man without woman.

*475.* What has been said about the absence of beauty and the feminine element from religion applies largely to Protestantism. Popular Catholicism, the religion of the less inhibited Latin peoples, has found a workable though at root unsatisfactory solution—the virtual deification of the Virgin Mary. We Christians know, in theory, that God has these symbolically feminine attributes of love, compassion, mercy, and beauty, but it has been hard for us to reconcile them with the image of the King of kings. Thus the demand of the heart for God as Mother as well as Father found an answer, adequate enough for the childlike mediaeval soul, in the gracious figure of the Queen of Heaven, although it meant, in practice, that the Holy Trinity became the Holy Quaternity. . . . Adam of St. Victor, her twelfth-century laureate, could hardly find enough divine attributes wherewith to adorn this "Mediatrix of all graces." She was the "Temple of Eternity," the "Ruler of the Angels," the "Empress of the Highest."

*476.* Whatever they may have meant to theologians, there can be no doubt as to the popular significance of such terms as Mother of God, Queen of Heaven, Mistress of the Angels, or of the hymnody which praised her as the "glorious Lady throned in rest amidst the starry host above," and as "she that riseth up as the morning, fair as the moon, clear as the sun." Mary, rather than Jesus, was the image where mediaeval man (as well as the simple Catholic of today) understood the love and beauty of God, the fertility and creative power of the divine nature. . . .

To her the most depraved sinner could pour out his heart in the certainty that he would be accepted in a loving embrace as infinite and all-inclusive as the sky that was symbolized by her star-decked robe of blue. . . .

Mary, we hail thee, Mother and Queen compassionate; Mary, our comfort, life, and hope, we hail thee. . . . To thee we are sighing as mournful and weeping we pass through this vale of sorrow. Turn thou, therefore, O our intercessor, those thine eyes of pity and loving-kindness upon us sinners [Final Antiphons, 4. Trinity Sunday to Advent].

In Mary, the Queen of Heaven, this tenderness is entirely beautiful, but thus far our attempts to mix it in with the image of the King of kings have been quite disastrous. . . . When we try to combine righteousness and love in one symbol the result is often that most unedifying type of moral tyrant who enforces his tyranny by constant harping on how much his children's misbehavior "wounds his love" for them, and administers judgment with the "this hurts me more than it's going to hurt you" line. We allow in God what we deplore in parents and teachers.

Our picture of Jesus has fared no better. With all the love and graciousness of God concentrated in the symbol of the Virgin, the mediaeval Christ was the Christus Victor—robed in glory, stately, austere, hardly human. But this conception was in fact Monophysite; the humanity was lost in the divinity, and after the rise of Humanism both the Catholic and the Protestant conceptions of Jesus attempted to realize his humanity—the former in order to counteract the false man-worship of Humanism, the latter in an effort to discover the Jesus of the Bible and of history. Yet the result was compromise. The humanity of the human and the divinity of the divine became muddled and clouded, as did likewise the two elements of justice and mercy, masculine strength and feminine grace. This compromise is the hermaphroditic Christ of popular Church art . . . solemn, effeminate, sanctimonious, moral-izing, ethereal, neither red-bloodedly human nor majestically divine.

*477.* All that we have managed to assimilate to our image of God and of his Christ is the tenderness of the feminine, but none of the beauty, the vitality or the allure.

*478.* Whoever is troubled by the present images . . . must go to that mystical center which is beyond all ordinary forms of symbolism, and there touch the Life which will, in due time, express itself in a nobler image of God and enable him to see a more splendid Christ in the pages of the Gospels.

[Sec. 458, Alan W. Watts, *Behold the Spirit: A Study in the Necessity of Mystical Religion* (New York: Pantheon Books, Inc., 1947), p. 132. Sec. 459, *ibid.*, pp. 133–35. Sec. 460, *ibid.*, p. 136. Sec. 461, *ibid.*, p. 137. Sec. 462, *ibid.* Sec. 463, *ibid.*, p. 139. Sec. 464, *ibid.*, p. 141. Sec. 465, *ibid.* Sec. 466, *ibid.*, pp. 141–46. Sec. 467, *ibid.*, pp. 146–47. Sec. 468, *ibid.*, pp. 147–48. Sec. 469, *ibid.*, pp. 148–49. Sec. 470, *ibid.*, pp. 158–59. Sec. 471, *ibid.*, pp. 160–61. Sec. 472, *ibid.*, pp. 162–63. Sec. 473, *ibid.*, pp. 164–65. Sec. 474, *ibid.*, pp. 165–67. Sec. 475, *ibid.*, pp. 168–69. Sec. 476, *ibid.*, pp. 170–72. Sec. 477, *ibid.*, p. 172. Sec. 478, *ibid.*, p. 173.]

## COMMENTS

That the literature of the Orient largely supports the grand conception elaborated by our author does not seem to us so clearly the case as it seems to him. The thesis, if substantiated, would be very welcome; and we have argued that in the *Upanishads* and *Vedantas* some support is to be found, as also in such individuals as Ramanuja and Radhakrishnan. To be sure, the pantheism which seemed present in much Eastern literature is not quite our Western variety; and, as we have stated, the issue in the East is between pantheism and panentheism; we are not aware that the issue has yet been resolved. However this may be, when one pays attention to Watts' principles rather than to their historical application, one becomes aware of the greater strength of his argument. If one believes that truth is attainable and that every datum can contribute to that truth, then from different bodies of data the same truth could be approached; this seems to mean that the concepts adequate within a given field of inquiry should exhibit possibilities of organic unity with the adequate concepts of any other field. That logic and aesthetics, the studies of thought and feeling, should employ similar principles is but a corollary of the foregoing. Consequently, the logically appropriate concepts and those aesthetically appropriate should not be, as Watts says they are not, in opposition. In its broadest application the above consequence would seem to require dipolarity within general conceptions; we think the requirement is present.

When Watts contends that a certain dipolarity of structure is needed for a conception of God sensitive to aesthetic concerns, the contention has some claim upon our logic. The close parallel between Watt's view derived from feeling and the panentheist view largely derived from a search for logical consistency tends to confirm them both.

It would little serve our purpose to comment upon the involved question of adequate religious symbolism with its masculine-feminine opposition which our author introduces in these pages; but the oppositions of freedom and necessity, transcendence and immanence, identity and difference, dualism and monism, unity and multiplicity, and the search for an all-inclusiveness which is not pantheistic, are quite to our purpose. Watts avers that oppositions should be included within the divine being rather than taken as contrasts between God and something extrinsic. It is our contention that the system of Whiteheadian metaphysics has the capacity to explain such oppositions within a single coherent scheme through differentiating concrete and abstract modes and that the concrete and abstract modes of the divine being represent the final explanation of inclusiveness without contradiction or external opposition. The emphasis Watts puts upon multiplicity as a perfection, not a privation, of being fixes his position outside that of classical theism; his emphasis upon the unity and freedom of God places him outside pantheism. So it seems to us that the conceptual correlate of the more adequate religious structure which Watts was seeking through an appraisal of mystic and religious experience is panentheism.

# Chapter VIII: *Limited Panentheism*

## JAMES (1842–1910)

Great as has been the influence of William James upon American philosophy, it may be questioned whether the full magnitude of his contribution not alone to American but to world thought has yet been appreciated. James was a great student of psychology as well as of philosophy, he was a literary genius, and he knew the world of men and of culture. Besides all that—and here he reminds us of Emanual Kant—he was a great man and not just a great intellect. Every atom of his being was devoted to search for the truth and promotion of the good. Unlike Kant, however, he was a man trained from his earliest youth to think for himself, from the outset sophisticated with regard to the diversity of doctrines and cultures, educated in various countries, son of a father who was himself an original thinker, and, something even rarer, one who wished his sons to be original in their own right and not mere copies of himself. And James had, what Kant also possessed in high degree, intellectual courage, which did not stop to ask. "Who will smile or rant over this truth I believe I have discovered?" but only sought to express the discovery as clearly and accurately as he could. What, then, was the upshot of all these rare qualities?

We suggest that William James, more than any other who has yet lived (unless we except Plato), was the psychologist of the philosophical mind, the great exponent of the "psychology of philosophers." He saw as few do, and expressed as none has, the basic drives, motivations, and human attributes and values that underlie or are at stake in the competing doctrines. But instead of deriving from this insight into motivations a futile relativism, according to which systems express merely the eccentricities of their originators, he saw that what a man's temperament enables him to see may actually be there and that what his temperament prevents him from seeing may also be there—in short, he did not forget that the influence of temperament upon doctrines is entirely compatible with the objectivity of truth itself. His pragmatism and will to believe, so far from being a flight into subjectivism, were really, certain excesses apart, a resolute and not by any means wholly unsuccessful effort to escape subjectivism.

There are two ways of trying to reconcile a sophisticated awareness of the origins of philosophical prejudice with faith in the possibility of arriving at universally valid truth. One is to attempt to denude one's self of (or render mild and harmless) all the emotions, desires, and aspirations which might deflect the course of pure intellectual curiosity. This is the way of intellectual puritanism, which issues in doctrines usually called "positivistic." This method works rather well in physics and mathematics, the objects of which really have no obvious relevance to emotions and aspirations. The other way is to strive toward a balance of all healthy emotions and all valid purposes, that is, toward as complete an emotional and practical nature as possible. Abundance and integration, not ascetic purification, of the sources of prejudice is here the aim. James plumped with all his energy for this second method. His theories about the relation of knowledge to action and emotion embody in technical form this basic decision. The world ultimately has to be for us what our whole nature is capable of recognizing. Doctrines indeed are thought, but they are also felt and enacted in living. The total meaning of a doctrine is this total role of it in our lives. And, since meaning is prior to truth, the truth we seek is the appropriateness of a doctrine to its total role. No philosophy is to be taken altogether seriously unless it can be lived out in the whole of our behavior, ultimately in the whole life of humanity through the generations. Here James and Albert Schweitzer are at one. But James is really less narrowly pragmatic than the European. For he does not demand such a radical renunciation of intellectual understanding with respect to the highest religious truths as Schweitzer seems to feel is obligatory. In *A Pluralistic Universe* especially, James wrestles valiantly with the metaphysical problems of God, man, and the universe and feels that he has achieved a measure of success in this endeavor.

What is his solution, so far as it goes —for James never pretends to have achieved complete and definitive results? James has the wit to see, what many overlook, that the primary problem is psychological rather than merely physical or even psychophysical. We start with the practically indubitable fact that we ourselves with our emotions, purposes, sensations, and thoughts exist. Now this means that a certain structure obtaining between psychological elements is constitutive of reality, whatever else may or may not be. There are various human selves related to one another and to their own states or experiences, total or partial. Let us call this given structure, using a word often employed by James as a fundamental philosophical category, "social." Reality is, whatever else it may be, a social structure. Now human society of course has a nonhuman environment. James never thought it worth while to question this, since all men live as though it

were so. Genuine doubt does not come in at that point. But doubt comes in as soon as we begin to characterize positively the nature of the nonhuman. It may be thought of as more or less remotely akin to the human, that is, another species of the genus, social structure, or not in the least thus akin or social. This is the issue between materialism (and the various forms of dualism and neutralism) and panpsychism. Materialism is always rejected when explicitly discussed by James, partly on the pragmatic ground that it says nothing to our emotional and aspirational nature and partly on the logical ground that it confuses the abstract and the concrete. The merely physical is not given to us as such but results from an abstraction from experiences which always, in their totality, contain emotions and purposes. James's point here is the same as that of Whitehead when the latter accuses materialism of the "fallacy of misplaced concreteness."

And yet, partly for pragmatic reasons and partly for reasons connected with his "radical empiricism," James did not commit himself to panpsychism, though it appealed to him. The extension of the social analogy to the lower levels of the subhuman did not appear pragmatically significant, and also he could not find a direct datum of experience upon which to base it. (Here his introspection may have been somewhat lacking in subtlety.)

The important question, to James, was whether or no there be something superhuman in our environment. That our nonhuman environment should be entirely subhuman was out of the question, pragmatically speaking. For the subhuman world is the morally neutral world, and if the cosmos, apart from man, is morally neutral, then man's moral aspirations—belonging, as they do, to a transitory creature ultimately helpless through himself alone to achieve universal and permanent values, yet as a thinking being able at any moment to raise the question of universality and permanence, and morally obligated to consider the long-run, universal good as decisive—are simple irrelevances, impertinences in the final perspective, while yet this perspective after all is our own humanly adopted one. Such a pretension to have achieved a perspective as men which nullifies our essential human nature seemed to James absurd, considering that the total meaning of human thought is a function of human living as· a whole.

Man's moral nature must either be treated as nothing in the final vision of things, or the cosmos itself must be viewed as other than morally neutral. But this means the cosmos must be viewed socially, for morality is social or nothing. A morally positive universe is one which stands over against us as a social other, making upon us demands or putting to us requests which we can in some measure fulfil, but demands or requests which are yet superhuman in their relevance to all the future, even beyond a possible or certain termination of human life itself, and in their ability to embrace the achievements of men everywhere in one significant Life. In short, we must come to the idea of God or to a theistic view of things.

But here James saw a great difficulty. The relation to God must, at least in some cases, be immediate or intuitive, not inferential or merely rational, for to James the testimony of the mystics, even when subjected to every pragmatic test, and with all due reservations, still sufficed to give cogent support to the notion of an immediate relation to deity. And, besides, how can the essential value of our lives lie in their contributions to a superhuman life, unless there is some direct contact of that life with ours? What "third term" could be worthy of mediating this contribution? For these and other reasons, James cannot be con-

tent with saying merely that God is a superhuman Other to our human selves. He is an other who is somehow one with us. How is that oneness to be conceived? The simplest way is to suppose that our and all experiences are parts of the divine experience, which is in this manner inclusive of all social reality, human or subhuman. This was the conception most current in philosophy at the time, as represented especiallly in the system of Royce.

But James saw difficulties in this view. These fell into two groups (which he does not always sharply contrast): the difficulties deriving from the mere idea of lower types of experience or social reality being included in higher types, or in James's phrase, the general idea of a "compounding of consciousness"; and the difficulties deriving from the extreme form of such supposed compounding according to which *all* experiences are parts of just *one* world-inclusive experience, that of God as omniscient. Now James, after many years of doubt tending toward sharp negation, comes to the conclusion that the first set of difficulties can be overcome, being due to a false "logical" or "intellectual" view of identity, while the second set cannot be overcome, so that, although God may indeed veritably include many of the lesser experiences, including our own, he cannot include absolutely all such experiences. He must, like other social beings, have an external as well as an internal environment. Otherwise, thinks James, he could not be a genuinely social or psychic being at all. So our conclusion is that God embraces us within his own conscious life, though not without residue.

A God genuinely inclusive of lesser individuals meets the religious requirement of our possible intimacy with deity and the moral requirement of the possibility of contributing to a life more permanent and universal than ours, without falling into the frustrations of pantheism, with its denial of the reality of temporal process and freedom of choice, in God or in man, or both. Thus a range of human interests is served to which more extreme doctrines cannot, it seems, do justice. It is another question whether James himself has not, at certain points, fallen into a one-sided extreme due, after all, to a temperamental bias of the very sort he is seeking to transcend. But the greatness of his discussion may be seen in the ease with which, as we shall show in our comment later, it is possible to enlarge the doctrine by appealing to his own criteria, somewhat more carefully applied at certain points.

## The Pragmatic Argument for God

*479.* For a philosophy to succeed on a universal scale it must define the future *congruously with our spontaneous powers.* A philosophy may be unimpeachable in other respects, but either of two defects will be fatal to its universal acceptance. First, its ultimate principle must not be one that essentially baffles and disappoints our dearest desires and most cherished powers. A pessimistic principle like Schopenhauer's incurably vicious Will-substance, or Hartmann's wicked jack-of-all-trades the Unconscious, will perpetually call forth essays at other philosophies. Incompatibility of the future with their desires and active tendencies is, in fact, to most men a source of more fixed disquietude than uncertainty itself. . . .

But a second and worse defect in a philosophy than that of contradicting our active propensities is to give them no object whatever to press against. A philosophy whose principle is so incommensurate with our most intimate powers as to deny them all relevancy in universal affairs . . . will be even more unpopular than pessimism. Better face the enemy than the eternal Void!

*480.* Small as we are, minute as is the point by which the cosmos impinges upon each one of us, each one desires to feel that his reaction at that point is congruous with the demands of the vast whole—that he balances the latter, so to speak, and is able to do what it expects of him.

*481.* Is the world a simple brute actuality, an existence *de facto* about which the deepest thing that can be said is that it happens so to be; or is the judgment of *better* or *worse,* of *ought,* as intimately pertinent as the simple judgment *is* or *is not?* The materialistic theorists say that judgments of worth are themselves mere matters of fact; that the words "good" and "bad" have no sense apart from subjective passions and interests which we may, if we please, play fast and loose with at will, so far as any duty of ours to the non-human universe is concerned. Thus, when a materialist says it is better for him to suffer great inconvenience than to break a promise, he only means that his social interests have become so knit up with keeping faith that, those interests once being granted, it *is* better for him to keep the promise in spite of everything. But the interests themselves are neither right nor wrong, except possibly with reference to some ulterior order of interests which themselves again are mere subjective data without character, either good or bad.

For the absolute moralists, on the contrary, the interests are not there merely to be felt—they are to be believed in and obeyed. Not only is it best for my social interests to keep my promise, but best for me to have those interests, and best for the cosmos to have this me. Like the old woman in the story who described the world as resting on a rock, and then explained that rock to be supported by another rock, and finally when pushed with questions said it was rocks all the way down—he who believes this to be a radically moral universe must hold the moral order to rest either on an absolute and ultimate *should*, or on a series of *shoulds* all the way down.

The practical difference between this objective sort of moralist and the other one is enormous. The subjectivist in morals, when his moral feelings are at war with the facts about him, is always free to seek harmony by toning down the sensitiveness of the feelings. Being mere data, neither good nor evil in themselves, he may pervert them or lull them to sleep by any means at his command. Truckling, compromise, time-serving, capitulations of conscience, are conventionally opprobrious names for what, if successfully carried out, would be on his principles by far the easiest and most praiseworthy mode of bringing about that harmony between inner and outer relations which is all that he means by good. The absolute moralist, on the other hand, when his interests clash with the world, is not free to gain harmony by sacrificing the ideal interests. According to him, these latter should be as they are and not otherwise. Resistance then, poverty, martyrdom if need be, tragedy in a word—such are the solemn feasts of his inward faith. Not that the contradiction between the two men occurs every day; in commonplace matters all moral schools agree. It is only in the lonely emergencies of life that our creed is tested: then routine maxims fail, and we fall back on our gods. It cannot then be said that the question, Is this a moral world? is a meaningless and unverifiable question because it deals with something non-phenomenal. Any question is full of meaning to which, as here, contrary answers lead to contrary behavior. And it seems as if in answering such a question as this we might proceed exactly as does the physical philosopher in testing an hypothesis. He deduces from the hypothesis an experimental action, *x;* this he adds to the facts $M$ already existing. It fits

them if the hypothesis be true; if not, there is discord. The results of this action corroborate or refute the idea from which it flowed. So here. . . . If this be an objectively moral universe, all acts that I make on that assumption, all expectations that I ground on it, will tend more and more completely to interdigitate with the phenomena already existing. $M + x$ will be in accord; and the more I live, and the more the fruits of my activity come to light, the more satisfactory the consensus will grow. While if it be not such a moral universe, and I mistakenly assume that it is, the course of experience will throw ever new impediments in the way of my belief, and become more and more difficult to express in its language. . . .

If, on the other hand, I rightly assume the universe to be not moral, in what does my verification consist? It is that by letting moral interests sit lightly, by disbelieving that there is any duty about *them* (since duty obtains only as *between* them and other phenomena), and so throwing them over if I find it hard to get them satisfied—it is that by refusing to take up a tragic attitude, I deal in the long run most satisfactorily with the facts of life. "All is vanity" is here the last word of wisdom. . . . While, on the other hand, he who contrary to reality stiffens himself in the notion that certain things absolutely should be, and rejects the truth that at bottom it makes no difference what is, will find himself evermore thwarted and perplexed and bemuddled by the facts of the world. . . .

*482.* For the sake of simplicity I have written as if the verification might occur in the life of a single philosopher—which is manifestly untrue, since the theories still face each other, and the facts of the world give countenance to both. Rather should we expect, that, in a question of this scope, the experience of the entire human race must make the verification, and that all the evidence will not be "in" till the final integration of things, when the last man has had his say and contributed his share to the still unfinished $x$. Then the proof will be complete; then it will appear without doubt whether the moralistic $x$ has filled up the gap which alone kept the $M$ of the world from forming an even and harmonious unity, or whether the non-moralistic $x$ has given the finishing touches which were alone needed to make the $M$ appear outwardly as vain as it inwardly was.

But if this be so, is it not clear that the facts $M$, taken *per se*, are inadequate to justify a conclusion either way in advance of my action? My action is the complement which, by proving congruous or not, reveals the latent nature of the mass to which it is applied. The world may in fact be likened unto a lock, whose inward nature, moral or unmoral, will never reveal itself to our simply expectant gaze. The positivists, forbidding us to make any assumptions regarding it, condemn us to eternal ignorance, for the "evidence" which they wait for can never come so long as we are passive. . . . If then the proof exist not till I have acted, and I must needs in acting run the risk of being wrong, how can the popular science professors be right in objurgating in me as infamous a "credulity" which the strict logic of the situation requires? If this really be a moral universe; if by my acts I be a factor of its destinies; if to believe where I may doubt be itself a moral act analogous to voting for a side not yet sure to win—by what right shall they close in upon me and steadily negate the deepest conceivable function of my being by their preposterous demand that I shall stir neither hand nor foot, but remain balancing myself in eternal and insoluble doubt? Why, doubt itself is a decision of the widest practical reach. . . . If I refuse to stop a murderer because I am in doubt whether it be not justifiable homicide,

I am virtually abetting the crime. If I refuse to bale out a boat because I am in doubt whether my efforts will keep her afloat, I am really helping to sink her.

*483.* Scepticism in moral matters is an active ally of immorality. Who is not for is against. The universe will have no neutrals in these questions. In theory as in practice, dodge or hedge, or talk as we like about a wise scepticism, we are really doing volunteer military service for one side or the other.

*484.* I confess that I do not see why the very existence of an invisible world may not in part depend on the personal response which any one of us may make to the religious appeal. God himself, in short, may draw vital strength and increase of very being from our fidelity. For my own part, I do not know what the sweat and blood and tragedy of this life may mean, if they mean anything short of this. If this life be not a real fight, in which something is eternally gained for the universe by success, it is no better than a game of private theatricals from which one may withdraw at will. But it *feels* like a real fight —as if there were something really wild in the universe which we, with all our idealities and faithfulnesses, are needed to redeem; and first of all to redeem our own hearts from atheisms and fears. For such a half-wild, half-saved universe our nature is adapted.

*God the Most Adequate Possible Object*

*485.* I . . . limit my ambition to showing that a God, whether existent or not, is at all events the kind of being which, if he did exist, would form *the most adequate possible object* for minds framed like our own to conceive as lying at the root of the universe. My thesis, in other words, is this: that *some* outward reality of a nature defined as God's nature must be defined, is the only ultimate object that is at the same time rational and possible for the human mind's contemplation. *Anything short of God is not rational, anything more than God is not possible. . . .*

Theism, whatever its objective warrant, would thus be seen to have a subjective anchorage in its congruity with our nature as thinkers; and, however it may fare with its truth, to derive from this subjective adequacy the strongest possible guaranty of its permanence. It is and will be the classic mean of rational opinion, the centre of gravity of all attempts to solve the riddle of life—some falling below it by defect, some flying above it by excess, itself alone satisfying every mental need in strictly normal measure.

486. We must not call any object of our loyalty a "God" without more ado, simply because to awaken our loyalty happens to be one of God's functions. He must have some intrinsic characteristics of his own besides; and theism must mean the faith of that man who believes that the object of *his* loyalty has those other attributes, negative or positive, as the case may be.

487. First, it is essential that God be conceived as the deepest power in the universe; and, second, he must be conceived under the form of a mental personality. The personality need not be determined intrinsically any further than is involved in the holding of certain things dear, and in the recognition of our dispositions toward those things, the things themselves being all good and righteous things. But, extrinsically considered, so to speak, God's personality is to be regarded, like any other personality, as something lying outside of my own and other than me, and whose existence I simply come upon and find. A power not ourselves, then, which not only makes for righteousness, but means it, and which recognizes us—such is the definition which I think nobody will be inclined to dispute. . . . In whatever other respects the divine personality may differ from ours or may re-

semble it, the two are consanguineous at least in this—that both have purposes for which they care, and each can hear the other's call.

Meanwhile, we can already see one consequence and one point of connection with the reflex-action theory of mind. Any mind, constructed on the triadic-reflex pattern, must first get its impression from the object which it confronts; then define what that object is, and decide what active measures its presence demands; and finally react. The stage of reaction depends on the stage of definition, and these, of course, on the nature of the impressing object. When the objects are concrete, particular, and familiar, our reactions are firm and certain enough—often instinctive. I see the desk, and lean on it; I see your quiet faces, and I continue to talk. But the objects will not stay concrete and particular: they fuse themselves into general essences, and they sum themselves into a whole—the universe. And then the object that confronts us, that knocks on our mental door and asks to be let in, and fixed and decided upon and actively met, is just this whole universe itself and its essence.

What are *they*, and how shall I meet *them*?

488. If I simply say, "Vanitas vanitatum, omnia vanitas!" I am defining the total nature of things in a way that carries practical consequences with it as decidedly as if I write a treatise De Natura Rerum in twenty volumes. The treatise may trace its consequences more minutely than the saying; but the only worth of either treatise or saying is that the consequences are there. The long definition can do no more than draw them; the short definition does no less.

489. By what title is it that every would-be universal formula, every system of philosophy which rears its head, receives the inevitable critical volley from one half of mankind, and falls to

the rear, to become at the very best the creed of some partial sect? Either it has dropped out of its net some of our impressions of sense—what we call the facts of nature—or it has left the theoretic and defining department with a lot of inconsistencies and unmediated transitions on its hands; or else, finally, it has left some one or more of our fundamental active and emotional powers with no object outside of themselves to react-on or to live for. Any one of these defects is fatal to its complete success. Some one will be sure to discover the flaw, to scout the system, and to seek another in its stead.

490. Well, just as within the limits of theism some kinds are surviving others by reason of their greater practical rationality, so theism itself, by reason of its practical rationality, is certain to survive all lower creeds. Materialism and agnosticism, even were they true, could never gain universal and popular acceptance; for they both, alike, give a solution of things which is irrational to the practical third of our nature, and in which we can never volitionally feel at home. ... The whole array of active forces of our nature stands waiting, impatient for the word which shall tell them how to discharge themselves most deeply and worthily upon life. "Well!" cry they, "what shall we do?" "Ignoramus, ignorabimus!" says agnosticism. "React upon atoms and their concussions!" says materialism. What a collapse! The mental train misses fire, the middle fails to ignite the end, the cycle breaks down halfway to its conclusion; and the active powers left alone, with no proper object on which to vent their energy, must either atrophy, sicken, and die, or else by their pent-up convulsions and excitement keep the whole machinery in a fever until some less incommensurable solution, some more practically rational formula, shall provide a normal issue for the currents of the soul.

Now, theism always stands ready with the most practically rational solution it is possible to conceive. Not an energy of our active nature to which it does not authoritatively appeal, not an emotion of which it does not normally and naturally release the springs. At a single stroke, it changes the dead blank *it* of the world into a living *thou*, with whom the whole man may have dealings.

491. This only is certain, that the theoretic faculty lives between two fires which never give her rest, and make her incessantly revise her formulations. If she sink into a premature, short-sighted and idolatrous theism, in comes department Number One with its battery of facts of sense, and dislodges her from her dogmatic repose. If she lazily subside into equilibrium with the same facts of sense viewed in their simple mechanical outwardness, up starts the practical reason with its demands, and makes *that* couch a bed of thorns.

492. Here let me say one word about a remark we often hear coming from the anti-theistic wing: It is base, it is vile, it is the lowest depth of immorality, to allow department Number Three to interpose its demands, and have any vote in the question of what is true and what is false; the mind must be a passive, reactionless sheet of white paper, on which reality will simply come and register its own philosophic definition, as the pen registers the curve on the sheet of a chronograph. "Of all the cants that are canted in this canting age" this has always seemed to me the most wretched, especially when it comes from professed psychologists. As if the mind could, consistently with its definition, be a reactionless sheet at all! As if conception could possibly occur except for a teleological purpose, except to show us the way from a state of things our senses cognize to another state of things our will desires! As if "science" itself were anything else than such an end of desire, and a most pe-

culiar one at that! And as if the "truths" of bare physics in particular, which these sticklers for intellectual purity contend to be the only uncontaminated form, were not as great an alteration and falsification of the simple "given" order of the world, into an order conceived solely for the mind's convenience and delight, as any theistic doctrine possibly can be!

493. So far as we can see, the given world is there only for the sake of the operation. At any rate, to operate upon it is our only chance of approaching it; for never can we get a glimpse of it in the unimaginable insipidity of its virgin estate. To bid the man's subjective interests be passive till truth express itself from out the environment, is to bid the sculptor's chisel be passive till the statue express itself from out the stone. Operate we must! and the only choice left us is that between operating to poor or to rich results.

494. Certain of our positivists keep chiming to us, that, amid the wreck of every other god and idol, one divinity still stands upright—that his name is Scientific Truth, and that he has but one commandment, saying, *Thou shalt not be a theist*, for that would be to satisfy thy subjective propensities, and the satisfaction of those is intellectual damnation.

495. Man's chief difference from the brutes lies in the exuberant excess of his subjective propensities—his pre-eminence over them simply and solely in the number and in the fantastic and unnecessary character of his wants, physical, moral, aesthetic, and intellectual. Had his whole life not been a quest for the superfluous, he would never have established himself as inexpugnably as he has done in the necessary. And from the consciousness of this he should draw the lesson that his wants are to be trusted; that even when their gratification seems farthest off, the uneasiness they occasion is still the best guide of his life, and will lead him to issues entirely beyond his present powers of reckoning. Prune down his extravagance, sober him, and you undo him.

496. If the religion of exclusive scientificism should ever succeed in suffocating all other appetites out of a nation's mind, and imbuing a whole race with the persuasion that simplicity and consistency demand a *tabula rasa* to be made of every notion that does not form part of the *soi-disant* scientific synthesis, that nation, that race, will just as surely go to ruin, and fall a prey to their more richly constituted neighbors, as the beasts of the field, as a whole, have fallen a prey to man.

## Theism and Monism

497. That sense of emotional reconciliation with God which characterizes the highest moments of the theistic consciousness may be described as "oneness" with him, and so from the very bosom of theism a monistic doctrine seems to arise. But this consciousness of self-surrender, of absolute practical union between one's self and the divine object of one's contemplation, is a totally different thing from any sort of substantial identity. Still the object God and the subject I are two. Still I simply come upon him, and find his existence given to me; and the climax of my practical union with what is given, forms at the same time the climax of my perception that as a numerical fact of existence I am something radically other than the Divinity with whose effulgence I am filled.

Now, it seems to me that the only sort of union of creature with creator with which theism, properly so called, comports, is of this emotional and practical kind; and it is based unchangeably on the empirical fact that the thinking subject and the object thought are numerically two. How my mind and will, which are not God, can yet cognize and leap to meet him, how I ever came to be so separate from him, and how God himself came to be at all, are problems that for the theist can remain unsolved and insoluble forever.

498. The highest flights of theistic mysticism, far from pretending to penetrate the secrets of the *me* and the *thou* in worship, and to transcend the dualism by an act of intelligence, simply turn their backs on such attempts. The problem for them has simply vanished—vanished from the sight of an attitude which refuses to notice such futile theoretic difficulties. Get but that "peace of God which passeth understanding," and the questions of the understanding will cease from puzzling and pedantic scruples be at rest.

## The Gnostical Attitude

499. But now, although to most human minds such a position as this will be the position of rational equilibrium, it is not difficult to bring forward certain considerations, in the light of which so simple and practical a mental movement begins to seem rather short-winded and second-rate and devoid of intellectual style. This easy acceptance of an opaque limit to our speculative insight; this satisfaction with a Being whose character we simply apprehend without comprehending anything more about him, and with whom after a certain point our dealings can be only of a volitional and emotional sort; above all, this sitting down contented with a blank unmediated dualism—are they not the very picture of unfaithfulness to the rights and duties of our theoretic reason?

500. Is not the unparalleled development of department Two of the mind in man his crowning glory and his very essence; and may not the *knowing of the truth* be his absolute vocation? And if it is, ought he flatly to acquiesce in a spiritual life of "reflex type," whose form is no higher than that of the life that animates his spinal cord?

501. And so, very naturally and gradually, one may be led from the theistic and practical point of view to what I shall call the *gnostical* one. We may think that department Three of the mind, with its doings of right and its doings of wrong, must be there only to serve department Two; and we may suspect that the sphere of our activity exists for no other purpose than to illumine our cognitive consciousness by the experience of its results. Are not all sense and all emotion at bottom but turbid and perplexed modes of what in its clarified shape is intelligent cognition? . . .

These questions fan the fire of an unassuageable gnostic thirst, which is as far removed from theism in one direction as agnosticism was removed from it in the other; and which aspires to nothing less than an absolute unity of knowledge with its object, and refuses to be satisfied short of a fusion and solution and saturation of both impression and action with reason, and an absorption of all three departments of the mind into one.

502. Like all head-long ideals, this apotheosis of the bare conceiving faculty has its depth and wildness, its pang and its charm. To many it sings a truly siren strain.

503. I confess that I myself have always had a great mistrust of the pretensions of the gnostic faith. Not only do I utterly fail to understand what a cognitive faculty erected into the absolute of being, with itself as its object, can mean; but even if we grant it a being other than itself for object, I cannot reason myself out of the belief that however familiar and at home we might become with the character of that being, the bare being of it, the fact that it is there at all, must always be something blankly given and presupposed in order that conception may begin its work; must in short lie beyond specu-

lation, and not be enveloped in its sphere.

Accordingly, it is with no small pleasure that as a student of physiology and psychology I find the only lesson I can learn from these sciences to be one that corroborates these convictions. From its first dawn to its highest actual attainment, we find that the cognitive faculty, where it appears to exist at all, appears but as one element in an organic mental whole, and as a minister to higher mental powers—the powers of will. Such a thing as its emancipation and absolution from these organic relations receives no faintest color of plausibility from any fact we can discern.

*504.* On the contrary, it is more than probable that to the end of time our power of moral and volitional response to the nature of things will be the deepest organ of communication therewith we shall ever possess. In every being that is real there is something external to, and sacred from, the grasp of every other. God's being is sacred from ours. To co-operate with his creation by the best and rightest response seems all that he wants of us. In such co-operation with his purposes, not in any chimerical speculative conquest of him, not in any theoretic drinking of him up, must lie the real meaning of our destiny.

### The Compounding of Consciousness

*505.* I wish to discuss the assumption that states of consciousness, so-called, can separate and combine themselves freely, and keep their own identity unchanged while forming parts of simultaneous fields of experience of wider scope.

*506.* The actual cannot be impossible, and what *is* actual at every moment of our lives is the sort of thing which I now proceed to remind you of. You can hear the vibration of an electric contact-maker, smell the ozone, see the sparks, and feel the thrill, co-consciously as it were or in one field of experience. But you can also isolate any one of these sensations by shutting out the rest. If you close your eyes, hold your nose, and remove your hand, you can get the sensation of sound alone, but it seems still the same sensation that it was; and if you restore the action of the other organs, the soul coalesces with the feeling, the sight, and the smell sensations again. Now the natural way of talking of all this is to say that certain sensations are experienced, now singly, and now together with other sensations, in a common conscious field. Fluctuations of attention give analogous results. We let a sensation in or keep it out by changing our attention; and similarly we let an item of memory in or drop it out.

*507.* Pray . . . recall what I said about the difficulty of seeing how states of consciousness can compound themselves. The difficulty seemed to be the same, you remember, whether we took it in psychology as the composition of finite states of mind out of simpler finite states, or in metaphysics as the composition of the absolute mind out of finite minds in general. It is the general conceptualist difficulty of any one thing being the same with many things, either at once or in succession, for the abstract concepts of oneness and manyness must needs exclude each other. . . .

On the principle of going behind the conceptual function altogether, however, and looking to the more primitive flux of the sensational life for reality's true shape, a way is open to us. . . . The concrete pulses of experience appear pent in by no such definite limits as our conceptual substitutes for them are confined by. They run into one another continuously and seem to interpenetrate. What in them is relation and what is matter related is hard to discern. You feel no one of them as inwardly simple, and no two as wholly without confluence where they touch. There is no datum so small as not to show this mystery, if mystery it be. The tiniest feeling that we can possibly have comes with an earlier and a later part and with a sense of their continuous procession. Mr. Shadworth Hodgson showed long ago that there is literally no such object as the present moment except as an unreal postulate of abstract thought. The "passing" moment is, as I already have reminded you, the minimal fact, with the "apparition of difference" inside of it as well as outside. If we do not feel both past and present in one field of feeling, we feel them not at all. . . . We realize this life as something always off its balance, something in transition, something that shoots out of a darkness through a dawn into a brightness that we feel to be the dawn fulfilled. In the very midst of the continuity our experience comes as an alteration. "Yes," we say at the full brightness, "*this* is what I just meant." "No," we feel at the dawning, "this is not yet the full meaning, there is more to come." In every crescendo of sensation, in every effort to recall, in every progress towards the satisfaction of desire, this succession of an emptiness and fulness that have reference to each other and are one flesh is the essence of the phenomenon. In every hindrance of desire the sense of an ideal presence which is absent in fact, of an absent, in a word, which the only function of the present is to *mean*, is even more notoriously there. And in the movement of pure thought we have the same phenomenon. When I say *Socrates is mortal*, the moment *Socrates* is incomplete; it falls forward through the *is* which is pure movement, into the *mortal* which is indeed bare mortal on the tongue, but for the mind is *that mortal*, the *mortal Socrates*, at last satisfactorily disposed of and told off.

Here, then, inside of the minimal pulses of experience, is realized that very inner complexity which the transcendentalists say only the absolute can genuinely possess. The gist of the matter is always the same—something ever goes indissolubly with something else.

*508.* If, with all this in our mind, we turn to our own particular predicament, we see that our old objection to the self-compounding of states of consciousness, our accusation that it was impossible for purely logical reasons, is unfounded in principle. Every smallest state of consciousness, concretely taken, overflows its own definition. . . . In the pulse of inner life immediately present now in each of us is a little past, a little future, a little awareness of our own body, of each other's persons, of these sublimities we are trying to talk about, of the earth's geography and the direction of history, of truth and error, of good and bad, and of who knows how much more? . . .

In *principle*, then, the real units of our immediately-felt life are unlike the units that intellectualist logic holds to and makes its calculations with. They are not separate from their own others, and you have to take them at widely-separated dates to find any two of them that seem unblent. Then indeed they do appear separate even as their concepts are separate; a chasm yawns between them; but the chasm itself is but an intellectualist fiction, got by abstracting from the continuous sheet of experiences with which the intermediary time was filled. It is like the log carried first by William and Henry, then by William, Henry, and John, then by Henry and John, then by John and Peter, and so on. All real units of experience *overlap*.

*509.* What is true here of successive states must also be true of simultaneous characters. They also overlap each other with their being. My present field of consciousness is a centre surrounded by a fringe that shades insensibly into a subconscious more. I use three separate terms here to describe this fact; but I might as well use three hundred, for the fact is all shades and no boundaries. Which part of it properly is in my consciousness, which out? If I name what is out, it already has come in. The centre works in one way while the margins work in another, and presently overpower the centre and are central themselves. What we conceptually identify ourselves with and say we are thinking of at any time is the centre; but our *full* self is the whole field, with all those indefinitely radiating subconscious possibilities of increase that we can only feel without conceiving, and can hardly begin to analyze. The collective and the distributive ways of being coexist here, for each part functions distinctly, makes connexion with its own peculiar region in the still wider rest of experience and tends to draw us into that line, and yet the whole is somehow felt as one pulse of our life— not conceived so, but felt so.

In principle, then, as I said, intellectualism's edge is broken; it can only approximate to reality, and its logic is inapplicable to our inner life, which spurns its vetoes and mocks at its impossibilities. Every bit of us at every moment is part and parcel of a wider self, it quivers along various radii like the wind-rose on a compass, and the actual in it is continuously one with possibles not yet in our present sight. And just as we are co-conscious with our own momentary margin, may not we ourselves form the margin of some more really central self in things which is co-conscious with the whole of us? May not you and I be confluent in a higher consciousness, and confluently active there, tho we now know it not?

*510.* We have now reached a point of view from which the self-compounding of mind in its smaller and more accessible portions seems a certain fact, and in which the speculative assumption of a similar but wider compounding in remoter regions must be reckoned with as a legitimate hypothesis. The absolute is not the impossible being I once thought it. Mental facts do function both singly and together, at once, and we finite minds may simultaneously be co-conscious with one another in a superhuman intelligence.

### God Not All-Inclusive: Fechner

*511.* Psychologically, it seems to me that Fechner's God is a lazy postulate of his, rather than a part of his system positively thought out. As we envelop our sight and hearing, so the earth-soul envelops us, and the star-soul the earth-soul, until—what? Envelopment can't go on forever; it must have an *abschluss*, a total envelope must terminate the series, so God is the name that Fechner gives to this last all-enveloper. But if nothing escapes this all-enveloper, he is responsible for everything, including evil, and all the paradoxes and difficulties which I found in the absolute at the end of our third lecture recur undiminished. Fechner tries sincerely to grapple with the problem of evil, but he always solves it ... by making his God non-absolute. ... His will has to struggle with conditions not imposed on that will by itself. He tolerates provisionally what he has not created, and then with endless patience tries to overcome it and live it down. He has, in short, a history. Whenever Fechner tries to represent him clearly, his God becomes the ordinary God of theism, and ceases to be the absolutely totalized all-enveloper. In this shape, he represents the ideal element in things solely, and is our champion and our helper and we his helpers, against the bad parts of the universe.

*512.* I propose to you that we should discuss the question of God without entangling ourselves in advance in the monistic assumption. Is it probable that there is any superhuman consciousness at all, in the first place? When that is settled, the further question whether its form be monistic or pluralistic is in order.

*513.* The numerous facts of divided or split human personality which the genius of certain medical men, as Janet, Freud, Prince, Sidis, and others, have unearthed were unknown in Fechner's time, and neither the phenomena of automatic writing and speech, nor of mediumship and "possession" generally, had been recognized or studied as we now study them, so Fechner's stock of analogies is scant compared with our present one. He did the best with what he had, however. For my own part I find in some of these abnormal or super-normal facts the strongest suggestions in favor of a superior co-consciousness being possible. I doubt whether we shall ever understand some of them without using the very letter of Fechner's conception of a great reservoir in which the memories of earth's inhabitants are pooled and preserved, and from which, when the threshold lowers or the valve opens, information ordinarily shut out leaks into the mind of exceptional individuals among us. But those regions of inquiry are perhaps too spook-haunted to interest an academic audience, and the only evidence I feel it now decorous to bring to the support of Fechner is drawn from ordinary religious experience.

*514.* To quote words which I have used elsewhere, the believer finds that the tenderer parts of his personal life are continuous with a *more* of the same quality which is operative in the universe outside of him and which he can keep in working touch with, and in a fashion get on board of and save himself, when all his lower being has gone to pieces in the wreck. In a word, the believer is continuous, to his own consciousness, at any rate, with a wider self from which saving experiences flow in. Those who have such experiences distinctly enough and often enough to live in the light of them remain quite unmoved by criticism, from whatever quarter it may come, be it academic or scientific, or be it merely the voice of logical common sense. They have had their vision and they *know*—that is enough—that we inhabit an invisible spiritual environment from which help comes, our soul being mysteriously one with a larger soul whose instruments we are.

One may therefore plead, I think, that Fechner's ideas are not without direct empirical verification. There is at any rate one side of life which would be easily explicable if those ideas were true, but of which there appears no clear explanation so long as we assume either with naturalism that human consciousness is the highest consciousness there is, or with dualistic theism that there is a higher mind in the cosmos, but that it is discontinuous with our own.

*515.* The analogies with ordinary psychology and with the facts of pathology, with those of psychical research, so called, and with those of religious experience, establish, when taken together, a decidedly *formidable* probability in favor of a general view of the world almost identical with Fechner's. The outlines of the superhuman consciousness thus made probable must remain, however, very vague, and the number of functionally distinct "selves" it comports and carries has to be left entirely problematic. It may be polytheistically or it may be monotheistically conceived of. . . . Only one thing is certain, and that is the result of our criticism of the absolute: the only way to escape from the paradoxes and perplexities that a consistently thought-out monistic universe suffers from as from a species of auto-intoxication—the mystery of the "fall" namely, of reality lapsing into appearance, truth into error, perfection into imperfection; of evil, in short; the mystery of universal determinism, of the block-universe eternal and without a history, etc.;—the only way of escape, I say, from all this is to be frankly pluralistic and assume that the superhuman consciousness, however vast it may be, has itself an external environment, and consequently is finite. Present day monism [Royce, for example] carefully repudiates complicity with spinozistic monism. In that, it explains, the many get dissolved in the one and lost, whereas in the improved idealistic form, they get preserved in all their manyness as the one's eternal object. The absolute itself is thus represented by absolutists as having a pluralistic object. But if even the absolute has to have a pluralistic vision, why should we ourselves hesitate to be pluralists on our own sole account? Why should we envelop our many with the "one" that brings so much poison in its train?

The line of least resistance, then, as it seems to me, both in theology and in philosophy, is to accept, along with the superhuman consciousness, the notion that it is not all-embracing, the notion, in other words, that there is a God, but that he is finite, either in power or in knowledge, or in both at once. These, I need hardly tell you, are the terms in which common men have usually carried on their active commerce with God; and the monistic perfections that make the notion of him so paradoxical practically and morally are the colder addition of remote professorial minds operating *in distans* upon conceptual substitutes for him alone.

Why cannot "experience" and "reason" meet on this common ground? Why cannot they compromise? May not the godlessness usually but needlessly associated with the philosophy of immediate experience give way to a theism now seen to follow directly from that experience more widely taken? and may not rationalism, satisfied with seeing her *a priori* proofs of God so effectively replaced by empirical evidence, abate something of her absolutist claims? Let God but have the least infinitesimal *other* of any kind beside him, and empiricism and rationalism might strike hands in a lasting treaty of peace. Both might then leave abstract thinness behind them, and seek together, as scientific men seek, by using all the analogies and data within reach, to build up the most probable approximate idea of what the divine consciousness concretely may be like.

### Pluralistic Panpsychism

*516.* If Oxford men could be ignorant of anything, it might almost seem that they had remained ignorant of the great empirical movement towards a pluralistic panpsychic view of the universe, into which our own generation has been drawn, and which threatens to short-circuit their methods entirely and become their religious rival unless they are willing to make themselves its allies. . . . Let empiricism once become associated with religion, as hitherto, through some strange misunderstanding, it has been associated with irreligion, and I believe that a new era of religion as well as of philosophy will be ready to begin.

*517.* Our philosophies swell the current of being, add their character to it. . . . As a French philosopher says, "Nous sommes du réel dans le réel." Our thoughts determine our acts, and our acts redetermine the previous nature of the world.

Thus does foreignness get banished from our world, and far more so when we take the system of it pluralistically than when we take it monistically. We are indeed internal parts of God and not external creations, on any possible reading of the panpsychic system. Yet because God is not the absolute, but is himself a part when the system is conceived pluralistically, his functions can be taken as not wholly dissimilar to those of the other smaller parts—as similar to our functions consequently.

Having an environment, being in time, and working out a history just like ourselves, he escapes from the foreignness from all that is human, of the static timeless perfect absolute.

Remember that one of our troubles with that was its essential foreignness and monstrosity—there really is no other word for it than that. Its having the all-inclusive form gave to it an essentially heterogeneous *nature* from ourselves. And this great difference between absolutism and pluralism demands no difference in the universe's material content—it follows from a difference in the form alone. The all-form or monistic form makes the foreignness result, the each-form or pluralistic form leaves the intimacy undisturbed.

No matter what the content of the universe may be, if you only allow that it is *many* everywhere and always, that *nothing* real escapes from having an environment; so far from defeating its rationality, as the absolutists so unanimously pretend, you leave it in possession of the maximum amount of rationality practically attainable by our minds. Your relations with it, intellectual, emotional, and active, remain fluent and congruous with your own nature's chief demands.

[Sec. 479, William James, *Essays on Faith and Morals* (New York: Longmans, Green & Co., 1943), pp. 82–83. Sec. 480, *ibid.*, p. 84. Sec. 481, *ibid.*, pp. 103–7. Sec. 482, *ibid.*, pp. 107–9. Sec. 483, *ibid.*, p. 109. Sec. 484, *ibid.*, p. 30. Sec. 485, *ibid.*, pp. 115–16. Sec. 486, *ibid.*, p. 121. Sec. 487, *ibid.*, pp. 122–23. Sec. 488, *ibid.*, p. 124. Sec. 489, *ibid.*, pp. 125–26. Sec. 490, *ibid.*, pp. 126–27. Sec. 491, *ibid.*, p. 128. Sec. 492, *ibid.*, p. 129. Sec. 493, *ibid.*, p. 130. Sec. 494, *ibid.*, p. 131. Sec. 495, *ibid.*, pp. 131–32. Sec. 496, *ibid.*, p. 132. Sec. 497, *ibid.*, pp. 134–35. Sec. 498, *ibid.*, p. 136 Sec. 499, *ibid.*, pp. 136–37. Sec. 500, *ibid.*, p. 137. Sec. 501, *ibid.*, pp. 138–39. Sec. 502, *ibid.*, p. 139. Sec. 503, *ibid.*, pp. 140–41. Sec. 504, *ibid.*, p. 141. Sec. 505, William James, *A Pluralistic Universe* (New York: Longmans, Green & Co., 1909), p. 181. Sec. 506, *ibid.*, pp. 268–69. Sec. 507, *ibid.*, pp. 281–84. Sec. 508, *ibid.*, pp. 285–87. Sec. 509, *ibid.*, pp. 288–90. Sec. 510, *ibid.*, p. 292. Sec. 511, *ibid.*, pp. 293–95. Sec. 512, *ibid.*, p. 295. Sec. 513, *ibid.*, pp. 298–99. Sec. 514, *ibid.*, pp. 307–8. Sec. 515, *ibid.*, pp. 309–12. Sec. 516, *ibid.*, pp. 313–14. Sec. 517, *ibid.*, pp. 317–19.]

## COMMENT

Whatever doctrine is true must give our practical energies something to press against, must have consistent and definite meaning, and must be capable of empirical support. James would have these three demands satisfied. Every nontheistic view fails, he thinks, to meet the three requirements: it withholds from practical activities their proper significance, and it probably contains also a confusion of theory. The problem then concerns the form of theism which can satisfy all three departments of the mind. The data of psychology and physiology support the view that consciousness can be compounded, and other data —that of religious experience and certain aspects of personality—can finally be understood, thinks James, only through a cosmic extension of this principle.

Now, James concludes that God is a being somehow-less-than-all-inclusive, limited in power or knowledge or both, and a creature of time. In reaching this view, demands of theory must have had a place; and he does argue that, on the one hand, an all-inclusive God cannot escape responsibility for evil and that, on the other hand, a God without a history, by canceling out the importance of time, drains our temporal concerns of their significance. But must one not conclude that these are practical decisions; and is James not here allowing the practical department of the mind to dictate a choice of theory without considering the needs of theory as such? (If this be the case, it would not be surprising inasmuch as James was so enthralled by the possibilities of his pragmatic approach.)

Defending the first and third departments of the mind against those who neglect them, he himself renders something less than full justice to the second department, where definition and the search for conceptual consistency and coherence are in order. His vague stipulation that God must be somehow less than all-inclusive is hardly an adequate alternative to the doctrines he opposed. Its lack of clarity exposes it to the contempt of the intellectually fastidious; further, the pragmatically thorough will remark that the moral argument of James himself is not unequivocally satisfied with so loose a conclusion. James rightly urges that the world must not be morally neutral at bottom. But polytheism, to which his doctrine opens the door, threatens us with such neutrality. For if the final fact is a plurality of wills, inevitably more or less at odds with one another (their perfection is not to be assumed), there can be no unequivocal cosmic demands to which we may respond, no ultimate interest or purpose we may serve or promote. Worse, there may, after all, be no permanence to our achievements, since a God only more or less supreme might (or even, in the infinite long run, must) be overwhelmed and destroyed by some aggregation of lesser wills or forces.

We think that James was clearest when he realized that what his reasoning led to was a God who is the deepest power in the universe, eminently good, and hence absolutely indestructible. But is this requirement met by the assertion that he is a being-somehow-less-than-all-inclusive, limited in power or knowledge, and perhaps (for all that is explicitly stated) entirely a creature of time? The theoretical problem is to render these variant themes clear and self-consistent. Certainly a temporal creature is not as such indestructible. The question is: Ought not James's "deepest power" (sec. 487) be taken to mean the categorically supreme power or being?

If categorical supremacy be interpreted in terms of the dipolar structure, all that our author has achieved can be retained but in a wider context. For example, it could then be seen that God's existence is not to be construed merely as an accidental fact, that is, merely as a fact (words being used properly), for then his permanence could not be assured (which James wants). That indeed the necessary is not to be discovered by searching among facts merely as such but is that without contrary possibility. Until the rights of theory are recognized, the strength of theory cannot be utilized, nor can any certainty attain to the mutual operation of the three departments of the mind. For example, we think James weakens the case for his social view of deity by giving up (or not consistently affirming) the social interpretation of matter ("panpsychism").

It is quite clear that James wished to avoid and did avoid the classical errors in their theistic and pantheistic forms. His pragmatic bent led him to see that the orthodox view (God is altogether immutable, absolute, wholly independent, and incapable of receiving any good from his creatures) betrayed the religious values it sought to embody. And James opposed the pantheistic doctrine of the unreality of freedom, individuality, and suffering with an emphatic rejection, tinged with ironic sympathy, on the ground that such an invitation to a "moral holiday" from the distinction between good and evil—along with all other distinctions—can only be viewed as an excessive yielding to one side of our natures, that which longs for harmony and peace at all costs. Had our author meditated further and more calmly, he must have seen that the poison of pantheism is not due to its attribution of universal inclusiveness to the supreme but to certain other assumptions, among these especially this: that time is to be treated like space, an order of entities real or unreal in the same sense, rather than an order of entities some actual and others only capacities for actualization, an order of creating-created. "God includes all things" need not mean that he includes future events; for perhaps there are no future events but only those that are present and past, with potentialities for further happening. This is just James's own view of time, but curiously he assumes pantheism's view of time in arguing against all-inclusiveness. That is, he confuses pantheism and panentheism, though his own categories permit of their distinction.

Further, James's discussion of the two possibilities open to logic is itself illogical. He says that either the supreme and inclusive experience just is the many experiences it includes or the supreme experience is an additional one not really inclusive of the others. But why is it not both additional or distinctive and inclusive? There are the ordinary experiences $x$, $y$, and $z$ and the superior experience $E$ which embraces $x$, $y$, and $z$ in its own unity of consciousness. What has logic or intellect against this? James is right in saying that for pantheism, following its own monopolar logic, the inclusive experience

just is the many experiences—unless, indeed, the latter are declared simply unreal, in which case there is nothing to include and no real inclusion. The third possibility, that the supreme experience is both inclusive and distinctive, the view of Whitehead and Fechner, James does not treat. That he misunderstood Fechner will be clear to anyone who compares section 511 with sections 338 ff., and also sections 317 ff.

Since many of James's ideas are retained and given greater strength and clarity in the system of Whitehead, one wonders how he would have reacted toward Whitehead's thought, which in its use of categorical distinctions preserves the rights of theory without neglecting either empirical or pragmatic concerns. Groping as James was toward the possibility of new and more penetrating concepts and toward a new and more adequate systematic expression, it is quite possible that, in Whitehead, James might have discovered that application of his own method toward which he was moving in his later years. So much is sure that he would not have found in Whitehead's thought (to the same degree at least) the lack of balance in applying the three aspects of mental functioning which turned him away from the systems of Royce, Bradley, and Aquinas.

# EHRENFELS (1859–1932)

Among the casualties of the first World War was a remarkable book by the man generally regarded as the founder of Gestalt psychology. Appearing in the gloomy year of 1916, *Cosmology* received almost no attention, and to this day its brilliant, deeply sincere, and original pages have been read, it seems, by but few. The basic argument of the book is that the temporal structure of the universe, as revealed by science, can only be explained if we

regard process as the interplay of two factors, one "chaos," or randomness, and the other a form-seeking, ordering factor which is called God. Christian von Ehrenfels was thus, with Peirce, one of the first to see, what is more and more becoming a commonplace, that scientific law is not reasonably to be viewed as an absolute orderliness but only as a certain measure or degree of regularity in a cosmic process which is everywhere also an affair of real chance and disorder. Very striking is the way in which our author, in spite of a rather intense hostility to Kant, develops a version of the Kantian argument that our ability to anticipate the order of nature is due to the fact that mind prescribes this order to nature—only it is not, says Ehrenfels, the human mind but the divine mind, of which we are integral parts, that does this. The current arguments about the "ground of induction" might gain by taking this discussion into account. It seems to agree substantially with what Peirce, no ill-equipped logician, came to on the same subject.

We classify the Ehrenfels doctrine as limited panentheism, for he says that individuals on their psychic side, which is not the whole of their natures, are integral to God. Noteworthy, in the passage which follows, is the lively sense displayed for the religious value of the doctrine that our sufferings too are within the divine life.

### Empiricism and Religious Transcendence

*518.* Behind the would-be loftiness of the distinction between problems of empiricism, which belong to human reason, and those of religious transcendence, in which all efforts of reason are to be prejudged as futile—there is nothing higher than a reluctance of the average man, essentially just as stupidly commonplace as that which, for example, up to the beginning of this century made him ridicule all attempts to construct a dirigible airship. There is no category which can actually be set apart as such, in which problems of religious import can be classified and set off from the other problems concerning human beings and dealt with by science. If human reason is considered able to cope with questions such as the origin of organic life on the earth, or the "extinction of heat" threatening the material world, or the question just now hanging

over the most advanced physics, whether, in view of entropy *and* the radioactivity of atoms, it is any longer possible to assume that matter has "never become," but exists from eternity; indeed, if we go so far as to consider rationally whether, in the deepest chloroform-induced trance of a sick man, something psychical still goes on—and if so, what it is—we can no longer reasonably deny to the same human reason the right to grapple with questions such as whether, after the cessation of all physiological functions in man, what was psychical in him has simply vanished from the world, or whether it continues to exist in some form or other—and if so, in what form? or the other question: If the hypothesis of a beginning of matter *should* prove to be inescapable, what then might have been the cause of that beginning? But now we are already in the midst of the realm of "transcendence," from which, by the Kantian decree, pure reason should remain absolutely banished. The prohibition cannot be enforced. The threads of thought run hither and thither. A separation cannot be carried out. This for the information of the kind reader, who otherwise may be taken aback by the strangeness of the title-words which here follow:

### The Scientific Hypotheses of Religious Dualism

Into the eternally causeless and uncontinuing, into the infinite which has neither order nor law, flows the unitary primal source of all necessity and form, of all that is beautiful, true and good in the world. We come nearest to a conceptual representation of it by the idea of a form-creating urge, existing from eternity to eternity, unbounded in might, which we call God. But the infinite something, in which God works, we can think of only negatively, indirectly, as the opposite of all that characterizes God. We call it Chaos. God and

Chaos constitute the world. Everything perceptually conceivable, even the most abstract of things, number, derives from both principles, unites in itself divine "henogenic" and "chaotogenic" contributions. All unity and universality come from God, all manifoldness from Chaos. Without Chaos God would be just as incapable of producing the world, as Chaos without God.

From eternity God is power, knowledge and impulse for higher and higher form-creation. God feels joy in creation, arising from eternal need to create. The world does not exist from eternity. The world had its origin when, after eternal need to create, God received from Chaos the stimulus for the first act of creation. But not "out of Chaos" did God make the world, but "out of himself," against chaotic resistances. But out of every deformation of his works God derives the impulse for new form-giving. We need not fear that out of Chaos may arise spontaneously a shape of terror, which would cause the destruction of even a part of our empirical world. That is infinitely improbable, therefore practically the same as impossible. The miracle of chance—the first excitation of God by Chaos—is conceivable only after an eternity of inaction and silence.

God experiences a reaction from each of his acts, and is therefore, as well as the world, engaged in an eternal evolution directed toward the future. In the beginning God had neither awareness of his works nor foreseeing consciousness. Now too he does not possess omniscience, and will never attain to it, even though he approximates it more and more. The world, therefore, has not been made with foresight after an eternal plan, but rather has arisen out of God's reactions to chaotic excitations and resistances. And this insight provides the true "theodicy," by which philosophy means the justification of God in view of the evil of the world, or the understanding which shows how the evil in this world is reconcilable with the nature of God.

Everything psychical in the world is "partially identical" with God; that is, with a part of its being it is also a part of God. God feels all pain and all joy in the world as his own pain and as his own joy. And God struggles in all and with all his creatures away from pain toward joy.

The preceding articles of belief are to be characterized as "dualistic theism," or simply as dualism. In opposition to them stands "solotheism," the worldview which recognizes God as the one and only world-principle, and culminates in the assertion, repeated again and again for centuries, dumbfounding in its defiant paradox, that "God produced the world out of nothing."

### Religious Values of Dualism

Eternal infinite Chaos is nothing bad, hateful, such as the devil is for devout Christians. Chaos is the epitome of all germs of reality, the prerequisite for a divine upward evolution into infinity, the possibility of surprises without end (for God also), which "eye hath not seen, nor ear heard." Chaos can be loved, and is loved by true dualists, no less than God. And to the solotheist's trust in God ("What God does is well done") corresponds the dualist's trust in the world. "Of the two principles on which the world depends, Chaos is without aim. God's aim, however, is directed toward the good. Therefore the good must conquer the world." What fundamentally makes the world lovable to the dualist is what may be called the "eternal allure," the "A new day beckons to new shores," a day undreamed-of by God himself, and again and again a new day, through all eternity; the "eternal allure" which rouses God himself to ever new creations, for every creative emanation is a venture for God, from which proceed undreamed-of raptures and also undreamed-of sorrows. This eternal venturer, "God," together with the inciter to ventures, "Chaos," can be loved just as much as, and perhaps even more than God the All-powerful, the All-knowing, was ever loved by devout solotheists.

Every psychical individual is an emanation of God, partially identical with God. The return to God of this emanation, with physical death, is a directly credible consequence of this view, and the expectation of this return is an equivalent in emotional life for the belief in immortality.

Dualism knows neither reward nor punishment in the life to come. But again, it is directly credible to the dualist, that the return to God, which confronts every individual, can bring nothing but joy to the good, whose work on earth was in conformity with God's, but that to the bad, who through chaotic forces were turned into ways opposed to God, it can bring only anxiety and grief. It is quite possible that this return to God, by virtue of a law in nature, may take place in a way analogous to that which Oriental religions have for centuries assumed and expounded in the doctrine of transmigration of souls.

To the countless number of all those unkindly dealt with by fate, pushed aside in the struggle for existence, burdened with care, down-trodden, to all the legions of the innocent who suffer, Christianity offers an unspeakable consolation in the doctrine, a seeming paradox to sound reason, that there is a merit in earthly sorrows borne with submission to God, which the Almighty will recompense by so much the greater joys in the life to come. Does the dualistic world-view know an equivalent for this article of belief, too, which perhaps millionfold, like no other, has won, wins and holds adherents to the church of the Crucified? Yes, dualism offers full compensation

too for this consolation of the soul, which it had been thought was lost. God, the eternal venturer, foresees well enough that every new act of creation, every emanation which enriches and beautifies the world, is in the last analysis a pushing forward into the chaotic, the uncertain, the unknowable even for God. He foresees that every act of creation must encounter resistance and may involve conflict, out of which will arise unforeseeable pain for the created, and therefore likewise for the creator himself. God has need of daring courage for each new emanation, of inner steeling against pain of every conceivable and inconceivable kind. God: that is, in part, we ourselves; and that is you too, you who are enslaved, down-trodden, rejected by fate. If only you bear your suffering unflinchingly, conscious of your oneness with God, and, in spite of your pain, affirming the world and life, you shall grow strong—no: the daring courage of God himself shall grow strong in you, and you shall have your share in all the coming miracles of life in this world!

With this awareness, even after the end of Christianity the word of Christ shall still hold good for you: "Come unto me, all ye that are weary and burdened, I will give you strength!"

He who professes himself a dualist, herewith bears witness that he believes the foregoing articles to be true.

But outside of this consensus, dualists may, without coming into conflict with their confession, differ greatly in their religious attitudes; and in these respects: (a) in cosmological hypotheses; (b) in moral convictions; (c) in the practice of religious rites and ceremonies, which at first will attach themselves to the ritual and ceremonial practices of religions already known and existing; (d) finally, in varying sympathy with intellectual trends having a connection with religious life.

a) In the realm of cosmology, particular importance here attaches to the hypotheses of over-souls based on humanity. By over-souls are to be understood psychical personalities which form themselves upon many individual human souls, and in range of consciousness, in intellect and power of deduction, and actual effective potentialities excel the individual souls in proportion to the number of these souls, while they also include the sense-impressions and experiences of the individual souls and correspondingly surpass them manyfold in emotional experience and scope of influence. The over-souls can form a totality on which as a base an over-soul of higher rank arises, and in all probability no limit is set to this step-by-step process. What each of us calls his individual consciousness is an over-soul, which is based, probably by the mediation of more than one step, on the millions of under-souls of our organism's cells.

It is highly probable that in mankind today the major number of the over-souls of higher rank are in process of coming into being (*in statu nascendi*), who press hard on one another in their respective spheres of influence, and have not yet arrived at any lasting equilibrium. Only conjectures may be made today as to this supra-human process, and hence it is understandable that the opinions even of convinced dualists may here diverge widely.

*b*) The morality of mankind is in constant process of evolution. The dualistic creed presupposes as foundation the humanitarian morality of the Western civilized world, without however committing itself as to details. Rather, it is probable that the present-day humanitarian morality is moving toward a radical change in two fields: first in the attitude taken toward the problem of killing oneself (suicide, voluntary death) as opposed to the killing of others (particularly in war), and second in sex-morality.

*c*) The ceremonial worship of religious dualism can be developed only gradually, in the course of generations, from germs existing at present in the ceremonial observances of the "positive religions" and in the fine arts. At the beginning, therefore—particularly in view of the division of civilized mankind into "common people," and "educated class"—in order to give expression to their high esteem for religion in general, before the "common people," it will be advisable for the "educated class" to take part passively and actively in the ceremonial worship of some one of the present-day positive religions, after the fashion of the naïvely devout adherents of the religion concerned.

*d*) In such a way the greatest variety in the religious attitudes of dualists can exist, on whose need for expression in words no limit should be imposed. But in this connection let us note the usefulness of the designations "observance" and "inclination." "Observance" as declaration of the intention of the one concerned, reserving his full conviction of the truth of the dualistic confession of faith, nevertheless to conform to the rites of a certain positive religion, hand in hand with which will generally go belief in the real existence of an over-soul based on the under-souls of those professing that positive religion. And "inclination" as expression of the sympathy of the one concerned with some one of the "trends" existing in the realms of cosmological theory or of practical morality. Accordingly designations such as "dualist of the Catholic, or Lutheran, or Russian-Orthodox, or even (if this might be) Israelitish observance" would be self-explanatory; and also characterizations such as "dualist of Buddhistic or Hellenistic or Old-German inclination," if not precisely standardized, would yet awaken specific ideas.

Religious dualism believes that its dogmas have been scientifically proved.

but does not fail to recognize the fact that in the course of scientific evolution much has already been thought proved, which nevertheless later had to be acknowledged as error. Should a like fate be appointed for the dogmatic basis of dualism, no supposed moral obligation will withhold its confessors from giving honor to truth, and adapting their convictions—and even should these be their most sacred ones—to the newly acquired knowledge. In this respect there is an essential difference between religious dualism and all hitherto existing positive religions, in what is called their confession of "faith."

[Sec. 518, Christian Ehrenfels, *Cosmogony*, trans. Mildred Focht (New York: Comet Press, 1948), pp. 216–23.]

### COMMENT

We have earlier encountered systems, and not that of Plato alone, in which some elements are not themselves concepts but rather images representing in dramatic form certain conceptual ultimates. Where this is the case, one presumes that the concepts themselves, and not the particular images, are the real interest of the author. Ehrenfels presents, we think, one such system. In opposition to "solotheism" (a derivation of all reality from God through creation) he feels the necessity for a dual principle of explanation; this duality is for him an opposition between God and an external environment, "Chaos," the two interacting as stimulus and resistance, accounting for the orderly and the novel aspects of reality.

What chiefly impresses one from the manner of Ehrenfels' expression is that the two principles are not really two but function as one. It is God-and-Chaos which makes possible novelty, advance, the lure of existence. Once

again, as in the case of Plato, it can be said that the meaning of two eternally operative and necessary principles is really a single meaning, however complex it may be. Ehrenfels' particular framework has its purpose in dramatizing the insights that (1) a lure, an ideal of harmony, within reality guarantees the continuing possibility of development, process, and worth-while change, (2) the values of life include freedom, but (3) they do not perish with the passage of time. Such insights were likewise important to Whitehead and were retained by, although not the principal determinants of, his decision to categorize eternal objects as a primordial divine nature and the immortality of events in process as a consequent nature. So for Whitehead these two ultimate features of reality become aspects of a single complex process.

Ehrenfels leads one rather to some unnecessary mystification in the exposition of his basically true insight. Chaos need not, after all, be hypostatized; it can be understood as multiple freedom. It is not itself a power but the interplay of powers none of which is wholly determined by any other. Also, the supreme or divine being may have a passive or receptive aspect by virtue of which it embraces all powers within itself, not by wielding them all, that is, making all decisions, but by sustaining and appreciatively enjoying-suffering them all. The admission of randomness or a chaotic aspect of existence, then, does not need to constitute a dualism; the duality may be between two aspects of a single being; and between this being and *many* others as included by it.

Concerning the eloquence of our author in regard to immortality and the consolations of the divine intimacy with our sufferings we can but express our appreciation.

# BRIGHTMAN (1884———)

Though he was influenced somewhat by James's *Pragmatism*, the opposing influences of traditional idealism and of the "scientific idealism" proposed in recent years by Eddington appear to weigh more heavily in the construction of E. S. Brightman's point of view. In at least one respect, Brightman has completely reversed the pattern set by James. Both thinkers have held that God must be regarded as partially inclusive and partially exclusive of reality; hence, "limitation" of the God-concept is a feature common to both systems. However, for James many at least of the nondivine selves are included in God's nature. This assertion that many, perhaps nearly all, sentient beings constitute part of a single consciousness—an assertion more than tentatively advanced by James—adds a type of psychic pluralism (limited by whatever degree of unity the divine contributes to this psychic realm) to his earlier statements of a more radical pluralism; while, as for inorganic nature, James never quite makes up his mind sharply whether it is really insentient or whether it is or is not contained in deity. Brightman, on the other hand, limits panentheism in a contrary manner, for Brightman holds that God comprehends within himself the *nonsentient* universe as his "given"; whereas, although conscious beings may communicate with God, they are apart from him, apparently in order to provide a categorical assertion of their individuality and freedom.

That the systems of James and Brightman present this rather surprising contrast may be accounted for, at least in part, by their differing views of perception. James believed that we experience the world of brute fact directly and unmistakably. Brightman believes

that we experience only our own mentality; all the rest is inferred, and every aspect of the inferred reality which does not belong to other localized or nondivine consciousness is part of a general or divine consciousness. This view is confirmed, in Brightman's opinion, not only by what he understands to be the nature of our direct experience, but also by the apparent ease with which an idealism is able to resolve the Cartesian problem (one's body can influence one's mind, avers Brightman, because one's body is part of another mind) and by the greater sensitiveness of idealism in interpreting poetic and religious insights.

And, indeed, Brightman's argument has some force behind it; his solution is neat; one wonders whether it is also sufficiently rigorous. In the following provocative and original selection the author moves toward his conception of a finite-infinite God through consideration of possible attributes which may apply to him.

## Expansion and Contraction in the Concept of God

*519.* . . . the combined testimony of science, religion, and philosophy all points in one general direction, namely, toward a broadening and enlarging conception of God, a conception vast enough to include all of the contributions of past and future science and all discoveries of every kind made by the human spirit. In fact, . . . we may say that one natural tendency of thought is toward pantheism, the view that all nature, all human life, all reality, together constitute God.

But, as Hegel has wisely pointed out, there are two opposite dangers into which thought may fall. We may, as he puts it, have too little of God and we may have too much of him.

*520.* How can there be too much of the best and most perfect? But that is just the point. If everything that is, just as it stands, is to be taken as a part of God, then the worst and the best equally belong to him. He thinks in our science, he aspires in our hopes; but he also sins in our sinning, fails in our failures, and is mistaken in our errors. A God who is everything is in danger of being everything but perfect, or only a perfect chaos. If he is everything in general, he is nothing in particular. Thus the expansion of the idea of God is in great danger of leading to its own nullification.

*521.* In fact, it is no special peculiarity of the idea of God that expansion, carried too far, ceases to be a gain and becomes a loss. . . . Expansion of any sort, whether of wealth, of population, or of armaments, carried to an extreme, tends to destroy its own value. Thus it is a rule that expansion turns into contraction. . . . This principle is universal in its scope. When any idea or principle of reality expands or seeks to expand beyond the limits set by the nature of things, it tends either to destroy itself or at least to become blurred and confused.

*522.* First of all, it is evident to any observer that the expansion of God into a Being of all-inclusive law has contracted our conception of his miracle-working power and his power to answer prayer. This statement is not intended in any way as a denial . . . that the interpretation of God in terms of natural law is a vast expansion in our thought of him. But that expansion involves a necessary limitation on uncritical belief in the miraculous and in answer to prayer. . . . The conception of a God of law is the conception of a God who is limited by his own principles, and who, so long as he remains what he is, is not able to violate them at our request or even at his own desire. If he did violate them, he would cease to be a God of principle. This is not merely a contraction in our idea of God; it is also a practical contraction in man's capacity for faith. In the presence of a God of law we find it more difficult than before to see how his unchanging laws are compatible with any special purpose to achieve value for individuals in the universe.

Secondly, the tendency of the expansion of the thought of God, as we found, was away from many tribal deities and national pantheons toward a single universal and perhaps all-inclusive God; and this expansion toward unity tends to contract God's relations with the conflicts of real life. The more perfect the unity of the divine nature is, the more marked becomes the contrast between God and the struggles of actual experience. The unitary spirit of God is at peace within itself; but the world is not at peace. God is perfectly self-consistent in his unity, but humanity is full of contradictions. It appears that we must either limit God's relations with the actual world or else we must limit the blissful unity of his nature. At least, we need to form a modified conception of his inner bliss in the light of the tragic limits to unity in the world of human struggle. Since we cannot surrender the facts of experience and retain the basis for any belief in anything, it turns out that a revised conception of the unity of God is necessary.

The shallower and more blindly optimistic thinkers have never been able to tolerate the thought of any compromise of the absolute unity of the divine nature. Even great and good men have been distressed by any idea of struggle or division within God's nature. Yet some of the most profound minds which have made the unity of God their central belief have found it necessary to conceive that unity in such a way as to provide for contrasts, for struggle, or even for suffering, within the life of God. Christian thought has been divided at this point. Many have exalted the absoluteness of God and his metaphysical unity to such an extent that they have thought of him as perfectly at peace within himself. But there has persisted an uneasy feeling that such peace is a peace without intellectual victory, involving an abstract separation of God from the real world in which we live and a retreat instead of a conquest on the part of God. The Christian doctrines of the Trinity and of the Atonement have been attempts to express the complex and even tragic nature of the inner life of God. They convey the impression not only of variety but also of definite limitations within the Divine Being. They present a God who struggles and suffers for the world's salvation. Whatever one may think of the traditional formulations of those doctrines, they certainly are closer to the facts of moral experience and to the experienced tragedy of life than is the notion of a blankly unitary God who has no genuine problems and no genuine diversity to deal with. Even Hegel, who has dwelt more emphatically on the absolute unity of God than most philosophers, makes the following profound remark:

The life of God and the Divine Knowledge may therefore perhaps be expressed as a play of Love with itself; but this idea sinks to the level of mere edification or even of inanity if there be absent from it the seriousness, the pain, the patience, and work of the Negative.

It is this seriousness and pain and patience and work of what Hegel calls the Negative that constitutes a necessary limitation on the absolute unity of the divine life. If there be a God at all, he must be a unitary person; but in his unity there is genuine opposition and struggle. Every person is a unitary experience of diverse and opposing

elements; the more excellent the person, the greater the inner diversity and hence the richer the unity that is attained.

Thirdly, the expansion of God into an all-inclusive being tends to contract his goodness. . . . He expands "beyond good and evil," and in so doing destroys the possibility of regarding him as good. We must either limit his expansion or deny his goodness. If God includes all the sins of men, as well as all their virtues, he is both sinful and virtuous; that is to say, neither one wholeheartedly. It may be said, as some philosophical absolutists have said—Royce in particular—that God includes the sin of man, and yet is good because he overcomes that sin and brings good out of it. But this leaves us with a hopeless contradiction on our hands. Here is this sin of mine. . . . If evil is truly evil, then it cannot be any part of an absolutely good being. Thus we have either to give up the absolute all-inclusiveness of God or his goodness. But if we give up his goodness, then he is no longer worthy of being regarded as God.

*523.* Fourthly, the expansion of God into an omnipotent being contracts his benevolence. . . . In reply to the question, If God is both all-powerful and all-good, why is there so much evil? traditional theism has answered that sin comes entirely from the free choice of man, while all other evils are disguised goods, intended as discipline for the perfection of character. To a certain extent, experience confirms this view. We have to acknowledge our responsibility for our own sins. Moreover, we cannot help perceiving that our best good often comes out of suffering and disaster. Nevertheless, the more frankly one thinks about the possibilities of omnipotent benevolence in contrast with the actualities of everyday human tragedies, the more superficial does this ordinary theistic answer seem.

*524.* If we ask ourselves about the

sources of belief in the omnipotence and the benevolence of God, it is clear that the former must be derived predominantly from abstract thought. It cannot be based on experience alone, although we do confront power in experience. Yet every experience is finite and as such cannot express omnipotence. But benevolence, on the other hand, is more plainly rooted in experience.

*525.* Moreover, it is religiously much more essential that God should be good than that he should be absolutely all-powerful. Hence, not a few thinkers have suggested the possibility of a God whose power is in some way limited. . . . Meanwhile it is all too evident that the attempt to combine the infinite expansion of divine power with the infinite expansion of divine goodness leads to a reaction. The only serious question is as to how far the reaction must go in the direction of recognizing limits in God.

Fifthly, the expansion of God into eternity contracts his relations with the world of experience in time. If we reduce time to its lowest terms, there are two points of certainty. The first is that we have actual experience of time, the consciousness of change and succession in our experiences. The second is that there must be something eternal in the universe. If we try to think of a beginning before which there was absolutely nothing or of an end after which there is nothing, we are thinking either of an effect without a cause or of a cause without an effect, and either idea is irrational. But to say that the temporal and the eternal must both be recognized is not to solve the problem of their relations. When God is regarded as the Eternal One, he is often thought of as above and beyond all time and change. But if his eternity be expanded to the point of eliminating all time from his nature, then, as was said a moment ago, his relations with

the world of our actual time experience are not only contracted, but are rendered remote and unintelligible.

*526.* Either the abstract idea of the divine eternity must in some way be modified, or else the Eternal One must surrender his dealings with the world of time. In one way or the other the idea of God must experience contraction.

Sixthly, the expansion of God's knowledge and power contracts human freedom and thus the attainment of a divine purpose. We have to show first how human freedom is affected and then how the divine purpose is involved.

It is conventionally asserted that the omniscience and omnipotence of God can be reconciled with the freedom of man in the following manner. A distinction is made between knowledge and causation. To know a thing is not identical with causing it. . . . No one would think of saying that God's or anyone's knowledge of past events could now be regarded as the cause of those events. "Why," it is asked, "should knowledge of future events be regarded as causing them?" . . . This is the traditional explanation of the difficulty.

But it is far from being satisfactory to all minds. . . . The objector asks: "If a free act can be known in advance of its happening, then must it not be in principle predetermined, even though the knowledge is not itself the ground of the predetermination?" If at any given time in advance of an act an absolutely certain knowledge of it is possible, then there must be some present grounds which render that knowledge necessary and nothing that can happen between the moment of knowledge and the moment of the act can in any way alter the nature of the act. Thus, foreknowledge inevitably involves a contraction of freedom.

When confronted with an objection

of this sort, America's greatest theist, Borden Parker Bowne, admitted that there was a difficulty. He suggested that it was connected with the nature of time. . . . Bowne admitted that there would be no way out of the difficulty, on the assumption that time is real, "unless we assume that God has modes of knowing which are inscrutable to us." But he held that on his own view of the ideality of time "the problem vanishes in its traditional form, and nothing remains but the general mystery which shrouds for us the epistemology of the Infinite." In spite of the fact that the foreknowledge of freedom is possible only on one of two conditions, the former of which is inscrutable and the latter general mystery, Bowne still accepted it. But we may well inquire whether an hypothesis that leads to such results is worth retaining. Even if Bowne is right, we shall have to say that the expansion of divine knowledge produces a contraction in our understanding of God. But it is very doubtful whether he is right. If he is not, then we must either deny human freedom or modify our view of the divine foreknowledge. The latter seems a more reasonable procedure than the former.

The second part of this sixth point was that the expansion of God's knowledge and power results in contraction in the very attainment of a divine purpose.

527. A God whose foreknowledge is absolute may enjoy Calvinistic sovereignty, he may issue eternal decrees which will eternally be fulfilled, he may embody the laws of mechanism, but he must forego a world of free beings who are morally self-determining. On the other hand, a God whose purpose it is to develop a society of free persons must forego some knowledge and some power if he is to attain his purpose. Expansion in either direction necessitates contraction in the other.

Seventhly, the expansion of God above reason contracts the reasonable basis for belief in his existence. In our previous discussions we have frequently found ourselves reaching a place where we were conscious of the mystery of things. We have found that great thinkers freely acknowledge the inscrutability of God's nature. And anyone who undertook to deny the mystery of things would not be bold, he would be ridiculous. . . . Nevertheless, it is the aim of thought to reach ever further into the darkness and to shed its rays as far as possible. If we choose to use the word God for the unknown or unknowable mystery of things, then such a God has the value of zero so far as concrete human values and problems are concerned. He could not be called good or beautiful or true; to say that he is utterly unknown is to deny that we have grounds for regarding him as worthy of worship or devotion. In short, it is to deny that God in any significant sense of the word exists at all.

528. These considerations lead to a plain conclusion, namely, that . . . if we . . . expand our idea of God by elevating it above all reason, we have contracted and even destroyed the grounds for belief in the existence of any God worth having. A known God must, therefore, be contracted within the limits of our reason. Thus we may say that the cause of reason and the cause of religion are inextricably bound up together. If reason fails, religion fails; and if religion fails, it will be because reason has failed.

### The Resultant Concept of God

529. God is a conscious Person of perfect good will. He is the source of all value and so is worthy of worship and devotion. He is the creator of all other persons and gives them the power

of free choice. Therefore his purpose controls the outcome of the universe. His purpose and his nature must be inferred from the way in which experience reveals them, namely, as being gradually attained through effort, difficulty, and suffering. Hence there is in God's very nature something which makes the effort and pain of life necessary. There is within him, in addition to his reason and his active creative will, a passive element which enters into every one of his conscious states, as sensation, instinct, and impulse enter into ours, and constitutes a problem for him. This element we call The Given. The evils of life and the delays in the attainment of value, in so far as they come from God and not from human freedom, are thus due to his nature, yet not wholly to his deliberate choice. His will and reason acting on The Given produce the world and achieve value in it.

[Sec. 519, Edgar Sheffield Brightman, *The Problem of God* (New York: Abingdon Press, 1930), p. 83. Sec. 520, *ibid.*, p. 84. Sec. 521, *ibid.*, pp. 87–88. Sec. 522, *ibid.*, pp. 92–96. Sec. 523, *ibid.*, pp. 96–97. Sec. 524, *ibid.*, p. 98. Sec. 525, *ibid.*, pp. 98–99. Sec. 526, *ibid.*, pp. 100–102. Sec. 527, *ibid.*, pp. 102–3. Sec. 528, *ibid.*, p. 105. Sec. 529, *ibid.*, p. 113.]

### COMMENT

In the foregoing the writer (1) treats as categorial contrasts the predicates judged to be appropriate to deity, (2) usually softens both poles of the opposition in conformity with a principle that the adequate concept will lie somewhere between the possible extremes, and (3) substitutes a radically different principle when considering the temporal-eternal and the good-evil contrasts.

Brightman does not, of course, treat the full range of categorial contrasts; but, in general, one can discover some aspect of the finite-infinite and inclusive-exclusive oppositions in most of the contrasts which he has discussed. Brightman decides that in principle God should be viewed as law-abiding but not such that all special purposes are sacrificed from his nature, that God should be unitary but not to such an extent that relation to diversity is ruled out, and that God should be as inclusive, powerful, and wise as is possible without making goodness impossible for him or freedom impossible for man. The whole question revolves about the procedure by which this is to be accomplished. His usual procedure is reminiscent of Aristotle in the *Nicomachean Ethics*. By means of the principle that categorial oppositions may be properly resolved by mutual qualification, Brightman arrives at a somewhat less general category—personality—which he finds properly applicable to God; his procedure leads to a conception similar in many respects to a very great human being. On this ground Brightman affirms the finitude of God.

But there are serious departures from the application of his principle. One would expect to find the temporal and eternal contraries modified into a being (not eternal, but) of immense temporal extent; instead, one finds both categories retained: God is eternal and yet related to time. Similarly, one would expect to discover the good-evil opposition resolved through the discovery of a morally neutral midpoint; once again, however, both categories remain: Gods' *purpose* is wholly good, although he *experiences* evil as a personal tragedy against which he must struggle. This instance has particular importance for our discussion inasmuch as our author's most distinctive view, that God is not a wholly blissful being but one in struggle against a "given" element in his nature, depends upon it. Brightman has, then, employed two principles: the ideal of the first leads one to a mean-between-extremes; the ideal of the second leads to a type of concept which characteristically embodies both of the initially opposed "extremes." It is to be carefully noted that the latter principle not only provides Brightman with the concept of the "given" but makes possible a finite-infinite contrast in God's nature. (The former principle, by contrast, leads only to the assertion that God is finite.) The principle involved in this latter case derives the personality of deity from a proper understanding of contraries which are in some manner more ultimate than he. But this in turn amounts to an arbitrary elevation of the "finite," or less than ultimate, categories.

It is our contention that Brightman could not have ended his analysis with "personality" as the final and adequate character of deity were he to have used the first principle, that of mutual qualification of extremes, consciously and consistently; for a personal-impersonal contrast is likewise possible. And, if the principle consists in resolving categorial oppositions by mutual qualification, "personality" would drop out, and our author's final conception of God's nature would perforce stand between personality and impersonality, with the question still pertinent which Brightman asked originally: "Is this too much or too little to grant of God?" It becomes evident that Brightman has exercised his religious feelings in determining where to stop. Substitution of the second determining principle when discussing the good-evil opposition was also dictated, one would suspect, by religious feeling which could not countenance either a wholly blissful or a morally neutral deity.

The principle of embodying both of these opposed and ultimate meanings

in the concept of deity, having led to his key concept, must be granted the more significant doctrine for his system. The reader will note that Brightman, when using this principle, avoided inconsistency by embodying each pole of an apparent opposition on a different level of abstraction; it is God's abstract purpose which is wholly good, and it is elements of his concrete experience which are evil. The retained temporal-eternal opposition has the same structure implicit within it, although Brightman did not here extend his discussion to the point where this structure would have become evident. The other contrasts might have been handled in the same manner. Had he followed this principle more assiduously, Brightman would have properly belonged not to the present chapter but to the one preceding, for in that case he would have had no need to qualify God's inclusiveness in order to retain individuality.

We have seen that the attempt to find a categorial mean is self-defeating. There remains the possibility of extending the use of Brightman's more basic principle, that of dipolarity, "eternal-temporal," "infinite-finite," etc. This alternative contains the advantage not only of greater clarity but of establishing an identity between the ultimate poles of all meaning and the being of religious worth. If Brightman's work does contain this equivocation (let us admit the difficulty of judging with finality work so variously derived and beginning from so many points), we suggest that the reason lies in his tendency to treat empirically or pragmatically what is in essence a question of conceptual order.

# Chapter IX: *Extreme Temporalistic Theism*

## ALEXANDER (1859–1938)

S. Alexander's thinking about the divine has many more facets than those contained in the following selection. He rejects outright a number of possible interpretations. God is not a "society of minds." The analogy from which such a view derives rests upon the fact that in man there may be separate personalities within a total personality; but the analogy breaks down when applied to the universe, for, while in man there is physiological connection between the separate centers, there is no evidence that our persons are joined in this manner to create a divine mind. Neither is God the "group mind," for a group mind is "not a new single mind." Alexander finds what he thinks to be the proper locus of the God-concept through a cautious extension of observed fact, assessing a range of "empirical" data as broad as human experience. On the assumption that space-time has the tendency to create progressively higher qualities, Alexander discovers two loci for the religious emotion: the first is the whole of infinite space-time; the second is that ultimate quality toward which space-time moves.

The first locus Alexander designates as God or, more exactly, the body of God; the second he terms "deity." Some difficulty may attend Alexander's use of these two terms, which have for him distinct yet supplementary meanings. By "deity," then, he means the quality of the divine. In one sense this is always the next quality in the series of qualities engendered by space-time; in another sense it is an ultimate quality, "perfection," toward which the whole of space-time is striving. In either sense deity is nothing actual but is merely

ideal. The full meaning of the term "God" is the whole of space-time with the quality of deity actual in it. Since that quality is nothing actual, even God is not wholly actual. What actually exists is this whole of space-time in *nisus* toward deity. Alexander sometimes refers to this whole space-time as the body of God, and the *nisus* then is toward the attainment of the divine mind. When thinking in this manner, he suggests that the quality of life akin to but less than mind now serves in the place of the mind of the universe, that is, serves this epoch as a substitute deity. Inasmuch as Alexander's terms have not become central to contemporary thinking, one might be disposed to dismiss the structure which the terms introduce as fanciful. And, since he grants that his view is necessarily expressed by figurative language, one may feel inclined to label his thinking as myth rather than metaphysics; but this serious man's thinking should not be dismissed lightly. If his terminology is unusual, his intent has often found expression in other writings. For example, his system has important analogies to that of Whitehead.

Each of Alexander's concepts has behind it some bloc of data or other. That the religious emotion requires an infinite object has its ground in data of religious experience which is, Alexander states, typically a recognition of a quality superior to that characterizing man (and the mind of man is infinite in some respects). The conceivability of God is grounded in a direction discerned in the processes of biological evolution—a movement toward higher forms through increased complexity of organization. That an infinite mind does not now exist has its ground in the doctrine that evolution proceeds from the less toward the more perfect. That such a mind is practically impossible rests on at least two kinds of evidence: (1) evolution habitually throws out classes of entities so that the next stage would have to be a polytheistic class of deities, and thus no one of them would be in every sense infinite; and (2) while an infinite deity whose mind contained the whole of space-time events could be only a unique individual, yet as actual its quality would be a universal (since every actual substance is a union of particular and universal), and a universal is capable of being repeated in various instances. Data can be advanced even for his application of the mind-body analogy to the universe. Mind and body in man exhibit themselves as a relation between a more specialized and a less specialized process; the relation between all of space-time and the quality engendered in its process is the same kind of relation; that is, a higher quality comes to be through further specialization of a portion of the general world process. It must be granted, then, that, if this is a figurative cosmology, at least it is composed of nonfigurative parts. He has written out a grand and complex analogy based upon what man can observe.

The result is a conception of God which, the reader will notice, hovers between reality and unreality. Alexander himself in writing seems to waver between a traditional and an empirical view of what one means by "possible." Since his deity is conceivable, it would seem to be possible; since observation directs otherwise, it seems impossible that the deity described can ever be a reality. A luminous possibility is advanced which, we are then told, is not really possible. In this form the view satisfies only partially, and perhaps does not satisfy at all, man's religious propensities. But it may be that the "im-possible possibility" which Alexander poses is resoluble even within the context of his careful affirmations. If this were to be found the case, our author might safely have affirmed far more than he does in the succeeding pages to which we now invite our reader.

### Space, Time, and Deity

530. God is the whole world as possessing the quality of deity. Of such a being the whole world is the "body" and deity is the "mind." But this possessor of deity is not actual but ideal. As an actual existent, God is the infinite world with its *nisus* towards deity, or, to adapt a phrase of Leibniz, as big or in travail with deity.

Since Space-Time is already a whole and one, why, it may be urged, should we seek to go beyond it? Why not identify God with Space-Time? Now, no one could worship Space-Time. It may excite speculative or mathematical enthusiasm and fill our minds with intellectual admiration, but it lights no spark of religious emotion. Worship is not the response which Space-Time evokes in us, but intuition. Even Kant's starry heavens are material systems, and he added the moral law to them in describing the sources of our reverence. In one way this consideration is irrelevant; for if philosophy were forced to this conclusion that God is nothing but Space-Time, we should needs be content. But a philosophy which left one portion of human experience suspended without attachment to the world of truth is gravely open to suspicion; and its failure to make the religious emotion speculatively intelligible betrays a speculative weakness. For the religious emotion is one part of experience, and an empirical philosophy must include in one form or another the whole of experience. The speculative failure of the answer is patent. It neglects the development within Space-Time of the series of empirical qualities in their increasing grades of perfection. The universe, though it can be expressed without remainder in terms of Space and Time, is not merely spatio-temporal. It exhibits materiality and life and mind. It compels us to forecast the next empirical quality or deity. On the one hand we have the totality of the world, which in the end is spatio-temporal; on the other the quality of deity engendered, or rather being engendered, within that whole. These two features are united in the conception of the whole world as expressing itself in the character of deity, and it is this and not bare Space-Time which for speculation is the ideal conception of God.

Belief in God, though an act of experience, is not an act of sight, for neither deity nor even the world as tending to deity is revealed to sense, but of speculative and religious faith. . . . Any attempt, therefore, to conceive God in more definite manner must involve a large element of speculative or reflective imagination. Even the description of God as the whole universe, as possessing deity, or as in travail with deity, is full of figurative language. If we are to make our conception less abstract we must try to represent to ourselves some individual in whom deity is related to its basis in the lower levels of empirical quality as far down as the purely spatio-temporal; and a being of this kind is, as we shall see, rather an ideal of thought than something which can be realized in fact in the form of an individual. What we have to do is to be careful to conceive the ideal in conformity with the plan of what we know of things from experience.

The simplest way of doing so is to forget for a moment that God being the whole world possessing deity is infinite, and, transporting ourselves in thought to the next level of existence, that of deity, to imagine a finite being with that quality, a god of a polytheistic system, or what we have called an angel. We must conceive such a being on the analogy of ourselves. In us a living body has one portion of itself specialized and set apart to be the bearer of the quality of mind. That specialized constellation of living processes, endowed with the quality of mind, is the concrete thing called mind. The rest of the body in its physiological, material, and spatio-temporal characters, sustains the life of this mind-bearing portion, which in its turn is said in the physiological sense to represent the rest of the body, because there is a general correspondence between the affections of the body and the excitements of the mind-bearing portion which are enjoyed as mental processes. In virtue of some of these mental enjoyments the mind contemplates the things outside its body, in virtue of others it contemplates its own bodily conditions in the form of organic sensa or sensibles, or of other sensibles of movement, touch, and the rest. In the superior finite which has deity, we must conceive the immediate basis of deity to be something of the nature of mind, just as the immediate basis of our mind is life, and the mind of the finite deity will rest on a substructure of life as with us. One part of the god's mind will be of such complexity and refinement as mind, as to be fitted to carry the new quality of deity. Thus whereas with us, a piece of Space-Time, a substance, which is alive, is differentiated in a part of its life so as to be mind, here a substance or piece of Space-Time which is mental is differentiated in a portion of its mental body so as to be divine, and this deity is sustained by all the space-time to which it belongs, with all those qualities lower than deity itself which belong to that substance. Moreover, as our mind represents and gathers up into itself its whole body, so does the finite god represent or gather up into its divine part its whole body, only in its body is included mind as well as the other characters of a body which has mind. Now for such a being, what for us are organic sensibles would include not merely the affections of its physiological body, but those of its mental "body," its mental affections. To speak more accurately, its mental affections, the acts of its mind-body, would take the place of our organic or motor sensa, while sensa, like hunger and thirst, which are the affections of its life-body, would fall rather into the class of sensa which with us are, like the feel and visual look of our bodies, contemplated by special senses. For such a being its specially differentiated mind takes the place of the brain or central nervous system with us. The body which is equivalent with the deity of the finite god, that is to say, whose processes are not parallel to but identical with the "deisings" or enjoyments of the god, is of the nature of mind.

Only this proviso must be added. The mental structure of which a portion more complex and subtle is the bearer of deity, must not be thought necessarily to be a human mind or aggregation of such, but only to be of the mental order. To assume it to be of the nature of human mind would be as if a race of seaweeds were to hold that mind when it comes (the quality of deity for seaweeds) must be founded on the life of seaweeds, and minds the offspring of seaweeds. What form the finite god would assume we cannot know, and it is idle to guess. The picture has been drawn merely in order to give some kind of definiteness to the vague idea of a higher quality of existence, deity as founded upon the highest order of existence we know. There is always a danger that such attempts at definiteness where precise knowledge from the nature of the case is out of the question may seem a little ridiculous. Fortunately when we leave the finite god and

endeavour to form a conception of the infinite God in his relation to things, we may avail ourselves of what is useful in the picture and avoid the danger of seeming to affect a prevision of how things in the future will come to be. We use the picture merely in order to understand how the whole world can be thought of as possessing deity.

We have now to think, not as before of a limited portion of Space-Time, but of the whole infinite Space-Time, with all its engendered levels of existence possessing their distinctive empirical qualities, as sustaining the deity of God. But when we imagine such an individual, we discover two differences which mark him off from all finites, including finite gods. The first is this. Our experience is partly internal and partly external; that is, the stimuli which provoke our enjoyments and through them are contemplated by us (and the same account applies with the proper extension of the terms to all finites) partly arise within our bodies and partly from external ones. The objects which we contemplate are partly organic or motor sensa and partly special sensa, in which are included our bodies as seen or touched or similarly apprehended. Now the body of God is the whole universe and there is no body outside his. For him, therefore, all objects are internal, and the distinction of organic and special sensa disappears. Our minds, therefore, and everything else in the world are "organic sensa" of God. All we are the hunger and thirst, the heart-beats and sweat of God. This is what Rabbi ben Ezra says in Browning's poem, when he protests that he has never mistaken his end, to slake God's thirst. For God there is still the distinction of enjoyment or deising and contemplation, for God's deity is equivalent only to a portion of his body. But it is only for the finites which belong to God's body, all the finites up to finites with mind, that the objects of contemplation are some organic and some external.

The second difference, and ultimately it is a repetition of the first, is this. God's deity is lodged in a portion of his body, and represents that body. But since his body is infinite, his deity (I allow myself to turn deity from a quality into a concrete thing just as I use mind sometimes for the mental quality, sometimes for the concrete thing, mental processes), which represents his body, is infinite. God includes the whole universe, but his deity, though infinite, belongs to, or is lodged in, only a portion of the universe. The importance of this for the problem of theism will appear later. I repeat that when God's deity is said to represent his body, that representation is physiological; like the representation on the brain of the different portions of the body which send nervous messages to the brain. Deity does not represent the universe in the mathematical sense, in which, for example, the odd numbers represent or are an image of the whole series of numbers. Such mathematical representation would require God's deity also to be represented in his deity; and it is not so represented in the same fashion as his body is represented.

The infinitude of God's deity marks the difference between him and all other empirical beings. Deity is an empirical quality, but though it is located in a portion only of the universe, which universe of Space-Time with all its finites of lower order is God's body, yet that portion is itself infinite in extent and duration. Not only is God infinite in extent and duration, but his deity is also infinite in both respects. God's body being the whole of Space-Time is omnipresent and eternal; but his deity, though not everywhere, is yet infinite in its extension, and though his time is a portion only of infinite Time, his deity is, in virtue of what corresponds in deity to memory and expectation in ourselves, infinite in both directions. Thus empirical as deity is, the infinity of his distinctive character separates him from all finites. It is his deity which makes him continuous with the series of empirical characters of finites, but neither is his "body" nor his "mind" finite.

For clearness' sake I must linger a little over this important and difficult matter; for in one sense our minds and all finite things are infinite as well. We are, however, finitely infinite; while deity is infinitely infinite. We are finite because our minds, which are extended both in space and time, are limited pieces of Space-Time. We are infinite because we are in relation to all Space-Time and to all things in it. Our minds are infinite in so far as from our point of view, our place or date, we mirror the whole universe; we are compresent with everything in that universe. . . . Though only a limited range of distinct things comes within our view, they are fringed with their relations to what is beyond them, and are but islands rising out of an infinite circumambient ocean. The whole of which they are parts may shrink in our apprehension into a vague object of feeling or be conceived more definitely as infinite. Still it is there. But this infinite world of Space-Time with its finite things engendered within it finds access to our minds only through our bodies and thence to our brains, and is cognised through our neuromental processes and the combinations of them. Our minds consist of our mental processes, which are also neural ones. If we follow a dangerous method of language, or of thinking, and fancy that the objects we know are the "content" of our minds we may be led into the belief that, since our minds contain representations of all things in the universe, our minds are infinite, in the same way as God's deity. If, however, we recollect that our minds are nothing but the processes of mind and have no contents but their process-characters we shall avoid this danger. We shall then understand how our minds can be finite in extent and duration and yet be compresent with and correspond to an infinite world.

We may distinguish two sorts of infinity, which I will call internal and external. An inch is internally infinite in respect of the number of its parts and corresponds to an infinite line of which it forms only a part. But it is itself finite in length. In the same way our minds, though finite in space-time, may be infinite in respect of their correspondence with the whole of things in Space-Time.

We said that our minds represented our bodies, because to speak generally the various parts of our body were connected neurally with their corresponding places in the cortex. External objects excite our minds through first impinging on our organs of sense. As such representations of our body, our mind is finite. But through that body it is brought into relation with the infinite world. Thus though finite in extent of space and time we are internally infinite. We are so as pieces of Space and Time. But also within the brain there is room for multitudinous combinations initiated from within and enjoyed as imaginations and thoughts, and, for all I know, these are infinitely numerous in their possibilities of combination. We have at least enough of them to comprehend the universe as a whole so far as such apprehension is open to our powers. It is sufficient for our purposes of argument that our minds as spatio-temporal substances are like all spatio-temporal extents internally infinite. Externally we are finite.

But there is nothing whatever outside the body of God, and his deity represents the whole of his body, and all the lower ranges of finites are for him "organic sensa." The spatio-temporal organ of his deity is not only internally but externally infinite. Deity, unlike mind, is infinitely infinite. . . .

We are now led to a qualification of the greatest importance. The picture which has been drawn of the infinite God is a concession to our figurative or mythological tendency and to the habit of the religious consciousness to embody its conception of God in an individual shape. Its sole value lies in its indication of the relation that must be understood upon the lines traced by experience to subsist between deity and mind. This is adequate for finite gods, supposing the stage of deity to have been reached. But the infinite God is purely ideal or conceptual. The individual so sketched is not asserted to exist; the sketch merely gives body and shape, by a sort of anticipation, to the actual infinite God whom, on the basis of experience, speculation declares to exist. As actual, God does not possess the quality of deity but is the universe as tending to that quality. This nisus in the universe, though not present to sense, is yet present to reflection upon experience. Only in this sense of straining towards deity can there be an infinite actual God. For, again following the lines of experience, we can see that if the quality of deity were actually attained in the empirical development of the world in Time, we should have not one infinite being possessing deity but many (at least potentially many) finite ones. Beyond these finite gods or angels there would be in turn a new empirical quality looming into view, which for them would be deity—that is, would be for them what deity is for us. Just as when mind emerges it is the distinctive quality of many finite individuals with minds, so when deity actually emerges it would be the distinctive quality of many finite individuals. If the possessor of deity were an existent individual he must be finite and not infinite. Thus there is no actual finite being with the quality of deity; but there is an actual infinite, the whole universe, with a nisus to deity; and this is the God of the religious consciousness, though that consciousness habitually forecasts the divinity of its object as actually realized in an individual form.

*531.* Infinite deity then embodies the conception of the infinite world in its straining after deity. But the attainment of deity makes deity finite. Deity is an empirical quality like mind or life. Before there was mind the universe was straining towards infinite mind. But there is no existent infinite mind, but only many finite minds. Deity is subject to the same law as other empirical qualities, and is but the next member of the series. At first a presage, in the lapse of time the quality comes to actual existence, animates a new race of creatures and is succeeded by a still higher quality. God as an actual existent is always becoming deity but never attains it. He is the ideal God in embryo. The ideal when fulfilled ceases to be God, and yet it gives shape and character to our conception of the actual God, and always tends to usurp its place in our fancy.

[Sec. 530, S. Alexander, *Space, Time, and Deity* (London: Macmillan & Co., 1920), II, 353–62. Sec. 531, *ibid.,* p. 365.]

COMMENT

The lucid sincerity of this attempt to explicate the nature of deity granted, one wonders at last whether metaphysics is indeed a matter of resting principle upon fact altogether. Or rather one wonders, since even Alexander does not in practice remain consistently factual, how one is to understand his careful extension of the observed fact, since such extension is not a statement of fact. Inasmuch as there is on his view no place for any "must be" in philosophic thinking, the most reasonable extension could in fact be untrue. But strangely there is a negative necessity which Alexander would like to retain in his system, for deity at least can never be. We have seen in our introduction how the reasons supporting his conclusions that deity can never exist are in every case extensions of observed fact. In so far the assertion cannot be maintained; that is, a negative necessity cannot issue from contingent fact alone.

But to say there can be no necessity of any kind, positive or negative, is itself a statement of at least one necessity. And, like many other such principles, this one negates itself. To assert so is not to engage in sophistry, any more than it is a sophism to point out that the logical positivist's principle of observation (in one, at least, of its forms) is not itself open to observation and so, in terms of the principle, is not itself meaningful. That Alexander's principle eventually negates itself leads to the plain conclusion that not every principle requires fact in a "scientific" sense in order to be called true. Alexander cannot have a universe "contingent" in every respect. The reason he cannot, we should insist, is that the meaning of a contingent principle must be in part determined by a contrasting principle which is necessary, and the place of contingency in the universe is determined in part by a contrasting necessity within that same universe.

It is of the highest importance in interpreting the tendency of Alexander's thought to recognize that he does find contrasting principles important. Examining in full his statements about God and deity, for example, one finds that he asserts the universe to be contained in God, while deity (eternally) transcends that universe; God is creative, while deity is in the order of the created; God is relative in that he contains the mixture of the whole, while deity is absolute and "of the order of perfection"; God is neither good nor evil, while deity transcends good and evil, is perfect. Some of these contrasts are clearly misleading, but in all the respects named God is the element in world process which is relative and inclusive; deity is the absolute and exclusive element.

Now, to preserve deity's absoluteness, Alexander decides that this factor should be regarded as sheerly ideal, a result of speculation, a nonexistent final cause. We, on the other hand, should insist that, if the contrast holds between God as contingent and deity as noncontingent, and between God as relative and deity as absolute, then the real contrary for God as actual (keeping the preceding contrasts in mind) is not deity as ideal (meaning imaginary) but deity as real-although-not-actual. This means that the noncontingency which Alexander sensed in deity should really be construed as the element of necessity in his cosmology. Returning then to our earlier statements, it would be no longer a fiction which leads the universe to higher forms, but an abstract yet real purpose contrasting with the totality of space-time and forming the other half of the principle of contingency and concreteness.

One is astonished that, after the extensive elaboration of the nature of deity, we should be told that this nature is nothing real. Alexander carefully pictures, taking his views together, a dipolar view of God which never quite becomes real under his hand. It would be well to know whether such a view was quite satisfactory even for Alexander; the only clear datum in this respect is Alexander's later judgment that Whitehead had gone beyond his own formulations. But other bits of evidence are present in *Space, Time, and Deity* itself which lead one to believe that, whatever his words, Alexander sometimes held, or at least could have held, to the reality of deity. In speaking of

point instants, the matrix of his evolutionary space-time, Alexander quite instructively states that these elements of reality "are real and actual just because they are ideal." And he strongly contends that deity is the form of the future; deity is a future event. In another connection Alexander makes the point that, if time is to be taken seriously, then we must grant that the past and future are just as real as the present moment. Thus he has within his system the needed contrast between the notion of the actual and the real and the needed equation of the ideal with the real which would make of his absolute deity a necessary element in space-time process. All that is lacking is a somewhat more consistent use of these basic distinctions.

Neglect of this distinction, although it led Alexander into an utter temporalism (for, somewhat inconsistently with other statements, he says that God and deity are both inherently temporal), did not prevent him from expressing many other rich insights. Discussing the conception of deity, Alexander points out that, while other beings have external environments, God's environment is wholly internal; that we are, on the organismic analogy, the "organic sensa" for deity; that values and disvalues are contained in God—the values of existence in the mind of deity, the evil of existence in God—and that the disvalues become subservient to that higher quality and are in some manner used thereby; and that our ultimate significance is not in personal immortality but in preparing the way for deity and producing enjoyment for God's being. These are panentheistic insights; and, indeed, panentheism seems to be implicit in the logical and conceptual framework of his thought, although it never quite became explicit in his writings.

# BERMAN (1893———)

It is Louis Berman's concern to trace out relevant lines of evidence in order to discover the point at which they tend to converge or to find in them some common suggestion concerning the superfact of God's existence. So to use the facts of science is not, one will admit, to use them scientifically; but Berman's aim is philosophic rather than scientific, is directed toward understanding rather than discovery. Notwithstanding this, he rises to his interpretation wholly from factual data. His facts are selected from the realms of physics, physiology, and mystical experience. The critical question is whether a collation of facts drawn from these areas can eventuate in a unified philosophic structure rather than in a merely interesting mosaic.

The collation consists of (1) the unity of the reports of mystical experience when adventitious elements are removed from them; (2) the presence of electrical phenomena in relation to consciousness particularly and to life generally, and the probability (in Berman's mind) of the truth of the converse: the presence of consciousness in electrical phenomena throughout the universe; (3) the manner in which such a view could explain the free variations which occur on the atomic level as minute conscious decisions; (4) the inadequacy of all mechanical explanations of evolution and hence the necessity for including a psychic factor in the explanation; and, finally, (5) the identity of the "germ plasm" of mankind leading to the suggestion that we as individuals are variant aspects of a common personality. The reports of mystical experience are perhaps more determinative for Berman than the other data.

It is doubtless the case that all evidence leads somewhere and means something; it is perhaps the case that the evidence leads in the general direction Berman so vividly describes. But, the reader will note, the author—taking the nearer side of things as a picture of their farther side—gained a concept of God which is just as contingent and destructible as the facts in which he discerned a common tendency. Was this result wholly accidental, or was the conclusion dictated by the method chosen? We shall discuss the question later. Meanwhile, the reader will discover that Berman writes of great ideas with commendable urgency, that his writing is richly suggestive, and that the cultural unity he seeks is admirable.

## The Psycho-continuum

532. The essence of the mystic participation consists of the establishment of certain psychic connections between the individual and the whole of life whereby he sees himself included as part of a collective enterprise. The individual's field of consciousness, and its penumbra of the unconscious, become linked with a network of oneness which cannot be explained by direct or indirect sensory contacts or associations such as are familiar to common sense and science. These connections are not merely projections and identifications by which the individual fails to distinguish between himself and his experiences. They are of the nature of continuities which may be called tele-participations to indicate that they take place and act at a distance and are definitely analogous to and suggestive of telepathy.

533. No hypothesis concerning these tele-connections can explain as many of the pertinent and verified findings in the field as does the conception of a psycho-continuum involving the collec-

tive unconscious and the collective superconscious. Energy is operative in their manifestations, a psychic energy or psycho-activity, concerning the properties of which we know little scientifically but enough empirically to compel us to recognize its existence and its interactions with other forms of energy such as heat, light and electricity. Psychic energy is at work in us and in all organisms as well as in the life-personality and the cosmos as a whole. The participation in the totality of that psycho-activity is the essence of the mystic participation.

534. The domain of the psychic extends throughout the universe. Flashes and momentary emanations of individual consciousness may occur in all molecular and atomic reactions, which may account for the fact of a certain degree of freedom and variation observed among them by physicists. In the larger and more permanent combinations of matter and energy in the cells of living protoplasm, psychic activity reaches a more stable habitat and the beginnings of memory for the psychic fixations of individuality, as a matrix of personality, are established. The excessively feeble psychic flashings of the individual atoms and molecules may be compounded, much as the electrical charges of tiny batteries may be arranged in series and accumulate considerable voltage.

535. How the psychergia [psychic energy] is transformed into other kinds of energy and how it then returns to its original state is the secret which probably contains the solution of the problem of mystic participation and its deliberate control. Though its operations cannot be identified with electricity, electricity seems to be generated wherever there are manifestations of psycho-activity. Along the fibers of nerves, for example, whenever they are stimulated, there flows an energy known as the nerve impulse or current which is always accompanied by manifestations of electricity designated by physiologists as the action current.

536. Altogether, it would seem possible that just as a group of electrons in motion, or a moving electrical field, begets magnetism, and magnetism induces electricity, psychergia and electricity are similarly related. The electrical field may have psychic properties while every psychic field has electromagnetic properties. Thus we may be able to understand how individual psychic fields of influence interlock in the cosmic psycho-continuum when we comprehend how individual electromagnetic fields participate in the space-time continuum.

*The Essence of Mystic Participation*

537. Throughout the ages, certain individuals here and there have reported a direct revelation of the basic affinities between humankind and the life-personality and the cosmic forces behind it. Their revelations have possessed an extraordinary and supernormal quality which has contrasted them with workaday life and psychation and so they have been called mystic as opposed to the rational. At the core of every such mystic revelation has been the direct perception, without the intervention of reasoning or logic or indeed any intermediary whatsoever, of an all-pervading ubiquitously operative supreme personality in whom all beings are united as one. Such a perception really amounts to a universal apperception, a perception which includes and transmutes all perceptions, past, present and future, into the single reality by means of an identification of the self with the cosmic: a cosmic communion.

It is the essence of the cosmic communion that it is a personal experience, like being in love, bearing a child, producing a poem, an experience at once profoundly illuminating and ultimately ineffable. It fills an aching void in the heart of the isolated individual, and completes the system of his psycho-reality in a pattern that extends into the infinite and lasts forever. It is accompanied by an emotion of cosmic ecstasy which provides it with an authority and sanction with which no other value can compete.

Interpreting the poetry, the metaphors and the music of the language in which the mystic struggles to convey the substance and meaning of his unique experience, there emerges a central nucleus in each of his communications: the establishment of communion with a personality larger than that of the communicant, the personality of the universe. That is the dominant fact upon which all agree, in spite of all differences of words, images, references, local conditionings and historical settings. . . . the common denominator of each, from ignorant peasant girl to learned scholastic is the same: that a new significance has been given human fellowship and human relations by the discovery of a link to the superhuman, in effect, the superconscious. It is as if a child seemingly deserted, an outcast from all that is warm and vitalizing, were to find again and return to a father and mother whom it thought forever lost, and to a multitude of kith and kin to whom it is blood-related and sympathetically attracted.

*538.* Philosophers and priests have created strange gods. They have made them magistrates of cosmic police courts to punish evil-doers and to reward the deserving. They have made them mathematicians, constantly thinking in formulas, no one knows for what reason. That word in the dictionary which stands for a word independent of all words, the Absolute, is also a god, an awesome abstraction in which all relatives are suspended in a state of arrested animation. The Absolute becomes the limbo for all queer psychological necessities of the human mind. But all these gods have proved themselves inadequate for the unification of humanity. Mankind behaves as if these gods were powerless. There can be no doubt that they have failed.

Indeed these ancient beliefs in the fatherhood of God and the brotherhood of man now sound like the most desiccated of platitudes because they no longer bear the pressure of dynamic realities. Yet there never was a time in the history of mankind when there was a more intense need for a validated conception of God to restore those bonds of unity and solidarity between men that religious beliefs provided in the past.

*539.* An assured conviction of the identity of their personalities and interests, rooted in the common blood and pscho-activity of a superpersonality which includes them all, must spread among all individuals, families, groups and classes. . . . Only utter obliviousness to the invisible fibers of flesh and memory, functioning and participation, which bind all human beings indissolubly together into a single organism, has made possible the fantastic extravaganza of self-torture and mutilation which is the present state of mankind.

### The Needed Synthesis

*540.* A tremendous synthesis of the known and the unknown is at hand and no one can gainsay its necessity. Out of the hopelessly contradictory and conflicting maelstrom of attitudes and customs, religions and philosophies, languages and governments, territories and boundaries, social institutions and economic systems in which so many individuals and nations have been wrecked, mankind must steer its course to the mainland of this synthesis and unification. And upon that land will arise the beginnings of a new humanity, linked with the visions of its early prophets, because it has recovered the meaning of their primeval oracles, and rediscovered them in that sound and critical approach to reality known as science.

Certain conceptions must be universalized in education and discourse as basic for every human being. First comes the fact that all human beings are descended from the same ancestors in the commingling of various ancestral strains in the past, and all will mingle their blood in their descendants. That is one of the prime teachings of biology. All human flesh fuses in a single mass as the materials of heredity are distributed and redistributed in the successive generations of interbreeding and crossbreeding. In the germ plasms of mankind, the psychic power of memory, never lost, has always stored and restored, held and reproduced the experience and personalities of ancestors as far back as the beginning of life. Viewed in its entirety, mankind is the history and the memory of one personality, that of the life-personality. The isolation of the individual, chained to his own limited consciousness by the self-protective necessities of his ego, can be broken down by revealing to him how blinded he has been to his vital continuity with the deepest reaches of the past and the dynamic sources of the future.

In the perspectives of time-space, the matrix of cosmic psychation, the individual is only a cross section in three dimensions of that stream of continuity which is a single superorganism and superpersonality. Life does not stand forlorn and lost on this planet, does not strive and suffer on this earth like a mariner marooned on an island never to be visited by a salvaging craft from a greater world. Life's habitat is but the fragment of a star, to be sure. It seems like a leaf swept by the wind in the face of the huge galaxies and supergalaxies, the inconceivable extent and duration of the universe. Yet life is no fluttering leaf, but a tree firmly rooted in the laws and purposes of the cosmic elements.

The second great awareness that should be spread to the ends of the earth is the idea that our planet was prepared for life. Chance could not have built its precarious but triumphant structure. It is no waif, lost in the streets of space and time, a voice crying in the wilderness. The correlations and integrations of life and environment and the conditions of their interadaptations can be traced to the very depth of the elements and atoms themselves. This preparation is not simply a rare curiosity of the cosmic adventure, nor a freak of its progeny. The properties of the elementary chemical constituents of the stuff of life, protoplasm, are uniquely fitted for its evolution. The era of prelife, the dance of the earth and the sun, and the other remarkable adjustments which maintain them in exquisite equilibrium, must be regarded as staging the scene for the appearance of life. Everything facilitates its emergence and its ascent to higher and more complex systems. . . .

That there is such a unique arrangement for and predisposition toward life in the intimate constitution of the cosmos, in the very heart of its deepest processes, can mean only that psychation, which is its most distinctive characteristic, is a manifestation of, in fact a continuation and extension of, a cosmic psycho-activity. This cosmic psycho-activity cannot be located in a defined three-dimensional body, as is human psychation in the brain. It can be conceived only as the organizing and directing energy of the continuum which modern physics has made of space, time and action. Dispersed in island universes which have evolved out of the original universe, it evolves that reality of ultrahuman dimensions of which human science is now beginning to have a glimpse.

All that we can say about this cosmic

psycho-activity is that it is set upon constructing ways and means of concentrating and stabilizing its energy in more and more complex systems. It can therefore be inferred that its dynamic activity is subject, like all other energies, to the universal law of degeneration, the law of entropy. It is possible thus to compare its fate with that of the other and lower forms of cosmic energy: electricity, magnetism, heat, and light. A slow but inevitable decay and death overcomes them all. That degeneration can be observed in the workings of our own psychic energy and in the span of our own lives.

*541.* Knowing the law of the degradation of all energy including its own, the cosmic godhead foresees the end of the universe in the total loss of all potentialities, and the cessation of all that is dynamic in a perpetually static level of inactivity. It foresees its own death in that changelessness. It is that logic which provides the clue to the underlying trends in the preparation for and evolution of life on earth. The long slow struggle of living things to evolve into dominators of their environment is really the history of the continuation of a cosmic struggle, the drive of the cosmic consciousness to save itself and renew itself, and, in the end, to immortalize itself.

In so far as we understand its history at all, life represents a reversal of the law of entropy. As species increased and multiplied, individuals have constructed themselves into systems of greater and greater energy content, which can bind energy into more and more complex, more and more stable and more and more durable forms. In man this tendency has reached its acme. For he has not only become conscious of the process, inventing and improving nonliving machines as aids to his purpose, but is seeking ways and means of penetrating into the ultimate secrets of energy, in all its combinations, degener-

ations and regenerations. All his researches are really directed to that objective, and thereby to the emancipation of consciousness from its material conditions and dependencies. This, the chief research of mankind, will mean in the end the attainment of a genuine immortality for the life-personality and the cosmic forces behind it.

Consequently there can be envisaged a ladder of individuation in the evolution of life forms as regards the consciousness of God. There are those on the lowest rungs, the entirely self-encapsulated, completely undifferentiated in their kinship with all of life and prelife; much like those vegetative cells in our own bodies which feed the brain and the unconscious. Then there are others who are barely conscious of their participation. A few here and there in human history have consciously participated. The time is coming when there will be more and more of the informed and inspired who are sharing, with fully opened eyes, in the growth of the greater personality of which they are parts.

*542.* The religion of the future, the religion of the life-personality within the cosmic consciousness, of the God of the universal evolution, need not be housed in stone or wood. It will rather be a fellowship of world order, a union of the participants in God.

*543.* We are not merely particles of stellar dust, but cells of the great cosmic being to whose history and preservation we are all essential. Each particular individual belongs to it, no matter how transiently and inadequately. Each acquires a new significance and dignity, a value and an importance of which he can never be deprived in the light of that relationship.

Religion and philosophy and science can, therefore, be conjoined in a union that will reverse the separative differentiations of the civilized ego. We revert once more to the union of all knowledge, all thought, all feeling, in the vision of the whole which was so natural to primitive man. For that vision is founded on the solid rock of the ultimate facts of the universe, life and psychation.

544. Groups may be formed as centers of symbiotic education. Their activities may vary from silent mediation to the arts of moving rhythmically in unison, as in the whirling dances of the East. All the techniques of music and poetry should be marshalled for the revival of the emotion of collective communion. Such group participation may not be necessary for some individuals but it will be absolutely essential for most. In time all will develop to some degree the power of communal communication which comes from association with the cosmic psycho-activity to which each is a contributing consciousness.

The mind of man is made in the image of the mind of God for good reasons. The evolution of mankind is the vanguard of all activities and events in the cosmos. The life-personality has reached the stage of universal knowledge in man, passing through intuition and instinct to intelligence and science in the pursuit of its ultimate aims. This knowledge will lead to an understanding of the mechanical (in the sense of blindly operating laws) in nature, life and the history of humanity as a reflection of God using the laws of energy: matter and logic—indeed, he is bound by them because involved in them, just as a poet or a musician or an engineer are held within the limitations of their crafts and materials.

The fundamental principles of the universe are the means by which the cosmic psycho-activity keeps itself together. The consequent necessity of mechanical laws and operations of matter and energy, time and space, systems and patterns in the basic continuum has consecrated the principle of individuation. But the individual has turned the

life consciousness into a multiple dissociated personality. Its reintegration by the renascence of the mystic participation will not only take the individual out of his solitariness—every man out of his isolation—but it will bring salvation to our species in its enlistments for the service of God, the God of evolution, and further his growth and his work for the continuation of his consciousness. God-consciousness must become the dominant, central, continuously operating idea of our lives.

He contributes to the consciousness of God who discovers truth, creates beauty, adds new treasures to the psychic possessions of mankind which are its only permanent possessions. The recognition of the God of evolution as *the ultimate fact of facts* and the identification of him with the cosmic drive of which the life-personality is the spearhead, is the only road to individual self-fulfillment.

545. Men will come to a new and grander conception of personal immortality. They persist and endure as patterns of memory, as psychic personalities, within God's being and becoming. That is the only everlasting life possible for them. Men will learn that God Himself is only potentially immortal, however inconceivably vast be His wisdom and power. But men will be heartened by the knowledge that they can, however infinitesimally, assist Him to immortality by adding all they are capable of to the great work and the great purpose. For they are now engaged in discovering the ways of energy and the means of life, the technics of organization and the emancipation of consciousness from its limiting conditions, a project which is in the end the drive of the cosmic Godhead itself— the final defeat of death, the only death that can really matter—the death of the mind of the universe.

[Sec. 532, Louis Berman, *Behind the Universe* (New York: Harper & Bros., 1943), p.

283. Sec. 533, *ibid.*, p. 283. Sec. 534, *ibid.*, p. 296. Sec. 535, *ibid.*, p. 284. Sec. 536, *ibid.* Sec. 537, *ibid.*, pp. 286–87. Sec. 538, *ibid.*, pp. 290–91. Sec. 539, *ibid.*, p. 292. Sec. 540, *ibid.*, pp. 293–95. Sec. 541, *ibid.*, pp. 296–97. Sec. 542, *ibid.*, p. 301. Sec. 543, *ibid.*, pp. 301–2. Sec. 544, *ibid.*, pp. 302–3. Sec. 545, *ibid.*, p. 303.]

### COMMENT

We freely grant that facts are suggestive of principles and, indeed, of the interpretation which the proper principles would demand. But an exclusive emphasis on fact can lead only to a suggested principle or a principle which has no more necessity in it than the facts which led thereto. Interpretation in terms of such principles, then, can be no other than contingent interpretation; its concepts can explain only contingent features of reality. It does indeed appear that Berman's contingent deity is a consequence more of his method than of his data. Indeed, in the absence of that unattainable totality of all fact, how can Berman insist that the facts lead to this particular theory? The data of future decades may shift their point of convergence or suggest a different superfact. To be sure, we have facts as the description of proximate and individual things; but does it follow that we can expect the characterization of their ultimate and inclusive nature to be nothing more than the superfact produced by their coupling? If the long history of metaphysics has shown anything, it is that principles are not identical to or exhausted by mere matters of fact.

The God which Berman finds implicit in mystic experience, evolution, and the psycho-continuum is a factual and so a concrete thing. A puzzling exception is, however, to be noted: apparently law (i.e., the law of entropy) has a necessity beyond that of fact, for even God is said to be subject to this law. Such relationship appears to deify the law of entropy rather than God. But if, as Berman thinks, God is truly all-inclusive, does he not include the law of entropy as well, and must this not add whatever necessity the law possesses to his nature? Berman does not consider the question. The ultimacy of this law in his thought seems to rest upon the scientific prestige with which it is, or was, regarded. But suppose this iota of necessity does constitute a problem for Berman's interpretation. Would not the problem commit him to the philosophic task; that is, to show that his view of God is in conformity with whatever facts we possess (as, presumably, he has done) and, in addition, that this concept can be placed in a consistent ideational context which is adequately descriptive of experience generally and capable of supporting the formal principles of specialized inquiries and of illuminating the interrelations of the concepts necessary to metaphysical inquiry such as the distinctions between contingent and necessary, cause and effect, time and space, internal and external relations, etc.? This is not to say that Berman as a popular writer should first have become a metaphysician; but Berman as a metaphysician insisting that deity is throughout contingent should certainly have faced metaphysical issues. Such data as he adduces may serve very well to illustrate a system, but they are not sufficient to establish that system.

Since Berman gives us no way of reasoning about necessity and contingency, the conclusion he reaches concerning an all-inclusive God, the directing energy of space-time, subject to growth and struggling against decay, is not to be accepted literally at the precise point where a judgment of necessity or contingency is concerned. And, if our general thesis is correct, a further elaboration of system should have led Berman to a sense of necessity not at all in conflict with the contingency he rightfully values as proper to God's nature.

# AMES (1870————)

The pragmatic test of meaning introduced by Peirce sometimes became in the practice of William James a test for truth; and in the hands of John Dewey this instrument worked more radically still in the fields of cosmology and ontology to reduce the realm of human discourse to actual and possible human experiences. Events replace things (although this is not Dewey's contribution), and any statement concerning a thing apart from or behind experience has no meaning. The force of this pragmatism and instrumentalism captured the mind of one of Dewey's associates at Chicago, Edward Scribner Ames. The reader will note in section 551 which follows that Ames, after insisting upon the importance of a personal judgment, asserts that such judgment "is in fact the only method of giving *meaning* to the world, and at last it is *meaning* which constitutes any world at all." The statement is typical of the system, emerges from a radical application of the pragmatic doctrine, intended initially as a test for meaning alone, and serves to blend the realm of meaning with that of significance. Even more than this, pragmatism leads Ames, in one frame of reference, to identify the significant with the real, so that reality comes almost to be identified, at such times, with the sum of our significant meanings.

The preceding judgments are not always applicable, for Ames also employs the term "reality" when he intends the common-sense objective meaning; but, in general, it seems to be the case that, while any adequate statement of reality must contain both fact and value, the value is for Ames more really real, more deserving of primary attention in describing the experience. Commonly value-statements—statements of appre-

ciation, aspiration, etc.—are held to be less objective than statements of fact. But, once an equation of the real with significant meaning has been effected, it becomes possible to reverse the common judgment concerning the relation of these types of expression. We should not then be surprised to discover that for Ames statements of value, expressing more of one's total experience, are more concrete and ultimately more objective than *mere* statements of fact. Science comes to be viewed as a very thin abstraction from the massive, many-faceted human experience. This is not to say that science is untrue; the factual basis, all of it, is implicit in and needed by any value statement, but, since reality is somehow experience, not only are the facts part of the experience but our response to the facts as well.

If a personal appreciative response must be fitted into the meaning of any experienced aspect of reality, then such response is a proper dimension of any or all reality. In conceiving the universe as a whole merely as a set of facts, one conceives the universe abstractly; one must here, as everywhere, conceive in a personal manner to conceive concretely and properly. The proper conception of the universe then is that of a personified reality. Ames elsewhere insists, by way of analogy, that one pictures one's alma mater more objectively as a gracious lady (knowing the figure has as its constituents many factual elements) or pictures the United States more properly as a kindly bearded gentleman, Uncle Sam (with its relevant factual background), than when a university is understood merely in terms of campus, personnel, endowment, and the like or than when the United States is conceived merely in terms of territory, institutions, tariffs, and the flow of trade. In the same manner God is man's figure for this whole universe made personal as every item of concrete experience is personal and idealized as one (rightly) selects the factual elements of order, love, beauty, and rationality as most significant and properly constitutive of its reality; and in the background the laws and facts of science, the brutality and struggle, become the facts supporting and the limitations qualifying the gracious figure characteristic of the whole. This, it seems to us, is the conceptual background against which the following selection is to be understood.

## The Attributes of God

*546.* If the understanding of a thing is sought in the concrete relations which it bears, it has within itself and in these relations all the values and all the reality which it signifies. The order and beauty found in the world and life are themselves inherent and actual, and give reality meaning and significance. Reality is in so far good, beautiful, and divine. Doubtless the reality we experience is in these respects limited and finite, and we are, on these grounds, required to be content with a finite God.

*547.* Reality is characterized by love; that is, love is present in the world and in life. It is the matrix of life in all orders of being, in mating, in friendship, in the good will which creates and binds together the higher forms of living beings. There is also hatred and envy and malice in reality, but love is pre-eminently identified with God. Here, as in other respects, God is not equivalent to all reality but to certain phases of it. Only where love is, God is. But wherever love is, in the higher and in the lower living forms, there God is manifest. Those who experience love, parental, filial, conjugal, communal, or cosmic, experience God. God, as love, is not far from any one of us. In love we live and move and have

our being. This love exists as personal, intelligent, and active in the living world of actual reality. Hence we say God is reality idealized. This idealization does not mean fabricated or imagined. It means selection. God is the world or life taken in certain of its aspects, in those aspects which are consonant with order, beauty, and expansion. That these features are present in reality as experienced, as known, is obvious. To assert that love is not present in rocks and tides and winds may be true but these do not exhaust reality, nor do they state the elements of reality which are of most dominant and pervasive importance. Love is present in animals and men and these belong to reality. It is manifest in lovers and families, in states and in world-societies, and these belong to the world and to the cosmos. Therefore reality, taken in its most inclusive and far-reaching significance, manifests love, and this empirical fact is the ground for the religious interpretations of reality as God.

*548.* In a similar way it may be shown that other attributes of reality are included in God. Intelligence and rationality are in life, not perfectly nor universally, but in degree. Modern psychology has greatly extended the recognition of intelligence in creation.

*549.* It is not the whole of life. There is much brute force, sheer impulse, blind activity, but a degree of rationality is present. To the rational beings who appreciate it, it is regarded as valuable beyond any quantitative relation in which it seems to stand to other measurable aspects of life. Religion thinks of this wisdom as a quality of reality conceived as God. God is reality manifesting the functions of intelligence. The world thinks, reasons, understands, in and through the rational beings which appear in it. For the argument now under consideration it is not necessary to show more than this. The very fact that there is an order of beings in the world and of it which manifests some degree of rationality is sufficient to justify the claim that reality includes this characteristic. The idealization of reality is illustrated by the tendency to select and magnify the significance of intelligence, and by including it in the nature of reality to identify it with God.

So conceived, God is found present in the daily and commonplace experience of living. Order, intelligence, and love are the qualities of his nature.

550. The values and the loyalties of religion are so engrossing that they allow little opportunity or tolerance for analytical and critical estimates. The religious view of the world, in its emotional intensity and affectionate appraisal, naturally employs vivid and intimate personal symbols of the most perfect and absolute kind. In religious appreciation, God is Reality idealized and glorified with the attributes of complete and flawless personality.

In lesser matters the human mind employs the honorific terms of perfection without confusion. A homely and humorous instance of this fact I have captured from our modern world of industry and trade. It is a trademark, stamped in metal, which I removed from an old oilstove still doing service in my summer cottage. The trademark reads: "New Perfection No. 62." Presumably the inventor of the stove, elated by the creation of such a convenient domestic device, was moved to call it "Perfection." When some improvement was developed, with no apology to the philosophical absolutists, he advertised his "New Perfection"; and with the successive inventions he boldly continued to number his growing perfections through the long series up to sixty-two!

Since God was first conceived in personal terms, he has been to religious souls the perfect Person. With the development of wisdom, mercy, justice, and love in the world, he has been the infinitely wise, merciful, just, and loving God. In spite of all evil in the world, regardless of the injustice, hatred, and falsehood which exist, God is to the hearts who love him, omniscient, omnipotent, complete and absolute perfection.

### The Sense in Which God Is Cosmic

551. There is a sense, surely, in which the scientific conception of the world is abstract and partial. No doubt it is legitimate for what it is, but to assume that it is the whole or that it is the truer conception is to surrender the only means of living a genuine human life. For that life is one of personal values, of imagination, purposes, and ends. To say that this is "merely," or "just," or "only" our human point of view, assumes that it is in some sense unreal and illusory, while from the side of the living, vital sense of things, it is far more "real" and important than anything else. In an empirical assessment of life as we live it, nothing is so actual and so meaningful. Why should an empiricist overlook or minimize these facts? They loom large and beautiful to our human estimate and therefore are for us actually large and beautiful.

It is important not to confuse transiency with insignificance. Human life need not be small because it is short. Value is not measured by time. Finite things in their little day may be the carriers of meanings and experiences which transcend their forms and limits. Even if the human race itself is destined to cease, are not our human loves and aspirations profoundly significant? The scope of life, by the calculations of the scientists, opens out towards a future of millions of years, and by the estimates of moral values, it acquires spiritual dimensions of more significant magnitudes. The individual knows that the end will come for him, yet he clings to life and enjoys it. May it not be the same for the whole of life?

It is good while it endures, and its values are great and wonderful beyond all such calculation. Life is good in the feel of it, even when mixed with pain and evil. Otherwise it would be abandoned. ... Actually, it goes on, under the shadow of smoking volcanoes, in the presence of danger and death, with an astonishing energy and joy. And when the brighter scenes are considered —domestic bliss, happy friendships, successful labor, achievements of discovery and creation—man appears as a happy, productive, and well adjusted child of Nature. What disturbs him most are his own dreams of something better yet to be, in contrast to which his present attainments are partial and inadequate. His "divine discontent" is itself prophetic and inspiring.

If "nature" includes man and all his works and aspirations, then the idea of God based upon it becomes cosmic in its significance. Here is found the answer to those objections which derive from the difficulties of interpreting God from the side of personality. These have their force only in that sharp dualism which conceives the physical universe on one side, and the human world as a little realm outside it. When nature is itself humanized by the inclusion of man, personality and the social process become legitimate in defining the entire picture. The physical becomes the abstract, partial aspect of the world, and the personal is the more adequate characterization. It is when we allow ourselves to be imposed upon by the natural-science point of view as more real, more actual, that the human sphere appears as subjective, illusory, or unreal. If we hold consistently to the facts of experience, empirically given, man has good ground for asserting the importance and centrality of his feeling for himself and his kind. It is just one of the interesting and impressive phenomena of human thought that it is able to take an outside look at the world, but that it is truer or more essential than the inside apprehension of reality through genuinely human estimates is a wholly gratuitous assumption. This may be a very vital instance of "the will to believe," but it is not merely arbitrary or fictitious. It is in fact the only method of giving *meaning* to the world, and at last it is *meaning* which constitutes any "world" at all. Starting with the richness and fullness of life as experienced through social and personal relations, it is possible to abstract certain aspects and treat them as the physical sciences do. But to assume that we can begin with the external, and the purely objective material realm, is to desert the empirical procedure and to lose grips upon the most immediate and worthful forms of reality. When this simple fact is realized, it may be seen that the abstract, natural-science interpretation of nature is indirect, round-about and exceedingly difficult of attainment; while the personal, social conception is more original, more real, and more appreciable.

*552.* Practical life constantly involves the use of objects, forces, and substances which are not wholly understood, and it is of the very genius of the scientific procedure to formulate conceptions of them in reference to their behavior and function. Life goes on under the pressure of wants and habits, with varying degrees of awareness of the factors involved. It is doubtful whether any knowledge of them is possible except in relation to that process and their use. Attitudes are evolved, values are cherished, and controls are effected without clear insight into all the events. Religious experience is no exception. Its gods are not to be understood apart from that experience, as abstract, isolated entities. They have their being in the action and outreaching of life itself.

God as Reality, inclusive and ideally evaluated, is not to be thought of apart from that Reality. It is no more strange that religion should have this general term than that science should have the word "Nature," or that politics should speak of "World" or that philosophy should conceive the "Cosmos." If these are "concrete universals" may not God also be a concrete universal? Any universal is used to gather up facts and experiences into a system, to designate the system in which they are known to stand. It is therefore more than a class term, indicating a number of particulars. Such a universal means an organization of factors into a whole. Thus "city" signifies more than "men," for a city presents associations of men in certain relations, geographical, political, and economic. The term God expresses order and purpose and moral values in the great Reality which we call Life or the World. Reality conceived as friendly, as furnishing support for man's existence and for the realization of ideal ends, is God.

[Sec. 546, Edward Scribner Ames, *Religion* (New York: Henry Holt & Co., 1929), p. 153. Sec. 547, *ibid.*, pp. 154–55. Sec. 548, *ibid.*, p. 155. Sec. 549, *ibid.*, p. 156. Sec. 550, *ibid.*, pp. 161–62. Sec. 551, *ibid.*, pp. 169–71. Sec. 552, *ibid.*, pp. 177–78.]

COMMENT

Ames habitually identifies God with two aspects of our experience: the inclusive whole is one important element of the conception, and the ideal aspect of that whole is the other. Were Ames to sacrifice either of these components, the word "God" would become a mere synonym for the other—either for "universe" or for "ideal." The two propositions are identified through the judgment—"God is reality idealized"—and we may presume that the act of judging has not itself changed the nature of that whole; reality is still the massive whole and ideal part which together furnish the elements making up this

judgment. It is worthy of note that just these two components are the ones which, again and again, in more metaphysical systems stand for God as inclusive totality (the relative aspect) and for God as abstract purpose (the ideal aspect).

The question is whether Ames's use of these metaphysical elements in any way saves his discussion from being a mere play of semantics; we think not. Ames wishes to view reality primarily as "significance," but in the background is to be found the more common meaning of reality as a real interplay of forces part only of which on his view are concerned with values. The meaning of his basic judgment depends upon its two components; and, taken together, these component meanings merely furnish a poetic solution for a metaphysical problem.

Certainly Ames would not wish to sacrifice the brute fact of the universe and to insist instead that reality is just the pictorial figure of something like Uncle Sam; this would lead to a species of idealism. Even to speak as though the position could be understood literally is to identify part with whole, deliberately blend real distinctions, and court the dangers of subjectivism. The view must then be understood poetically or as in some sense less than literal; and this brings with it a renewed demand for the literal statement of what has here been said poetically. It is a demand for metaphysics.

We contend that meaning cannot be identified as such with significance; and significance can be identified with reality only in a very personal and nonliteral sense. Of course it is true that any significant statement requires a kernel of meaning, and any meaning carries at least a minimal significance. But systems of meaning are more highly structured than what we may term "systems of significance." For meaning needs precision, is dipolar, and could never lead to an identification of the concrete with the abstract, of the real with the ideal; while significance tends often to blend such distinctions, the emphasis resting upon richness of metaphor and not upon precision. Now, inasmuch as "God" has often appeared in both kinds of system—in the systems of meaning (the classical philosophies) as a concept implicit in its most general principles; in systems of significance (the popular religions) as the ultimate sanction concerning values—it is not surprising that someone should attempt to identify the two realms, as Ames has done. But the attempt is ultimately unwise and unworkable, for there is no exact correspondence between them. Significance sacrifices other concerns for practicality, while some meaning systems have no direct,

or at best minimal, practical bearing. And, although ultimately there must be some connection between meaning and significance, a facile identification is not likely to aid in its discovery.

If what Ames desired was the right to apply significant terms to reality no matter what the nature of that reality may be, we tend to grant this right. If he intended a minimal statement of the kind of quality one would associate with God for purposes of social organization, then the force of the statement is in question, or its unitive power, or its relevance for a specified background and tradition, none of which questions is within our province. But, where the issue is one of meaning as such, a metaphysics beyond these usages is requisite to explicate the precise relations of that universe.

## CATTELL (1905——)

Raymond B. Cattell, like others in this chapter, centered his attention upon an area of contingent fact. Whereas Alexander utilized the data of biological emergence, and Berman emphasized physics and physiology, Cattell accepts the relations between individual and group as being of pivotal importance for the question of God. Here the factual yield of social psychology is advanced as the key to the solution of our problem, although Cattell grants that the discipline is still in an exploratory stage. Once again the reader will be confronted with an attempt to reach principles through the manipulation of fact. Certain of the difficulties standing in the way of such attempts have been noted earlier.

Cattell seems to find in social psychology a principle similar to the *gestalten* of psychologists Köhler, Wertheimer, and others; that a group is more than the sum of its individuals constitutes his principle. What this

means the author elaborates patiently and extensively. Much of what he says in elaborating this basic insight is doubtless true; and certainly the factual data of Cattell's field, as well as those of the other disciplines represented in the present chapter, have bearing upon the final shape of an adequate philosophic scheme. But has Cattell, in the saying, remained within the field—as he thinks he has—of his own discipline? If he has not, that fact merely serves to introduce our contention (which will be elaborated in the commentary) that the discipline of metaphysics is needed to aid in interrelating the themes he so convincingly advances. The argument as it stands is rich and stimulating; we ask the reader to judge concerning its self-sufficiency.

### The Conception of a Group Mind

553. While clinical psychology has been destroying religious beliefs, social psychology has been holding out the

possibility of new religious foundations. But since the claims of clinical psychology have been more spectacular and the growth of a painstaking experimental social psychology has been slow, the public has not yet perceived that what psychology takes away with one hand it more than gives back with the other.

Elements of the modern conception of a group mind are found in Hobbes, Hegel, Bosanquet, and others. The essence of the notion is that in any organized group of human beings there exists a super-individual mind, built up from, yet greater than, the sum of the individual minds.

For some reason a habit of verbal thinking persists in the average layman, and even among some physical scientists, which makes such a notion seem absurd when it is first encountered. Yet the evidence is open to the observation of everyone, and, as I shall show, it is irrefutable.

*554.* What do we mean when we speak of any individual mind? We mean that the individual is alive, that he responds to stimulation, that he has emotions and appetites, that he acts and wills to do certain things, that he decides between different courses of action, that his behaviour shows evidence of memory and of some constant habits and sentiments which constitute his personality. If we are not behaviourists—it is of no great relevance to the detection of mind—we also assume that he is conscious. Further, as biologists, we expect the behaviour characteristic of mind to be invariably associated with some physical grey matter, either in one mass as in the vertebrates or in more scattered masses as in the invertebrates.

Now consider any group—from a ship's crew or a football team to a nation. The group, if in a healthy state, acts in a unified way towards some definite end, as an individual does when

sane. It responds as a whole to external stimuli. It shows evidence of emotion and heightened excitability, which you can perceive in an individual by his pulse or his language. Similarly you can perceive in a football crowd a common wave of emotion, reddening a thousand faces, or read in the newspapers of a nation the more wild expressions which mirror a heightened feeling tone. The behaviour of a nation reveals idiosyncrasies of habit and native temperament as does that of individuals. There is a memory of its past and of incidents occurring between itself and other groups. The "group memory" is stored partly in individual minds and partly in the archives of libraries. There are persisting sentiments, partly in the form of national traditions, which mould each new generation of group protoplasm, and which issue in behaviour giving character to the group mind. And the conflicting feelings and attitudes of a group issue, through newspaper discussions, ballots, and organized political committees in acts of will which alter the face of the earth.

Just how memories are stored, feelings excited, or actions expressed we need not expound in any detail here. A parallel could not in any case be worked out because we do not know these things of the individual mind either. All we know are the manifestations of stimulation, emotion, memory, and will. The question of group mind structure, though a fascinating one, cannot be approached here more than to observe that most mental features of the group mind are carried in the individual minds. The individual mind mirrors in miniature the group mind, yet no individual mind, not even the comprehensive minds of politicians, or of literary or scientific men, can subtend the whole range of awareness of the group mind. Nor can any individual mind, however great its feeling or desire to act, equal the power and intensity and richness of feeling included in the group mind.

The objection commonly raised to the use of the same term for both the group and the individual manifestations of mind is that the individual mind has a greater unity than the group mind. In the former there is supposed to be one consciousness and one mass of nerve tissue. But such an assertion merely shows ignorance of the individual mind. We now know that there can be two or more separate consciousnesses—co-consciousnesses—in one mind, and that even the unity of consciousness and action in the healthy individual is only the result of binding together many would-be-independent impulses and feelings. In this respect the study of the individual mind has been helped by our knowledge of the group mind, for the structure of contending subordinate group minds, of repressing and repressed elements, and of a hierarchy of functions, observed in the group mind, has proved an enlightening model for exploring the individual mind.

As for the trivial objection that the physical elements—the individual brains and records—of the group brain are in no fixed geographical relation to each other, whereas those of the individual mind are localized in one cranium, it is scarcely worthy of discussion. The physical elements of a group mind may be physically bunched together as in a ship, and may vanish together at its sinking. The same cells of the individual brain, on the other hand, as Lashley has shown, may work in different combinations at different times. But the important thing is that the elements of the group mind should be in communication, by sight, speech, writing, telephone, or other means, so that each portion of nervous tissue can react appropriately to whatever is affecting all the others. Whether the portions of

grey matter are separated by interstitial tissue and communicate by nerve threads as in the brain or are separated by brick walls and communicate by electric wires as in the group mind is of little consequence. Nor are the idioms of communication important providing they are appropriate to the mental experience to be transmitted: lovers may communicate by hand pressures and mathematicians by symbols: each maintains a group awareness of some form of initially individual excitation.

Naturally there are different types of group mind just as there are different kinds of individual mind, and the less organized kind of group mind, the crowd, is lower than any individual mind, unless we look for the latter far down in the scale of animal evolution.

555. The voice of the crowd is not even an echo of the voice of God, but it is equally certain that the highly organized and integrated self-conscious group mind, containing more individuals than any brain has cells, exceeds quantitatively and qualitatively any performance of which an individual mind is capable.

A most interesting study could be made of the parallels between various types of individual mental structures and group structures. For instance, "split personalities" are observable in both. In both there are changes of mood, for just as different instinctive drives dominate the individual at different times, so the mood and policy of nations alters as different thrusts of political demand come to power in the government. In both there are distinct kinds of breakdown to which particular types of internal organization are particularly prone. There are hysterics and manic depressives, obsessionals and anxiety neurasthenics among the nations. The cycle of confidence and depression in the business activity of the group which now puzzles the economist may well depend on a similar mechanism to that which causes alternations of confidence and depression in the energies of the individual of cyclothyme temperament.

556. The more complex properties of the group mind can be understood only after we have classified the relation of the individual to the group mind. The individual gives to it and he takes away, but what he gives often stays, and what he takes away generally leaves the group mind unimpoverished. Practical psychological observations are best made at first on small groups, e.g., the school. Now it is a commonplace among teachers that a school spirit or tone exists which is not entirely attributable to any single boy or collection of boys. The "gestalt" or pattern psychologists have long argued convincingly that, especially in psychological matters, the whole is more than a sum of its parts. There is either something new in the pattern of the elements or some "creative synthesis" whereby new qualities are produced from the fusion of the given qualities.

As yet we know nothing about the alchemy whereby this group spirit is distilled from the character of individual minds, but we do know that the group mind acts powerfully in moulding individual minds. It is a devastating yet salutary experience to take a piece of paper and list those ideas which are genuinely our own creations, and those which we have taken over as our own from parents, teachers, friends, and books. Our thoughts, our ways of feeling, our pleasures, our type of humour, even our most intense convictions are commonly grafted upon us, as gently as a mother clothes a naked child, by the group mind.

557. For the slow gains of history, the discoveries of scientists, the phrases of poetry and song, the patterns of human nature hewn out by dramatists, and all the accumulated experience of man about life and the universe are an intrinsic part of each individual mind. Each can rearrange a little the furniture he has been given, but in the vast majority of people individuality is the name given to their inability to grasp more than a small fraction of all that the group mind covers. To each is given some power of selection, a possibility, generally no more than unconsciously used, to invest ideas with new patterns of emotional force—that, plus a little intellectual inventiveness, generally used in nothing but conversational wit. Environment, from the day of our birth, tends to treat us as vessels, of varying capacities, into which can be poured the social heritage that has its sources in Plato and Jesus, Galileo and Newton, Confucius and Shakespeare, and indeed in all the greater and lesser contributors to culture since culture began.

### The Forms of Immortality

558. In every man there is the possibility of contributing something new through his own true individuality, i.e., through that part of his individuality that is not merely passive. Therein lies our personal immortality. This gift to the group mind may be on the intellectual level—Spearman has shown in detail how such entirely new mental constructions come about. On the other hand, it may be a new emotional adjustment through which society benefits. As yet we know little more than that some processes of trial and error, through courageous life experiment, may produce such increments of growth of the group mind. But they also serve who only preserve in their own lives the good features in the group mind against the constant battering of disintegrative forces.

From a broad scientific standpoint our immortality is plainly of two kinds. We have a biological, physical immortality in our children, who perpetuate the dispositions, temperaments, and intelligences of their parents. Through this similarity they are living forces tending to foster the same kinds of values as those which we have ourselves most naturally loved. It could reasonably be maintained that this biological immortality alone is more satisfying than any of the internally contradictory phantasies of traditional religion. For certain features of the desire for immortality persist because we have never tasted of its fulfillment. Most religious sects imagine they would be perpetually entertained by the novelty of wings and harps. A representative of more sophisticated opinion, Mr. Winston Churchill, thinks of the entertainment he would get from a dialogue between Plato and his friend Lord Balfour. "When I go to heaven," he confidently banters, "I shall try to arrange a chat between these two on some topic not too recondite for me to follow." It is possible, however, that they would quarrel continually, or that the dialogue would be drowned by the roar of football crowds or radio enthusiasts likewise pursuing perpetual happiness in their own way.

When all is said, the only thing we lose by avoiding this kind of immortality, is the satisfaction of contact with old friends. It may be objected that we also lose, in merely biological immortality, the satisfaction of our own entirely unique personal continuity, since in each generation there is a break, a reshuffling of the germinal genes and chromosomes, a slight reorientation of the living forces of the next individual. But are we so sure that the pattern of our own living personality remains so very fixed? The individual arrested in immortality at fifteen would be very different from the "same" individual translated to immortality at fifty. The continuity of our consciousness is destroyed even by each night's sleep and the individual awakes each day in some way altered. Is this so different from his dying in sleep and continuing as his children?

*559.* There is something in all but the simplest minds that strives for a more direct and individual persistence than is given in biological immortality; for a persistence of the things concerning which the individual strives and hopes and fears, and for a persistence of those strivings themselves. This desire may or may not be met by the second form of immortality which scientific observation is able to recognize. To understand this second form one must note that in the group mind every individual's words and actions, every precept, emotional expression or example of conduct, spreads out in a widening circle of consequences in the lives of his contemporaries and his posterity.

The laws of physics, which permit energy neither to be created nor destroyed, and the principle of determinism, of inevitable cause and effect, running throughout the universe, ordain that every mental state or physical occurrence shall be a consequence of all that has gone before. Every kind of thoughtful action, every act characterized by truth and beauty, generates similar acts in others, and contributes something to the growing heart of goodness in the group mind.

Acts and ideas and feelings reverberate down the ages, and coalesce and favour the development of their own forms. The hard and honest thinking of the scientist and his devotion to truth, wring discoveries from the stubborn grasp of Nature, which continue in the service and thought of man, a beneficent immortality increasing human power, and favouring the realistic ways of thinking originally found in the scientist. The new visions and heightened experiences of artist, poet, and musician continue like melodies played on the instruments of each new generation of brains. They persist as experiences in a living, immortal group mind. The vitality and joy which invests them does not end. As Cicero observed long ago, "A short life is given us by Nature, but the memory of a well-spent life is eternal." Actually we have to deal with the persistence of something more than memories: the immortality of attitudes, of joys, and aesthetic experiences, of heroisms and modes of self-expression.

Surely this immortality is as superb in conception as any conceived in primitive forms of religion! It omits only an integrated self-activity in the ideas that go on. It adds the possibility of ideas expanding in intensity and influence till they far surpass their first glowing in an individual mind. But its relation to biological immortality is a close and organic one. A system of ideas sits most comfortably on minds similar in structure to those which created the ideas, so that the aristocrat and the Chinaman are correct in emphasizing the importance of familial persistence. On the other hand, whatsoever is good and true and beautiful will last in all group minds. Furthermore, it is certain that ideals and ways of thinking can, over many generations, mould a population by Darwinian selective survival towards a biological type suited to those ideals. The two kinds of immortality interact. To ask which is "more important" for the group mind is to pose a question which is insoluble in that form; but it is evident that men of great vision, religious leaders, scientists, and artists have regarded their spiritual immortality as of more value to society than their biological survival, and a whole Church, by insisting on celibacy in its priesthood, has embraced the same view. Research might answer the question for particular classes of individuals, yet one is tempted to say meanwhile that there can be few whose contribution to society is so increased by their freedom from family cares that they are justified in sacrificing biological immortality.

The suggestion has been implied above that the structure of the group mind is such as to favour in some way the preservation of good as opposed to evil actions and thoughts. To justify that suggestion would require a great assembly of instances. So brief a treatment as this will have to content itself with the assertion that evil actions, by the very nature and definition of evil as that which is opposed to group welfare, must in time, if not immediately, mutually cancel and destroy each other. Actions are evil because they are noncontributory, untrue to life, mutually contradictory, selfish rather than outwardly directed, tending naturally to become null and void. I think Whitehead is asserting the same view when he says, "There is self-preservation inherent in that which is good in itself."

560. As one examines this notion of immortality within the group mind it becomes evident that different individuals achieve widely varying degrees of immortality. Since we do not survive as a whole, since the evil elements are arrested and only the unselfishness and that which is of value to the group mind lives on, it is true to say that the evil man has little or no immortality, but that the saint becomes almost pure immortality. The immortality of Christ pervades almost all our lives, moulding them towards happiness and peace and love. The immortality of Shakespeare in the spoken word, the thought and wit and wisdom over a large part of the earth is only a little less striking. In our modern realistic modes of reasoning and in our powers over Nature we enjoy the immortality—indeed we are the immortality—of the thought and will of great scientists from Newton to Pasteur, and of all whom they have inspired.

Immortality is a matter of degree,

but that degree is far from being decided by the talents which a man is given at birth. The humblest men and women may achieve great immortality. For it seems reasonable to conjecture that the cohesion of the group mind is the prerequisite of all else, and that cohesion is maintained by the love and self-abnegation of every individual in his daily life. The devoted mother, the common soldier giving his life for the group ideals upon the battlefield, are equally essential to the group development and share in great measure the foundational elements in its immortality. If we accept the intuitions of Christ in this as in other fields as being contingently the nearest approximation to truth that human wisdom may attain, it is evident that love and humility, sincerity and faith in fellow-men, have as great an immortality value as power, mental capacity, or creativeness.

### The Group Mind and the Concept of God

To commence an investigation of the group mind in what purports to be a study of religion may have seemed to the reader at first somewhat strange, but the reasons for doing so must have become increasingly clear as the qualities of the group mind emerged. It is evident that many of its properties are undoubtedly those which in intuitive and traditional literature have been repeatedly ascribed to God.

This mind is a super-individual consciousness with which the individual can maintain communion. He depends upon it, and it exercises a benevolent intervention in his life. He is, spiritually, and in some sense physically, created by the group mind. In serving it he is doing precisely what has been defined as the worship and service of God. It is the cumulative reservoir of super-individual wisdom and it defines, by the conditions of its existence, the commandments of morality. It is the assurance of immortality, which is to be obtained only by giving one's life to it. It gives to the individual faith to carry out those tasks valuable to the community which chance and accident and evil may interrupt in the individual's life.

There is not a phrase or metaphor in the essential scriptures of great religions which do [not] ring true when applied to the group mind. Seeking to define more precisely the qualities of the group mind one finds oneself compelled to resort to words hitherto used in theology rather than in science. For example, how should one characterize the individual qualities that have immortal value from those which disappear each generation in the dross of mere individual animal life? Precisely the word we want exists in the term "divine." If we assign the term divinity to the "group mindedness" of things, then it is obvious that personalities such as those of Christ are almost wholly divine. But there is some measure of divinity—of godlikeness—in Buddha and Plato, Michelangelo or Beethoven, and in every individual, however insignificant, who has some concern for the good aspirations of his fellow-men.

*561.* So far it is possible to proceed noting only the great gains which the psychology of religion acquires through considering the group mind. But it would be no service to our study to slur over the difficulties which now begin to accrue. For instance, it is whispered that the group mind is not always possessed of qualities greater or more noble than those of the average man. The mind of a mob is indeed notably inferior in all but emotional intensity. What size and structure are necessary in a group before the higher characteristics of group spirit emerge? If God emerges from the group mind, at what point of its evolution does this significant event occur; or have we to deal wholly with a continuous change, only to be described appropriately by the formulae of mathematical covariation? Again, is the group mind for all practical purposes to be identified with our living fellow-men, so that the modern tendency to substitute service to the group for service to God will receive support from our present analysis? Furthermore, are there no items in the traditional references to God, and His functional relation to man, which fail to conform with, or cannot be derived from, the notion of the group mind?

Since psychologists have yet failed to investigate the group mind, since its most able sponsor, McDougall, in his highly original introductory study has stopped short of these issues, there are no ready-made authoritative answers. . . . Suffice it if the present chapter has demonstrated that a great positive contribution concerning the realities behind religious thought can be made by psychology. All man's religious efforts are not lost; all his thinking of God has not been a delusion; at worst it has been the substitution of simple and childlike symbols for a reality too complex long to be held in the focus of attention. We work with no lesser margin of illusion than when we salute a flag or accept paper money in lieu of real wealth.

The social and psychological benefits which are so rich a reward for belief in God may not therefore be as ill-founded and spurious as we feared. Had Freud been as good a social psychologist as he was a clinician he would not, therefore, have been forced to deny the psychological viewpoint itself. For this is what he did when he asserted that since the religious man is still as much a prey as the irreligious to ills and disasters, and still subject to the powers of Nature, he gains nothing but the cold conclusion that the God which he has found is merciless or powerless or inscrutable. Freud cannot see what Job gained by refusing to curse such a God. Yet from the psychological viewpoint the gain is enormous, namely, the absence of fretting and bitter recrimination in the face of irremediable evils, in increased social solidarity, in peace of mind and assurance of ultimate victory through God in man's long struggle with his environment.

[Sec. 553, Raymond B. Cattell, *Psychology and the Religious Quest* (New York: Thomas Nelson & Sons, 1938), p. 62. Sec. 554, *ibid.*, pp. 63–65. Sec. 555, *ibid.*, pp. 65–66. Sec. 556, *ibid.*, pp. 70–71. Sec. 557, *ibid.*, p. 71. Sec. 558, *ibid.*, pp. 72–73. Sec. 559, *ibid.*, pp. 73–76. Sec. 560, *ibid.*, pp. 76–78. Sec. 561, *ibid.*, pp. 80–81.]

## COMMENT

The parallel drawn with such care in the preceding pages would seem to be some form of analogical reasoning; but clearly we have no ordinary form of analogy presented here. Cattell has not insisted, after the fashion of a causal analogy (the *analogia entis* would be an example), that a conscious being must have *caused* those aspects of society which parallel certain functions in us. Nor does it seem that he intended an ordinary analogy of properties; to be sure two entities—an individual and a group—are placed in comparison, and it is discovered that response to stimulation, emotion and appetite, action and will, decision, memory, and habit are present in them both; but the argument does not conclude that a further property of consciousness, discernible in the individual, is likely to have its analogue in a superindividual group consciousness.

Consciousness, Cattell argues, is of no great moment to his analysis. In so far as analogical reasoning is employed, such argument seems to take place on the semantic level. And it is on the whole closer, we feel, to Cattell's purpose to regard him as arguing: mentality means a certain quality of activity of the kind expressed in the functions cited above; society meets the conditions of the concept quite as neatly as does an individual; one may therefore speak properly of a group mind. Up to this point one can judge only that the view is somewhat ambiguous, but certainly one should not deny freedom in the use of words. However, had Cattell been content with this argument alone, the only issue of his thought would have been such as his suggestion to the economist that business cycles and the alternating confidence-depression cycle in an individual are highly similar mechanisms and should be subject to similar treatment.

In fact, Cattell, having fixed the meaning of mentality, moves beyond the conditions of his semantic analogy. He is a half-step beyond the proper limitations of analogy when he suggests that because of the greater richness of the group mind it may be viewed as a kind of superindividual; when he suggests that the group mind fulfils the functions of deity, he suggests a position which can be seen by analysis to be far outside the scope of his original argument. He does insist that his conclusions rest on "scientific" observation; but, as his discussion expands, it becomes clear that he cannot properly stop short of metaphysics. He seems to believe that metaphysical considerations have no pertinence for his argument; yet, although assuming that mind—whether individual or societal—is wholly contingent, he indulges in subtle and interesting qualifications.

Within the range of contingent fact alone it appears obvious that, if society remembers, it also forgets; if it contributes beneficial elements to us, it likewise allows harmful elements to ingress into our being; if it is the source and receptacle of our goodness, it is both of these for our evil tendencies as well. And doubtless there is no ultimate necessity in the life of an individual

(although his purpose is more abstract, hence less contingent, than the more particular details of his experience) or in the "life" of a society; but does this not mean that necessity is couched elsewhere? Cattell urges that it is the nature of evil to negate itself and that even forgotten influences continue in the group mind. But let the reader note that this view of evil is metaphysical (his citation of Whitehead in this regard should be proof enough), and to answer the charge of "perpetual perishing" by use of the group mind is to make of it a metaphysical entity of some sort. Certainly observation has not furnished these concepts.

The extent of God's inclusiveness and his status with respect to contingency are here in question. Now Cattell is willing to pose the question: Has God arisen from group interaction at some point? While he does not himself answer this question, the further his thinking continues, the more it appears that the answer should be in the negative. The initial elements of the societal-individual analogy have been drawn from a modern industrial society, perhaps that of a national unit. We learn, however, that the group mind has "lived" through and contains a past which includes the excellences of many both successive and coexistent partially independent societies; the conception of the group mind is in this manner extended to include all culture and in the process becomes somewhat less dependent upon the structure of any particular society and something other than identical with that society. Finally, the metaphysical insistence, as we termed it, that man as such is immortal both biologically and by virtue of the way his ideas, attitudes, experiences, and actions are forever a part of God broadens the view to the point where at least all of humanity and even the most personal aspects of man's existence are included within deity.

This final extension (if "immortality" is given any clear meaning) introduces a certain element of necessity into the idea of God. The term does, indeed, seem to have more than rhetorical import for Cattell; if at last, however, he would retain the term while insisting upon the sheer contingency of God, it would be proper, because of the presence of contradictory assertions, to point out the meaninglessness of this aspect of his thought. An apparent guaranty of immortality is to be found in the ability of the group mind to transcend the failures of particular societies; but this is insufficient. What of the possible failure of the whole human quest which becomes a necessary failure, ironically enough, when the view remains wholly contingent and an immeasurable future time is contemplated? The only answer is that the view implicit in the writer's affirmations, but never unequivocally expressed, needs to become an explicit affirmation of the system—the view, namely, that necessity as well as contingency must be granted among the ascriptions proper to God's nature.

The question of inclusiveness has not yet been answered, but it may be noted that the concept gained in inclusiveness as it gained in adequacy; no firm line is drawn between what is included and what excluded from God's nature. And it seems that, had Cattell wished, he could have used his analogy to provide a cosmic extension of "mentality." If one is to think of mentality as characterizing whatever evinces habit, decision, appropriateness of reaction (and consider Whitehead's emphasis upon appetition), memory, and the like, why may not the universe as such with its orderly processes, new events, and movement into the past be judged from a naturalistic perspective as a cosmic mind? To argue so is to extend Cattell's analogy. The argument would be no more convincing than his, but, in fact, the cosmos fits the conditions of a superindividual at least as well as does society and in some respects (taking the total past as the analogue of memory) fits those conditions more neatly.

We would argue, then, that Cattell needs both necessity and inclusiveness in his concept of God, that one implies the other, and that Cattell's discussion moves toward a view which, implying these elements, implies also the dipolar conception of deity rather than the sheerly contingent deity suggested by the initial framework of his thought.

# Chapter X: *Extreme Temporalistic Theism*

## WIEMAN (1884———)

For H. N. Wieman, God, or "creativity," or "the creative event," whatever else he or it may be, is the producer, or the production or emergence, or the manner of production or emergence, of unexpected, unpredictable good. In specifying the nature of the creative event, Wieman is eloquent and powerful and often very illuminating with regard to important life-problems. He is at his best when dealing with the human behavior and experiences involved in significant value-emergence in our lives. Some see in his explication of divine creativity a stroke of genius. The term is obviously Whiteheadian but the concept is not.

While recognizing the need for some modicum of metaphysical undergirding, Wieman is generally skeptical of its validity. It follows that one cannot hope to understand Wieman by way of Whitehead. In fact, Wieman's penchant for naturalism and empiricism is more reminiscent of John Dewey than of any metaphysician. Both speak of processes of creation, both describe the production of good as issuing from a context of events, and Dewey—like Wieman—is willing to use the term "God" in this connection. Dewey influenced Ames profoundly, and yet it is Wieman's description of God which bears the greater resemblance to these words of Dewey:

The process of creation is experimental and continuous. The artist, scientific man, or good citizen, depends upon what others have done before him and are doing around him. The sense of new values that become ends to be realized arises first in dim and uncertain form. As the values are dwelt upon and carried forward in action they grow in definiteness and coherence. Inter-action between aim and existent conditions improves and tests the ideal; and conditions are at the same time modified. Ideals change as they are applied in existent conditions. The process endures and advances with the life of humanity. What one person and one group accomplish becomes the standing ground and starting point of those who succeed them. When the vital factors in this natural process are generally acknowledged in emotion, thought and action, the process will be both accelerated and purified through elimination of that irrelevant element that culminates in the idea of the supernatural. When the vital factors attain the religious force that has been drafted into supernatural religions, the resulting reinforcement will be incalculable.

These considerations may be applied to the idea of God, or, to avoid misleading conceptions, to the idea of the divine. This idea is, as I have said, one of ideal possibilities unified through imaginative realization and projection. But this idea of God, or of the divine, is also connected with all the natural forces and conditions—including man and human association—that promote the growth of the ideal and that further its realization. We are in the presence neither of ideals completely embodied in existence nor yet of ideals that are mere rootless ideals, fantasies, utopias. For there are forces in nature and society that generate and support the ideals. They are further unified by the action that gives them coherence and solidity. It is this *active* relation between ideal and actual to which I would give the name "God." I would not insist that the name *must* be given. There are those who hold that the associations of the term with the supernatural are so numerous and close that any use of the word "God" is sure to give rise to misconception and be taken as a concession to traditional ideas.[1]

1. John Dewey, *A Common Faith* (New Haven: Yale University Press), pp. 49-51.

The naturalism expressed in the foregoing passage is unequivocal, however inadequate it may be. Wieman, while adhering to naturalism, differs sharply from Dewey in his emphasis. Man is regarded by Wieman as a passive factor in the event from which good emerges so that it is not really man who clarifies, carries forward, and implements the ideal; this is the function of God or creativity. Where Dewey would attribute the emergence of value to the co-working of men plus more general factors, Wieman would say that this emergence is the work of God. It would be more traditional and more Whiteheadian to think of this emergence as due to man's co-working with God rather than regarding it either as literally God's working or man's working. There are other differences of emphasis which we shall allow the reader to discover for himself. Disagreeing both with Whiteheadian metaphysics and Dewey's somewhat truncated naturalism, Wieman's thought lies between these systems, containing a few features similar to Whitehead's system, others resembling Dewey's, and some few emphases foreign to both of them.

To do justice to this author, we must bear in mind his methodological intent. He wishes to deal with religious questions by the observational method of science, properly extended to cover the more subtle aspects of value and purpose, which are also in some sense empirical facts. His theory has been termed an "operational view of God." It is a characteristic manifestation of our times, and it is presented (as the reader will soon see) with great courage and candor as well as with much ingenuity.

## The Creative Event

562. No knowable cause or explanation for anything that happens can reach deeper than events and their structure and qualities. This view claims to be able to take account of all the intricacies and subtleties—all the height, breadth, and depth of human existence—omitting, explaining away, flattening out, or truncating nothing. We shall have no recourse to any "transcendental grounds, orders, causes or purposes" beyond events, their qualities, and relations. Naturalism bases this claim on thorough analysis of the method by which any knowledge whatsoever can be obtained. We shall interpret value, in the following pages, entirely in terms of events, their qualities and relations (structure). The richest and highest values sought and found by religion and morals are interpreted as structured events and their possibilities.

In selecting this naturalistic version of reality, we have had to choose between two great traditions which Western civilization has inherited. Each presents its own interpretation of what is supremely important for all human living. One is Jewish Christian, the other Greek Christian. The Jewish tradition declares that the sovereign good works creatively in history. While this ruling creativity is said to have form, the importance of it lies in its creative potentialities and not in its form. The Greek tradition, on the other hand, declares that the sovereign good is essentially a system of Forms or a Supreme Form. The one tradition gives supreme authority to the creative event, the other to the Form. Our interpretation follows the Jewish tradition in giving priority to the creative event.

But there is one respect, being naturalists, in which we depart from both traditions: we ignore the transcendental affirmation in the Jewish Christian tradition of a creative God who not only works in history but resides beyond history. The only creative God we recognize is the creative event itself. So also we ignore the transcendental affirmation in the Greek Christian tradition of the reality of Forms of value, uncreated and eternal, having causal efficacy to constrain the shape of things without themselves being events at all. The only forms of value we recognize are produced by the creative event. Even possibilities, so far as relevant to actual events, are created. The form of the creative event itself at our higher levels of existence is determined by the creative process at more elementary levels. In our view the higher levels of existence spring from, rest upon, and are undergirded by the lower.

Thus the active God derived from the Jewish tradition and the forms derived from the Greek tradition are both brought down into the world of time, space, and matter and are there identified as events displaying a definite structure with possibilities. When we insist that nothing has causal efficacy except material events, by "material" we mean not merely pellets of inanimate matter but also events that include the biological, social, and historical forms of existence. These, however, never cease to be material. Nothing has value except material events, thus understood, and their possibilities.

*563.* Creative good is distinguished from two kinds of created good, one of which is instrumental and the other intrinsic. Instrumental and intrinsic created good are alike in the sense that both are made up of events meaningfully connected; but in the instrumental kind the quality of the events is either negligible or irrelevant to their positive value. Eating tasteless or nauseating food might have the instrumental value of providing me with energy for participation later in events yielding intrinsic value. If the food is tasteless, the quality is negligible; if nauseating, there is quality, but the quality is irrelevant to the instrumental value. The eating of such food might, however, take on intrinsic value through other meaningful connections then and there experienced—the friendliness of associates, memories recalled, and happy anticipa-

tions. All these qualities flood in upon me from near and far and are experienced in the very act of eating with these people at this time and place. In such an event the eating ceases to be instrumental by taking on rich quality through meaningful connection with many other happenings. The same system of events may be in one reference an instrumental, and in another reference an intrinsic good.

*564.* Therefore, intrinsic value may be defined as a structure of events endowing each happening as it occurs with qualities derived from other events in the structure. On the other hand, instrumental value is a structure of events whereby each happening as it occurs does not acquire qualities from other events in the structure, or, if it does, these qualities are irrelevant to the value of the structure in the reference under consideration.

When there is a break between two or more systems of events such that the qualities of the one system cannot get across to the other, the only meaningful connection between the two must be nonqualitative and instrumental. It is nonqualitative either because the qualities of these connecting events are negligible or because they are irrelevant to the good that is served.

*565.* When good increases, a process of reorganization is going on, generating new meanings, integrating them with the old, endowing each event as it occurs with a wider range of reference, molding the life of a man into a more deeply unified totality of meaning. The wide diversities, varieties, and contrasts of all the parts of a man's life are being progressively transformed into a more richly inclusive whole. The several parts of life are connected in mutual support, vivifying and enhancing one another in the creation of a more inclusive unity of events and possibilities. This process of reorganization is what we shall call the "creative event." It is creative good, standing in contrast to both kinds of created good we have been considering. By means of this creative good, systems of meaning having intrinsic value, previously disconnected so that the qualities of the one could not get across to the other, are so unified that each is enriched by qualities derived from the other. Meaningfully connected events, once instrumental, now become component parts of a total meaning having intrinsic value.

566. The creative event is so basic to all our further interpretation of value that we must examine it with care. It is made up of four subevents; and the four working together and not any one of them working apart from the others constitute the creative event. Each may occur without the others and often does, but in that case it is not creative. We have to describe them separately, but distinctions made for the purpose of analysis must not obscure the unitary, fourfold combination necessary to the creativity.

The four subevents are: emerging awareness of qualitative meaning derived from other persons through communication; integrating these new meanings with others previously acquired; expanding the richness of quality in the appreciable world by enlarging its meaning; deepening the community among those who participate in this total creative event of intercommunication. We shall examine each of these subevents in detail.

## The First Subevent*

Let us remember that qualitative meaning consists of actual events so related that each acquires qualities from the others. Every living organism so reacts as to break the passage of existence into units or intervals called "events" and to relate these to one another in the manner here called "qualitative meaning." So long as this is done by the organism without the aid of linguistic communication, the range and richness of qualitative meaning is very limited. Not until the single organism is able to acquire the qualitative meanings developed by other organisms and add them to its own can the world of meaning and quality expand to any great compass. Therefore the first subevent in the total creative event producing value distinctively human is the emerging awareness in the individual of qualitative meaning communicated to it from some other organism.

Interaction between the organism and its surroundings, by which new qualitative meaning is created without communication or prior to communication, is certainly creative. If we were studying the creative event as it occurs at all levels of existence, this creativity at the subcommunicative level would be included. But we have chosen to give attention to what creates value at the human level. What creates value at the biological level is basic to human existence, but it is not distinctively human. We shall give some attention to it, but only for the purpose of seeing more clearly the character of the creative event as it works through intercommunications in human society and history. It is here, where one organism can acquire the meanings gathered by a million others, that the miracle happens and creativity breaks free from obstacles which elsewhere imprison its power. Only at this level can the creative event rear a world of quality and meaning expanding beyond any known limit, sometimes by geometrical progression.

## The Second Subevent*

The individual becomes more of a personality when these meanings derived from others are integrated with what he already has. His thoughts and feelings are enriched and deepened. This integrating does not occur in every case of communicated meaning, since there is much noncreative communication in our modern world by way of radio, television, movies, newspapers, and casual interchange between individuals. The mere passage through the mind of innumerable meanings is not the creative event. These newly communicated meanings must be integrated with meanings previously acquired or natively developed if the creative event is to occur. This integrating is largely subconscious, unplanned and uncontrolled by the individual, save only as he may provide conditions favorable to its occurrence. This integrating is, then, the second subevent in the four, which together make the total event creative of all human value.

It is in this second subevent that man seems most helpless to do what must be done. The supreme achievements of this internally creative integration seem to occur in solitude, sometimes quite prolonged. When many meanings have been acquired through communication and through much action on the material world, there must be time for these to be assimilated. If one does not for a time draw apart and cease to act on the material world and communicate with others, the constant stream of new meanings will prevent the deeper integration. A period of loneliness and quiet provides for incubation and creative transformation by novel unification. If new meanings are coming in all the time, the integration is hindered by the new ingressions. The creative integration may be greatly aided by worship when worship allows a supreme good to draw into a unity of commitment to itself all the diverse values that have been received from many sources.

567. The creative event, in all four of its stages, is going on all the time in human existence. When we speak of prolonged solitude, on the one hand, and intensive and profound communication, on the other, as being prerequisite to creative transformation, we refer only to the more striking examples of it.

In obscure and lowly form it is occurring continuously in human life, even when decline and disintegration also occur. The latter might be more rapid than the creative process until human life itself disappeared. Nevertheless, the creative event must continue so long as human life goes on because it is necessary to the human level of existence.

### The Third Subevent*

The expanding and enriching of the appreciable world by a new structure of interrelatedness pertaining to events necessarily follow from the first two subevents. It is the consequence of both the first two, not of either one by itself. If there has been intercommunication of meanings and if they have been creatively integrated, the individual sees what he could not see before; he feels what he could not feel. Events as they happen to him are now so connected with other events that his appreciable world has an amplitude unimaginable before. There is a range and variety of events, a richness of quality, and a reach of ideal possibility which were not there prior to this transformation.

568. One important thing to note is that this expanding of the appreciable world may make a man more unhappy and more lonely than he was before; for now he knows that there is a greatness of good which might be the possession of man but is not actually achieved. One is reminded of the man who preached through all his life: "God is my Father and all you are my brothers," declaring continuously the blessedness of all-encompassing love and yet living in a world so barren of love that he must have been heartbreakingly lonely through all the days of his life. This loneliness comes to agonized expression in the story of the temptation, Gethsemane, and the cry on the Cross.

Such a profound sense of loneliness is difficult for any man to bear, and yet it is the hope of the world because the man who feels it is aware of a greatness of love that might be but is not. Such loneliness indicates a vast emptiness which love between men might fill. This loneliness might become so deep and so intense that a man could not endure it unless he were permitted to die upon a cross for love; he might then fill an emptiness no actual love can fill by a sacrificial expression of love. This seeking for a love that is never fulfilled might become so deep and so intense that a man would spend all his life preaching the principles of a kingdom of love that would sound like the beatitudes of madness in a world like this. They could be made intelligible only by attributing them to an illusion that the world was shortly to come to an end and would be transformed miraculously into such a kingdom. Perhaps such loneliness, born of such craving for love between men, would drive a man to that desperate madness in which he dreamed that by dying on a cross he could somehow bring this kingdom of love into existence.

This expanding of the appreciable world, accomplished by the third subevent, is not, then, in its entirety the actual achievement of an increase of value in this world, although it will include that. But it is also, perhaps even more, an expansion of the individual's capacity to appreciate and his apprehension of a good that might be, but is not, fulfilled. It is the awakening of a hunger and a longing which, in one aspect at least, is a craving for more love between men than ever can be in the compass of this life.

### The Fourth Subevent*

Widening and deepening community between those who participate in the total creative event is the final stage in creative good. The new structure of interrelatedness pertaining to events, resulting from communication and integration of meanings, transforms not only the mind of the individual and his appreciable world but also his relations with those who have participated with him in this occurrence. Since the meanings communicated to him from them have now become integrated into his own mentality, he feels something of what they feel, sees something of what they see, thinks some of their thought. He may disapprove, deny, and repudiate much that has been communicated to him from them, but this is a form of understanding and community. Perceptions and thoughts that are denied are as much a part of one's mentality as those affirmed. They may contribute as much to the scope and richness of one's mind, to one's appreciable world, and to the depth of one's community with others as perspectives which we affirm and with which we agree.

This community includes both intellectual understanding of one another and the feeling of one another's feelings, the ability to correct and criticize one another understandingly and constructively. It includes the ability and the will to co-operate in such manner as to conserve the good of life achieved to date and to provide conditions for its increase.

Paradoxical as it may sound, this increased community between persons may bring with it a sense of alienation and wistful hunger and even anguish, because one is now aware of misunderstandings in the other. He apprehends in the mind of the other, as he could not before, bitterness, fear, hate, scorn, pride, self-concern, indifference, and unresponsiveness when great need and great issues call. Likewise, the other may apprehend in him in somewhat different areas these ailments of the human spirit. Increase in genuine community, which is not mere increase in back-slapping geniality, will include all this discernment of illness and evil in one another. Increase in community is not necessarily pleasant; the good produced by the creative event brings increase in suffering as well as increase in joy; community brings a burden as well as a release. Those who cannot endure suffering cannot endure the increase of human good. Refusal to take suffering is perhaps the chief obstacle to increase in the good of human existence.

These are the four subevents which together compose the creative event. They are locked together in such an intimate manner as to make a single, total event continuously recurrent in human existence. The creative event is one that brings forth in the human mind, in society and history, and in the appreciable world a new structure of interrelatedness, whereby events are discriminated and related in a manner not before possible. It is a structure whereby some events derive from other events, through meaningful connection with them, an abundance of quality that events could not have had without this new creation.

If by "new creation" one simply means something new in the world, a new event that never occurred before, then, of course, every event is creative. But that is not what is here meant. We are limiting our study chiefly to creative event as it occurs in communication between human individuals. . . . It is true that there is a creative process that has worked through many centuries to bring forth the kind of organism that can participate in the creative event of human communication. . . .

The thin layer of structure characterizing events knowable to the human mind by way of linguistic specification is very thin indeed compared to that massive, infinitely complex structure of events, rich with quality, discriminated by the noncognitive feeling-reactions of associated organisms human and nonhuman. This infinitely complex structure of events composing this vast society of interacting organisms and their sustaining or destructive environment is like an ocean on which floats the thin layer of oil representing the structures man can know through intellectual formulation. These structures knowable to the human mind can have depth and richness of quality only if they continue conjunct and integral with this deep complex structure of quality built up through countless ages before even the human mind appeared and now accessible to the feeling-reactions of the human organism. But when the human mind in its pride tries to rear its knowable structures as supreme goals of human endeavor, impoverishment, destruction, conflict, and frustration begin because these structures are then cut off from the rich matrix of quality found in organic, nonintellectual reactions.

Any meaning loses depth and richness of quality derived from this unknown depth of structured events with quality determined by noncognitive feeling-reactions of the organism, when it is treated as an end instead of as a servant to creativity and all that creativity may produce below the level of human cognition. Man can use his knowledge and the truth he seeks to know to serve this creativity. Also he can so live as to keep his achieved meanings closely bound to the rich matrix of qualified events that cannot be known in their specific detail. When he does live thus, he experiences an uncomprehended depth and richness which give content to the abstractions of rationally comprehended structures. When he does not, life loses quality and value.

### Creative Good Is Supra-human*

569. The creative event is supra-human, not in the sense that it works outside of human life, but in the sense that it creates the good of the world in a way that man cannot do. Man cannot even approximate the work of the crea-

tive event. He would not come any closer to it if his powers were magnified to infinity, because the infinite increase of his ability would have to be the consequence of the prior working of the creative event.

The work of the creative event is different in kind from the work of man. Any attempt to measure the power of man against the power of the creative event is defeated at the start because one cannot compare the two. It is true that man can set up conditions that obstruct the work of the creative event so that the good it produces will be much less than it would have been if men had met its demands. Also, he can serve it by removing obstacles. Men can do this in their personal conduct, in the organization of society, in the physical and biological regime which they maintain. When men do meet its demands, the creative event faithfully produces a far greater abundance of human good. But the actual creative event is never the work of man and cannot be. In that sense it is supra-human. . . . Since creativity is not readily accessible to awareness, we can speak of creativity as "transcendent." But it is not transcendent in the sense of being nontemporal, nonspatial, and immaterial. It can be discovered in this world by proper analysis.

### Creative Good Is Absolute Good*

570. The claim that creative good is the only absolute good can be defended only after we are clear on what is meant by "absolute" in this context. When we speak of "absolute good" we shall mean, first of all, what is good under all conditions and circumstances. It is a good that is not relative to time or place or person or race or class or need or hope or desire or belief. It is a good that remains changelessly and identically the same in character so far as concerns its goodness. It is a good that would continue to be so even if all hu-

man beings should cease to exist. It is a good that retains its character even when it runs counter to all human desire. It is a good that continues to be identically the same good even when it works with microscopic cells prior to the emergence of any higher organism.

Creative good meets all these requirements pertaining to absolute good. Its goodness is not relative to human desire, or even to human existence, although it is also good when desired and when working in the medium of human existence.

On the other hand, created good—the structure of meaning connecting past and future that we feel and appreciate— is relative value in all the senses that stand in contrast to the absolute as just described. The particular chains of qualitative meaning having value for man do not necessarily have value for microbes. The structure of interrelatedness pertaining to events which increases quality and meaning relative to one organism or race or class or culture will not ordinarily be equally good for another. Thus created good does not retain the same character of goodness under all circumstances and conditions and in relation to every different sort of organism, human person, or social culture. The creative good which does retain its character of goodness under all these changing conditions is, then, the only absolute good.

A second mark of absolute good is that its demands are unlimited. A good is absolute if it is always good to give myself, all that I am and all that I desire, all that I possess and all that is dear to me, into its control to be transformed in any way that it may require. If there is some point beyond which the cost is too great to justify the claim that a good makes upon me, then it is relative in that respect. Creative good is absolute in this sense for there is no amount of created good opposed to it which can diminish the claim that it makes upon me. The value of the creative source of all good is immeasurable compared to any particular instance of good derived from this source.

Thus in a third way, inseparable from the second, creative good is absolute. It is unlimited in its demands because it is infinite in value. Its worth is incommensurable by any finite quantity of created good. No additive sum of good produced in the past can be any compensation for the blockage of that creativity which is our only hope for the future. And the created good of the past sinks into oblivion when not continuously revitalized by the recurrent working of the creative event.

Fourth, absolute good is unqualified good. There must be no perspective from which its goodness can be modified in any way. Always, from every standpoint, its good must remain unchanged and self-identical, whether from the worm's view or the man's view, whether under the aspect of eternity or under the aspect of time, whether viewed from the standpoint of the beginning or the ending, whether judged by its origin or by its final outcome, whether viewed as means or as end. In respect to created good one can always find some standpoint from which its value disappears or changes; it must be qualified. But in this sense, too, creative good is absolute.

Finally, creative good is absolute in that it is entirely trustworthy. We can be sure that the outcome of its working will always be the best possible under the conditions, even when it may seem to us to be otherwise. Even when it so transforms us and our world that we come to love what we now hate, to serve what we now fight, to seek what now we shun, still we can be sure that what it does is good. Even when its working re-creates our minds and personalities, we can trust it.

We can also be sure that creative good will always be with us. When all

other good is destroyed, it springs anew; it will keep going when all else fails. In this dual sense creative good is absolutely trustworthy: it always produces good; it never fails.

*571.* We have identified God with the creative event, but this requires some qualification. Any intellectual formulation about a concrete reality is never more than a meager, sketchy abstraction pertaining to it. The concrete event is infinitely complex and rich in quality. The intellectual formulation about it is not. Even this does not make plain the full disjunction between the true concept of a concrete reality and the concrete reality itself.

*572.* Truth is a form of apprehension (1) fitted to the capacities of the human mind and (2) fitted to guide the human being in dealing with other concrete events. The mind is not fitted to apprehend the concrete events which we immediately experience in feeling, but it is fitted to apprehend structures of possibility, which may approximate to various degrees the demarcations and interrelations of actual events. If such approximation is the best we can say for so simple an event as a falling body, the approximation must be more remote and more meager for such a reality as the concrete source of all human good. In such a sense only, can we call creativity a true concept about God. If it is a better concept than others (as we believe it to be), it can be so only in the sense that it is better fitted to intellectual formulation by way of the tests of truth; is a concept which is not the structure of the actual events of God's reality as these are accessible to feeling but is a possibility which can be made to approximate one feature of this concrete reality, and, most important of all, is better fitted than other concepts to guide practical action in meeting the demands of the source of all human good.

These are very severe qualifications

of the claim that the kind of event we have described is identical with God. In one sense it is not identical at all. But in whatsoever sense any concept of God can be identified with the reality of God, this concept can be. God, according to this interpretation, is immediately accessible to human living and human feeling in all the fulness of his concrete reality. He is not immediately accessible to the intellectual formulations of the human mind, but, for that matter, neither is any other concretely existing reality. Truth about concrete events, including truth about God, is not identical with the structure of those events, nor is it even one ingredient in that structure. The concrete events are qualities immediately apprehended by feeling. The truth about them is a structure of possibility which the human mind can formulate and use to guide those events called "human beings" in their meaningful relations to that kind of event called "God."

[Sec. 562, Henry N. Wieman, *The Source of Human Good* (Chicago: University of Chicago Press, 1946), pp. 6–8. Sec. 563, *ibid.*, p. 54. Sec. 564, *ibid.*, p. 55. Sec. 565, *ibid.*, p. 56. Sec. 566, *ibid.*, pp. 57–60. Sec. 567, *ibid.*, pp. 61–62. Sec. 568, *ibid.*, pp. 62–67. Sec. 569, *ibid.*, pp. 76–77. Sec. 570, *ibid.*, pp. 79–81. Sec. 571, *ibid.*, p. 305. Sec. 572, *ibid.*, pp. 305–6.]

### COMMENT

Wieman's proposition belongs to a class of propositions whose common class property is expressed in the formula, "There Is Production of Unexpected Good." There are certain questions which arise in regard to this notion, no matter how it be further specified.

1. Let us consider Production (emergence). We are told that this is an event and also that it is a kind of event. It is surely not meant that there is one actual occurrence or operation which, once for all or eternally, produces good. And even that, or in what sense, there is *at a*

*given moment* one world-wide divine operation is not made clear. Suppose—and there is scientific reason for supposing—that the universe contains many more than one inhabitable planet and suppose that the "work of God" is going on on several such planets. In what sense is it one God who is thus working rather than several "Gods" of more or less similar natures? And, of course, the same problem arises with respect to more or less isolated communities even on this planet. What, then, is the oneness of deity that distinguishes the Wieman doctrine from polytheistic conceptions? (For it seems certain that there is intended to be such a distinction.)

It may be well to explain that our difficulty is not with the idea that deity is a class of occurrences or events. Accepting as we do the Whiteheadian idea that an individual, such as John Jones, is (whatever else or more he may be) a class of experiences, we should be willing to say the same of God. But, since Mr. Wieman refuses to allow consciousness, memory, or purpose to deity, the "more" that distinguishes him as an individual from a mere class is not too apparent. One feels the need for some doctrine of analogy which would posit for God something corresponding to "personal integrity." And, if God is a class, it is hard to see just what are the members of the class. They cannot be divine experiences, for apparently there are none. Are they human experiences? It sometimes seems from what is said that they must be. Perhaps they are events behind or back of human experience, or they are certain features of human experiences. Is God simply a characteristic (value-emergence as such) found in many experient events?

2. Production of good, we are told, is also destruction of good. New goods displace old. This is insisted upon and forms an important and valuable part of the ethos of the system. But what about the displaced goods? Are they

simply nullified and as though they had never been? In that case all our specific objectives must in the long run prove vain, according to the probabilities. True, there is held to be some provision for conservation of past values, stored up in works of art and in many forms of conscious and unconscious memory. Yet, in the long run, it seems inevitable that any given value must be lost. Even if the earth were to be inhabitable forever—an astronomical impossibility, one gathers—or if man may hope to escape to another planet, still there just is not room, with the limitations of the human attention span, for any appreciable *proportion* of the values of past generations, and their billions of experiences per diem, to house themselves in the consciousness of any given human present. Wieman's view is that this is simply a tragic fact of life that we must accept. But perhaps it is absurd rather than tragic if taken as the last word about the question of the permanence of value. It would really mean that our efforts are worthless, that no act can in the long run have better consequences than any other. If the common destiny is nullification, the rivalry of values is meaningless.

Furthermore, this view seems to make fact as unintelligible as value. That a certain value "was realized" is fact, whether any human being is now aware of the having-been of this value or not. This is involved in the mere idea of fact, or the mere idea of "past." The idea of God, whatever else it may be, is the clarification of this having-been, as independent of any present human experience. It is, we hold, fully as reasonable to identify God with the indestructibility of fact and value as with the production or emergence of them. Indeed, that it is important to produce new values seems one with the truth that, as produced, they become added to the treasury of accomplished goods where "neither moth nor rust doth cor-

rupt and where thieves do not break through and steal." This does not mean that we have no reason to combat moths. For the persistence of structures which moths would destroy can aid in the production of further *new* values (experiences, with their intrinsic qualities), which may then be added to the treasury. But if no experiences can be preserved, and in merely human terms they cannot be, then all concrete values (for only experiences are concrete values) are doomed, bound for nullification.

3. The good, according to our author, is in principle Unexpected. That the emergence of value is not wholly foreseeable is a doctrine in good standing. But Wieman's inferences from this are puzzling. He says that human beings do not produce the emerging values, since (for he gives no other reason) they neither foresee nor intend them. Therefore, something else, call it "deity," produces them. What is the logic of this argument? Is it this? What produces values must foresee them. We do not foresee; therefore, we do not produce. Then does God foresee the values? No, this Wieman denies. God neither sees nor foresees. He is not a conscious being at all. So the major premise must be altered. Is the argument rather this: What a *conscious* being produces, it must foresee. We, who are conscious, do not foresee certain values; therefore, we do not produce them, and something else produces them which is either conscious of them in advance or is not conscious at all. This is the only form of the argument that seems to allow the conclusion drawn. However, it would leave the question open whether or not God is conscious.

Our author, however, seems to reason further: since, in us, consciousness does not foresee values, in no case can consciousness do so. This is making short work of the old problem of "eminence." Of course God is not conscious (or anything else) *merely as we are.* Furthermore, if our consciousness is the criterion, why be so sure that consciousness can have no effects except those it foresees? We should have thought our consciousness had many unforeseen effects. And why make such an ungraduated dichotomy between foresee and not foresee? A poet who, having composed the first stanza of a poem, begins to compose the second both does and does not foresee the values he is to produce. He foresees poetic, not musical, value; lyric, not epic; etc. And in the art of creative conversation, which Wieman rightly stresses, here too our intentions go part of the way toward defining what is to come. Now it may be granted that this does not warrant the notion of consciousness as, in the ideal case, fully and exactly foreseeing, or eternally seeing, the values of all moments of time. That such an assumption would nullify the very meaning of time and creative freedom we do believe; and we have tried to read every argument of note on the question.

But, still, is there here or anywhere else a basis for the dictum that consciousness can have only such effects as it foresees? Suppose that God is a conscious being and that he does not foresee values in their concrete particularity, these being, for him, too, an emergent in each case. Does it follow that there must be something additional to his consciousness, and to human and other experiences also, as explanation of this emergence? Why may not the emerging consciousness, with the antecedent experiences as data (Whitehead), *determine its own value?* Self-determination, the "self-created creature," seems the answer to this problem. And, if one denies this, he is denying emergence. The antecedents do either all the determining or not all of it. If they do all, then there is no emergence. If not all, then there is self-determining of the present by the present (or by

something in it and not in the past). Why not, then, regard the present consciousness as self-determining? Foresight is not implied. Whitehead's "creativity," which some think has been turned into Wieman's God (with qualifications as to the kind and degree of resulting value), seems, rather, quite left out of Wieman's thought. The main point of "creativity," self-creation, must be denied to give the argument for the divine nonconsciousness such plausibility as it has.

There seems occasion here for the general remark that no doctrine of God can avoid the problem of analogy. Either the divine nature is totally incomparable, and then all words about God have only the meaning that direct religious intuition, sheer experience of deity, can give them—hardly meanings available for "scientific method" perhaps—or else, when we ascribe properties to deity, we can point to analogous properties, say, in man. But then will it not be arbitrary to pick out "creativity" and proceed, perhaps, as follows: the poet, in a sense, is creative; God is creative eminently (or in some more radical or better sense), but nevertheless God is not, even eminently, conscious or qualified by will and feeling. For these aspects there is no analogy. There is analogy only for the bare creativeness. Allow this procedure, and you will equally have to allow the selection of "will" without consciousness (Schopenhauer) or of "feeling" without will (Bradley) and in either case with or without creativity. The basic dimensions of experience make no sense in isolation from each other, and no doctrine of analogy will ever have weight until we cease indulging in arbitrary choices among the dimensions to be dealt with.

It is nothing new for a theologian to favor activity over passivity, cause over effect, production over reception. God pours out values; we receive them. We (or such as we) are the final recipients of all (created) actual satisfactions. This used to mean that God does not *receive* satisfaction, because he eternally *has* all satisfaction without needing to receive it. For Wieman, it means that God is simply without satisfaction, experience, feeling, either eternal or received. On both the old and this new view it is false that God is love. For love (according to any definition that makes sense in terms of our experiences) means at least satisfaction in and because of the satisfaction of others, partly contingent upon or receptive to their satisfaction. It is, some of us hold, a catastrophic mistake to favor the outgoing over the receptive aspects of love as a theological category. The supreme love is exactly as much, we suggest, the supreme "receptacle" as it is the supreme "source" of good. Moreover, the insight that love is ultimate, with no concept going deeper, seems implicit in much of what Wieman writes about the social nature of creativity. Yet, so long as he is unable or unwilling to give God himself social character and *individuality*, must it not be impossible to furnish a clear logic for the distinction of God from man and for the relations between them?

Professor Wieman has expressed with great eloquence the common doctrine that God is infinitely above such categories as personality or consciousness or mind. But, no more than the others, has he been able to tell us what "above" (or "superior to") can possibly indicate except in terms of consciousness, except in terms of experiences of joy, satisfaction, and love, whose continuity and coherence we call "personality." If there is no experience, there is no actual value. Consciousness is the final measure and estimate of value and only through confusion can it think of looking "beyond" itself for a more ultimate measure. The more adequate is conscious evaluation to its given values, the more incomparable it will be with merely

ordinary consciousness such as ours, which is never adequate to its data. And, finally, the categorically supreme form of consciousness can only coincide with all that can be meant by a categorically supreme individual consciousness, that is, a supreme personality. For, if it lacks the unity which is connoted by "person," then it will not contain the adequate realization of its own internal relationships and structure. These are reasons why we cannot conceive that Wieman is right.

It has been held, with considerable cogency, that Wieman has given us the outstanding expression of an experimentalist-instrumentalist theory of deity.[2] Yet can it really be correct to say that God is creative action, while we are merely receptive or permissive of this action; and, on the other hand, that we more or less consciously enjoy the created values, while God has no feeling or consciousness of joy but only something infinitely "better"—which, however, only we, not he, know to be better, and in which superiority only we, not he, can take satisfaction. "Operationism" here means setting aside the social structure of experience, which is all the clue there is, we suggest, to the meaning of life, particularly in its higher reaches, at just the point where the spiritual insights of the ages (embodied in the doctrine that God is love), and simple logic as well, favor making the maximal use of it. Only by love do we transcend our individual limitations, only by participation (Wieman himself eloquently testifies to this truth) in the experiences of others. Is it likely that we can transcend love itself as a principle, taking into account the categorically supreme as well as ordinary forms? Of course love is "creativity," but not bare creativity; it is also joy, memory,

2. See Huston Smith's admirable article, "The Operational View of God," *Journal of Religion*, XXXI (1951), 94–111.

sympathy, etc. It is more or less conscious creativity, and in the supreme case it must be supremely conscious, for this only means that there is adequate realization of the contrast between actual and potential values, which contrast is the final measure of good, whether created or creative.

Yet we wish to close with the expression of our sincere and vivid appreciation of the worth of Wieman's vision of the creative, inexhaustible, emergent, aspects of good, forever transcending all previous achievements, more or less confuting previous (human) convictions, ideals, and expectations, shattering old habits, even highly venerated ones, and calling for flexibility, humility, willingness to learn and unlearn, to dare and adventure, in community with others and yet also, in a certain sense, alone with God.

# PART THREE

*Skeptical or Atheistic Views, Ancient
and Modern*

# Chapter XI: *Religio-pragmatic Skepticism*

## BUDDHISM

It is frequently held that the possibility of a great religion without a theistic belief is established by the example of Buddhism. Certainly Buddha is one of the greatest of the nontheistic thinkers of all time. As the following passages make clear, he was a religious pragmatic skeptic who set aside metaphysical beliefs as irrelevant to man's basic concern. Whereas the Hindu mystics had sought attainment through union with the universal spirit, made possible by purification from all distracting desires and attachments and involving the perception of the unreality of diversity and becoming, Buddha appears to hold that it is not necessary to characterize attainment of Nirvana in metaphysical terms. We need to know only that it is freedom from the desires that lead to suffering and misery.

### Irrelevance of Certain Questions

573. The religious life, Māluṅkyāputta, does not depend on the dogma that the world is eternal. . . . Whether the dogma obtain, Māluṅkyāputta, that the world is eternal, or that the world is not eternal, there still remain birth, old age, death, sorrow, lamentation, misery, grief, and despair, for the extinction of which in the present life I am prescribing.

. . . Accordingly, Māluṅkyāputta, bear always in mind what it is that I have not elucidated. . . . I have not elucidated . . . that the world is eternal; I have not elucidated that the world is not eternal. . . . I have not elucidated that the saint neither exists nor does not exist after death. And why, Māluṅkyāputta, have I not elucidated this? Because, Māluṅkyāputta, this profits not, nor has to do with the fundamentals of religion, nor tends to aversion, absence of passion, cessation, quiescence, the supernatural faculties, supreme wisdom, and Nirvana. . . .

And what, Māluṅkyāputta, have I elucidated? Misery, Māluṅkyāputta, have I elucidated; the origin of misery have I elucidated; and the path leading to the cessation of misery. . . . This does profit, has to do with the fundamentals of religion, and tends to aversion, absence of passion, cessation, quiescence, knowledge, supreme wisdom, and Nirvana. . . .

### Brahma the Unknown

574. Then you say, Vàsettha, that none of the Brahmans, or of their teachers, or of their pupils, even up to the seventh generation, has ever seen Brahmà face to face. And that even the Rishis of old, the authors and utterers of the verses, of the ancient form of words which the Brahmans of today so carefully intone and recite precisely as they have been handed down—even they did not pretend to know or to have seen where or whence or whither Brahmà is. So that the Brahmans versed in the Three Vedas have forsooth said thus: "What we know not, what we have not seen, to a state of union with that we can show the way, and can say: 'This is the straight path, this is the direct way, which makes for salvation. . . .'"

"Now what think you, Vàsettha? Does it not follow, this being so, that the talk of the Brahmans, versed though they be in the Three Vedas, turns out to be foolish talk?"

411

## Denial of Soul-Substance

575. "What is a chariot?" asked Nāgasena. "Is the ornamental cover the chariot? Are the wheels, the spokes . . . the chariot? Are all these parts together . . . the chariot? If you leave these out, does there remain anything which is the chariot?"

. . . "No."

"Then I see no chariot, it is only a sound, a name. In saying that you came in a chariot, you have uttered an untruth. . . ."

"No untruth have I uttered, venerable monk. The cover, wheels, seat, and other parts all united or combined (chariot-wise) form the chariot. . . ."

"And just so," said Nāgasena, "in the case of man. . . . 'As the various parts of a chariot form, when united, the chariot, so the five Skandhas [physical mass, perception, sensation, consciousness and predispositions],[1] when united in one body, form a being, a living existence.'"

576. "This soul of mine can be perceived, it has experienced the result of good and evil actions committed here and there: now this soul of mine is permanent, lasting. . . .

"This, brethren, is called the walking in delusion, the jungle of delusion . . . the writhing of delusion, the fetter of delusion."

577. "How, Bhante Nāgasena, does rebirth take place without anything transmigrating? . . ."

"Suppose, your majesty, a man were to light a light from another light; pray, would the one light have passed over (transmigrated) to the other light?"

"Nay, verily, bhante."

"In exactly the same way, your majesty, does rebirth take place without anything transmigrating."

"Give another illustration."

"Do you remember, your majesty,

1. According to John R. Everett, *Religion in Human Experience* (New York: Henry Holt & Co., 1950), p. 115.

having learnt, when you were a boy, some verse or other from your professor of poetry?"

"Yes, bhante."

"Pray, your majesty, did the verse pass over (transmigrate) to you from your teacher?"

"Nay, verily, bhante."

"In exactly the same way, your majesty, does rebirth take place without anything transmigrating."

[Sec. 573, Henry Clarke Warren, *Buddhism in Translation* (Cambridge: Harvard University Press, 1922), pp. 121–22; see also Robert O. Ballou, *The Bible of the World* (New York: Viking Press, 1944), pp. 256–57. Sec. 574, *Sacred Books of the Buddhists*, trans. Rhys Davids (London: Henry Frowde [succeeded by Oxford Press], 1899), pp. 304–5. Sec. 575, Rhys Davids, *Buddhism* (London: Society for Promoting Christian Knowledge, 1917), pp. 96–97. Sec. 576, Max Müller (ed.), *Sacred Books of the East*, Vol. XI: *Buddhist Suttas*, trans. Rhys Davids (London: Oxford Press, 1881), p. 299; see also John R. Everett, *Religion in Human Experience* (New York: Henry Holt & Co., 1950), p. 115. Sec. 577, Warren, *op. cit.*, p. 234; see also John B. Noss, *Man's Religions* (New York: Macmillan Co., 1949), p. 159.]

### COMMENT

How shall we interpret these striking rejections? First of all, is it not significant that the religious metaphysics with which the great religious founder is dealing is illusionistic classical pantheism? Buddha is here not judging the theistic question so much as the question of acosmic pantheism.

But still, some may say, Buddha did get along without theism, and this shows that theism is at least not necessary. However, we may ask, "How *well* and how *completely* did Buddha get along without theism?" In fact, he presented his followers with some difficult dilemmas which apparently forced them to depart more or less widely from his own doctrine. If Nirvana is not union with deity, what is it? Mere escape from suffering, mere nonsuffering? The great teacher refused to assert rebirth or personal immortality, except for those who do not wholly succeed in attaining superiority to desire. He did not, then, identify Nirvana with personal happiness beyond this life. Is it merely such contentment as we can enjoy on earth by taking all attachments lightly? There is no denying the negative cast of much Buddhistic thought: the object seems not primarily the good but the avoidance of evil. To destroy the sources of misery, more than to nourish the sources of joy and happiness, seems to be the procedure. Does this mean that joy automatically ensues when misery is removed?

Again, one is to love all beings, all life; but this seems at times more a means of weakening special attachments than of extending the scope of affection as itself a good. Good will is "the heart's release." There is "ripening" in sharing gifts. The emphasis remains upon the self and its inner possession of value. In popular Buddhism, however, even in the stricter or Hinayana branch, the doctrine is partly transformed. And in Mahayana Buddhism, even the more esoteric theories themselves undergo transformation. What happens is that love is made a cosmic principle; the whole universe is seen as suffused with divine beings, Buddhas and Bodhisattvas, to whom prayer is made, who are filled with benevolence toward men and sympathy for their sufferings. And in some forms of the doctrine there is an explicit theory of a cosmic consciousness which is the primal reservoir from which all these streams of benevolence proceed.

Is this defection from pure humanism a merely historical fact? Is there not rather a logical ground for it? The goal is simply the negative one of escape from suffering, or else a positive good is sought. Since a negative goal is not enough, the humanism or skepticism of

Buddha can be appealed to only if it can be shown to have positive bearings. Are we simply to destroy the "attachments" to others, and to our own earthly values, which inevitably expose us to anxiety and frustration; or are we rather to generalize attachment and thus overcome the selfish element in it, leaving it still attachment, positive treasuring of human potentialities and achievements? (An implication might be that, as many modern Buddhists recognize, one need not become a monk to live Buddhistically.) In that case some of the sufferings will indeed be mitigated. I shall no longer feel it to be intolerable that a man should insult me or treat me unfairly, for I shall have accepted the principle that an insult to me is simply an insult to a member of the human race, an evil which is not worse because that member is myself. But, while this will mitigate the bitterness of such an insult, it will at the same time expose me to a share in sufferings that selfish men could escape—those that arise in me as I see the injustices with which multitudes of men about me are afflicted or the catastrophes which overwhelm them. Only the root of suffering in narrow self-regard will be cut off; but is that the only root?

It is a Buddhistic saying that we are to love the whole world as a mother loves a child. But then we enter sympathetically into *all* the sufferings of life. Is this the sheer escape from sorrow which sometimes seems to be what is meant by Nirvana? If not, and surely it is not, then it is either higher or lower than that wholly serene state. If it is lower, then not humanism but mere personal escape is what the doctrine finally comes to. Buddha himself, and then his followers, practice love; but do they give any clear doctrine of the relation of love to Nirvana?

Ultimately (as Schweitzer and Berdyaev insist), either one must accept tragedy as inherent in life and in all good or one cannot take love as the highest principle. However, it is notable that many Buddhistic tenets may be embraced in a suitable version of the doctrine that God is love. Such tenets include: there is a good beyond all selfish attachments, those involving arbitrary exclusions; this good is not canceled out by death, and yet neither is it dependent upon personal immortality in the conventional sense of rebirth to new adventures after death; it is not a matter of a soul-substance of which all experiences are predicates; it is not a sheer identity with the pure Absolute. These are largely negative characterizations of Buddhism. How can positive content be given the doctrine save as follows? Nirvana is our glimpse of and participation in the Love which is not so much unattached as universally attached to all of life, universally participant in the sorrows, joys, and overarching beauty of things. Through our sense of echoing and contributing to this Love we are saved from fretful or agonized clinging to egoistic, partisan, or petty claims and aspirations, and we triumph over the transience of all experience not by virtue of living beyond death but by virtue of the experiences we even now feel ourselves contributing to the Love which does outlive all death and all forgetfulness.

The cosmic response to which Mahayana and all popular Buddhism permit us to appeal is the only way to solve the antinomies between the universality and the personal sincerity of love, between transience and permanence, between negative and positive conceptions of the good. As human beings we cannot wholly overcome selfishness by positive universality. Special attachments are inherent in our natures. But we can have, as it were, a special attachment to the divine; we can accept our roles as abiding moments in the life of deity. We can see escape from intolerable tragedy in the vision of the

tolerable tragedy which full participation in all of life, with all its beauty as well as its suffering, brings to deity. Deity has indeed all troubles but no "troubles of its own," no jealousies, no fears, no partisan aims. It has rather its own beauty of synthesis whereby all this is held together in a divine flux of experience. And it has all the most secret joys and beauties, wherever they are. This is the true Nirvana. It cannot literally be ours. But it can be ours to whatever extent human possession of the perfect or superhuman attainment makes logical sense. Just so far as we *can* love unselfishly, participate richly, synthesize beautifully, and satisfy our longing for perfection by cultivating the sense of harmony with the one truly perfect mode of living, the "consequent nature of God," just so far the peace that transcends all mere sorrow, frustration, anxiety, transience, can be ours.

A few days after the above lines were written, a representative of Japanese Buddhism, Dr. Suzuki, declared in a lecture that in his opinion the mature Buddhist philosophy, the Kegon, implies an idea of God. He stressed two points: God can be conscious of himself only in relation to the world, not in sheer independence of it; and God suffers in and with all creatures. A panentheist would agree but would insist upon a clear distinction between "God can be conscious only in relation to some world or other" and "God can be conscious only in relation to this world." The latter view is that of classical pantheism. As Dr. Suzuki has expounded Kegon Buddhism, it is somewhat ambiguous as between pantheism and panentheism. Its theory that the One is identical with the Many because the total system of terms and relations constituting reality is present in each term (each monad, as Leibniz later put it, mirroring the universe) requires qualification to safeguard the openness of the future and the reality of creative freedom.

A striking feature of much Buddhistic literature is its insistence that the terms entering into the universal network are events, not things or persons in the ordinary sense.[2] Our question, however, is whether the supreme reality in its inclusive aspect is an ever fixed eternal system of events or whether there is not an inexhaustible creation of inclusive events (divine experiences), each with its own system of relations, rather than a system inclusive of process once for all. It is well to attenuate the notion of the self-identity of ordinary things and persons sufficiently so that their unity with their neighbors in space will be somewhat comparable to their own unity through time. And it may seem that, since the divine unity is all-inclusive spatially, there is no reason why it should not be so temporally. However, the analysis of reality into event-sequences has other grounds than the laudable one of overcoming the contrast (favorable to egoism) between self-identity and sheer otherness with respect to neighbors, or the presumptuous attribution to one's own "soul" of perpetual persistence such as may be one of the unique privileges of the One transcending ourselves. The ultimate ground of the primacy of events is that what becomes is logically inclusive of what does not become rather than conversely. Process is given as the concrete from which all merely fixed elements are abstracted.

The melancholy aspect of process which seems to have impressed Buddha can be overcome by seeing that the poverty of our retention of the past in the pitiful echoes we call "memory" is a negative or privative feature of our experience which can very well be transcended on a higher level or in divine experience. What cannot be transcended, since it is positive, is creativity, freedom, inexhaustible further actualization. This inexhaustibility is no mere privation distinguishing one level of experience from another. It is the very essence of possibility that there are incompossible ways of actualizing it. To do everything is indistinguishable from doing nothing. But there is no logical absurdity in the idea that what has been done has been done; hence cannot in itself (even perhaps for us) be now lost and as though it had never been done. The apparent transitoriness of all created values is indeed a sign that the meaning of life embraces something transcendent of human, and all ordinary, process, but the creation of ever new values is itself a transcendent principle presupposed by all apparent loss and by all fixity of meaning. As a Zen Buddhist said: "The immovable is in the moving itself." What seems to have been hard both for Christians and for Buddhists to believe is that the supreme reality is infinitely more than the merely eternal and is the ever moving eminent Process which contains eternity and, in addition, all actualized time.

2. D. T. Suzuki, *The Essence of Buddhism* (Kyoto, 1948), p. 57 n.

# Chapter XII: *Logico-metaphysical Skepticism*

## CARNEADES AND HUME (*ca.* 215–125 B.C.; 1711–76)

An anticipator of Hume and one of the greatest critics of metaphysical and theological constructions was the leader of the second Platonic academy, Carneades. We therefore preface our introduction to Hume with the following from Zeller's account of Carneades (whose writings, being lost, are known to us only through references in other authors):

According to the usual conception, God is the infinite being, which at the same time is a particular individual, endowed with life and personality. Carneades shows that these two requirements contradict each other; that it is impossible to ascribe the characteristics of personal existence to deity without limiting its infinity. However we think of God, we must in any case think of him as living; now every living being is ... capable of destruction. Further, every living being has necessarily a sensory nature, and so far from denying senses to deity, we must rather, in the interest of divine omniscience, attribute to God more than our five senses alone. But to be capable of sensation is to be capable of change, for sensation is a change in the soul; it is also to be capable of pleasure and displeasure, since sensation without this is inconceivable. Everything changeable is mortal; everything subject to suffering is subject to corruption, which is the cause of suffering. ... To be alive is further to desire that which is according to nature and to avoid that which is contrary to nature; but the contrary to nature is that which has power to destroy the being. ... Passing from the concept of life to that of rationality, we see that we must attribute to deity not only bliss but all virtues. But how, asks Carneades (with Aristotle) can one attribute a virtue to the divine? Every virtue presupposes a defect, in whose overcoming it consists: temperate is only he who can also be intemperate; ... brave only he who

is threatened with danger; ... a being for whom pleasure had no charm, and pain and danger no terrors, is one to whom none of these virtues could be attributed. Just as little could we ascribe wisdom to a being insensitive to pleasure and pain; for wisdom is the knowledge of good and evil; how could one know these if one had never experienced pleasure or pain? Or how can one conceive, as is alleged of God, a being capable of pleasure only but not of pain, inasmuch as the one is known only through its contrast with the other, and inasmuch as the possibility of what is favorable to life involves the possibility of what is unfavorable? For similar reasons we cannot attribute to God skill in the choice of means, for this implies conditions imposed by a partly unknown environment. ... Finally, the inconceivability of deity is seen if we simply ask whether God is limited or unlimited, bodily or not bodily. Deity cannot be unlimited, for the unlimited, since it has no location, is immovable, and without soul, since owing to its infinity it cannot form a besouled totality; yet we think of deity as movable and besouled. Deity cannot be limited, for then it would be defective; it cannot be incorporeal, for soul belongs to a body with senses and motions; deity cannot be corporeal for the corporeal is either composite and corruptible, or simple (fire, water, etc.) and without life or consciousness.[1]

Carneades, in these and other arguments, anticipates much of the skepticism of Hume. The basic difficulty of theism which he, perhaps, was the first to state clearly may be put into a dilemma: any notion of deity is either anthropomorphic or meaningless. God either is just a "magnified non-natural

1. E. Zeller, *Die Philosophie der Griechen* (Leipzig: Reising Verlag, 1909), III, Part I, 525–28.

man" (Matthew Arnold) or is nothing conceivable, mere emptiness, without physical reality, and no less without life, personality, or consciousness. The distinctive trait of deity, which alone makes him more than a supernaturally powerful and excellent human being, is his infinity or absolute independence of all conditions or limits. But this trait is purely negative, and the moment we try to conceive some positive character, such as consciousness or will or goodness, to relieve the emptiness of mere "nonlimitedness" as such, we encounter contradiction between the negative and the positive aspects of our thinking.

There are three modes of escape: we may give up infinity entirely, we may give up positive attributes of life or consciousness entirely, or, finally, we may find some way to harmonize the two elements of the God-idea by taking each to characterize an aspect of God. This is the plain answer—we suggest the only one that is not evasion—to Carneades. To take a remote analogy: there is no contradiction in saying that a man is unchanging in honesty and yet changing in his particular utterances. For diverse utterances can be equally honest. Contradiction arises only if we affirm that the man is *in all respects* unchanging and, yet, that he says now this and now that. Again, there is no contradiction in saying that a being is unlimited in what it might experience but limited in what it actually does experience. Actuality is in essence limited, for it is essentially decision as among mutually exclusive possibilities. But the possibilities for decision are not limited in the same sense, for the very meaning of limitation is relative to the unlimited possibilities, failure to actualize some of which constitutes "limitation."

In some of his arguments Carneades merely assumes that there can be no categorically supreme case of a category. Not all change or suffering need

be that of something corruptible. Unlimited power to assimilate actual values implies, because of the inexhaustibility of possibility and the permanence of past achievement, an endless increase in value but not at all a possible decrease. The latter is always due to lack of power to assimilate. The suffering that accrues through sympathy with the suffering of others is not, it may be held, essentially a sense of one's own insecurity or personal danger. One must distinguish between arguments which turn on the essentially dipolar character of life, consciousness, and the like and those which merely take it for granted that only ordinary cases, without essential superiority, are conceivable.

Hume's analysis is roughly similar to that of Carneades. It is more elaborate (than the form in which we have Carneades), and it takes account of classical theism, which had not been sharply formulated in ancient times. The same basic dilemma is involved. Either God is infinite and immutable, and therefore without will or consciousness, or he is finite and changeable, and therefore his will and consciousness are imperfect and corruptible. Like Carneades, also, Hume argues that the survey of the world cannot demonstrate a God unless it be one as imperfect as the world seems to be. But Hume takes account of the possibility, urged by Anselm and others, of an a priori proof for the divine perfection. He admits that, were such a proof valid, the imperfection of the world would not be decisive counterevidence. For we cannot tell whether the world, imperfect as it may seem to our ignorant vision, is really as a whole unworthy of a perfect creator. Perhaps the whole world is as perfect, or nearly so, as any that a perfect cause could produce. Hume, however, denies that the a priori (ontological) proof is valid, giving essentially Kant's reason that "existence" is not a special property, such as might be included in the property "perfection." Moreover, Kant's famous contention, that all the arguments for God presuppose the ontological proof, is substantially that of Hume. For the empirical arguments cannot reach the perfection of deity, which only a priori considerations could justify our asserting, the world being, for our knowledge, not perfect. This is just what Kant maintains, but he put the matter more formally and systematically.

Hume's attack on theism is much more penetrating than Kant's in some respects, for he does not arbitrarily limit himself to classical theism but tries to exhaust the possible "theisms" and to show that none can be made secure against attack.

Like Kant, and with even less qualification, Hume assumes that causal order is absolute in the world of nature and that determinism is a true account of temporal process. The consequence of this assumption is that evils cannot be explained as due to the free choice of the creatures; for these choices are wholly predetermined by events occurring in the remotest past, so that responsibility must belong to any creator of the world whole.

Hume also maintains that we have no insight whatever into any power of the mind to control either its own ideas or the motions of bodies. It is vain to imagine a supreme mind ordering the world, if it is a complete mystery to us how any mind orders even its own thoughts. Our thoughts fall into order; but we do not order them, for all we can tell. No more can we understand how our minds control our bodies or anything outside these bodies; and hence we have no rational basis for a theory of a divine mind controlling the world.

## The Deity Incomprehensible

578. [Demea speaking:] The ancient Platonists, you know, were the most religious and devout of all the Pagan philosophers; yet many of them, particularly Plotinus, expressly declare, that intellect or understanding is not to be ascribed to the Deity; and that our most perfect worship of him consists, not in acts of veneration, reverence, gratitude, or love; but in a certain mysterious self-annihilation, or total extinction of all our faculties. These ideas are, perhaps, too far stretched; but still it must be acknowledged, that, by representing the Deity as so intelligible and comprehensible, and so similar to a human mind, we are guilty of the grossest and most narrow partiality, and make ourselves the model of the whole universe.

All the *sentiments* of the human mind, gratitude, resentment, love, friendship, approbation, blame, pity, emulation, envy, have a plain reference to the state and situation of man, and are calculated for preserving the existence and promoting the activity of such a being in such circumstances. It seems, therefore, unreasonable to transfer such sentiments to a supreme existence, or to suppose him actuated by them; and the phenomena besides of the universe will not support us in such a theory. All our *ideas*, derived from the senses, are confessedly false and illusive; and cannot therefore be supposed to have place in a supreme intelligence: And as the ideas of internal sentiment, added to those of the external senses, compose the whole furniture of human understanding, we may conclude, that none of the *materials* of thought are in any respect similar in the human and in the divine intelligence. Now, as to the *manner* of thinking; how can we make any comparison between them, or suppose them anywise resembling? Our thought is fluctuating, uncertain, fleeting, successive, and compounded; and were we to remove these circumstances, we absolutely annihilate its essence and it would in such a case be an abuse of terms to apply to it the name of thought or reason. At least if it appear more pious and respectful (as it really is) still to retain these terms, when we mention the Supreme Being, we ought to acknowledge, that their meaning, in that case, is totally incomprehensible; and that the infirmities of our nature do not permit us to reach any ideas which in the least correspond to the ineffable sublimity of the Divine attributes.

## Coincidence of Mysticism and Atheism

It seems strange to me, said Cleanthes, that you, Demea, who are so sincere in the cause of religion, should still maintain the mysterious, incomprehensible nature of the Deity, and should insist so strenuously that he has no manner of likeness or resemblance to human creatures. The Deity, I can readily allow, possesses many powers and attributes of which we can have no comprehension: But if our ideas, so far as they go, be not just, and adequate, and correspondent to his real nature, I know not what there is in this subject worth insisting on. Is the name, without any meaning, of such mighty importance? Or how do you Mystics, who maintain the absolute incomprehensibility of the Deity, differ from Sceptics or Atheists, who assert, that the first cause of all is unknown and unintelligible? Their temerity must be very great, if, after rejecting the production by a mind, I mean, a mind resembling the human (for I know of no other), they pretend to assign, with certainty, any other specific intelligible cause: And their conscience must be very scrupulous indeed, if they refuse to call the universal unknown cause a God or Deity; and to bestow on him as many sublime eulogies and unmeaning epithets as you shall please to require of them.

## Mystic and Anthropomorphite

Who could imagine, replied Demea, that Cleanthes, the calm philosophical

Cleanthes, would attempt to refute his antagonists by affixing a nickname to them . . . ? Or does he not perceive, that these topics are easily retorted, and that Anthropomorphite is an appellation as invidious, and implies as dangerous consequences, as the epithet of Mystic, with which he has honoured us? In reality, Cleanthes, consider what it is you assert when you represent the Deity as similar to a human mind and understanding. What is the soul of man? A composition of various faculties, passions, sentiments, ideas; united, indeed, into one self or person, but still distinct from each other. When it reasons, the ideas, which are the parts of its discourse, arrange themselves in a certain form or order; which is not preserved entire for a moment, but immediately gives place to another arrangement. New opinions, new passions, new affections, new feelings arise, which continually diversify the mental scene, and produce in it the greatest variety and most rapid succession imaginable. How is this compatible with that perfect immutability and simplicity which all true Theists ascribe to the Deity? By the same act, say they, he sees past, present, and future: His love and hatred, his mercy and justice, are one individual operation: He is entire in every point of space; and complete in every instant of duration. No succession, no change, no acquisition, no diminution. What he is implies not in it any shadow of distinction or diversity. And what he is this moment he ever has been, and ever will be, without any new judgment, sentiment, or operation. He stands fixed in one simple, perfect state: nor can you ever say, with any propriety, that this act of his is different from that other; or that this judgment or idea has been lately formed, and will give place, by succession, to any different judgment or idea.

I can readily allow, said Cleanthes, that those who maintain the perfect simplicity of the Supreme Being, to the extent in which you have explained it, are complete Mystics, and chargeable with all the consequences which I have drawn from their opinion. They are, in a word, Atheists, without knowing it. For though it be allowed, that the Deity possesses attributes of which we have no comprehension, yet ought we never to ascribe to him any attributes which are absolutely incompatible with that intelligent nature essential to him. A mind, whose acts and sentiments and ideas are not distinct and successive; one, that is wholly simple, and totally immutable, is a mind which has no thought, no reason, no will, no sentiment, no love, no hatred; or, in a word, is no mind at all. It is an abuse of terms to give it that appellation; and we may as well speak of limited extension without figure, or number without composition.

Pray consider, said Philo, whom you are at present inveighing against. You are honouring with the appellation of *Atheist* all the sound, orthodox divines, almost, who have treated of this subject; and you will at last be, yourself, found, according to your reckoning, the only sound Theist in the world. But if idolaters be Atheists, as I think may justly be asserted, and Christian Theologians the same, what becomes of the argument, so much celebrated, derived from the universal consent of mankind?

But because I know you are not much swayed by names and authorities, I shall endeavour to show you, a little more distinctly, the inconveniences of that Anthropomorphism, which you have embraced; and shall prove, that there is no ground to suppose a plan of the world to be formed in the divine mind, consisting of distinct ideas, differently arranged, in the same manner as an architect forms in his head the plan of a house which he intends to execute.

## Mind Not Self-explanatory

*579.* . . . a mental world, or universe of ideas, requires a cause as much as does a material world, or universe of objects; and, if similar in its arrangement, must require a similar cause. For what is there in this subject, which should occasion a different conclusion or inference? In an abstract view, they are entirely alike; and no difficulty attends the one supposition, which is not common to both of them.

Again, when we will needs force *Experience* to pronounce some sentence, even on these subjects which lie beyond her sphere, neither can she perceive any material difference in this particular, between these two kinds of worlds; but finds them to be governed by similar principles, and to depend upon an equal variety of causes in their operations. We have specimens in miniature of both of them. Our own mind resembles the one; a vegetable or animal body the other. Let experience, therefore, judge from these samples. Nothing seems more delicate with regard to its causes, than thought; and as these causes never operate in two persons after the same manner, so we never find two persons who think exactly alike. Nor indeed does the same person think exactly alike at any two different periods of time. A difference of age, of the disposition of his body, of weather, of food, of company, of books, of passions; any of these particulars, or others more minute, are sufficient to alter the curious machinery of thought, and communicate to it very different movements and operations. As far as we can judge, vegetables and animal bodies are not more delicate in their motions, nor depend upon a greater variety or more curious adjustment of springs and principles.

*580.* To say, that the different ideas which compose the reason of the Supreme Being, fall into order of themselves, and by their own nature, is really to talk without any precise meaning. If it has a meaning, I would fain know, why it is not as good sense to say, that the parts of the material world fall into order of themselves and by their own nature. Can the one opinion be intelligible, while the other is not so?

We have, indeed, experience of ideas which fall into order of themselves, and without any *known* cause. But, I am sure, we have a much larger experience of matter which does the same; as, in all instances of generation and vegetation, where the accurate analysis of the cause exceeds all human comprehension. We have also experience of particular systems of thought and of matter which have no order; of the first in madness, of the second in corruption. Why, then, should we think, that order is more essential to one than the other? And if it requires a cause in both, what do we gain by your system, in tracing the universe of objects into a similar universe of ideas? The first step which we make leads us on for ever.

*581.* It was usual with the Peripatetics, you know, Cleanthes, when the cause of any phenomenon was demanded, to have recourse to their *faculties,* or *occult qualities;* and to say, for instance, that bread nourished by its nutritive faculty, and senna purged by its purgative. But it has been discovered, that this subterfuge was nothing but the disguise of ignorance; and that these philosophers, though less ingenuous, really said the same thing with the sceptics or the vulgar, who fairly confessed that they knew not the cause of these phenomena. In like manner, when it is asked, what cause produces order in the ideas of the Supreme Being, can any other reason be assigned by you, Anthropomorphites, than that it is a *rational* faculty, and that such is the nature of the Deity? But why a similar answer will not be equally satisfactory in accounting for the order of the world, without having recourse to

any such intelligent creator as you insist on, may be difficult to determine. It is only to say, that *such* is the nature of material objects, and that they are all originally possessed of a *faculty* of order and proportion. These are only more learned and elaborate ways of confessing our ignorance; nor has the one hypothesis any real advantage above the other, except in its greater conformity to vulgar prejudices.

## Indefinite Results of Experimental Theism

*582.* But to show you still more inconveniences, continued Philo, in your Anthropomorphism, please to take a new survey of your principles. *Like effects prove like causes.* This is the experimental argument; and this, you say too, is the sole theological argument.

*583.* Now, Cleanthes, said Philo, with an air of alacrity and triumph, mark the consequences. *First,* By this method of reasoning, you renounce all claim to infinity in any of the attributes of the Deity. For, as the cause ought only to be proportioned to the effect, and the effect so far as it falls under our cognisance, is not infinite; what pretensions have we, upon your suppositions, to ascribe that attribute to the Divine Being?

*584. Secondly,* You have no reason, on your theory, for ascribing perfection to the Deity, even in his finite capacity, or for supposing him free from every error, mistake, or incoherence, in his undertakings. There are many inexplicable difficulties in the works of Nature, which, if we allow a perfect author to be proved *a priori,* are easily solved, and become only seeming difficulties, from the narrow capacity of man, who cannot trace infinite relations. But according to your method of reasoning, these difficulties became all real; and perhaps will be insisted on, as new instances of likeness to human art and contrivance. At least, you must acknowledge, that it is impossible for us to tell, from our limited views, whether this system contains any great faults, or deserves any considerable praise, if compared to other possible, and even real systems. Could a peasant, if the Aeneid were read to him, pronounce that poem to be absolutely faultless, or even assign to it its proper rank among the productions of human wit, he, who had never seen any other production?

But were this world ever so perfect a production, it must still remain uncertain, whether all the excellences of the work can justly be ascribed to the workman. If we survey a ship what an exalted idea must we form of the ingenuity of the carpenter, who framed so complicated, useful, and beautiful a machine? And what surprise must we feel, when we find him a stupid mechanic, who imitated others, and copied an art, which through a long succession of ages, after multiplied trials, mistakes, corrections, deliberations, and controversies, had been gradually improving? Many worlds might have been botched and bungled, throughout an eternity, ere this system was struck out; much labour lost, many fruitless trials made; and a slow, but continued improvement carried on during infinite ages in the art of world-making.

*585.* And what shadow of an argument, continued Philo, can you produce, from your hypothesis, to prove the unity of the Deity? A great number of men join in building a house or a ship, in rearing a city, in framing a commonwealth; why may not several deities combine in contriving and framing a world? This is only so much greater similarity to human affairs. By sharing the work among several, we may so much farther limit the attributes of each, and get rid of that extensive power and knowledge, which must be supposed in one deity, and which, according to you, can only serve

to weaken the proof of his existence. And if such foolish, such vicious creatures as man can yet often unite in framing and executing one plan, how much more those deities or demons, whom we may suppose several degrees more perfect!

*586.* In a word, Cleanthes, a man who follows your hypothesis is able perhaps to assert, or conjecture, that the universe, sometime, arose from something like design; but beyond that position he cannot ascertain one single circumstance; and is left afterwards to fix every point of his theology by the utmost license of fancy and hypothesis. This world, for aught he knows, is very faulty and imperfect, compared to a superior standard; and was only the first rude essay of some infant deity, who afterwards abandoned it, ashamed of his lame performance: it is the work only of some dependent, inferior deity; and is the object of derision to his superiors: it is the production of old age and dotage in some superannuated deity; and ever since his death, has run on at adventures, from the first impulse and active force which it received from him. You justly give signs of horror, Demea, at these strange suppositions; but these, and a thousand more of the same kind, are Cleanthes's suppositions, not mine. From the moment the attributes of the Deity are supposed finite, all these have place. And I cannot, for my part, think that so wild and unsettled a system of theology, is in any respect preferable to none at all.

*587.* It must be a slight fabric, indeed, said Demea, which can be erected on so tottering a foundation.

## God as the Soul of the World-Organism

*588.* To render it still more unsatisfactory, said Philo, there occurs to me another hypothesis, which must acquire an air of probability from the method of reasoning so much insisted on by Cleanthes. That like effects arise from like causes: this principle he supposes the foundation of all religion. But there is another principle of the same kind, no less certain, and derived from the same source of experience; that where several known circumstances are observed to be similar, the unknown will also be found similar. Thus, if we see the limbs of a human body, we conclude that it is also attended with a human head, though hid from us. Thus, if we see, through a chink in a wall, a small part of the sun, we conclude that, were the wall removed, we should see the whole body. In short, this method of reasoning is so obvious and familiar, that no scruple can ever be made with regard to its solidity.

Now, if we survey the universe, so far as it falls under our knowledge, it bears a great resemblance to an animal or organized body, and seems actuated with a like principle of life and motion. A continual circulation of matter in it produces no disorder: a continual waste in every part is incessantly repaired: the closest sympathy is perceived throughout the entire system: and each part or member, in performing its proper offices, operates both to its own preservation and to that of the whole. The world, therefore, I infer, is an animal; and the Deity is the SOUL of the world, actuating it, and actuated by it.

You have too much learning, Cleanthes, to be at all surprised at this opinion, which, you know, was maintained by almost all the Theists of antiquity, and chiefly prevails in their discourses and reasonings. For though, sometimes, the ancient philosophers reason from final causes, as if they thought the world the workmanship of God; yet it appears rather their favourite notion to consider it as his body, whose organization renders it subservient to him. And it must be confessed, that, as the universe resembles more a human body

than it does the works of human art and contrivance, if our limited analogy could ever, with any propriety, be extended to the whole of nature, the inference seems juster in favour of the ancient than the modern theory.

There are many other advantages too, in the former theory, which recommend it to the ancient theologians. Nothing more repugnant to all their notions, because nothing more repugnant to common experience, than mind without body; a mere spiritual substance, which fell not under their senses nor comprehension, and of which they had not observed one single instance throughout all nature. Mind and body they knew, because they felt both: an order, arrangement, organization, or internal machinery, in both they likewise knew, after the same manner; and it could not but seem reasonable to transfer this experience to the universe; and to suppose the divine mind and body to be also coeval, and to have, both of them, order and arrangement naturally inherent in them, and inseparable from them.

Here, therefore, is a new species of *Anthropomorphism*, Cleanthes, on which you may deliberate; and a theory which seems not liable to any considerable difficulties. You are too much superior, surely, to *systematical prejudices*, to find any more difficulty in supposing an animal body to be, originally, of itself, or from unknown causes, possessed of order and organization, than in supposing a similar order to belong to mind. But the *vulgar prejudice*, that body and mind ought always to accompany each other, ought not, one should think, to be entirely neglected; since it is founded on *vulgar experience*, the only guide which you profess to follow in all these theological inquiries.

*589.* This theory, I own, replied Cleanthes, has never before occurred to me, though a pretty natural one; and

I cannot readily, upon so short an examination and reflection, deliver any opinion with regard to it. You are very scrupulous, indeed, said Philo: were I to examine any system of yours, I should not have acted with half that caution and reserve, in starting objections and difficulties to it. However, if anything occur to you, you will oblige us by proposing it.

Why then, replied Cleanthes, it seems to me, that, though the world does, in many circumstances, resemble an animal body; yet is the analogy also defective in many circumstances the most material: no organs of sense; no seat of thought or reason; no one precise origin of motion and action. In short, it seems to bear a stronger resemblance to a vegetable than to an animal, and your inference would be so far inconclusive in favour of the soul of the world.

## Philo's Hypothesis

590. [Philo] . . . were I obliged to defend any particular system of this nature, which I never willingly should do, I esteem none more plausible than that which ascribes an eternal inherent principle of order to the world, though attended with great and continual revolutions and alterations. This at once solves all difficulties; and if the solution, by being so general, is not entirely complete and satisfactory, it is at least a theory that we must sooner or later have recourse to, whatever system we embrace. How could things have been as they are, were there not an original inherent principle of order somewhere, in thought or in matter? And it is very indifferent to which of these we give the preference. Chance has no place, on any hypothesis, sceptical or religious. Everything is surely governed by steady, inviolable laws. And were the inmost essence of things laid open to us, we should then discover a scene, of which, at present, we can have no idea. Instead of admiring the order of

natural beings, we should clearly see that it was absolutely impossible for them, in the smallest article, ever to admit of any other disposition.

## Equality of Action and Reaction between Mind and Body

591. In all instances which we have ever seen, ideas are copied from real objects, and are ectypal, not archetypal, to express myself in learned terms: You reverse this order, and give thought the precedence. In all instances which we have ever seen, thought has no influence upon matter, except where that matter is so conjoined with it as to have an equal reciprocal influence upon it. No animal can move immediately anything but the members of its own body; and indeed, the equality of action and reaction seems to be an universal law of nature: But your theory implies a contradiction to this experience. These instances, with many more, which it were easy to collect (particularly the supposition of a mind or system of thought that is eternal, or in other words, an animal ingenerable and immortal); these instances, I say, may teach all of us sobriety in condemning each other, and let us see, that as no system of this kind ought ever to be received from a slight analogy, so neither ought any to be rejected on account of a small incongruity. For that is an inconvenience from which we can justly pronounce no one to be exempted.

## The Argument a Priori

592. But if so many difficulties attend the argument a posteriori, said Demea, had we not better adhere to that simple and sublime argument a priori, which, by offering to us infallible demonstration, cuts off at once all doubt and difficulty? By this argument, too, we may prove the INFINITY of the Divine attributes, which, I am afraid, can never be ascertained with certainty from any other topic.

593. You seem to reason, Demea, interposed Cleanthes, as if those advantages and conveniences in the abstract argument were full proofs of its solidity. But it is first proper, in my opinion, to determine what argument of this nature you choose to insist on; and we shall afterwards, from itself, better than from its *useful* consequences, endeavour to determine what value we ought to put upon it.

The argument, replied Demea, which I would insist on is the common one. Whatever exists must have a cause or reason of its existence; it being absolutely impossible for anything to produce itself, or be the cause of its own existence. In mounting up, therefore, from effects to causes, we must either go on in tracing an infinite succession, without any ultimate cause at all; or must at last have recourse to some ultimate cause, that is *necessarily* existent: Now, that the first supposition is absurd may be thus proved. In the infinite chain or succession of causes and effects, each single effect is determined to exist by the power and efficacy of that cause which immediately preceded; but the whole eternal chain or succession, taken together, is not determined or caused by anything; and yet it is evident that it requires a cause or reason, as much as any particular object which begins to exist in time. The question is still reasonable, why this particular succession of causes existed from eternity, and not any other succession, or no succession at all. If there be no necessarily existent being, any supposition which can be formed is equally possible; nor is there any more absurdity in Nothing's having existed from eternity, than there is in that succession of causes which constitutes the universe. What was it, then, which determined Something to exist rather than Nothing, and bestowed being on a particular possibility, exclusive of the rest? *External causes*, there are supposed to

be none. *Chance* is a word without a meaning. Was it *Nothing?* But that can never produce anything. We must, therefore, have recourse to a necessarily existent Being, who carries the REASON of his existence in himself, and who cannot be supposed not to exist, without an express contradiction. There is, consequently, such a Being; that is, there is a Deity.

### Weakness of the Same

I shall not leave it to Philo, said Cleanthes, though I know that the starting objections is his chief delight, to point out the weakness of this metaphysical reasoning. It seems to me so obviously ill-grounded, and at the same time of so little consequence to the cause of true piety and religion, that I shall myself venture to show the fallacy of it.

I shall begin with observing, that there is an evident absurdity in pretending to demonstrate a matter of fact, or to prove it by any arguments *a priori*. Nothing is demonstrable, unless the contrary implies a contradiction. . . . Whatever we conceive as existent we can also conceive as non-existent. There is no being, therefore, whose non-existence implies a contradiction. Consequently there is no being whose existence is demonstrable. I propose this argument as entirely decisive, and am willing to rest the whole controversy upon it.

It is pretended that the Deity is a necessarily existent being; and this necessity of his existence is attempted to be explained by asserting, that if we knew his whole essence or nature, we should perceive it to be as impossible for him not to exist as for twice two not to be four. But it is evident that this can never happen, while our faculties remain the same as at present. It will still be possible for us, at any time, to conceive the non-existence of what we formerly conceived to exist; nor can the mind ever lie under a necessity of supposing any object to remain always in being; in the same manner as we lie under a necessity of always conceiving twice two to be four. The words, therefore, *necessary existence,* have no meaning; or, which is the same thing, none that is consistent.

But farther, why may not the material universe be the necessarily existent Being, according to this pretended explication of necessity? We dare not affirm that we know all the qualities of matter; and for aught we can determine, it may contain some qualities, which, were they known, would make its nonexistence appear as great a contradiction as that twice two is five. I find only one argument employed to prove, that the material world is not the necessarily existent Being; and this argument is derived from the contingency both of the matter and the form of the world. "Any particle of matter," it is said, "may be *conceived* to be annihilated; and any form may be *conceived* to be altered. Such an annihilation or alteration, therefore, is not impossible." But it seems a great partiality not to perceive that the same argument extends equally to the Deity, so far as we have any conception of him; and that the mind can at least imagine him to be non-existent, or his attributes to be altered. It must be some unknown, inconceivable qualities which can make his non-existence appear impossible, or his attributes unalterable: And no reason can be assigned, why these qualities may not belong to matter. As they are altogether unknown and inconceivable, they can never be proved incompatible with it.

Add to this, that in tracing an eternal succession of objects, it seems absurd to inquire for a general cause or first author. How can anything, that exists from eternity, have a cause, since that relation implies a priority in time and a beginning of existence?

In such a chain, too, or succession of objects, each part is caused by that which preceded it, and causes that which succeeds it. Where then is the difficulty? But the WHOLE, you say, wants a cause. I answer, that the uniting of these parts into a whole, like the uniting of several distinct countries into one kingdom, or several distinct members into one body, is performed merely by an arbitrary act of the mind, and has no influence on the nature of things. Did I show you the particular causes of each individual in a collection of twenty particles of matter, I should think it very unreasonable, should you afterwards ask me, what was the cause of the whole twenty. This is sufficiently explained in explaining the cause of the parts.

## Evil and the Moral Attributes of Deity

*594.* [Cleanthes] If you can . . . prove mankind to be unhappy or corrupted, there is an end at once of all religion. For to what purpose establish the natural attributes of the Deity, while the moral are still doubtful and uncertain?

*595.* Whence can any cause be known but from its known effects? Whence can any hypothesis be proved but from the apparent phenomena?

*596.* The only method of supporting Divine benevolence, and it is what I willingly embrace, is to deny absolutely the misery and wickedness of man. Your representations are exaggerated; your . . . inferences contrary to fact and experience. Health is more common than sickness; pleasure than pain; happiness than misery. And for one vexation which we meet with, we attain, upon computation, a hundred enjoyments.

Admitting your position, replied Philo, which yet is extremely doubtful, you must at the same time allow, that if pain be less frequent than pleasure, it is infinitely more violent and durable. One hour of it is often able to outweigh a day, a week, a month of our common insipid enjoyments. . . . Pleasure, scarcely in one instance, is ever able to reach ecstasy and rapture; and in no one instance can it continue for any time at its highest pitch and altitude. The spirits evaporate, the nerves relax, the fabric is disordered, and the enjoyment quickly degenerates into fatigue and uneasiness. But pain often, good God, how often! rises to torture and agony; and the longer it continues, it becomes still more genuine agony and torture. Patience is exhausted, courage languishes, melancholy seizes us, and nothing terminates our misery but the removal of its cause, or another event, which is the sole cure of all evil, but which, from our natural folly, we regard with still greater horror and consternation.

But not to insist upon these topics, continued Philo, though most obvious, certain, and important; I must use the freedom to admonish you, Cleanthes, that you have put the controversy upon a most dangerous issue, and are unawares introducing a total scepticism into the most essential articles of natural and revealed theology. What! no method of fixing a just foundation for religion, unless we allow the happiness of human life, and maintain a continued existence even in this world, with all our present pains, infirmities, vexations, and follies, to be eligible and desirable! But this is contrary to everyone's feeling and experience: It is contrary to an authority so established as nothing can subvert. No decisive proofs can ever be produced against this authority; nor is it possible for you to compute, estimate, and compare all the pains and all the pleasures in the lives of all men and of all animals: And thus, by your resting the whole system of religion on a point, which, from its very nature, must forever be uncertain, you tacitly confess, that that system is equally uncertain.

But allowing you what never will be believed, at least, what you never possibly can prove, that animal, or at least, human happiness, in this life, exceeds its misery, you have yet done nothing: For this is not, by any means, what we expect from infinite power, infinite wisdom, and infinite goodness. Why is there any misery at all in the world? Not by chance surely. From some cause then. Is it from the intention of the Deity? But he is perfectly benevolent. Is it contrary to his intention? But he is almighty.

*597.* . . . I will be contented to retire still from this intrenchment: For I deny that you can ever force me in it. I will allow, that pain or misery in man is *compatible* with infinite power and goodness in the Deity, even in your sense of these attributes: What are you advanced by all these concessions? A mere possible compatibility is not sufficient. You must *prove* these pure, unmixed, and uncontrollable attributes from the present mixed and confused phenomena, and from these alone. A hopeful undertaking! Were the phenomena ever so pure and unmixed, yet being finite, they would be insufficient for that purpose. How much more, where they are also so jarring and discordant!

Here, Cleanthes, I find myself at ease in my argument. Here I triumph. Formerly, when we argued concerning the natural attributes of intelligence and design, I needed all my sceptical and metaphysical subtility to elude your grasp. In many views of the universe, and of its parts, particularly the latter, the beauty and fitness of final causes strike us with such irresistible force that all objections appear (what I believe they really are) mere cavils and sophisms; nor can we then imagine how it was ever possible for us to repose any weight on them. But there is no view of human life, or of the condition of mankind, from which, without the greatest violence, we can infer the moral attributes, or learn that infinite benevolence, conjoined with infinite power and infinite wisdom, which we must discover by the eyes of faith alone. It is your turn now to tug the labouring oar, and to support your philosophical subtilities against the dictates of plain reason and experience.

### The Finitude of Deity

I scruple not to allow, said Cleanthes, that I have been apt to suspect the frequent repetition of the word *infinite*, which we meet with in all theological writers, to savour more of panegyric than of philosophy; and that any purpose of reasoning, and even of religion, would be better served, were we to rest contented with more accurate and more moderate expressions. The terms, *admirable, excellent, superlatively great, wise,* and *holy;* these sufficiently fill the imaginations of men; and any thing beyond, besides that it leads into absurdities, has no influence on the affections or sentiments. Thus, in the present subject, if we abandon all human analogy, as seems your intention, Demea, I am afraid we abandon all religion, and retain no conception of the great object of our adoration. If we preserve human analogy, we must forever find it impossible to reconcile any mixture of evil in the universe with infinite attributes; much less can we ever prove the latter from the former. But supposing the Author of Nature to be finitely perfect, though far exceeding mankind, a satisfactory account may then be given of natural and moral evil, and every untoward phenomenon be explained and adjusted. A less evil may then be chosen in order to avoid a greater; inconveniences be submitted to, in order to reach a desirable end; and in a word, benevolence, regulated by wisdom, and limited by necessity, may produce just such a world as the present. You, Philo, who are so prompt

at starting views, and reflections, and analogies, I would gladly hear, at length, without interruption, your opinion of this new theory; and if it deserve our attention, we may afterwards, at more leisure, reduce it into form.

### The Imperfections of Creation

My sentiments, replied Philo, are not worth being made a mystery of; and therefore, without any ceremony, I shall deliver what occurs to me with regard to the present subject. It must, I think, be allowed, that if a very limited intelligence, whom we shall suppose utterly unacquainted with the universe, were assured, that it were the production of a very good, wise, and powerful Being, however finite, he would, from his conjectures, form *beforehand* a different notion of it from what we find it to be by experience; nor would he ever imagine, merely from these attributes of the cause, of which he is informed, that the effect could be so full of vice and misery and disorder, as it appears in this life. Supposing now, that this person were brought into the world, still assured that it was the workmanship of such a sublime and benevolent Being; he might, perhaps, be surprised at the disappointment; but would never retract his former belief, if founded on any very solid argument; since such a limited intelligence must be sensible of his own blindness and ignorance, and must allow, that there may be many solutions of those phenomena, which will forever escape his comprehension. But supposing, which is the real case with regard to man, that this creature is not antecedently convinced of a supreme intelligence, benevolent, and powerful, but is left to gather such a belief from the appearances of things; this entirely alters the case, nor will he ever find any reason for such a conclusion. He may be fully convinced of the narrow limits of his understanding; but this will not help him in forming an inference concerning the goodness of superior powers, since he must form that inference from what he knows, not from what he is ignorant of.

*598.* Did I show you a house or palace, where there was not one apartment convenient or agreeable; where the windows, doors, fires, passages, stairs, and the whole economy of the building were the source of noise, confusion, fatigue, darkness, and the extremes of heat and cold; you would certainly blame the contrivance, without any farther examination. The architect would in vain display his subtility, and prove to you, that if this door or that window were altered, greater ills would ensue. What he says may be strictly true: The alteration of one particular, while the other parts of the building remain, may only augment the inconveniences. But still you would assert in general, that, if the architect had had skill and good intentions, he might have formed such a plan of the whole, and might have adjusted the parts in such a manner as would have remedied all or most of these inconveniences. His ignorance, or even your own ignorance of such a plan, will never convince you of the impossibility of it. If you find any inconveniences and deformities in the building, you will always, without entering into any detail, condemn the architect.

In short, I repeat the question: Is the world, considered in general, and as it appears to us in this life, different from what a man, or such a limited Being would, *beforehand*, expect from a very powerful, wise, and benevolent Deity? It must be strange prejudice to assert the contrary. And from thence I conclude, that however consistent the world may be, allowing certain suppositions and conjectures, with the idea of such a Deity, it can never afford us an inference concerning his existence. The consistence is not absolutely de-

nied, only the inference. Conjectures, especially where infinity is excluded from the Divine attributes, may perhaps be sufficient to prove a consistence, but can never be foundations for any inference.

There seem to be *four* circumstances, on which depend all, or the greatest part of the ills, that molest sensible creatures; and it is not impossible but all these circumstances may be necessary and unavoidable. We know so little beyond common life, or even of common life, that, with regard to the economy of a universe, there is no conjecture, however wild, which may not be just; nor any one, however plausible, which may not be erroneous. All that belongs to human understanding, in this deep ignorance and obscurity, is to be sceptical, or at least cautious, and not to admit of any hypothesis whatever, much less of any which is supported by no appearance of probability. Now, this I assert to be the case with regard to all the causes of evil, and the circumstances on which it depends. None of them appear to human reason in the least degree necessary or unavoidable; nor can we suppose them such, without the utmost licence of imagination.

The *first* circumstance which introduces evil, is that contrivance or economy of the animal creation, by which pains, as well as pleasures, are employed to excite all creatures to action, and make them vigilant in the great work of self-preservation. Now pleasure alone, in its various degrees, seems to human understanding sufficient for this purpose. All animals might be constantly in a state of enjoyment: but when urged by any of the necessities of nature, such as thirst, hunger, weariness; instead of pain, they might feel a diminution of pleasure, by which they might be prompted to seek that object which is necessary to their subsistence. Men pursue pleasure as eagerly as they avoid pain; at least, they might have been so constituted. It seems, therefore, plainly possible to carry on the business of life without any pain.

599. But a capacity of pain would not alone produce pain, were it not for the *second* circumstance, viz., the conducting of the world by general laws; and this seems nowise necessary to a very perfect Being. It is true, if everything were conducted by particular volitions, the course of nature would be perpetually broken, and no man could employ his reason in the conduct of life. But might not other particular volitions remedy this inconvenience? In short, might not the Deity exterminate all ill, wherever it were to be found; and produce all good, without any preparation, or long progress of causes and effects?

Besides, we must consider, that, according to the present economy of the world, the course of nature, though supposed exactly regular, yet to us appears not so, and many events are uncertain, and many disappoint our expectations. Health and sickness, calm and tempest, with an infinite number of other accidents, whose causes are unknown and variable, have a great influence both on the fortunes of particular persons and on the prosperity of public societies; and indeed all human life, in a manner, depends on such accidents. A being, therefore, who knows the secret springs of the universe, might easily, by particular volitions, turn all these accidents to the good of mankind, and render the whole world happy, without discovering himself in any operation. A fleet, whose purposes were salutary to society, might always meet with a fair wind. Good princes enjoy sound health and long life. Persons born to power and authority be framed with good tempers and virtuous dispositions. A few such events as these, regularly and wisely conducted, would change the face of the world; and yet would no more

seem to disturb the course of Nature, or confound human conduct, than the present economy of things, where the causes are secret, and variable, and compounded. Some small touches given to Caligula's brain in his infancy might have converted him into a Trajan. One wave, a little higher than the rest, by burying Caesar and his fortune in the bottom of the ocean, might have restored liberty to a considerable part of mankind. There may, for aught we know, be good reasons why Providence interposes not in this manner; but they are unknown to us; and though the mere supposition, that such reasons exist, may be sufficient to *save* the conclusion concerning the Divine attributes, yet surely it can never be sufficient to *establish* that conclusion.

If everything in the universe be conducted by general laws, and if animals be rendered susceptible of pain, it scarcely seems possible but some ill must arise in the various shocks of matter, and the various concurrence and opposition of general laws; but this ill would be very rare, were it not for the *third* circumstance, which I proposed to mention, viz. the great frugality with which all powers and faculties are distributed to every particular being. So well adjusted are the organs and capacities of all animals, and so well fitted to their preservation, that, as far as history or tradition reaches, there appears not to be any single species which has yet been extinguished in the universe. Every animal has the requisite endowments; but these endowments are bestowed with so scrupulous an economy, that any considerable diminution must entirely destroy the creature. Wherever one power is increased, there is a proportional abatement in the others. Animals which excel in swiftness are commonly defective in force. Those which possess both are either imperfect in some of their senses, or are oppressed with the most craving wants. The human species, whose chief excellency is reason and sagacity, is of all others the most necessitous, and the most deficient in bodily advantages; without clothes, without arms, without food, without lodging, without any conveniences of life, except what they owe to their own skill and industry. In short, nature seems to have formed an exact calculation of the necessities of her creatures; and, like a *rigid master*, has afforded them little more powers or endowments than what are strictly sufficient to supply those necessities. An *indulgent parent* would have bestowed a large stock, in order to guard against accidents, and secure the happiness and welfare of the creature in the most unfortunate concurrence of circumstances. Every course of life would not have been so surrounded with precipices that the least departure from the true path, by mistake or necessity, must involve us in misery and ruin. Some reserve, some fund, would have been provided to ensure happiness; nor would the powers and the necessities have been adjusted with so rigid an economy.

*600.* In order to cure most of the ills of human life, I require not that man should have the wings of the eagle, the swiftness of the stag, the force of the ox, the arms of the lion, the scales of the crocodile or rhinoceros; much less do I demand the sagacity of an angel or cherubim. I am contented to take an increase in one single power or faculty of his soul. Let him be endowed with a greater propensity to industry and labour; a more vigorous spring and activity of mind; a more constant bent to business and application.

*601.* Almost all the moral, as well as natural evils of human life arise from idleness; and were our species, by the original constitution of their frame, exempt from this vice or infirmity, the perfect cultivation of land, the improvement of arts and manufactures, the exact execution of every office and

duty, immediately follow; and men at once may fully reach that state of society which is so imperfectly attained by the best-regulated government. But as industry is a power, and the most valuable of any, Nature seems determined, suitably to her usual maxims, to bestow it on men with a very sparing hand.

*602.* The *fourth* circumstance, whence arises the misery and ill of the universe, is the inaccurate workmanship of all the springs and principles of the great machine of nature. It must be acknowledged that there are few parts of the universe which seem not to serve some purpose, and whose removal would not produce a visible defect and disorder in the whole. The parts hang all together; nor can one be touched without affecting the rest, in a greater or less degree. But at the same time, it must be observed, that none of these parts or principles, however useful, are so accurately adjusted as to keep precisely within those bounds in which their utility consists; but they are, all of them, apt, on every occasion, to run into the one extreme or the other. One would imagine that this grand production had not received the last hand of the maker; so little finished is every part, and so coarse are the strokes with which it is executed. Thus, the winds are requisite to convey the vapours along the surface of the globe, and to assist men in navigation: but how oft, rising up to tempests and hurricanes, do they become pernicious? Rains are necessary to nourish all the plants and animals of the earth: but how often are they defective? how often excessive?

*603.* What more useful than all the passions of the mind, ambition, vanity, love, anger? But how oft do they break their bounds, and cause the greatest convulsions in society? There is nothing so advantageous in the universe but what frequently becomes pernicious by its excess or defect; nor has Nature guarded, with the requisite accuracy, against all disorder or confusion.

*604.* On the concurrence, then, of these *four* circumstances does all, or the greatest part of natural evil depend. Were all living creatures incapable of pain, or were the world administered by particular volitions, evil never could have found access into the universe: and were animals endowed with a large stock of powers and faculties, beyond what strict necessity requires; or were the several springs and principles of the universe so accurately framed as to preserve always the just temperament and medium; there must have been very little ill in comparison of what we feel at present. What then shall we pronounce on this occasion? Shall we say that these circumstances are not necessary, and that they might easily have been altered in the contrivance of the universe? This decision seems too presumptuous for creatures so blind and ignorant. Let us be more modest in our conclusions. Let us allow, that, if the goodness of the Deity (I mean a goodness like the human) could be established on any tolerable reasons *a priori*, these phenomena, however untoward, would not be sufficient to subvert that principle; but might easily, in some unknown manner, be reconcilable to it. But let us still assert that as this goodness is not antecedently established, but must be inferred from the phenomena, there can be no grounds for such an inference, while there are so many ills in the universe, and while these ills might so easily have been remedied, as far as human understanding can be allowed to judge on such a subject.

### Unity versus Goodness in the First Cause

*605.* Look round this universe. What an immense profusion of beings, animated and organized, sensible and active! You admire this prodigious variety and fecundity. But inspect a little more narrowly these living existences, the only beings worth regarding. How hostile and destructive to each other! How insufficient all of them for their own happiness! How contemptible or odious to the spectator! The whole presents nothing but the idea of a blind Nature, impregnated by a great vivifying principle, and pouring forth from her lap, without discernment or parental care, her maimed and abortive children!

Here the Manichean system occurs as a proper hypothesis to solve the difficulty.

*606.* But if we consider, on the other hand, the perfect uniformity and agreement of the parts of the universe, we shall not discover in it any marks of the combat of a malevolent with a benevolent being. There is indeed an opposition of pains and pleasures in the feelings of sensible creatures: but are not all the operations of Nature carried on by an opposition of principles, of hot and cold, moist and dry, light and heavy? The true conclusion is that the original Source of all things is entirely indifferent to all these principles, and has no more regard to good above ill than to heat above cold, or to drought above moisture, or to light above heavy.

There may *four* hypotheses be framed concerning the first causes of the universe: *that* they are endowed with perfect goodness; *that* they have perfect malice; *that* they are opposite and have both goodness and malice; *that* they have neither goodness nor malice. Mixed phenomena can never prove the two former unmixed principles; and the uniformity and steadiness of general laws seem to oppose the third. The fourth, therefore, seems by far the most probable.

### The Convergence of Theism and Atheism

*607.* I ask the Theist, if he does not allow that there is a great and immeasurable, because incomprehensible difference between the *human* and the *di-*

*vine* mind: The more pious he is, the more readily will he assent to the affirmative, and the more will he be disposed to magnify the difference: He will even assert that the difference is of a nature which cannot be too much magnified. I next turn to the Atheist, who, I assert, is only nominally so, and can never possibly be in earnest; and I ask him, whether, from the coherence and apparent sympathy in all the parts of this world, there be not a certain degree of analogy among all the operations of Nature, in every situation and in every age; whether the rotting of a turnip, the generation of an animal, and the structure of human thought be not energies that probably bear some remote analogy to each other: It is impossible he can deny it: He will readily acknowledge it. Having obtained this concession, I push him still farther in his retreat; and I ask him, if it be not probable, that the principle which first arranged, and still maintains, order in this universe, bears not also some remote inconceivable analogy to the other operations of Nature, and, among the rest, to the economy of human mind and thought. However reluctant, he must give his assent. Where then, cry I to both these antagonists, is the subject of your dispute? The Theist allows, that the original intelligence is very different from human reason: The Atheist allows, that the original principle of order bears some remote analogy to it. Will you quarrel, Gentlemen, about the degrees, and enter into a controversy which admits not of any precise meaning, nor consequently of any determination?

*608.* Consider then, where the real point of controversy lies; and if you cannot lay aside your disputes, endeavour, at least, to cure yourselves of your animosity.

And here I must also acknowledge, Cleanthes, that as the works of Nature have a much greater analogy to the effects of *our* art and contrivance than to those of *our* benevolence and justice, we have reason to infer that the natural attributes of the Deity have a greater resemblance to those of men, than his moral have to human virtues. But what is the consequence? Nothing but this, that the moral qualities of man are more defective in their kind than his natural abilities. For, as the Supreme Being is allowed to be absolutely and entirely perfect, whatever differs most from him departs the farthest from the supreme standard of rectitude and perfection.

These, Cleanthes, are my unfeigned sentiments on this subject.

*609.* If the whole of Natural Theology, as some people seem to maintain, resolves itself into one simple, though somewhat ambiguous, at least undefined proposition, *That the cause or causes of order in the universe probably bear some remote analogy to human intelligence:* If this proposition be not capable of extension, variation, or more particular explication: If it affords no inference that affects human life, or can be the source of any action or forbearance: And if the analogy, imperfect as it is, can be carried no farther than to the human intelligence, and cannot be transferred, with any appearance of probability, to the other qualities of the mind; if this really be the case, what can the most inquisitive, contemplative, and religious man do more than give a plain, philosophical assent to the proposition, as often as it occurs, and believe that the arguments on which it is established exceed the objections which lie against it? Some astonishment, indeed, will naturally arise from the greatness of the object; some melancholy from its obscurity; some contempt of human reason, that it can give no solution more satisfactory with regard to so extraordinary and magnificent a question. But believe me, Cleanthes, the most natural sentiment which a well-disposed mind will feel on this occasion, is a longing desire and expectation that

Heaven would be pleased to dissipate, at least alleviate, this profound ignorance, by affording some more particular revelation to mankind, and making discoveries of the nature, attributes, and operations of the Divine object of our faith.

[Sec. 578, David Hume, *Dialogues concerning Natural Religion*, Vol. II of *Philosophical Works* (London, 1827), pp. 457–62. Sec. 579, *ibid.*, pp. 462–63. Sec. 580, *ibid.*, p. 464. Sec. 581, *ibid.*, pp. 464–65. Sec. 582, *ibid.*, p. 467. Sec. 583, *ibid.*, pp. 468–69. Sec. 584, *ibid.*, pp. 469–70. Sec. 585, *ibid.*, p. 470. Sec. 586, *ibid.*, p. 472. Sec. 587, *ibid.*, p. 474. Sec. 588, *ibid.*, pp. 474–76. Sec. 589, *ibid.*, pp. 476–77. Sec. 590, *ibid.*, pp. 479–80. Sec. 591, *ibid.*, pp. 494–95. Sec. 592, *ibid.*, p. 496. Sec. 593, *ibid.*, pp. 496–500. Sec. 594, *ibid.*, p. 510. Sec. 595, *ibid.*, p. 511. Sec. 596, *ibid.*, pp. 511–13. Sec. 597, *ibid.*, pp. 512–17. Sec. 598, *ibid.*, pp. 517–19. Sec. 599, *ibid.*, pp. 519–22. Sec. 600, *ibid.*, p. 522. Sec. 601, *ibid.*, pp. 522–23. Sec. 602, *ibid.*, pp. 523–24. Sec. 603, *ibid.*, pp. 524–25. Sec. 604, *ibid.*, p. 525. Sec. 605, *ibid.*, p. 526. Sec. 606, *ibid.*, pp. 526–27. Sec. 607, *ibid.*, pp. 535–36. Sec. 608, *ibid.*, pp. 536–37. Sec. 609, *ibid.*, pp. 547–48.]

## COMMENT

If the outstanding merit of Hume's critique of theism is that it avoids arbitrarily narrowing the choice to that between classical theism and atheism and, above all, that it sees clearly the tendency of classical theism to coincide with atheism (by depriving the idea of God of positive or definite content), the chief defect of the critique is that, after all, Hume does not entirely succeed in his apparent aim of exploring all the major theoretical possibilities open to theology. Arbitrary restrictions are still imposed. What are these? We see at least three.

First, Hume tends to contrast two monopolar forms of theism and to overlook the dipolar synthesis which would avoid the one-sidedness common to both. Thus we are offered the dilemma: mysticism (purely negative conception of deity) or anthropomorphism (affirmation of a positive but wholly imper-

fect, contingent, divine nature). But if there be two aspects of the divine nature, one aspect may be infinite, simple, necessary, and eternal, much as the mystics say God as a whole is, and the other aspect may be "finite," complex, contingent, in process, and in so far (though only in a highly abstract sense) comparable to man. And yet, by virtue of the other and infinite aspect, God may not be manlike in the unfortunate senses which Philo points out. In addition, there may be two categorically different ways of being finite or in process, one of which applies to the creatures and the other to the creator. And the latter or divine way may be incompatible with the corruptibility, possible plurality, wickedness, or weakness of deity which render the experimental theism of Cleanthes so unsatisfactory in outcome. What Hume here overlooks, like many before and after him, is that categorical perfection can be defined in dipolar fashion, so that there may be a perfect or ideally supreme form of finitude, complexity, change, and contingency, as well as of infinity, simplicity, eternity, and necessity. In only one phrase does Hume throw out the idea of a God "perfect in his finite capacity." But the idea is not developed, on the ground that empirical evidence cannot establish perfection in this, or any other, sense; and that a priori evidence is not available. But here again, in respect to the dilemma, a priori or a posteriori, the synthetic possibility is overlooked.

One may grant to Hume (or Cleanthes) that no actuality can be known a priori. Any actuality, for instance, any actual knowing, even divine, may be conceived not to exist. But the question, "Does an all-knowing God exist?" is not, in dipolar thinking, a question about this or that divinely cognitive actuality. It is the question, "Is there any actuality with certain divine cognitive attributes?" or "Is a certain infinite class of possible actualities, any of which would be all-knowing, a null class or no?" Now if the question can be answered affirmatively a priori, this means that the class could not conceivably be null. But, for all that, any particular instance of the class which exists might not have existed, but its place would then have been taken by another member.

Had Hume clearly conceived this doctrine, his criticism must have taken a different form and perhaps would not have appeared so devastating. Thus, for example, it would not have been possible to declare triumphantly that, for all Demea can show, the world itself is the necessary being. For, on our analysis, this could only mean that the class of possible worlds could not have been null, and this is a corollary of panentheism, not an alternative to it. The panentheistic or dipolar view here is that the necessary existent is not just God or just world, but God-with-world.

We are now ready to deal with the objection of Hume that a mental world requires a cause no less than a physical. We grant that any particular actuality, however mental, requires an antecedent cause. But that God exists is no particular actuality but merely the being of some divine actuality or other, the necessary nonnullity of a class of actualities. Thus the existence of God requires no cause, even though every actuality, even divine, requires one. The antecedent cause of a particular divine mental state is the preceding state of God-world, including the eternal class-essence of all such states. And the order of the cosmos, which Hume takes to be the essential premise of theism, points to God simply because personal order is the only form of order able to constitute a world. But God, who orders the world, orders himself in relation to the world, and there is no regress of ordering powers.

Here we must indicate the second major arbitrary assumption of Hume. He speaks repeatedly as though mind and matter were given to us as alike mysterious and incomprehensible systems of particulars. But actually nothing is directly given to us as a nonmental entity. The idea of matter, as something to be contrasted to mind, is a verbal construct. Hume recognizes that matter is not a datum, for, according to his *Treatise and Enquiry*, all we know are impressions and ideas derived therefrom. But in the *Dialogues* this falls into the background, and it appears that we have on our hands two sorts of entities, minds and nonminds or bodies. Apparently, the reasoning is that neither minds nor bodies are known to us but only impressions whose unity into any kind of coherent reality, whether that of personality and conscious identity, or of some impersonal and unconscious substance, remains problematic. And since God or the ultimate ground of order is assuredly not a mere heap of impressions, it makes no difference whether we say the ground is a mind or a body; in either case we make a blind leap beyond the given. But here Hume is failing to observe experience sufficiently freely and subtly. True, if some arbitrarily defined notion of immortal "soul" or "spiritual substance" is to be looked for, experience will not exhibit such an entity. But experience does exhibit itself as coherent in certain ways and degrees. There is such a thing as memory, uniting present with past, or as expectation, uniting present with future; there is a *gestalt* integrity of each momentary experience in its various simultaneous functions. Such coherence as we directly and vividly intuit is psychical, and we do (some of us think) intuit such coherence. But the coherence which makes an atom one entity, through time, or even in one of its momentary states, is no datum of direct experience at all. Thus we do, in spite of Hume, have reason for employing psychical concepts in our world interpretation rather than nonpsychical ones (which are necessarily merely negative and empty).

To maintain the foregoing thesis, we need not go so far as Hume himself goes in reducing the data of knowledge to mere human impressions. We can admit that man is directly aware of something other than just his own mental states. But the point is, while this nonhuman reality is actually given as nonhuman, as something not ourselves which acts upon us, it is not for all that given as nonmental or merely material. The rage of the wounded lion is no mere mental state of the hunter, but it is nevertheless something psychic. It is not mere insentient stuff. In the case of an inanimate object (or of microscopic entities, such as single cells) any such psychic character is, if present, not obvious. Does it follow that it is not there at all? How can this follow, inasmuch as every evidence of common sense and science points toward the view that the nature of rocks and fluids (not to mention that of their microscopic constituents) is not on the surface of our sensory experience but is exceedingly recondite and almost wholly hidden from us as we immediately experience these things? The highly recondite natures of minerals or cells may be a psychic nature. And, since no alternative nature attributable to them is clearly given directly, we have no positive alternative mode of conceiving the recondite natures of things. Physics does not offer such an alternative, for it merely establishes certain mathematical patterns of spatiotemporal order, leaving the qualitative aspects of the things thus ordered, whether psychic or no, entirely open.

The third arbitrary assumption underlying Hume's treatment is his adoption of strict determinism. With all his skepticism, Hume here is a dogmatist.

The order of nature, he insists, is absolute and unbroken. What follows for theism? That the Cosmic Orderer is responsible for all evils. But suppose determinism to be false, in the radical sense that not only human beings but all individuals, nay more, all events, have some degre of self-determination not wholly controllable by any cosmic principle or power. Then the cosmic order consists, not in a determination of all events just as they occur, but in the setting of limits to the self-determination inherent in each event. Order is thus the limit imposed upon chaos. It is not the alternative to or the absence of chaos but its qualification as limited or partial, rather than absolute or pure, chaos. That evils take place is then due to the chaotic element. And if it be asked, "Why does God not eliminate the chaos entirely?" the reply is, "Because this is meaningless." Order just is the limiting of chaos, as a river is the channeling (not the absence) of water. God's power cannot be exercised upon nonentity or upon the powerless but only upon lesser powers. "Being is power" (Plato); if there are beings besides God, there are powers other than the divine. If God is supremely free, then men also are free in some measure and even in relation to God. God cannot absolutely determine what his creatures do; for then they would not exist as creatures, and he would not exist as ruler of creatures or as actual creator.

What, then, is the perfection of the divine power, thus "limited" or rendered "finite" by the creaturely powers? Simply that the limits God imposes upon the creatures are ideal or optimal limits, in the sense that, were the creatures given more freedom, the gain in vitality would be more than overbalanced by the increase in discord; and, were they given less freedom, the gain in concord would be more than overbalanced by the loss of vitality, of depth of individuality, and of the zest arising from creative capacities. Thus providence is not the elimination of chance but its confining within judicious limits.

Hume's thought does not attain the subtlety of such conceptions. Schelling, Fechner, Whitehead, and others have put us today in a different position from any easily possible in the eighteenth century. Hume was haunted, like so many others, by the fallacious notion of a perfectly contrived world. Such a world would be totally dead and in fact would be nonentity. Reality is essentially living, sentient, creative; and manipulation or contrivance consists only in channeling this vital creativity within more or less judicious limits. Even if we suppose that the divine performance of this function is perfect, this does not mean the elimination of conflict and tragedy. These cannot be eliminated, since they spring from a principle which inheres in reality as such or in the eternal essence of God as such. They can be limited only in such a way that the vitalities of which they are the price are worth that price. This is a tragic view of existence which is hard to accept but which is symbolized by the Cross and made tolerable by the companionship of the Divine, who shares in our suffering.

## SCHOPENHAUER (1788–1860)

Schopenhauer, whose literary talents were comparable to, if not surpassing, Hume's, combined something like comparable intellectual penetration with a much more pronounced hostility to the religious ideas of his time. He is not content to attack the arguments for theistic belief but aggressively develops the counterarguments. Of course, Carneades, and Hume, too, to some extent, had done this; but Schopenhauer shows a zest for discrediting religious tenets which had been rare up to his time. He really hates theism, in whatever form.

The premises of Schopenhauer's criticisms include, as do Hume's, the assumption of determinism. But Schopenhauer, unlike the Scotch skeptic, offers a metaphysical reason for the doctrine rather than relying merely upon the considerable success of science in unraveling causal laws. Like Hume, he is not content with criticism of classical orthodoxy but seeks to discredit pantheistic doctrines as well. Unlike Hume's, his opposition to religious beliefs is not motivated solely by his conviction of the indemonstrability or unintelligibility of *any* conclusion in regard to religious matters. Rather, he fights them as rivals to a definite view to which he is himself committed, his well-known theory of the universe as manifestation of an essentially blind or unconscious striving, Will, which is insatiable and incurably wretched, and from which the only relief (never complete) is to be had through artistic contemplation and Buddhistic renunciation. Pity for other individual manifestations of the Will, like ourselves deeply unhappy, is the basic moral attitude. Men are brothers, not in hope, but in hopelessness. They are one—on the level of an absolutely unconscious Impetus which is prior to all individual differences. This is the doctrine which our author prefers to theism. And he seems greatly to enjoy it.

For he who likes a gloomy hour
Should love the works of Schopenhauer.

And how his works were enjoyed by a whole generation! Let us see how this author dealt with the question of theism.

## Optimism Implicit in Theism as Well as Pantheism

*610.* ... the origin of evil is the rock on which Theism, no less than Pantheism, splits, for both imply Optimism. But evil and sin, both in their fearful magnitude, are not to be explained away, while the threatened punishments for the latter only increase the former. Whence all this, now, in a world which is either itself a God, or the well-intentioned work of a God? If the theistic opponents of Pantheism exclaim against it, "What! all evil, terrible, abominable entities are God?" the Pantheists may reply: "How! all these evil, terrible, abominable entities have been produced by a God *de gaieté de coeur.*"

*611.* Or else free will is to blame for it. God has indeed created this, but created it free, and therefore it concerns him not what it does afterward. For it was *free,* that is, it could act so and otherwise; it might therefore be just as well good as bad. Bravo! but the truth is that free being and created being are two mutually destructive and therefore contradictory qualities; hence the assumption that God has created beings, and has at the same time imparted to them freedom of will, is as much as to say that he has created them, and at the same time he has not created them. For *operari sequitur esse,* i.e., the effects or actions of any possible thing can never be anything else than the consequences of its nature, which is only known through them. Hence a being, in order to be free in the sense here required, must have no nature, that is, must be nothing, or, in other words, must both be and not be at once. For what *is* must also be *something;* an existence without essence cannot even be thought. If a being is created, it is created as it is created, and therefore it is badly created if it *is* badly created, and badly created if it acts badly, *i.e.,* its effects are bad. As a consequence the guilt of the world, which

is just as little to be explained away as its evil, always shifts itself back on its originator.

*612.* If, on the other hand, a being is morally free, it cannot have been created, but must have aseity, that is, must be an original thing existing by virtue of his own power and completeness, and not referable to another. Its existence is then its own act of creation, which unfolds and expands itself in time, exhibiting once for all the distinct character of this being, which is, nevertheless, its own work, for all of whose manifestations the responsibility rests upon itself alone. If, now, a being is responsible for its action—if it is to be accountable—it must be free. Thus, from the responsibility and imputability which our conscience declares, it follows very certainly that the will is free, but from this, again, that it is the original thing itself, and hence, that not merely the action, but also the existence and essence of man are his own work.

## "God" an Anthropomorphic Product of the Will

*613.* Theism requires not only a cause distinct from the world, but an intelligent, a knowing and willing, that is a personal, in short, an individual cause; such a cause alone does the word God connote.

An impersonal God is no God at all, but merely a misapplied word, a misconception, a contradiction *in adjecto,* a shibboleth for professors of philosophy who, after having given up the thing, are anxious to smuggle in the word. The personality, on the contrary, that is, the self-conscious individuality which first knows, and then in accordance with the knowledge wills, is a phenomenon known to us solely from the animal nature which is present on our small planet, and is so intimately connected with this that we are not only not justified in thinking it as separate and independent, but are not even capable of doing so. But to assume a being of such a kind, as the origin of nature herself and of all existence is a colossal and daring conception which would startle us if we heard it for the first time, and if it had not by dint of earliest teaching and continuous repetition become familiar to us as a second nature, I might also say a fixed idea.

*614.* According to the foregoing, Anthropomorphism is an essential characteristic of Theism, and it is expressed not merely in the human form nor even in human affections and passions, but in the fundamental phenomenon itself, to wit, in the one will furnished with an intellect for its guidance, which phenomenon, as already said, is known to us only in animal nature and most perfectly in human nature, which is only thinkable as Individuality, and which when it is endowed with reason is called Personality. This is confirmed by the expression, "as truly as God lives"; He is indeed a living being, that is, one willing with knowledge. Hence a God requires a heaven in which he is enthroned and whence he governs. Much more on this account than because of the expression in the Book of Joshua was the Copernican system at once received with distrust by the Church, and we find accordingly a hundred years later Giordano Bruno as the champion at once of this system and of Pantheism. The attempts to purify Theism from Anthropomorphism, notwithstanding that they are only meant to touch the shell, really strike at the innermost core. In their endeavor to conceive its object abstractly they sublimate it to a dim cloud-shape whose outline gradually disappears entirely in the effort to avoid the human figure; so that at last the whole childish idea becomes attenuated to nothing. But besides all this the rationalistic theologians, who are especially fond of these attempts, may be reproached with contradicting the Holy Scriptures, which

say, "God created man in his own image; in the image of God created he him." Let us then away with the jargon of the professors of philosophy! There is no other God than God, and the Old Testament is his revelation—especially the Book of Joshua. From the God who was originally Jehovah, philosophers and theologians have stripped off one coating after the other, until at last nothing but the word is left.

One might certainly, with Kant, call Theism a practical postulate, although in quite another sense to that which he meant. Theism is indeed no product of the Understanding but of the Will. If it were originally theoretical, how could all its proofs be so untenable? But it arises from the Will in the following manner: the continual need with which the heart (Will) of man is now heavily oppressed, now violently moved, and which keeps him perpetually in a state of fear and hope, while the things of which he hopes and fears are not in his power—the very connection of the chain of causes which produce them only being traceable for a short distance by his intelligence—this need, this constant fear and hope, causes him to frame the hypothesis of personal beings on whom everything depends. It is assumed of such that they, like other persons, are susceptible to request and flattery, service and gift—in other words, that they are more tractable than the iron Necessity, the unbending, the unfeeling forces of nature, and the mysterious powers of the world-order. At first, as is natural, and as was very logically carried out by the ancients, these Gods were many, according to diversity of circumstances. Later on, owing to the necessity of bringing sequence, order, and unity into knowledge, these Gods were subordinated to one, which, as Goethe once remarked to me, is very undramatic, since with a solitary person one can do nothing. The essential, however, is the impulse of anxious humanity to throw itself down and pray for help in its frequent, bitter, and great distress and also in its concern for its eternal happiness. Man relies rather on external grace than on his own merit. This is one of the chief supports of Theism. In order therefore that his heart (Will) may have the relief of prayer and the consolation of hope, his intellect must create a God; and not conversely, because his intellect has deduced a God, does he pray. Let him be left without needs, wishes, and requirements, a mere intellectual will-less being, and he requires no God and makes none. The heart, that is the Will, has in its bitter distress the need to call for almighty and consequently supernatural assistance. Hence, because a God is wanted to be prayed to he is hypostatized, and not conversely. For this reason the theoretical side of the theology of all nations is very different as to the number and character of their gods; but that they can and do help when they are served and prayed to, thus much is common to them all, since it is the point upon which everything depends. It is at the same time the birth-mark by which the descent of all theology is recognizable, to wit, that it proceeds from the Will, from the heart, and not from the head or the intelligence, as is pretended.

## The Apagogic Counterdemonstration

*615.* In order to mitigate the heterodoxy of his "Critique of all Speculative Theology," Kant added thereto not only moral theology, but also the assurance that even though the existence of God had to remain unproven, it would be just as impossible to prove the opposite, an assurance with which many have consoled themselves, without observing that he, with pretended simplicity, ignored the *affirmanti incumbit probatio*, as also that the number of things whose existence cannot be proved is infinite. He has naturally taken still more care not to bring forward the arguments which might be employed for an apagogic counter-demonstration when once one ceased to adopt a merely defensive attitude, and began to act on the aggressive. The proceeding would be somewhat as follows:—

1. In the first place the unhappy constitution of a world in which living beings subsist by mutually devouring each other, the consequent distress and dread of all that has life, the multitude and colossal magnitude of evil, the variety and inevitability of grief often attaining to horror, the burden of life itself hurrying forward to the bitterness of death cannot honestly be reconciled with its being the work of a united All-Goodness, All-Wisdom, and All-Power. To raise an outcry against what is here said is just as easy as it is difficult to meet the case with solid reasons.

2. There are two points which not only occupy every thinking man, but also which the adherents of every religion have most at heart, and on which the strength and persistence of religion is based; firstly, the transcendent moral significance of our conduct; and secondly, our continuance after death. When once a religion has taken care of these two points everything else is secondary. I will therefore test Theism here in respect of the first, and later on in that of the second point.

With the morality of our conduct Theism has a double connection, *viz.*, one *a parte ante,* and one *a parte post,* that is, with respect to the causes and consequences of our action. To take the last point first; Theism indeed gives morality a support, albeit one of the roughest kind, one indeed by which the true and pure morality of conduct is fundamentally abolished, inasmuch as every disinterested action is at once transformed into an interested one by means of a very long dated but assured bill of exchange which is received as payment for it. The God, *viz.*, who was in the beginning the Creator, appears in the end as an avenger and paymaster. Regard for such an one can certainly call forth virtuous actions, but these are not purely moral since fear of punishment, or hope of reward are their motive, the significance of such virtue being reducible rather to a wise and well-considered egoism. In the last resort it turns solely on the strength of belief in undemonstrable things; if this is present no one will certainly stick at accepting a short period of sorrow for an eternity of joy, and the really guiding principle of morality will be "we can wait." But every one who seeks a reward for his deeds, either in this or in a future world, is an egoist. If the hoped-for reward escape him, it is the same thing, whether this happens by the chance which dominates this world, or by the emptiness of the illusion which builds for him the future one. For these reasons Kant's Moral Theology, properly speaking, undermines morality.

Again, *a parte ante*, Theism is equally in contradiction with morality, since it abolishes freedom and responsibility. For with a being which in its *existentia* and *essentia* alike, is the work of another, neither fault nor merit can be conceived.

*616.* That the creator made man *free*, that he gave him an *existentia* without an *essentia*, in other words, an existence merely *in abstracto*, inasmuch as he left it to him to be what he would, is an impossible proposition.

*617.* 3. On the assumption of Theism it does not fare much better with our continuance after death than with the freedom of the will. That which has been created by another has had a beginning of existence. Now that that which for an infinite time has not been, should from all eternity continue to be, is an outrageously bold assumption. If at my birth I have come from nothing and been created out of nothing, then it is the highest probability that at death I shall again become nothing. Endless continuance *a parte post*, and nothing *a parte ante*, do not go together. Only that which is itself original, eternal, uncreated, can be indestructible.

*618.* On the other hand, why should he fear death who recognizes himself as the original and eternal being, the very source of all existence, who knows that outside him nothing, properly speaking, exists at all—he who closes his individual existence with the saying of the Holy Upanishads, *hae omnes creaturae in totum ego sum, et praeter me ens aliud non est*, on his lips or even in his heart. He alone, can with logical consistency, die peacefully. For, as already said, *aseity* is the condition of immortality as of accountability. In accordance with the foregoing, contempt of death and the most complete indifference to, or even joy in dying, is thoroughly at home in India. Judaism, on the contrary, originally the sole and only pure monotheistic religion, teaching a real God-creator of heaven and the earth, has with perfect logicality no doctrine of immortality, and hence no recompense after death, but only temporal punishments and rewards, whereby it distinguishes itself from all other religions, though possibly not to its advantage. The two religions sprung from Judaism, in so far as they took up the doctrine of immortality, which had become known to them from other and better religious teaching, and at the same time retained the God-creator, acted illogically in doing so.

### Pantheism Tautologous and Theism Unproved

*619.* Against Pantheism I have chiefly this objection only, that it says nothing. To call the world God is not to explain it, but only to enrich language with a superfluous synonym of the word "world." Whether it says "the world is God," or "the world is the world," comes to the same thing. If indeed we start from God as the given thing to be explained, and say, "God is the world," there we have to a certain extent an explanation, in so far as we return from the unknown to the known; still it is only a verbal explanation. But if we start from the really given, viz, the world, and say "the world is God," it is as clear as daylight that we have said nothing thereby, or that at least *ignotum* is explained *per ignotius;* hence Pantheism presupposes Theism as having preceded it. For only in so far as one starts with a God, and therefore has him already in advance, and is intimate with him, can one finally bring oneself to identify him with the world, in order to put him on one side in a decent manner. We have not started impartially from the world as the thing to be explained, but from God as the given thing; after we did not know what to do with the former, the world had to take over his *rôle.* This is the origin of Pantheism. For on a first and impartial view it would never occur to anyone to regard the world as a God. It must obviously be a very ill-advised God who knew no better amusement than to transform himself into a world such as this: into a hungry world, in order there to endure misery, suffering, and death, without measure or end, in the shape of countless millions of living, but anxious and tormented beings, who only maintain themselves for a while by mutually devouring each other: *e.g.,* in the shape of six million negro slaves, who daily on an average receive sixty million blows of the whip on their bare bodies, and in the shape of three million European weavers who, amid hunger and misery, feebly vegetate in stuffy attics or wretched workshops, etc. That would indeed be a pastime for a God! who as such must be accustomed to things very different.

The supposed great progress from Theism to Pantheism, if taken seriously and not merely as a masked negation, as above suggested, is accordingly, a progress from the unproven, and hardly thinkable to the actually absurd. For however unclear, vacillating, and confused may be the conception which one associates with the word God, two predicates are at all events inseparable from it—the highest power and the highest wisdom. But that a being armed with this should have placed himself in the position above described, is an actually absurd idea; for our position in the world is obviously such as no intelligent, let alone an all-wise being, would place himself in. Theism, on the other hand, is merely unproven, and even if it is difficult to conceive that the infinite world should be the work of a personal, and therefore individual being, such as we only know from animal nature, it is nevertheless not exactly absurd. For that an almighty and, at the same time, an all-wise being should create a tormented world is always conceivable, although we may not know the wherefore of it. Hence, even if we attribute to him the quality of the highest goodness, the incomprehensibility of his judgment is always the refuge by which such a doctrine escapes the reproach of absurdity. On the assumption of Pantheism, however, the creating God is himself the endlessly tormented, and on this small earth alone dies once in every second, and this of his own free will, which is absurd. It would be much more correct to identify the world with the devil, as has been actually done by the venerable author of "The German Theology," inasmuch as on p. 93 of his immortal work (according to the restored text, Stuttgart, 1851), he says: "Therefore are the evil spirit and nature one, and when nature is not overcome there also is the evil one not overcome."

[Sec. 610, *Selected Essays of Schopenhauer,* trans. E. Belfort Bax (London: George Bell & Sons, 1914), pp. 71–72. Sec. 611, *ibid.,* pp. 72–73. Sec. 612, *ibid.,* p. 73. Sec. 613, *ibid.,* pp. 134–

35. Sec. 614, *ibid.*, pp. 136–39. Sec. 615, *ibid.*, pp. 141–43. Sec. 616, *ibid.*, p. 145. Sec. 617, *ibid.* Sec. 618, *ibid.*, p. 147. Sec. 619, *ibid.*, pp. 192–93.]

## COMMENT

Our author's attack upon theism in all its forms involves two assumptions: (1) what individuals do, and in general how things act, is determined by their original natures; (2) all life is essentially unhappy. From the first, it follows that a divine author of our natures must be responsible for our deeds and misdeeds as well as all our misfortunes. From the second, it follows that, whether God is distinct from the world and its responsible author or identical with the world, he either is discredited by his wretched creation or is himself a wretched being. And in neither case can freedom be imputed to the human individual.

Schopenhauer's argument is: A being which is produced by another, by causes of any kind, must be whatever those causes have made it. Hence only a being that is uncaused, and never began to be, can be free. But if all reality is the One blind Will, only in appearance split into many personalities—the old monistic idea, save that blind will is here substituted for consciousness, the Self, or some other word emptied of its normal meaning—then each of us can say, Schopenhauer suggests, "I am really eternal, uncreated, for my separate individuality, which had a birth and will die, is appearance only." In his real, or in Kant's phrase *noumenal*, self, a person is independent of causes and circumstances and in this sense free. (If this seems a completely empty sort of freedom, it is fair to Schopenhauer to add that Kant's view is scarcely less so, since for him too all the phenomena of space and time are appearance only; and in abstraction from space-time what is left of individuality in any positively conceivable sense?)

If, in spite of Schopenhauer, it is conceivable that individuals, in some sense created, should nevertheless be self-determined, or in part self-created, then God would not necessarily be responsible for our misdeeds or for our misfortunes. It would still follow, however, that on the pantheistic assumption of our forming parts of deity he would suffer from our pains and sorrows. And Schopenhauer thinks the absurdity of a God who would turn himself into such a world as ours is more complete than that of one who would merely bring such a world into being outside himself. Here he agrees with the main theological tradition of the West, in so far as pantheism has generally, in theological circles, been thought open to graver objections than classical theism. But note that Schopenhauer does not admit any advantage of theism so far as God's responsibility for evil goes. And, in truth, to have the misdeeds in himself would not make him responsible for them, unless it be granted that a whole must be responsible for all its constituents. Perhaps there are self-determined constituents! Perhaps ideal power over constituents would consist rather in ability to mold a suitable whole-form around whatever constituents might, in part spontaneously develop, and this ability would include power to keep the diversity of constituents within such bounds as were required to make an integrated whole-form always possible.

Whether individuals are in God or merely produced by him, the problem of freedom has two aspects, only one of which is seen by Schopenhauer. Negatively, freedom means not being wholly determined by another. Schopenhauer takes this to mean not being originated or caused at all. But this is the monopolar assumption that "caused by another" is something absolute, out of all tension with its contrary, "self-active," originative, free. Perhaps (as Peirce, Berdyaev, and many other philosophers have held) all causation is a mixture of chance and necessity, a channeling of spontaneity within certain limits set by another or others, inside which limits a thing decides itself. This is the positive side of freedom. But if one adopts this un-Schopenhauerian view of causality, one must also break with some of the language of classical theism. One must not suppose that a man's full actual nature is established by divine fiat. One must say with Whitehead (and Sartre) that man is *causa sui,* cause of himself, self-created in a certain measure, as well as caused by another, or created.

Schopenhauer's argument that a man can only act according to his nature, his being or essence, is a clear instance of the monopolar prejudice that being is prior to becoming. According to this view, we derive action from nature, becoming from being. We do not, in fact. A man's "nature" is a cross-section of his acting and not something with prior status. It is an explanation after the fact, an abstract of the concrete reality which is process, and never mere being or essence. From this, however, it follows that we are to some extent new beings every moment, born anew as somewhat different entities. Furthermore, theism should construe divine power as an eliciting of, and a setting of limits to, our self-creation. We must not put God in the position of being literally, for each of us, the one who "made me what I am today," in the words of the vulgar song. He made it possible (but not inevitable) for us to make ourselves what we are and also made it possible for us to make ourselves something else, that is, possible that a somewhat different self might have made itself or, better, might have self-actively or spontaneously become real.

This does not "limit" divine power, as though the basic concept of power were sheer making, and the mixture of making and self-making spoken of above were a restriction upon this concept. Just the contrary, "making" in the normal sense is a restriction upon what power in general is. Mere making is power so far as the thing upon which the power is exercised or in which it issues is negligibly endowed with self-activity (as in the famous "potter's clay"). This means that the result of the power is in itself trivial (mere "stuff" or "matter") or to us appears so. This is not the ideal of power but merely power manifested in inferior kinds of effect! God's power is actually greater than sheer "omnipotence," sheer making by fiat, whose products could only be lifeless and without individuality. The divine power is the fostering of other wills, other powers, other self-active agents, endowed with a measure of self-creativity. The ability to foster the becoming and growth of such agents is incomparably greater than this matter of sheer fiat of which we have heard so much. (The latter is really only a limiting zero case.)

From the nature of power as just analyzed it follows that the only alternative to a trivial creation is a tragically dangerous one. For if beings, the more so the higher their value, must be self-created, then no providence can prevent them from more or less conflicting with one another. Freedom of many beings interrelated in a society or world is bound to involve all sorts of risk—and, in the aggregate, certainty —of multitudes of conflicts between incompatible desires. These need not be sinful but will often be innocently incompatible, as when two men desire the primary place in the affections of one girl, or two girls in those of one man. It is inevitable that individuals should have preferences, and, if no providence can fully determine these preferences, then neither can it guarantee their compatibility.

The question is not, "Shall there be

tragedy?" but "Shall the tragedy be simply external to the deity, or shall he rather accept it into his own Life?" Now Schopenhauer seems to grant to classical theism that it makes some sense to think of the world as wholly extrinsic to God. But here he leaves untouched such questions as how, if God knows the world he has created, one can suppose X to be not a constituent of knowledge-of-X; or can suppose that in God there is merely knowledge-of, and outside this knowledge just X. We think that the slight advantage here conceded to theism over pantheism (and by implication panentheism) is entirely illusory and that, tragedy or no tragedy, the world could not be simply extrinsic to deity.

But if the creation must be tragic, and if, as follows from what has just been said, the creation is divine self-creation, then is not God a wretched being? However, "tragic" (as here employed) is one thing, "wretched," another. For Schopenhauer the world is an unredeemed, unrelieved tragedy, or virtually so. Here he goes beyond the mere fact that all sorts of suffering and wickedness occur and maintains that these evils form the essentials of existence. His principal argument is ingenious: life is actual only in the present moment; past experience is dead, future experience is not yet possessed; the essential worthlessness of the present is shown by the fact that we are never content with it, for do we not always abandon it for another present, the future, which in turn becomes a new present? And this new present satisfies us as little as its predecessors. The truth that change never ceases is just this very fact that the given present never satisfies the will. If the will were ever satisfied, change would cease. To this a priori argument Schopenhauer adds a marvelous wealth of empirical illustration and apparent confirmation. Life, he reminds us, oscillates between

pain and ennui. Either we have burdens to bear or we become burdens to ourselves.

The a priori argument is easier to meet than the empirical. The past is dead in the sense that we in the present no longer possess its fulness of experience. But it need not be dead for God, who may yet fully possess it. Now, if we love God, then it does not follow that it "must be a matter of indifference" to us whether the past experiences were happy or otherwise; for we wish to have made our contribution to the divine life as valuable as possible. The consciousness of having done this can give present satisfaction. For similar reasons, the worthlessness of the present is not proved by the fact that we never rest content with it, that change always proceeds. For if every present is preserved entire in God, what we do when we supplant such a present with a new experience is not to throw the old present on the rubbish heap but to pour it into the treasure-house into which no thieves can ever break. Because possible values are partly incompatible, and possibility as a whole is an inexhaustible infinity, no contribution could make further contribution superfluous. This may be offered as definite refutation of the a priori argument, in the sense that, to establish the pessimistic conclusion, it must first be proved that no divine treasure-house of all experience exists or that, if it does, we cannot find our joy in contributing to it; in other words, we cannot love God conceived as perfect in memory. These negations have not been proved by Schopenhauer, and hence neither has his pessimism.

The empirical argument is more complicated, but it is at best inconclusive. True, there is a tendency for life to take the form of flight either from pain or from ennui. But what does that prove? The inescapable element of tragedy inherent in freedom makes pain always a possibility. The possibility of boredom has the same basis. If the chances of freedom bring about too great a divergence between individuals (including microscopic as well as macroscopic, nonhuman and indeed nonanimal as well as human and animal), there is pain; if it brings about an excess of sameness in some region of experience, there is monotony or boredom. Negatively the business of life is to escape (and to help others to escape) these two forms of failure to achieve beauty, or rich harmony, of experience. But it is a fallacy to think of the goal as essentially negative. Success is only illogically defined as the avoidance of failure; rather, failure is the missing of success. We wish to avoid missing because we wish to hit the target. The proof is that, if merely avoiding pain and ennui were the aim, we should only have to die. Schopenhauer retorts that the will itself would not die but only one of its appearances. But the answer is that the notion of a will that is in itself completely nonindividual, devoid of conscious aim, and incapable of achieving anything on the whole is empty of meaning, a mere assemblage of words.

Thus we seem safe in concluding (and this is our own a priori argument, for which we also can find factual illustrations!) that volition is essentially love of the good, not dislike of evil. The fact that volition goes on thus means that living essentially, or primarily, realizes good and only secondarily is tinged with evil. As for pain and ennui, they are the two poles of failure to achieve good, and we use them as signs marking out the limits within which we may expect to find that good.

Schopenhauer makes a good deal of the idea that all life is a process of dying and of seeking to avoid what cannot be avoided, death. But one may reply: a fully sane and wise man, or a healthy animal, is not really trying to live for-

ever. One does not wish to die prematurely, with some of the main possibilities of one's career unexploited, one's dearest purposes not put into effect. But an elderly man (or even perhaps an elderly animal in its fashion) may lie down, peacefully content to die. One's contribution to the cosmic treasures of experience has been completed. Only superstition of one sort and another, or moral perversity, prevent this from being the normal attitude of those who have reached fruition of their human capacities, have done for life what one individual can do, and are ready to take their final places in the immortality of the divine recollection.

How far Schopenhauer can be effectively answered from the standpoint of classical theism we leave to the proponents of that doctrine. But he has not refuted panentheism. Consider his contention that, if we are in God, then God lives a miserable life. If our point is valid, that one lives because living is good, if even for scourged slaves life is dear, as a rule, then for the God who suffers with them in this scourging, life must be incomparably more dear and indeed categorically and for all eternity worth living. (Schopenhauer indulges in literary tricks here by adding together the millions of blows that fell, he affirmed, upon the totality of slaves daily but not adding together the billions of satisfactions also experienced daily by slaves, whose value to their masters would have been slight had they not had such.)

Not only does the normal balance of good over evil that makes premature death from lack of interest in living the rare exception accrue to God, since he lives through all our joys no less than all our sufferings, but, in addition, God has his own integral qualities of experience, his enjoyment of his own incomparably beautiful synthesis of all experience. It still remains true that a tragic tinge is not absent from the divine happiness. But this does not justify Schopenhauer in representing God as foolishly or weakly submitting to such tragedy. Foolishness or weakness always means that a wiser or stronger course is conceivable. Now, on our doctrine, no conceivable God faces the alternative—world with its tragedy, or divine life in sheer solitude?

But Schopenhauer's critique of theology has a third premise. This is that God must be a conscious individual and that this can only mean a besouled animal. Thus, as Hume also contended, and Carneades before him, either God is genuinely living and intelligent—and this means animal-like—or he is a dead, impersonal, abstract something or other equivalent to nonentity. Either anthropomorphism (more correctly, zoömorphism) or meaninglessness: the old dilemma! As against the theisms Schopenhauer knew, it has great force. But not because all consciousness must be animal-like or manlike in a sense dangerous for every sort of theism. An analogy is not the same as a close similarity. If striking a dog "hurts" him, and yet dog-feelings are through and through canine, not human, then the question arises, "May there not be superhuman as well as subhuman forms of feeling?" And if even microbes may plausibly be viewed as sentient, then it may be in order to try to formulate the concept of a form of sentience and consciousness which is in principle in some sense or senses the "highest possible" form.

What logic requires is only that we should have some explicit principles for our analogy. If man has a body as well as a mind, then perhaps "divine mind" does entail as its correlate "divine body." But since, by definition, it is a question of a·mind in principle superior to all others, it will also be a question of a body in principle superior to all others. The universe is

conceivably such a body (it can be argued it is not conceivable as anything else). Not that it is actually the best possible state of affairs but that any better state would be another state of itself, the divine body.

As against Schopenhauer, this argument is particularly pertinent, since he seeks to generalize the notion of "will" infinitely beyond the animal and human forms to make it the essence of reality as such, while refusing to the theist the right to generalize other psychological conceptions, those of feeling and thought and body, equally broadly.

It seems, then, that Schopenhauer unwittingly serves excellently as an ally of panentheism, which alone is left undamaged by his sharp arrows. For his blows fall not alone upon religious doctrine, striking some of them at least with good effect, but unintentionally they are even more deadly in their impact upon atheistic views. For how can an atheist deny that, in very truth, every present is immediately thrown away in favor of something else which is itself no more acceptable as worth keeping? Without the divine treasure-house to retain them, experiences in falling into the past must really become as nothing. The usual answer of atheism, that our achievements live on in posterity, looks rather strange in the light of Schopenhauer's analysis. If a man's own personal memory cannot, even while he lives, prevent his joys of other days and years from being now out of his possession—apart from the infinitesimal scraps and palest of pale echoes of these joys which are all that he just now enjoys and which do not all taken together make his present experience appreciably richer than many a one which he had ten or twenty years ago —how then can the matter be remedied by referring to other persons who may live later on who will know or care little or nothing about these past joys of his? It is such considerations that seem to bring out the shallowness of the cheerful kind of atheism that nowadays likes to call itself "naturalism." It is Schopenhauer, who with unerring skill located the weak spot in optimism on a naturalistic basis, whom these gentlemen ought to refute and just where he is least vulnerable! We here leave them to each other.

# FEUERBACH (1804–72)

An experiment which logically should have been made sooner or later was that of Feuerbach, who attempted to find in the general field of possibilities as open to man as such, in his racial essence, the "unlimitedness" which, misinterpreted, had given rise to the idea of God. If we consider, not what this or that man actually is, but all that men sometime somewhere, under some conditions or other, might be, we have (Feuerbach thinks) an unlimited scope of possible thoughts, experiences, and acts of will or of love. So, then, the omnipotence of God is really the omnipotence of man taken in this indeterminate way. The extraordinary fervor, eloquence, clarity, and confidence with which Feuerbach expounds his theory are due in no small measure, we suggest, to the large elements of truth which it contains.

We think it no credit to the classical theists that, apart from Barth, so little effort has been made to reply to Feuerbach. Barth's reply seems a measure of desperation. Feuerbach says that God is simply man in his indeterminate potencies; Barth (at least in his earlier phase) says that God is wholly other than man and in no rationally explicable relation to him, either as alike or as different. This seems almost tantamount to admitting all that Feuerbach charges (that the intelligible meaning of "God" is "humanity"), with the additional and dubiously helpful contention that theology has the alternative of refusing to present any intelligible account of its meanings. If that is the alternative, then,

we submit, Feuerbach's case is strong indeed.

## The Essence of Religion

*620.* . . . religion, expressed generally, is consciousness of the infinite; thus it is and can be nothing else than the consciousness which man has of his own— not finite and limited, but infinite nature. A really finite being has not even the faintest adumbration, still less consciousness, of an infinite being, for the limit of the nature is also the limit of the consciousness. The consciousness of the caterpillar, whose life is confined to a particular species of plant, does not extend itself beyond this narrow domain. It does, indeed, discriminate between this plant and other plants, but more it knows not. A consciousness so limited, but on account of that very limitation so infallible, we do not call consciousness, but instinct. Consciousness, in the strict or proper sense, is identical with consciousness of the infinite; a limited consciousness is no consciousness; consciousness is essentially infinite in its nature. . . . in the consciousness of the infinite, the conscious subject has for its object the infinite of his own nature.

What, then, *is* the nature of man, of which he is conscious, or what constitutes the specific distinction, the proper humanity of man? Reason, Will, Affection. To a complete man belong the power of thought, the power of will, the power of affection. The power of thought is the light of the intellect, the power of will is energy of character, the power of affection is love. Reason, love, force of will, are perfections—the perfections of the human being—nay, more, they are absolute perfections of being. To will, to love, to think, are the highest powers, are the absolute nature of man as man, and the basis of his existence. Man exists to think, to love, to will. Now that which is the end, the ultimate aim, is also the true basis and principle of a being. But what is the end of reason? Reason. Of love? Love. Of will? Freedom of the will. We think for the sake of thinking; love for the sake of loving; will for the sake of willing—i.e., that we may be free. True existence is thinking, loving, willing existence. That alone is true, perfect, divine, which exists for its own sake. But such is love, such is reason, such is will. The divine trinity in man, above the individual man, is the unity of reason, love, will. Reason, Will, Love, are not powers which man possesses, for he is nothing without them, he is what he is only by them; they are the constituent elements of his nature, which he neither has nor makes, the animating, determining, governing powers—divine, absolute powers —to which he can oppose no resistance.

*621.* Man is nothing without an object. . . . But the object to which a subject essentially, necessarily relates, is nothing else than this subject's own, but objective, nature. If it be an object common to several individuals of the same species, but under various conditions, it is still, at least as to the form under which it presents itself to each of them according to their respective modifications, their own, but objective, nature.

*622.* In the object which he contemplates, therefore, man becomes acquainted with himself; consciousness of the objective is the self-consciousness of man. We know the man by the object, by his conception of what is external to himself; in it his nature becomes evident; this object is his manifested nature, his true objective *ego.* And this is true not merely of spiritual, but also of sensuous objects. Even the objects which are the most remote from man, *because* they are objects to him, and to the extent to which they are so, are revelations of human nature.

*623.* The *absolute* to man is his own nature. The power of the object over him is therefore the power of his own nature. Thus the power of the object of feeling is the power of feeling itself; the power of the object of the intellect is the power of the intellect itself; the power of the object of the will is the power of the will itself. The man who is affected by musical sounds is governed by feeling; by the feeling, that is, which finds its corresponding element in musical sounds.

*624.* Every limitation of the reason, or in general of the nature of man, rests on a delusion, an error. It is true that the human being, as an individual, can and must—herein consists his distinction from the brute—feel and recognize himself to be limited; but he can become conscious of his limits, his finiteness, only because the perfection, the infinitude of his species, is perceived by him, whether as an object of feeling, of conscience, or of the thinking consciousness.

*625.* No being can deny itself, *i.e.,* its own nature; no being is a limited one to itself. Rather, every being is in and by itself infinite. . . . Every limit of a being is cognisable only by another being out of and above him.

*626.* The discrepancy between the understanding and the nature, between the power of conception and the power of production in the human consciousness, on the one hand, is merely of individual significance and has not a universal application; and, on the other hand, it is only apparent. He who, having written a bad poem, knows it to be bad, is in his intelligence, and therefore in his nature, not so limited as he who, having written a bad poem, admires it and thinks it good.

It follows that if thou thinkest the infinite, thou perceivest and affirmest the infinitude of the power of thought; if thou feelest the infinite, thou feelest and affirmest the infinitude of the power of feeling. The object of the intellect is intellect objective to itself; the object of feeling is feeling objective to itself. If thou hast no sensibility, no feeling for music, thou perceivest in the finest music nothing more than in the wind that whistles by thy ear, or than in the brook which rushes past thy feet.

627. Music is a monologue of emotion. But the dialogue of philosophy also is in truth only a monologue of the intellect; thought speaks only to thought. The splendours of the crystal charm the sense, but the intellect is interested only in the laws of crystallization. The intellectual only is the object of the intellect.

### The Conception of God

All therefore which, in the point of view of metaphysical, transcendental speculation and religion, has the significance only of the secondary, the subjective, the medium, the organ—has in truth the significance of the primary, of the essence, of the object itself. If, for example, feeling is the essential organ of religion, the nature of God is nothing else than an expression of the nature of feeling. The true but latent sense of the phrase, "Feeling is the organ of the divine," is, feeling is the noblest, the most excellent, i.e., the divine, in man. How couldst thou perceive the divine by feeling, if feeling were not itself divine in its nature? The divine assuredly is known only by means of the divine—God is known only by himself. The divine nature which is discerned by feeling is in truth nothing else than feeling enraptured,

in ecstasy with itself—feeling intoxicated with joy, blissful in its own plenitude.

It is already clear from this that where feeling is held to be the organ of the infinite, the subjective essence of religion—the external data of religion lose their objective value. And thus, since feeling has been held the cardinal principle in religion, the doctrines of Christianity, formerly so sacred, have lost their importance. If, from this point of view, some value is still conceded to Christian ideas, it is a value springing entirely from the relation they bear to feeling; if another object would excite the same emotions, it would be just as welcome. But the object of religious feeling is become a matter of indifference, only because when once feeling has been pronounced to be the subjective essence of religion, it in fact is also the objective essence of religion.

628. What, then, makes this feeling religious? A given object? Not at all; for this object is itself a religious one only when it is not an object of the cold understanding or memory, but of feeling. What then? The nature of feeling—a nature of which every special feeling, without distinction of objects, partakes. Thus, feeling is pronounced to be religious, simply because it is feeling; the ground of its religiousness is its own nature—lies in itself. But is not feeling thereby declared to be itself the absolute, the divine? If feeling in itself is good, religious, i.e., holy, divine, has not feeling its God in itself?

But if, notwithstanding, thou wilt posit an object of feeling, but at the same time seekest to express thy feeling truly, without introducing by thy reflection any foreign element, what remains to thee but to distinguish between thy individual feeling and the general nature of feeling;—to separate the universal in feeling from the disturbing, adulterating influences with which feeling is bound up in thee, under thy individual conditions? Hence what thou canst alone contemplate, declare to be the infinite, and define as its essence, is merely the nature of feeling. Thou hast thus no other definition of God than this: God is pure, unlimited, free Feeling.

*629*. In the perceptions of the senses consciousness of the object is distinguishable from consciousness of self; but in religion, consciousness of the object and self-consciousness coincide. The object of the senses is out of man, the religious object is within him, and therefore as little forsakes him as his self-consciousness or his conscience; it is the intimate, the closest object. "God," says Augustine, for example, "is nearer, more related to us, and therefore more easily known by us, than sensible, corporeal things." The object of the senses is in itself indifferent—independent of the disposition or of the judgment; but the object of religion is a selected object; the most excellent, the first, the supreme being; it essentially presupposes a critical judgment, a discrimination between the divine and the non-divine, between that which is worthy of adoration and that which is not worthy. And here may be applied, without any limitation, the proposition: the object of any subject is nothing else than the subject's own nature taken objectively. Such as are a man's thoughts and dispositions, such is his God; so much worth as a man has, so much and no more has his God. Consciousness of God is self-consciousness, knowledge of God is self-knowledge. By his God thou knowest the man, and by the man his God; the two are identical.

*630*. What was at first religion becomes at a later period idolatry; man is seen to have adored his own nature. Man has given objectivity to himself, but has not recognised the object as his own nature: a later religion takes this forward step; every advance in religion is therefore a deeper self-knowledge. But every particular religion, while it pronounces its predecessors idolatrous, excepts itself—and necessarily so, otherwise it would no longer be religion—from the fate, the common nature of all religions: it imputes only to other religions what is the fault, if fault it be, of religion in general. . . . it fancies its object, its ideas, to be superhuman.

*631*. The denial of determinate, positive predicates concerning the divine nature is nothing else than a denial of religion, with, however, an appearance of religion in its favour, so that it is not recognised as a denial; it is simply a subtle, disguised atheism. The alleged religious horror of limiting God by positive predicates is only the irreligious wish to know nothing more of God, to banish God from the mind. Dread of limitation is dread of existence. All real existence, *i.e.*, all existence which is truly such, is qualitative, determinative existence. He who earnestly believes in the Divine existence is not shocked at the attributing even of gross sensuous qualities to God. He who dreads an existence that may give offence, who shrinks from the grossness of a positive predicate, may as well renounce existence altogether. A God who is injured by determinate qualities has not the courage and the strength to exist. Qualities are the fire, the vital breath, the oxygen, the salt of existence. An existence in general, an existence without qualities, is an insipidity, an absurdity.

*632*. There is, however, a still milder way of denying the divine predicates than the direct one just described. It is admitted that the predicates of the divine nature are finite, and more particularly, human qualities, but their rejection is rejected; they are even taken under protection, because it is necessary to man to have a definite conception of

God, and since he is man he can form no other than a human conception of him. In relation to God, it is said, these predicates are certainly without any objective validity; but to me, if he is to exist for me, he cannot appear otherwise than as he does appear to me, namely, as a being with attributes analogous to the human. But this distinction between what God is in himself, and what he is for me destroys the peace of religion, and is besides in itself an unfounded and untenable distinction. I cannot know whether God is something else in himself or for himself than he is for me; what he is to me is to me all that he is. . . . I can make the distinction between the object as it is in itself, and the object as it is for me, only where an object can really appear otherwise to me, not where it appears to me such as the absolute measure of my nature determines it to appear—such as it must appear to me. It is true that I may have a merely subjective conception, *i.e.*, one which does not arise out of the general constitution of my species; but if my conception is determined by the constitution of my species, the distinction between what an object is in itself, and what it is for me ceases; for this conception is itself an absolute one. The measure of the species is the absolute measure, law, and criterion of man.

*633*. What the subject is lies only in the predicate; the predicate is the *truth* of the subject—the subject only the personified, existing predicate, the predicate conceived as existing. Subject and predicate are distinguished only as existence and essence. The negation of the predicates is therefore the negation of the subject. What remains of the human subject when abstracted from the human attributes? Even in the language of common life the divine predicates—Providence, Omniscience, Omnipotence—are put for the divine subject.

The certainty of the existence of God, of which it has been said that it is as certain, nay, more certain to man than his own existence, depends only on the certainty of the qualities of God —it is in itself no immediate certainty. To the Christian the existence of the Christian God only is a certainty; to the heathen that of the heathen God only. The heathen did not doubt the existence of Jupiter, because he took no offence at the nature of Jupiter, because he could conceive of God under no other qualities, because to him these qualities were a certainty, a divine reality. The reality of the predicate is the sole guarantee of existence.

*634*. The identity of the subject and predicate is clearly evidenced by the progressive development of religion which is identical with the progressive development of human culture. So long as man is in a mere state of nature, so long is his god a mere nature-god—a personification of some natural force. Where man inhabits houses, he also encloses his gods in temples.

*635*. The Homeric gods eat and drink;—that implies eating and drinking is a divine pleasure. Physical strength is an attribute of the Homeric gods: Zeus is the strongest of the gods. Why? Because physical strength, in and by itself, was regarded as something glorious, divine. To the ancient Germans the highest virtues were those of the warrior; therefore their supreme god was the god of war, Odin—war, "the original or oldest law." Not the attribute of the divinity, but the divineness or deity of the attribute, is the first true Divine Being. Thus what theology and philosophy have held to be God, the Absolute, the Infinite, is not God; but that which they have held not to be God is God: namely, the attribute, the quality, whatever has reality. Hence he alone is the true atheist to whom the predicates of the Divine Being—for example, love, wisdom, justice—are nothing; not he to whom merely the subject of these predicates is nothing. And in no wise is the negation of the subject necessarily also a negation of the predicates considered in themselves. These have an intrinsic, independent reality; they force their recognition upon man by their very nature; they are self-evident truths to him; they prove, they attest themselves. It does not follow that goodness, justice, wisdom, are chimæras because the existence of God is a chimæra.

636. The fact is not that a quality is divine because God has it, but that God has it because it is in itself divine: because without it God would be a defective being. Justice, wisdom, in general every quality which constitutes the divinity of God, is determined and known by itself independently, but the idea of God is determined by the qualities which have thus been previously judged to be worthy of the divine nature.

637. Now, when it is shown that what the subject is lies entirely in the attributes of the subject; that is, that the predicate is the true subject; it is also proved that if the divine predicates are attributes of the human nature, the subject of those predicates is also of the human nature. But the divine predicates are partly general, partly personal. The general predicates are the metaphysical, but these serve only as external points of support to religion; they are not the characteristic definitions of religion. It is the personal predicates alone which constitute the essence of religion—in which the Divine Being is the object of religion.

638. But here it is also essential to observe, and this phenomenon is an extremely remarkable one, characterizing the very core of religion, that in proportion as the divine subject is in reality human, the greater is the apparent difference between God and man; that is, the more, by reflection on

religion, by theology, is the identity of the divine and human denied, and the human, considered as such, is depreciated. The reason of this is, that as what is positive in the conception of the divine being can only be human, the conception of man, as an object of consciousness, can only be negative. To enrich God, man must become poor; that God may be all, man must be nothing. But he desires to be nothing in himself, because what he takes from himself is not lost to him, since it is preserved in God. Man has his being in God; why then should he have it in himself? Where is the necessity of positing the same thing twice, of having it twice? What man withdraws from himself, what he renounces in himself, he only enjoys in an incomparably higher and fuller measure in God.

639. Wherever, therefore, the denial of the sensual delights is made a special offering, a sacrifice well-pleasing to God, there the highest value is attached to the senses, and the sensuality which has been renounced is unconsciously restored, in the fact that God takes the place of the material delights which have been renounced. The nun weds herself to God; she has a heavenly bridegroom, the monk a heavenly bride. But the heavenly virgin is only a sensible presentation of a general truth, having relation to the essence of religion. Man denies as to himself only what he attributes to God. Religion abstracts from man, from the world; but it can only abstract from the limitations, from phenomena; in short, from the negative, not from the essence, the positive, of the world and humanity: hence, in the very abstraction and negation it must recover that from which it abstracts, or believes itself to abstract. And thus, in reality, whatever religion consciously denies—always supposing that what is denied by it is something essential, true, and consequently inca-

pable of being ultimately denied—it unconsciously restores in God. Thus, in religion man denies his reason; of himself he knows nothing of God, his thoughts are only worldly, earthly; he can only believe what God reveals to him. But on this account the thoughts of God are human, earthly thoughts: like man, he has plans in his mind, he accommodates himself to circumstances and grades of intelligence, like a tutor with his pupils; he calculates closely the effect of his gifts and revelations; he observes man in all his doings; he knows all things, even the most earthly, the commonest, the most trivial. In brief, man in relation to God denies his own knowledge, his own thoughts, that he may place them in God. Man gives up his personality; but in return, God, the Almighty, infinite, unlimited being, is a person; he denies human dignity, the human *ego;* but in return God is to him a selfish, egoistical being, who in all things seeks only himself, his own honor, his own ends; he represents God as simply seeking the satisfaction of his own selfishness, while yet he frowns on that of every other being; his God is the very luxury of egoism. Religion further denies goodness as a quality of human nature; man is wicked, corrupt, incapable of good; but, on the other hand, God is only good—the Good Being. Man's nature demands as an object goodness, personified as God; but is it not hereby declared that goodness is an essential tendency of man? If my heart is wicked, my understanding perverted, how can I perceive and feel the holy to be holy, the good to be good? Could I perceive the beauty of a fine picture if my mind were aesthetically an absolute piece of perversion? Though I may not be a painter, though I may not have the power of producing what is beautiful myself, I must yet have aesthetic feeling, aesthetic comprehension, since I perceive the beauty that is presented to me external-

ly. Either goodness does not exist at all for man, or, if it does exist, therein is revealed to the individual man the holiness and goodness of human nature. That which is absolutely opposed to my nature, to which I am united by no bond of sympathy, is not even conceivable or perceptible by me. The holy is in opposition to me only as regards the modifications of my personality, but as regards my fundamental nature it is in unity with me. The holy is a reproach to my sinfulness; in it I recognize myself as a sinner; but in so doing, while I blame myself, I acknowledge what I am not, but ought to be, and what, for that very reason, I, according to my destination, can be; for an "ought" which has no corresponding capability does not affect me, is a ludicrous chimæra without any true relation to my mental constitution.

*640.* I can perceive sin as sin, only when I perceive it to be a contradiction of myself with myself—that is, of my personality with my fundamental nature. As a contradiction of the absolute, considered as another being, the feeling of sin is inexplicable, unmeaning.

*641.* Man—this is the mystery of religion—projects his being into objectivity, and then again makes himself an object to this projected image of himself thus converted into a subject; he thinks of himself as an object to himself, but as the object of an object, of another being than himself. Thus here. Man is an object to God. That man is good or evil is not indifferent to God; no! He has a lively, profound interest in man's being good; he wills that man should be good, happy—for without goodness there is no happiness. Thus the religious man virtually retracts the nothingness of human activity, by making his dispositions and actions an object to God, by making man the end of God—for that which is an object to the mind is an end in action; by making the divine activity a means of human salvation. God acts, that man may be good and happy. Thus man, while he is apparently humiliated to the lowest degree, is in truth exalted to the highest. Thus, in and through God, man has in view himself alone. It is true that man places the aim of his action in God, but God has no other aim of action than the moral and eternal salvation of man: thus man has in fact no other aim than himself. The divine activity is not distinct from the human.

*642.* God is the highest subjectivity of man abstracted from himself; hence man can do nothing of himself, all goodness comes from God. The more subjective God is, the more completely does man divest himself of his subjectivity, because God is, *per se,* his relinquished self, the possession of which he however again vindicates to himself. As the action of the arteries drives the blood into the extremities, and the action of the veins brings it back again, as life in general consists in a perpetual systole and diastole; so is it in religion. In the religious systole man propels his own nature from himself, he throws himself outward; in the religious diastole he receives the rejected nature into his heart again. God alone is the being who acts of himself —this is the force of repulsion in religion; God is the being who acts in me, with me, through me, upon me, for me, is the principle of my salvation, of my good dispositions and actions, consequently my own good principle and nature—this is the force of attraction in religion.

*643.* Religion is the disuniting of man from himself; he sets God before him as the antithesis of himself. God is not what man is—man is not what God is. God is the infinite, man the finite being; God is perfect, man imperfect; God eternal, man temporal; God almighty, man weak; God holy, man sinful. God and man are extremes: God is the absolutely positive, the sum of all realities; man the absolutely negative, comprehending all negations.

But in religion man contemplates his own latent nature. Hence it must be shown that this antithesis, this differencing of God and man, with which religion begins, is a differencing of man with his own nature.

*644.* This nature is nothing else than the intelligence—the reason or the understanding. God as the antithesis of man, as a being not human, *i.e.,* not personally human, is the objective nature of the understanding. The pure, perfect divine nature is the self-consciousness of the understanding, the consciousness which the understanding has of its own perfection. The understanding knows nothing of the sufferings of the heart; it has no desires, no passions, no wants, and, for that reason, no deficiencies and weaknesses, as the heart has. Men in whom the intellect predominates, who, with one-sided but all the more characteristic definiteness, embody and personify for us the nature of the understanding, are free from the anguish of the heart, from the passions, the excesses of the man who has strong emotions; they are not passionately interested in any finite, *i.e.,* particular object; they do not give themselves in pledge; they are free. "To want nothing, and by this freedom from wants to become like the immortal gods";—"not to subject ourselves to things, but things to us";—"all is vanity";—these and similar sayings are the mottoes of the men who are governed by abstract understanding. The understanding is that part of our nature which is neutral, impassible, not to be bribed, not subject to illusions—the pure, passionless light of the intelligence.

*645.* Only by the understanding can man judge and act in contradiction with his dearest human, that is, personal feelings, when the God of the understanding—law, necessity, right—commands it.

The father who, as a judge, condemns his own son to death because he knows him to be guilty, can do this only as a rational, not as an emotional being. The understanding shows us the faults and weaknesses even of our beloved ones; it shows us even our own. It is for this reason that it so often throws us into painful collision with ourselves, with our own hearts. We do not like to give reason the upper hand: we are too tender to ourselves to carry out the true, but hard, relentless verdict of the understanding. The understanding is the power which has relation to species: the heart represents particular circumstances, individuals—the understanding, general circumstances, universals; it is the superhuman, *i.e.*, the impersonal power in man.

646. Religious anthropomorphisms, therefore, are in contradiction with the understanding; it repudiates their application to God; it denies them. But this God, free from anthropomorphisms, impartial, passionless, is nothing else than the nature of the understanding itself regarded as objective.

God as God, that is, as a being not finite, not human, not materially conditioned, not phenomenal, is only an object of thought. He is the incorporeal, formless, incomprehensible—the abstract, negative being: he is known, *i.e.*, becomes an object, only by abstraction and negation (*viâ negationis*). Why? Because he is nothing but the objective nature of the thinking power, or in general of the power or activity, name it what you will, whereby man is conscious of reason, of mind, of intelligence. There is no other spirit, that is (for the idea of spirit is simply the idea of thought, of intelligence, of understanding, every other spirit being a spectre of the imagination), no other intelligence which man can believe in or conceive than that intelligence which enlightens him, which is active in him. He can do nothing more than separate

the intelligence from the limitations of his own individuality. The "infinite spirit," in distinction from the finite, is therefore nothing else than the intelligence disengaged from the limits of individuality and corporeality—for individuality and corporeality are inseparable—intelligence posited in and by itself. God, said the schoolmen, the Christian fathers, and long before them the heathen philosophers—God is immaterial essence, intelligence, spirit, pure understanding. Of God as God no image can be made; but canst thou frame an image of mind? Has mind a form? Is not its activity the most inexplicable, the most incapable of representation? God is incomprehensible; but knowest thou the nature of the intelligence? Hast thou searched out the mysterious operation of thought, the hidden nature of self-consciousness? Is not self-consciousness the enigma of enigmas?

647. "The reason cannot rest in sensuous things"; it can find contentment only when it penetrates to the highest, first necessary being, which can be an object to the reason alone. Why? Because with the conception of this being it first completes itself, because only in the idea of the highest nature is the highest nature of reason existent, the highest step of the thinking power attained: and it is a general truth, that we feel a blank, a void, a want in ourselves, and are consequently unhappy and unsatisfied, so long as we have not come to the last degree of a power, to that *quo nihil majus cogitari potest*—so long as we cannot bring our inborn capacity for this or that art, this or that science, to the utmost proficiency. For only in the highest proficiency is art truly art; only in its highest degree is thought truly thought, reason. Only when thy thought is God dost thou truly think, rigorously speaking; for only God is the realised, consummate, exhausted thinking power. Thus in conceiving God,

man first conceives reason as it truly is, though by means of the imagination he conceives this divine nature as distinct from reason, because as a being affected by external things he is accustomed always to distinguish the object from the conception of it.

*648.* The understanding is that which conditionates and co-ordinates all things, that which places all things in reciprocal dependence and connection, because it is itself immediate and unconditioned; it inquires for the cause of all things, because it has its own ground and end in itself. Only that which itself is nothing deduced, nothing derived, can deduce and construct, can regard all besides itself as derived; just as only that which exists for its own sake can view and treat other things as means and instruments. The understanding is thus the original, primitive being. The understanding derives all things from God as the first cause; it finds the world, without an intelligent cause, given over to senseless, aimless chance; that is, it finds only in itself, in its own nature, the efficient and the final cause of the world—the existence of the world is only then clear and comprehensible when it sees the explanation of that existence in the source of all clear and intelligible ideas, *i.e.*, in itself.

*649.* Thus the understanding is the *ens realissimum*, the most real being of the old onto-theology. "Fundamentally," says onto-theology, "we cannot conceive God otherwise than by attributing to him without limit all the real qualities which we find in ourselves." Our positive, essential qualities, our realities, are therefore the realities of God, but in us they exist with, in God without, limits. But what then withdraws the limits from the realities, what does away with the limits? The understanding. What, according to this, is the nature conceived without limits, but the nature of the understanding releasing, abstracting itself from all limits? As

thou thinkest God, such is thy thought; —the measure of thy God is the measure of thy understanding. If thou conceivest God as limited, thy understanding is limited; if thou conceivest God as unlimited, thy understanding is unlimited. If, for example, thou conceivest God as a corporeal being, corporeality is the boundary, the limit of thy understanding; thou canst conceive nothing without a body. If, on the contrary, thou deniest corporeality of God, this is a corroboration and proof of the freedom of thy understanding from the limitation of corporeality. In the unlimited divine nature thou representest only thy unlimited understanding.

*650.* Unity is involved in the idea of the understanding. The impossibility for the understanding to think two supreme beings, two infinite substances, two Gods, is the impossibility for the understanding to contradict itself, to deny its own nature, to think of itself as divided.

The understanding is the infinite being. Infinitude is immediately involved in unity, and finiteness in plurality. Finiteness—in the metaphysical sense—rests on the distinction of the existence from the essence, of the individual from the species; infinitude, on the unity of existence and essence. Hence, that is finitude which can be compared with other beings of the same species; that is infinite which has nothing like itself, which consequently does not stand as an individual under a species, but is species and individual in one, essence and existence in one. But such is the understanding; . . . it is incapable of being compared, because it is itself the source of all combinations and comparisons; immeasurable, because it is the measure of all measure—we measure all things by the understanding alone.

*651.* Lastly, the understanding or the reason is the necessary being. Reason exists because only the existence of the reason is reason; because, if there were no reason, no consciousness, all would be nothing; existence would be equivalent to non-existence. Consciousness first founds the distinction between existence and non-existence.

*652.* Of all the attributes which the understanding assigns to God, that which in religion, and especially in the Christian religion, has the pre-eminence, is moral perfection. But God as a morally perfect being is nothing else than the realised idea, the fulfilled law of morality, the moral nature of man posited as the absolute being; man's own nature, for the moral God requires man to be as he himself is: Be ye holy for I am holy; man's own conscience, for how could he otherwise tremble before the Divine Being, accuse himself before him, and make him the judge of his inmost thoughts and feelings?

But the consciousness of the absolutely perfect moral nature, especially as an abstract being separate from man, leaves us cold and empty, because we feel the distance, the chasm between ourselves and this being;—it is a dispiriting consciousness, for it is the consciousness of our personal nothingness, and of the kind which is the most acutely felt—moral nothingness. The consciousness of the divine omnipotence and eternity in opposition to my limitation in space and time does not afflict me: for omnipotence does not command me to be myself omnipotent, eternity, to be myself eternal. But I cannot have the idea of moral perfection without at the same time being conscious of it as a law for me. Moral perfection depends, at least for the moral consciousness, not on the nature, but on the will—it is a perfection of will, perfect will. I cannot conceive perfect will, the will which is in unison with law, which is itself law, without at the same time regarding it as an object of will, *i.e.*, as an obligation for myself. The conception of the morally perfect being is no merely theoretical, inert conception, but a practical one, calling

me to action, to imitation, throwing me into strife, into disunion with myself; for while it proclaims to me what I ought to be, it also tells me to my face, without any flattery, what I am not. And religion renders this disunion all the more painful, all the more terrible, that it sets man's own nature before him as a separate nature, and moreover as a personal being, who hates and curses sinners, and excludes them from his grace, the source of all salvation and happiness.

Now, by what means does man deliver himself from this state of disunion between himself and the perfect being, from the painful consciousness of sin, from the distressing sense of his own nothingness? How does he blunt the fatal sting of sin? Only by this; that he is conscious of *love* as the highest, absolute power and truth, that he regards the Divine Being not only as a law, as a moral being, as a being of the understanding; but also as a loving, tender, even subjective human being (that is, as having sympathy with individual man).

The understanding judges only according to the stringency of law; the heart accommodates itself, is considerate, lenient, relenting, κατ᾽ ἄνθρωπον. No man is sufficient for the law which moral perfection sets before us; but, for that reason, neither is the law sufficient for man, for the heart. The law condemns; the heart has compassion even on the sinner. The law affirms me only as an abstract being—love, as a real being. Love gives me the consciousness that I am a man; the law only the consciousness that I am a sinner, that I am worthless. The law holds man in bondage; love makes him free.

Love is the middle term, the substantial bond, the principle of reconciliation between the perfect and the imperfect, the sinless and sinful being, the universal and the individual, the divine and the human. Love is God himself, and apart from it there is no God. Love makes man God and God man. Love strengthens the weak and weakens the strong, abases the high and raises the lowly, idealises matter and materialises spirit. Love is the true unity of God and man, of spirit and nature. In love common nature is spirit, and the preeminent spirit is nature. Love is to deny spirit from the point of view of spirit, to deny matter from the point of view of matter. Love is materialism; immaterial love is a chimæra.

### Incarnation and Trinity

*653.* If in the Incarnation we stop short at the fact of God becoming man, it certainly appears a surprising, inexplicable, marvellous event. But the incarnate God is only the apparent manifestation of deified man; for the descent of God to man is necessarily preceded by the exaltation of man to God. Man was already in God, was already God himself, before God became man, *i.e.,* showed himself as man. How otherwise could God have become man? The old maxim, *ex nihilo nihil fit,* is applicable here also. A king who has not the welfare of his subjects at heart, who, while seated on his throne, does not mentally live with them in their dwellings, who, in feeling, is not, as the people say, "a common man," such a king will not descend bodily from his throne to make his people happy by his personal presence. Thus, has not the subject risen to be a king before the king descends to be a subject? And if the subject feels himself honoured and made happy by the personal presence of his king, does this feeling refer merely to the bodily presence, and not rather to the manifestation of the disposition, of the philanthropic nature which is the cause of the appearance? But that which in the truth of religion is the cause, takes in the consciousness of religion the form of a consequence; and so here the raising of man to God is made a consequence of the humiliation or descent of God to man. God, says religion, made himself human that he might make man divine.

That which is mysterious and incomprehensible, *i.e.,* contradictory, in the proposition, "God is or becomes a man," arises only from the mingling or confusion of the idea or definitions of the universal, unlimited, metaphysical being with the idea of the religious God, *i.e.,* the conditions of the understanding with the conditions of the heart, the emotive nature; a confusion which is the greatest hindrance to the correct knowledge of religion. But, in fact, the idea of the Incarnation is nothing more than the human *form* of a God, who already in his nature, in the profoundest depths of his soul, is a merciful and therefore a human God.

*654.* Can I love man without loving him humanly, without loving him as he himself loves, if he truly loves? Would not love be otherwise a devilish love? The devil too loves man, but not for man's sake—for his own; thus he loves man out of egotism, to aggrandise himself, to extend his power. But God loves man for man's sake, *i.e.,* that he may make him good, happy, blessed. Does he not then love man as the true man loves his fellow? Has love a plural? Is it not everywhere like itself? What then/is the true unfalsified import of the Incarnation but absolute, pure love, without adjunct, without a distinction between divine and human love? For though there is also a self-interested love among men, still the true human love, which is alone worthy of this name, is that which impels the sacrifice of self to another. Who then is our Saviour and Redeemer? God or Love? Love; for God as God has not saved us, but Love, which transcends the difference between the divine and human personality. As God has renounced himself out of love, so we, out of love, should renounce God; for if we do not sacrifice God to love, we sacrifice love to God, and, in spite of the predicate of love, we have the God—the evil being—of religious fanaticism.

*655.* Love does not exist without sympathy, sympathy does not exist without suffering in common. Have I any sympathy for a being without feeling? No! I feel only for that which has feeling, only for that which partakes of my nature, for that in which I feel myself, whose sufferings I myself suffer. Sympathy presupposes a like nature. The Incarnation, Providence, prayer, are the expression of this identity of nature in God and man.

It is true that theology, which is preoccupied with the metaphysical attributes of eternity, unconditionedness, unchangeableness, and the like abstractions, which express the nature of the understanding—theology denies the possibility that God should suffer, but in so doing it denies the truth of religion.

*656.* What, then, is it that I love in God? Love: love to man. But when I love and worship the love with which God loves man, do I not love man; is not my love of God, though indirectly, love of man? If God loves man, is not man, then, the very substance of God? That which I love, is it not my inmost being? Have I a heart when I do not love? No! love only is the heart of man. But what is love without the thing loved? Thus what I love is my heart, the substance of my being, my nature. Why does man grieve, why does he lose pleasure in life when he has lost the beloved object? Why? because with the beloved object he has lost his heart, the activity of his affections, the principle of life. Thus if God loves man, man is the heart of God—the welfare of man his deepest anxiety. If man, then, is the object of God, is not man, in God, an object to himself? is not the content of the divine nature the human nature? If God is love, is not the essential content of this love man? Is not the love of God to man—the basis and central point of

religion—the love of man to himself made an object, contemplated as the highest objective truth, as the highest being to man? Is not then the proposition, "God loves man" an orientalism (religion is essentially oriental), which in plain speech means, the highest is the love of man?

*657.* . . . from a solitary God the essential need of duality, of love, of community, of the real, completed self-consciousness, of the *alter ego*, is excluded. This want is therefore satisfied by religion thus: in the still solitude of the Divine Being is placed another, a second, different from God as to personality, but identical with him in essence— God the Son, in distinction from God the Father. God the Father is *I*, God the Son *Thou*. The *I* is understanding, the *Thou* love. But love with understanding and understanding with love is mind, and mind is the totality of man as such— the total man.

Participated life is alone true, self-satisfying, divine life:—this simple thought, this truth, natural, immanent in man, is the secret, the supernatural mystery of the Trinity. But religion expresses this truth, as it does every other, in an indirect manner, *i.e.*, inversely, for it here makes a general truth into a particular one, the true subject into a predicate, when it says: God is a participated life, a life of love and friendship. The third Person in the Trinity expresses nothing further than the love of the two divine Persons towards each other; it is the unity of the Son and the Father, the idea of community, strangely enough regarded in its turn as a special personal being.

*658.* . . . the mystery of the Trinity was to the ancient Christians an object of unbounded wonder, enthusiasm, and rapture, because here the satisfaction of those profoundest human wants which in reality, in life, they denied, became to them an object of contemplation in God.

It was therefore quite in order that, to complete the divine family, the bond of love between Father and Son, a third, and that a feminine person, was received into heaven; for the personality of the Holy Spirit is a too vague and precarious, a too obviously poetic personification of the mutual love of the Father and Son, to serve as the third complementary being. It is true that the Virgin Mary was not so placed between the Father and Son as to imply that the Father had begotten the Son through her, because the sexual relation was regarded by the Christians as something unholy and sinful; but it is enough that the maternal principle was associated with the Father and Son.

*659.* Personality, individuality, consciousness, without Nature, is nothing; or, which is the same thing, an empty, unsubstantial abstraction. But Nature, as has been shown and is obvious, is nothing without corporeality. The body alone is that negativing, limiting, concentrating, circumscribing force, without which no personality is conceivable. Take away from thy personality its body, and thou takest away that which holds it together. The body is the basis, the subject of personality. Only by the body is a real personality distinguished from the imaginary one of a spectre. What sort of abstract, vague, empty personalities should we be, if we had not the property of impenetrability—if in the same place, in the same form in which we are, others might stand at the same time? Only by the exclusion of others from the space it occupies does personality prove itself to be real. But a body does not exist without flesh and blood. Flesh and blood is life, and life alone is corporeal reality. But flesh and blood is nothing without the oxygen of sexual distinction.

*660.* All the glory of Nature, all its power, all its wisdom and profundity, concentrates and individualises itself in distinction of sex. Why then dost thou shrink from naming the nature of God by its true name? Evidently, only because thou hast a general horror of things in their truth and reality; because thou lookest at all things through the deceptive vapours of mysticism. For this very reason then, because Nature in God is only a delusive, unsubstantial appearance, a fantastic ghost of Nature—for it is based, as we have said, not on flesh and blood, not on a real ground—this attempt to establish a personal God is once more a failure, and I, too, conclude with the words, "The denial of a personal God will be scientific honesty:"—and, I add, scientific truth, so long as it is not declared and shown in unequivocal terms, first *à priori*, on speculative grounds, that form, place, corporeality, and sex do not contradict the idea of the Godhead; and secondly, *à posteriori*—for the reality of a personal being is sustained only on empirical grounds—what sort of form God has, where he exists—in heaven—and lastly, of what sex he is.

*661.* The Divine Being is the human being glorified by the death of abstraction; it is the departed spirit of man. In religion man frees himself from the limits of life; he here lets fall what oppresses him, obstructs him, affects him repulsively; God is the self-consciousness of man freed from all discordant elements; man feels himself free, happy, blessed in his religion, because he only here lives the life of genius, and keeps holiday.

*662.* The divine being is the pure subjectivity of man, freed from all else, from everything objective, having relation only to itself, enjoying only itself, reverencing only itself—his most subjective, his inmost self.

*663.* "Where Nature ceases, God begins," because God is the *ne plus ultra*, the last limit of abstraction. That from which I can no longer abstract is God, the last thought which I am capable of grasping—the last, *i.e.*, the highest, *Id quo nihil majus cogitari potest, Deus est.*

## God as Personal

664. In general, the need of a personal God has its foundation in this, that only in the attribute of personality does the personal man meet with himself, find himself. Substance, pure spirit, mere reason, does not satisfy him, is too abstract for him, *i.e.*, does not express himself, does not lead him back to himself. And man is content, happy, only when he is with himself, with his own nature. Hence, the more personal a man is, the stronger is his need of a personal God. The free, abstract thinker knows nothing higher than freedom; he does not need to attach it to a personal being; for him freedom in itself, as such, is a real positive thing. A mathematical, astronomical mind, a man of pure understanding, an objective man, who is not shut up in himself, who feels free and happy only in the contemplation of objective rational relations, in the reason which lies in things in themselves—such a man will regard the substance of Spinoza, or some similar idea, as his highest being, and be full of antipathy towards a personal, *i.e.*, subjective God. Jacobi therefore was a classic philosopher, because (in this respect, at least) he was consistent, he was at unity with himself; as was his God, so was his philosophy—personal, subjective. The personal God cannot be established otherwise than as he is established by Jacobi and his disciples. Personality is proved only in a personal manner.

Personality may be, nay, must be, founded on a natural basis; but this natural basis is attained only when I cease to grope in the darkness of mysticism, when I step forth into the clear daylight of real Nature, and exchange the idea of the personal God for the idea of personality in general. But into the idea of the personal God, the positive idea of whom is liberated, disembodied personality, released from the limiting force of Nature, to smuggle again this very Nature, is as perverse as if I were to mix Brunswick mum with the nectar of the Gods, in order to give the ethereal beverage a solid foundation.

665. . . . the idea of deity coincides with the idea of humanity. All divine attributes, all the attributes which make God God, are attributes of the species—attributes which in the individual are limited, but the limits of which are abolished in the essence of the species, and even in its existence, in so far as it has its complete existence only in all men taken together. My knowledge, my will, is limited; but my limit is not the limit of another man, to say nothing of mankind; what is difficult to me is easy to another; what is impossible, inconceivable, to one age, is to the coming age conceivable and possible. My life is bound to a limited time; not so the life of humanity. The history of mankind consists of nothing else than a continuous and progressive conquest of limits, which at a given time pass for the limits of humanity, and therefore for absolute insurmountable limits. But the future always unveils the fact that the alleged limits of the species were only limits of individuals. The most striking proofs of this are presented by the history of philosophy and of physical science. It would be highly interesting and instructive to write a history of the sciences entirely from this point of view, in order to exhibit in all its vanity the presumptuous notion of the individual that he can set limits to his race. Thus the species is unlimited; the individual alone the limited.

But the sense of limitation is painful, and hence the individual frees himself from it by the contemplation of the perfect Being; in this contemplation he possesses what otherwise is wanting to him. With the Christians God is nothing else than the immediate unity of species and individuality, of the universal and individual being. God is the idea of the species as an individual—the idea or essence of the species, which as a species, as universal being, as the totality of all perfections, of all attributes or realities, freed from all the limits which exist in the consciousness and feeling of the individual, is at the same time again an individual, personal being. *Ipse suum esse est.* Essence and existence are in God identical; which means nothing else than that he is the idea, the essence of the species, conceived immediately as an existence, an individual. The highest idea on the standpoint of religion is: God does not love, he is himself love; he does not live, he is life; he is not just, but justice itself; not a person, but personality itself—the species, the idea, as immediately a concrete existence.

Because of this immediate unity of the species with individuality, this concentration of all that is universal and real in one personal being, God is a deeply moving object, enrapturing to the imagination; whereas, the idea of humanity has little power over the feelings, because humanity is only an abstraction; and the reality which presents itself to us in distinction from this abstraction is the multitude of separate, limited individuals. In God, on the contrary, feeling has immediate satisfaction, because here all is embraced in one, *i.e.,* because here the species has an immediate existence—is an individuality. God is love, is justice, as itself a subject; he is the perfect universal being as one being, the infinite extension of the species as an all-comprehending unity. But God is only man's intuition of his own nature.

666. In order to make God free and independent of all that is human, he is regarded as a formal, real person, his thinking is confined within himself, and the fact of his being thought is excluded from him, and is represented as occurring in another being. This indifference or independence with respect to us, to our thought, is the attestation of a self-subsistent, *i.e.,* external, personal existence. It is true that religion also makes the fact of God being thought into the self-thinking of God; but because this process goes forward *behind* its consciousness, since God is immediately presupposed as a self-existent personal being, the religious consciousness only embraces the indifference of the two facts.

Even religion, however, does not abide by this indifference of the two sides. God creates in order to reveal himself: creation is the revelation of God. But for stones, plants, and animals there is no God, but only for man; so that Nature exists for the sake of man, and man purely for the sake of God. God glorifies himself in man: man is the pride of God. God indeed knows himself even without man; but so long as there is no other *me*, so long is he only a possible, conceptional person. First when a difference from God, a nondivine is posited, is God conscious of himself; first when he knows what is not God, does he know what it is to be God, does he know the bliss of his Godhead. First in the positing of what is other than himself, of the world, does God posit himself as God. Is God almighty without creation? No! Omnipotence first realises, proves itself in creation. What is a power, a property, which does not exhibit, attest itself? What is a force which affects nothing? a light that does not illuminate? a wisdom which knows nothing, *i.e.,* nothing real? And what is omnipotence, what all other divine attributes, if man does not exist? Man is nothing without God; but also, God is nothing without man; for only in man is God an object as God; only in man is he God. The various qualities of man first give difference, which is the ground of reality in God. The physical qualities of man make God a physical being—God the Father, who is the creator of Nature, *i.e.,* the personified, anthropomorphised essence of Nature; the intellectual qualities of man make God an intellectual being, the moral, a moral being.

667. But if it is only in human feelings and wants that the divine "nothing" becomes something, obtains qualities, then the being of man is alone the real being of God—man is the real God. And if in the consciousness which man has of God first arises the self-consciousness of God, then the human consciousness is, *per se*, the divine consciousness. Why then dost thou alienate man's consciousness from him, and make it the self-consciousness of a being distinct from man, of that which is an object to him? Why dost thou vindicate existence to God, to man only the consciousness of that existence? God has his consciousness in man, and man his being in God? Man's knowledge of God is God's knowledge of himself? What a divorcing and contradiction! The true statement is this: man's knowledge of God is man's knowledge of himself, of his own nature. Only the unity of being and consciousness is truth. Where the consciousness of God is, there is the being of God—in man, therefore; in the being of God it is only thy own being which is an object to thee, and what presents itself *before* thy consciousness is simply what lies *behind* it. If the divine qualities are human, the human qualities are divine.

668. The necessary turning-point of history is therefore the open confession, that the consciousness of God is nothing else than the consciousness of the species; that man can and should raise himself only above the limits of his individuality, and not above the laws, the positive essential conditions of his species; that there is no other essence which man can think, dream of, imagine, feel, believe in, wish for, love and adore as the *absolute,* than the essence of human nature itself.

669. God is the highest being; therefore, to feel God is the highest feeling. But is not the highest feeling also the highest feeling of self? So long as I have not had the feeling of the highest, so long I have not exhausted my capacity of feeling, so long I do not yet fully know the nature of feeling. What, then, is an object to me in my feeling of the highest being? Nothing else than the highest nature of my power of feeling. So much as a man can feel, so much is (his) God. But the highest degree of the power of feeling is also the highest degree of the feeling of self. In the feeling of the *low* I feel myself lowered, in the feeling of the *high* I feel myself exalted. ... Thus God, as an object of feeling, or what is the same thing, the feeling of God, is nothing else than man's highest feeling of self. But God is the freest, or rather the absolutely only free being; thus God is man's highest feeling of freedom. How couldst thou be conscious of the highest being as freedom, or freedom as the highest being, if thou didst not feel thyself free? But when dost thou feel thyself free? When thou feelest God. To feel God is to feel oneself free. For example, thou feelest desire, passion, the conditions of time and place, as limits. What thou feelest as a limit thou strugglest against, thou breakest loose from, thou deniest. The consciousness of a limit, as such, is already an anathema, a sentence of condemnation pronounced on this limit, for it is an oppressive, disagreeable, negative consciousness. Only the feeling of the good, of the positive, is itself good and positive—is joy. Joy alone is feeling in its element, its paradise, because it is unrestricted activity.

670. Hence thou strivest to escape from the sense of limitation into unlimited feeling. By means of the will, or the imagination, thou negativest limits, and thus obtainest the feeling of freedom. This feeling of freedom is God.

[Sec. 620, Ludwig Feuerbach, *The Essence of Christianity*, trans. Marian Evans (London: Kegan Paul, Trench, Trübner & Co., Ltd., 1893), pp. 2–3. Sec. 621, *ibid.*, p. 4. Sec. 622, *ibid.*, p. 5. Sec. 623, *ibid.* Sec. 624, *ibid.*, p. 7. Sec. 625, *ibid.* Sec. 626, *ibid.*, pp. 8–9. Sec. 627, *ibid.*, pp. 9–10. Sec. 628, *ibid.*, pp. 10–11. Sec. 629, *ibid.*, p. 12. Sec. 630, *ibid.*, p. 13. Sec. 631, *ibid.*, p. 15. Sec. 632, *ibid.*, pp. 15–16. Sec. 633, *ibid.*, p. 19. Sec. 634, *ibid.*, p. 20. Sec. 635, *ibid.*, p. 21. Sec. 636, *ibid.*, pp. 21–22. Sec. 637, *ibid.*, p. 25. Sec. 638, *ibid.*, pp. 25–26. Sec. 639, *ibid.*, pp. 27–28. Sec. 640, *ibid.*, p. 28. Sec. 641, *ibid.*, pp. 29–30. Sec. 642, *ibid.*, p. 31. Sec. 643, *ibid.*, p. 33. Sec. 644, *ibid.*, p. 34. Sec. 645, *ibid.*, pp. 34–35. Sec. 646, *ibid.*, pp. 35–36. Sec. 647, *ibid.*, pp. 36–37. Sec. 648, *ibid.*, p. 37. Sec. 649, *ibid.*, pp. 38–39. Sec. 650, *ibid.*, p. 42. Sec. 651, *ibid.* Sec. 652, *ibid.*, pp. 46–48. Sec. 653, *ibid.*, pp. 50–51. Sec. 654, *ibid.*, p. 53. Sec. 655, *ibid.*, p. 54. Sec. 656, *ibid.*, pp. 57–58. Sec. 657, *ibid.*, p. 67. Sec. 658, *ibid.*, p. 70. Sec. 659, *ibid.*, pp. 91–92. Sec. 660, *ibid.*, pp. 92–93. Sec. 661, *ibid.*, pp. 97–98. Sec. 662, *ibid.*, p. 98. Sec. 663, *ibid.* Sec. 664, *ibid.*, pp. 99–100. Sec. 665, *ibid.*, pp. 152–54. Sec. 666, *ibid.*, pp. 227–28. Sec. 667, *ibid.*, p. 230. Sec. 668, *ibid.*, p. 270. Sec. 669, *ibid.*, p. 284. Sec. 670, *ibid.*

COMMENT

Our objection to Feuerbach's theory is that in the very essence of human thinking as such, or human experiencing and volition as such, lies limitation, even with respect to possibilities, with respect to all that men could be or do. To be man means, in purely general terms and without regard to this man as distinguished from that, or these circumstances as distinguished from those, to be a consciousness localized in a body forming but part of the whole of nature as consisting of bodies. Thus it means to see the world from the perspective of a locus arbitrarily selected among possible loci. It means to see other persons "externally," their bodies being outside one's own, through which one perceives the world. If it be objected that there is nothing in the idea of having a body which conflicts with the idea of knowing by supersensory means, say, telepathy, what others are thinking and feeling, the answer is that, if telepathy were of unlimited scope, it would be impossible to mean anything by limitation to a particular body. That I have this body and you have that is only a brief way of summarizing the manifold limitations of our experiences, yours as perspectively focused over there, mine here. It is accordingly not simply in what men actually are that they are limited but in what they could be and still be men (with localized bodies and with knowledge always shot through with ignorance and illusion).

Whatever might exist would, if it existed, be known and enjoyed by deity. This cannot be said of man. Take the entire detail of the world as it is now. It is inconceivable that any man (or all men collectively) could ever perceive this total complex of details, which must have its own beauty as a single over-all pattern. But God may perceive it. Nonetheless, he is in one sense limited. Think of all the world complexes that might exist and which, if they did, he would perceive as existent, but which do not exist and therefore are not perceived as existent even by deity. But the difference between divine and human knowing is that, whereas deity perceives as actual only the worlds that are actual and only potentially perceives the possible worlds as actual, no man can ever perceive *any* actual world, or any part of it, with clarity and adequacy, and there are possible worlds which *no man could* perceive, such as those which may follow the death of the human race itself. In such fashion the dipolar theory can meet Feuerbach's ingenious arguments, which are the ultimate development of the old contentions of Carneades, that the infinity or absoluteness of deity are irreconcilable with his concreteness, individuality, and actual consciousness. Can any man ever know what it feels like to be an ant? What it felt like to be a dinosaur? What it feels like to be a rational inhabitant of some other planet whose leading species have reached a level of superhuman intelligence? The individual limitations of consciousness are not the only limitations; there are the racial ones also, the restriction to certain senses as avenues of information, the small attention span, etc. These racial limitations are vaguely bounded; but this is infinitely far from there being no limitations. Of course we must be in some sense "beyond" any perfectly specific limitation to be aware of it but only in a fashion itself severely limited. If I know I am not so skilful as one might be, this may be made possible by a sense of power to increase my skill. But infinite power or skill is not involved, whether as a personal or as a human possibility. Only deity can have infinite skill, that is, skill to know the world, or otherwise respond to it, adequately for the highest ends.

In a word, Feuerbach has a strong case against monopolar theism, but he is guilty of systematic exaggeration of "indefinite" into "infinite" or "absolute." Consciousness is infinite in power, but not human consciousness, if "human" is to retain any definite meaning. It is obvious enough that Feuerbach is an unintentional witness to the mystic unity of man with God—for, indeed, we could not know our limitations did we not in some intimate and direct fashion know the consciousness which is definitive of consciousness itself, as unlimited in potentiality—and he is a witness to the human value of this our sense of divine consciousness and love.

# Chapter XIII: *Motive-Torque or Psychological Skepticism*

## NIETZSCHE (1844–1900)

It might be argued that Nietzsche, despite all the explosive violence in his form of expression, is attempting the same kind of identification made by Schopenhauer and Feuerbach. A certain amount of similarity is obvious. Schopenhauer exhibits an energy in his writing comparable to, although more effectively controlled than, the aphoristic style of Friedrich Nietzsche. But Schopenhauer is arguing for a metaphysics of his own. Feuerbach argues that God is to be identified with the concept of humanity. Both Schopenhauer and Feuerbach for the most part rest their arguments, as had Hume, upon questions of logic or metaphysics. In this respect Nietzsche marks a difference of approach, for Nietzsche is not concerned with pointing out a mistaken logical identification or with replacing an inadequate metaphysics by a metaphysics of his own. Instead, he engages in a psychological analysis: God is an instrument of self-torture, a consequence of man's twisted motives, a way of saying "No" to life. For this reason we have classed Nietzsche, together with Freud, who did effectively explore this possibility, as an exponent of a skepticism based on motive-torque —on motives repressed and twisted, achieving their satisfaction in another form.

### God as a Delusion of the Will

671. This will to self-torture, this restrained cruelty of the internalized animal-man, withdrawn into himself, shut up behind bars by the state in order to tame him, who has invented the bad conscience to punish himself, the nat-

ural expression of the will to punish having been prohibited—this man of the bad conscience has made use of the religious presupposition in order to carry his self-martyrdom to its dreadful extreme of severity and sharpness. A guilt toward God: this idea becomes his instrument of torture. He supposes in God the final oppositions which he finds in his own ineradicable animal-instincts, he interprets these instincts themselves as guilt toward God (hostility, rebellion in relation to the "Lord," the "Father," the ancestor and origin of the world), he agitates himself with the contradiction "God" and "Devil," he takes every No, which he has said to himself, to his own nature, and views it as a Yes outside himself, as something real and concrete, as God, divine holiness, divine judgment, divine hanging, as the Beyond, the Eternal, as martyrdom without end, as Hell, immeasurability of punishment and guilt. This is a kind of delusion of the will, a form of spiritual cruelty, with which nothing else compares: that the *will* of man should find itself guilty and contemptible beyond possibility of reconciliation; that his *will* should believe it is being punished, with no possibility that the punishment could ever atone for the guilt; that his *will*, the last ground of things, should infect and poison itself with the problem of punishment and guilt in order to bar to itself forever any escape from this labyrinth of "fixed ideas"; that his *will* should construct an ideal—that of the "holy God"—so that by comparison with this its own absolute unworthiness may become palpable! Oh this deluded, sad animal, man. What . . . paroxysms, what *bestiality of ideas*, break forth, when he is hindered ever so little from being animal in act! . . . Here is without doubt the most fearful illness that has ever raged in men:—and whoever is still able to hear . . . how in this night of martyrdom and nonsense the cry of Love, the cry of the most intense rapture, of salvation in love, has sounded, he turns away, gripped by an ungovernable horror. . . .

So much once for all for the origin of the "holy God."

[Sec. 671, Friedrich Nietzsche, *Werke* (Leipzig: Alfred Kröner Verlag, 1923), pp. 386–88.]

### COMMENT

Viewed from the aspect of our author's general purpose, this brief selection is part of the destruction, the sifting, inherent in the philosopher's task of gaining new value perspectives. Nietzsche seems to have wished to replace the attitude of hatred for life and disparagement of things human with a positive attitude of acceptance and appreciation for the human dimension. It is somewhat paradoxical that Nietzsche pursued the life-denying concepts with such evident hostility. And one wonders whether there are to be found in Nietzsche's work any really new perspectives of greater strength. And yet it would not be to the point to speculate here about his success or failure in achieving this goal.

The proper question is: What has been destroyed? Nietzsche's very forcefulness leads him to overstate even his genuine insights. It is true that God can be, has often been, an instrument of self-torture; it seems to be true that such a conception of God has been the dominant conception in some times and places. But, granting this, the evidence discredits not the "holy God" but the individuals, times, and places where the idea of God has been so used. Nietzsche's destructive intent reaches only to a life-denying conception of God, God as cosmic policeman, as immutable judge. He has shown the dangers of monopolarity in theology just where the theological conception touches human life.

Elsewhere, of course, writing as a philosopher, he does insist that the idea of God is too crude an answer to the problem of existence, too much of a restriction upon thinking. But it is not clear that the objection applies to all ideas about God; it is not even clear that it applies to any other than the concept he disavows for psychological reasons. We really know, then, only what he is against; and in our judgment his opposition to this twisted concept is proper. That he does not state an alternative conception of God means only that he did not arrive at one; it does not mean that there is no concept which can successfully withstand his criticism. The force of Nietzsche's probing is here essentially negative; and an idea of God implicit in thought and the completion of thought would be neither crude nor a restriction upon thinking.

Nonetheless, our author's outcry on this matter has real depth, detract from it what one may. It is essentially the thesis elaborated by Freud into a powerful explanation of human behavior. And further aspects of this issue will be treated in connection with our selection from his writings.

## FREUD (1856–1940)

There is something to be said for the thesis that Freud was the first man to show with some definiteness what the mixture of "animality" and "rationality" in man really is. One of the main points of his analysis might be put thus: The mighty forces which oppose or distort the operations of intelligence in grown-up human beings are not simply, or even perhaps chiefly, their present animal nature, the direct influences of their bodily organs. The forces are rather primarily the not consciously recalled, but still vitally present, feelings which came into being through earlier instances of the blended animal and rational functionings which characterize the small child. It is men, not animals, who suffer from Oedipus complexes and the like, whose love for the mother finds in the father a rival as well as also a protector and sometimes a punisher. Such troubles are due to the fact that even the small child in his way thinks as well as senses and feels. He has theories about his relatives and emotions connected therewith. And Freud's truly great discovery is that the earliest manifestations of the cognitive-spiritual side of man become from then on part of the vague but potent background of all the later ones. What this amounts to is that the emotional-sensory past of man is the main material to which his later life gives ever new form. Past experience is the very substance of the present self—not some "matter" or stuff which in the past received form and now receives another one instead; no, just the past experiences themselves with their own very forms. Freud shares with Bergson the honor of discovering the great secret of process itself, which is memory in its primary sense of the direct possession of past events by present ones. Except at the very beginning of life, to be happy in the human sense is largely to have been happy in the human sense, though in a more childish way; and to be unhappy is largely to have been unhappy. Time is not essentially substitution of one state for another but accretion of state superimposed upon state.

If this is true, then the religion of adults, like all their forms of living, especially those which are strongly emotional, cannot well be understood until we see the great emotional configurations of childhood that they express—whatever else, later acquired, they may also embody. With admirable ingenuity and brave candor Freud searches out these connections of religion with childhood. The child must, in order to grow into a member of society, renounce numerous instinctual gratifications whose indulgence would not be acceptable to others; and the child must do this largely without being able to understand why. Thus not rational insight but something else, some anxiety in most cases, some fear, must furnish the motive. This amounts to saying that the child must pass through some degree of neurosis, which, except in unfortunate cases, can ultimately be outgrown.

But we must think not only of the development of the child into adult but also of the race, from its childhood into a more mature form of culture. In the childhood of the race there was not enough intelligence to give potency to the simple recognition of the reasons of social utility against murder and other unsocial acts; instead, blind emotional compulsions and fears were brought into play. God has prohibited the undesirable actions and will punish their performance with dreadful efficiency, as he will reward good acts with equal effectiveness. Thus God is for the adult what the father is for the child today and also even for grown sons, and the whole family group, in primitive times. God is the prolongation into adulthood, individual and racial, of the function of the father. And religion is the prolongation of neurosis whereby the insufficient supply of intelligence in most men (as in all children) for their needs is eked out by illusory, emotionally toned beliefs. But the religious neurosis has the great advantage of social objectivity; that is, it is shared with many others, who thus aid one another to sustain and enjoy the "delusional transformation of reality" in which religion essentially consists. So religion is a form of mass delusion.

With much resourcefulness and, for all we know, with much truth, Freud sets forth the powerful forces that produce and sustain this delusion. The plight of man is serious, at best, in civilization as we know it. His means of happiness are all highly precarious, and the most reliable, alas, do not offer intense forms of gratification. It is too much for most of us: we fall back upon a wishful transformation of our reality picture; dreams of heavenly rewards compensate for suffering and uncertainty; our sense of guilt, originally produced by identification with disapproving parents whose disapproval and aggression toward us is thus internalized and made into an aspect of our superego, is extended into the vision of a divine punisher of sin, and thus we regress to or live over again the child's situation in relation to parent, the unconscious memory of which is too strong for any radically different approach to life to be possible for us in our troubled and difficult position. Moreover, religion has been taught to us from our early years, and credulity taught as a duty, reinforced with threats of hell if we disbelieve.

Nevertheless, Freud believes, as other neuroses can be outgrown, so likewise eventually the racial neurosis of religion. At least, the hope is legitimate, and we can but try to contribute to the ultimate triumph of intelligence and the reality principle over the mere pleasure principle and its wishful extension into illusion and delusion. And the process of emancipation seems already under way. "Man cannot remain a child forever; he must venture at last into the hostile world."

It is not Freud's contention that psychoanalysis of itself suffices to disprove the truth of religious doctrines. Only at one point does this occur: the claim of religion that its beliefs derive directly from God himself seems untenable in view of the cogent genetic explanation which analysis offers of the individual and racial origin of religious ideas. In calling religion "illusion," Freud means not that it is certainly a false picture of reality but that the origin of belief is in wish and need, not in any perception of evidence or rational inference from facts. In calling religion "delusion," as he sometimes does, he is going further and is asserting that the rational probabilities are against there being any significant degree of truth in the creeds. Here he appeals not to psychoanalysis but to what has, he says, been apparent to critics of religion for a long time when they have dared to speak plainly: the manifest indifference of the forces of nature to human wishes, the impossibility of reconciling the evils of life with the goodness of God, the inconsistencies of religious thinking, etc. And, in any case, if there be truth in religious doctrine, it is science alone which could tell us that this is so. "Intuition" is always particular and private; it gives no reliable clues to truth. Philosophy is but science eked out illegitimately with elements of intuition; or it is religion fighting a rearguard action, giving up the substance of belief while retaining some of its labels.

Freud also holds that religion has many harmful effects upon conduct. Whereas individuals have widely different capacities from which should result widely different methods of securing such happiness as is open to them, religion, says Freud, tries to reduce all to a single method, which involves "decrying of the value of life" and seeking for satisfaction in imaginary substitutes for life, in both respects exerting "a preliminary intimidating influence upon intelligence." The positive value thus achieved is that "religion succeeds in saving many people from individual neuroses. But little more." Thus, even apart from the question of truth, and with reference to all other values, religion can hardly be justified, save as a transitory phase of culture. The indictment is vigorous, massively supported. It is presented in three different works, from which the following passages are taken.

## The Function of Religion

672. If one wishes to form a true estimate of the full grandeur of religion, one must keep in mind what it undertakes to do for men. It gives them information about the source and origin of the universe, it assures them of protection and final happiness amid the changing vicissitudes of life, and it guides their thoughts and actions by means of precepts which are backed by the whole force of its authority. It fulfils, therefore, three functions. In the first place, it satisfies man's desire for knowledge; it is here doing the same thing that science attempts to accomplish by its own methods, and here, therefore, enters into rivalry with it. It is to the second function that it performs, that religion no doubt owes the greater part of its influence. In so far as religion brushes away men's fear of the dangers and vicissitudes of life, in so far as it assures them of a happy ending, and comforts them in their misfortunes, science cannot compete with it. Science, it is true, teaches how one can avoid certain dangers and how one can combat many sufferings with success; it would be quite untrue to deny that science is a powerful aid to human beings, but in many cases it has to leave them to their suffering, and can only advise them to submit to the inevitable. In the performance of its third function, the provision of precepts, prohibitions, and restrictions, religion is furthest removed from science. For science is content with discovering and stating the facts. It is true that from the applications of science, rules and recommendations for behaviour may be deduced. In certain circumstances they may be the same as those which are laid down by religion, but even so the reasons for them will be different.

673. One can only understand this remarkable combination of teaching, consolation and precept in religion, if one subjects it to genetic analysis. We may begin with the most remarkable item of the three, the teaching about the origin of the universe—for why should a cosmogony be a regular element of religious systems? The doctrine is that the universe was created by a being similar to man, but greater in every respect, in power, wisdom, and strength of passion, in fact by an idealized superman. . . . It is interesting to notice that this creator of the universe is always a single god, even when many gods are believed in. Equally interesting is the fact that the creator is nearly always a male, although there is no lack of indication of the existence of female deities and many mythologies make the creation of the world begin precisely with a male god triumphing over a female goddess, who is degraded into a monster. This raises the most fascinating minor problems, but we must hurry on. The rest of our enquiry is made easy because this God-Creator is openly called Father. Psychoanalysis concludes that he really is the father, clothed in the grandeur in which he once appeared to the small child. The religious man's picture of the creation of the universe is the same as his picture of his own creation.

If this is so, then it is easy to understand how it is that the comforting promises of protection and the severe ethical commands are found together with the cosmogony. For the same individual, to whom the child owes its own existence, the father (or, more correctly, the parental function which is composed of the father and the mother), has protected and watched over the weak and helpless child, exposed as it is to all the dangers which threaten in the external world; in its father's care it has felt itself safe. Even the grown man, though he may know that he possesses greater strength, and though he has greater insight into the dangers of life, rightly feels that fundamentally he is just as helpless and unprotected as he was in childhood and that in relation to the external world he is still a child. Even now, therefore, he cannot give up the protection which he has enjoyed as a child. But he has long ago realized that his father is a being with strictly limited powers and by no means endowed with every desirable attribute. He therefore looks back to the memory-image of the over-rated father of his childhood, exalts it into a Deity, and brings it into the present and into reality. The emotional strength of the memory-image and the lasting nature of his need for protection are the two supports of his belief in God.

The third main point of the religious programme, its ethical precepts, can also be related without any difficulty to the situation of childhood. . . . The same father (the parental function) who gave the child his life and preserved it from the dangers which that life involves, also taught it what it may or may not do, made it accept certain limitations of its instinctual wishes, and told it what consideration it would be expected to show towards its parents and brothers and sisters, if it wanted to be tolerated and liked as a member of the family circle, and later on of more extensive groups. This child is brought up to know its social duties by means of a system of love-rewards and punishments, and in this way it is taught that its security in life depends on its parents (and, subsequently, other people) loving it and being able to believe in its

love for them. This whole state of affairs is carried over by the grown man unaltered into his religion. The prohibitions and commands of his parents live on in his breast as his moral conscience; God rules the world of men with the help of the same system of rewards and punishments, and the degree of protection and happiness which each individual enjoys, depends on his fulfilment of the demands of morality; the feeling of security, with which he fortifies himself against the dangers both of the external world and of his human environment, is founded on his love of God and the consciousness of God's love for him. Finally, he has in prayer a direct influence on the divine will, and in that way insures for himself a share in the divine omnipotence.

### Critical Examination of Religion, the Illusion

*674.* The scientific spirit, strengthened by the observation of natural processes, began in the course of time to treat religion as a human matter, and to subject it to a critical examination. This test it failed to pass. In the first place, the accounts of miracles roused a feeling of surprise and disbelief, since they contradicted everything that sober observation had taught, and betrayed all too clearly the influence of human imagination. In the next place, its account of the nature of the universe had to be rejected, because it showed evidence of a lack of knowledge which bore the stamp of earlier days, and because, owing to increasing familiarity with the laws of nature, it had lost its authority. The idea that the universe came into being through an act of generation or creation, analogous to that which produces an individual human being, no longer seemed to be the most obvious and self-evident hypothesis; for the distinction between living and sentient beings and inanimate nature had become apparent to the human mind, and had made it impossible to retain the original animistic theory. Besides this, one must not overlook the influence of the comparative study of different religious systems, and the impression they give of mutual exclusiveness and intolerance.

Fortified by these preliminary efforts, the scientific spirit at last summoned up courage to put to the test the most important and the most emotionally significant elements of the religious *Weltanschauung*. The truth could have been seen at any time, but it was long before any one dared to say it aloud: the assertions made by religion that it could give protection and happiness to men, if they would only fulfil certain ethical obligations, were unworthy of belief. It seems not to be true that there is a power in the universe, which watches over the wellbeing of every individual with parental care and brings all his concerns to a happy ending. On the contrary the destinies of man are incompatible with a universal principle of benevolence or with—what is to some degree contradictory—a universal principle of justice. Earthquakes, floods and fires do not differentiate between the good and devout man, and the sinner and unbeliever. And, even if we leave inanimate nature out of account and consider the destinies of individual men in so far as they depend on their relations with others of their own kind, it is by no means the rule that virtue is rewarded and wickedness punished, but it happens often enough that the violent, the crafty and the unprincipled seize the desirable goods of the earth for themselves, while the pious go empty away. Dark, unfeeling and unloving powers determine human destiny; the system of rewards and punishments, which, according to religion, governs the world, seems to have no existence. This is another occasion for abandoning a portion of the animism which has found refuge in religion.

The last contribution to the criticism of the religious *Weltanschauung* has been made by psychoanalysis, which has traced the origin of religion to the helplessness of childhood, and its content to the persistence of the wishes and needs of childhood into maturity. This does not precisely imply a refutation of religion, but it is a necessary rounding off of our knowledge about it, and, at least on one point, it actually contradicts it, for religion lays claim to a divine origin. This claim, to be sure, is not false if our interpretation of God is accepted.

The final judgment of science on the religious *Weltanschauung*, then, runs as follows. While the different religions wrangle with one another as to which of them is in possession of the truth, in our view the truth of religion may be altogether disregarded. Religion is an attempt to get control over the sensory world, in which we are placed, by means of the wish-world, which we have developed inside us as a result of biological and psychological necessities. But it cannot achieve its end. . . . Its consolations deserve no trust. Experience teaches us that the world is not a nursery. The ethical commands, to which religion seeks to lend its weight, require some other foundations instead, for human society cannot do without them, and it is dangerous to link up obedience to them with religious belief. If one attempts to assign to religion its place in man's evolution, it seems not so much to be a lasting acquisition, as a parallel to the neurosis which the civilised individual must pass through on his way from childhood to maturity.

*675.* . . . the reproaches made against science for not having solved the riddle of the universe are unfairly and spitefully exaggerated. Science has had too little time for such a tremendous achievement. It is still very young, a recently developed human activity.

*676.* And it must not be forgotten that the last century has brought with it such a quantity of new discoveries and such a great acceleration of scientific progress that we have every reason to look forward with confidence to the future of science. . . . it is true that the path of science is slow, tentative and laborious. That cannot be denied or altered. No wonder that the gentlemen of the opposition are dissatisfied; they are spoilt, they have had an easier time of it with their revelation.

677. . . . what is the purpose of all these passionate disparagements of science? In spite of its present incompleteness and its inherent difficulties, we could not do without it and could not put anything else in its place. There is no limit to the improvement of which it is capable, and this can certainly not be said of the religious *Weltanschauung*. The latter is complete in its essentials; if it is an error, it must remain one for ever. No attempt to minimise the importance of science can alter the fact that it attempts to take into account our dependence on the real external world, while religion is illusion, and it derives its strength from the fact that it falls in with our instinctual desires.

678. . . . the human intellect is weak in comparison with human instincts. . . . But nevertheless there is something peculiar about this weakness. The voice of the intellect is a soft one, but it does not rest until it has gained a hearing. Ultimately, after endlessly repeated rebuffs, it succeeds. This is one of the few points in which one may be optimistic about the future of mankind, but in itself it signifies not a little. And one can make it a starting-point for yet other hopes. The primacy of the intellect certainly lies in the far, far, but still probably not infinite, distance. And as it will presumably set itself the same aims that you expect to be realized by your God —of course within human limits, in so far as external reality, Ἀνάγκη, allows it—the brotherhood of man and the reduction of suffering, we may say that our antagonism is only a temporary

and not an irreconcilable one. We desire the same things, but you are more impatient, more exacting, and—why should I not say it—more selfish than I and those like me. You would have the state of bliss to begin immediately after death; you ask of it the impossible, and you will not surrender the claim of the individual. Of these wishes our God Λόγος[1] will realize those which external nature permits, but he will do this very gradually, only in the incalculable future and for other children of men. Compensation for us, who suffer grievously from life, he does not promise. On the way to this distant goal your religious doctrines will have to be discarded, no matter whether the first attempts fail, or whether the first substitute-informations prove to be unstable. You know why; in the long run nothing can withstand reason and experience, and the contradiction religion offers to both is only too palpable. Not even the purified religious ideas can escape this fate, so long as they still try to preserve anything of the consolation of religion. Certainly if you confine yourself to the belief in a higher spiritual being, whose qualities are indefinable and whose intentions cannot be discerned, then you are proof against the interference of science, but then you will also relinquish the interest of men.

## Man's Search for Happiness

679. It sounds like a fairy-tale, but not only that; this story of what man by his science and practical inventions has achieved on this earth, where he first appeared as a weakly member of the animal kingdom, and on which each individual of his species must ever again appear as a helpless infant—O inch of nature!—is a direct fulfilment of all, or of most, of the dearest wishes in his fairy-tales. All these possessions he has

1. I.e., the twin gods Λόγος-Ἀνάγκη of the Dutchman *Multatuli*.

acquired through culture. Long ago he formed an ideal conception of omnipotence and omniscience which he embodied in his gods. Whatever seemed unattainable to his desires—or forbidden to him--he attributed to these gods. One may say, therefore, that these gods were the ideals of his culture. Now he has himself approached very near to realising this ideal, he has nearly become a god himself. But only, it is true, in the way that ideals are usually realised in the general experience of humanity. Not completely; in some respects not at all, in others only by halves. Man has become a god by means of artificial limbs, so to speak, quite magnificent when equipped with all his accessory organs; but they do not grow on him and they still give him trouble at times. . . . Future ages will produce further great advances in this realm of culture, probably inconceivable now, and will increase man's likeness to a god still more. . . . we will not forget, all the same, that the human being of to-day is not happy with all his likeness to a god.

*680.* [One way of seeking happiness] . . . strives to bring about independence of fate—as we may best call it—and with this object it looks for satisfaction within the mind, and uses the capacity for displacing libido which we mentioned before, but it does not turn away from the outer world; on the contrary, it takes a firm hold of its objects and obtains happiness from an emotional relation to them. Nor is it content to strive for avoidance of pain—that goal of weary resignation; rather it passes that by heedlessly and holds fast to the deep-rooted, passionate striving for a positive fulfilment of happiness. Perhaps it really comes nearer to this goal than any other method. I am speaking, of course, of that way of life which makes love the centre of all things and anticipates all happiness from loving and being loved. This attitude is familiar enough to all of us; one of the forms in which love manifests itself, sexual love, gives us our most intense experience of an overwhelming pleasurable sensation and so furnishes a prototype for our strivings after happiness. What is more natural than that we should persist in seeking happiness along the path by which we first encountered it? The weak side of this way of living is clearly evident; and were it not for this, no human being would ever have thought of abandoning this path to happiness in favour of any other. We are never so defenceless against suffering as when we love, never so forlornly unhappy as when we have lost our love-object or its love.

*681.* A small minority are enabled by their constitution nevertheless to find happiness along the path of love; but far-reaching mental transformations of the erotic function are necessary before this is possible. These people make themselves independent of their object's acquiescence by transferring the main value from the fact of being loved to their own act of loving; they protect themselves against loss of it by attaching their love not to individual objects but to all men equally, and they avoid the uncertainties and disappointments of genital love by turning away from its sexual aim and modifying the instinct into an impulse with an *inhibited aim.* The state which they induce in themselves by this process—an unchangeable, undeviating, tender attitude —has little superficial likeness to the stormy vicissitudes of genital love, from which it is nevertheless derived. It seems that Saint Francis of Assisi may have carried this method of using love to produce an inner feeling of happiness as far as anyone; what we are thus characterizing as one of the procedures by which the pleasure-principle fulfils itself has in fact been linked up in many ways with religion; the connection between them may lie in those remote fastnesses of the mind where the distinctions between the ego and objects and between the various objects become matters of indifference. From one ethical standpoint, the deeper motivation of which will later become clear to us, this inclination towards an all-embracing love of others and of the world at large is regarded as the highest state of mind of which man is capable. . . . I will not withhold the two principal objections we have to raise against this view. A love that does not discriminate seems to us to lose some of its own value, since it does an injustice to its object. And secondly, not all men are worthy of love.

*682.* My love seems to me a valuable thing that I have no right to throw away without reflection. It imposes obligations on me which I must be prepared to make sacrifices to fulfil. If I love someone, he must be worthy of it in some way or other.

*683.* He will be worthy of it if he is so like me in important respects that I can love myself in him; worthy of it if he is so much more perfect than I that I can love my ideal of myself in him; I must love him if he is the son of my friend, since the pain my friend would feel if anything untoward happened to him would be my pain—I should have to share it. But if he is a stranger to me and cannot attract me by any value he has in himself or any significance he may have already acquired in my emotional life, it will be hard for me to love him. I shall even be doing wrong if I do, for my love is valued as a privilege by all those belonging to me; it is an injustice to them if I put a stranger on a level with them. But if I am to love him (with that kind of universal love) simply because he, too, is a denizen of the earth, like an insect or an earthworm or a grass-snake, then I fear that but a small modicum of love will fall to his lot and it would be impossible for me to give him as much as by all the laws of reason I am entitled to retain for myself. What is the point of an injunction promulgated with such solemnity, if reason does not recommend it to us?

When I look more closely I find still further difficulties. Not merely is this stranger on the whole not worthy of love, but, to be honest, I must confess he has more claim to my hostility, even to my hatred. He does not seem to have the least trace of love for me, does not show me the slightest consideration. If it will do him any good, he has no hesitation in injuring me, never even asking himself whether the amount of advantage he gains by it bears any proportion to the amount of wrong done to me. What is more, he does not even need to get an advantage from it; if he can merely get a little pleasure out of it, he thinks nothing of jeering at me, insulting me, slandering me, showing his power over me; and the more secure he feels himself, or the more helpless I am, with so much more certainty can I expect this behavior from him towards me.

*684.* . . . men are not gentle, friendly creatures wishing for love, who simply defend themselves if they are attacked, but . . . a powerful measure of desire for aggression has to be reckoned as part of their instinctual endowment.

*685.* The existence of this tendency to aggression which we can detect in ourselves and rightly presume to be present in others is the factor that disturbs our relations with our neighbours and makes it necessary for culture to institute its high demands. Civilized society is perpetually menaced with disintegration through this primary hostility of men towards one another. Their interests in their common work would not hold them together; the passions of instinct are stronger than reasoned interests. Culture has to call up every possible reinforcement in order to erect barriers against the aggressive instincts of men and hold their manifestations in check by reaction-formations in men's minds. Hence its system of methods by which mankind is to be driven to identifications and aim-inhibited love-relationships; hence the restrictions on sexual life; and hence, too, its ideal command to love one's neighbour as oneself, which is really justified by the fact that nothing is so completely at variance with original human nature as this. With all its striving, this endeavour of culture's has so far not achieved very much.

### Eros and the Death Instinct

*686.* On the basis of speculations concerning the origin of life and of biological parallels, I drew the conclusion that, beside the instinct preserving the organic substance and binding it into ever larger units, there must exist another in antithesis to this, which would seek to dissolve these units and reinstate their antecedent inorganic state; that is to say, a death instinct as well as Eros; the phenomena of life would then be explicable from the interplay of the two and their counteracting effects on each other.

*687.* Those who love fairy-tales do not like it when people speak of the innate tendencies in mankind towards aggression, destruction and, in addition, cruelty. For God has made them in his own image, with his own perfections; no one wants to be reminded how hard it is to reconcile the undeniable existence—in spite of all the protestations of Christian Science—of evil with his omnipotence and supreme goodness. The devil is, in fact, the best way out in acquittal of God; he can be used to play the same economic role of outlet as Jews in the world of Aryan ideals. But even so, one can just as well hold God responsible for the existence of the devil as for the evil he personifies.

*688.* . . . the process [of culture] proves to be in the service of Eros, which aims at binding together single human individuals, then families, then tribes, races, nations, into one great unity, that of humanity. . . . These masses of men must be bound to one another libidinally; necessity alone, the advantages of common work, would not hold them together. The natural instinct of aggressiveness in man, the hostility of each one against all and of all against each one, opposes this programme of civilization. This instinct of aggression is the derivative and main representative of the death instinct we have found alongside of Eros, sharing his rule over the earth. And now, it seems to me, the meaning of the evolution of culture is no longer a riddle to us. It must present to us the struggle between Eros and Death, between the instincts of life and the instincts of destruction, as it works itself out in the human species. This struggle is what all life essentially consists of and so the evolution of civilization may be simply described as the struggle of the human species for existence. And it is this battle of the Titans that our nurses and governesses try to compose with their lullaby-song of Heaven!

*689.* In our investigations and our therapy of the neuroses we cannot avoid finding fault with the super-ego of the individual on two counts: in commanding and prohibiting with such severity it troubles too little about the happiness of the ego, and it fails to take into account sufficiently the difficulties in the way of obeying it—the strength of instinctual cravings in the *id* and the hardships of external environment. Consequently in our therapy we often find ourselves obliged to do battle with the super-ego and work to moderate its demands. Exactly the same objections can be made against the ethical standards of the cultural super-ego. It, too, does not trouble enough about the mental constitution of human beings; it enjoins a command and never asks whether or not it is possible for them to obey it. . . . The command to love our neighbours as ourselves is the strongest defence there is against human aggressiveness and it is a superlative example of the unpsychological attitude of the cultural super-ego. The command is impossible to fulfil; such an enormous inflation of love can only lower its value and not remedy the evil. Civilization pays no heed to all this; it merely prates that the harder it is to obey the more laudable the obedience. The fact remains that anyone who follows such preaching in the present state of civilization only puts himself at a disadvantage beside all those who set it at naught. What an overwhelming obstacle to civilization aggression must be if the defence against it can cause as much misery as aggression itself! "Natural" ethics, as it is called, has nothing to offer here beyond the narcissistic satisfaction of thinking oneself better than others. The variety of ethics that links itself with religion brings in at this point its promises of a better future life. I should imagine that as long as virtue is not rewarded in this life ethics will preach in vain. I too think it unquestionable that an actual change in men's attitude to property would be of more help in this direction than any ethical commands; but among the Socialists this proposal is obscured by new idealistic expectations disregarding human nature, which detract from its value in actual practice.

*690.* Men have brought their powers of subduing the forces of nature to such a pitch that by using them they could now very easily exterminate one another to the last man. They know this—hence arises a great part of their current unrest, their dejection, their mood of apprehension. And now it may be expected that the other of the two "heavenly forces," eternal Eros, will put forth his strength so as to maintain himself alongside of his equally immortal adversary.

[Sec. 672, Sigmund Freud, *A New Series of Introductory Lectures on Psycho-analysis,* trans. W. J. H. Spratt (New York: W. W. Norton & Co., 1933), pp. 220–21. Sec. 673, *ibid.,* pp. 222–24. Sec. 674, *ibid.,* pp. 227–30. Sec. 675, *ibid.,* p. 236. Sec. 676, *ibid.,* pp. 237–38. Sec. 677, *ibid.,* pp. 238–39. Sec. 678, Sigmund Freud, *The Future of an Illusion,* trans. W. D. Robson (London: Hogarth Press, 1943; New York: Scott, Liveright Publishing Corp., 1949), pp. 93–94. Sec. 679, Sigmund Freud, *Civilization and Its Discontents* (London: Hogarth Press and the Institute of Psychoanalysis, 1943), pp. 52–53. Sec. 680, *ibid.,* pp. 36–38. Sec. 681, *ibid.,* pp. 69–71. Sec. 682, *ibid.,* p. 81. Sec. 683, *ibid.,* pp. 82–83. Sec. 684, *ibid.,* p. 85. Sec. 685, *ibid.,* pp. 86–87. Sec. 686, *ibid.,* p. 97. Sec. 687, *ibid.,* pp. 99–100. Sec. 688, *ibid.,* pp. 102–3. Sec. 689, *ibid.,* pp. 139–41. Sec. 690, *ibid.,* p. 144.]

## COMMENT

We have no intention of defending religion "all along the line" against the foregoing criticisms. That there has been much infantilism and wishful illusion in religion seems manifest. If what Freud calls "religion" is the only alternative now available to a philosophy of life drawn solely from the results of present-day science, then we face a desperate dilemma. But is it the only alternative?

Freud thinks that religion consists in the notion that there is a supernatural Father who guards us from injury and suffering, save so far as he punishes us, otherwise giving us all manner of good things, and finally bringing us, if we obey him, to a lasting happiness in which no need shall be without its satisfaction. Any attempt to refine upon this truly infantile conception our author scornfully rejects as an effort to keep the religious labels without their essential meaning. But with what right does he do this and insist that the religious view, as he interprets it, is fixed forevermore, while science can endlessly improve the subtle accuracy of its hypotheses? The question is this:

Has Freud proved that the entire human value of religion consists in the "nursery" conception of reality? Is it really so that every introduction of greater rationality and evidential truth value into religious ideas will mean just so much subtracted from their emotional appeal, so that the limit of the process can only be a vacuous conception concerning which controversy is idle?

There is another view of God and religion than that which Freud has in mind, and for some of us at any rate it offers certain "consolations" (Freud's term). It also seems to us probably true, or (in Plato's words) "something like the truth." According to this view, God is not a power whose function is to keep us from all harm, for his "rule" of the world is not a sheer determining of events but an inspiring influence upon events that are in part always self-determined or free. On this view, tragedy is inherent in process, and God is not outside the tragedy, bringing it about as punishment or for some other end, but is undergoing it also himself. In this respect there is indeed a remote analogy between God and an earthly father who suffers in and with the family misfortunes. But surely (and Freud, though grudgingly, concedes this) it is no disproof of an adult idea that it has some analogy or other to a childish idea. But Freud systematically understates and misstates the *categorical* contrast between the functions of deity (as most reasonably conceived) and any human, even fatherly, functions. In some ways, a much better analogy is that between God and an organism. We are as cells in the inclusive organism. (A psychiatrist who had studied with Freud once defended this conception of God in conversation with one of the authors of this book.) Say, if you will, that this recalls the womb experience. What of that? We think in terms of analogies with past experi-

ence. But no one is saying that God is just like the mother, only vastly larger. Just as science has refined upon primitive ideas derived from external, particular perceptions, so philosophy has refined upon ideas derived from more internal and pervasive experiences.

Let us return to the question of the emotional value of religion. Freud admits that the "riddle of death" probably admits no scientific solution. But he sees as the religious solution simply an awakening of the human individual to new adventures and joys after death. There is another conception which just as definitely deals with the riddle of personal destruction. It can appeal for strong support to Freud's own work. This conception sees as the essential immortality the preservation beyond death, not just of some abstract core of individuality, or self-identity, which runs through human experiences, but of the very experiences themselves in their concreteness; and it sees the clue to this preservation in memory. Even in terms of merely human memory, it seems that experiences do not simply undergo extinction but live on with a sort of highly subdued life, so long as the individual, or even, in some slight measure, perhaps, so long as the race, survives. But nothing like effective and permanent preservation of the full vividness of living can be ascribed to human memory. Only a radically superhuman, a divine, memory could accomplish this. But such a memory, it seems logically clear, certainly could accomplish it, and must do so, if it exists.

At the moment we are discussing not the truth of the idea but its human interest, for Freud's multiple argument must be met point by point. And he claims that all emotional and practical interest evaporates from religious doctrines if they are altered from their infantile form. Now the idea that immortality is essentially divine memory can hardly be infantile. Most of mankind, including most theologians and philosophers of the past, if not of the present, seem scarcely to have dreamed of this solution of the riddle of death. On Freudian principles, then, the idea is far from childish; otherwise, many men would have it, considering what a simple direct answer to the riddle in question it furnishes. And with this idea of immortality, there is no question of selfish rewards in heaven or of escape from life's tragedies into a transcendental nursery to make up for the fact that the planet is not a nursery. Yet upon this view death ceases to be a riddle in any reasonable sense. For, according to this doctrine, experiences are the final concrete actualities, and the problem of their preservation is the fundamental problem of immortality. Such preservation is not accomplished effectively by human means even in this life and prior to death. Death is but the bringing to a close of a particular sequence of experiences which are to be immortalized, and which, according to panentheism, in the moment of death are already immortal. Why, then, should there be death? Why not? Why should a particular sequence, such as a human life, go on forever? Life begins already to lose some of its zest, which is always due partly to novelty, when youth is over; the finiteness of our life-span is thus aesthetically appropriate, and we find death an intolerable thought only because we imagine that the essential preservation must be of self-identity rather than of experiences, or because we are so "narcissistic" that we see in our own self-identity, or so anthropomorphic that we see in human personality as such, the sole thread of coherence binding past, present, and future into meaningful relation.

What then of reward and punishment? If we realize that each moment of our lives, once it is past, has its reality in divine memory and nowhere else, so that our present consciousness represents vastly less than 1 per cent of our total reality in God, and this consciousness itself will have abiding reality only as contribution to the divine life, then we see that self-love is a comic or tragic absurdity, save as it is embraced in love for God. The sense of sin, in its full religious meaning, is the tragic side of this absurdity. It is the realization that we have failed to love the One who is our own reality and infinitely more and thus have not even consistently loved ourselves. In this light we can see the point of such old sayings as: "The reward of a good deed is the good deed itself"; "Paradise and hell . . . are only metaphors for the agony of sin and the happiness of virtue"; "Not for the sake of attaining bliss shall we love God and practice virtue, but to love God and practice virtue is itself true bliss. . . . There is no need of any other reward than this, and there is no greater punishment than to be deprived of this boon forever."

Freud remarks that naturalistic ethics in some cases offers us only the narcissistic satisfaction of thinking one's self better than others, while religion promises a better future life; and he suggests that the way to make ethics effective is to find means, probably through altering the institution of property, of rewarding virtue in this life. Now, if any alteration of property would better reward virtue, a reasonable religion will advocate it; but Freud here disregards the possibility that God as locus of our reality, as the one who still vividly cares for the more than 99 per cent of our experiential actuality which we have lost, the one who thus loves us incomparably more truly and completely than we can love ourselves, can therefore offer us an object to love which alone is absolutely worthy, and thus give us indeed a reward of virtue in this life. We shall return to this topic of love.

Suppose a Freudian were to reply to

us that it is just the appeal to narcissism and anthropomorphism that gives religion its function and power and that this power would be lost were it admitted that providence (1) does not guard us against tragedy or (2) reward (or punish) us with a prolongation of our life-histories after death under more (or less) favorable circumstances but can only (3) give our moments of living and those of our children and of all human posterity imperishable vividness in the divine memory. What would we say? We should say that (3) is not yet all of the consolations of purified religion and that, in any case, if men cannot learn to satisfy themselves with these consolations, much less can they learn to make shift with the meager fare offered them by Freud's program for the future of man! For, on the one hand, he offers men nothing that purified religion cannot also offer. Since this religion makes human living intrinsic to the divine life, contributory to its value, such religion does not "decry the value of life"; just the contrary, it will seek ways to achieve human happiness and will avail itself of all the resources which Freud so well summarizes in *Civilization and Its Discontents*, including all the methods of science. But, on the other hand, purified religion has additional resources of its own. As we have seen, it shows (and mere science cannot show this) that death need not be the frustration of our deepest purposes, provided these purposes are freed from narcissism. Freud wishes for this transcendence of narcissism or selfishness, but he cannot show on the basis of his beliefs that even with this transcendence we can escape ultimate frustration of all our purposes and even of our deepest or most general and disinterested purposes.

There is something more. Purified religion can offer a sense of the meaning of life and the unity of reality satisfying not only to our emotions but also to our intelligence. Freud says that science aims at intellectual unification but only as an aim indefinitely postponed to the future. But perhaps one does not need to wait for the future of science to see that the problem of unity transcends the scientific fact-searching method in principle. For it is not merely facts but possibilities that require unification. And it is not merely natural stabilities, or laws, valid for long cosmic periods, but the primordial and everlasting that must be included in our concept of reality if it is to meet the essential human interest. The problem is irreducibly metaphysical. Man is a metaphysical animal as well as a scientific one.

Freud says frankly that he knows less than almost anyone about metaphysical systems and their history. But his belief is that they rely illegitimately upon intuition and that they "over-estimate the epistemological value of our logical operations." In short, Freud is and was from the outset a positivist. He sees nothing except the intellectually rigorous investigation of mere facts, on the one side, and irresponsible toying with dreams, fancies, intuitions, on the other. But perhaps there is a third thing, the intellectually rigorous investigation, not of facts, actualities, but of the deepest level of experience which lies beneath the alternative actual-possible, and reveals the ground of this alternative itself, and is therefore neither actual nor merely possible but necessary and eternally real. Freud assumes throughout that religion is concerned with a great pseudo-fact, in competition with the genuine facts of science.

Now, in our panentheistic view God in his concrete, superrelative actuality is indeed a great fact, inclusive of the facts of science and infinitely more. To know this side of God in its particular qualities, we should need to be at the end of the development of science; and this goal must indeed be indefinitely postponed. But there is an abstract essence of God which is no fact at all, since it is rather a principle expressed in possibilities as truly as in actual facts. To ascertain what this is, or whether or not the idea of such a thing has any validity and truth, it is vain to employ a method whose aim is merely to decide which among "possible worlds" is the actual one. For just this discrimination is irrelevant to the question at issue. Yet Freud has merely assumed, with other positivists, that the question does not exist or is illegitimate. He certainly cannot pretend to have dealt with it by a method which is logically irrelevant. His insistence that science deals with mind as well as matter, with life as well as the inorganic, may be justified; but it fails to bear on the metaphysical question, which concerns the principle or principles common to all possible matter or mind, the level of matter or mind lying beneath the dichotomy into what is and what might be.

As to the "proofs for the existence of God," the more clearly they are worked out, the more obviously do they take this form. Freud barely mentions the proofs and says only that they come down to us from primitive times in documents full of contradictions, revisions, interpolations—from which one gathers that he does not mean metaphysical proofs but proofs from miracles, prophecies, and the like. Once more he is dismissing metaphysics as insignificant or as at best offering us a "vague abstraction" in place of the "mighty personality of religious doctrine."

Now, according to our own theory, the "essence" of God is abstract. But it is to be borne in mind that this essence is not the whole story of our doctrine; for this essence is one that makes it necessary or certain that there be something concrete and actual which is expressive of the essence, a "consequent nature of God" as well as a primordial nature. Moreover, the dipolar theory of deity makes God in a definite sense a person, with a life of experiences embodying a persistent personality trait or character, and with *de facto* particular purposes and appreciations as well as a fixed general purpose or goal, with percepts as well as concepts, passive reception or sympathetic sensitivity as well as active influence upon others. What this means is that the program of life so eloquently expounded by Freud as that which makes love central is elevated to a higher plane upon which the difficulties he points out are no longer so desperate. In God we have an object of love which cannot die or shut us out from its life; and this object includes all our objects within itself. Thus, without turning away from life in this world as it really is, we can always be loving the universal Person, the Thou in the relation to which every I-Thou relation is embraced, as Buber says.

How is it, then, with the problem of loving one's neighbor if, as is all too likely, he is not a lovable individual? This is a most difficult matter indeed, and we have no easy answer. But the religious injunction is to love God first and above all and the neighbor as in God. The sense of the divine unity actually embracing self and neighbor alters the feeling of the relation with him. Freud (but also many preachers, no doubt) leaves out much in religious teaching here. To love neighbor as self is not a simple command, like "Do not commit murder," but a statement of the religious ideal. Moreover, "salvation is by faith, not by works," that is, love of God is the presupposition of adequate love of men.

Freud's admission that we have reason to love the son of a friend seems logically to apply to all creatures in relation to God, for the very reason Freud gives—if God is viewed panentheistically as sharing in our experiences! Loving neighbor as self means that, like the Good Samaritan, we are to take his needs seriously, in spite of the fact that his pains are inside his skin, not ours. Neighborly love is realization of the actual situation and feelings of the other, so far as responsibility for him is thrust by circumstances upon us, and so far as such realization is within our power; and, according to our doctrine, it is action designed to further the good of the other as, with ourselves, embraced in the life of God. Neighborly love is not in competition with the delight in special friends, or in particularly fine personalities; but it is opposed to the tendency to look upon men whose lives we have power to help or hinder, as though they had no vivid feelings or needs of their own but were mere foils for our feelings and means to our needs.

The patterns for living set forth by Freud under the heading of work, cooperation for the common good, and creative action in art and science can be fully embraced under purified religion as love of God—conceived as Father, if you will, but in a sense in which the infantile cannot conceive of fatherhood. We create in and for the divine life, which is itself supremely creative but also supremely able to appropriate the creative achievements of others. We are fellow-workers with and for God and with and for other men in God. Thus all the diverse patterns among which Freud says religion will not allow us to choose freely according to our individual capacities are in fact open to us in purified religion. But they are shown as aspects of one pattern with great alternative possibilities of emphasis.

Concerning the death instinct and the aggressiveness of men, we remark that if the experience is the unit of actuality,

and if death is the aesthetically appropriate termination of a given personal sequence of actualities, without prejudice to their immortality, and if this immortality of experiences amounts to the preservation of all the reality that the human person in question has ever possessed in life, then death is in all truth a goal of life and not in principle its frustration. So perhaps there is a deep truth in the notion that death is an "instinct." Whether morbid distortions or displacements of this instinct account in part for the remarkable destructiveness of man is a question we do not attempt to answer. (One may suspect that the incompatibility among possible values is more to the point.) As for the suggestion that this destructiveness contradicts the religious teaching that man is made in the image of God, it seems strange that no mention is made of the doctrine of the Fall of Man. The image is a distorted image, according to the teaching. True enough, the role of the devil is hardly explanatory of this situation, and no doubt religious doctrine has been less than luminous at this point. But still, granted the freedom of the creature, its self-creative capacity, one can see that there might be failure to image God in the optimal way indicated for the given species of creature.

Here it is important to note that Freud not only is a positivist but, like his predecessor Hume, is (it seems) a determinist. He is so impressed with causality, for which however he can have no ontological basis, that he never achieves a conception of self-creativity, free from compromise with an assumed absolute determination by antecedent conditions. In an age in which the most exact science, physics, has attenuated its determinism, it is annoying to hear psychologists tell us that Freud has shown how even mental phenomena are rigorously determined. A science so far from absolute rigor in its methods as psychology would show a more becoming modesty if it refrained from such pronouncements. Of course mental phenomena reflect their conditions. Who ever doubted it save undisciplined minds? But "reflect" is one thing; "are fully determined by" is another.

Concerning the Freudian use of the term "illusion," there is the following to be said. Such a belief as that a person will awaken after death to find departed friends still in continued existence ready to welcome him and will possess a body immune to injury or disease or suffering has perhaps no basis other than wishes. But the decisive point is not simply that they embody wishes rather than evidence; the decisive philosophical point is that the values they envisage are not indispensable values; the wishes they embody are not inevitable wishes. Life can have an intelligible aim which does not imply such benefits. Other wishes can be put in the place of the wish for heaven as above characterized. But suppose there are elements of purpose implied in all purposes or of wishing implied in all wishes. Then it is impossible to wish or will to accept the denial of such elements, such values inherent in all values. For example, the scientist's faith in the reality of an order of nature which is there for his discovering—is this faith wishful? If one insists upon certain special reqirements for the order, that it be absolute, totally exclusive of any disorder or creative novelty, then we are faced indeed with a wishful distortion of the faith in order. But that there is some principle of order, along with whatever principle of chaos or creativity there may be, is not a wishful thought, since it has no alternative that can genuinely be chosen. Now, similarly, that the value of experience be not destroyed by the passage of time, that our achievement have some sort of abidingness, is an equally indispensable belief. No matter what value we wish for in particular, we do not wish this value to be first something and then nothing.

To see how absurd "illusion" is in such a context, consider the question: What constitutes "truth" about experience which is past and humanly forgotten—say, the myriads of experiences of forgotten and unrecorded generations of men in prehistoric times? If these experiences simply do not exist, then how is there truth about them? Can definite truth be about something so indefinite as nothing? Or is the sum of facts we or any human minds can definitely know about the past equal to the sum of truths about it? Surely in some humanly transcendent sense the past is still real, its very having-been somehow still is. What is such a having-been which still is? The only positively intelligible answer is the simple one: divine memory.

In all these matters we are dealing with metaphysical, not scientific, questions; and in metaphysics the distinction between what satisfies desire and what does not is meaningless, for this distinction concerns alternative possible facts, not principles common to all possible facts. Any world would have order, and any world would provide for the permanence of truth and hence of value, once achieved. These are not special values, with alternatives, but the way in which there is any real value at all. If in the long run all achievement is to be as though it had not been, then "achievement" has no meaning. Again, the objection to Freud's determinism is not simply that it interferes with some special value of freedom but that it implicitly denies even the value of order, which is significant because there is something to be ordered, and this something is spontaneity, creation of novelty. Causality is the imposing of due limits upon unpredictable novelty, not the negation of such novelty. Once more we confront the Law of Polarity.

In sum, we think that Freud has drawn up a tremendous indictment, partly sound, of traditional religion.

But we deny his right to impose a veto upon the growth and purification of religion, and we assert that the dipolar concept of deity offers genuine human values fully compatible with a realistic devotion to life on this earth as it is but additional to any which science alone can furnish. These additional values are not those of mere emotion but rather and essentially of the intelligence. It is man's intelligence which makes death a problem for him and which makes him seek a unity transcendent of mere self-interest or altruism, a unity of meaning which in principle embraces all life in a single goal—the goal of enriching the inclusive experience of the universal person. (Incidentally, Freud's remark that there can be no "meaning of life" plausibly inclusive of animals is untrue, for the inclusive experience can savor the vividness of sensation and feeling actualized in animals and integrate it into a higher synthesis along with human feeling and thought.)

Granted that there is much wishful distortion, much infantilism, much neurosis, in existing religion, which one may hope mankind will outgrow, it still remains a distinct question, confused with the first by Freud, whether such a religious idea as that of God will disappear in the process. That family and civilized life imposes distortions upon the idea may have been proved by psychoanalysis; but the basic issue is metaphysical and not scientific or factual. It seems also not to occur to Freud that an eternally real divine love would naturally manifest itself in its creations through more or less remote analogies and that the existence of family life may have for one of its purposes the very development in its members of the sense of cosmic parenthood which Freud analyzes. One needs only to add that the purification of this sense from infantile crudities and pathological distortions may also be a divine goal, despite our author's almost angry denunciation of the attempts at such purification. His grasp of their direction and intent is much too vague and incorrect to justify his attitude.

# Chapter XIV: *A Skepticism Based on Analysis of Meaning*

## DENNES (1898———)

In our general Introduction we pointed out that God, as the categorically supreme and necessary being, is not a mere fact and that the question of his existence and essential nature is a question of meaning. The emphasis in contemporary philosophy upon questions of meaning is thus favorable to a clarification of the theistic issue. Logical positivists (or, as they prefer to be called, logical empiricists) who say that "God" is a meaningless symbol are more worthy opponents for a theologian than the atheist who says that there is no God. For the atheist, as Anselm proved, is talking nonsense. It is vastly more difficult to prove that he who says, " 'God' stands for nonsense," is himself uttering nonsense—or a falsehood. (Nonsense here means: without consistent meaning, such as could be true or false.)

The question of meaning is the question of our own human meanings. We can mean something by words only through our experience. If "empirical" be taken broadly enough, then, as Dennes says, the empirical theory of meaning "has no alternative." If everything in our experience could be exactly the same whether "there is a God" were true or false, then the statement is no statement, is meaningless. Our author here seeks to show that no difference in either the facts or the values in our experiences is implied by the acceptance or the denial of theism. Hence the theistic question is nonsensical.

Order in the world does not and could not prove God; for any possible world would be ordered. That the future is humanly predictable does not and could not prove God; for the future is predictable or unpredictable by us only on the basis of our knowledge, not that of the divine. That some things are more valuable than others does not and could not prove God; for we mean by "valuable" only that we and other men take delight in and treasure these things. If we do this, we do it regardless of the assertion or denial of a God.

To say that God delights in what men hate is to make God a devil and to rob of all meaning the proposition, "God is good." So reference to God is only a detour; we must always come back to the one essential question, "Do we men reasonably predict or prize the thing or not?" The challenge is subtle and forceful. What can the theist say in reply?

### The Criterion of Meaning

*691. The meaning of a statement or proposition . . .* is the state of affairs the occurrence of which would make the statement true, its non-occurrence, false. Now, since terms mean experienced or experienceable objects (including relations, qualities, orders), it follows that the combinations of terms which are statements can only mean the observable states of affairs which they assert or predict. (Observable, *nota bene*, not necessarily actually observed).

*692.* It follows at once from this account that there is no strict meaning in discourse about deity if deity is taken both as beyond all possible experience and (what amounts to the same) as having no effect on, as making no difference in, what can be experienced.

*693.* The notion of deity we shall consider will be (like the Platonic, Judaic, Catholic, and all but the most modernistic Protestant notions) the notion of a deity who is not just the world, and whose existence and action does not fail to make some difference in the observable world.

694. We come now to the central questions: (1) What may we regard as evidence for belief in such a god. . . ? (2) In what ways would belief in such a god contribute to the explanation of anything in nature or history? (3) Can religion, as we have defined it [an insight that purports to relate nature to a god], be regarded as "grounding values" or as determining what conduct is right? (4) In what sense, if in any, does religion give meaning and richness to experience?

## The Arguments for God

There is a striking circularity in most treatments of these questions. The orderliness, the organic relatedness, the human usefulness of examined stretches of nature, are represented as understood by us and as constituting evidence of the existence of a divine intelligence controlling nature, whether as creator, as director, or as final cause. But then it is said that the very phenomena which we used as evidence of a god's existence (and we could not have used them as evidence if we had not understood them) cannot themselves be understood, or indeed exist at all, except by reference to the deity whose character and existence we inferred from them. Again, we are told that types of value, graded and ordered as they are in our appreciation, are evidence of the existence and nature of god; but in turn, the deity, whose character and existence were inferred from the order of values, not only guarantees the validity of the types of value and determines their order, but constitutes their valuableness itself. From the vast number of accounts of the gods—their ways, their laws, their preferences—we are advised

to select that account as worthy of belief which represents god as good, or as the best; and then we are told that the ground—indeed the very essence—of goodness is constituted by the will or law or preference of the deity.

695. As evidence for the existence of god as a controlling intelligence, people have considered the coherence, the organic relatedness, of natural processes; and also what is called the purposefulness of some of these. It is interesting here to remember that the coherent order of nature was used by the Epicureans as "proof" that the world is a machine, and by the Stoics (their contemporaries) as "proof" that the world is, not a machine, but a living intelligent animal. As a matter of fact, it is proof of neither of these theories, nor of any other. The fact is that, with or without a god, with or without "mechanism" or "organism," no entities can exist together or comprise a "world," except such as do not annul one another. That is, any possible complex of events will be such that all are adjusted to the others, and none is ruled out as "contradictory." Some sorts of complex order suit human purposes better than others —e.g., an order in which on the surface of the earth there are regions with what we call temperatures between the freezing and boiling points of water. But a state of affairs in which there were no "temperate zones" would be just as coherent and orderly—every factor in it would be as well adjusted to all others as in that "coherent order" which most men prefer. No, coherence in things is no evidence of a controlling intelligence, for *with or without such an intelligence there could be nothing that was not coherent.* And the existence of some *particular* sort of coherent order, suitable, e.g., to human life, is no evidence of a controlling intelligence, for no such thing as disorder or chaos is possible with or without god (there could only be various orders, more or

less "complex"); and among orders we cannot say that any one is as such more or less intelligible, more or less congenial to a divine theoretic intelligence, than is any other.

But if the order of nature does, in certain stretches, suit man, is that evidence that not merely a theoretic intelligence, but an intelligence interested in man, produced it or controls it? Logically, of course, it no more constitutes such evidence than does the "suitableness" of the distintegration of a comet to the being and career of the derivative meteors, constitute such evidence. All stretches of natural process that occur at all are perfectly suited to their ingredients and their "environment," and to say so much of any existent is to say no more than that it exists as what it is. Logically, reference of the order of nature, or of any area of nature, to a divine intelligence adds nothing, as explanation, to the scientific description of nature.

*696.* Certainly power as such will not distinguish gods from devils, as the mediaeval theologians clearly saw. And the exhibition of power to divide the waves, halt the sun, or raise the dead would be no ground for supposing, with respect to him who exhibited such power, that whatever he said was true, and whatever he commanded, right for men. If any person—a prophet, a priest, a seer, or one claiming a nearer intimacy, or even identity, with deity—should by his words or acts halt, or divert, or accelerate the usual processes of nature in such a way as to serve human good, we should prize that person as we do, for example, the skilled and generous surgeon or the enlightening teacher. But if the person, or his interpreters, told us that he had no merely human or natural or limited power to produce goods, but could, if he chose, abolish all evil—if he told us that, but did not proceed to acts of universal benevolence, and to a satisfactory explanation of the merely occa-

sional character of his past benefactions, we should either doubt his truthfulness, his power, or his benevolence. Of course, theodicies (at least since the Book of Job) have argued that evils are right as being indispensable to the chastening, discipline, and perfecting of souls. But on such a view, we have no way to distinguish the acts of devils from the work of gods, since there is no conceivable degree or duration of what we men call evil of which we may not, logically, quite as well as of the smallest difficulty or obstacle, say that it supplies the test and discipline necessary to our perfecting. On such a view, there is no difference between right and wrong. Everything that happens we must say ought to happen. And hence our words "right," "wrong," and "ought" lose all significance save as synonyms for "whatever happens in the world."

It is sometimes said that the world is only intelligible by reference to deity because prediction would be nonsense save in a "law-bound world," and that the conception of deity is precisely the conception of the power able to bind the world ineluctably by law. We meet here the confusion between law as command that processes follow a certain pattern, and law as description of a pattern of events joined with advice to expect further instances of the pattern. Now if god's laws (as commands) are never broken, there is no way of distinguishing a world bound by them from a world whose configuration exhibits whatsoever particular factual regularity that it does. But those who insist that god is in this sense a presupposition of intelligibility probably mean, not that predictions would mean nothing save in a law-bound world, but rather that we could not, except in such a world, know in advance that our predictions would turn out to be true. But this we could not know anyway, since a deity could by no sign to us guarantee the future. If he enjoyed a knowledge *totum simul,* he might know that his promises would be kept, but *he could not make us know it* unless he gave us the vision *totum simul* too—*in which case our "knowledge of the future," and not god's guarantee, would be our assurance.* Short of our appropriation of universal vision, it would be only by the postulate that particular regularities, or patterns of growth, will pervade all nature that we could say this would be the case. And the postulate remains postulate whether or not it is cast in theistic terms.

Historically, the great philosophical theologies that have been constructed as metaphysical groundings of nature have all turned out to be either *a* descriptions of the world in a novel language; or *b* truisms or tautologies (some important, some unimportant); *c* irrelevant;—and usually they have been combinations of all three. Aristotle's deity is the illegitimately inferred and quite irrelevant ground of unending process. Whitehead's theory of the primordial and consequent natures of god seems to tell us no more than that: (1) Everything is possible; (2) Some part of what is possible has occurred or is occurrent; (3) Nothing ever can occur which should undo or annul any actual occurrence. These are all truisms. Far from being an inference of god from nature, or an explanation of nature in terms of god, they are merely exhibitions of (very appropriate) definitions of "possibility" and "existence." But the language in which they are cast raises very different hopes—or even convictions—in most readers.

### Deity and the Question of Value

But perhaps we are looking in the wrong direction for the grounds of theism when we examine cosmologies and their alleged theistic presuppositions. God's laws, we are often told, are moral commandments, rather than descriptions or prescriptions of natural or-

der (if such prescriptions are taken as anything but moral). Here we must face two related questions. The first (Plato's question in the *Euthyphro,* and Kant's in his *Religion Innerhalb der Grenzen der Blossen Vernunft*): Can the commands, or the will, of deity make anything right that would not be right irrespective of such commands? or add anything to the rightness of what is right irrespective of them? The second is the question: How do we recognize moral commands as proceeding authentically from deity?

We cannot consider these questions without some explanation of what we shall mean by "value" or "good," and by "right." I understand "valuable" to mean that in which man (or plants or animals) are positively interested, that in which delight is taken. And "right" I take to be the adjective that designates such actions as will probably yield (in their particular situation) the most valuable results, in the sense of "valuable" just defined.

*697.* But if interest or delight make their objects valuable, should we then have to say that the objects of God's interest or delight or love have at least as good (for the religious, incomparably better) claims to be called valuable as have any objects or acts or institutions in which men may delight? No. Not only are we not obliged to say this, but should we try to say it we should be making a verbal distinction which expressed no distinction of meaning. For *the only ground any of us could have for sincerely accepting certain revealed preferences as the preferences of gods and not of devils, is the ground that the preferences agree with our own.* Hence we are unable to say that what we call divine preferences can institute, or can enhance, values so as to distinguish them in any way from the objects of human love. If divine preferences differed from our own, we could not sincerely describe them as determining what we should call valuable. Of course, we may trust a friend's, or an expert's, or a prophet's judgment rather than our own. But in matters of value, such trust is reasonable only as expressing the hope and expectation that, if we had the wider experience of him whose judgment we trust, we should share his preference. We can have no grounds for such expectation except the knowledge that our preference and the expert's agree with respect to some (or all) of those objects with which we are both acquainted, plus the evidence that the expert is probably acquainted with a wider range of objects than we are. And nothing could verify our expectation or justify our trust except the discovery that, in the event, we do come actually to agree with the expert's preference as we become conversant with the situations about which he advised us when we were ignorant of them. The expert's, or the god's, preference, therefore, can never be recognized as binding upon us until it becomes our preference. And, once it becomes our own preference, it constitutes its object valuable in the only sense in which we can significantly or honestly call anything valuable for us, quite independently of any expert or authoritative preference. The new values which, following upon expert advice, we may come to appreciate are, in their status as valuable, independent of whatever influences may have led us to discover them.

698. . . . the value of what we love is just the same, no matter who introduces us to it, or with what promises or persuasion or commands—no matter, indeed, whether we are unable to specify anybody or anything as having done the introducing.

699. If we reject the definitions of "right" and "valuable" which I have employed, and define "the right" as simply "what God commands," how are we to determine which of the various commands, offered to us by diverse religions as having divine origin and authority, are actually what their sponsors say they are? We have here a difficulty precisely analogous to that which faced us when we tried to find a way of distinguishing such cosmic laws as were divine, from merely human descriptions and predictions. Plato seems here unanswerable, though his own asserted criteria of rightness are unsatisfactory. His view (in the *Euthyphro*) is that unless we know what is right by some mark other than that a god (or even all the gods) commands it, we shall be unable to distinguish the commands of gods from the commands of imposters. For although a command is punctuated by thunderbolts, or miraculously written on stone tablets, or spoken insistently in the hearts of men, it does not follow that it would be right to obey the command—unless we mean by "right" nothing more than obedience to the thunderer, or the carver of stone tablets, or the still small voice. If we have reason for obeying any of these, it can only be that its expressions have seemed to us true and righteous in terms of *our* norms of truth and right. And, if the expressions were thus, and upon such grounds, true and righteous, then they were (and are) true and righteous whether they are said to be the voice of God or the voice of conscience, or are given no such reference to anything beyond what they themselves convey or advise.

We seem to be driven to the conclusion, foreshadowed in Plato's *Euthyphro*, and expressed in our time by Benedetto Croce in his *Filosofia dello Spirito*, and by Professor Dewey in his article, "Is There a God?" in a recent issue of the *Christian Century*. It is the conclusion that religious experience and theological doctrine add nothing to the meaning or truth of any statement or to the validity of any rule of conduct—add nothing which is not finally traceable to, and which does not owe its meaning and its probability to, observations and loves and preferences which remain what they are, and mean all that they do, whether or not they are referred to, or taken as evidence of, deity. As Dewey expresses it, the term "God" cannot be given meaning save as designating some experienceable processes—such as the "multitude of factors and forces which are brought together simply with respect to their coincidence in producing one undesigned effect—the furtherance of good in human life." The confused notion that reference to deity confers validity has sometimes fired men's hearts to great undertakings. Unfortunately we must judge many of those undertakings to have been intolerant, mean-spirited, full of a persecuting zeal the more hideous because it pretended to an assurance of impeccable righteousness. And of the undertakings, those we regard as noble and fine, we so regard because they were aimed towards, or contributed to, the things we love—not because they were commanded by any sort of authority—terrestrial or celestial.

It remains true, of course, that some religious geniuses have been among the wisest and noblest of men. That from their sayings, and from the example of their lives, we have a great deal to learn. Indeed, about some aspects of the conduct of life, many of the most accomplished of our moralists seem as innocent babes when compared with some of the "saints." But if our analysis has been acceptable, there is very great danger in confusing the truth and the rightness of what any man says, with the alleged authority of the speaker or of the speaker's source or inspiration. The nub of the whole matter is that such confusion leaves us no way whatever to distinguish the better from the worse, or "false gods from true."

The great danger to values in our time—to the very values which the greatest religious geniuses have loved—is that we may far too insufficiently perceive those values (perceiving them requires much study, much discipline, much labor), far too little appreciate them, and serve them. If we think their whole validity rests upon a theological sanction, then the moment that sanction is thrown into doubt (as it is to-day upon all sides, and for cogent reasons), at that very moment our confidence in the values themselves is destroyed. But if we took seriously what is actually the case, viz., that "whatsoever things are true, whatsoever things are honest, whatsoever things are just, whatsoever things are pure, whatsoever things are lovely, whatsoever things are of good report," are lovely and good for those who delight in them, and will be for all persons who may be brought to know and delight in them, irrespective of reference to authority—then no doubts could assail us, except the very proper and fruitful doubt whether we are taking the likeliest means to spread among men for their happiness, an appreciation of the fair practices, the beautiful objects and interesting techniques, and the knowledge, which we may love and know to be good.

*700.* Religion has been a great and precious symbol for much that is dearest to us. Its scriptures, its liturgy, its poetry and building and music and painting, are among the finest achievements of man. It was once sincerely believed that, without reference to deity, all these achievements must lose their worth. It is a great and tragic irony that this very belief should now be a source of danger to the values it was supposed to establish. For thoughtful men are coming to see that, irrespective of questions as to their truth or probability, references to deity cannot have the meanings once supposed. Hence, so far as they should hold the belief that divine sanction is the ground of excellence, they are now likely to become, not only skeptical of, but even cynically indifferent to, the values that have been dear to the religious.

*701.* The various goods the religions have enshrined stand on their own feet in human experience. All that we must give up is the meaningless conviction that we had reached absolutes—absolute truths about the whole cosmos, absolute duties irrespective of their results in experience, absolute values "valid" irrespective of human preference. This conviction added nothing to the preciousness of anything. All too often it lulled men's efforts by a false sense of security, and blinded them to the pains that must be taken if what is valuable is to be defended against its enemies, and developed and extended in the lives of men.

[Sec. 691, William R. Dennes, "Preface to an Empiricist Philosophy of Religion," *College of the Pacific Publications in Philosophy*, ed. Paul Arthur Schilpp (Stockton, Calif.: College of the Pacific, 1934), III, 114. Sec. 692, *ibid.*, p. 115. Sec. 693, *ibid.* Sec. 694, *ibid.*, p. 113. Sec. 695, *ibid.*, p. 117. Sec. 696, *ibid.*, pp. 119–21. Sec. 697, *ibid.*, pp. 121–22. Sec. 698, *ibid.*, p. 122. Sec. 699, *ibid.*, pp. 123–24. Sec. 700, *ibid.*, p. 125. Sec. 701, *ibid.*]

## COMMENT

The first question is, "Does God make a difference in experience?" On the dipolar view we must distinguish two aspects of God: his contingent factual reality and his necessary or essential reality. The former does indeed make a difference, since it consists of actual divine responses to the world which in turn become stimuli to which the world responds. But these actual responses of God cannot be clearly discerned. The difference they make is hidden in the subtle depths of motivation. To see what God is now doing to me would be to see an all-knowing evaluation of my world as stimulus to my response to life, and in seeing this I would myself be all-knowing. I can subconsciously feel the stimulus—if theism is correct, I do feel it—but I cannot clearly discern it, even definitely imagine it.

This does not make the idea meaningless. For, if theism is correct, what I might be able to see is that there must be *some* such all-knowing evaluation. The generic essence of omniscience may be accessible in a purely abstract and general way. For this essence is no mere fact. It does not make a difference as between one possible experience and another; for it is (if anything whatever), the common categorical feature of any experience and any world. The idea of an "adequate knower" is that of an individual whose content of knowing is coincident with reality, an individual to whom any actual fact is known as actual, and to whom any possible fact, *were* it actual, *would* be known as actual. Dennes may think this is nonsense. But he cannot prove it by insisting that it should make a factual difference. By definition, the mere existence of God cannot make a factual difference, since this existence is conceived as an aspect of every possible fact. That or nothing! If the existence and the nonexistence of a being with unrestricted power of knowing are both to be conceived as possible facts, then we have the paradox that one of these possible facts *could not* be known as actualized by the unrestricted power of knowing—which therefore is restricted after all! The conclusion is that, if the idea of such a power has consistent meaning, its existence cannot be factual but only categorical, necessary. Only the accidental states and content of the all-knowing can be matters of fact or "make a difference" in experience.

Our author does not entirely ignore the view of God as categorical, but he tries to show that such a view must be empty, abstract, and without religious significance (sec. 696). What he seems to overlook here is that ultimate categories belong together and that they express experience, not mere being or events—whatever these might be apart from experience. (That experience consists of events we do not dispute.) One difference between our author and, say, Whitehead, to whom he refers, is that the latter is more careful to avoid the "fallacy of misplaced concreteness." For Whitehead, such terms as "possibility," "fact," "past," are mere words except in relation to the modes or aspects of experience which they indicate. Also the basic modes of experience are mutually integral to one another. "God" stands for the unity of the basic ideas and for their inseparability from experience as such; he is that unity of experiential modes which is universal to reality as such and *is* its universality.

The "hopes" which Dennes speaks of as irrelevant are indeed so if they go beyond what is implicit in the mere idea of God as just characterized; for instance, if they involve some arbitrary notion of personal immortality or heavenly rewards and punishments. But if they merely mean that the basic category of *actuality* is not to be divorced from the equally basic experiential mode of *value*, or that past is not separable from memory, or future from anticipation, so that the inclusive actuality must be an inclusive value and the indelible past must be an all-embracing memory, then they merely amount to our enjoyment of that unity of thought and meaning and experience in which all universal categories have their validity.

The piecemeal treatment of categories, in which their relations to one another never really come into focus, is what seems to separate a positivistic treatment, such as Dennes' from a metaphysical one, such as that of Whitehead. To say "God" is indeed to say that there (necessarily) is a general store of possibility which is everlasting and inexhaustible, but it is also to say that the past is indelible and also that each thing has some inherent value thanks to which it contributes value to other things and to the inclusive reality, and so on and so on—all these general truths being focused into unity through the idea of a universal experience whose total richness coincides with that of the total reality and is the same thing. (Distinguishing them as really diverse can only, we affirm, amount to the fallacy of misplaced concreteness.)

Says our author: "With or without God, any possible complex of events will be such that all are adjusted to the others" or such that they "do not annul one another"—that is, they will be ordered. This we grant. But what it shows is that "the existence of God" as orderer of all things does not describe one possible state of affairs rather than another; it is an interpretation of what is common to all possible states of affairs. Order is indeed something thus common; but the theist sees, as the full meaning of this, that the coherence of the divine life is bound, in any possible world, to express itself in an orderliness of that world's events. God is not something simply additional to the order; he is the order most deeply and clearly understood, in relation to other categorical features common to all possible world states. Similarly, a human personality is not something simply additional to the order in the events of the human body; the personal coherence and the bodily coherence are two inseparable aspects of one reality. But the human personality is a merely factual order, which dissolves at death and largely dissolves temporarily in extreme illness. Divine personality (in its essential rather than accidental features) is a categorical order, the order of any and all possible world arrangements. This is the only such categorical order or coherence there is and, therefore, the only categorical personality.

Consider again the question of values. If we find a deep joy in the love of our children and in fostering their growth into happy and loving personalities, then I at least should agree emphatically with the statement that these experiences contain genuine values, whatever beings may exist or not exist. But since the existence of God, by definition, is categorical, to say that the values are genuine "whether there be a God or not," is to talk nonsense. It is contrary to meaning to speak of God's not existing. We are not comparing two hypotheses, experience in a world without God and experience in a world with God. We are comparing two ways of conceiving all experience and reality, one or the other of which (as we know a priori or from meanings alone) must be absurd: (1) experiences of value such as ours, limited, imperfect in space and time, in wisdom and generosity, constitute all the experience there is; (2) these experiences are in intuitive (often, or usually, largely unconscious) contact with experience which is categorical in its excellence and mode of existence.

Whichever of these conceptions is correct, the other must be absurd, a pseudo-conception only. This means that it violates all our meanings. If the nontheistic alternative is thus absurd, then not even Dennes can really entertain it except verbally. Of course, then, he feels that he could not be forced to give up his values by his refusal to espouse theism; his values, and all his meanings, must already implicitly or intuitively give him in principle what the theist has. All he can lack is the full awareness of the relations of these values to the categorical features of reality. He lacks the conscious expression of his intuitions.

Thus it is notable that Dennes says nothing about the question of the long-run goal of endeavor, whether the expanding human good he envisages will expand and endure forever or perhaps end in some final race catastrophe, and nothing about the transitoriness of all particular values as inhering in particular experiences which themselves, apart from theistic interpretation, seem utterly transitory phenomena, destined to vanish into oblivion. This transitoriness is not something significant merely because some superhuman being worries himself about it; it is we men who are interested in the relation of the present to the future and who prize permanence, some sort of ultimate abidingness, in achievement. And we cannot, apart from the idea of God, consciously conceive any such abidingness. But also in terms of space, as well as time, there is something frustrating and baffling about our value-experiences, if not taken theistically. We feel that two happy men, one here, one there, are better than one. But what does this mean? How can two joys be added to make a greater value, if value is joy and if no actual joy includes both my happiness and yours? If there is a divine joy thus inclusive, the puzzle is solved. True, we ourselves will then take delight in the thought of this inclusive delight. But we will not actually and effectively possess its inclusiveness.

Dennes reminds us that all value we can recognize must be somehow expressible in human terms. But the necessity for a human correlate of all our values does not eliminate the necessity for a divine correlate. There is such a thing as our delight in the delight of another, and why not a superhuman other?

In section 697 ("Of course, we may trust a friend's . . . judgment . . .") our author is close to seeing the theist's point. In so far as we come to experience what a wiser friend, not we, is at present aware of, our valuations will tend to take on similarities to his which they now lack. But the question at issue here, not mentioned by the author, is whether or not we could be in an analogous relation to a friend or expert whose superiority to us is categorical and not factual only, and whether, and how, we could recognize this superiority! There is needed here a distinction between abstract and concrete valuation. Abstractly, we value what God values, namely, joy and love and richness of experience in all sentient beings (according to Dennes even in plants). But only in principle, in utmost vagueness. When we think calmly about it, and reach genuine self-understanding, what we approve of is, in a vague general way, the very thing God approves of. Otherwise, as Dennes rightly says, we could not meaningfully say, "God is good." But we also know that in moments of specific decision we tend to forget about the universal welfare and to think chiefly about that of ourselves and our special favorites; and we know also that at best we never concretely and accurately grasp the joy or sorrow of others, even of one other, let alone all sentient creatures!

If then we feel ourselves related to one who can concretely and accurately value what we only abstractly, vaguely, more or less incorrectly apprehend in our valuations, why should we not also feel that it is his valuations which are inclusive of all real value? If we can conceive these inclusive valuations as preserved in an indestructible memory, then we need no longer feel puzzled or baffled by the sense of life's transitoriness. It still can seem as important as

before to record history and life in documents and works of art; for the value of these things is in the *new* experiences they produce in posterity, who will derive from them not simply duplicates of the original experiences but new syntheses of feeling and thought through the contrast between the bygone and the contemporary.

Is it not clear that one who has the feelings above described has also values that cannot be had—we do not say "without God," for that is nonsense—but without theism as a conscious belief? For to feel that our valuations are included in a concretely, effectively, and accurately all-embracing love is to enjoy a feeling that cannot be enjoyed to the full by a nontheist. Now, either this feeling contains a delight or satisfaction peculiar to itself or it does not. If it does, then it is false that all the values religion cherishes can be had without (consciousness of) God. And how is Dennes to prove that the feeling does not contain its unique value? Or that the value which it contains is not fundamental to all our life, inspiring and sustaining it in such a way that it is not an accident but a principle that the "Saints" have tended to be exceptionally wise and noble? Admittedly much can be said against this supposition, but also much for it.

So we submit that the theistic question is at the least still open and meaningful, for all that skepticism, ancient and modern, has shown.

*Epilogue*

# Epilogue

## THE LOGIC OF PANENTHEISM[1]

702. Mathematics, pure logical form, is almost as important in knowledge as observation. One reason for this is particularly significant for philosophy. The function of observation is not merely to decide for or against some hypothesis but ultimately to decide among possible hypotheses. We do not merely test explanations one at a time against the facts; we bring to the facts a system of possible explanations to be evaluated against each other. The cogency of the procedure obviously depends, in part, upon whether or not the possibilities for explanation have been exhausted. To be sure of having surveyed all the possibilities, one must arange them in a formal way, by means of a mathematical diagram, algebraic or geometrical. When Kepler saw that the orbits of the planets were not circular, he had available the theory of conic sections—largely worked out long before by other mathematicians—which systematically displayed all the forms of simple curves of the class to which circles belong. When we argue about a philosophical problem, we are too little in the habit of looking for a similarly rigorous system of possibilities.

In philosophy we all too customarily employ loose, nonformal, and hence, for all we know, inexhaustive, divisions of doctrines or else the trivial formal division of positive and negative—as idealism and nonidealism, realism and nonrealism—where the negative case may conceal distinctions quite as relevant as that between it and the positive case. One then forces one's self

to believe the "best" theory one happens to hit upon or finds in the history of philosophy, with no guaranty that the really best, or true, theory has even been considered. And since errors may deviate from the truth in diverse directions to a roughly equal extent, it may be that, of the theories surveyed, there are several best ones which, though differing sharply from one another, are yet equally good (or bad) —so that only prejudice or taste can produce a decision among them. In view of the stubbornness of philosophical argument, who can fail to suspect that this has frequently occurred?

The purpose of this essay is to provide for one crucial philosophical problem an equivalent (or, at least, some indications of an equivalent) of the theory of conic sections in astronomy. Such a "mathematics of the theistic possibilities," of some aspects of which this will be a rough sketch, is not dependent for its value upon whether or not any form of theism is true or even meaningful. For the time to consider that question is after we know, in some formally exact way, what the possibilities are, even if they are only possible ways of falling into unmeaning. The blanket assertion in advance that none of the conceptions is capable of experiential verification begs the question. Indeed, as can be shown, the very meaning of "experiential" shifts according as one supposes the existence or nonexistence of a being corresponding to the diverse conceptions.

The various forms of theism differ from each other mainly in their attitude toward two questions: (1) Is God independent of the universe of entities other than himself, capable of existing

1. A revision of "A Mathematics of Theism," from *Review of Religion*, VIII (1943), 20–38.

without them, or is he not thus capable? (2) Is God a perfect being, and in what sense? Each of these questions has a formal structure by which it and its possible answers can be made more precise. In combination, the two approaches yield nine formally possible, exactly defined versions of "supreme being" (additional to any usual idea of "finite" or "imperfect" God). Most of these versions are missing from the classical discussions; and, indeed, the classical arguments for God, as well as the counterarguments, can be shown to depend for their apparent cogency upon restricting attention to some only of the nine cases. Also, there is reason to think that the neglected cases include one which, more than any other, is supported by religious insight. Thus the analysis serves to rectify not only formal errors in the interrelating of concepts but a material error in the interpretation of religion. This error concerning religion has recently been widely recognized as such by philosophers and theologians.

Let us consider first the question of independence. For orthodox theism, God is the independent universal cause or source; the universe, his extrinsic effect or outcome. The universe is "outside" the divine actuality, not a qualification or constituent of it. For pantheism (commonly supposed to be the alternative doctrine), God is the inclusive reality, and there is no ultimate cause distinct from and independent of the cosmic totality. The universe is within the divine actuality and qualifies its very essence or irreducible nature. Must a theist choose one or the other of these positions? Do they constitute a "Yes" and "No" in response to the same question? Or are they answers to several questions, which deserve separate consideration? Since at least three concepts appear to be involved—"independent," "cause," and "all-inclusive"—we may well suspect

that more than one issue is at stake. But, then, theism might be right on one of these issues, and pantheism on another! That is, there may be a "higher synthesis." If theism holds that God is independent and cause but not all-inclusive, and pantheism holds that God is all-inclusive but not independent, and perhaps not (at least in the sense intended by theism) cause, then the two theories are extreme opposites or contraries. But contraries may both be false! Perhaps God is in some manner all three—independent, cause, and all-inclusive? It is time to examine our three concepts in order to see how far they are logically compatible with one another.

What is the exact meaning of "cause" in theology? The term means at least this: something whose existence is requisite for, implied by, inferable from, the existence of its "effect"—in the theological case, all reality other than God. But is there a converse relation? If the effect requires the cause, does the cause also require the effect? The main theological tradition denies this of God. It holds that he is independent of the world, could exist without it, and is in no way qualified by its existence. The world is qualified by its utter dependence upon God, but God could have been himself, exactly as he is, without any world whatever. This makes God different in principle from what is ordinarily meant by a cause. From a cause one expects to derive consequences, make predictions; but from God, it seems, nothing follows. He has "made" the world, but, if he had made a different world or none at all, he would yet have been exactly what he is. Thus his effects do not seem in any sense to "follow from" their cause. We may call this a "radically asymmetrical" conception of causal necessity.

Modern thought suggests an alternative view. In current science a cause is sometimes conceived as related to its effect, not by necessity but by probability; and this means that the existence of the cause involves that there shall be some one of a class of more or less likely outcomes. The cause necessitates the occurrence of some effect or other with a specified range of variability. In physics this relation is even convertible, the effect necessitating not any uniquely specifiable cause but only a class of causes as variously probable. However, recent philosophy has marshaled evidence for the view that time is asymmetrical in its logical structure, so that, while the "earlier" never entails the "later" in its individual details, the later does strictly entail the earlier. A man's childhood is essential to his manhood, but not his manhood to his childhood. Not every child becomes a man at all, but every man has been a child. History, biology, and psychoanalysis support the view that the present involves the past at least more completely than it involves the future; and an attractive philosophy of time holds that this "asymmetrical involvement" inheres in the very meaning of earlier and later and that the past is involved absolutely (the past is "immortal"—Whitehead, Bergson), while the future involvement requires only some member or other of a given class. But this it does require. Let us call such asymmetry "moderate" rather than "radical." If such be the cause-effect relation, then there can be a formal analogy between divine and other causation. God's existence would make it inevitable that there be a world but only possible that there be just this sort of world. Deity would be independent of (would not require or necessitate) any particular world, but he would not be independent of world-as-such. The "supreme cause," as pure or universal cause, would be that which, being required by all other things, itself requires only that the class "possible worlds" has some actual member.

We may now face the time-honored query: Is not every cause itself an effect, so that a cause of all things other than itself is an absurdity? To be effect, we have decided, is to require something else which does not in turn require the given thing, unless in the moderate sense of requiring the nonnullity of its class. That "causes are always also effects" means then that, besides being required as antecedents by certain things, they themselves require still other things as their antecedent conditions. The regress seems infinite, at least if time has had no beginning. Let us not dispute this infinity. But note that the causes ere in question are concrete events. That there could be a concrete cause not itself effect of anything, I do not wish to affirm. But our definition of cause does not limit itself to concrete factors or conditions. Anything (abstract or concrete) required by, but not (unless in the "moderate" sense defined) requiring, something is a cause of that something, by our terminology. It is left open whether it is all that is required, whether it is "the" cause or "sufficient condition" of it. We have not wished yet to raise the question of whether deity is to be conceived as in this sense "the" cause of things.

We have so far only formulated a possible definition: God as supreme (in the sense of universal) cause is what is universally required by other things and which itself requires only that the class of other things be not null. What is there inconsistent in this definition? Perhaps it does imply that God, *qua* universal or supreme cause, is not concrete but abstract. Very well, I have no objection. I have not said that God is *only* the supreme cause; therefore, though this cause may be abstract, God in his total reality may yet be concrete. (Something concrete may have an abstract aspect.) In this concreteness he may indeed be effect as well as cause, which means that he may require other things than himself to be just what he concretely and in fact is. In this his concrete total actuality God may interact with the world, receiving as well as imparting influence. Such a reactive being could not simply be identified with the supreme cause. But still it might, in an aspect of itself, be this cause.

Taken concretely, deity would not be merely supreme cause but rather supreme power or agency, in the sense in which a man is a power or agency. A man as a power is not a single cause but a stream of causes, each of which is also an effect. God as an agent or power is not, perhaps, to be conceived as *a* cause of all things, nor yet as *the* cause of all things, but rather as a (or *the*) supreme stream of causation which at the same time is the supreme stream of effects. Thus, the criticism of the cosmological argument that it takes "cause" out of the chain of causation in which alone it has meaning is justified only if the cosmological argument is taken as reducing God's causal role to a single type of relationship. We have to take account of the possibility that the divine is cause in two senses, analogously to the double sense in which a man is cause. (1) A man at each moment makes decisions, responses to the world, which in turn become stimuli to which other individuals respond. Here all meaning is lost if we try to isolate "being cause" from "being effect." Perhaps, in this aspect, the deity is as truly acted upon as acting. (2) But suppose a man throughout the years is inspired by a certain persistent idea or ideal, which also, as his ideal, influences others. Once he has acquired the ideal, it functions from thenceforth as cause rather than as effect, even though the original acquisition was an effect. Could there not be a primordial mind with an *un*acquired ideal, thus one which was never an effect? And would

this ideal not have effects? In its mere possession of this ideal, the primordial mind would be purely cause rather than effect. But it in no way follows that all the mind's experiences, perceptions, of concrete actualities would be purely causative rather than themselves effects. Ideas and ideals, being abstract, have, in proportion to their abstractness, a certain independence of the concrete alternatives of existence; but true perceptions of the concrete and actual, on the contrary, cannot disagree with the particular features which the actual happens to have. They are thus not independent; they are effects. But they will also have effects and be themselves causes. In this way, the reader can perhaps see why I maintain that, on the one hand, universal cause, pure cause, need not exhaust the sense in which God is cause, while, on the other hand, there is no absurdity in this idea of pure cause, provided its concreteness is not asserted.

The correctness of all this is not assumed in what follows but only the possibility of its correctness. We are seeking the views that cannot be ruled out offhand as impossible, in order, among the not obviously impossible views, to find the true one. Yet we shall assume, as a matter of word usage, that a "cause" in the widest meaning of the term is always independent of its particular effect, while this always depends upon the cause. Thus we shall assume an asymmetry in causal necessity; but, whereas radical asymmetry leaves open the possibility that not even the class or kind of effect is implied, "moderate asymmetry" holds the nonnullity of a class of effects—though no particular member of the class—to be rendered necessary by the existence of the cause. On either view, causes are always independent of particular effects, effects always dependent upon particular causes. That causes can exist temporally prior to effects is, one may suggest, the temporal aspect of the asymmetrical logical relation. The present exists by virtue of the past, which it requires, but not by virtue of the future. Whatever the future may become, this, we may say, is the present. But we cannot say, whatever the past may have been, this is the present. For we are, as adults, those who have been such-and-such children. It is included in our very being that we have been what we have been. Psychiatry gives concreteness to this proposition. We here take it as the universal nature of being an effect.

To suppose that pantheism and theism are two mutually exclusive and exhaustive ways of conceiving the causal relations of God and world is to forget that there are two senses in which God may be "independent cause" of the world, even if we speak here of this world, not merely of world-as-such, worlds as a class. "$X$ is the independent cause of $W$" might mean only that $X$ in some aspect of itself is, or has, something independent and causative of $W$; it does not necessarily mean that $X$ is or has nothing else besides, in being or having which it, in turn, depends upon $W$. A man may be independent of his friends—and support them—financially but be heavily dependent upon them emotionally. Or he may be emotionally self-sufficient but financially dependent. True, by "God is independent" we might choose to mean he is merely or purely that, so that the "something independent" in God would be God in all aspects, or in his entirety. But then we should be assuming, not one of two, but one of three formally possible positions: God is, in all his being, independent; he is, in some aspect of his being, independent; he is, in no aspect, independent. Is it really self-evident that to exert independent power one must, besides possessing something independent, avoid possessing anything dependent? If, in-

deed, God is wholly "simple," without diversity of aspects, then his independent aspect must be all there is. But the problem of simplicity is only the question at issue in another form (see below). Similarly, if God has no "accidents" distinct from his "essence," then he is either wholly dependent or wholly independent. But we need not here refute the alleged proofs that God cannot have accidents. We are at the stage of formulating the doctrines among which such demonstrations have to decide.

Let us now employ some simple symbols for the ideas we have been discussing. Let $C$ stand for universal Cause, i.e., for something that everything else requires, or upon which everything else depends, but which itself requires no other thing (leaving it open whether the class of "other things" is or is not required to be non-null, that is, whether "moderate" or "radical" asymmetry of causal necessity is involved). Let $W$ stand for the all-inclusive something, the Whole of reality (leaving it open whether or not there is a fixed totality of the real, or an ever growing one containing new items each time it is referred to). We then have three possible assertions about God (setting aside the purely negative one that he is neither universal cause nor all-inclusive reality). (1) God is (whether as a whole or in some aspect of himself only) universal cause, or *God is $C$;* (2) God is all-inclusive reality, or *God is $W$;* (3) God is both universal cause and all-inclusive reality, or *God is $CW$.* What are the logical relations of these three propositions? If the second alternative in the parentheses of (1) is excluded, then (1) becomes contradictory of (2), and (3) becomes self-contradictory. This is the basis of the idea that we must choose between theism, positing deity as independent cause, and pantheism, positing him as all-inclusive reality. For, indeed, an independent cause of all things cannot contain or include them, since, had there not been just those things to include, there must have been a more or less different total reality. An inclusive reality does require whatever it includes. But there is no reason why an inclusive reality may not contain an independent cause of things, or why God may not only in his total actuality be identical with this inclusive reality, but also, in an aspect of himself, identical with the independent cause. (It might, as we have suggested, be an ideal which he entertains, or a character or essence which he can never lack, even though he is always also more than just this ideal or this essence.)

The situation then is that, by virtue of the parenthetical qualification of (1), (1) and (2) are compatible with one another, and therefore, if theism only means that there is a divine independent cause of all things and pantheism, that there is a divine all-inclusive reality, both may be true. Not that there may be two Gods but that one God may have both an independent essence and dependent accidents, somewhat as a man has both his relatively fixed and unmodifiable character and also his varying actual experiences. Thus the positive content of theism and pantheism can be consistently combined in *God is CW;* for the contradiction between theism and pantheism arises only from the denial of any possible distinction between God as independent cause and God in his total actuality.

The whole positive content of (1), it may be argued, is that God will exist and will be himself (and would have existed and been himself) no matter what particular world exists (or had existed) or fails (or had failed) to exist; while the positive content of (2) is that God includes all reality in his own reality. So far there is no conflict between the two assertions. But classical theism insists that, not only would God exist and be himself, he would exist in the very same state, or, rather, there is here no possible distinction between existence and state, or between essence (what makes God always himself) and accidents. This is an arbitrary negation added to the positive assertion in (1). Does it not contradict the assertion? For where there is no distinction between essence and accidents, between "himself" and "his states," there (as all the history of philosophy testifies) is no intelligible meaning for essence or existence or selfhood or any other concept.

Classical pantheism unwittingly connived with classical theism in insisting upon the same arbitrary negation added to the positive doctrine of each. For, not content with affirming the all-inclusiveness of deity, pantheists often insisted also that his total actuality could not have been otherwise, that there are no divine accidents. This is not inferable from all-inclusiveness. Rather, the contrary is inferable; for, since the total reality must contain all there is, whether necessary or contingent, and since to deny the contrast between necessary and possible is to destroy the meaning of both, this contrast must be preserved and must fall within deity; and there must be divine accidents. But then there is no reason for denying that there is also a divine essence, independent of the accidents, and necessary. In this way, the polar nature of basic concepts (Morris Cohen's Law of Polarity) is properly expressed. Thus not merely is it not imperative to interpret (1) and (2) as mutually contradictory; there is even reason to suspect that, when so interpreted, they become *self*-contradictory. Accordingly, (3), *God is CW*, not only deserves no such neglect as it has received but has, if anything, the best claim of all to our consideration.

Assertion (3), which I call "panentheism," affirms God as containing both an all-independent all-causative factor *and* the totality of effects. In *God is CW*, God *as C* conforms to classical theism, *as W*, to classical pantheism—except for the negative absolutism whereby each doctrine adds to its own distinctive content the denial of that of the other. "God is truly independent and truly dependent" is no absurdity, unless by "truly" one means, in all that he is, rather than in something that he is. There is good reason for not initially meaning this. To impute to God a distinctive excellence such as is lacking to all ordinary things, it is enough to say that he is, in some aspect, independent of all; for ordinary things are in no aspect independent of all. Further, to depend, in some aspect, upon all other things, is likewise a unique maximum, since ordinary things depend only upon some other things (according to nearly all philosophers). Thus there is no reason for supposing that Washington required your existence or mine for his own existence or nature. But God, as knowing that you and I exist, has knowledge that he could not have had had we not existed, and, therefore, in this knowledge, he requires our existence and so, as we have been using words, "depends" on us in that respect. Note that only God thus depends, for some aspect of himself, upon literally *all* others. Thus dependence can be maximized as definitely as independence. And, accordingly, each of our three forms, C, CW, and W, marks off a being strictly maximal compared to all conceivable others (outside the three). They are rival versions of "supreme being" in a strict sense. One cannot be more universally independent than independent of all, more universally inclusive than inclusive of all, or simultaneously more independent-and-inclusive than, in some aspect, wholly the one, and for the rest wholly the other.

That inclusiveness means dependence is self-evident; for a whole that could be, in all respects, just what it is were its parts otherwise than they are is nonsense. (The differences may be minor, as when one of my cells is destroyed, but—assuming that "I" genuinely includes that cell—it is real.) Accordingly, *as* independent, God is exclusive, not inclusive; and, if this independent factor be all of God, then God-and-what-is-other-than-God must be a total reality greater (more inclusive) than God. This desperate paradox is removed by construing "God-*and*-not-God" as meaning: "God in all his aspects (independent and dependent) *and* the parts or included factors entering into the dependent aspects." (As we have seen, only the dependent can be inclusive.) We may speak of "the whole *and* its parts"; but this is no more than just the whole itself.

In scope, then, CW is no more than W alone, for either implies "all reality." And nothing can be more than the totality of being and value. But the W in CW refers to all reality as involving *one* universally causal factor which, by our definition of cause, is independent of the rest, while W in isolation would mean all reality as in no factor independent. Pantheism, or *God is W* (in isolation), contains therefore (to repeat) no positive factor lacking in *God is CW* (best called panentheism). And likewise, all that separates *God is C* (in isolation), classical theism or deism, from *God is CW* is the former's denial that God has in himself or in his total actuality anything from which he (in his independent aspect) is independent. The contention that the beings from which God (in some essential aspect) is independent are not parts of him (in his total reality) is sheer negation. And though "independence" itself is verbally negative, it can be construed positively. It means: "self-identical no matter how other things vary." But that the varying things are not in the independent being as a whole, or that the self-identity is the whole content of the being, making it merely the same, and not the same in a partly different state (or experience), is again sheer negation. Of such negations, arbitrary at the initial stage of formulating alternatives of doctrine, the stubborn conflict of theism and pantheism is the offspring.

If our earlier "moderately asymmetrical" view of causality be applied, the C in CW implies the nonnullity of the class, "realities differing from God," but does not imply just the nondivine realities which in fact do exist. Thus W is really a variable, and between C and any actual values of the variable the implication runs only toward C (the cause is necessary to the effect but not vice versa). God in his essence is independent of any world in particular, though not of world-assuch; God in his concrete total being at a given moment (a certain value of W and so of CW) contains just the actual world that then exists or at least has existed.

It is popular to say that God is immanent as well as transcendent; but this largely misses the point. The cause is of course in the effect, since it is logically necessary to it. Only thus could it be inferable from it. But is God merely cause, merely C, or is he CW? This is the critical question; and it is not answered by asserting both world immanence and world transcendence of God. The important question, as Fechner remarked, is whether the world is immanent in God.

God as CW "transcends" the world, not only as every whole transcends each and every one of its parts, but in the uniquely radical way of containing an essence or element of self-identity absolutely independent of whichever among possible contingent things are actual as parts of the Whole. The genuine issue is thus triadic: is the world in relation to God (1) wholly extrinsic; (2) wholly intrinsic; or (3) wholly extrinsic to *something in* God but intrinsic to God *as a whole?*

We now turn to the evaluative approach to the idea of God, his "perfection." What is the formal structure of this idea? The perfect, one often hears, is what lacks no possible value, so that all possibility of increase in value is cut off. But we must be cautious here. For "all the value possible," or "the sum of all perfections," may not itself be a possible value, since there seem to be "incompossibles" (Leibniz) among possible values. Hence "that whose value leaves no possibility of value unrealized" may be a self-contradictory definition. But it may be that we can find some other formula sufficiently related to this one to deserve its name, "perfection," but sufficiently different to avoid its, at least apparent, self-contradiction.

"Perfection" at least means: excellence in some emphatic or pre-eminent sense. To excel is to surpass others in value. An emphatic, if not the most emphatic, case is to surpass all conceivable others in value. Such a being need not actualize all possible value. For suppose a being so related to others, and to the very possibility of others, that it (and it alone) contains *all* the values that actual beings contain, and suppose also that it is certain to acquire *all* new values actualized anywhere, if and as they are actualized. Then the superiority which it already enjoys— for all other values are but parts of its value—cannot conceivably be overcome. Is the supposition fantastic? Suppose a mind truly cosmic, able to enjoy the universe as content of its knowledge. Then every new beauty of experience realized anywhere will be added to the cosmic experience, plus any emergent values due to the synthesis of the various values, new and old, in the cosmic experience. True, this supposes that the cosmic mind does not know its experiences in advance, or "eternally." But this would not necessarily mean that it was inferior to some other conceivable mind. For it may be held that no conceivable knowledge can eternally embrace what is not eternally in being; that novelty is real, and the knowledge of it must itself be novel.

What I have been saying implies that the perfect, the surpasser of all others, may also surpass itself. And, indeed, by "others" we may very well mean entities more radically distinguishable from the given being than would be other states (experiences?) of itself; and in such other states the being might potentially surpass itself as it actually is. Then (you may object) must not the actual state lack something? I remind you that we have not defined perfection as all possible value. However, the alleged idea of a being lacking no possible value can be produced as a (doubtfully consistent) special case under our own definition. One has only to refuse to restrict, as above, the meaning of "others" to "other individuals" (in the definition "necessarily surpasses all others") in order to find one's self confronted with the idea or pseudo-idea of a being which cannot improve and which surpasses all other conceivable beings. It must then have all possible values (and be an immutable, "pure actuality"); for any value which it lacked (supposing there could be such) would be impossible for it to attain, and yet possible for reality as a whole, which would then be a conceivable other surpassing the unsurpassable being, a reduction to absurdity of the supposition. Thus the classical concept (or pseudo-concept) of perfection is but a special case of the idea of the all-other-surpassing—the case in which the exclusion of an unsurpassed "other" is permitted (perhaps with loss of consistency) to extend even to other states

of the same being," or alternatively, in which, to the positive prescription, "surpassing others," is added the dubious negative one, "not conceivably surpassing self."

The basic idea of other-surpassing has three forms, according as it is applied to zero, some, or all (conceivable) others. The first gives the idea of minimal or least being; the second, that of middling or imperfect ("finite") being; the third, that of maximal, supreme, or perfect being. This division is mathematical or purely formal, since the nonformal aspects of the relation of "surpassing" do not function to create the distinctions but only the notion of relation to all, some, or no terms other than the term in question.

If we include the distinction between self-relation and relation to others, we find that each of the three forms of other-surpassing subdivides into two, making six forms in all—as follows. (By "nonreflexive" will be meant, not surpassing or being surpassed by self, that is, with no possibility of change for better or worse. By "reflexive" will be meant, with some possibility of change —whether for better, for worse, or both, being left open by the table, though I shall hold that in the case of R only change for the better is plausible.)

Minimal Being (superiority to *no* others)

| | |
|---|---|
| *n:* nonreflexive form | Null, zero, as static abstraction |
| | The negative absolute, or absolutely small |
| *i:* reflexive form | Infinitesimal, the dynamic, concrete diminutive |
| | The negative relative, or infinitely small (e.g., the life of a dying man as near death as you please) |

Middling or Imperfect Being (superiority to *some* others)

| | | |
|---|---|---|
| *a:* nonreflexive form | Ordinary abstractions, e.g., manliness | The little absolute |
| *r:* reflexive form | Ordinary concretes, e.g., a man | The little relative |

Maximal or Perfect Being (superiority to *all* others)

| | |
|---|---|
| *A:* nonreflexive form | The Supreme Abstraction. (God as merely self-identical?) The Great Absolute or Absolutely Superior |
| *R:* reflexive form | The Supreme Concrete. (God as living personality, self-contrasting as well as self-identical?) The Great Relative, or the Great, Relatively to all others and to (past states of) itself. The Super-Relative or Reflexively Transcendent—Transcendental Relativity |

This table, the skeleton of which could be put into purely mathematical form (but for the inconvenience of printing it thus), shows that the ordinary contrast, perfect versus imperfect, as usually construed, is a misleading (or imperfect) distinction. Thus the perfect is usually taken as incapable of increase in value, so that "imperfect" lumps together the reflexive forms of minimal, middling, and maximal superiority! Again, the habit of identifying "absolute" and "perfect" conceals the cardinal truth that ordinary abstractions have a kind of absoluteness or independence of relations and of change and that reflexive maximal superiority,

though relative, or varying with relations and change, is just as radically superior to ordinary concrete things as is nonreflexive or absolute perfection to ordinary abstractions.

A certain species of quality is always just that species, trivial or exalted; but a concrete being can take on new, additional, perhaps better species. It can become better than its previous self, whereas, by the very meaning of abstraction, what a given abstractive act discerns is the same wherever and whenever it be found. This suggests that A, nonreflexive or classical perfection, is the supreme object of abstraction, not the supreme object of concrete or total awareness.

Many considerations support this. One is that R implies A as an abstractable aspect of its own meaning. For what is R improves upon itself, and what improves upon *itself* must retain some kind of self-identity; it must become X better than X. But if a being in *all* respects was R or improved, it could in no respect remain the same or identical; moreover, the required non-R aspect of the R being must conform to the definition of A, since, as superior to *all* others, the R being already possesses an absolutely perfect or A quality, the quality of being universally other-superior, of surpassing absolutely all others. Thus A is required as self-identical aspect of what, in the respects in which it is not A, is R. (Of course R itself, as such, is self-identical in that the quality of being R is always that quality. But this is like the fact that change as such never changes but is always—change. R—as we saw of W earlier—is really a variable, the abstract variable of which A is the abstract constant, the latter being like "sameness" abstracted from concrete samenesses-and-differences, the former like "difference" abstracted from the same concrete.

The above account fits the obvious

fact that we get such ideas as identity, being, absolute, by abstracting from that aspect of novelty in experience by which the given is more than mere being but is also becoming, more than mere actuality but also actualization, more than a being-good but a freely becoming-better, an adding of novelty to treasured and funded experience. "To be less at one time and more at another" presupposes the ideas of time and of dynamic self-identity, and these can never be derived from that of mere being. How could we reach the *concrete* ultimate by omitting process from the process of experience, or diversity from the unity in diversity? True enough, it was often said that God is equally above unity and diversity, being and becoming, in our human sense; for he escapes all our categories. But the partiality for unity, identity, being, over plurality, diversity, becoming, oozes from nearly every page written on this subject for some twenty centuries (until Kant and later).

Being and becoming are not the only factors in the "process" from which both are abstracted. There is also the having-become, by which the real, as self-surpassing, is still what it previously became, while becoming more besides. It became $p$, it now becomes $q$, additional to (and involving) $p$. Thus we have: (1) becoming; (2) having-become, or earlier becoming as involved in later; (3) the primordial and fixed aspect of mere being constituting the abstract self-identity of process at *any* and every time.

An old objection to conceiving of God as subject to increase is that then he must also be in danger of decrease, decay, even of total destruction. This is a *non sequitur*. We might as well say that to be able to act well is to be able to act badly; therefore, either God cannot act well or he may act badly. Increase in value is good change, decrease is evil change; the capacity for one does

not imply capacity for the other, unless anything good implies the correlative evil. And if the *ultimate* process is not one of net gain, why process at all? In any case, an R being cannot be conceived to decay; for one reason, because then another R being (it could not be the same one) must be conceivable as its superior, namely, an incorruptible R being. And an incorruptible R being is conceivable, since we need only suppose one with complete memory of past actuality, and the ability to maintain self-integrity while becoming aware of each addition to actuality as it occurs. If the past once for all "has been what it has been," then *something* does preserve, and as it were remember, all that happens. Why not a literal memory? Is there a beter explanation? Thus, new experiences, additional values, need not mean losing any of the old. "Time is creation or nothing" (Bergson). Destruction is not co-ordinate with creation. (For us men, who forget nearly everything, past values are, it is true, mostly lost. Also, enduring sources of values, like buildings or bodies, may "cease to endure," but this only means that they no longer add new chapters to their histories; it does not mean that the old chapters are abolished. As parts of the past, they are all fully there, if it be true that the past is real in spite of our forgetting.)

Another objection is that God is simple, and so cannot be A merely in one aspect, while as a whole being R. Now, the A aspect itself may indeed be simple; for instance, God's knowledge as A is the same as his goodness as A, and so on. But his knowledge as A is not the same as his knowledge as R, or as his happiness as R. The axiom of simplicity has been deduced as end result from reasoning that starts with such pseudo-axioms as that a cause must contain the equivalent of its effect. No panentheist will admit this axiom.

The formula AR is no more self-contradictory than the formula *ar*. A happy man may acquire a higher species of happiness, although neither one of these species becomes higher. *The abstract and immutable qualifies the concrete and mutable.* When the perfect was supposed an exception, it was because the conceptual structure of maximal superiority was not clearly stated, and the overlooking of the concept R illegitimately assumed the functions of a refutation of that concept.

AR seems more promising than A alone as descriptive of the creative source and sustainer of things, since AR contains the principle of relativity, which cannot be derived from the merely absolute. Relation is a positive idea; unlike ignorance, or "inattention to the interests of others," it cannot be equated with the partial absence of some positive element. If relation is simply not in God, then no magic can explain its presence anywhere.

In order to avoid positing relations, even though of "superiority to others," in God, it has been customary to define him negatively as unrivaled and unsurpassed by others, so that he was not related as superior, but only they, as inferior. Thus Anselm's "that than which none greater can be conceived" may at least appear to avoid relating God. But it is of no consequence, for the same divisions of minimal, middling, and maximal, and of reflexive and nonreflexive, forms, arise as much from this negative definition as from our positive one. And this is true for all the other stock concepts, such as completeness, pure actuality, aseity, or infinity. On any showing (had I space to go into this) the neglected alternative, R, would present itself and demand a hearing, and there would be the same indications as we have found that the non-R form of perfection is abstract.

Furthermore, on any assumption, God must be related to have knowledge. Knowledge of $x$ is relation-to-$x$ as possessed by the knower. The possession is contingent if $x$ is contingent; for if $x$ had happened not to be actual, then it could at most have been known as a possibility, not as an actuality. It may be answered that divine knowledge has only a formal analogy, not a concrete similarity, to ours. But it is on the most formal, analogical level that the difficulty arises. God's knowing that proposition P is true cannot be an accident of his being, if (as alleged) his being is without accidents, absolute, relationless. Hence none of his knowledge could have been other than it is. But if P affirms the existence of a contingent being, then P *could* have been false, though God must, if his knowledge is necessary, have "known" it as true. Thus something could have been which, had it been, would have meant false knowledge in God. This is simple, formal contradiction of the infallibility of his knowledge. It is not a mere inability on our part to imagine a knowing concretely so different from ours as the divine.

The contradiction is not mitigated by urging that God's knowledge does not have to conform to things, since it conforms things to itself. Read the conformity either way; you contradict it in saying that, on the one side things could have been different, but, on the other, all is as it must be. In addition, if things alone are conformed, then when a man sins he is only being conformed to God's knowledge.

Again, God is said to know his own all-causative essence, and in this he sees all that can be produced by it. But can he see which among the things he can produce he actually does, and which not? It is a contradiction if something contingent is involved in something wholly necessary.

No doubt divine knowledge is radically different from ours and surpasses ours not merely as ours surpasses that of the animals. We may say, indeed, that

God is the being who transcends others while surpassing himself; whereas we surpass ourselves and others but transcend no one. God's knowledge, accordingly, is analogous, not similar, to ours. But analogy should be honestly carried through. It should set some requirements that are adhered to; and, when one removes from classical theology all that covertly implies superrelativity and accidents in God, nothing is left of divine "knowledge" (as Maimonides in his recklessly candid moments said) but a word.

The absolute cannot know or have any relation to the relative, but only the relative to the absolute. Thus AR does not relate A to any relative things, but it relates God, as R or transcendentally relative, to A as well as to ordinary relative things. Since whatever contains a relation contains its terms (relation-of-$x$-to-$y$ being only a relational type apart from $x$ and $y$), therefore whatever includes relations is, in so far, concrete and comprehensive, and whatever excludes relations is in so far abstract and noncomprehensive. Whatever has the relations of absolute and relative has all the reality that is in either and is a relative which is more than the absolute. This is no paradox, except by misuse of terms. Absolute does not mean inclusive, concrete, or supreme. It means independent; and what guarantees that the independent must or even can be inclusive? True, the inclusive must depend only upon its parts; but that is a very real dependence, for, given different parts, the whole must be correspondingly different.

Nothing, of course, can be more than what is "absolute *in all respects*," "absolutely absolute"—save as a consistent conception means more than a self-contradictory one. "A in all respects" means no more than round-square. For what it describes must have all actual values while yet having no actuality. Determination, definite actuality, is lim-

itation, negation. But to be indeterminate, indefinite, inactual, is also limitation of another kind. The purely and all-ways unlimited is mere nonsense.

In one sense A, absoluteness, includes relationship. Among abstractions, as Russell has remarked, are "abstractness" and "concreteness." The property of being concrete is not a concrete thing. Now R is the over-all abstraction, divine concreteness as such. And the A in AR means that the reflexively perfect must, in some abstract aspect, be non-reflexively or immutably perfect. A has relation to R in that its only meaning is as abstract aspect of concrete perfection. But this is relation to R as a mere suchness, the generic property of "having accidents," by which the perfect transcends all and surpasses itself, and this "having accidents" as such includes no accidents, but only demands that there be some. So A, though related to R, is not related to anything contingent but to the necessary category of accidentality—there shall be accidents. God as a concrete whole, AR in character, is the one who is related to accidental things themselves.

God is a whole whose whole-properties are distinct from the properties of the parts. This is so of every whole, but most radically so of the supreme whole. The parts are *ar*, the whole, AR. A whole of relative parts can never be merely absolute, for there can always be additional parts. But a whole of *ar* parts can very well be AR. What is in the parts is in the whole; so, for example, our misdeeds are in God; but not as his misdeeds, or his deeds at all—rather as his misfortunes. They make his overall satisfaction less than it otherwise would be, but not his goodness of decision. For if a part decides something, the whole permits, suffers, endures, the decision, it does not make it. It is orthodox doctrine that God does not enact our sins, and this is just as tenable if we are parts of God, since to be is to have power; therefore, to be distinguishable from the whole, though within it, is to have power which is not the whole's as its own whole-quality. In this whole-quality, the power of parts is something suffered, not enacted—as, in general, what is active in the other is passive in the self. This Fechnerian principle is the only self-consistent view of dynamic wholes and parts and of the relations of human and divine freedom.

Let us now combine our two classifications of ideas of God, the one made in terms of causality together with totality, and the other in terms of perfection; or C, CW, W, and A, AR, R. In combination these become:

| | | |
|-----|------|-----|
| A-C | A-CW | A-W |
| AR-C | AR-CW | AR-W |
| R-C | R-CW | R-W |

The first column contains three forms of transcendental theism; the second, three forms of what is best called *panentheism;* the third, three forms of pantheism. The first row contains three forms of nonreflexive perfectionism; the second row, three forms of reflexive-nonreflexive perfectionism; the third row, three forms of reflexive perfectionism. The middle member of the middle row (or column) AR-CW, has the advantage of synthesizing all the positive principles of the entire table. If there be a "higher synthesis" or golden mean with respect to the extremes, it seems this must be it. The first row is God as the extreme of pure absoluteness, with nothing positive from which relativity can be derived; the third row is God as the extreme of pure relativity with nothing stable that can be asserted once for all, even relativity itself. The first column is God as the extreme of sheer causality divorced from any of its effects, power with nothing that power does; the third column is God as the extreme of contingent phenomena with no element of independence, necessity, or self-existence. Is it hard to see that

these are all broken fragments of truth rather than the truth? Only AR-CW avoids all the extremes. Of the others, four, such as A-C, are in two extremes at once; the remaining four, such as A-CW, suffer from the special absurdity of positing a profound duality in terms of one category and sheer unity in terms of the other, in spite of the evident truth that the two categories are so closely interrelated as to forbid such differential treatment.

The argument which our analysis furnishes for the conclusion AR-CW is the stronger in that it is not isolated but is the type of argument that alone offers any hope of producing agreement in philosophy. For who imagines that the classical extremes of doctrine, such as monism versus pluralism, pure transcendentalism versus pure immanentalism, pure atemporalism versus a temporalism that can point to no ultimate identity in process—who imagines that these mighty opposites can ever fight their battles to a definitive triumph of either side? Surely only a doctrine which can say to all such extremes, "You are all of you right and all of you in error, right in refusing to accept your opponent's position, wrong in supposing the choice lies between you"—only such a doctrine can resolve the conflicts.

Of course, atheists will suppose that all nine theistic doctrines are erroneous (or absurd) and that there is no cosmic or perfect being, in any such strict sense as these doctrines agree in supposing. But this is to suggest that one of the most extreme doctrines of all, a relativism more radical than R by itself, ought to gain final assent. What a counsel of despair! It would mean that the totality of things (or, again, that the most universal causal factor) was in no way formally different from items which it contains (or effects which it produces), or that the totality of values is surpassable in all senses in which values short of the totality are surpassable, or, again, that the element in being or existence which makes being to be itself, or existence existence, is in every sense as contingent as anything else.

But is AR-CW a religious doctrine? It implies a God more knowing, more benevolent, more powerful, more happy or blessed than any other conceivable being. So far, surely, so good; but, then, R means that God can somehow increase in value. Yet as "omniscient" already, the God of religion cannot increase in knowledge, if that means overcoming previous error or ignorance; as "holy" or entirely righteous, he cannot overcome previous selfishness or meanness; nor, as "all-powerful," can he overcome previous weakness. But this leaves ample room for an R factor of improvement! For the things God knows to exist, and deals righteously and powerfully with as existent, are not all the things that can exist (it is logically impossible that all possible things should coexist). Accordingly, suppose that something which does not but can exist subsequently does so. There will then be a new existent for God to know and deal with as such; and his total life, as inclusive of his knowledge and its content, will be enriched.[2]

Since the new objects of God's knowledge include new states of happiness in the creatures, and since God cares for this happiness, he must obviously derive satisfaction, and new satisfaction, from these states. Denying this is hardly an imperative of religion, since it makes nonsense of the alleged love of God.

But I shall perhaps be told that religion has thought of God as beyond and

exclusive of the world, rather than as, according to W, its receptacle. I think this is an illusory impression of religion, due to inattention to the meaning of words. Religion has not emphasized the bare idea that we are in God but has stressed how we are in God. We are in God by being objects of his love and knowledge. As Whittier says:

> I only know I cannot drift
> Beyond his love and care.

There is no need to multiply quotations. But, it will be said, this does not literally mean we are inside God. I ask: What, then, does it mean? Do you seriously suppose that God's actuality is one thing, and his knowledge with its immediate contents, or his love with its direct objects of concern, just another? What, then, unites God with "his" knowledge or love, or these with "their" objects, if it is not God's actuality? It scarcely seems that those who make such proposals can have thought of what they are saying.

True, our human knowledge and love may not seem to embrace things within our own being. But human knowledge and love are radically imperfect, especially where their objects are the most indirect or external to our being. It seems strange to try to conceive God's knowledge and love by supposing that the indirectness and externality of the most fallible forms of our experience are the models for conceiving his infallible form!

But can dead matter be part of God? I reply that no one has proved there is any mere dead matter, and many of the best scientific and philosophical minds have thought the notion a pseudo-concept. Again, can human freedom be part of God? As indicated above, the Fechnerian principle justifies an affirmative. Once more, can human ignorance and error be part of divine wisdom? The answer is much the same. Believing is

2. It has been admitted in the general Introduction that, since this doctrine seems to involve a series of cosmic states as presented to God, and so the absolute simultaneity physics now denies (perhaps not in the relevant sense), there is an unresolved problem. Cf. D. H. Parker, *Experience and Substance* (Ann Arbor: University of Michigan Press, 1941), for one attempt to deal with it.

an act, and this may be our act but not God's, except as the whole endures the acts of its parts, as precisely their acts not the whole's. It has our beliefs as ours, and as ours parts of itself—but not as its beliefs would be parts of itself. That this is conceivable has been affirmed by two great psychologist-philosophers who meditated long on the matter, James and Fechner.

Thus AR-CW seems to stand out as the truth, if there is an ascertainable truth, of theism. The absolute, nonreflexive or merely identical, factor in God, God as A-C, is the pure cause which neither is nor contains any effect; the unmoved mover which, as Jacob Boehme was one of the first to see, is *in* God but is not God (in his concreteness). The superrelative or reflexively transcendant perfection of God is the fulness of his being, his wholeness as always self-identical, but self-identical as self-enriched, influenced but never fully determined by (and never fully determining) others—in short, a living, sensitive, free personality, preserving all actual events with impartial care and forever adding new events to his experience. The absolute is the One merely as One; the superrelative is the many as also one, or the one as also many. The world as not God is the many merely as many—an abstraction from the many as one, as the integrated, active-passive content of omniscience.

*Indexes*

# Index of Names

Akiba ben Joseph, 158
Alexander, S., ix, 17, 18, 365–72, 385
Ames, E. S., ix, 17, 380–85, 395
Anaxagoras, 71
Anselm, 17, 25, 96–106, 111, 112, 134, 148, 417, 486, 510
Aquinas, Thomas, ix, 17, 23, 106, 108, 111, 112, 119–42, 155, 176, 327, 328, 352
Aristotle, ix, xi, 1, 14, 17–18, 31, 55, 58–75, 76, 84, 111, 112, 118, 119, 121, 122, 123, 127, 211, 212, 276, 314, 315, 321, 363, 416, 489
Arnauld, Antoine, 112, 138–39, 142
Arnold, Matthew, 155, 417
Ashari, al-, 297
Asvagosha, 165, 167–69
Athanasius, St., 325
Augustine, 17, 23, 25, 85–96, 122, 123, 131, 156, 158, 197, 306, 451
Aurelius, Marcus, 158, 166
Avicenna, 75

Baker, Augustine, 325
Balfour, Lord, 389
Barth, Karl, vii, 306, 448
Bautain, Louis Eugène Marie, 229
Beethoven, Ludwig, 391
Berdyaev, Nicolas, vi, vii, 15, 84, 149, 153, 164, 176, 187, 209–10, 228, 230, 234, 259, 285–94, 298, 303, 413, 443
Bergson, Henri, 85, 95, 228, 294, 297, 310, 469, 501, 509
Berkeley, George, 188
Berman, Louis, ix, 373–79, 385
Bernard, St., 158
Boehme, Jacob, 164, 188, 233, 285, 288, 514
Boethius, 225
Bosanquet, Bernard, 386
Bowne, B. P., 362
Bradley, F. H., 174, 352, 406
Brahmachari, Mahanam Brata, v
Breasted, James Henry, 77
Brightman, E. S., ix, 17, 18, 227, 358–64
Broad, C. D., 295
Browning, Robert, 156, 368
Brunner, Heinrich Emil, 306
Bruno, Giordano, 439
Buber, Martin, 176, 302–6, 482
Buchler, Justus, 258
Buddha, 262, 391, 411

Campanella, Tommaso, 137
Cardanus, Hieronymus, 137 n.
Carneades, 277, 416–17, 437, 447, 465
Cattell, Raymond B., ix, 17, 385–94
Channing, W. E., 150–52
Churchill, Winston, 389
Cicero, 390
Cohen, Morris R., 2, 504

Confucius, 262, 388
Cornford, F. M., 5, 56
Crell, Johannes, 225
Croce, Benedetto, 490

Damascene, John, 122
Damien, Father, 153–54, 160
Dante Alighieri, 158
Darwin, Charles, 260
Dawani, Jaluluddin, 296
Dekker, Eduard Douwes (Multatuli), 474 n.
Democritus, 61
Demos, Raphael, 38, 211–12
Denis, the Carthusian, 325
Dennes, W. R., 486–95
Descartes, René, 97, 133–37, 358
Dewey, John, 111, 380, 395–96, 490–91

Eckhardt, Meister, 325
Eddington, Arthur, 358
Ehrenfels, Christian von, ix, 17, 352–57
Eliot, George (Evans, Mary Anne), x
Erigena, Johannes Scotus, 164, 169
Evans, Mary Anne; see Eliot, George
Everett, John R., 412 n.

Farabi, al-, 75
Fechner, Gustav T., vi, ix, 15, 17, 23, 140, 152, 153, 161, 229, 234, 243–57, 269, 270, 275, 310, 347–48, 352, 437, 506, 512, 513, 514
Feibleman, James, 258
Feuerbach, Ludwig, ix, x, 448–66, 467
Fock, Otto, ix, 225
Francis, St., 158
Freud, Sigmund, 348, 392, 468–85

Galileo, 388
Garvie, A. E., 153, 270
Gaunilo, 97, 100
Gersonides (Levi ben Gerson), 75, 106, 112, 118, 189, 225
Ghazzali, al-, xi, 15, 17, 23, 106–11, 176
Gilson, É. H., 57, 119
Goethe, J. W. von, 10, 439
Goudge, T. A., 258

Hartmann, Eduard von, 338
Hegel, G. W. F., 2, 177, 188, 234, 242, 266, 269, 291, 300, 358–59, 360, 386
Heraclitus, 2
Hinton, James, 153, 154–55, 161, 162
Hisham, 109
Hobbes, Thomas, 386
Hodgson, Shadworth, 346
Horten, M., 109 n.
Hügel, Friedrich von, 152–63
Hume, David, x, 142, 145, 148, 416–37, 447, 483

517

# General Index

[Since "God" is the principal item of the Index, look for any topic both under its own name and under the "God" entry.]

Chance, 153, 354
and law, 424
as meaningless, 425
Change, 59, 72, 93, 211; *see also* Becoming
serial, 295–96
Chaos, as principle opposed to God, 354
Christ, 252, 355, 390, 391; *see also* Jesus
as "Christus Victor," 333
Monophysite conception of, 333
two natures of, 156, 159
Christianity, 162, 297, 299, 324, 329–30
doctrines of, 366, 450
and sorrow, 355
and suffering, 291–92
Christology, 163
Circularity
in Descartes's reasoning, 133–34
in theistic argument, 487
Civilization, 478
Co-creation, 140
Cognition, 181–82, 344; *see also* Thought; Reason; Understanding
Coherence, concept of, 236
Commands, moral, 489; *see also* Ethics; Good; Value
Community, idea of, 460
Complex, requiring principle of simplicity, 213–14
Conception
and the principle of expansion and contraction, 359
subjective, 452
and substance, 194
Concepts
correlative, 293–94
and images, 357
Concrete, the; *see also* Abstract
and abstract, 116, 189
containing the abstract, 131–32
Conscience, 472, 491
and guilt toward God, 467
Consciousness, 179–81, 255, 373, 392–93, 447; *see also* God
and atomic reactions, 374
compounding of, 337, 345–47, 348, 374, 501
as continuous, 373
cosmic, 413
and duality, 211–12
as essentially infinite, 448
as a field of overlapping states, 346–47
human and divine, 464
individual, 389
and instinct, 448
nature of, 248–49
states of, 345
superindividual, 391
universal, 278
Contingency, 195; *see also* Necessity
absence of, in God and world, 192–94
denial of, 209
of fact, and intuition, 13

and freedom, 222
in God, 19–20
and imperfection, 97
and necessity, 13, 97, 101–3, 119, 130–31, 189–90, 216, 221, 233, 379
Continuity
personal, 389
as relational generality, 266
Continuum
psychic, 374
space-time, 374
Contradiction, 133, 138; *see also* Antinomy; Paradox
of corporeality and incorporeality in God, 416
the essential, 236–37
in the idea of God, 417
of limitation and limitlessness in God, 416
of personality and infinity in God, 416
in primal nature, 237
principle of, 236
and process, 241–42
and truth, 120
and unity, 237
Contraries; *see also* Dipolarity; Polarity
admitting of a supercase, 5
polar, 176, 197, 273
in Aristotle, 58–60
in theistic conceptions, 500
Contrariety, 33
and levels of abstraction, 364
Contrasts
categorical, 2, 197, 363
as correlative, 2
eternal, 235
Cosmogony, 471
Cosmology, 258, 281, 335, 380, 489
Cosmos, and psychic activity, 376–78
Creation, 34–35, 291, 304–5, 401
*ex nihilo*, 23, 270–71, 274
and God, 23, 463
imperfections of, 428–32
as play, 309
play as its motive, 186, 187
process of, 395–96
and self-creation, 147–210
Creative event
and four subevents of, 398–401
and God, 403–4
as growth of value, 398
as suprahuman, 401–2
as transcendent, 402
Creativity, 228, 276, 398, 406, 407, 415
as absolute, 402–3
divine, 395
four phases of, 282
and God, 286–87
and meaning, 401
and potentiality, 277
social, 149
Creature, as partly self-determining, 273
Culture, evolution of, 477